Michael C. LeMay
California State University, San Bernardino

THE PERENNIAL STRUGGLE

RACE, ETHNICITY,

and

MINORITY GROUP POLITICS

in the

UNITED STATES

PRENTICE HALL, UPPER SADDLE RIVER, NEW JERSEY 07458

Library of Congress Cataloging-in-Publication Data

LeMay, Michael C., 1941–
    The perennial struggle : race, ethnicity, and minority group politics in the United States
/ Michael C. LeMay
      p. cm.
    Includes bibliographical references and index.
    ISBN 0-13-020547-8
    1. Minorities—United States—Political activity.   2. Minorities—United States—Political
activity—Case studies.   3. Political participation—United States.   4. Political
participation—United States—Case studies.   5. United States—Politics and
government—Case studies.   I. Title

E184.A1 L435 2000
305.8'00973—dc21

                                    99-058622

Editorial Director: Laura Pearson
Executive Editor: Beth Gillett Mejia
Senior Marketing Manager: Christopher DeJohn
Project management and interior text design: Serena Hoffman
Prepress and Manufacturing Buyer: Ben Smith
Cover Art Director: Jayne Conte
Cover Designer: Bruce Kenselaar
Cover art: Mathew McFarren, Stock Illustration Source

This book was set in 11/12 Garamond
by Stratford Publishing Services, Inc., and was
printed and bound by RR Donnelley & Sons Company.
The cover was printed by Phoenix Color Corp.

Printed in the United States of America

10 9 8 7 6 5 4 3 2 1

ISBN 0-13-020547-8

Prentice-Hall International (UK) Limited, *London*
Prentice-Hall of Australia Pty. Limited, *Sydney*
Prentice-Hall Canada Inc., *Toronto*
Prentice-Hall Hispanoamericana, S.A., *Mexico*
Prentice-Hall of India Private Limited, *New Delhi*
Prentice-Hall of Japan, Inc., *Tokyo*
Pearson Education Asia Pte. Ltd., *Singapore*
Editora Prentice-Hall do Brasil, Ltda., *Rio de Janeiro*

To my wife, Lynda,
who makes it all worthwhile

CONTENTS

Preface ix

CHAPTER ONE

The Language of the Struggle:
The Basic Concepts of Majority/Minority Relations 1

We/They and Group Identity 1
    Majority Group 4
    Minority Group 4
    Ethnicity 6
    Race 7
    Racial Minority Groups 8
    Prejudice 9
    Discrimination 11
    Segregation 14
    Social Stratification 15
Minority Status 16
    Political Implications 17
Coping Strategies 18
    Acculturation and Assimilation 19
    Integration 20
    Amalgamation and Accommodation 20
    Pluralism 22
SUMMARY 23
KEY TERMS 23
REVIEW QUESTIONS 24
NOTES 25
SUGGESTED READINGS 25
CASE STUDY 1.1 IS AMERICA STILL A MELTING POT? 26

CHAPTER TWO

Strategies of the Struggle: Theories of Race Relations and Methods of Coping with Minority Status   28

Theories of Assimilation   30
    The Psychological Approach   33
    The Social-Psychological Approach   34
    The Sociological Approach   35
    The Economic Approach   36
The Systems Dynamic Perspective   37
    A Systems Model of Assimilation   37
    Operational Indicators of the Model   40
Strategies for Coping with Minority Status   45
    Accommodation   45
    Separatism   53
    Radicalism   54
SUMMARY   60
KEY TERMS   61
REVIEW QUESTIONS   61
NOTES   62
SUGGESTED READINGS   62
CASE STUDY 2.1   THE ARAB-AMERICAN MARKET   63

CHAPTER THREE

The Strategy of Accommodation: The Economic Route   67

Asian Americans   67
    Chinese Americans   68
    Japanese Americans   73
    Korean Americans   82
European Immigrants   84
    German Americans   84
    Scandinavian Americans   87
    Greek Americans   89
Hispanic Americans   94
    Chicano Americans   95
    Puerto Rican Americans   98
    Cuban Americans   99
Black Americans   101
SUMMARY   107
KEY TERMS   107
REVIEW QUESTIONS   108
NOTES   108
SUGGESTED READINGS   109
CASE STUDY 3.1   BOOKER T. WASHINGTON'S ATLANTIC COMPROMISE ADDRESS   110

CHAPTER FOUR
The Strategy of Accommodation: The Political Route   112

Irish Americans   113
Italian Americans   116
Greek Americans   122
Slavic Americans   125
      Polish Americans   126
      Russian Americans   128
Jewish Americans   129
Hispanic Americans   131
Black Americans   134
SUMMARY   137
KEY TERMS   137
REVIEW QUESTIONS   138
NOTES   138
SUGGESTED READINGS   138
CASE STUDY 4.1   URBAN MACHINES AND ETHNIC MINORITIES   140

CHAPTER FIVE
The Strategy of Separatism: Physical Separatism   143

The Amish and Mennonites   144
The Mormons   151
Native Americans   160
Black Nationalism: Marcus Garvey and "Back to Africa"   172
SUMMARY   177
KEY TERMS   177
REVIEW QUESTIONS   178
NOTES   178
SUGGESTED READINGS   178
CASE STUDY 5.1   KINGDOM COME   179

CHAPTER SIX
The Strategy of Separatism: Psychological Separatism   185

The Black Muslims   185
Hasidic Jews   197
SUMMARY   202
KEY TERMS   202
REVIEW QUESTIONS   202
NOTES   203
SUGGESTED READINGS   203
CASE STUDY 6.1   THE NATION OF ISLAM REACHES OUT   204

CHAPTER SEVEN
Old-Style Radicalism   207

Socialism   207
Communism   214
Fascism   225
Nazism   230
SUMMARY   233
KEY TERMS   234
REVIEW QUESTIONS   235
NOTES   235
SUGGESTED READINGS   235
CASE STUDY 7.1   THE COMMUNIST PARTY AND THE SCOTTSBORO DEFENSE   236

CHAPTER EIGHT
New-Style Radicalism   239

The Modern Black Civil Rights Movement   240
Brown Power: The Hispanic Protest Movement   252
Red Power: The Native American Protest Movement   262
SUMMARY   269
KEY TERMS   270
REVIEW QUESTIONS   270
NOTES   270
SUGGESTED READINGS   270
CASE STUDY 8.1   MARTIN LUTHER KING, JR., "LETTER FROM A BIRMINGHAM JAIL"   272

CHAPTER NINE
Arenas of the Struggle   281

Education   282
Employment   287
Housing   296
Immigration   300
Law Enforcement   310
Political Participation   314
SUMMARY   321
KEY TERMS   321
REVIEW QUESTIONS   322
NOTES   322
SUGGESTED READINGS   322
CASE STUDY 9.1   AMERICAN DIVERSITY INTO THE TWENTY-FIRST CENTURY   324

Bibliography   327
Photo Credits   339
Index   340

PREFACE

The struggle among ethnic groups is a highly persistent and nearly worldwide phenomenon. Its resurgence in recent years to the forefront of world concerns is evidenced by such recent events as the breakup of the former Yugoslavia, culminating in the tragedy of ethnic cleansing in Bosnia and Kosovo; the civil war in Rwanda, resulting in the genocidal slaughter of thousands of innocent Tutsi civilians and the mass exodus of millions of refugees; the announcement of a cease fire by the Irish Republican Army after three decades of bloody terrorism on both sides of the conflict; and the rapid breakup of the former Soviet Union into various republics, often driven by a sense of ethnic pride and a yearning for national identity and autonomy, as in Chechnya. Turkey has struggled for years with its Kurdish separatist movement, and India with Kashmir rebels seeking independence; Liberia has had a seven-year war with deep ethnic overtones. All these ethnic conflicts have resulted in a cumulative death toll of several millions. One can truly characterize the conflictual relationships between ethnic minority groups and a majority society as a "perennial struggle."

In the United States we see both the persistence and the renewed strength of minority group politics. Continual examples of hate crimes demonstrate that racism is far from over in the United States. Yet the Black and Hispanic Congressional Caucuses have increased in size and have played key roles in molding a critical compromise in recent immigration policy reforms, in the Haitian refugee policy of the Bush and Clinton Administrations, and in recent compromises made in welfare reform, to cite but a few examples of its importance.

The Perennial Struggle is about race and ethnic relations and how they play out in minority group politics in the United States. Understanding these relationships is critical to understanding American politics generally. Understanding these relationships is key to a grasp of American society generally, because of the rich diversity of our racial and ethnic composition. The United States is a *nation of nations;* it receives more immigrants to its shores than does the rest of the world combined.

Some years ago historian Oscar Handlin (1951) wrote a Pulitzer Prize winning book, *The Uprooted.* In it Handlin related that he had started out to write a history of the immigrants to America, but soon discovered that the immigrants *were* American history! To paraphrase his observation, the perennial struggle of minority groups in America is enduring; it displays a richness of styles, methods, and techniques. Ethnic politics can no longer be understood as just the old-style urban political machine.

In the past several decades much has appeared in books, periodicals, newspapers, and the mass media—both television and the cinema—about ethnic groups and their problems. The recent civil rights movements of blacks, Hispanics, Native Americans, the elderly, women, and gay Americans have impressed upon American society an acute awareness of the presence of many minority groups—of their discontent with their status and of their struggle to cope with and overcome, or at least mitigate, the effects of that status.

Early works by social scientists raised expectations of more or less complete assimilation as the processes of industrialization and urbanization reduced the salience of ethnicity. The explosive decades of the 1960s and 1970s laid to rest the myth of the "melting pot" nature of American society. Recent scholarly examinations of ethnic relations have largely rejected such expectations. New studies have demonstrated the richness and complexity of racial and ethnic relations with majority society and have underscored the persistence of those relations and their relevance for political, social, and economic behavior.

As various minority groups developed into interest groups struggling to get "their fair share of the pie," it has become increasingly evident that the perspectives of all the social science disciplines need to be applied to the study of ethnic relations. The perspectives of the anthropologist, the historian, the political scientist, the sociologist, the social psychologist, and the economist all add to our theoretical knowledge of the ethnic question. Integration of these perspectives is essential to better understand the rich complexity of race and ethnic relations—how public policy may limit minority group conflict, and how better to promote a healthy pluralism in our society. Such broader and deeper understanding may help limit minority group conflict, either among minority groups or between them and the majority society.

Many colleges and universities are themselves struggling with issues of diversity. They have integrated the various perspectives of the social science disciplines into courses such as Race and Racism, Roots of American Racism, or Minority Group Politics in the United States. If American society is to avoid the woes of a Bosnia, Kosovo, Northern Ireland, or Rwanda, or even to prevent the development of separatist movements as in French-speaking Canada, we need to better understand the perennial struggle of ethnic relations and its impact on politics and policy. We need to understand the history, contribution, and special problems of minority groups in American society. In short, we need to understand the how and the why of their perennial struggle.

This book, then, has several goals. It uses historical examples to illustrate how the United States came to its rich mixture of minority subcultures, how race and ethnicity interact with class status to form persistent patterns. It applies the insights of the various social sciences to an analysis of racial and ethnic relations to clarify their similarities and differences. It examines social mobility in the United States, developing a systems model of assimilation to view the wide variety of factors that influence the rate, degree, and type of assimilation of various minority groups struggling within our society. It also examines why some groups reject assimilation or are largely excluded from such assimilation by the majority. Using the examples of a rich array of group experiences, it develops a typology of the strategies employed by minority groups to cope with their status—from assimilation to separatism to radicalism. It distinguishes two tactical approaches to each of the strategies employed by minority groups. It examines various public policy areas, describing how policy is used by the majority to channel access and routes of assimilation of the various minority groups. The book also describes how public policy can be used by minority groups to change their role and status in the majority culture, or at least to mitigate some of the vexing problems they face as a result of their minority status. It shows how groups seek to change or use immigration policy to influence the relations of the United States with their countries of origin.

THE STRUCTURE OF THIS BOOK

This book is intended to serve as a core text in such courses as Race and Racism, Ethnic Politics, or Minority Group Politics. Hopefully, it loses none of the richness of insight the various social science perspectives offer to the study of ethnic and racial relations, while integrating those perspectives into a consistent viewpoint that a core textbook can bring to such a rich and complex area of study.

Chapter One concerns the language of race and ethnic relations. It discusses the basic concepts of the struggle between minority and majority groups and provides definitions for all the key terms or concepts used in the study of racial and ethnic relations.

Chapter Two presents various theories about race relations and then develops a typology of strategies that minority groups use in their perennial struggle with majority society. It outlines three major strategies and two tactical approaches to each strategy and presents a systems dynamic model of the assimilation process.

Chapter Three then examines in detail the strategy of economic accommodation. It reviews the experience of many minority groups who have adopted this strategy to cope with their minority status. It looks at national-origin minority groups and subgroups of Hispanic, Asian, and African Americans who adopted economic accommodation in one or another of its tactical approaches as the best method to survive and prosper.

Chapter Four continues the discussion of the strategy of accommodation, focusing on the use of the political route. It discusses Irish Americans, Italian Americans, Greek Americans, Slavic Americans, Jewish Americans, and African Americans and how they used politics to pursue their perennial struggle.

Chapter Five examines the strategy of separatism, with a review of several groups practicing the tactic of physical separatism to isolate themselves from the majority culture. It examines the Amish and Mennonites, the Mormons, Native Americans, and those African Americans who followed Marcus Garvey and his "Back to Africa Movement."

Chapter Six then looks at separatism from the perspective of the psychological tactic to achieve isolation from the majority culture. It examines the Black Muslims and Hasidic Jews and how they used this tactical approach to separatism.

Chapter Seven examines the strategies of old-style radicalism. It covers the "isms" of socialism, communism, fascism, and nazism and shows how these political ideologies sought to enroll minority group members in an effort to radically reform American society, its values, and its politics. It explains how each attempted, with little success, to gain the adherence of racial and ethnic minorities to their ideological and political cause.

Chapter Eight discusses the politics of new-style radicalism—the civil rights movements from W. E. B. DuBois to Dr. Martin Luther King, Jr., from Black Power to Brown and Red Power. It looks at their use of nonviolent protest to drastically alter United States society.

Chapter Nine looks at the use of public policy to place groups into minority status, and how such groups seek to alter public policy to change their status and roles in society. It examines the major arenas of conflict between majority society and minorities: education, employment, immigration, housing, law enforcement, and political participation.

To enhance its educational value as a core textbook for a highly complex and controversial subject area, this book uses various pedagogical devices that enrich the discussion, provide special or extra insight, and make the study and review of the material more "user friendly." Each chapter has a summary, a glossary of the key terms introduced in the chapter, photographs, graphs, figures, and even some cartoons to illustrate and enlighten various topics in each chapter. Review Questions are listed at the end of each chapter to provide a special means of study. Finally, each chapter closes with a list of Suggested Readings and a Case Study. There is an extensive bibliography at the back of the book and both an author and subject index to facilitate the reader's access to the material.

ACKNOWLEDGMENTS

I wish to thank several individuals at Prentice Hall for their assistance with this project. Executive Editor Beth Gillett Mejia, who originally reviewed the manuscript and decided to do the project; Serena Hoffman, the Senior Project Manager for the book; and Mary Louise Byrd, an excellent copy editor whose careful editing of the manuscript improved my efforts considerably. Mirella Signoretto did some fine art work turning my poor hand-drawn illustrations into usable figures.

A debt of gratitude is owed to several readers who improved the manuscript by their suggestions: James Button, University of Florida; N. Hart Nibbrig, George Mason University; Robert C. Smith, San Francisco State University; and Theodore J. Davis, Jr., University of Delaware. Any faults that remain are solely those of the author.

Several colleagues at California State University-San Bernardino read the manuscript and offered helpful suggestions. I wish to thank Professors David Decker, Cecilia Julagay, Mary Texeira, and Elsa Valdez in the department of sociology. I wish to thank the CSUSB Foundation for its support of a sabbatical leave that enabled me to complete the manuscript. Two students who deserve special thanks are Stephanie Fairman, who drew the cartoons, and Kevin Grisham, who researched some of the photographs via the Internet. The departmental secretary, Mrs. Debbi Fox, was helpful in many ways as always. I would especially like to thank the many students in my Race and Racism class with whom I classroom-tested much of this material. Finally, special thanks to Carey Van Loon, in Instructional Media and Graphics, who helped me to produce Figures 2.1 and 2.2.

Michael C. LeMay

CHAPTER ONE

THE LANGUAGE OF THE STRUGGLE
The Basic Concepts
of Majority/Minority Relations

When embarking on any field of study, a fundamental task with which one must begin is the development and refinement of the key concepts to be used. This task is all the more problematic and important when the key concepts are emotionally charged and when common vernacular and scholarly discussion use different definitions of those key concepts. In a diverse society such as the United States, we are all members of either a majority or minority group, and that affiliation shapes the emotionally charged attitudes we have toward the basic concepts central to this book—concepts such as majority and minority group, ethnicity, prejudice, stereotyping, discrimination, racism, assimilation, and pluralism, to name but a few. A common understanding of each basic concept and analytical distinctions about the manner in which it is used is essential to grasp subjects as complex and rich as racial and ethnic relations and minority group politics in the United States.

A clear focus on these basic concepts is necessary to understand American politics because much of the practical political behavior of the American system reflects prejudice and discrimination and minority groups' reactions to them. As well, a great deal of American political behavior reflects the majority's attempts to deal with the presence of so many and varied groups.

WE/THEY AND GROUP IDENTITY

In 1963, sociologist Peter Rose first published his ground-breaking book on race relations entitled *They and We*. Now in its fourth edition, Rose's book explicates the concept of *ethnocentrism* (the belief that one's own group is unique and right), wherein a people exaggerate and intensify everything in their own folkways that is peculiar to them and that sets them apart from others. He quotes a Rudyard Kipling verse that captures the essence of such ethnocentric thinking:

1

> All good people agree,
> And all good people say,
> All nice people like Us, are We
> And everyone else is They.

Individuals within any group vary in the extent to which they identify with that group. For some members, and for certain types of groups, belonging to the group becomes central to their own identity. For others, their social and patterned behavior and most of their internalized norms and values are deeply dependent upon the group. Still others may be but tangentially involved with a group, and internalize that connection only weakly.

Joseph Fichter (1954) developed a typology for his study of members of a parish that can be usefully adapted to almost any minority group. It helps us to understand the individual's relation both to the group and its members (the "we") and to those outside the group (the "they"). Fichter's distinctions help us grasp the dynamics of intergroup relations and why some groups vary in the degree of intensity of their members' group-relatedness. This, in turn, helps us to understand the rate at which members of a group shed a sense of "we-ness" and merge into a group of "theys."

Fichter categorizes four types of persons in terms of their group-relatedness: nuclear, modal, marginal, and dormant. A *nuclear member* of a group is one whose self-identity is totally involved in the group. Such an individual exhibits all the norms, values, and physical or cultural traits associated with that group. For the sake of an example, if we applied this concept to a national-origins group, say, Italian Americans, our nuclear member might be a 72-year-old Italian grandmother who immigrated to the United States at age 16. Though widowed for many years now, she still dresses in all black every day. She attends mass daily, praying the rosary often. She speaks Italian almost exclusively, her English being very broken and with a heavy Italian accent. She lives in an Italian-American neighborhood, say, in South Boston, above a little Italian delicatessen that she and her late husband operated for some 30 years. All of her friends are Italian American. Her social life revolves totally around her parish and her family. Her married children still come over virtually every Sunday for a big family meal. She eats Italian food three times a day, every day. One could pick her up and deposit her into some village in Italy and she would hardly notice except for the absence of her family and friends. She is, in short, more Italian than American.

The *modal type* is one who accepts most of the norms and values of the group and who manifests nearly all of the physical or cultural traits of the group. For our hypothetical case, it might be the 55-year-old son of the Italian grandmother. He speaks Italian fluently, but having been born in the United States, he also speaks English as a native language and with no accent. He married an Italian-American woman from the neighborhood, a childhood sweetheart. He owns and operates an Italian-American restaurant, where he and his wife and several of his nine children and other relatives all work. He is a practicing Catholic, attending mass on Sunday and all holy days. He eats Italian-style food at least once a day. His social life, too, revolves largely around his family and friends, except for two close non-Italian-American buddies with whom he served in the U.S. army and who have remained close ever since. His clothing and physical features are such that even a total stranger seeing him would likely guess him to be an Italian American. You could pick him up and drop him in Italy and he would survive and adjust fairly well. He is, in short, very "*Italian* American." He thinks of himself in precisely those terms.

The *marginal type* manifests only a few traits and internalizes only some of the norms and values of the group. Such a person might be the 30-year-old grandson of our Italian immigrant. He has left home and the neighborhood to attend a university, majoring in business administration. He recently joined a major corporation as an assistant personnel manager and is working at a branch office located in a small midwestern town that has few Italian Americans. He married a non-Catholic and non-Italian woman (of Norwegian American background). He no longer practices Catholicism regularly, attending church only a few times a year (at Christmas and Easter and for weddings and funerals). He occasionally attends his wife's Lutheran church services. But when he does, he harbors guilty feelings about that fact. He speaks a little Italian with a heavy American accent. He reads the language poorly, and now that he has so little chance to use it, he is fast becoming rusty in Italian. His new wife cannot cook very well, and certainly cannot cook traditional Italian dishes. He eats Italian food only occasionally, when out at a restaurant or when visiting his family in Boston. He dresses like all the other rising young executives of the company. A stranger meeting him might guess him to be of Italian American heritage, judging from his features, but not necessarily so. In order to rise more readily in the corporation, he legally changed his name from Antonio Marcconi to Tony Marks. If asked to do so, he describes himself as "an American of Italian descent."

Tony's daughter, who will grow up with a non-Italian-sounding name and acquire yet another name upon marriage, and who will be raised in a non-Italian environment, exemplifies the *dormant type*. She exhibits few if any of the physical characteristics typical of the group and internalizes in a latent manner only some of the norms and values of the group. By adulthood, she will be a person who will speak about as much Italian as the typical American, that is, only a few words picked up from the popular culture. She will not practice Catholicism and will rarely attend the service of any denomination. She also will marry a non-Catholic, let us say of German-American heritage. She can neither read, write, speak, nor really understand Italian. She knows, of course, that her grandparents on her father's side are Italian Americans and that her paternal great-grandmother was an immigrant from Italy. She loves her grandparents dearly, even though she only met them on a few occasions for a week or so when she was younger and went on family vacations to visit her father's family back east. She has some emotional ties, as a result, however, and they are strong if largely subconscious. Given the right stimulus, they do surface. She does, for example, react strongly to any "dumb Italian" or "cowardly Italian" jokes. If asked to do so, she would describe herself as "an American of Norwegian and Italian descent."

Although these examples employ a generational gap to illustrate the differing degrees or types of group-relatedness, the reader should understand that such a time continuum is not essential. A person could be an immigrant stepping off the ship and be, psychologically speaking, a marginal type. The type of group-relatedness depends on a person's internalized self-identity with the relevant group. A third-generation

Greek American might behave as a modal or a nuclear type. Religious groups often provide good examples of this effect. Adult converts to a religious denomination often behave in a more modal or even nuclear way than one born and raised in a given denomination.

Majority Group

For our purposes here, the **majority group** in any society is defined as one that is superordinate in a superordinate/subordinate relationship. It need not be a numerical majority; it simply must have sufficient power to determine the values and norms of society to set public policy. Such a group, by definition, is the "discriminator" rather than the subject of discrimination.

In American society, that group is the WASP—the White/Anglo-Saxon/Protestant majority. They emerged out of the colonial era as the dominant group along the Atlantic seaboard as the "host" or "native" group of the United States. They replaced the Native American and surpassed in influence all other West European immigrant groups. English language and customs, and their ideas regarding commerce, law, government, and religion came to predominate. By 1815, Anglo conformity had become dominant and unchallenged.

The emergence of Anglo conformity came during a time when intellectual credence, based on biblical and pseudo-scientific support, was increasingly given to the concept of *white supremacy*—that is, to the belief that the military and economic success of the whites were the result of biologically inherited differences among racial groups. Anglo conformity held that the more nearly a person approximated the Anglo-American model, the more nearly "American" that person was judged to be. Immigrant groups were seen as more or less desirable according to how closely they resembled the Anglo-American pattern, how rapidly they departed from their own cultural patterns, and how successfully they became socially invisible within the newly emerging WASP-American society.

Any group that was either unwilling or unable to fit into the developing American majority pattern was viewed as a "problem" group. Either a group's clannish refusal to accept the "superior" ways of life of the majority, or its possession of some undesirable physical trait that made it difficult or impossible to become "WASP-like," was sufficient to brand such a group in some way deficient, and the group was subjected to discrimination.

Minority Group

Common usage of language emphasizes the numerical aspect of minority. Webster defines minority, for instance, as "the smaller in number of two groups constituting the whole," or "a group having less than the number of votes necessary for control." Here, minority is a political concept referring to a *power relationship*. It is a group on the subordinate end of a superordinate/subordinate relationship, viewed as differing from others in some characteristic and subjected to differential treatment. Thus, until 1994, the blacks of South Africa were the minority even though they made up roughly

80 percent of the population. Women are a minority in the United States, although they constitute just over 52 percent of the population.

The concept of minority is a power status concept. Relationships between dominant and minority groups are not determined by numbers but rather by the distribution of power. The minority's presence in a society implies the existence of a corresponding dominant group with higher social status and greater privileges. The minority is excluded from full participation in the life of society. **Minority groups** may be described as subordinate groups in a social/political hierarchy with inferior power and less secure access to resources than has the majority (Kottak and Kozaitis 1999).

Self-image is an important distinction in understanding American minority group politics since many "groups" did not become such with a self-conscious group identity until they arrived in the United States and found themselves being treated differentially. The Irish immigrant arriving in 1848 from Dublin, for example, likely thought of himself as a "Dubliner." After being treated in the United States in an unequal manner, being refused jobs on the basis of "No Irish Need Apply" signs, the immigrant began to think of himself as an "Irishman" or as "Irish American." His group identity was in response to the discriminatory treatment.

Thus, the majority "creates" the minority group *as a group* by seeing all persons evidencing a certain characteristic as being "different" from them and subjecting that person to negative differential treatment on the basis of that perceived difference. What characteristic is singled out as constituting a significant "difference" varies from society to society and even from time to time or place to place within a society. In the United States there have been various characteristics upon which minority status has been based.

The concept of group is not a simple one. When does a collection of individuals constitute a group? A *group* consists of persons of varying status whose behavior is determined by the expectations of its members. As long as all individuals follow the expected pattern of behavior, the group is at equilibrium. If individuals are forced or allowed to deviate from their accustomed pattern, equilibrium is destroyed, and the group no longer exists as a group.

We can distinguish various types of groups. **Ethnic groups** are *primary groups,* those characterized by intimate face-to-face association and cooperation. A primary group involves a mutual identification for which "we" is the natural expression. The very essence of a primary group is that sense of "we-ness" that develops among its members.

Groups may be seen from an internal versus external perspective. The external tradition is more commonly employed by sociologists. This perspective views groups as a whole and stresses the relationship to other groups in society. But we can also view groups, as does Gordon Allport (1958), from an internal perspective. Groups are assemblages of individuals. This view stresses factors of solidarity and anomie; the pressures and positive or negative rewards that induce individuals to comply with the group's wishes, to form social relationships that strengthen group solidarity. The forces of anomie are those factors that induce individuals to avoid social contact and to behave independently of one another. Groups are collections of people with significantly interdependent relations.

Ethnicity

Minority status in the United States is based on many characteristics. The two primary bases for such status in the United States have been *race* and *ethnicity*. The distinction between the two is important because the differing base for minority status affects the manner in which a group copes with the resulting problems. It also affects the manner in which the majority will accept or reject a group, and the way the majority society channels the options open to that minority group. It affects the methods and tactics used by a minority group in coping with its status. Race is institutionalized and structured in ways that public policy creates patterns of racial distinction in politics and society. The institutional structure of the welfare state played a central role in transforming the racial structure of American politics and society (Lieberman 1999: 7).

Members of an ethnic group show cultural similarities and differences from other groups that foster a sense of peoplehood. Such groups may be viewed by their members and/or outsiders as religious, racial, national, linguistic, and/or geographic. Ethnic group members have in common their **ethnicity**, or sense of peoplehood, which represents a part of their collective experience. As Rose notes: "In a society made up of many cultural groups, like the United States, the intensity of ethnic identity or ethnicity is apt to be determined by the attitude of the members of the 'host' society toward the 'strangers' in their midst" (p. 7).

If the majority society is tolerant of an ethnic group, that acceptance may loosen the bonds of ethnic identity, as in the case of the Scottish and German immigrants to America. By contrast, rejection and subordination strengthen those bonds.

Ethnic minority groups develop a sense of "symbolic ethnicity." That is, they use the symbols of their ethnic group—eating certain foods, observing certain ceremonial holidays, supporting specific political issues confronting the old country—as cultural

Max Weber (1864–1920).

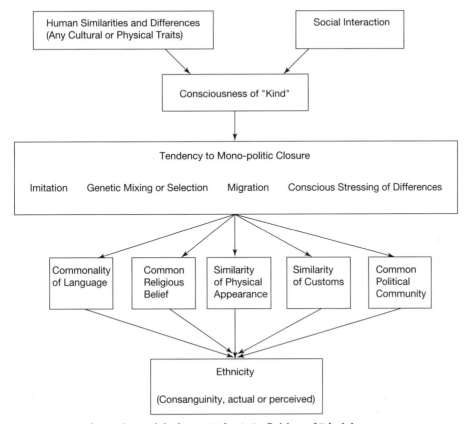

FIGURE 1.1 A Schematic Model of Max Weber's Definition of Ethnicity

SOURCE: Adapted from Howard Bahr and Bruce Chadwick, *American Ethnicity* (Lexington, MA: D.C. Heath, 1979), p. 5.

markers that show outsiders as well as their fellow ethnics that they belong. These characteristics are often *ascribed,* that is, acquired at birth. These perceptions of the concept of ethnicity are summarized in Figure 1.1, a schematic model of Max Weber's concept of the origins of ethnicity or sense of peoplehood.

Race

Race refers to the differential concentrations of gene frequencies for certain traits that, so far as we know, are confined to physical manifestations such as skin color, hair texture, and facial features. Race is a socially constructed concept. It has no intrinsic connection with cultural patterns or institutions (Gordon 1964: 27). **Racism** refers to an ideology that considers the unchangeable physical characteristics of a group to be linked in a direct, causal way, to their psychological and intellectual functioning, and on that basis, distinguishes between superior and inferior races.

When racism permeates a society, it may result in *institutionalized racism*, in which society's norms and values so reflect the racism of the majority society that *racial stratification*—the system of distributing social rewards on the basis of racial discrimination—occurs. In its extreme form, such structurally institutionalized racism may establish a racial caste system.

Racial Minority Groups

Racial groups are a subcategory of ethnic groups in that racial identity can be and usually is a basis for "commonly shared cultural traditions," or a sense of "peoplehood." Yet a distinction between ethnic and racial groups is analytically useful since racial groups often experience special barriers. Pierre Van den Berghe provides a social definition of a racial group:

> A human group that defines itself and/or is defined by other groups as different from other groups by virtue of innate and immutable physical characteristics. These physical characteristics are in turn believed (by the racist society) to be intrinsically related to moral, intellectual, and other non-physical attributes or abilities. (1967: 5)

Table 1.1 lists the various racial and ethnic groups found in the United States in rank order of their declared ancestry and by their percentage of the total population.

TABLE 1.1   Rank Order of Persons by Claimed Ancestry, 1990

Ancestry Claimed	1990 Population	Percentage of Total Population	Ancestry Claimed	1990 Population	Percentage of Total Population
German	57,986,000	23.3%	Greek	1,110,000	0.4%
Irish	38,740,000	15.6	Swiss	1,045,000	0.4
English	32,556,000	13.1	Austrian	871,000	0.4
Italian	14,715,000	5.9	Japanese	847,562	0.3
French	10,321,000	4.1	Indian	815,447	0.3
Polish	9,266,000	3.8	Lithuanian	812,000	0.3
Dutch	6,227,000	2.5	Korean	798,849	0.3
Scottish	5,394,000	2.2	Ukrainian	741,000	0.3
Swedish	4,681,000	1.9	Finnish	659,000	0.3
Norwegian	3,869,000	1.6	Vietnamese	614,000	0.2
Russian	2,953,000	1.2	Canadian	561,000	0.2
French Canadian	2,167,000	0.9	Hawaiian	211,014	0.1
Welsh	2,034,000	0.8	Laotian	149,014	0.1
Slovak	1,883,000	0.8	Cambodian	147,411	0.1
Chinese	1,645,000	0.7	Thai	91,275	0.0*
Danish	1,635,000	0.7	Hmong	90,082	0.0*
Czech	1,615,000	0.6	Samoan	62,964	0.0*
Hungarian	1,582,000	0.6	Guamanian	49,345	0.0*
Filipino	1,406,770	0.6	Tongan	17,606	0.0*
Portuguese	1,153,000	0.5			

*Less than one-tenth of a percent.

SOURCE: U.S. Bureau of the Census, *1990 Census of Population, Social and Economic Characteristics, United States* (Washington, DC: U.S. Government Printing Office, 1991), p. 12.

Prejudice

In everyday usage, prejudice and discrimination are often treated as if they were synonymous. Such usage obscures some very important distinctions having significant impact upon public policy that help us toward a clearer understanding of general political behavior.

Gordon Allport, in his classic *The Nature of Prejudice*, defines prejudice simply as "an antipathy based upon faulty generalizations" (1958: 10). Rose defines it as "a system of negative beliefs, feelings, and action-orientations regarding a group of people" (1990: 86). As Rose notes, that definition involves the three major dimensions of all attitude systems: the cognitive (beliefs), the affective (feelings), and the connotative (predisposition to act in particular ways, or policy orientations).

Prejudice is best understood as a mind-set whereby the individual or group accepts as valid the negative social definitions that the majority society forms in reference to some minority group and is predisposed to apply those negative social definitions to all individuals who are perceived of as belonging to that group simply on that basis. Prejudice is a highly emotionally charged attitude toward an outgroup (that is, majority members may be prejudiced against minority members, and vice versa). It is directed in negative and stereotypical terms based upon a social definition of the group. A person is hated, feared, shunned, and avoided merely because that person is seen, not as an individual to be judged on his or her own merits, but rather as a member of that outgroup.

Stereotypes differ from rational generalizations in that they are oversimplistic and overexaggerated beliefs about a group, most often acquired secondhand. These images are highly resistant to change. Today, for example, Arabs, a minority in the United States, are often subjected to negative stereotyping. Arab-American stereotypes include their being "all fabulously wealthy," "barbaric and uncultured," "sex maniacs with a penchant for white slavery," and that they "revel in acts of terrorism" (Shaheen 1984).

An individual often learns or acquires prejudicial attitudes at a preconscious or subconscious level. He or she has virtually no control over such attitudes. They are deeply ingrained or internalized and often connected with very primary feelings or emotions. Given a certain stimulus, an individual will unconsciously or almost automatically react in a given—that is, a prejudicial—way. The attitude may not be overtly manifested. One may be prejudiced but not discriminate.

Prejudice can become so widely accepted that it begins to underlie the values and norms of a society. Prejudice becomes structured or *institutionalized*. Prejudicial values become structured to the detriment of some for the benefit of others. Blacks may be forbidden from joining certain labor unions, which cuts off their access to certain occupations. This may benefit the employers of blacks by holding down pay scales for the jobs they are allowed to enter and ensures the majority society of a large pool of cheap labor. It benefits whites by allowing them to hold disproportionately the more desirable occupations. A racist society is one that has prejudicial attitudes permeating the norms and values of that society. Prejudice will be manifested in behavior, since the societal values determine the norms of behavior of individuals within that society.

Many early studies of prejudice tried to find a simple, single-factor explanation of it.[1] That focus shifted when it became increasingly clear that groups differ in the degree and direction of the prejudice they exhibit, and that the target groups of prejudice may shift over time and/or place within a society. Harry Kitano (1997) stresses four categories of how prejudice develops: exploitation, ignorance, racism/ethnocentrism, and symbolism.

- *Exploitation* involves theories wherein one group dominates another sexually, economically, and socially. The "inferior" group must be kept in its place so that the "superior" group members can enjoy advantages of better employment, social status, and life styles. For instance, through subtle or even overt means, a particular group may be forced to take certain jobs to ensure employers among the dominant group of a large pool of cheap labor, or so that there will be a group of individuals who will perform necessary but socially undesirable tasks. A classic example of such an explanation is Marxian theory.

- *Ignorance* is often viewed as a simple explanation for prejudice.[2] Lack of information and knowledge leads to *stereotyping:* "an overgeneralization associated with a racial or ethnic category that goes beyond existing evidence" (Feagin and Feagin 1996: 10). Stereotyped images, in turn, are projected through the mass media and permeate the popular culture of the society. The process of *selective perception* often works to reinforce such stereotyping by validating the attitudes. A group may be labeled "overly avaricious," always concerned with making a buck. If a member of a minority seems to fit the stereotyped image (and the society often generates pressures upon individuals of the minority inducing them to behave in ways that fit that very image), then the majority group member sees evidence to confirm the stereotype. If the minority group member's behavior does not fit the image, such behavior is explained away as an exception, which does nothing to upset the basic prejudice.

- *Ethnocentrism,* or the belief that one's own group is unique and right, is viewed as being almost universal.[3] This concept is used to explain prejudice as a weapon in intergroup conflict. Ethnocentrism serves the group in power. A racist society, for example, develops an ideology of white supremacy based upon a biblical and/or "scientific" theory that justifies the white supremacy and the institution of slavery.

- *Symbolic* explanations view prejudice as a by-product stemming from other concerns.[4] Freudian theory, for example, views all behavior as psychically determined. Prejudice is seen as a symptom reflecting a deeper, intrapsychic phenomenon. Social-psychological theory, following this perspective, emphasizes frustration and aggression as critical variables behind prejudice. Frustrated individuals feel hostility. Often they are blocked in directing that hostility toward the true source of that frustration and deal with hostility by directing it toward a convenient target—a *scapegoat.* Minority groups, because of their relative powerlessness in society, become convenient scapegoats. In czarist Russia, for example, peasants could not take out their aggression against the nobility who exploited them, so in frustration they turned their aggression against the Jews.

The sociological perspective emphasizes the link between change and prejudice.[5] The more static the society, the less its prejudice; the more diverse and changing the society, the greater its prejudice. In this view, prejudice is an attempt to conserve the existing social order. Anti-Semitism or antiblack prejudice would rise in the United States during periods of economic turmoil, such as severe recessions or depressions, or during periods of rapid social change brought on, for instance, by the nation's involvement in a war. This perspective views prejudice as a "social problem."

This view focuses on the linkage between attitude and behavior. Prejudiced attitudes do not predetermine prejudicial behavior. An individual's behavior may be determined more by the social situation at any particular time than by that person's preexisting mind-set. Both attitude and behavior are highly susceptible to situational change.

The sociological perspective places a new focus on how prejudice (as a person's attitudinal set) is learned. In this view, prejudicial behavior (an act of discrimination) shapes and alters prejudice as a mind-set. The learning of prejudice is affected by social situations. The complex prejudicial practices within a community provide the family and similar traditional and peer groups with the frame of reference that perpetuates such practices and sustains or even extends prejudice. Jim Crow laws in the South, for instance, were viewed as being a necessary underpinning of societal norms designed to enforce the continuation of the existing social order by which the white elite ruled. If a society wishes to change or reduce the degree of prejudice, it must begin by changing such institutional bases of prejudice. Such a society must begin by repealing its Jim Crow laws.

But precisely how a society might employ public policy in an attempt to reduce or mitigate prejudice is shaped by its perceptions of prejudice. The "cure" is designed to fit the perceived "illness." If one believes prejudice is caused by ignorance, then public policy would involve various forms of education designed to alleviate that ignorance. If one accepts prejudice as being caused by exploitation, a far different set of policy options is suggested: affirmative action programs or some set of quotas to end systematized occupational prejudice. If prejudice is viewed as some sort of psychological disorder, the result of flawed personality development producing people who need scapegoats or who have authoritarian personality types and are susceptible to a rigid dogmatism, then policy enacting health care programs designed to "prevent" their development would be advocated.

These varied sources of prejudice are summarized in Figure 1.2. This framework views the combination of societal, psychological, and economic factors as determining social background factors that shape the level and focus of the resulting prejudice.

Discrimination

Discrimination is analytically distinct from prejudice. A person can have a prejudiced attitude without exhibiting overt discriminatory behavior. Likewise, a person, given a certain social milieu, may routinely behave in a discriminatory manner even if he or she does not possess the relevant prejudicial attitude. **Discrimination** is defined as applied prejudice. Negative social attitudes are translated into action. Public policy enforces the subordination of a minority's political, social, and economic rights.

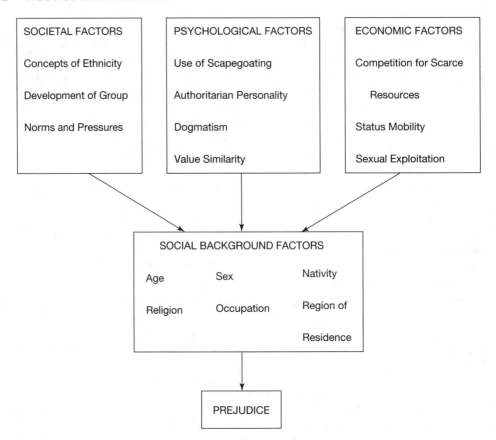

FIGURE 1.2 The Sources of Prejudice

SOURCE: Adapted from Howard Bahr and Bruce Chadwick, *American Ethnicity* (Lexington, MA: D.C. Heath, 1979), p 25.

Kitano distinguishes various types of racist behavior as overt, aversive, and institutional. In a more elaborate scheme, Robert Merton (1949) describes the relationship between prejudice and discrimination in a paradigm that involves four types of persons and their typical response patterns. Merton's typology is summarized in Box 1.1.

While both majority and minority group members can and often do develop prejudice, usually only the majority group member is able to translate prejudice into action, to discriminate, since only majority group members have the power to determine the norms of acceptable behavior. Discrimination connotes the *institutionalization* of expressions of prejudicial attitudes in order to socially control a minority group. Employers in a society who are of the dominant group may develop the practice of a "glass ceiling"—a barrier that blocks the promotion of a qualified worker in a multiracial work environment.

BOX 1.1: Merton's Typology of Prejudice and Discrimination

THE UNPREJUDICED NONDISCRIMINATOR

Merton calls them "all-weather liberals." They are persons who do not have individual prejudice, nor are they willing to behave in a discriminatory manner because of societal norms or pressure. They believe in the American creed of freedom and equality for all and practice it fully. They are vigorous champions of the underdog, take the Golden Rule quite literally, and cherish American egalitarian values.

UNPREJUDICED DISCRIMINATORS

Merton calls them "fair-weather liberals." They are persons who do not have prejudiced attitudes, but give in to social pressures and discriminate, often without thinking of it or being consciously aware of the discriminatory behavior they are manifesting. An example would be the home-owners of the urban North who deny having any personal feelings versus blacks, yet steadfastly try to keep them out of their neighborhoods for fear of altering the character of those neighborhoods. More pragmatic than the "all-weather liberals," they discriminate when such behavior is socially called for, seems to be appropriate, or is in their own self-interest. Merton suggests that the "fair weather liberals" are often the victim of guilt because of the discrepancy between their personal beliefs and their actual conduct. They are especially amenable to the pressure of the liberal.

PREJUDICED NONDISCRIMINATORS

Merton calls this type a "fair-weather illiberal," or a sort of timid bigot. Many people of prejudice are not activists. They feel hostility toward members of an outgroup and they subscribe to conventional stereotypes of others, but they, too, react to the social situation. If the situation, by law or custom, forbids open discrimination, they comply. They would serve black customers, sit next to them on public transportation, send their children to integrated schools, and yet complain about the system that compels them to do so. The "fair-weather illiberal" does not accept the moral legitimacy of the creed. He conforms if he must, and will fail to conform when the pressure to do so is removed.

PREJUDICED DISCRIMINATOR

Merton calls this type the "all-weather illiberal." He or she is the active bigot, the "redneck" or Archie Bunker type of bigot who manifests prejudice in discriminatory behavior almost instinctively and consistently. He or she is the overt racist. "All-weather illiberals" neither believe in the American creed nor act in accordance with its principles. Like the "all-weather liberal," the prejudiced discriminator conforms to a set of standards, but in this case those standards proclaim the right, even the duty, to discriminate. He or she does not refrain from expressing prejudiced attitudes and is willing to defy the law, if need be, in order to protect his or her beliefs and vested self-interests.

Discrimination is typically manifested in several ways. The majority will try to control the numbers of the minority group to better ensure their remaining powerless. It is manifested economically by barring minority members from unions or professional associations or by otherwise excluding them from certain occupations. This is accomplished by making minorities the last hired and first fired among those occupations they do manage to enter. Discrimination is shown in education, demonstrated in a reluctance to educate "inferiors," or by providing them with inferior education. Discrimination is seen in restrictions on political participation by using devices such as the white primary, the grandfather clause, the literacy test, the poll tax, or by unequal application of registration requirements or in the gerrymandering of electoral districts. Social discrimination is seen in limiting the minority's access to hotels, restaurants,

---

BOX 1.2:   Defamation Behavior: Ethnophaulisms and Ethnic Jokes

---

Ethnophaulisms: All racial and ethnic groups use them. The greater the number used against a group, the greater the prejudice. Ethnophaulisms seem to be important, if not essential, to the spread of ethnocentrism. Examples of such would be to refer to blacks as "jigaboo," "nigger," "nap-head," and the like; or to refer to Jews as "hebe" or "kike"; or to refer to Puerto Ricans as "spics," Polish-Americans as "Polacks," and the like.

Ethnic humor is typically based on some exaggerated, stereotyped trait that negatively characterizes entire groups. The "dumb Polack" joke, for example, as in: "Did you hear about the Polack who bought a snow tire? It melted before he got home!" Or the cowardly Italian joke, such as: "What is the shortest book in print? Great Italian War Heroes."

---

public transportation, and other public facilities. Parks, pools, libraries, and even churches may be closed to them. Intermarriage is at least socially isolated and often legally proscribed. The Jim Crow laws of the South sought to segregate African Americans in all areas of life. Ghettoization of blacks and Jews and forcing Native Americans to live on reservations exemplify the use of public policy to enforce geographic segregation to isolate a minority.

A common manifestation of prejudice is the use of *defamation* or *derogation*,[6] directed at the outgroup members. Such derogation involves the use of **ethnophaulisms**, defamatory terms used by members of one ethnic group to refer to members of others (Rose 1990). Ethnic humor, based on negative stereotypes, is another such practice. Box 1.2 gives examples of these types of derogatory behavior.

Segregation

We may define **segregation** as the act of separating and isolating members of a racial or ethnic minority group from members of the majority society. Such isolating may be done more or less formally; that is, by custom or by law. *De facto segregation* is based on fact or social customs rather than by law (which is *de jure segregation*), resulting from more subtle processes. An example is *gerrymandering,* the drawing of electoral district lines in such a way that a social group is disadvantaged. This might be done to ensure that a school district, for example, is racially homogeneous (all white, all black, etc.). It might be done to split or dilute the votes of a racial group so they will be less able to elect one of their own to public office. Housing segregation, another example, is often maintained through such devices as redlining districts by mortgage lenders, or by real estate practices resulting in buying, selling, or renting housing in segregated patterns. Since public education is often based on the principle of the neighborhood school, de facto segregation in housing effectively segregates public schools as well.

Segregation may involve the separation of public facilities, such as drinking fountains, waiting rooms, and rest rooms, as done by Jim Crow laws. They were designed to isolate the majority member from contact with the despised minority group member in as many points of contact as was possible. More institutionalized segregation is exemplified in urban housing programs in which racial groups are ghettoized. Segregation may be so extensive that it involves the complete geographic separation of a racial or ethnic group, for example, the reservations for Native Americans and the use of concentration camps for Japanese Americans during World War II. Segregation is but one of the more blatant aspects of social stratification, an elaborate system that structurally institutionalizes racial and ethnic segregation.

Social Stratification

Social inequality involves the distribution of "rewards, goods and services, benefits and privileges, honor and esteem, or power and influence available to the incumbents of the different social roles and positions and associated with different roles and positions" (Matras 1975: 11–12). **Social stratification** refers to the methods and procedures used to assign individuals and groups to different roles and positions. Most societies exhibit inequalities in honor, status, or prestige; in economic influence and material rewards; and in access to military, political, and bureaucratic power. This structural ranking perpetuates unequal rewards and power in a society. Such inequalities may lead to the establishment of strata or social classes—that is, division of whole societies or communities within societies—that represent the division of a combination of such rewards. When such class divisions are organized along racial or ethnic lines, a society reflects ethnic stratification found among *all* multiethnic societies.

Sociologists who study stratification often place societies along a continuum from caste systems to class systems. A *caste system* has two or more rigidly defined and unequal groups in which membership is passed from generation to generation. Where one is born totally dictates the lifestyle and opportunities of the individual throughout his or her life. In a *class system,* inequality of status is not determined solely by birth. A class system allows for some degree of *achieved status,* where one gains in status through one's own actions. Both caste and class systems are ideal types. In the real world, most societies fall within that continuum and may change their position along it over time. Sociologist William Wilson (1987) has popularized the concept of *underclass*—the long-term poor who lack the training and skills to function well in the modern postindustrial society.

Functional sociologists view a manageable amount of ethnic stratification as functional.[7] They see society as needing a consensus and shared identity or "we-ness" to encourage cooperation within society among members who share certain basic values and a shared sense of identity. They see ethnocentrism as a natural tendency within society. They recognize, however, that while functionally necessary, such ethnocentrism can cause conflict and often lead to ethnic stratification.

Ethnic stratification is a problem that ought to be minimized, even if it is somewhat inevitable. Joe Feagin (1996) distinguishes four basic types of discriminatory practices within societies evidencing ethnic stratification: isolate discrimination, small-group discrimination, direct institutionalized discrimination, and indirect institutionalized discrimination.

1. *Isolate discrimination* is harmful action taken with intent by a member of the dominant group against a member of a subordinate racial or ethnic group. Such discrimination is not socially embedded in a larger organization or community setting. A young person who goes out "gay-bashing" and intentionally beats up some person he believes to be homosexual would illustrate this type.

2. *Small-group discrimination* is harmful action taken by a small number of dominant group members acting together against members of a racial or ethnic minority group, without the support of the norms or rules of the larger society. The Aryan Nation and skin-heads terrorizing blacks and bombing black churches, for instance, illustrate this type.

3. *Direct institutionalized discrimination* refers to organizationally prescribed action that by intent has a negative differential impact on members of a racial or ethnic minority group. Discrimination by real estate agencies to create the ethnic ghetto is an example of this type.

4. *Indirect institutionalized discrimination* consists of practices having negative differential impact on members of minority groups even though they are carried out with no intent to harm members of those groups. An example of this type would be nonwhite workers suffering from seniority practices even though the seniority system was not originally set up to harm them.

MINORITY STATUS

A variety of characteristics may be singled out by a society as being "significantly different" from the dominant group's self-image to provide a reason for placing a group or groups in minority status. These bases vary from society to society and from time to time or place to place within a society.

One of the leading theorists of ethnic relations, Richard A. Schermerhorn (1970), has argued persuasively that *how* a minority becomes such is critically important to our understanding of resulting factors, such as the degree to which pressure is applied against them, the avenues opened or closed to them, and their resources to deal with their minority status. He distinguishes five inter-group sequences. First is the emergence of pariahs, such as the untouchables in India or the Eta in Japan. Then there is the emergence of indigenous isolates, exemplified by certain tribes in Africa who follow traditional lifestyles while the dominant elite, usually from another tribe, moves the rest of the nation toward modernization. A third sequence results from annexation, through military conquest or by economic means such as treaty purchase. A fourth is by migration in some manner, either forced migration such as slave transfer, the movement of forced labor, contract labor, or the displacement of persons, or by voluntary migration. A fifth sequence is that of colonization.

In the United States minority status has been based on national origin, religion, race, gender, sexual preference, age, and physical disability. It is important to remember that prejudice may be cumulative, stronger against persons exhibiting two or more characteristics upon which such status is based. The severity of prejudice and discrimination against a group greatly influences the ways in which a minority copes with its status. It has implications for political behavior by both the dominant and the subordinate groups.

Political Implications

The presence of so many and varied minority groups in American society profoundly impacts their political behavior. Ultimately, this entire book is devoted to those implications. We highlight a few here that will be discussed more fully in later chapters.

The need to absorb so many millions of persons of various subcultures and to deal with "other-group loyalties" has a significant impact on the majority culture. Elite groups in the majority have attempted to shape public policy in ways that directly respond to the influx of minority groups. The majority is often split into factions depending on how differing viewpoints about the best policy for dealing with the "problem minority group" affects them. Some, such as the Know Nothing Party, respond with nativist reactions, advocating restrictionist immigration policy. Others, such as the Ku Klux Klan, attempt to totally isolate by violence and severe social segregation despised groups like blacks, Catholics, and Jews. Other elite factions react in just the opposite way. They may reach out to minority groups, advocating an "open-door" immigration policy and lobbying to spend public monies to recruit immigrants to the United States. This elite faction is often mixed in its pro-minority stance, actively seeking some "desired" minority group while being less than enthusiastic about certain religious or racial groups.[8]

The latter faction of the dominant society has been among the economic elite and the more politically powerful. Their views prevailed in public policy. Sometimes they have pursued economic policy through nonpublic institutions of the majority society, such as railroads, steamship lines, or corporations that hired immigrant agents. They favored the large supply of cheap labor afforded by an open-door immigration policy. Others have acted through public policy, especially the leaders of several political parties. The Republican and Democratic political parties emerged as the dominant parties in the two-party system of the United States precisely because they did reach out to immigrants, building their parties as vast coalitions of various voting blocs.

Minority groups, too, were greatly influenced in their political behavior by their status, and continue to be so even today. Most groups exhibit at least an initial period of relatively low political participation. The length of time for an initial phase varies. In general, nationality groups become politically active to a higher degree and more quickly than do religious or racial groups. The minority's reaction is in large measure influenced by the majority's stance toward them. A period of relative inaction is typically followed by a stage in which they use politics very consciously to seek social and economic gains or to reduce the effects of discrimination.

Political party identification often becomes linked with ethnic loyalties, producing persistent patterns of voting behavior. Nationality groups tend to develop this linkage more quickly than do racial groups, perhaps because the former see a faction of the elite seeking their vote and rewarding their participation, which it is more reluctant to do with racial minorities. Those political parties that responded to the opportunity afforded by ethnic voting blocs that could be manipulated on the basis of ethnic loyalties thrived and became dominant. Those political parties that rejected such coalition building soon declined and disappeared (Welch et al. 1998).

Both majority and minority groups form political interest groups that seek to influence public policy. Policy questions often take on ethnic relevance. The majority develops factions seeking to pass restrictive immigration laws or to legally force certain racial groups into geographic or social isolation through such means as reservation policy, the anti-Chinese land laws, the ghettoization of blacks, Jews, and Chicanos, and the enactment of Jim Crow segregation laws. Other elite factions soon learn that stands on public policy issues of both domestic and foreign policy concerns can become convenient means to politically manipulate large blocs of voters.

Minority groups respond to domestic legislative proposals designed to reduce discrimination or that otherwise socially and economically benefit them as a group. Often the mere psychological benefit accrued by simple recognition—naming a school or public park after an ethnic hero, for example—is enough to cement the loyalty of a minority group to a political party.

Minority groups have a keen interest in foreign policy when such policy can influence the government or nation to which they feel an ethnically based loyalty or antipathy. The Greek, Irish, Chinese, and Jewish lobbies have been significant forces influencing U.S. foreign policy vis-a-vis Greece, Ireland and Great Britain, Cyprus, Taiwan, and Israel.

COPING STRATEGIES

Minority groups develop strategies to cope with their status that determine the degree and manner of their political activity. Each strategy exhibits various tactical approaches to pursue that strategy. A given minority may develop factions and engage in more than one strategy at a given time, just as the majority may form factions over how to deal with minority groups within its culture. Edgar Litt (1970) suggests that all minorities will respond in one of three ways: *accommodation*, which we distinguish as being pursued by either an economic or political tactical approach; *separatism*, which may be either physical or psychological; and *radicalism*, which may be either old style or new style in its tactics. Martin Marger (1997) similarly classifies racial minorities into assimilationist, secessionist, and militant ones. As articulated by Booker T. Washington, black Americans advocated accommodating to racial discrimination by attempting to find an economic niche that would be nonthreatening to the middle class. Over time, he argued, they could themselves move into the middle class and be accepted. Other blacks, such as Marcus Garvey with his "Back to Africa" movement or the Black Muslims, preached separatism. Still others, from W. E. B. Du Bois to Dr. Martin Luther King, Jr., have advocated a radical approach by attempting to change the basic value system of the dominant culture. These strategies and tactics are discussed in the chapters that follow.

Each strategy inevitably involves the minority in the perennial struggle characterizing minority group politics in America. The dilemma about how difficult it is for

Peaceful coexistence at last!

racial and ethnic minorities to get along with one another is illustrated by the recent cases of ethnic cleansing in Bosnia and Kosovo and in the intertribal genocide in Rwanda.

Acculturation and Assimilation

Two related concepts need to be discussed here. Various racial and ethnic groups coming into contact with a dominant culture that assigns them to minority status have experienced discrimination to keep them in a low socioeconomic level. The minority group must react to this situation. It is the type and quality of interaction that characterize minority group politics.

Acculturation is the process by which a member of a minority subculture gradually absorbs the norms, values, and lifestyle of the dominant culture, or at least that portion of majority society within which it operates regularly. A certain degree of acculturation will take place simply as a result of the sustained contact between two cultures. It is not all one-sided. In turn, the dominant culture will absorb some aspects of the subordinate culture. The majority Anglo-American culture, for example, acquired the Christmas tree and kindergarten from German immigrants. Another example is the Americanization of pizza, tacos, and similar ethnic foods now so broadly accepted as part of the American diet. Indeed, the American two-party system was forged and greatly shaped by the influx of so many millions of immigrants who needed to be accommodated. Much acculturation, however, is from the subordinate to the dominant culture. Minority group members gradually adopt the norms and values of Anglo-American culture. They begin to speak English, adopt the economic and political methods used in the United States, and may even change their names or religious affiliation to be more compatible to the dominant culture.

A related concept is that of **assimilation**, the subjectively felt or psychological identification with the majority. In total assimilation, the former minority group member feels a part of the majority, and the majority accepts him or her as such. Not all minorities can or even want to assimilate. Acculturation may be viewed as a type of assimilation—cultural assimilation (Gordon 1964).

Integration

Michael Banton (1967) distinguishes six "orders" of interracial contact between groups. We mention four here: The first order is that of "peripheral contact" involving minimal interaction between the two cultures. If the two are of roughly equal power, such interaction tends to be formal—involving the exchange of ambassadors and consulates, and instituting formal cultural exchanges and the like. Such interaction leaves the majority of each culture autonomous and independent of one another. Institutionalized contact between unequal power groups Banton calls "paternalism" or "colonialism." Under paternalism, role and status are sharply defined, and social distance is maintained through etiquette, regulations, and repeated demonstrations of power by the dominant group. Paternalistic societies are rigidly stratified by racial castes. His third type of interaction is acculturation.

Banton's fourth type is **integration**. In this order racial distinctions are disregarded or given only minor consideration. The primary interactions among the two races on most levels (in housing, schooling, employment, interest group affiliation, friendship, and social relations) are conducted on an equal basis. Rigid definitions and racially prescribed roles are discarded or greatly modified, so there is more freedom for voluntary choice and movement across racial lines. Integration may also take place on a less than equal basis. Integrated army units may be led by white officers; an integrated company may have all of its top echelon of managers be all white males, even though its labor force may be fairly equally mixed. In such a case, integration may be but little evidenced in the more intimate social relationships, such as intergroup marriage.

Amalgamation and Accommodation

Milton Gordon (1964) distinguishes seven kinds of assimilation: cultural behavioral, structural, marital, identificational, attitude receptional (the absence of prejudice), behavioral receptional (the absence of discrimination), and civic (the absence of value or power conflict). He presents certain hypotheses about the relationships among these dimensions of assimilation: (1) that in majority/minority contact, cultural assimilation will take place first; (2) that acculturation may take place even if none of the other types of assimilation occurs, and that the situation of "acculturation-only" may continue indefinitely; and (3) that if structural assimilation occurs, along with or subsequent to acculturation, the other types will inevitably follow.[9] According to Gordon, prejudice and discrimination will disappear from a society only when civic assimilation has been reached. It is possible for a good deal of cultural assimilation, and even some structural assimilation to occur, without further stages developing, or doing so only slowly. In the United States, structural assimilation is evident with respect to Euro-American minorities, but little has yet occurred with respect to racial minorities.

The capacity of a specific minority to achieve the more advanced dimensions of assimilation, according to Gordon, is determined by what he labels "competitive power," the ability of individuals to compete in the reward system of a society, and by "pressure power," the ability to effect change in society in a collective fashion. Such power pressure may be manifested in one of two ways: (1) political pressure involving actions appropriate to the standard political behavioral norms of that society, for instance, actions via voting, litigation in courts, lobbying the legislature, and the like; or (2) disruptive pressures, involving acts that disrupt normal and expected routines of social intercourse, ranging from peaceful but unconventional demonstrations to violent revolution.

To return to Banton's orders of interracial contact, his fifth order is **amalgamation**. As an example, Banton refers to interracial marriage and its variations (intimate social interaction, living together as a couple but not legally married, etc.). Amalgamation can occur without much acculturation (for example, war-bride marriages between American servicemen and Japanese, Korean, or Vietnamese during those respective wars). Such assimilation is frequently thought to be the inevitable result of integration, which is why it was so resisted in the South. Gordon maintains that once members of a minority could freely enter into social clubs, organizations, and similar institutions of majority society on an equal footing, then intermarriage and the remaining stages of assimilation would follow. Fear of amalgamation is not only found among members of the dominant group. Members of the minority racial group often resent and resist such assimilation as well.

American society is clearly witnessing a much greater degree of interracial marriage. The profusion of couples breaching once impregnable barriers of color, ethnicity, and faith is startling. Over a period of roughly two decades, the number of interracial marriages in the United States has escalated from 310,000 to more than 1.1 million; 72 percent of those polled by *Time* magazine know married couples who are of different races. The incidence of births of mixed-race babies has multiplied 26 times as fast as that of any other group. Among Jews the number marrying out of their faith has shot up from 10 to 52 percent since 1960. Among Japanese Americans, 65 percent marry people who have no Japanese heritage; Native Americans have nudged that number to 70 percent. In both groups the incidence of children sired by mixed couples exceeds the number born into uni-ethnic homes. Such amalgamation does not come without pain. The child of one such union stated, "I know that people are tolerating me, not accepting me" (*Time*).[10]

A common image of such amalgamation, the *melting-pot theory*, was especially popular during the twentieth century. It envisioned a unique American character emerging out of the intermingling of different people in this new environment. It assumed that structural assimilation would take place. While the concept is a noble one, it has never accurately depicted minority group experience in the United States, although the trend toward increasing racial intermarriage already noted may yet bring about such a society in the distant future.

Accommodation is another term that refers to the relations between the dominant society and its various racial/ethnic minority groups. In **accommodation**, the minority accepts the value system of the dominant culture and wants to be accepted into it. The dominant culture recognizes the legitimacy of the minority's attempts to assimilate. The progression to assimilation is gradual, however, with some degree of conflict and competition. The friction is on both sides of the racial/ethnic lines. Depending on the reactions of both sides, accommodation could result in amalgamation or pluralism.

Pluralism

Banton's sixth order is pluralism, in which racial differences indicate much wider variation in expected behavior than is the case with integration. **Pluralism** has been likened to separate nation states, in which groups live side by side with different languages and cultures and with a minimum of social interaction, integration, or assimilation. In place of the "melting-pot" image of society, a "salad-bowl" image might be more appropriate with cultural pluralism. As in a tossed salad, each ingredient remains distinct and identifiable, yet all contribute to the ultimate mix.

Cultural pluralists view the need to maintain subsocietal separation as key "to guarantee the continuance of the ethnic tradition and the existence of the group, without at the same time interfering with the carrying out of standard responsibilities to the general American civic life" (Gordon 1964: 158). For a pluralist society, wide-scale intermarriage and extensive primary-group relations across racial or ethnic lines pose a grave threat to its existence. Gordon maintained that the reality of American life is one of structural pluralism rather than cultural pluralism, although some degree of cultural pluralism still obviously remains, especially with regard to racial subcultures.

Cultural pluralism refers to the maintenance of ethnic subcultures with their traditions, values, and styles. *Structural pluralism* refers to the structural compartmentalization into analogous and duplicative but culturally alike sets of institutions. The United States, for instance, has two major racial castes, black and white, sharing the same Western culture and the same language. To be white is to belong to the upper half of the system, with its corresponding social-psychological perspectives. Members of the white power structure feel superior and responsible. They emphasize law and order and gradualism in race relations, and place a high value on rational discussion and scientific studies. They feel that if the "other" would only become more like them, the ethnic stratification and boundaries would soon disappear. Those in the subordinate position, however, view the world differently. They may try to escape their minority status by changing their names or exterior appearances or by altering reality. They sometimes overidentify with the dominant group, or vent their frustrations on members of other minority groups, or even among others in their own. They often feel great impatience with the racial status quo and demand immediate action to change it.

Kitano adds yet another model to Banton's six stages—*biculturalism,* which he describes as a variant of both acculturation and pluralism based on the observation that exposure to several cultures can be additive. A person can acquire and be comfortable with both the dominant culture and his or her own ethnic heritage. A bilingual person is one who has acquired one of the skills important to such bicultural adaptation, although language is but one such skill or factor. An individual with a bicultural orientation would have friends in several cultures, enjoy various foods, appreciate and speak at least two languages, and be able to interact with various groups with an appropriate sensitivity to the different cultures. A bicultural perspective assumes the desirability of a variety of cultural styles. Such a response, however, is difficult in any society where one culture is thought to be superior or better than the other(s). Marger (1997) distinguishes a typology of multiethnic societies as being either colonial, corporate, pluralistic, or assimilationist. Within that typology he distinguishes various types of pluralism: egalitarian, cultural, corporate, and inegalitarian.

These models assume that both groups are relatively equal in power. Yet, by definition, for racial/ethnic minorities, power is not equal. It is the more powerful, the dominant, group that determines the direction of the interaction between them. In acculturation, as we stated earlier, the minority changes more and more like the majority, rather than vice versa. Thus, while in America the many groups learn from each other, acculturation generally means the acquisition of the "American way," although to do so does not necessarily mean the shedding of all of the ancestral heritage. Indeed, ethnic (ancestral heritage) identification has been and remains strong and surprisingly persistent. Some have advocated that for the 2000 census a category of "mixed-race" or "multiracial" be added (see, for example, Wright 1994).

SUMMARY

This chapter introduced the key terms and concepts that make up the "language" of the struggle between majority and minority groups. It introduced the jargon of ethnic and racial relations by discussing the contributions to that field by a number of important scholars of racial and ethnic relations. It focused on the sociological perspective, with added insights from anthropology, economics, political science, and social psychology. It laid the groundwork for later chapters that explore the theories and strategies of racial and ethnic relations more fully, and that use the experiences of a multiplicity of such groups to illustrate key aspects of their struggle as they cope with minority status in the United States. It developed important analytical distinctions among basic terms used to study racial and ethnic relations, and presented some graphical figures to illustrate those distinctions.

The vexing issues of whether or not the United States should be a "melting pot" or a more pluralistic "salad bowl" were raised in the popular press over concern about America's continued immigration and the problems it poses to the nation.

KEY TERMS

Accommodation: the minority group accepts the value system of the dominant culture and seeks inclusion.

Acculturation: a process by which a member of a subculture gradually absorbs the norms, values, and lifestyle of the dominant culture.

Amalgamation: interracial marriage or marriage-like intimate social interaction (living together as a couple but not legally married).

Assimilation: the subjectively felt or psychological identification with the majority.

Discrimination: applied prejudice in which negative social definitions are translated into action, including public policy, through the subordination of a minority's political, social, and economic rights.

Ethnic group: a self-perceived group of people who hold a common set of traditions not shared by others with whom they are in contact, including religion, language, history, and common ancestry, giving them a sense of "peoplehood."

Ethnicity: a sense of peoplehood.

Ethnophaulism: a type of derogation involving the use of defamatory terms for members of one ethnic group by another.

Integration: society disregards or gives but minor consideration to racial distinctions.

Majority group: the superordinate group in a superordinate/subordinate relationship.

Minority group: the subordinate group in a superordinate/subordinate relationship; they are viewed as unique on the basis of perceived physical, cultural, economic, or behavioral characteristics and are treated negatively as a result.

Pluralism: social pattern where groups live side by side with different language and culture and with a minimum of social interaction, integration, or assimilation.

Prejudice: a set of attitudes that causes, supports, or justifies discrimination; a mind-set whereby individuals or groups accept negative social definitions that the majority forms in reference to some minority group as valid, predisposing them to apply those definitions to all in the group.

Race: the differential concentration of gene frequencies for certain traits that are confined to physical manifestations, such as skin color, hair texture, and facial features.

Racism: an ideology that considers the unchangeable physical characteristics of a group to be linked in a direct, causal way to their psychological and intellectual functioning, and thereby to distinguish superior and inferior races.

Segregation: the act of separating and isolating members of a racial or ethnic group from members of the majority society. May be by law (de jure) or by custom (de facto).

Social stratification: the distribution of rewards, goods, services, benefits and privileges, honor and esteem, or power and influence according to different social roles and positions; methods to assign individuals to different roles and positions.

Stereotypes: oversimplistic and exaggerated beliefs about a group, most often acquired secondhand.

REVIEW QUESTIONS

1. What are Fichter's four types of group-relatedness?

2. Discuss what is meant by, and the purposes of, various Jim Crow laws.

3. Discuss how discriminatory practices contribute to ethnic stratification.

4. In the United States, what have been the various bases used to assign minority status to various groups?

5. Discuss intergroup sequences used to account for how a group comes to be confined to minority status.

6. Can you describe the three strategies for coping with minority status?

7. What are Banton's six orders of interracial group relations?

8. What are Gordon's seven stages or kinds of assimilation?

9. Besides the United States, what other countries exemplify ethnic stratification?

10. Contrast the "melting-pot" with the "salad-bowl" image of interracial relations. What theory of race relations best fits each of these images?

NOTES

1. For a general discussion on the causes of prejudice, including all these explanations, see Allport (1954), Berry (1958), and Williams (1947). In addition to the economic theory of Karl Marx, others argue the economic exploitation approach. See, for example, Bonacich (1976), Fox-Piven and Cloward (1975), Ralf Dahrendorf (1939), Fushfield (1973), Tabb (1970), Cox (1948), and Wilson (1987).

2. Both sociologists and social psychologists stress this view. See, for instance, Emory Bogardus (1950), Feagin and Feagin (1996), Allport (1950), and Collins (1970). In the early twentieth century, social scientists rejected the doctrine of racial superiority, but some held the view that people *instinctively* dislike the strange and different. They saw xenophobia (the dislike of foreigners) as an inborn trait. See, for example, such sociologists as E. B. Reuter (1934) and the early work of Robert Park (1924).

3. For sources that emphasize ethnocentrism as an underlying factor in social/ethnic relations, see Rose (1990), Feagin and Feagin (1996), Simpson and Yinger (1965), and Levine and Campbell (1972).

4. See Freud (1950), Allport (1954), Dollard et al. (1939), and Bettleheim and Janowitz (1950).

5. See, for instance, the later work of Park (1939, 1950), Gordon (1964), Davis and Moore (1945), and Durkheim (1964).

6. Derogation refers to several types of verbal behavior that are defamatory in nature: ethnophaulisms, unintentional references to color and verbal slips that are derogatory (color-laden phrases), ethnic jokes and ethnic accents, and ethnic labeling. See Rose (1990) and Palmore (1962).

7. Various social scientists represent the functional school. See such sociologists as Talcott Parsons (1953), Kingsley Davis and Wilber Moore (1945), and Emile Durkheim (1964). An example of a functional economist would be Adolph Berle (1959). Functional psychologists include Herrnstein (1971) and Jensen (1969). For criticism of the functional school approach, see Anderson (1974) and Matras (1975).

8. For a discussion of immigration policy as it relates to the influx of national-origins groups employing various "door" images, see LeMay (1987).

9. See also Kottak and Kozaitis (1999).

10. "Intermarried . . . with Children," *Time,* Special Issue, November 15, 1993, p. 64.

SUGGESTED READINGS

ALLPORT, GORDON. *The Nature of Prejudice.* New York: Addison-Wesley, 1954.

BANTON, MICHAEL. *Race Relations.* London: Tavistock, 1967.

FEAGIN, JOE R., AND CLAIRECE FEAGIN. *Racial and Ethnic Relations,* 5th ed. Upper Saddle River, NJ: Prentice Hall, 1996.

GORDON, MILTON. *Assimilation in American Life.* New York: Oxford University Press, 1964.

KITANO, HARRY. *Race Relations.* Upper Saddle River, NJ: Prentice Hall, 1997.

LEMAY, MICHAEL. *From Open Door to Dutch Door.* New York: Praeger, 1987.

ROSE, PETER. *They and We.* New York: McGraw-Hill, 1990.

SCHERMERHORN, RICHARD. *Comparative Ethnic Relations.* New York: Random House, 1970.

VAN DEN BERGHE, PIERRE. *Race and Racism.* New York: Wiley, 1971.

CASE STUDY 1.1

Is America Still a Melting Pot?

The melting-pot imagery comes to our lexicon from the steelmaking industry, so important to the nation at the beginning of the twentieth century when immigration hit its zenith. The image evokes the cauldron in which the various ores are placed to produce the new alloy—steel. The term comes from a 1908 play by Israel Zangwill, a poet, novelist, dramatist, political activist, ardent suffragist, and a leading figure in the Zionist movement. His play, *The Melting Pot,* coined the phrase that has been with us ever since.

Immigration was at its height in the 1900–1910 decade when Zangwill wrote his play. In the 1980s–1990s, immigration was once again running full blast, leading the nation again to question its policies and how able the country and its economy was to absorb the millions of new arrivals. Many question the desirability of accepting so many newcomers and the very idea of the melting-pot culture. Many feel that the United States has lost control of its borders. Many are frightened by the long-term prospects for the economy and are worried about their own jobs. Many believe, erroneously, that immigrants are flooding the welfare rolls and causing high crime rates. A 1993 *Newsweek* poll revealed that 60 percent of the population saw immigration as bad, and 59 percent thought many immigrants end up on welfare. A mere 20 percent still viewed America as a melting pot.

In 1994, California passed an anti-immigrant initiative, Proposition 187. In 1996, Congress and the Clinton Administration revised legal immigration policy and enacted welfare reform law with provisions intended to discourage immigration. Even proponents of immigration have largely distinguished between illegal immigration (bad) and legal immigration (good). Congress attempted to control illegal immigration in 1986 with passage of a law that is commonly known as IRCA, the Immigration Reform and Control Act. IRCA attacked the problem of illegal immigration with a two-pronged approach: it offered amnesty and eventual citizenship to 3.7 million illegal aliens, but at the same time it aimed at demagnetizing the draw of the U.S. labor market by making it illegal to hire undocumented aliens. IRCA failed to reduce illegal immigration, however, which, after a brief dip, surged once again to the 2 million to 4 million undocumented immigrants estimated in the United States in the pre-IRCA period. Economists such as Donald Huddle, at Rice University, and George Borjas, at the University of California, San Diego, have studied the economic impact of immigration on the nation's economy. They document short-term economic effects, although the long-term benefits of immigrant labor and business enterprise have been established by other studies (the Rand Corporation).

Today, the United States is the world's leading receiving nation of immigration. It accepts more immigrants than all of the other industrialized nations of the world combined. Annually the United States takes in over a million immigrants—mostly going to seven states that together absorb 90 percent of the new influx: California, Arizona, Texas, Illinois, New York, Florida, and New Jersey. The nature of the flow has shifted markedly since 1965 as well. Prior to the 1965 Immigration Act (often called the Kennedy Immigration Act), two-thirds of immigrants to the United States came from northern and western Europe. Today, 90 percent come from Latin America (especially Mexico and Central America) and Asia. Up to 80 percent of these newest immigrants are people of color—so much for the myth that America's immigration policy is racist. While the current levels in numbers rival the 1900–1920 decades, in terms of percentage of the population, the levels are far lower: about 1 percent of the population in 1900–1920 as opposed to about a third of 1 percent today. Nonetheless, the numbers are immense and cause strains in absorbing so many—both economic and social strains.

Many of the native population fear the changes this influx will bring about. In California, for example, which receives by far the greatest number of the newest immigrants, the Los Angeles school district now has a majority of its students of minority racial backgrounds (black, Asian, Hispanic).

Immigration policy today struggles with a dichotomy of aims. On the one hand, it tilts toward accepting immigrants who contribute to the nation's economic progress. Clearly the United States has the advantage of the "brain drain," attracting immigrants from Asia and the developing nations who are among their most talented and educated. On the other hand, the United States has accepted literally millions of refugees since 1970—Vietnamese, Laotians, Cambodians, Cubans, Russians, and other oppressed nationalities.

Immigration today accounts for fully a third of the nation's population growth, and projections into the future put the population in 2050 at 383 million. Those projections have in part refueled concerns for limiting immigration. Politicians have questioned whether America can absorb so many people with such different languages, cultures, economic, and political backgrounds. In the Southwest, where Hispanics account for 70 to 80 percent of the newcomers, fears are aroused that the United States will develop a separatist political movement akin to the Parti Separatist in Quebec, Canada. Calls for replacing bilingual education with "English only" have gained strength and have been on a number of ballot initiatives. These same states have enacted laws to end affirmative action programs as well.

The extensive diversity of ethnic America argues for a policy of multicultural and political pluralism. It suggests that the United States is more a "salad bowl" than a melting pot. The continued relevance of ethnicity and the steady stream of newcomers clearly pose challenges to the nation's political and social structures.

CHAPTER TWO

STRATEGIES OF THE STRUGGLE
Theories of Race Relations
and Methods of Coping
with Minority Status

The resurgence of immigration, both legal and illegal, has renewed old fears and concerns about how able the new immigrants will be to assimilate and how willing American society should be to absorb these new immigrants. In 1996, Congress passed a revised immigration law that contained a number of provisions designed to restrict illegal immigration and otherwise discourage immigration. It increased the border patrol, strengthened the law to deal with document fraud and alien smuggling, tightened detention and deportation and employee verification procedures, restricted access to a number of public benefits, and tightened asylum, parole, and short-term visa provisions (HR3610–PL104-208, signed into law by President Clinton on September 30, 1997, as part of an omnibus spending bill). The Congress and the Clinton Administration adopted reform legislation for welfare that also contained a number of provisions aimed at legal and illegal immigrants. (See Box 2.1 for a summary of those provisions.)

The number of refugees during the 1990s has been over 130,000 a year, and the number of illegal aliens entering the United States has been estimated at 200,000 annually. The nation again faces the task of absorbing roughly a million new arrivals a year. The fact that the vast majority of the newest arrivals are either Hispanic or Asian raises additional concerns about how prepared they are to successfully "melt" and who will pay the cost for programs designed to assist them in the process of assimilation. Some Americans fear a "Hispanic separatist movement" developing in the United States, along the lines of the French-speaking separatist political movement in Quebec.[1]

BOX 2.1:   The Personal Responsibility and Work Opportunity Act, August 1996

The new welfare law imposes new restrictions on both legal and illegal immigrants.

ILLEGAL ALIENS

1. *Restrictions:* Restricts the federal benefits for which illegal aliens and legal nonimmigrants, such as travelers and students, could qualify. The benefits denied are those provided by a federal agency or federal funds for

   - Any grant, contract, loan, professional license, or commercial license
   - Any retirement, welfare, health, disability, food assistance, or unemployment benefit

2. *Exceptions:* Allows illegal aliens and legal non-immigrants to receive

   - Emergency medical services under Medicaid; no coverage for prenatal or nonemergency delivery assistance
   - Short-term, noncash emergency disaster relief
   - Immunizations and testing for treatment for the symptoms of communicable diseases
   - Noncash programs identified by the attorney general and delivered by community agencies such as soup kitchens, counseling, and short- term shelter, that are not conditioned on the individual's income or resources and are necessary for the protection of life/safety
   - Certain housing benefits (for existing recipients only)
   - Licenses and benefits directly related to work for which a nonimmigrant has been authorized to enter the United States
   - Certain Social Security retirement benefits protected by treaty or statute

3. *State and local programs:* Prohibits states from providing state or local benefits to most illegal aliens, unless a state law was enacted after August 22, 1996, the day the bill was enacted, that explicitly made illegal aliens eligible for the aid. However, illegal aliens are entitled to participate in school lunch and/or breakfast programs if they are eligible for a free public education under state or local law. A state can also opt to provide certain other benefits related to child nutrition and emergency food assistance.

LEGAL IMMIGRANTS

4. *Current immigrants:* Makes most legal immigrants, including those already in the United States, ineligible for Supplemental Security Income (SSI) and food stamps until they become citizens; existing recipients needed an eligibility review by August 1997. This ban is exempt for

   - Refugees, those granted asylum, and aliens whose deportation was being withheld
   - Those who had worked in the United States for ten years.
   - Veterans and those on active military duty, as well as their spouses, and unmarried children

5. *Future immigrants:* Bars legal immigrants who arrived in the United States after August 22, 1996, from receiving most low-income federal benefits for five years after their arrival. Individuals exempt from this ban are:

   - Refugees and those granted asylum and aliens whose deportation has been withheld, as well as Cuban and Haitian entrants
   - Veterans and those on active military duty, their spouses, and minor children

   Programs exempt from this ban are:

   - Emergency medical service under Medicaid
   - Short-term, noncash emergency disaster relief
   - Child nutrition, including school lunch programs, Women, Infants, Children (WIC), and the like.
   - Immunization and testing for treatment of symptoms of communicable diseases
   - Foster care and adoption assistance
   - Noncash programs identified by the attorney general (soup kitchens, short-term shelter, and the like)
   - Loans and grants for higher education
   - Elementary and secondary education
   - Head Start programs for pre-school children
   - Assistance from the Job Training Partnership Act

continued

BOX 2.1:   The Personal Responsibility and Work Opportunity Act, August 1996

---

6. *State options:* Allows states to deny benefits from the welfare block grant and Medicaid and social service block grants to most legal immigrants; exemptions are the same as for SSI and food stamps. Future immigrants subject to the five-year ban noted above.

   • Existing recipients to be continued until January 1, 1997

   • Exemptions granted to refugees, those granted asylum, and so on; those who worked in the United States for ten years; veterans and those on active military duty, their spouses, and minor children.

7. *Sponsors:* Expands circumstances under which an immigrant's sponsor would be financially responsible for that individual; generally affecting those entering the United States sponsored by a member of their immediate family. Affidavits of support would be legally enforceable

for up to ten years after the immigrant last received benefits. Programs exempted are the same as those exempted from the five-year ban on benefits to future immigrants.

8. *Reporting and verifying:* Requires agencies that administer SSI, housing assistance, or the welfare block grant to report quarterly to the Immigration and Naturalization Service (INS) the names and addresses of people they knew were unlawfully in the United States. Charges the attorney general to issue regulations within 18 months requiring that anyone applying for federal benefits be in the United States legally, and that states administering federal benefits would have to comply with the verification system within 24 months after they were issued.

SOURCE: *Congressional Quarterly Almanac,* LII, 1996 (Washington, DC: Congressional Quarterly, 1997), pp. 6-18 (Re: HR3734–PL104-193).

THEORIES OF ASSIMILATION

When groups find themselves treated differently, they have to cope with that different status. This chapter will discuss the coping strategies available to minority groups. For example, some groups reject the dominant culture. Others seek to radically alter the norms and values of that society in order to improve their status and better their lives. Most groups seek some accommodation with the dominant culture, attempting to get their fair share of the pie and to move up the economic ladder.

Minority groups seeking to assimilate vary in the degree to which they desire to do so, and the various groups clearly differ in the rate at which they do achieve some degree of acculturation and assimilation. Historically, such national-origins groups as the Scandinavians, the Germans, and the Scots and Welsh moved up quickly and with little friction. Other national-origins groups, such as the Irish, Italians, Greeks, and Slavs, faced stiff resistance and moved slowly. Religious minorities sometimes reject assimilation, but even those who do accept it generally move slower than do nationality groups. Some religious groups faced severe persecution. The Mormons, for example, were forced to give up a basic tenet of their faith before they could assimilate into the dominant culture. Racial groups experienced the greatest resistance. They were subjected to greater degrees of prejudice and discrimination and have moved the slowest of all (Feagin and Feagin 1996; Omi and Winant 1996). Many reacted to that discrimination by rejecting assimilation for separatism. Some have attempted to radically change some aspects of the value system of the dominant culture so as to be better received. Those racial groups that strove to assimilate found it difficult. Even among the various racial minority groups found in the United States, great variation is evident in the means and rate of their assimilation.

The question of why the variations in the rates of assimilation and their causes is by no means an easy one to answer. Several theories have been advocated by scholars of racial and ethnic relations to explain variations in the rate of assimilation among different subcultures. Scholars from the various social sciences emphasize different variables as to how and why subcultures merge into the majority culture at varying rates and routes of access.

This chapter will focus first on single-factor explanations for the rate of assimilation. It will then present a system's model of assimilation. It will also present the strategies a minority group adopts to cope with its status, including why many groups reject assimilation in favor of other strategies. The chapter essentially previews subsequent chapters that will describe in greater detail the experiences of some minorities who have used the accommodation strategy.

Stanley Lieberson (1980) presents a sophisticated analysis of the causes and nature of the gap between South, Central, and East European groups and black Americans in their respective rates of assimilation. He attempts to account for why those who migrated to the United States during and after the 1880s fared so much better than did black Americans (for briefer but more recent studies, see also Hollifield 1989; Schmidt 1989; Stowers, 1989).

Assimilation is best viewed as a gradual process of transformation, either within an individual or within a group as more and more of its members begin to change individually. This gradual transformation involves persons typical of a given subculture becoming more and more like individuals typical of the dominant culture. It is the complex process in which a person from a minority subculture gradually merges into another culture. It manifests itself in a number of dimensions or subprocesses: cultural, structural, marital, identificational, attitude receptional, behavioral receptional, and civic (Gordon 1964: 71; Kottak and Kozaitis 1999: 48–49; for a critical discussion of the assimilation model and alternative theories, see Feagan and Feagin 1996: 30–56). The continued absorption into the majority culture depends on both the minority members seeking to assimilate and the majority's acceptance of their doing so. The pace of assimilation varies from person to person and group to group. It is possible for individuals and thus for groups to move to the cultural and even the structural stage and remain there for some time. A group may regress for a time if hostility toward it suddenly increases, as it did against German Americans during World War I. Once the stage of marital assimilation occurs, the pace increases rapidly; and Milton Gordon suggests that after structural assimilation occurs, the other stages are inevitable.

In Chapter 1, we briefly sketched Joseph Fichter's (1954) four categories of group-relatedness. These four categories—nuclear, modal, marginal, and dormant—are useful in examining the degree to which members of a group are assimilating. If a group has many marginal-member types, it will change or shed some of the distinguishing characteristics, norms, values, or traits that set it apart from the majority culture, and the pace of acculturation/assimilation will quicken. A dormant-member type is obviously well on the way toward total assimilation—one who has reached at least the identificational stage in Gordon's typology.

Table 2.1 shows the acculturation/assimilation process as a continuum with Gordon's typology arrayed along it. It demonstrates the gradual absorption by either the person or the entire group as many members individually acculturate, moving the whole group toward civic assimilation. Once total assimilation takes place (Gordon's stage of civic assimilation), the former minority subculture ceases to be readily identified as such. All the individuals would have become so assimilated that neither its former members nor the majority society realistically distinguish the group existing as a separate subcultural group. Civic assimilation is viewed as the end stage of the process.[2] It means that while a former minority group may still maintain some minor measure of cultural identity (for example, Irish Americans celebrating St. Patrick's Day by the wearing of the green), their doing so elicits no prejudice or discrimination from members of the dominant culture. In fact, they may be so acceptable that even some dominant group members adopt the identity for the day and celebrate with them. There are no barriers in politics, jobs, or intimate social contact. While members of

TABLE 2.1   A Continuum of Acculturation/Assimilation

Subcultural Group	The Group as a Whole						Majority Culture
Begins to shed some cultural norms (e.g., food, clothing style) typical of the subculture and acquire those of the majority.	Begins to enter job market structure, voluntary associations, etc., of working-class and lower-middle-class levels.	Outgroup marriage becomes common (greater than 50%).	Most group members begin to think of themselves as "hyphenated" Americans, or Americans of "n-descent."	Majority no longer shows prejudice against the group.	Absence of discrimination against the group.		Group participates fully in the civic life of the majority culture; no value and power conflict.

Gordon's Continuum

Cultural	Structural	Marital	Identificational	Attitude Receptional	Behavioral Receptional	Civic
Name change (anglicized); acquires some norms typical of the new culture (food, clothing style, some language) and begins to shed those of the subculture.	Gets job on working-class or higher level; begins to join voluntary associations of that level (unions, Lions Club, etc.).	Marries out of own group into the majority group.	Thinks of himself/herself as belonging to majority but still recognizes the subcultural heritage.	Feels no prejudice on the basis of subcultural background.	Individual no longer experiences discrimination.	Individual participates fully in the civic life of the majority.

the group occasionally manifest "subgroup relatedness," they identify with the majority culture. A classic example would be a woman describing herself as "an American of German-French ancestry."

The Psychological Approach

A variety of perspectives or explanations of assimilation stress a single variable as *the* factor that best accounts for differing rates of assimilation. Scholars stressing psychology, for instance, might emphasize the minority group members' ability to cope with the stress of minority status. A scholar adopting this perspective might focus on the ability or inability of the minority group member to change, stressing the motivation to change. Dale McLemore, for example, offers a psychological explanation to account for variations between Italian and Jewish immigrants in their rate of assimilation.

> Two other differences between the Italian and Russian Jew are noteworthy. The first of these has to do with the psychological impact of American urban living on the members of the two groups. It is an understatement to say that thousands of people in all of the new immigrant groups were bitterly disappointed by the conditions they found in the New World. . . . Both the Italians and the Jews were subject to these tremendous pressures. The Jews, however, were somewhat more insulated than the Italians. Bad as conditions were, the Jews found in America a degree of freedom from persecution unimagined under the rulers of Eastern Europe. They were extremely eager to make use of their new freedom and, consequently, embraced the opportunities that existed in public education and politics much more rapidly than did the Italians. (1983: 64)

Another application of this perspective would be the achievement motivation studies of Bernard Rosen. Rosen stresses the individual's psychological and cultural orientation toward achievement: the person's need to excel, his or her desire to enter the competitive race for social status, an initial willingness or not to adopt the high valuation placed on personal success. Rosen believes that racial and ethnic groups differ in their orientation toward achievement, especially as expressed in the drive for upward social mobility, and that those differences in orientation have been a singularly important factor contributing to the dissimilarities in their social mobility rates (Rosen and Crockett 1969). He describes what he calls the *achievement syndrome,* composed of three components. The purely psychological factor is achievement motivation, the individual's internal impetus to excel. The other two components are cultural. Value orientations, determined by the group's subculture, implement achievement-motivated behavior. Culture also influences the educational/vocational aspirations of the members of that subculture. This view sees these three factors as variously affecting one's status achievement by moving the individual to excel and organizing and directing his or her behavior toward high-status goals.

A similar emphasis on the psychological dimension underlies those studies that account for prejudice and discrimination of the majority society's members by focusing on personality types. The "frustration/aggression" personality studies exemplify this approach (Dollard et al. 1939). Childhood patterns are viewed as contributing to the development of a pathological personality type. Early childhood restrictions and later adult limitations can create an inordinate need for power and prestige. When an individual fails to achieve perceived needs, the person may become highly frustrated. Sustained frustration leads to the development of an authoritarian personality type compelling the person to aggression and scapegoating against a highly visible and readily accessible minority. The individual with such a personality disorder uses the minority as a means of displacing frustration. Similarly, certain minority members may develop psychological disorders. Social blindness, self-hatred, and identification dilemmas lead to high frustration levels. These may lead some minority members into an aggressive response. Their powerlessness enables the majority's power elite to exploit or control them. The minority's sense of being controlled or exploited leads to further frustration, and the cycle goes on (Kinloch 1974).

The Social-Psychological Approach

Closely related is the social-psychological approach, which includes a psychological factor but stresses the social milieu within which that factor operates. Prejudice is seen as a function of the individual's position in the social structure, which is to say that it is determined by a person's degree of socioeconomic security. It is further influenced by the racial socialization to which one is exposed, and is subject to family, peer, and regional pressures. This view sees racial prejudice as a function of the extent and quality of interracial contact to which a person has been exposed (Kinloch 1974). The social-psychological view sees several factors affecting the "speed of inclusion": whether or not people have migrated voluntarily, whether or not they desire to integrate, the racial identification of the individual or group, and the extent to which the majority is willing or not to accept the minority group members for inclusion (McLemore 1983: 6–8).

The mixture of social structural elements with psychological orientations is important in Milton Gordon's theoretical work. He discusses the variables needed to study the type and degree of assimilation and the degree of intergroup conflict. He argues that a general theory of ethnic relations must integrate all such variables. *Biosocial* variables would include a measure of the sense of self and the tendency toward protection of self. These variables would recognize that a man defending the honor or welfare of his ethnic group is a man defending himself. Likewise, there are variables Gordon calls *interaction process* factors, dealing with stereotyping, frustration/aggression, felt-dissatisfactions, goal attainments, and conflict-reducing mechanisms. A measure of the level of felt-dissatisfaction is necessary for understanding the prevailing ideologies and value systems of both the majority and the minority. Perceived sanctions determine how the minority assesses its chances for success. The tendency for conflict to escalate leads to the need for the majority to develop conflict-reducing mechanisms. Gordon's third type is what he labels *social variables:* the absolute and relative sizes of the majority and minority, their comparative rates of natural increase, their territorial dispersion, and the value consensus or lack thereof among both the majority and minority groups. For social variables, Gordon would focus on the nature of ideologies about race, religion, and ethnic groups; on the distribution of relative power resources; and on the political nature of the majority society along a democratic to totalitarian scale (Gordon 1964; see also Glazer and Moynihan 1975: 91–107; Lieberman 1998: 10–11).

Nathan Glazer views social-psychological aspects of the minority group as being the more important factors affecting the rate of assimilation. He emphasizes whether or not the minority is concentrated (that is, rural versus urban settlement patterns) and whether or not the group comes from "nations struggling to become states" (such as the Poles, Lithuanians, or Slovaks) or from "states struggling to become nations" (such as Italy, Turkey, and Greece) (in Kurokawa 1970: 74–86).

Social-psychological studies focus on the minority's orientation toward majority society, coupled with a structural assessment of the group's reaction to its minority status: whether the group is assimilationist or pluralist. Irwin Rinder suggests three types of pluralism: (1) *accommodated pluralism,* in which moderately deprived minorities such as the Chinese and the Jews meet moderate barriers with a group identity that contains some important centripetal strengths, such as high morale, continuity, and economic versatility; (2) *segregated pluralism,* in which severely disadvantaged minorities, stigmatized as either culturally primitive, racially different, or both, are able to sustain their members' identity by maintaining a strong traditional social order isolated from the majority society; and (3) *exotic pluralism,* in which minorities are neither severely disadvantaged nor moderately deprived but, rather, are temporarily advantaged by their distinctiveness from the dominant group—for example, immigrants from the British Isles. Their differences seem to be rewarded rather than penalized because they create no obstacles at the same time that they afford a marginal differentiation which is considered to be exotic without being unsettling (Kurokawa 1970: 43–54).

The Sociological Approach

The sociological perspective was the first model employed in analyzing assimilation because sociologists were among the first to become concerned with explaining the process. Robert Park (1950), for instance, posited the idea of a race relations cycle. He argued that when different racial/cultural groups come into sustained contact, they cannot avoid falling into competition. He argued that the race relations cycle of contact, competition, accommodation, and eventual assimilation is progressive and irreversible. Its rate may vary, but its direction cannot be reversed. Several other sociologists have followed Park's lead in constructing variations of cycles they believe are sociologically determined.[3] This view forms the basis of the entire ethnic stratification literature that emphasizes the socially structured nature of intergroup relations. Donald Noel states:

> Ethnic stratification will emerge when distinct ethnic groups are brought into sustained contact *only* if the groups are characterized by a high degree of ethnocentrism, competition, *and* differential power. Competition provides the motivation for stratification; ethnocentrism channels the competition along ethnic lines; and the power differential determines whether either group will be able to subordinate the other. (1968: 157–172; Noel's italics)

The sociological perspective is implicit in Ralf Dahrendorf's (1939) discussion of class conflict in industrial societies. He stresses that the greater the deprivation of a group in its economic, social status, and social power resources, the more probable it is that it will resort to intense and violent conflict to achieve gains in any of those areas. As the social class position of the subordinate group rises, intergroup conflict will become less intense and less violent. Lloyd Warner and Leo Srole (1945) likewise maintain that when similarities between the minority group and the majority group exist, the probability is greater that the relationship between the two will be relatively harmonious and that assimilation will eventually occur. The greater and the more visible the cultural differences between the groups, the greater the likelihood that conflict will occur (see also Blalock 1967).

Pluralist theorists disagree with Park's notion of an "inevitable and irreversible cycle." Pluralism recognizes that minorities can maintain their distinctiveness and simultaneously interact with the larger society (Barth and Noel 1972; Kottak and Kozaitis 1999). Although arriving at far different conclusions, pluralists share Park's basic sociological perspective on how to explain differences among groups and their rates of assimilation.

The Economic Approach

The economic perspective is an equally important approach to concerns about assimilation and racial/ethnic relations. Marxian theory claims that economic determinism explains all intergroup relations. Numerous scholars have used various forms of economic analysis to explain acculturation and assimilation. Vincent Parrillo (1985) notes that sometimes economic and technological conditions facilitate minority integration. When the economic conditions are healthy and jobs are plentiful, newcomers find it easier to work their way up the socioeconomic ladder of a society. *Occupational mobility,* the ability to improve one's job position, becomes the key to rapid assimilation. This approach notes that downward socioeconomic mobility increases ethnic hostility among that portion of the majority suffering the greatest economic decline. Numerous studies show that upward social mobility is linked to tolerance, whereas downward social mobility is linked to prejudice and discrimination (see Gallagher 1998).

Some scholars focus on the occupational rank and skills level of groups to explain variations in their rates of assimilation. They maintain that the higher the immigrant's former occupational status and the more transferable those skills are, the greater the rate of assimilation. The less positive value placed on ethnic identity by members of the host society and the more equal the prestige of the occupational fields of the two societies, the greater the rate of acculturation (Kurokawa 1970; Weinstock 1963).

Another use of an economic perspective to explain rates of assimilation is the split-labor-market analysis of Edna Bonacich (1976). She argues that dominant group workers realize economic gains by "keeping down" some minority group workers. The antagonism that white workers feel toward black and other minorities stems from the fact that the price of labor in the two groups differs initially, and that the capitalist class does not create, but rather is faced with, a "split labor market." Such a market is characterized by conflict among three groups: the capitalists (those doing the hiring), higher paid labor, and cheap labor. The economic interests of the two labor groups are fundamentally different. Higher paid labor is genuinely threatened by cheap labor groups, which undercut the dominant, higher paid labor group by doing the same work for lower wages. Since the business class gains by substituting cheap labor for higher paid labor, the attempt by the latter to improve their wages and working conditions by organizing and striking can be broken by the "reserve army" of cheap laborers.

Implicit in each of these perspectives is a different theory of discrimination. The psychological and social-psychological perspectives imply a cultural transmission theory of discrimination; the economic perspective reflects a group-gains theory of discrimination; and the sociological view reflects a situational-pressures theory of discrimination. The value of each of these perspectives is in its focus on a *necessary* factor to explain assimilation. While each adds a bit of the truth in explaining varying rates of assimilation, no single view adequately accounts for all variations nor is equally applicable to all minority groups.[4] A system's model involves consideration of all these perspectives.

THE SYSTEMS DYNAMIC PERSPECTIVE

The concept of a **system** emerged as a major focus in the social sciences after World War II.[5] Such a concept reflects the understanding that many things, from a car or a computer to an entire universe, are more than a collection of parts. The car is more than a bunch of steel, plastic, rubber, wires, and glass parts; its parts are assembled so that people can be moved from place to place. The computer is more than a plastic cabinet and boards or chips with programmed paths for electronic messages and storage. It is a highly sophisticated system to facilitate communication between or among individuals. Moreover, one system can be viewed as being related to other, higher order systems. The car, for example, is part of a transportation system that may also be viewed as part of the ecosystem. Similarly, the computer affects our government, business, education, and mass media systems. Each of these systems is markedly affected by a change from the typewriter to the word processor, as the technological system impacts upon them all. Every system may be viewed as being a part of a larger system (a subsystem) or an encompassing one (a suprasystem).

A Systems Model of Assimilation

The systems perspective (Easton 1965) focuses on the many factors that influence the rate of assimilation. One must recognize the fact that assimilation is inherently *reciprocal,* that is, simultaneously involving the actions of both the majority society and the minority. It reflects the interactions—the feedback effect—among the various factors that influence the process. Figure 2.1 illustrates Michael LeMay's (1985) systems model of assimilation. The model graphically portrays the following relationships. The rate of assimilation varies in speed according to the level of acculturation that a given minority group has achieved at any given point in time. That level of acculturation is determined by two variables: (1) tolerance, the majority's willingness to accept

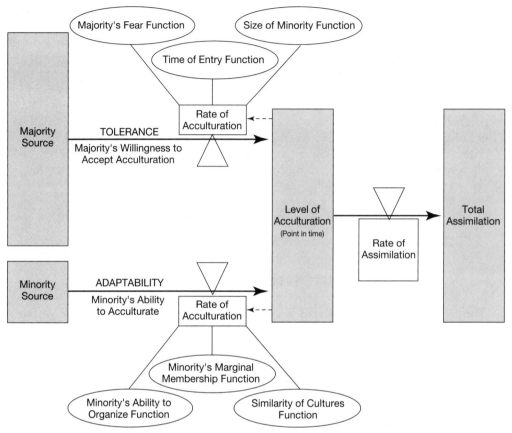

FIGURE 2.1 A Systems Model of Assimilation

SOURCE: Michael LeMay, *The Struggle for Influence* (Lanham, MD: University Press of America, 1985), p. 263.

acculturation by the members of the minority; and (2) adaptability, the minority members' ability to acculturate. Each of these variables is determined by three functions.

The **majority's fear function** represents the degree to which the majority society perceives the minority subculture as a threat. The threat may be economic, value-based, cultural, and so on. The model states that the greater the degree of fear felt within the majority society, the less willing it is to accept acculturation by the minority group members.

Closely linked is the influence of the **size of minority function**. This function must be understood as a relative one; the size of the minority in relation to the majority is the key aspect of how that size function influences the majority society's willingness or not to allow the minority to acculturate. We are dealing here with a function that refers to the majority's *perception* of the size of the minority. The visibility of the minority to the majority (highly visible physical features, geographic concentration versus dispersal, and so on) influences the majority's sense of the size of the minority. The perception of threat implicit in the size function also means that if the majority feels the potential size of the minority is a source of threat, it will adversely affect the majority's willingness to accept the minority's acculturation attempts (as we will see in the case of Chinese Americans). Thus, a religious minority that is small but growing rapidly through intense proselytism (such as the Mormons, discussed in Chapter 5) will be viewed as a larger and more threatening group than a relatively small one not aggressively seeking new converts. Likewise, a minority that is small but is experiencing a large influx or a rapid birth rate relative to the majority society's birth rate is viewed as a larger threat (for example, Mexican Americans in the 1980s).

Finally, the model states that the majority's willingness to accept the minority's acculturation is also a function of the "time of entry" of the minority subculture into the majority society. This function is dependent upon the majority's perception of the minority. A group entering during economic recession or depression, or of social upheaval and instability, will be less accepted by the majority than one coming during an economic boom. The "new" immigrant groups, who entered during the decades of the 1870s and 1880s, which experienced depressions like the Panic of 1873, were less well received than those coming prior to the Civil War. "Entry" means the beginning of initial and sustained contact between the two cultures. It may be the time when an immigrant group arrives in substantial numbers to a new country or when an indigenous religious sect emerges. It may be the result of internal migration from one region to another within the majority's geographic area. How sustained is the influx of the new group determines the majority's perception and willingness to accept acculturation of the minority.

The second major element determining the level of acculturation of the minority is the adaptability variable, that is, its ability to acculturate rate. That rate results from three functions that cause it to vary over time. The first is the "minority's ability to organize function." Groups cannot cope with prejudice and discrimination or develop new values among their members unless they are well organized. The more organized the group desiring to acculturate (Jews, Greeks, Chinese), the faster its rate of doing so. The less organized a group (Mexicans, Puerto Ricans), the slower its rate of acculturation.

The second function of the adaptability rate is its **marginal membership function**. The greater the number of a group's marginal members, the faster its rate of acculturation. The more nuclear or modal the membership, the slower its rate of acculturation. The more rapid intermarriage rates among Japanese Americans than among Chinese Americans, for instance, illustrate this function.[6]

Finally, the minority's adaptability rate is influenced by the **similarity of cultures function**. The closer in basic norms, customs, and values two cultures are, the easier it is for members of the minority culture to acquire the majority culture and the more likely it is that the dominant culture will adopt some aspects of the incoming subordinate culture. An incoming group using a language vastly different from English acquires the norms and values of American culture more slowly than an English-speaking group. A foreign language linguistically closer to English enables the group to learn more readily. This function also concerns such cultural aspects as urban living patterns, clothing styles, child-rearing practices, religious beliefs and practices, and so on. The Scotch Irish and Welsh assimilated more rapidly than did the Greek or Slavic groups (for an excellent but critical discussion of the cultural similarities effect, see Min 1995).

The model specifies the level of acculturation is *simultaneously influenced* by these two major variables. The model incorporates an informational feedback process. The feedback flow indicates that as a group acculturates, it becomes easier and more desirable for its members to do so. Likewise, the dominant culture members become more willing to accept the subordinate group members, allowing further accultura-tion. The majority may begin to accept as an aspect of its own culture some norms and values from the minority subculture. Acculturation is a sharing process, a two-way street. Therefore, even without changing, the minority may become more like the majority and thus more acceptable to it. Italian, Chinese, and Mexican foods, for example, have become "Americanized." A dominant culture may drastically alter its perceptions of some aspect of the subordinate subculture. Norms and customs may suddenly become more acceptable without changing. Since World War II many Chi-nese norms and customs are viewed as charming, quaint, or desirably exotic. The feed-back influence increases the willingness of the majority to accept the minority's acculturation, reinforcing the minority's desire and capability to do so, raising the level of acculturation, and speeding up the rate of assimilation.

LeMay's systems model of assimilation focuses on the multiplicity of variables and stresses the dynamic interrelationship of those variables. Its usefulness will increase once it has been operationalized. It is helpful to show empirical indicators for each of the rates and functions that have been specified here. Only then can the model be tested for its explanatory or predictive value. While the development and opera-tional testing of the model is beyond the scope of this chapter, some suggestions of operational measures are sketched here to further clarify the model.

The ability to develop measures is often hampered by a lack of data. Some of the groups to which we might wish to apply the model began their acculturation/assimila-tion process long before such possible data were routinely kept, or whose reliability is seriously questioned. Sometimes the data are unavailable because we do not know how to measure something or we do not have agreement among scholars as to whether or not some set of data accurately reflects a given variable. The "similarity of cultures function," for example, depends on judgment about the compatibility, or lack thereof, concerning certain cultural norms, values, or practices. We may often need to rely on surrogate measures for certain functions specified in the model. The following, then, should be viewed as tentative suggestions regarding the nature or type of empirical data needed to operationalize the model's various rate, level, and function elements.

Operational Indicators of the Model

Because the rate of assimilation is the dependent variable, we will begin our discussion of operational measures with that concept. What we need to measure this element of the model are some readily accessible data that indicate civic assimilation. An index comprised of three or four indicators might be the most fruitful way to measure civic assimilation. We are attempting here to indicate the assimilation rate achieved by a group in a civic sense, so election data would be the most obvious manner to operationalize it. We would probably construct an ordinal-level index (high, medium, low rate of civic assimilation). The degree to which a group bloc votes would be one part of such an index. The closer the group votes, as measured by percent split in votes between the competing major parties in, for instance, presidential elections, to that of the split among the majority population, the more assimilated is the minority group; the more the group cohesively bloc votes, the less assimilated is the group. Equally important, the index would need to have a component that measured the turnout rate, that is, the percentage of the group actually voting from among those eligible to do so. Again, the closer the group in question was in turnout to the general population turnout rate, the more assimilated the group is, and vice versa. The index might also employ a negative indicator, such as the willingness of some group to cross ethnic lines and vote against one of its own for some other electoral reason. An illustration of this effect would be conservative black voters voting for a George Bush for President when a Jesse Jackson is on the ballot. Such **cross-group voting**, for whatever reason, indicates a degree of civic assimilation. Finally, such an index might include the number of members from a minority group to have been elected to national-level office (for instance, to the U.S. Congress or nominated or elected President). Because to get such a candidate elected to that level of office requires a fair degree of acceptance of that minority member by voters of the majority, it seems logical to include such data in a civic assimilation index (Schmidt 1989; Stowers 1989).

The "majority's fear function" could be measured indirectly. The fear of a group is difficult to measure directly at any time and would be impossible for the historical past—we can no longer "opinion-poll" persons from the 1880s. Several surrogate measures are possible, however, and could be used to develop an index (again ordinal-level) of the majority's fear function. Presuming that a threat of unemployment is a major cause of fear among the dominant or majority society members, the percentage unemployed at any given time might be used. Likewise, sociological literature suggests several methods of measuring segregation (both residential and social) of a given group. A degree of segregation measure could be a possible indicator of the majority's fear of the minority. The use of **ethnophaulisms** (a racial or ethnic group's derogatory nickname for another) might also be a component of a fear function index. A high degree of association between the amount of prejudice against an outgroup and the number of ethnophaulisms for a group has been shown on a limited basis (Palmore 1962).

Similarly, the number and types of racial stereotypes have been shown to correlate highly with levels of prejudice (Katz and Braley 1958). Another surrogate measure might be one of ethnic violence—perhaps indicated by the number of race riots or race-based lynchings. The size and strength of organized opposition groups might be useful. Estimated membership in hate groups such as the Ku Klux Klan, or percent vote for avowed nationalistic groups such as the Know Nothing Party or the American Party, might be developed. For more recent periods, perhaps an index of white flight to the suburbs might be employed.

The "size of minority function" could be measured simply by the relative percentage of a minority group in the total population. Since this function concerns the majority's willingness to accept the acculturation of the minority, however, the *perception* by the majority of the size of the minority is the key aspect of this function. Thus, relative birth rates might be used as an element of this function, since a rapidly growing minority (i.e., with high natural birth rates relative to women of childbearing age among the dominant group) would be seen as a larger threat than would be one whose birth rate was comparable to or lower than the majority society's birth rate. In the case of a religious minority group, a "conversion rate" indicating growth due to proselytism would have to be added to the natural birth rate data for the group.

Likewise, the "time of entry function" would have to include not only the peak decade for the relevant group's emergence within the dominant culture but also the length of the immigration or emergence period. Stanley Lieberson (1980) notes the importance of the flow of migrants in his analysis of differences between South/Central/East European groups and blacks. A continuous influx of a group over a long period of time adversely affects its occupational queuing and its ability to employ a special niche in the occupational structure of society. Sizable continuous numbers of newcomers raise and maintain a level of ethnic and/or racial consciousness between and among members of both the majority and minority groups. The long-term migration of a group may also cause a shift in ethnic and racial group boundaries. If, for instance, the large and continuous migration of blacks to the north takes place while the previously discriminated against white ethnic immigration flow basically stops, then the negative dispositions toward those white ethnic immigrants would be muffled and modified as they come to be viewed as relatively more desirable neighbors, co-workers, political candidates, and so on, than were blacks.

This effect seems relevant to account for the differences in rates of assimilation between Asian Americans and African Americans. Although both are racial minorities, the rate and patterns of their assimilation are very diverse. The fact that the Asian immigration influx was comparatively small (until recent years at least) and of a brief duration may be an exceedingly important difference to account for their widely divergent rates of assimilation.

With respect to measuring the minority's adaptability—its willingness to acculturate rate—each of these functions would be measured by an ordinal-level index composed of several elements. The "minority's marginal membership function" might be measured by the percentage of "outgroup" marriage. Another indicator might be the number and relative size of clearly identifiable ethnic associations for a given group.

Likewise, the "minority's ability to organize function" might be tapped by several indicators that could serve as surrogate measures. The size of the ethnic press, indicated by the number and circulation of newspapers catering to a given ethnic group, might be one such component of this function. The number and size of ethnic associations for a given group is a possible measure. The relative wealth at the time of entry are data of possible use with respect to immigration groups. Similarly, the formal educational levels and percent literacy of a group are possible surrogate indicators of a group's ability to organize. Job skills at the time of entry might also so serve, since the immigration service has some fairly good data on occupational status at the time of entry for most groups since 1900. Lieberson suggests the use of "life expectancy" as a surrogate for the relative social status of a group at the time of entry. Presuming the higher the status of a group's members the greater the ability to organize themselves, such data might serve as a component of this index.

The "similarities of cultures" function might be measured by a similar index of several elements. Agreement in settlement patterns might be one component. A rural-to-rural or urban-to-urban settlement pattern would be a positive indicator, whereas an urban-to-rural or rural-to-urban pattern would be a negative one. The linguistic closeness of the language group to English would also show cultural closeness. Protestant faith (measured by percentage of a group adhering to a Protestant denomination) would be a likely component of any cultural closeness index. The group's being of the Caucasian race or not would also be included. A skin-color weighting of the closeness or distance from the dominant group's white color would be suggested by an extensive body of sociological literature.

Such empirical measures, when developed, would allow the model to be tested using statistical measures. The applicability of the model to explain past groups' assimilation could be measured. Ideally, the model would ultimately be refined so as to predict future assimilation rates. The important point here is that the very attempt to measure these variables and functions exemplifies the value of such modeling. The process of developing the model forces us to think about the assimilation process in a manner that lends itself to developing some specific empirical measures of what is occurring in the very complex real world. It may suggest the future collection of data not presently available that could more accurately or directly serve as indicators of the process and the interrelationships suggested by the model. Just as the development of

"It occurs to me that none of this would have happened if our forefathers had stricter immigration laws."

BOX 2.2:   Research-Substantiated Propositions Concerning Rates of Assimilation

1. The greater the difference between the host and the immigrant cultures, the greater the subordination, the greater the strength of the ethnic social system, and the longer the period necessary for the assimilation of the ethnic group (Warner and Srole 1945). [similarity of cultures function]

2. The larger the ratio of the incoming group to the resident population, the slower the rate of assimilation (Williams 1947). [size of minority function]

3. The more rapid the influx of an incoming group, the slower the rate of assimilation (Williams 1947). [time of entry function]

4. The greater the dispersion of the immigrant group, especially in the same territorial pattern as the dominant group, the more rapid the immigrants' assimilation (Schermerhorn 1949). [similarities of cultures function]

5. The higher the educational, income, and occupational levels of the incoming group, the more rapid its assimilation (Weinstock 1963). [minority's ability to organize function]

6. The greater the predisposition of the incoming group to change, the more rapid the rate of assimilation (Borrie 1959). [minority's marginal membership function]

7. The greater the disposition of the receiving community to recognize differences as legitimate, the more rapid the rate of assimilation (VanderZanden 1983). [negative of the majority's fear function]

8. The greater the degree of economic competition between the native and immigrant groups, the slower the rate of assimilation (VanderZanden 1983; Lieberson 1980). [majority's fear function]

9. The greater the proximity and access to the homeland, the slower the rate of assimilation (VanderZanden 1983; see also Burma 1970; Fitzpatrick 1971). [a negative way of expressing the minority's willingness to acculturate rate and/or the marginal membership function]

10. In situations of continuous intergroup contact, subordinate migrants (newcomers who are politically and economically dominated by an established indigenous population) tend to be more rapidly assimilated than subordinate indigenous populations (native groups who are subjected to political and economic domination by a migrant group) (Acuna 1972; Blauner 1969, 1972; Burma 1970; Schermerhorn 1949; VanderZanden 1983). [Relevant to both the minority's willingness to acculturate rate and to the majority's willingness to accept acculturation rate]

a consensus about the concept of gross national product contributed significantly toward the expansion of economic theory, perhaps a comparable effect might be achieved within the social sciences for the development of a general theory of ethnic and race relations.

James VanderZanden (1983), in his review of the literature on American minority relations, has identified a number of propositions that he found to be "research substantiated." He uses different terminology, but all ten of his propositions parallel the expectations of the model described here. Box 2.2 lists his ten propositions about influences of the rate of assimilation, noting references to the previous studies from which they are drawn and how they relate to the model presented here.

STRATEGIES FOR COPING WITH MINORITY STATUS

As stated earlier, when a group finds itself placed in minority status, it must react. Be it quickly or slowly acculturating, a group that experiences discrimination simply cannot ignore that fact. Various scholars have suggested different typologies for minority group reaction to the dominant group's treatment of them. Harry Kitano (1997) developed a typology of reaction that includes conflict, acceptance, aggression, and avoidance. Race riots would be a form of conflict. Kitano discusses forms of acceptance being ritualistic behavior, superpatriotism, and the internalization of stress. He also posits four kinds of aggression: direct, such as insurrection, strikes, boycotts, and race rioting; indirect, such as use of the arts, ethnic humor, or passive resistance; displaced aggression, such as scapegoating; and the change of goals, avoidance, retreatism, or withdrawal manifested by such behavior as drug or alcohol addiction, schizophrenia, or suicide.

Our discussion draws heavily on the work of Edgar Litt (1970) and employs a schema that is a modification of Litt's analysis of American ethnic politics. He includes the politics of accommodation, separatism, and radicalism. We employ his typology as three strategies. For each of these strategies, we further distinguish two basic tactical approaches for pursuing that overall strategy. The strategy of accommodation may be pursued primarily through an economic or a political route. The strategy of separatism may rely on physical or psychological methods of isolation from the majority culture. Finally, the strategy of radicalism may be either an old style or new style of radicalism. Each of these strategies and their associated tactical approaches will be briefly discussed here. Subsequent chapters will deal with each in greater detail, using the experiences of various ethnic and racial minorities to illustrate them.

Accommodation

When using the strategy of **accommodation**, members of the minority group accept the value system of the dominant culture. They simply want their "fair share" of what the majority society has to offer. They want to be accepted by the dominant group, eventually to become virtually indistinguishable from it. Whether a group desiring accommodation follows an economic or political route to that end depends on several factors.

Groups most likely to use an economic approach are those who voluntarily migrate to the area of the dominant culture. They want to assimilate and accept the majority's value system, which is why they migrated to that society to begin with. If they have some desired economic skills or arrive with sufficient means to be able to use the economic approach, this tactical approach to the accommodation strategy is especially appealing (see the discussion of Asian-American groups in Chapter 3).

Timing is an important factor in the choice of economic accommodation. If an immigrant group arrives during a period of an expanding economy, it is more likely to find available points of access. During such periods, moreover, the majority's fear of the foreign *(xenophobia)* is likely to be reduced, thereby reinforcing their desire to accommodate.

Groups who possess desirable job skills will not only be welcomed; they also have a means for climbing the socioeconomic ladder. If they have the financial means to get to rural areas, for instance, they can more readily acquire cheap land and be more socially acceptable in the frontier regions where their labor is a more needed commodity. Some groups have sufficient capital to start their own businesses or to establish special economic niches for themselves. These often involve occupational areas viewed by the majority as noncompetitive or nonthreatening. Such groups are often called "middle-man minorities" (Schaefer 1998). The Scandinavian and German immigrant groups used this approach. They arrived in the United States when the frontier was still open. Many came with enough resources to reach the interior farmland or to gain desirable jobs in urban areas during the early stages of America's industrialization process. Improved economic status was followed by improved social status, and political involvement largely followed their socioeconomic acculturation.

The Greeks, East European Jews, Chinese, and Japanese also used this approach, particularly relying upon the **occupational niche** route. That concept is closely related to that of **occupational queuing**—the ranking of jobs by order of their desirability for a given group. Members of the majority, by definition, enjoy a favorable situation among employers. They fill as much as they can of society's more desirable jobs, leaving the less attractive ones to the minority population. If the minority population is subdivided by race or ethnic origin in terms of their "worthiness" in the eyes of the dominant group, then members of that group will open access to the remaining desirable jobs first to those ethnic groups deemed most worthy by the dominant group. Thus, one may proceed downward, ranking jobs until all groups have attained their positions. If there are more potential workers than there are total jobs available, then those minorities at the bottom will experience the highest rates of unemployment or underemployment.

The dominant group tends to perpetuate its dominance. Since majority members are more likely to be employers, key co-workers, union officials, and so on, they and their offspring will be in the best position to secure the more desirable jobs. Although such a system is not entirely rigid, occupational queuing is evident in the United States. A group at the bottom of the racial/ethnic hierarchy will tend to fill the least desirable positions in rough proportion to the group's percentage of the total population. If that minority is large, it will find some opportunities higher on the occupational hierarchy, since the majority would not be pushing as far down. If the minority is a small percentage of the total population, there will be room only at the very bottom because the majority will tend to compete successfully for the other jobs. This queuing effect makes the shift in unemployment most radical for the lowest-ranking minorities. When the economy is sluggish or in recession, the minority groups at the bottom are pushed out of jobs as the majority members are forced to "push downward." On the other hand, the minority finds new job opportunities open when the economy is booming because a labor shortage is created. In that case, the majority members cannot fill all of their traditional employment opportunities. In occupational queuing, minorities are the last hired and the first fired.

Tables 2.2, 2.3, and 2.4 illustrate such occupational queuing. Table 2.2 shows the percentage employed in a variety of occupations for females, blacks, and Hispanics as of 1997. Table 2.3 details their relative unemployment as of 1996, and Table 2.4 gives their median and personal income data. A clear pattern of queuing is reflected in the tables.

TABLE 2.2   Percentage of Females, Blacks, and Hispanics Employed in Specified Occupations, 1997

Occupation	Female	Black	Hispanic
Total in work force	46.2%	10.8%	9.8%
Personnel/labor relation managers	63.4	7.5	2.9
Administrators, education and related	61.3	10.7	5.8
Managers, medicine and health	76.8	7.4	4.3
Architects	17.9	1.7	5.1
Engineers	9.6	3.9	3.8
Mathematical, computer scientists	30.4	7.5	3.1
Chemists, except biochemists	25.5	5.5	4.2
Dentists	17.3	2.6	1.1
Health assessment/treating occupations	86.5	8.4	3.3
Registered nurses	93.5	8.3	2.9
Dietitians	88.7	28.5	6.0
Speech therapists	95.0	3.6	3.7
Teachers—colleges/university	42.7	6.5	3.4
Pre- and kindergarten teachers	97.8	13.2	9.7
Elementary school teachers	83.9	10.9	5.4
Special education teachers	82.9	10.8	3.2
Lawyers and judges	26.7	2.8	3.8
Actors and directors	38.2	7.3	5.1
Public relations specialists	65.7	7.4	6.7
Dental hygienists	98.2	1.5	2.3
Licensed practical nurses	94.1	15.4	5.6
Legal assistants	83.9	9.8	5.8
Securities, financial services sales	31.2	5.5	2.6
Sales workers, retail/personal services	65.7	11.9	10.0
Cashiers	78.4	15.6	12.1
Secretaries, stenographers, typists	97.9	9.8	6.9
Receptionists	96.5	8.8	9.7
Financial records processing	92.2	7.1	6.4
Billing clerks	93.8	12.2	6.0
Telephone operators	83.5	21.5	8.4
Weighers, measurers, and checkers	56.2	11.9	10.9
Eligibility clerks, social welfare	86.9	15.1	13.1
Bank tellers	90.1	9.8	9.0
Data entry keyers	81.9	18.3	9.8
Teacher's aides	93.1	15.2	12.6
Service occupations	59.4	17.6	14.6
Private household service	95.4	16.2	25.6
Child-care workers	96.8	11.8	17.4
Cleaners and servants	94.9	17.8	31.3
Food preparation/service occupations	56.8	12.4	16.4
Food counter, fountain service	69.4	12.4	8.5
Kitchen workers, food preparation	72.6	9.8	14.2
Health service occupations	88.2	30.8	9.2
Dental assistants	96.7	6.1	11.5
Personal services occupations	80.9	14.3	9.6
Barbers	22.8	36.6	7.8
Hairdressers, cosmetologists	90.3	10.2	8.7
Family child-care providers	98.2	11.0	11.2

continued

TABLE 2.2   Percentage of Females, Blacks, and Hispanics Employed in Specified Occupations, 1997

Occupation	Female	Black	Hispanic
Early childhood teacher's assistants	95.6%	17.2%	10.8%
Precision crafts and repairers	8.9	8.1	12.1
Mechanics and repairers	3.9	7.9	10.2
Automobile mechanics	1.5	7.8	13.2
Construction trades	2.4	7.1	13.7
Operators, fabricators, laborers	24.7	15.1	15.4
Textile sewing machine operators	82.0	16.0	33.8
Pressing machine operators	70.6	22.4	44.1

SOURCE: U.S. Bureau of the Census, *Statistical Abstract of the United States, 1998* (Washington, DC: U.S. Government Printing Office, 1998), Table 672, p. 417.

TABLE 2.3   Unemployment, by Sex, Race, Age, and Hispanic Origin, 1997

Percent Unemployment Rate, 1997						
Male:	4.9%					
Female:	5.0					
White:	4.2	Black:	10.0%	Hispanic:	7.7%
16–19 years old:	13.6	16–19:	32.4	16–19:	21.6
20–24 years old:	6.9	20–24:	18.3	20–24:	10.3

TABLE 2.4   Income and Poverty Level Rates, by Race and Hispanic Origin, 1996

Median Income in Constant (1996) Dollars		Per Capita Dollars	Percent Below Poverty
All races	$12,815.00	$18,136.00	13.7%
White	12,961.00	19,181.00	11.2
Black	11,772.00	11,899.00	28.4
Asian/Pacific Islanders	14,634.00	17,921.00	NA
Hispanic	9,484.00	10,048.00	29.4

SOURCE: U.S. Bureau of the Census, *Statistical Abstract of the United States, 1998* (Washington, DC: U.S. Government Printing Office, 1998), Tables 753–756, pp. 476–477.

Minority group members sometimes use "special niches," concentrating in certain occupations first open to them either because of special skills and interests or because the majority considered that job undesirable or nonthreatening to its favored positions. These minority members develop a network of ethnic contacts and experience that attracts others of their group to those occupational opportunities.

When immigration of a minority rapidly accelerates, however, the ability of that group to exploit the special niche is reduced markedly. Such specialties can absorb only a relatively small portion of the group's work force when that group is experiencing rapid population growth. Not all Chinese men can open a restaurant or laundry in a city where they are a sizable faction of the total population. Not all Jews can own their own stores or garment businesses in New York. Not all Greeks can be confectioners or restaurant owners in Baltimore. In cities where a given group suddenly becomes a sizable part of the total population, it is more difficult for occupational niches to provide adequate opportunity for many of the group's members.

For those groups that are able to develop special niches, especially if their immigration then ceases or tapers off, they can exploit such jobs to climb the socioeconomic ladder. The job stability associated with such niches enables the group members to plan ahead and save more of their resources to enable their children to achieve greater educational levels. After a generation or two, the entire group rises up the status ladder of the society.

The availability of such niches is a key factor in a group's viewing economic accommodation as desirable. The majority, in turn, views the minority as being less threatening to its favored-job-status positions. The minority sees that approach as being more likely successful and thus a more desired strategy for them to pursue.

For some groups, even if they do desire assimilation, economic opportunities are not sufficiently open to them to be the more attractive tactic. They may enter society when expanding job opportunities are not available. They may lack the necessary job skills or resources (capital to open one's own restaurant, retail store, garment business, or import/export firm) or farming skill and the capital needed to get to where free or cheap farmland is in abundance.

For some immigrant groups reliance on the economic route is blocked. Then the tactic of political action becomes an option for coping with minority status. As with economic accommodation, political accommodation is favored by a group as its overall strategy only when certain conditions pertain. Generally speaking, the political path will be all the more attractive when a group's economic path is blocked by relatively strong occupational discrimination. "No Irish Need Apply" signs preceded the development of the Irish urban political machine.

For political accommodation to work, a minority group must have the organizational skills and experience to develop a base to deliver a cohesive voting bloc. It needs such political organization to direct its political activity toward specific group goals. And, of course, the group must be able to vote. Another critical ingredient is that the majority society must be politically divided into several factions. One or another of such factions will desire a coalition with the minority in order to consistently win in its electoral struggle with the other dominant group faction(s). If the minority can demonstrate its ability to move in organized voting blocs, it becomes a desirable coalition partner. In order for the majority faction to acquire the sustained electoral loyalty of the minority bloc, it will have to grant some rewards to the minority members, enabling them to use politics as a means to climb the socioeconomic ladder.

The political tactic of accommodation is the most attractive alternative to a minority group having a psychological need for the rewards that political recognition can bring. If the economy is expanding sufficiently to provide for many unskilled jobs that can be dispensed by the political elite, the dominant faction can easily reward its minority coalition partners. The political strategy must rely upon a political organization capable of distributing these rewards for political loyalty (an urban political machine). The Irish used this tactical approach most successfully to pursue accommodation. The Slavic and Italian groups also employed this approach, although less successfully and less often than did the Irish.

Native politicians soon recognized the value of appealing to ethnic groups to attract their votes in massive and easily manipulated voting blocs. They saw that ethnic voters were likely to vote for a co-ethnic and responded by offering an ethnically balanced slate. Including an Irish immigrant as a council member, a Jew as city auditor, a Greek as city clerk, and so on assured the party of loyal support from those groups. Erecting a statue to Columbus in an Italian-heavy ward or naming a new high school in a Polish area after General Pulaski were easy ways to appeal to these groups for their vote.

Fred Greenstein (1970) identified five factors that propelled the development and operation of the classic urban machine. First was the explosive rate of growth of the nation's cities. Prior to the flood of immigration, only one city in the country, Philadelphia, exceeded 250,000 in population. By 1890, eleven cities had attained that size, three of which were over 1 million. In four decades the urban population had increased sixfold, while the rural population had only doubled. Chicago, in 1850, was under 10,000 in population; by 1900, it had reached 1,690,000.

The explosive growth rate of those cities meant an increase in demand for basic public services essential for survival. Large cities needed highly developed transportation systems to supply food and other essential resources. Cities needed extensive streets, lighting, bridges, and mass transit. Massive sewer systems had to be installed and tons of garbage removed. Police and fire stations had to be built and manned. Building codes and inspection programs had to be put in place. Hospitals, health services, and school systems led to nearly overwhelming demands being placed on city governments. All of those needs meant there were a substantial number of unskilled jobs.

A related factor was the disorganized municipal government structure prevalent at the time. City governments were structurally ill prepared to meet the challenges created by an explosive rate of growth. Hundreds of officials were individually elected, sometimes annually, and thus had little incentive to work together. Power was fragmented still more by large and unwieldy city councils, and a host of boards and commissions. The urban machine developed, in part, as an informal and extralegal means to unify what the formal structure so fragmented.

A third factor was the flow into the cities of millions of immigrants who formed a highly dependent population. The machine politicians soon realized the value of catering to this population through their ethnically based organizations. A fourth factor was the needs of businessmen. Businesses varied in size from the very large to the very small. All had needs to which the politician could cater. Some needed the government services: street maintenance, sewer and water expansion. Some needed government permits to build or expand. Some sought relief from government restrictions on plant operations, safety conditions, disposal of waste, and so on. For them, their prime need was to operate without government interference. Yet other businessmen had the opposite need. They did business with government itself: contractors, utility producers, and mass transit operators were all engaged in the profitable pursuit of serving the very process of massive and rapid urban growth. Such businesses provided the machine politicians with graft in return for favored treatment. The politicians, in turn, used the graft money not only to enrich themselves but also to fund the material incentives of welfare-type services that they dispensed to needy immigrants in exchange for their loyal electoral support. This system enabled the machine to dispense private sector jobs to many of their loyal supporters. The *patronage system* became the oil that greased the machine's smooth operation.

The final factor was relatively unrestricted suffrage. Since even the lowliest citizen could vote, machine politicians catered to those groups who could provide bloc voting. The political party apparatus performed the valuable service of initiating immigrants into citizenship and teaching them the value of participating in politics. Despite the machine's raw and at times corrupt and inefficient policy process, it accepted and welcomed immigrants and provided them with an invaluable commodity—the vote. Machine workers greeted disembarking immigrants. They were soon naturalized and registered to vote by judges controlled by the machine. Although corrupt, the urban political machine did much to reduce the hopelessness of the immigrants' conditions. In return, the immigrant responded with loyal and easily manipulated electoral support to the machine's endorsed candidates.

Patronage was crucial to the machine's development because the immigrants were desperate for steady jobs. There were no government programs for employment or to pay unemployment benefits. The machine's provision of jobs was sorely needed and much appreciated. The explosively expanding cities provided many job opportunities to be filled by loyal party workers: jobs in police, fire, sanitation, and street construction and maintenance. Private jobs in the many businesses and industries indebted to the machine politicians became part of the patronage system. The machine also provided a host of welfare services to the immigrant. In the words of Tammany Hall Boss George Washington Plunkitt, the philosopher-king of the old-style urban machine:

> What holds your grip on your district is to go right among the poor families and help them in different ways they need help. I've got a regular system for this. If there's a fire in Ninth, Tenth, or Eleventh Avenue, for example, any hour of the day or night, I'm usually there with some of my district captains as soon as the fire engines. If the family is burned out I don't ask whether they are Republicans or Democrats, and I don't refer them to the Charity Organization Society, which would investigate their case in a month or two and decide if they are worthy of help about the time they are dead from starvation. I just get quarters for them, buy clothes for them if their clothes were burned up, and fix them up til they get things runnin' again. It is philanthropy, but it's politics too—mighty good politics. Who can tell how many votes one of these fires brings me? The poor are the most grateful people in the world, and, let me tell you, they have many more friends in their neighborhoods than the rich have in theirs. (cited in Greenstein 1970: 49)

The "boss," or party official, helped immigrants with all of their dealings with government. He personified government for the newcomer who desperately needed that service. The party was friend and intermediary in dealing with the broader, majority society: the courts, police, and local bureaucracy.

The machine gave the immigrant group a much needed psychological boost simply by recognizing them and the value of their culture. Politicians appealed to their sense of group loyalty and bound that loyalty to a party attachment. Whether running an entire slate of officials representing a wide variety of ethnic groups living in the city or erecting a statue or naming a school, park, or other public building after some ethnic hero, or simply attending ethnic group gatherings such as weddings, funerals, dances, or similar social occasions, the machine politician appealed to the minority group's members because such activities showed that the politician cared for the group. It made minority group members feel valued. And the immigrants responded with loyal bloc voting.

After a generation or so, recognition politics were no longer sufficient to keep ethnic group loyalties attached to the party. Ethnic group members began pressing for more. They sought and could extract from the machine and the political system a number of collective welfare benefits. Litt refers to this as the "rule of expansion," namely, get more benefits. Where the old boss might have found a place to live for the family that was burned out, the new system demanded public housing projects, which were soon filled with members of the relevant minority group.

The final phase of successfully employed political accommodation is what Litt calls *preferment politics.* In this stage the minority group has achieved sufficient access and power within the political machinery that the group is able to influence the fundamentals of the system. It is generally able to determine the allocation of political claims made within its framework. A group like the Irish Americans not only can succeed in getting a few divisible rewards allocated to them, they can even go beyond demanding a public housing program and bureaucracy. In this final stage, they capture the political party machinery, take over the bureaucracy, and determine the policies by which it will distribute a general welfare benefit such as public housing.

As Litt notes:

> This sticky phase of ethnic political claims may be handled by party leaders in several ways. A major factor in stable accommodation is the extent to which heretofore dominant groups have secured preferments outside of their political positions. If the dominant group is secure enough to yield the social and economic benefits of party preferments to assertive ethnic claimants, accommodation is facilitated; the most difficult problems are likely to arise when relative newcomers must displace others who have not yet come to securely reap the social and economic benefits of political preferments. (p. 72)

Irish Americans used their ability to capture urban political machines as a means to get ahead. They nudged aside nativist politicians when the latter were no longer needed. Once they gained control, they used the political power to control positions to achieve a broader social and economic status. An Irish immigrant eventually became mayor of Boston. The son of an immigrant went on to become governor of Massachusetts. The Ivy League schools and prestigious business enterprises, and even the more elitist social clubs, accepted a governor's son. And, in the instance of John F. Kennedy, a grandson of an immigrant went on to become President of the United States. The Boston Brahman, having a wide variety of social and economic opportunity open to them, were more willing to yield and move aside when the aspiring Irish politician applied pressure to move up the ladder.

Those same Irish politicians were less likely to step aside for the aspiring Italian- or Greek- or Polish-American politician. The Irish Americans were too new, too psychologically insecure of their place on the ladder to move aside easily. The Irish-American politician forced the later arriving ethnic politicians to seek access to upward social and economic mobility by means of economic accommodation, or through the Republican Party (see, for example, Levy and Kramer 1973).

Separatism

Sometimes the minority group rejects the value system of the dominant society. It may seek not to acculturate but simply to be left alone. It does not seek to impose its values on the majority, nor does it want the majority to do so to it. It wants the dominant groups to respect its differing values, to allow it to hold those values, and to practice its norms, values, and lifestyle without discrimination. Often such groups are ones that have come into sustained contact with the majority society in some largely involuntary manner.

Forced migration, such as the importation of slaves, can bring two such cultures together. The minority rejects its status and position. Often internally developing minority groups, such as a new religious minority, come to reject the value system of the dominant society. The Mormons, as we shall see in greater detail in Chapter 5, are a classic example. Sometimes the minority subculture finds itself in such status because of boundary absorption, as in the case of many Hispanic Americans and the various Native American tribes. When a minority group, for whatever reason, adopts separatism, it may attempt to do so in one of two ways: physical separatism or isolation, or the psychological separatism of its members from the norms, values, customs, and lifestyles of the dominant culture.

The choice of the physical route depends on the group's ability to physically isolate itself. This may be done by going to frontier or rural areas where low density enables them to be a numerically superior group. The Amish and Mennonites, who are clustered in rural enclaves, are an example. Reducing their contacts with majority society to a bare minimum helps. Often the majority society rejects contact with the group, reinforcing the isolating effects of rural settlement. The Mormons' fleeing to ever more isolated frontier areas in response to majority society is a classic example. So too is Marcus Garvey's Back to Africa movement.

Sometimes physical separatism is not really a matter of choice. It may be forced upon the group by the majority culture. Ghettos, barrios, Chinatowns, and the Mormons' flight to isolated areas to avoid persecution exemplify this effect. The military forced Native American survivors of an earlier policy of near-annihilation to ever-decreasing areas of "reservation."

A critical ingredient for successful separatism is the group's maintaining an economic system capable of supporting its members in isolation. Generally, necessary economic interactions with the majority group hasten the decline of the group's use of separatism by bringing about subtle changes in their values that gradually signal a degree of acculturation.

The use of the psychological tactic of separatism is more often the choice of millennial movements whose strong ideology is the means by which a sort of psychological shell is built around the individual member, isolating each member from the influence of the dominant society, even though they may be living in the midst of that society. Good examples of this are the Black Muslim and Hasidic Jew. As in all separatist politics, the Black Muslims exhibit distinct organization and cultural norms specifically designed to compensate for the effects of discrimination by the dominant society. The group withdraws from the ongoing polity. In Litt's words, "Ethnic separatism is to a political system as third parties are to the American two-party monopoly" (p. 76).

Radicalism

A third and final strategy for minorities involves rejecting the value system of the majority and seeking to replace those values with their own. This *radical strategy* exhibits two major tactical approaches: old style and new style radicalism.

In *old-style radicalism* the ideology is very different from the prevailing one of the majority culture, but the behavior remains standard. Groups following this route attempt to use standard political behavior, such as electoral politics, to win over the majority to its new ideology and value system. It is the politics of radical third-party movements. The American Communist Party, attempting to win support among blacks, exemplifies this approach. While never very successful in winning electoral support, even among alienated blacks, its indirect impact was important.

Similarly, the American Socialist Party used the old-style radical approach. A small faction of German Americans sought to win over a large immigrant following. In a few places with large German-American populations such as Milwaukee, Socialists achieved a short-term, local electoral success. Their influence was strongest in its impact upon the trade union movement, especially where Jewish influence in the union was strong. The Socialist influence pervaded important trade unions, the Yiddish press, and Jewish social activities such as the Socialists Workingmen's Circle. From their experience with Socialism, Jewish communal leaders of three decades acquired the political skills and style that influenced the American trade union movement (for instance, the International Ladies Garment Workers), the development of American intellectual life (through numerous academic and political accomplishments of "ex-radicals"), and American national politics (for instance, the role of New York's American Labor Party and the Liberal Party in electing Franklin D. Roosevelt in 1936, 1940, and 1944).

The American Alliance of Polish Socialists tried to appeal to the larger Polish immigrant group, although never as successfully as the more accommodationist Polish National Alliance. Those interested in American Socialism joined the Polish section of the American Socialist Party. A small faction of Italian Americans flirted briefly with radical politics. A few were attracted to the American Communist Party, and another small faction supported the American Fascist Party. Neither group achieved much size or electoral strength.

The task of the old-style radical was a difficult one. The ideologue had to convince the ethnic member that future rewards would outweigh the benefits to be gained from the present system. The radical ideologue had to convince the ethnic masses that attachments based on principle were more important in the long run than the short-term satisfactions obtained through membership in ethnic fraternal and social associations. The ideology's success depended on a degree of political awareness and sophistication in response among ethnic groups that in reality had low to moderate political interest, experience, or inclination. Old-style radical leaders had to forge a common bond between "blood and believer." They had to promote the ideological premises themselves.

Because of these difficulties, radical ideological politics of the old style never really caught on among the various ethnic groups. The religious beliefs and ethnic organizations of many groups provided their members with the emotional and structural support needed to cope with their strange new environment in the "New World." The ethnics' desire for social acceptance was often too strong for many to be attracted to the radical political party platforms. Accommodation politics won them sufficient material gains to undercut the ideological appeal. They simply preferred the immediate gratification and emotional and psychological ties to their "own" groups to the long-term and doubtful rewards of an alien ideology.

The major political parties, moreover, undercut the appeal of radical third-party movements whenever such splinter groups won some electoral strength. The major parties adopted a few aspects of the radical party's platform, bringing a few of their more popular concerns into conformity with majority society goals.

The greatest success of old-style radicalism was to focus attention on some problems, ideas, or concerns stressed by the third-party movement in its campaigns. Their political impact was indirect: inducing majority parties to adopt, albeit in some modified form, their more radical planks. Today's minority groups use new-style radicalism, perhaps best exemplified by the militant black civil rights movement of the late 1950s to mid-1960s. Under this approach, the minority espouses less radical ideological points but employs what is at the time considered to be radical behavior.

For such new-style radicalism to emerge, three elements must converge. The first element is a widespread feeling of anomie among minority group members. This anomie means that deprived persons, united only by common location or color, are more likely to view normal accommodation politics as ineffective and meaningless. The second element is when a group has a weak social base. Anomie among ethnic group members becomes politically potent when it is built into enduring social relations, when the individual's frustrations are no longer screened or adequately controlled by social mechanisms. Then personal anomie is likely to produce the politics of passion. History shows that isolated social groups are the most susceptible to mass movements and extreme volatility in political behavior. Isolated factory worker groups participated in the more violent and volatile aspects of the labor movement. Ethnic groups developed the politics of radical passion. The third element leading to new-style radicalism is the broad and direct intervention of federal institutions in the core urban areas. The nationalization of ethnic politics led to tactics that encouraged passionate political activity.

Radical behavior may range along the full spectrum of nonviolent, direct-action protest to full-scale revolution. Figure 2.2 shows such a continuum.

NONVIOLENT ◄─────────────────────────────────► VIOLENT

Direct-Action Protests	Boycotts	Paramilitary Posturing	Sporadic Riots	Urban Guerilla Tactics	Small-Scale Revolution
(Sit-ins, freedom rides)	(Rent strikes stopping construction)	(Weapons patrols)	(Political riots)	(Small to large-scale urban units)	(Coups, full-scale revolution)

FIGURE 2.2 A Continuum of Radical Behavior Tactics

Michael Lipsky (1968) has developed a schematic model of how and why such groups can sometimes use protest activity as a political resource. Relatively powerless groups—ethnic "have-nots," for instance—lack the traditional power resources of society: money, access to insiders, knowledge of the policy process, and so on. The protest situation works something like a credit card, enabling the protest group to "borrow" or use the power resources of other group(s)—what Lipsky labels the "reference publics"—in the majority society by getting them to apply pressure on government decision makers (the target group) who would otherwise be unavailable to the protestors. Figure 2.3 shows Lipsky's model in graphic form.

A minority group selects some unconventional protest situation designed to attract mass media coverage. A lunch counter sit-in, a freedom ride, a "wade-in" at a segregated beach, a "fish-in" by a local Native American tribe are all typical examples of such behavior. The Montgomery, Alabama, bus boycott was among the first and

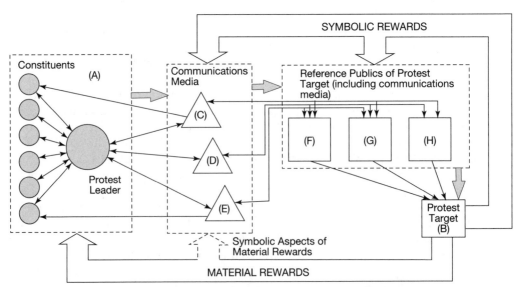

FIGURE 2.3 Schematic Representation of the Process of Protest by Relatively Powerless Groups

SOURCE: Michael Lipsky, "Protest as a Political Resource," *American Political Science Review* 61(4): 1145.

serves well to illustrate the workings of the model. Blacks in Montgomery in the mid-1950s were subject to discrimination in many forms, including the local ordinance segregating the city's public bus system. The local city council (the target group) would be the authoritative decision-making body that had the power to change local segregation laws. Blacks lacked access to the city council. They had no voting capacity. They had no money. They were objects of bigotry, thus lacking prestige, inside connections, or other similar power resources. But blacks did make up over 75 percent of the bus company's daily riders. By boycotting the bus system, they attracted local and eventually national media coverage: television, radio, newspapers, and national magazines. The boycott was newsworthy precisely because it was so unconventional for that time.

News coverage and the economic threat implicit in the boycott aroused fear among several of the city's social/economic elites (the reference publics). Executives of the local bus company felt a threat to their profits (it hit them in the pocketbook, where it hurts most). After a year of drastically reduced revenues, the executives responded by pressing the city council to change the law. Downtown businessmen—retail store owners and managers, theater and restaurant owners—began to feel the economic pinch. Their profits dropped because of the boycott. An economic elite trying to attract national business investment to Montgomery was aroused, fearing the harm national publicity about "bad relations with their colored folk" had on their efforts to attract new investment. These elites eventually pressured the city council to change the law to end the boycott. The boycott not only resulted in a positive change, as segregation laws were rescinded, it marked the emergence of Dr. Martin Luther King, Jr., as a national civil rights leader.

Lipsky discusses typical responses of the target group (government decision makers) to the protest situation. The target group may offer symbolic satisfaction. In response to protest over police brutality, for example, a local police department might hire a token minority group member. The press will cover the officer's graduation from the police academy, and the department will publicly emphasize its hiring of that minority person, symbolically stating an end to brutality. Such symbolic rewards are easy to give since they cost the target group next to nothing. They are really aimed more at the media and the reference public(s) than at the protest group members. If either or both of the former react favorably to the symbolic rewards, it relieves the target group from the pressure arising from the protest situation.

A second common response is to try to buy off the protestors with some token material rewards. The target group dips into its slack resources. Such a response is far cheaper than seriously reallocating its benefits in the direction of the protest group's goals. Imagine a group of welfare mothers on AFDC protesting the lack of allotments to buy winter clothing in a cold, northern city such as New York. The welfare office cannot increase the amounts given to every family on its rolls, but it can buy clothing for the children of the few protesting mothers. This may end the demonstrations, the media coverage, and any resulting political pressure on the agency.

A third typical response may be the target group reorganizing and innovating internally to blunt the impetus of the protest efforts. By reorganizing to act quickly in the worst cases, the target group may preempt protest efforts by responding to the cases that best dramatize the protestors' goals. The agency may designate all efforts that harm its reputation as "worst" cases and devote special efforts in the most heavily dramatized cases. Such special efforts wear down the "cutting edge" of the protest situation. Many large city agencies developed informal "crisis" arrangements to project the publicity the agencies desired and mobilized their resources for solving "crisis" cases. They also developed policy innovations allowing them to respond quickly when confronted with a protest situation.

A fourth reaction is the target group appearing constrained to act on the protest goals. The target group may extend its sympathies but claim the lack of resources or legal authority to respond to the protest demands. If successful in this response, the target group takes the heat off itself by diverting the protest group's attention to another, usually higher and geographically distant, government agency. This response is often effective with established civic agencies because they are known to have an undeniable element of truth; such agencies often are financially underfunded or constrained in their policy-making powers by directives from state or federal level agencies. Target groups attempt to diminish the impact of protest demands by claiming relative impotence.

A fifth response involves the target group using its extensive resources to discredit the protest leader or the protest group. The FBI's attempt to discredit Dr. King, by bugging him to uncover "dirt" about his sex life in order to blackmail him, or to publish such information in order to discredit him as a "man of the cloth," is a classic instance of this response. The civil rights movement and many of its leaders were portrayed as "communist dupes." Protests by local blacks were shrugged off as the efforts of "outside agitators." The Black Panthers were effectively discredited as violent radicals advocating revolution and violent change. Even when there is little validity to the allegations, this tactic may be effective if it results in the media either ceasing to cover the protest or changing the tone of its coverage, eliminating the protest group's effectiveness in reaching the reference publics and activating their resources. If the protest group is discredited, the target group no longer feels pressured, even if the media continue to cover the protest. The reference publics either ignore the protest situation or respond by approving the repression of the protest group.

Another classic response is to postpone action. A blue-ribbon commission is appointed to study the problem. Months later it issues a report that promptly gathers dust on some shelf. The protest situation is sometimes time-bound in its effectiveness. If the target group can postpone action, real pressure is removed. Welfare mothers protesting the need for more winter clothing allotment cannot effectively do so in the summer. Protest against inadequate numbers of minority employees on public construction projects cannot effectively be carried out once the job is three-fourths completed. The American Indian Movement's seizure of Wounded Knee was symbolically effective because it was bound to a centennial anniversary of the massacre. Postponing policy commitments is often an effective way for the target group to remove any real pressure to change its manner of allocating resources.

Any or several of these responses may be used by the target group, sometimes simultaneously. They should not be understood as serial responses; that is, first try option one, then if it fails, option two, and so on. The target group may try option one first, then six, and if that fails, number three.

A seventh logical response, although one only implied by Lipsky, is for the target group to grant some or all of the protest group's goals. Protest leaders sometimes include a few easy-to-grant goals within a list of demands in order to induce a quick favorable response. Such "success" at winning even a few slices of the loaf they are seeking can then be used to strengthen group cohesion, win new supporters, encourage the reference publics to keep up the pressure, and generally increase pressure on the target group to grant even more of the protestors' demands. This tactic partly accounts for why the civil rights movement was more successful against de jure segregation than against de facto segregation. It is easier to change Jim Crow laws than to change broadly accepted societal norms and customs. The successful use of this approach by the black civil rights movement inspired other groups to imitate the tactic. Black Power inspired Red, Brown, Gray, and Gay Power movements, all of which employed variations of the direct-action protest tactic. One of the best philosophical justifications for civil disobedience is the eloquent "Letter from a Birmingham Jail," written by Dr. King. (See Case Study 8.1.)

When peaceful protest tactics fail to work, groups using new-style radicalism may be driven to increasingly more violent radical behavior. The need to continue to attract mass media coverage imposes a pressure toward increasingly radical rhetoric, if not violent behavior. The first time a freedom ride or sit-in is used, it is hot news. Direct-action protests soon become old-hat. The national media's and the nation's attention span to any one problem is short-lived. Protest leaders are compelled to use more radical rhetoric and behavior to "keep the cameras rolling." Expressions like "burn, baby, burn" inspire violent reactions among some in the majority. This may instill violent reaction among minority group members. The radical approach contains a strong though not inevitable tendency toward more violent tactics.

The sporadic riots of the late 1960s were logical extensions of the approach. The targeted political rioting that rocked some 150 American cities during the summers of 1967–1968 were the emotional outbursts predicted by Dr. King. The use of gun sniping, occasional bank heists, or kidnapping by the Symbionese Liberation Army (SLA) exemplifies the more radical, violent spectrum of this approach. When less violent tactics seem to fail, or bring results many feel are too little or too late, more violent tactics may be used. The two approaches may work in tandem. The radicalness of the Black Panthers may lead city representatives to bargain with the NAACP.

This trend toward increasingly more radical behavior is neither inevitable nor irreversible. The winning of specific goals through unconventional and nonviolent protest may bring about sufficient changes in the rules of the game under which standard politics are conducted that a group previously rejecting accommodation politics as useless might change and adopt that strategy. After the civil rights movement used its nonviolent protest politics to end Jim Crow laws, blacks developed a substantial voting force in southern politics. By the late 1970s and continuing to the present, blacks used standard electoral politics to win a considerable number of elective and appointive positions via the polling booth instead of the streets.

A given minority may pursue any one of these three basic approaches. It may employ one approach at one time, and another at some other time. Some of the larger minority groups may fragment into factions, each of which pursues a different strategy

TABLE 2.5   Strategies and Tactics of Minority Groups' Responses to Discrimination and Placement in Minority Status

Strategy	Tactics and Groups Employing Them	

Accommodation	*The Economic Approach*
	Occupational queuing and use of special niches.
	Groups using:
	    Scots, Welsh, Germans, Scandinavians, Dutch, Japanese, Chinese, Korean, blacks (Booker T. Washington followers).
		The Political Approach
		Machine politics and coalitions, electoral-generated gains.
		Groups using:
		    Irish, Italians, Greeks, Jews, Slavs, Women (e.g., NOW).

Separatism	*Physical Separatism*
	Moving to isolated areas.
	Groups using:
	    Chinese, Amish, Mennonites, Mormons, Native Americans, blacks (Marcus Garvey followers).
		Psychological Separatism
		Building shell around members.
		Groups using:
		    Black Muslims, Hasidic Jews, millennial religious groups.

Radicalism	*Old-Style Radicalism*
	Ideological "isms."
	Groups using:
	    Socialism—Jews, Poles, Germans, Slavs, Russians
	    Communism—same as Socialism
	    Fascism/Nazism—Germans, Italians, White Russians, radical agrarianism, Utopian movements.
		New-Style Radicalism
		Nonviolent to violent protest actions.
		Groups using:
		    SCLC, SNCC, CORE, Black Panthers, SLA, AIM, UFW of Cesar Chavez.

at the same time. Blacks in the 1960s, for example, showed all three approaches were possible. The Black Muslim faction advocated separatism while the Urban League followed an accommodationist approach. Dr. King and his Southern Christian Leadership Conference (SCLC) preached and used new-style radicalism. His success inspired others: the Congress on Racial Equality (CORE) and the Student Nonviolent Coordinating Committee (SNCC); even the National Association for the Advancement of Colored People (NAACP) began using similar tactics. The Black Panthers and more radical groups such as the SLA used more violent tactics in their approach to new-style radicalism. By the late 1970s, the civil rights movement changed to a predominantly accommodationist approach.

SUMMARY

This chapter discussed various theoretical perspectives to study racial/ethnic relations among various minority groups. It highlighted insights to the assimilation process offered by the psychological, social-psychological, economic, and sociological views of the process. It presented a systems dynamic model of the assimilation process.

The chapter discussed typical responses by minority groups to their status. Three major strategies were distinguished: the politics of accommodation, separatism, and radicalism. The chapter developed two main tactical approaches for each strategy: the economic or political route to accommodation, the physical or psychological route to separatism, and the old-style and new-style routes to radicalism.

Table 2.5 summarizes these strategies and their tactical approaches, suggesting examples of various groups that used one or more of these strategies in response to discrimination. Different groups employed different strategies over time. While the accommodationist strategy is by far the most common, new-style radicalism has become the more popular approach in recent decades. The chapter discussed Michael Lipsky's model of protest politics to show why direct-action protest politics may effect changes in the political system.

Some groups fragmented into factions employing the various approaches at the same time. The chapter briefly discussed choice of which strategy is the more attractive alternative for any given group at any particular time. The characteristics of various minorities and the resources available to them are major determinants in their choice of strategy and tactical response.

KEY TERMS

Accommodation strategy: a minority group accepts the values of the majority and seeks "entrance" and its fair proportion of societal rewards.

Cross-group voting: when members of a minority group vote for someone other than a co-ethnic when they have a choice. It is a prime indicator of civic assimilation.

Ethnophaulism: a racial or ethnic group's derogatory nickname for another group.

Majority's fear function: the degree to which majority society perceives the minority subculture as a threat.

Marginal membership function: the number of marginal members within the minority group, which influences its rate of acculturation/assimilation.

Occupational niche: job roles or positions open to a minority because they are viewed as non-threatening by the dominant group. Minority groups show high concentrations in particular occupations.

Occupational queuing: the rank-ordering of jobs by their socioeconomic desirability.

Similarity of cultures function: the closeness of fit between the majority and minority subcultures.

Size of minority function: the perceived relative size of the minority to the majority group.

System theory: theory that views relationships as being integrally related parts of a whole wherein the sum is greater than the parts. Each system may be viewed as being part of another larger system (a subsystem) or as an encompassing system (a suprasystem).

REVIEW QUESTIONS

1. What are Milton Gordon's seven stages of assimilation?

2. Discuss the three strategies that minorities use to cope with their status and give examples of groups using each strategy. Which strategy/tactics are Arab Americans likely to use? Why so?

3. What are the stages of political accommodation?

4. Describe the characteristics typical of a millennial movement. What are some typical groups exemplifying it? Why do such movements favor separatism?

5. Compare and contrast old-style and new-style radicalism.

NOTES

1. Elections held in Quebec, Canada, in September 1994 returned to power the Separatist Parti Quebecois by giving it a solid majority in the provincial legislature, winning 77 of 125 seats. The party leader promised a referendum within a year on the question to secede. See Craig Turner, "Separatists Party Headed for Victory in Quebec Election," *Los Angeles Times,* September 13, 1994, pp. A1, A3.

2. Other scholars have suggested similar stages. See, for example, E. S. Bogardus, who suggests the following stages in acculturation: curiosity, economic welcome, industrial and social antagonism, legislative antagonism, fair play tendencies, quiescence, and second-generation difficulties. See his "Race Relations Cycle," *American Journal of Sociology* 35 (January 1930): 613. W. O. Brown states that race relations have a "natural history" of initial contact, emergence of conflict, temporary accommodation, struggle for status, mobilization, and solution. See his "Cultural Contacts and Race Conflicts," in E. B. Reuter, ed., *Race and Cultural Contacts* (New York: McGraw-Hill, 1934), pp. 34–37. E. C. Glick posits a sequence of phases: precontact, contact and predomination, domination, and accommodation. See his "Social Roles and Types in Race Relations," in A. W. Lind, ed., *Race Relations in World Perspective* (Honolulu: University of Hawaii Press, 1955), pp. 239–241.

3. Not all scholars view assimilation as inevitable or even likely. Barth and Noel, for instance, argue that in addition to assimilation, there are at least four other possible stable outcomes of intergroup contact: exclusion (including both expulsion and annihilation), symbiosis, stratification, and pluralism. See, for example, their "Conceptual Frameworks for the Analysis of Race Relations: An Evaluation," *Social Forces* 50 (1972): 333–347; see also Conrad Kottak and Kathryn Kozaitis, *On Being Different* (Boston: McGraw-Hill, 1999), pp. 48–51.

4. This section draws heavily from William Davisson and John J. Uhran, Jr., "Modeling and Simulation: A Systems Science Approach," mimeo., University of Notre Dame, 1976.

5. See the seminal work of David Easton, *A Framework for Political Analysis* (Englewood Cliffs, NJ: Prentice Hall, 1965).

6. Rates of intergroup marriage have been shown to be important in numerous studies. See, for example, B. R. Bugelski, "Assimilation Through Intermarriage," *Social Forces* 40 (1961): 148–153; Joseph P. Fitzpatrick, "Intermarriage of Puerto Ricans in New York City," *American Journal of Sociology* 71 (1968): 395–406; C. Peach, "Which Triple Melting Pot? A Re-Examination of Ethnic Intermarriage in New Haven, 1900–1950," *Ethnic and Racial Studies* 3 (1980): 1–16; and B. B. Wessel, *An Ethnic Survey of Woonsocket, Rhode Island* (Chicago: University of Chicago Press, 1931).

SUGGESTED READINGS

BLALOCK, HUBERT M., JR. *Race and Ethnic Relations.* Englewood Cliffs, NJ: Prentice Hall. 1982.

EASTON, DAVID. *A Framework for Political Analysis.* Englewood Cliffs, NJ: Prentice Hall, 1965.

GORDON, MILTON. *Assimilation in American Life.* New York: Oxford University Press, 1964.

KITANO, HARRY. *Race Relations,* 5th ed. Upper Saddle River, NJ: Prentice Hall, 1997.

KOTTAK, CONRAD, AND KATHRYN KOZAITIS. *On Being Different: Diversity and Multiculturalism in the North American Mainstream.* Boston: McGraw-Hill, 1999.

LIEBERMAN, ROBERT C. *Shifting the Color Line: Race and the American Welfare State.* Cambridge, MA: Harvard University Press, 1998.

LIEBERSON, STANLEY. *A Piece of the Pie.* Berkeley: University of California Press, 1980.

LIPSKY, MICHAEL. "Protest as a Political Resource," *American Political Science Review* 62, no. 4 (December 1968): 1144–1158.

LITT, EDGAR. *Ethnic Politics in America.* Glenview, IL: Scott, Foresman, 1970.

SCHERMERHORN, RICHARD. *Comparative Ethnic Relations.* New York: Random House, 1970.

VANDERZANDEN, JAMES W. *American Minority Relations.* New York: Ronald Press, 1983.

WHITE, JOHN. *Black Leadership in America: From Booker T. Washington to Jesse Jackson,* 2nd ed. New York: Longman, 1990.

CASE STUDY 2.1

The Arab-American Market

Samia El-Badry, president of International Demographic
and Economic Associates (IDEA) of Austin, Texas.

Real Arab Americans don't fit into media stereotypes. They are people we know and respect, like consumer advocate Ralph Nader. Singer Paula Abdul and deejay Casey Kasem prove that Arab Americans can be as American as rock and roll. Heart surgeon Michael De Bakey and Heisman Trophy winner Doug Flutie place Arab Americans among our heroes. Secretary of Health Donna Shalala, Senate majority leader George Mitchell, and many other Arab Americans rank among our leaders.

The vast majority of Arab Americans are citizens. They are much like other Americans, except younger, more educated, more affluent, and more likely to own a business. The demographics of Arab Americans make them an important consumer market.

According to the Census Bureau's definition, Arab Americans are people who trace their ancestry to the northern African countries of Morocco, Tunisia, Algeria, Libya, Sudan, and Egypt, and the western Asian countries of Lebanon, occupied Palestine, Syria, Jordan, Iraq, Bahrain, Qatar, Oman, Saudi Arabia, Kuwait, United Arab Emirates, and Yemen. While these nations vary somewhat in their cultures and traditions, the common ground is an "Arabic heritage" and the Arabic language.

Arab Americans may be olive-skinned, white, or black. Some have blue eyes; others have brown. Some are Moslems, some are Christians, and a small share are Jews.

They can dress in traditional attire, but most favor Western garb.

Arab immigration to the U.S. began in the late 19th century. Early arrivals were mostly Christians from Syria and Lebanon who established themselves as merchants.

Since World War II, Arab immigration has been characterized by people from capitalist classes, landed gentry, and influential urban families fleeing from countries where the leadership was overthrown. Many postwar immigrants were Palestinians displaced when Israel was established in 1948. Others were Egyptians whose land was taken by the Nasser regime, Syrians fleeing a country overthrown by revolutionaries, or Iraqi royalists escaping republican regimes . . .

Immigration from the Middle East picked up dramatically in the 1960s. In fact, more than 75 percent of foreign-born Arab Americans in 1990 had immigrated after 1964, compared with 52 percent of the total foreign-born U.S. population. The largest share (44 percent) came to the U.S. between 1975 and 1980, compared with just 24 percent of all foreign-born persons. This recent flood is due in large part to the Immigration Act of 1965, which ended a quota system that favored immigrants from Europe. Most post-1965 Arab immigrants have been Moslems with even more education than their predecessors. However, a 1991 survey suggests that about half of Arab Americans identify themselves as Christians. . . .

The 1990 census found 870,000 Americans who list an Arab country among their top two ancestries. The census definition is not the only one, however, and it has not been consistent. . . . Yvonne Haddad of the University of Massachusetts estimates that if all 1990 census undercounts were corrected, the tally would run to more than 1 million Arab Americans.

Census data show that 82 percent of Arab Americans are U.S. citizens, and 63 percent were born in the U.S. Fifty-four percent of Arab Americans are men, compared with 49 percent of the total U.S. population. This is partly due to the fact that men of all nationalities are more likely to immigrate first, while women tend to follow.

Arab Americans tend to be younger than the overall American population. Again, this is probably because younger people are more likely than older people to immigrate. As a result, a large proportion of Arab Americans are in their childbearing years, and another large proportion are native-born children and teenagers.

As with many other minorities, Arab Americans are a geographically concentrated group. Over two-thirds live in ten states; one-third live in California, New York, and Michigan. They are also more likely than other Americans to live in metropolitan areas. Thirty-six percent of Arab Americans live in ten metros, led by Detroit, New York, and Los Angeles–Long Beach.

In general, Arab Americans are better educated than the average American. The share who did not attend college is lower than average, and the share with master's degrees or higher is twice the average. Because a larger-than-average share of Arab Americans are highly educated people of working age, their work force rates are high. Eighty percent of Arab Americans aged 16 and older were employed in 1990, compared with 60 percent of all American adults.

ARAB-AMERICAN WORKERS

Sixty percent of Arab Americans work as executives, professionals, salespeople, administrative support, or service personnel, compared with 66 percent of the general American population. . . . They are more likely than average to be entrepreneurs or self-employed (12 percent versus 7 percent).

Arab Americans hold different occupations in different cities. For example, 23 percent of those who live in Washington, D.C., and Anaheim are executives, and 18 percent of those in Houston and Washington are professionals. Arab Americans are most likely to do sales work in Anaheim and Cleveland, while administrative support jobs are relatively more important in Bergen–Passaic, New Jersey, and New York City. Service jobs like education and health care are most important to Arab Americans in Cleveland and Boston.

In Detroit and Chicago, the above-mentioned mostly white-collar occupations only account for about half of Arab-American employment. In manufacturing-dominated Detroit, 16 percent of the Arab-American labor force works in precision, production, and craft occupations, or as machine operators and assemblers.

Only 35 percent of Arab Americans work in manufacturing, finance, and service industries, compared with 57 percent of all U.S. workers. Regardless of occupation, one in five Arab-American workers is engaged in the retail-trade industry, slightly higher than the 17 percent U.S. average. Of these, 29 percent work in eating and dining facilities, as everything from franchise managers to waiters. Eighteen percent work in grocery stores, 7 percent in department stores, and 6 percent in apparel and accessory outlets. Retail trade is the biggest employer of Arab Americans in every major metro except Boston—where a greater share are employed in health and educational services.

As occupation and industry vary, so does income. Among the ten metros with the most Arab Americans, median Arab-American household income in 1990 ranged from $32,300 in the Detroit metropolitan area to $53,600 in Washington, D.C. Median household income for all Arab-American households in 1990 stood at $39,100, compared with the U.S. average of $30,100.... Arab Americans are numerous, affluent, and often misunderstood. Like the gay population and Asian Americans, they suffer from stereotyping and negative press. Yet all are significant and distinct niche markets.

A glance through the advertising pages of Arab-American publications reveals a mix of specialized and mainstream products and services, such as medical and legal services, Middle Eastern foods, books, crafts, and jewelry, as well as "regular" videotapes, home electronics, travel, and restaurants. Like any other immigrant group, Arab Americans want to enjoy America's riches while preserving the important parts of their native culture....

The American Arab Chamber of Commerce provides a service called Arab-Link that helps businesses market to both Arab Americans and Arabs abroad....

Huntington Bank actively markets to Arab Americans. Almost the entire staff in its East Dearborn branch speaks Arabic, according to Mary Short, vice president in charge of marketing at Huntington's headquarters in Troy. East Dearborn is an area heavily populated by people of Arabic descent, and the bank has successfully recruited many of its employees from the neighborhood. The bank advertises in Arabic-language publications and uses other media to reach its customers, but Short says that the best advertising is word-of-mouth recommendations from people who live and work nearby.

Last September, the Dearborn branch opened a small business service center in conjunction with Wayne State University. Wayne State has been working with minority business owners in other cities, but this new center represents its first outreach to the Arab-American community. Short says practically all of the branch's customers are self-employed and "doing a cash business."

Because Arab Americans are more likely than others to be entrepreneurs, business-to-business marketers would do well to learn more about this community.

Immigrants coming from Arab nations still represent less than 3 percent of all immigrants coming to the United States, but their numbers are growing. In 1992, more than 27,000 people from Arab nations immigrated to the United States—68 percent more than those who came ten years earlier. These figures do not include Palestinians migrating from Israel or from the occupied territory. Among the 78,400 immigrants who arrived between 1990 and 1992, 17,500 are from Lebanon. That's more than one in every five recent Arab immigrants. People from Egypt (13,300) and Jordan (12,700) each account for about one in six Arab immigrants. Those coming from Syria (8,700) ranked fourth, accounting for one in nine recent arrivals. And Iraq (7,400) ranked fifth, making up less than one in ten immigrants. Although the order has changed somewhat, these same nations were also in the top five in 1982.

The fastest-growing Arab-immigrant group is from Sudan. While it accounted for only 675 immigrants in 1992, that's nearly nine times more than the number that arrived ten years earlier. The number of people coming from Qatar, Saudi Arabia, United Arab Emirates, and Yemen all grew more than fourfold between 1982 and 1992. But the largest of these rapidly growing segments, people from Yemen, accounted for just 2,100 immigrants in 1992. There were fewer than 600 immigrants from Saudi Arabia, fewer than 200 from the United Arab Emirates, and just 59 from Qatar. Other nations that have at least doubled the number of immigrants that they send to America include Algeria, Morocco, Tunisia, Bahrain, and Kuwait. . . .

Businesses that want to reach Arab Americans should be aware that this is a sensitive market. They are tired of the negative press surrounding international issues. And they are tired of thoughtless portrayals in the media. Donald Bustany, president of the Los Angeles chapter of the American-Arab Anti-Discrimination Committee (ADC) told the *Dallas Morning News:* "Even with people of good faith, it takes awhile to turn attitudes around."

SOURCE: Adapted from *American Demographics,* January 1994, pp. 22–27, 30–31. © 1994 by American Demographics, Inc. Reprinted with permission.

CHAPTER THREE

THE STRATEGY OF ACCOMMODATION
The Economic Route

When an ethnic or racial group is assigned to minority status by the dominant society, it must react. Historically many such groups developed out of the immigration process. They came voluntarily to the United States seeking a better life: more economic opportunity and greater religious and political freedom. They desired assimilation. Their choice of tactics to pursue a strategy of accommodation was either an economic or political route. This chapter discusses the economic route to accommodation. Since more immigrants came for economic opportunity than for any other reason, many groups pursued an economic path. Groups who immigrated during a period of an expanding economy, or who arrived with special skills or resources, were more able and willing to use this approach. This chapter will discuss in some detail the accommodation patterns of Asian Americans and several European groups. The chapter closes with the pattern of economic accommodation pursued by Hispanic Americans and the faction of African Americans who followed the philosophy of Booker T. Washington.

Of all the racially based minority groups, the most successful in their struggles have been the various Asian-American groups who employed the economic route. A significant proportion of Asian Americans have achieved middle-class status. Since they desired assimilation and often pursued entrepreneurial opportunities, achieving middle-class status, given their goals, can be considered a successful use of the strategy. It is to their "success story" we turn our attention.

ASIAN AMERICANS

Asian Americans make up one of the nation's smallest racial minorities—2.9 percent of the total. According to 1990 census data, there are 4,979,000 foreign-born residents in the United States from Asian nations of origin, of whom over 56 percent came to the United States during the 1980–1990 decade. They are well educated; as of 1997, 76 percent had high school degrees and over 42 percent had four years of college or more. Although as of 1990 Asian Americans (whether native or foreign-born) made up only 2.9 percent of the total U.S. population, they earned 3.8 percent of the bachelor's degrees awarded during the 1980–1990 decade, 3.4 percent of the master's degrees, 3.8 percent of the doctoral degrees, and 5.3 percent of the "first-professional" degrees. Occupationally, 20 percent are professionals, 15 percent are in service occupations, and 12.5 percent are operators, fabricators, or laborers. As of 1993, among Asian Americans, 65.3 percent were employed (compared to 54.4 percent of whites), and only 3.8 percent were unemployed (as compared to 8.0 percent of whites). Their median personal income in 1996 dollars was $14,634 (as compared to $12, 961 for whites), and their per capita income in 1996 constant dollars was $17,921 (as compared to $19,181 for whites).

Tables 3.1, and 3.2 present statistical data that provide an overview of their numbers, origins, and economic status. Table 3.1 presents their relative percentage of the total population by selected countries of origin. Table 3.2 compares Asian-American family incomes, as of 1997, with that of blacks and whites.

Chinese Americans

At nearly 23 percent of all Asian Americans, Chinese Americans are the largest Asian-American group. They were the first Asian immigrants to come to the United States in significant numbers. After the discovery of gold in California in 1848, Chinese laborers surged into the state. The largest groups came from Kwantung and Fukien provinces, in southern China. In part, they fled economic depression and resulting local rebellions, but also floods, famine, and the general social discontent in their homeland. They were also pulled by the demand for labor created by the California gold boom. Railroad and steamship companies recruited them heavily.

TABLE 3.1   Percentage of U.S. Population of Asian Origin by Selected Nations of Origin, 1990

	Number (thousands)	Percent
Total U.S. population	248,710	100%
Asian	7,274	2.9
Chinese	1,645	.06
Filipino	1,407	.05
Japanese	848	.003
Asian Indian	815	.003
Korean	799	.003
Vietnamese	615	.008
Laotian	149	.005
Cambodian	147	.005
Thai	91	.0003
Hmong	90	.0003

SOURCE: U.S. Bureau of the Census, *Statistical Abstract of the United States, 1998* (Washington, DC: U.S. Government Printing Office, 1998), Table 30, p. 31.

TABLE 3.2   A Comparison of Asian-American, Black, and White Family Income, 1997

Income Level	Asian	Black	White
Less than $5,000	3.9%	7.8%	2.0%
5,000 to 9,999	3.8	11.1	3.9
10,000 to 14,999	5.3	10.7	5.4
15,000 to 24,999	11.4	17.6	13.0
25,000 to 34,999	10.9	14.3	13.5
35,000 to 49,999	15.8	15.1	18.3
50,000 or more	48.7	23.3	44.1
Families below the poverty level	11.9	26.1	8.6
Persons below the poverty level	14.1	28.3	11.2

SOURCE: U.S. Bureau of the Census, *Statistical Abstract of the United States, 1998* (Washington, DC: U.S. Government Printing Office, 1998), Tables 51, 52, pp. 51–52.

Chinese laborers were welcomed for the first few years after their arrival in America. They were initially viewed as industrious, thrifty, adaptable to many types of tasks, and willing to perform labor unattractive to the majority white males. Chinese immigrants quickly became essential to the California economy. They were organized, so an employer could secure any number of workers by negotiating with a single contractor. This placed them in a comparatively advantageous position. Once employed, Chinese laborers stayed on the job, agreeing to do the most undesirable tasks. With the lack of labor generally, and especially the lack of women, they found work in the mines, building railroads, and as ranch hands, farm laborers, and domestic servants. The Central Pacific Railroad, for example, employed some 9,000 Chinese immigrants a year. By 1860, they made up about 10 percent of California's population and roughly 25 percent of its work force (Thompson 1996).

Their warm welcome was short-lived. By the mid-1850s, growing hostility was evident. In the mining regions especially, the Chinese were often robbed and beaten and occasionally murdered. By 1849, a Know Nothing judge of the California Supreme Court had ruled that the Chinese could not testify in courts against white men. Crimes against them often went unpunished.

Their problems reflected resentment against them because they were viewed as threats to white labor. The Chinese immigrants were overwhelmingly males who came to the United States as **sojourners**—intending to work here only for a few years to save money and then return to their native land to buy land. The Chinese male–female ratio from 1860 to 1900 was a few thousand to one. This problem was exacerbated when 14 states passed *antimiscegenation laws* (forbidding marriage between the white and Asian races). Those laws, coupled with the scarcity of Chinese females, left the men with no alternative but total abstention or the use of prostitutes. Prostitution was usually associated with the opium traffic, which soon led to a severe image problem of "criminality" concerning Chinese immigrants. Difficulty in importing Chinese females contributed to the long-lasting nature of the imbalance. By 1882, Chinese labor immigration was greatly reduced. As of 1890, only 2.7 percent of Chinese were American-born. The ratio began to be redressed during the 1920s when

30 percent were native-born. But real parity was not achieved until after a 1943 law ended the total ban on Chinese labor immigration and provided a quota that allowed Chinese women to enter the country. By 1960, two-thirds of Chinese Americans were native-born, and the male–female ratio was finally nearly balanced.

Miscegenation laws were but one manifestation of the legal constraints imposed on the Chinese in America. By the 1850s, California expelled them from the mining work camps, forbade their entry into public schools, denied their right to testify against whites in court, and barred them from obtaining citizenship. By 1865, calls for restrictions on their immigration began. In 1867, the Democratic Party swept into California's elective offices running on an anti-Chinese platform. The Panic of 1873 brought on economic conditions that greatly increased the sense of competition from Chinese immigrant labor, and calls against the "Yellow Menace" broadened. In 1887, the Workingmen's Party, led by Dennis Kearny running on a blatantly anti-Chinese campaign, scored political success in several cities. The party called for an end to all Chinese immigration. By the 1870s, such sentiment was so strong on the West Coast that it was virtually political suicide to take the Chinese side. This anti-Chinese legal action culminated nationally in the passage of the Chinese Exclusion Act of 1882.

The impact of that law, first passed with a provision imposing a ten-year ban and amended in 1884 to further tighten the ban, was immediate and drastic. In 1881, 11,900 Chinese labor immigrants entered the United States and over 39,500 came in 1882. But that figure dropped to a paltry 8,031 in 1883, and by 1885 a mere 23 Chinese laborers managed to enter. In 1892, Congress renewed the Exclusion Act for another ten years, and in 1902 the law was extended indefinitely.

Laws were not the only method used to restrict Chinese life and work opportunities. Violence and social segregation were common. Anti-Chinese feelings reached a fever pitch by the mid-1870s. Many turned from law to violence. In 1871, 21 Chinese were killed in a Los Angeles riot. In 1880, Denver also experienced a severe anti-Chinese riot. A typical example of the use of violence was the Trukee Raid of 1876; whites burned a Chinese home and shot and killed the residents as they attempted to flee the flames. White citizens tried for the crimes were acquitted. The Order of Caucasians advocated the elimination of the Chinese through the use of violence. They raided and burned various sections of Chinatowns. In 1885, at Rock Springs, Wyoming, a mob killed 28 Chinese and drove hundreds of others from their homes. In Tacoma, Seattle, and Oregon City, mobs expelled hundreds of Chinese from those cities. Unionized labor, particularly the Teamsters, became a major force behind the violently anti-Chinese movement. The violence subsided after the restrictions laws were passed, but strong prejudice and discrimination remained, especially in jobs and housing, well into the 1890s. Newspapers spread the stereotyped images of the Chinese with stories about prostitution, gambling, and opium dens in Chinatowns. "Chinks" and "John Chinaman" were names used as racial slurs.

Job discrimination was prevalent. Violence kept many out of the mine fields, but so too did legislation. In 1855, the Foreign Miners' Tax was enacted in California. It required foreign miners to pay a four-dollar-per-month tax. In addition, the tax increased each year the miner did not become a citizen. Since the Chinese were legally excluded from naturalization, they were forced to pay ever higher rates. This legislation and the violence soon forced them to seek other areas of employment.

The general lack of women in the frontier, however, opened up the area of domestic services to the Chinese as one field in which they would not be viewed as a competitive threat to the white male labor force. Laundries, restaurants, and other domestic services required little capital or job skills. The increasing job discrimination and violence encouraged their tendency to cluster together in urban Chinatowns. Even there, however, they could not escape legislative harassment. San Francisco passed ordinances between 1876 and 1880 aimed solely at the Chinese. A special tax was placed on small hand laundries, all of which were operated by the Chinese at the time. A "Cubic Air Act" was passed that jailed the occupants of overcrowded housing rather than the landlords, if each person did not have 500 square feet of living space. The city also enacted a "Queu Tax," that is, a tax on pigtails—a hairstyle worn exclusively by the Chinese. An ordinance was passed restricting the shipment of human bones, aimed at the Chinese custom of sending a deceased person's bones home for burial. Although these laws were nearly impossible to enforce very widely and were ultimately found to be unconstitutional, they contributed to the atmosphere and the institutionalization of a rigid social and geographic segregation of the Chinese in America.

When the Chinese did enter an industry, pay discrimination forced further segregation. The Chinese virtually took over the San Francisco shoe industry. The cigar industry became over 90 percent Chinese. They made up 64 percent of California's textile industry workers. In these occupations, wages fell dramatically from $25 to $9 per week (Kitano 1997).

Chinatowns developed in Los Angeles, San Francisco, New York, Boston, Pittsburgh, and St. Louis, and this pattern continues today. Chinese Americans are overwhelmingly urban and concentrated in several large Chinatowns.

The Chinese reacted to the discriminatory pressures by forming organizations for self-protection, for social and economic benefits, and for pooling their scant economic resources. The older organizations, such as the Six Companies of San Francisco, were highly specific, limited in scope and membership, and conservative. They offered education and medical services, settled disputes among members, and gave legal aid to members involved in lawsuits with whites. During the period of heightened violence against them, they hired their own private policemen to guard property in Chinatown. They fought legal cases to overturn the anti-Chinese laws passed at local, state, and even the national level. The Six Companies helped bury their dead and cared for their graves. Before the establishment of official diplomatic and consular offices in America, the Six Companies served as the unofficial voice of the Chinese Imperial Government on behalf of Chinese residents in America (Kung 1962).

Newer Chinese organizations reflect American patterns—Chinese golf clubs, boy scout troops, and Lions Clubs. Organized religion plays a minor role. A more confrontational stance has been adopted by the Asian-American Political Alliance, a group of Chinese-American and Japanese-American youth who reject the accommodationist posture of their elders. A middle-of-the road position was taken by the

Chinese American Citizens League. Founded in 1895, the league promotes mutual interests among Americans of Chinese ancestry.

A major factor in easing the situation of the Chinese Americans was the basic attitude shift within the majority society during the 1940s, when China became a U.S. ally against the Japanese. Suddenly the mass media began stressing the Chinese people's peace-loving nature, how valiantly they fought against the "sly, tricky Jap," how different they were from their more aggressive neighbor. They were viewed as honest, hardworking, gentle, and compliant. The alliance between the United States and China against Japan led to the repeal of the Chinese Exclusion Act. A citizens committee was formed to advocate for repeal. That law was passed on December 13, 1943. The McCarren-Walter Act of 1952 further codified the many immigration laws into one statute, and Chinese labor quotas for immigration, though small, were set, and restrictions against naturalization were repealed. Increased Chinese immigration was enabled by the refugee law enacted under President Kennedy in 1962. Finally, in 1965, President Johnson signed into law an act that abolished the national-origins quota system and pooled all unused nationality quotas into one group. Chinese immigration rose substantially after 1970.

Even in California the attitude against the Chinese changed dramatically during and after World War II. They were praised for their high ethical standards in faithfully meeting their contractual and other obligations and for their commercial abilities. The personal word of the Chinese merchant was accepted by American bankers, businessmen, lawyers, and even customs officials. They had a reputation for paying their bills, taxes, rents, and other debts.

The war period opened up other avenues for more rapid economic accommodation. Because of manpower shortages during the war, Chinese Americans entered skilled as well as unskilled positions in industry. They proved to be hardworking employees. They soon competed in many occupational fields, although today there is still evidence of more subtle discrimination in employment in that they are underrepresented in executive, managerial, academic, sales, and personnel positions and in the more highly paid crafts, such as ironworkers, operating engineers, plumbers, and electricians (Parrillo 1996).

The cohesive and extended family structure of Chinese-American society is seen as a contributing factor to their more rapid acculturation. Their heritage stresses education. Third-generation Chinese Americans were able to get good educations after the post–World War II economic gains made by the first- and second-generation cohorts. With improved educations, they entered the professional job market. They have done well in formal education, now ranking among the highest educated of minority groups. The third generation has completely acculturated in its style of clothing, observance of American holidays such as Christmas, Easter, and the Fourth of July—although they still commonly celebrate the Chinese New Year. The typical Chinese American eats with a knife and fork rather than chopsticks, and more often than not eats traditional American dishes.

Chinese laundries and restaurants are still highly popular and profitable forms of business. Quantitatively, the laundry business surpasses all others, but the amount of revenue received is less than that of the Chinese restaurant industry. The hand laundry still predominates, but laundries that perform specific functions, such as shirt process-ing, are more mechanized. The Chinese restaurant has grown into an American favorite and produces good profits for its owners, most of which are either run by a partnership or a single owner. Other popular Chinese-American businesses are the Chinese grocery and the import-export gift shops. The very image of Chinatown has changed. Once despised as dirty, crime-ridden dens of iniquity, Chinatowns are now viewed as bits of quaint old China set down in our streets, providing the tourist with a unique and pleasurable cross-cultural experience.

Today's Chinese Americans are well acculturated and largely middle class. Being native-born, they speak English as their native tongue. With few exceptions they are Americanized in almost all cultural aspects. Structural assimilation has been far less achieved. Individual incomes are still below the national white average, although their family income exceeds that of the average white family. They still exhibit a higher than average rate of mental illness, and tuberculosis remains a nag-ging health problem. In housing, they remain clustered in the Chinatowns of Hawaii, San Francisco, Los Angeles, and New York. Delinquency and gang behavior are serious problems. Social contacts between Chinese Americans and whites still reflect a degree of racial prejudice. While the Chinese are no longer feared in the job market, there are still indicators of prejudice operating against them there. Their greatest success comes when they own and operate their own businesses. Their rate of intermarriage, another indicator of assimilation, remains low. While becoming more common, intermarriage is still frowned upon on the mainland, as opposed to Hawaii, by members of both races. That is less of a problem among Japanese Ameri-cans, to whom we next turn.

Japanese Americans

At 12 percent of all Asian Americans, Japanese Americans are the third largest Asian group in the United States, according to the 1990 census. Japanese immigration to the United States began in 1868, when 148 contract workers came to Hawaii as planta-tion workers, but most came during the period between 1890 and 1924, and since 1965. It was not until the Meiji Restoration in 1868 that the Japanese were allowed to emigrate. Initially they were encouraged to do so and were well received in Hawaii. They first came expecting their stay to be temporary, working under a three-year con-tract that had been arranged by the Hawaiian government. They were viewed as a source of cheap labor and an alternative to the Chinese "coolie" labor force.

After the initial three-year period, some migrated to the mainland, concentrat-ing on the West Coast, especially in California. In 1870, there were only 56 Japanese immigrants on the mainland, but by 1890, they exceeded 24,000 and totaled just over 72,000 by the 1910 census. In 1920, they exceeded 110,000, at which level they basi-cally stabilized because of the Immigration Law of 1924, which specifically barred them until it was rescinded in 1952. By 1941, when the Japanese attacked Pearl Har-bor, there were only 127,000 Japanese aliens and Japanese Americans on the main-land, some 94,000 of whom lived in California, and among whom 63 percent were native-born citizens.

The Japanese adapted well to working conditions in the United States. The majority were young males (the ratio of male to female was about 4 to 1 from the farming class, which in Japan placed them in the middle class). They were highly literate; nearly 99 percent were able to read, exceeding by far the literacy of the majority population and clearly distinguishing them from their West and East European immigrant counterparts. In Hawaii, most worked in farming, usually in all-male work gangs under the supervision of an agent. Those who went to the mainland established a more diversified occupational pattern. Their most typical job was working on the western railroads, but they were also employed in canneries, in the mines, as domestic servants, cooks, and waiters, and in groceries and dry goods establishments. Their low wage scale troubled them as they evidenced a strong desire for upward mobility. They soon turned to agriculture on the mainland, particularly truck farming, and they became strong economic competitors. Prior to World War I, although Japanese immigrants farmed less than 1 percent of the agricultural land in California—and that often the most marginal land—they produced 10 percent of the state's total crop.[1]

The Japanese faced immediate hostility and some violence upon coming to the mainland, when anti-Chinese sentiment was extended to them. The shoemakers' union attacked Japanese cobblers in 1890. Similar attacks by cooks' and waiters' union members followed in 1892. Fears of the Japanese "Yellow Peril" grew markedly after the success of Japan in the Russo-Japanese War of 1905. In May of that year the Japanese and Korean Exclusion League was formed. It was soon renamed the Asiatic Exclusion League. Labor and the *San Francisco Chronicle* led the protest movement in 1905.

As with the Chinese, legal action against them soon followed. In 1906, San Francisco adopted an ordinance segregating them into "Chinese" schools. In 1907, President Theodore Roosevelt issued an order, lasting until 1948, which barred their entry into the United States from a bordering country or U.S. territory (that is, Canada, Mexico, or Hawaii). Opposition to their immigration rose.

In 1908, the Roosevelt Administration used diplomatic and economic pressure to force the Japanese government to accept the "gentleman's agreement" to restrict emigration voluntarily. The importing of Japanese wives was excluded from that agreement, so the peak year of Japanese immigration was 1907–1908, after which it sharply declined except for the "picture-bride" marriage system that brought in brides. From 1911 to 1920, 87,000 Japanese were admitted, but 70,000 returned to Japan, for a net gain of a mere 17,000 for that decade.

Legal action continued against them. In 1913, the Webb-Henry bill, better known as the California Alien Land Act, was passed. This law restricted Japanese aliens from owning land. It limited their leasing of land to three years and forebade land already owned or leased from being bequeathed. California Attorney General Webb frankly described the law he authored as follows:

> The fundamental basis of all legislation . . . has been and is, race undesirability. It seeks to limit their presence by curtailing their privileges which they may enjoy here, for they will not come in large numbers and long abide with us if they may not acquire land. And it seeks to limit the numbers who will come by limiting the opportunities for their activities here when they arrive. (cited in Kitano 1976: 17)

Although most Japanese got around the law by placing ownership in the names of their native-born children, who held citizenship, or in the names of their Caucasian friends, the racist nature of the law foreshadowed the troubles to come.

In 1921, the Supreme Court ruled, in *Ozawa* vs. *the United States,* that the Japanese were not Caucasoid and therefore were subject to the Asian restrictive laws. In 1923, California attempted to plug the loopholes in its Alien Land Act by prohibiting aliens from being the guardians of a minor's property. When the United States upheld the constitutionality of that law, similar laws were quickly passed in New Mexico, Arizona, Louisiana, Montana, Idaho, and Oregon.

The Immigration Act of 1924 was the final legal restriction aimed at totally blocking Asian immigration. Restrictions on their acquiring citizenship complicated their acculturation process. The Japanese government was especially upset by this law for its blatant manifestation of racism. Not only did it feel the law was a "slap in the face" to a people for whom "face," or honor, was all important, but they considered it a direct violation of the gentleman's agreement that specified that the United States would not adopt any discriminatory laws against the Japanese (Kitano 1976: 28).

The effect of this law was to develop an unusually pronounced generation gap among the Japanese Americans. They can be categorized by age/generation. The *Issei* were born in Japan and immigrated here. They were prevented by law from becoming citizens until 1954, and were unable to vote or to own land and were subject to miscegenation laws. The *Nisei* were the generation born between 1910 and 1940. They are native-born citizens who could vote, own land, and the like. They have been characterized as the "quiet generation" who are now in their 70s and 80s. The *Sansei* were born after World War II and are now middle-aged. A final group, the *Kibei,* were Nisei children sent to Japan to be raised in a traditional culture, who, by the time the war broke out, were desperately trying to return to the United States (see Hosokawa 1969; Kitano 1976).

During the 1930s, as Japan extended its "co-prosperity sphere," tension between Japan and the United States increased, and anti-Japanese sentiment on the West Coast continued to rise alarmingly until culminating in racial hysteria after the Japanese attack on Pearl Harbor on December 7, 1941. That attack began a virtual nightmare for Japanese Americans living on the mainland. Nearly 120,000 Japanese Americans, some 70,000 of whom were native-born citizens, were sent to "relocation camps" in the interior for what was termed "military necessity." The relocation camps were a euphemism for what were, in fact, concentration camps. Their conditions were grim. Surrounded by 15-foot-high barbed-wire fences, the camps were guarded by armed troops stationed around the perimeter and on spotlight towers. Residents lived in crude barracks where stalls a mere 18 feet × 21 feet housed families of six or seven. They were partitioned off with 7-foot-high walls with 4-foot openings affording no privacy. Residents used outside latrines and camp mess halls. They were locked in by nine o'clock with a ten o'clock lights-out curfew. The camps were located in seven states as shown in Table 3.3, run by the War Relocation Authority and the War Relocation Work Corps. Below is a description of Poston in Arizona, whose peak population reached 17,867 by August 1942.

TABLE 3.3   Japanese-American Relocation Camps and Their Capacities

Camp Name/Location	Dates of Operation	Numbers
Gila River, Arizona	Aug. 1942–Nov. 1945	13,400
Granada, Colorado	Sept. 1942–Oct. 1945	7,600
Heart Mountain, Wyoming	Sept. 1942–Nov. 1945	11,100
Jerome, Arkansas	Nov. 1942–June 1944	8,600
Manzanar, California	June 1941–Nov. 1945	10,200
Minidoka, California	Sept. 1942–Oct. 1945	9,900
Poston, Arizona	June 1942–Nov. 1945	18,000
Rohwer, Arkansas	Oct. 1942–Nov. 1945	8,500
Topaz, Utah	Oct. 1942–Oct. 1945	8,300
Tule Lake, California*	June 1942–Mar. 1946	18,800
Total†		114,490

*There were two camps at Tule Lake. The second was a high-security prison for the 3,500 Japanese Americans believed to pose individual threats to the U.S. war effort. None was ever charged with or convicted of spying or sabotage. Still, this small group was not released until the war was over.

†Some prisoners were released before others were interned. The total number of "evacuees" was more than 120,000.

SOURCE: Peter Wright and John Armor, *Manzanar* (New York: Times Books, 1988). Copyright © 1989 by Peter Wright and John C. Armor. Reprinted by permission of Random House, Inc.

The barracks were flimsily constructed. Sometimes as many as eight people lived in one room. Mattresses were made by stuffing cloth bags with straw. There was hardly any furniture. The heat was intense in the summer, and the minimum temperature during the winter occasionally fell below the freezing mark. And then there were the barbed wire and the guards. It is little wonder that some people felt betrayed at having been sent to such a place and either actively resisted or failed to cooperate fully with the administration's plans. (McLemore 1982, 179)

Table 3.3 lists the internment camps, their dates of operation, and the numbers interned at each camp. The accompanying photograph of the barracks at Manzanar shows their bleakness. Only racial prejudice can adequately explain the internment policy. Its chief author, General De Witt, provided a blatantly racist rationale for the camps:

In the war in which we are engaged racial affinities are not severed by migration. The *Japanese race is an enemy race* and while second and third generation Japanese born on United States soil and possessed of United States citizenship have become "Americanized," *the racial strains are undiluted.* (cited in McLemore 1982: 184; italics added)

In the succinct words of one scholar, "One hundred thousand persons were sent to concentration camps on a record which couldn't support a conviction for stealing a dog (Rostow 1945: 184).[2]

Paradoxically, on Hawaii, which was in a much more vulnerable position, authorities did not attempt a mass evacuation of the 120,552 Japanese-American citizens living there. The war passed without a single proven act of espionage or sabotage by a Japanese American there or on the mainland. The army announced that "the

An evacuated Japanese American family dines in a large mess hall at Manzanar.

shipping situation and the labor shortage make it a matter of military necessity to keep the people of Japanese blood on the Island." Yet the army had used the very words of "military necessity" to justify the West Coast evacuation plan (Hosokawa 1969: 457–467). The failure to evacuate Japanese Americans on Hawaii was a matter of manpower and logistics. Their skills and energies were desperately needed in Hawaii. The government did not have the ships to move 100,000 Japanese Americans, plus 20,000 military dependents, to the mainland and bring back an equal number of workers to take their place. Given an opportunity to do so, the Japanese Americans in Hawaii demonstrated that nothing needed to be done to restrict them. On the mainland they were not given that chance, although the danger of attack was more remote.

Anti-Japanese activity was particularly widespread and intense on the West Coast. Newspaper headlines, editorials, political speeches, as well as mob actions and nativist organizations, reflected the prejudice against the Japanese. Politicians struck out against them, exploiting the tensions of the average voter and avoiding reference to more critical issues. Even before World War II, many politicians used that prejudice to help win elections. There were strong correlations between waves of anti-Japanese agitations and election years. The Japanese-American group was small, economically and politically weak, and an ideal scapegoat. Politicians running for office could attack them without fear of reprisal. There were economic as well as political motives for such activities. Trade unions and small landowners took part in the agitation, but much of the organized opposition stemmed from the owners of huge estates. Large landowners diverted attention from their own control by attacking the Japanese farmer as the cause of everyone's problems.

The racial homogeneity of the Japanese Americans made them easy targets of stereotyping. The stereotype of the Japanese as a "buck-toothed, bespectacled, monkey-faced sneak" was easily applicable to the Issei and the Nisei, whose physical characteristics made them easy to segregate. A Nisei was instantly a "Jap," no matter how removed his family, interests, and culture were from Japan. Japanese Americans were caricatured as the schoolboy, the farmer, the gardener, and the corner grocer in a Japanese military uniform. By contrast, German Americans and Italian Americans had become more or less indistinguishable. They had different heights, different shades of white skin, and hair coloring ranging from blond to brunette. Whereas the "German Nazi" and the "Italian Fascist" were verbally distinguished from German Americans and Italian Americans, the term "Jap" was applied to all of Japanese ancestry, be they long-term resident aliens, native-born citizens, friends, or enemies.

The climate of opinion created by those who saw economic and political gain in anti-Japanese agitation was an important factor in the evacuation. Those few alien Japanese who truly were a military danger were already known to the FBI and were taken into custody within a few days. That all the rest, including some 70,000 native-born citizens, should be treated as a military threat was an act of official racism. There was never a single act of convicted sabotage or related criminal activity connected to the war effort by a Japanese American. By contrast, although there were efforts of sabotage by some German Americans and Italian Americans, they were never considered for evacuation.

Japanese Americans accepted the evacuation and internment surprisingly peacefully. There was one strike at Poston and a riot at Manzanar during the very early period when conditions were especially grim. But once the immediate period of hysteria passed, Japanese-American evacuees of proven loyalty were allowed to leave the camps and join the U.S. Army. Some 20,000 did so, 6,000 of whom served in the Pacific. Most were in the famed 442nd Regimental Combat Team, which became the most highly decorated unit in the European theater.

In *Hirabayashi* vs. *the United States,* in 1943, and in *Korematsu* vs. *the United States,* in 1944, the U.S. Supreme Court upheld the constitutionality of the evacuation order. In the latter decision, approved by a 6–3 vote, the dissenting justices rendered sharp dissents. In *Endo* vs. *the United States* (1944), the Court revoked the West Coast Evacuation Order. Effective January 2, 1945, Japanese Americans were no longer under forcible detention. By June 1946, all the camps were closed.

Ironically, the forced geographic segregation in the internment camps ultimately contributed to a more rapid acculturation of Japanese Americans and advanced their assimilation process in several ways. The wartime relocation forced them out of their ghettos; it broke up the Little Tokyos of San Francisco and Los Angeles and it ended the nearly feudalistic control that the Japanese father held over his children. It emancipated the Japanese-American woman. Power within the ethnic community shifted from the Issei to the Nisei and propelled them into the mainstream of American life. The Nisei entered new occupations, improved their economic status, and helped pull down the legalized racial barriers against them.

Educational barriers particularly began to fall. By May 1942, the National Student Relocation Council was organized. That fall, hundreds of Nisei were enrolled in interior schools. By 1942–1943, 928 students in the relocation centers were enrolled in colleges and universities, in addition to 650 Nisei students who were not evacuees. Over 280 colleges and universities in 38 states accepted them. About 20 percent were able to finance their own educations; the colleges, universities, and various church boards and foundations aided the other 80 percent. They did well. Reports from the receiving institutions were highly commendatory. The Nisei students demonstrated an encouraging desire and ability to assimilate once freed from the oppressive strictures of life on the West Coast.

A related spur to their dispersal was the increasing need for manpower. Sugar producers and processors created an insistent cry for evacuees to be released as laborers in the beet fields of the states outside the restricted military zones. Seasonal work permits were granted to approximately 1,700 evacuees, most of them young men, during the spring and summer months. They were effective workers, and during the fall harvest the demand was even greater—nearly 10,000 evacuees went out on seasonal work permits.

By the fall of 1942, work permits granting indefinite leave were given to those not found to be "security risks." As manpower needs grew desperate, employers in the Midwest began to call for Nisei help. Many Nisei urged others in the camps to move out. This completely altered the prewar employment patterns. On the coast they were farmers, produce merchants, fishermen, gardeners, and domestic helpers. In Chicago and other midwestern cities, they worked in factories and in such diverse areas as social work, teaching, chemistry, and engineering and as dental and lab technicians, draftsmen, and mechanics. Soon they were earning two to ten times as much as they had received in prewar employment. Some Nisei were supervising persons of other races, a situation unheard of on the coast. Less than 10 percent were employed domestically. Many soon had their own businesses. Nisei women were hired as stenographers, at first reluctantly, then enthusiastically, as their good qualities became known. They rarely had a chance at secretarial jobs in California. Many of the women found well-paying jobs in the clothing industry, operating sewing machines.

In Chicago, Japanese-American–owned stores were interspersed with others, and they had to cater to the general public, in contrast to Los Angeles where they had to look to their own for such employment and as customers. In the Midwest, instead of setting up their own churches, they attended more than 100 of Chicago's established churches and found themselves welcomed. This new atmosphere, in part due to the regional shift, in part made possible by the careful work of the Relocation Authority in soliciting the approval of responsible citizens, contributed to the success of relocating the evacuees. Usually a War Relocation Authority (WRA) officer would spend two to three weeks conferring with local government officials, union leaders, heads of civic organizations, and ministers before authorizing any resettlement.

The Japanese American Citizens League (JACL), founded in 1930, began during the war to lobby quietly but effectively against the prejudice and discrimination facing their community. The JACL worked with the WRA, the American Civil Liberties Union, the Common Council for American Unity, Norman Thomas of the Post-War Council, the American Baptist Home Mission Council, the YWCA, and the Friends Service Committee to help evacuees find jobs and housing. The JACL held the Nisei together and kept them in touch with one another through its paper, *The Pacific Citizen.* It gave the Nisei a strong, clear editorial voice when most newspapers were either against or simply ignoring them. It was through its paper that the JACL expressed its goal as an organization for Japanese Americans: the emancipation of all Japanese Americans from the stigma of limited citizenship and the cloak of questioned loyalty through their total assimilation into the general culture and their complete acceptance as co-Americans by their fellow citizens.

The wartime dispersal was fairly widespread. Nearly 43,000 had resettled in nine states: Illinois, 15,000; Colorado, 6,000; Utah, 5,000; Ohio, 3,900; Idaho, 3,500; Michigan, 2,800; New York, 2,500; New Jersey, 2,200; and Minnesota, 1,700.[3] The Nisei liked their new homes, as they had job challenges and opportunity unknown to them in California. After the war, the JACL continued its work. It led the fight for naturalization of the Issei, recognizing that only as citizens would the Issei have equal protection under the law. It fought to remove the discriminatory aspects of U.S. immigration law.

Congress moved slowly. An amendment to the Soldiers' Brides Bill was passed allowing the Japanese spouses and children of American servicemen to enter the United States without regard to the Oriental Exclusion Act. Individual congressmen sponsored more than 200 private bills benefiting the Issei and Nisei. Tenure, which had been canceled as a result of the evacuation, was restored to Nisei under the federal civil service. The JACL found strong support in Congress from Representative Francis E. Walter of Pennsylvania and Senator Pat McCarren of Nevada. The McCarren-Walter Immigration and Naturalization Act of 1952 provided for the repeal of the Oriental Exclusion Act of 1924, extending to Japan and other Asian countries a token immigration quota. It also eliminated race as a bar to citizenship. Truman vetoed the bill for reasons not linked to Japanese Americans, but the JACL made a determined effort to override the veto. The Nisei sought editorial support in local newspapers, and Nisei veterans got in touch with men they had known while in uniform. Congress passed the bill over the presidential veto by a vote of 278–113 in the House and 57–26 in the Senate.

The McCarren-Walter Act was a big step for the Issei. Hundreds of them enrolled in citizenship courses sponsored by local churches, JACL chapters, and other organizations. Further JACL legal successes came with passage of the Immigration Act of 1965, which ended the national-origins quota system. Since 1970, Japanese immigration has averaged about 4,000 annually.

Since the 1960s, Japanese Americans, and more especially the Sansei, have achieved remarkable success. By nearly any criterion they have become the most successful of all minority groups. As one scholar wrote: "Perhaps the model choice for handling the problem of visibility has been 'psychological passing': identifying and acquiring the American culture at such a rapid rate that they have been termed as America's model minority" (Kitano 1976: 200; see also Marger 1997: 353).

The Nisei and Sansei have higher average formal education than any other group in the United States, including whites. They have been very upwardly mobile. In occupational choice, they have concentrated in the professions, particularly architecture, medicine, dentistry, engineering, teaching, and pharmacy. They have moved into highly technical fields. Their average income exceeds that of all other nonwhites and is comparable in amount and distribution to that of whites. As a group, and in contrast to Chinese Americans, they have exhibited low rates of juvenile delinquency, divorce, and mental illness. They overwhelmingly live in middle-class housing. Their out-marriage rate exceeds 50 percent. More than 15 percent of them hold professional jobs, far higher than any other minority group and on a par with whites. Over 88 percent have high school degrees and over 35 percent graduated college. At under 3 percent below the poverty level, they exceed the national average and the rate of whites in poverty. A Japanese-American child can expect to live six to seven years longer than a white child, and ten to twelve years longer than a black child.[4] Crime figures are even more telling. While arrest rates for white, black, Hispanic, and Native American adults have soared during the past three decades, those for Japanese-American adults, which were never high, declined sharply.

They exhibit considerable evidence of secondary and even primary cultural assimilation. Their record in business, the professions, housing, joining voluntary associations, and dating is remarkable. Their out-marriage rate is higher than that for any other racial minority, changing from 11 percent in 1949 to 20 percent in 1959, to 33 percent in the 1960s. A 1973 study found 50 percent of Sansei married outside their race. It peaked at 63.1 percent in 1977. By 1989, another study found their out-marriage rate was 51.9 percent.

Several theories have been advanced to account for their remarkably successful assimilation. The **value-compatibility theory** holds that traditional Japanese values are highly compatible with white middle-class values and stress upward social mobility. Politeness, respect for authority, attention to parental wishes, and duty to the community, plus the stress on hard work, cleanliness, neatness, and honesty coupled with an emphasis on formal education, are traditional Japanese values that mirror traditional values of Anglo Americans, and their acceptance of these values played an important part in the relationship of the two groups. The **community cohesion theory** accounts for why these values were so effectively socialized among the Nisei and Sansei generations, stressing the way their values were transmitted to the entire ethnic group (McLemore 1982).

Despite this impressive record there are gaps. While third and fourth generations are rapidly entering the professions, Japanese Americans remain heavily concentrated in agriculture. Gardening is still dominated by them in California. In business they have yet to achieve the higher corporate levels, and they are significantly underrepresented in the art and entertainment fields. Outside of Hawaii, where they compose about 37 percent of the population, they have comparatively little political power, and their impact on mainland politics has been minor. All of Hawaii's delegation to Congress is Asian American. There are four Asian Americans serving in the House from California.

Korean Americans

At 11 percent of the Asian-American population, Korean Americans rank in fourth place. They exhibit a classic case of the economic route to accommodation. They often play the role of the "middleman minority"—acting as a sort of buffer between the dominant society and other minority groups, especially blacks and Hispanics, among whom they live and work. Though small in total numbers (currently just over 820,000), they are a very important segment of the Asian-American community and illustrate a pattern of accommodation typical of that wider community, even as they present some characteristics that differ from those of other Asian Americans, particularly Chinese Americans and Japanese Americans.

Korean immigration can be described in terms of three distinct phases or waves. Their early immigration was brief: 1903–1905. The second wave was between 1951 and 1965; the third, and largest, wave has occurred since 1965.

The earliest group of Korean immigrants, like the Chinese and Japanese before them, came first to the territory of Hawaii. From 1902 to 1905, just over 7,000 Koreans migrated to Hawaii to work on the islands' plantations. This migration was organized by the Hawaii Sugar Planters Association. They typically were young males between 18 and 35 years of age. The ratio of male to female was 6 to 1. About 1,000 of those original immigrants went on to the mainland, mostly California, in 1905. Unusual for Asian immigrants, a significant portion were Christian, which aided in their acculturation and acceptance by white Americans (Kim 1977). Their involvement in Christian churches not only assured them a more sympathetic reception by whites, it gave members of the Korean community who were not in clan associations or sworn to a brotherhood group a chance to engage in social intercourse outside of their work camps. Even non-Christian Korean parents saw the value of sending their children to Christian schools.

The first group of Korean immigrants was from the lower class in Korea. They were contracted to work in Hawaii as cheap labor to replace the Chinese and Japanese, and their wages were lower than that paid to the latter two groups. In the American labor force, the early Korean immigrants were concentrated in agriculture as laborers, or in urban areas as dishwashers, kitchen helpers, and janitors. They largely devoted whatever political activity they engaged in around issues relating to their homeland.

At the time of their original migration, Korea was under the influence of both diplomatic and economic pressure from Japan. The Japanese government went so far as to induce the Korean government to appoint the Japanese consul in Hawaii, Saito Kan, as the honorary Korean consul in May 1905. The Korean community did not accept the consul, however, and continued to petition the government to appoint a Korean national as their consul. After 1905, the Korean government bowed to Japanese pressure and no longer allowed Koreans to emigrate. Some in Hawaii returned home; others moved on to the mainland. By 1910, Korea was colonized by Japan, and further immigration was limited to about 1,000 "picture brides," who came between 1910 and 1924.

The second wave of Korean immigrants came during 1951–1965. Numbering about 25,000, they were mostly wives of American servicemen, Korean War orphans adopted by Americans, and students. Instead of being located mainly in one area, they were geographically widely dispersed.

The third wave of Korean immigration, the largest and most significant influx, came after 1965, when the U.S. government repealed the national-origins quota system that was the basis of U.S. immigration policy since 1924. This latest wave averaged over 15,000 Korean immigrants per year from 1965 to 1980 and over 33,000 per year since 1980.

The 1990 census data put the Korean-American population at 799,000, among whom 568,000 were foreign-born, and over 56 percent of whom had entered during the 1980–1990 decade. As with other recent Asian immigrants, Korean immigrants are decidedly middle to upper class with high levels of education. By 1993, their median family income, at $33,909, approached the national average of $35,108. Over 80 percent of Korean Americans are high school graduates (compared to the national average of 58.8 percent), and 34.4 percent have college degrees (compared to the national average of 20.4 percent). Their employment patterns reflect that higher educational background and family income status. While 13 percent of Korean Americans were employed as operators, fabricators, and laborers (as compared to the national average of 18.6 percent of the 1990 labor force), and 15 percent were employed in service jobs (compared to the national average of 18.1 percent), over 13.3 percent worked in the professions, exceeding the national average of 12.3 percent. A study of the Korean-American community in Los Angeles found that over 40 percent of the heads of households were self-employed (as compared to 8 percent of the general population), and 80 percent worked in Korean-owned firms, mostly in the service and retail trades. The Korean settlement in Los Angeles, historically the nation's largest, grew tenfold in the decade after 1965. The Korean-American community is fairly dispersed geographically.

The large influx of Korean immigrants since 1970 led to an organizational resurgence among Korean Americans. The explosive growth of the Korean-American population in the Los Angeles metropolitan area, for example, gave rise to over 50 nonprofit community organizations, 50 church groups, 4 Buddhist temples, and more than 50 high school alumni groups (Kim 1977).

Among Korean-American business enterprises, major-sized firms are concentrated in oriental foods, packing, and truck farming. Most Korean-American businesses, however, involve small firms, concentrated mostly in retail and service enterprises. Among retail businesses, they are most often found in grocery, market, and liquor stores; in hardware and electric appliance shops; in software retail stores; in gift shops; and in wholesale trading, especially wig shops and grocery wholesalers. Among service businesses, Korean Americans are concentrated in food and entertainment; in semiprofessional services such as travel, insurance, and real estate; in professional services such as accounting, income tax preparation, medicine, and dentistry; in such small-scale service enterprises as photography and art studios, printing shops, beauty shops, and shoe repair shops; and in larger-scale services such as auto repair and garages.

As mentioned earlier, in their role as small businessmen, and because of the location of their business enterprises, Korean Americans have become the "middleman minority," the buffer between the dominant white society and other racial minorities, especially blacks and Hispanics (Blalock 1967; Bonacich 1973; Bonacich and Modell 1980; Marger 1997; Turner and Bonacich 1980; Zenner 1991). That role has led them typically to being cast as scapegoats and the target of interracial violence. Among the black communities in Los Angeles and New York, where Korean Americans operate one-quarter of the small businesses, they are resented by blacks, who commonly accept the stereotypical image of Koreans getting help in starting such enterprises from the government and at the expense of the black community. In reality, the base of Korean capital for such ventures comes from pooling family resources.

Korean-American immigrant success in their business ventures has undoubtedly contributed greatly to their achieving middle-class economic status in the United States. The degree of Korean-American assimilation correlates significantly with the following characteristics: education, length of residence, present occupation, religion, and proficiency in the English language (Hurh 1977).

EUROPEAN IMMIGRANTS

German Americans

Immigrants from Germany exceed those from any other nation. According to the 1990 census, nearly 58 million persons reported German ancestry. At 23.3 percent of the total U.S. population, they rank first among all Euro-American ancestry groups. Their migration has been long and consistent, going back to colonial times and before the government started counting persons entering. The 1990 census reports that 712,000 Americans were born in Germany. Over 11 percent of all persons legally entering the United States during the 1980–1990 decade came from Germany. Total German legal immigration exceeds 7 million. Given the size of their migration, German Americans naturally exhibit the use of several coping strategies. Most came when their job skills were desired and opportunities were abundant. Most pursued economic accommodation. Their experience serves as a case study for most European immigrants to the United States.

Three major currents of German immigration are commonly distinguished: the colonial period, when they came mostly for religious and economic reasons; from 1848 to the Civil War, when they came for political and economic reasons; and post-Civil War, when they came primarily for economic opportunity, often having been recruited by the various state governments, the railroads, several industries, and by friends or relatives already here.

In one sense, German immigrants were never one nationality; their distinctive "Germanness" developed here, when they were treated alike, as German Americans. Until 1870, there was only a loose federation of many German states. Indeed, for much of modern history, the Germans have been a hybrid people of German-speaking states in Central Europe and Austria, Hungary, Luxembourg, Switzerland, Poland, Czechoslovakia, and Russia. In America, they were all considered the same, categorized for immigration purposes based on their common language. Although the native stock viewed them as a single people, they were a fairly diverse group splintered by regional strife and along religious lines.

During the colonial period, German-American immigration patterns were distinguished by the movement of entire communities bound together in religious sects. They sought and cultivated some of the richest farmland in colonial America. Their granaries served as the "breadbasket" for the Revolutionary forces. Scattered thinly among the total population, they were united only by language and had little political clout or interest beyond their local affairs. They had high intermarriage rates with the Anglo native stock, facilitating a rapid assimilation. Geographically, they came from Europe as Palatinates, Salburgers, Wurttenburgers, and Hanoverians. Religiously, they were Mennonites, Dunkers, Lutherans, Calvinists, and (a few) Jewish.

The outbreak of the Revolutionary War changed attitudes toward Germans. Though widely scattered, they still made up the single largest nationality group after the British. They felt no special loyalty to the British crown and were unfriendly to the Tories, who favored continued union with England. At first reluctant to become involved in colonial politics, they did become converted to the cause of independence. Several German regiments were raised and fought prominently and well in the Revolutionary War. That service was widely recognized and helped develop a spirit of respect. Several states even passed laws that translated statutes and other government proceedings into German. Their wartime service was a major step toward being accepted and toward their assimilation. As their general social and economic conditions improved, they began to take a more active part in public affairs. In partisan politics, they tended to align with the Democrats, since, as small farmers, they never were at home with the eastern establishment.

During the 1830s and 1840s, Germans immigrated for different reasons. The agricultural revolution hit Central Europe, and inheritance laws requiring land to be equally divided among all children led to small subsistence farms that became too small to support them in tough times, forcing many off the land. They turned to manufacturing—clocks, tools, and the like—but even this left them overly vulnerable to economic change. When the potato famine struck, their choice was to emigrate or starve. Fortunately, this coincided with the opening of the American Midwest. Texas, the Great Lakes region, and the Ohio River valley all became home to these new settlers. As midwestern cities exploded in population, they attracted large German migrations. Chicago, Detroit, Milwaukee, Cincinnati, and St. Louis led the way to a swath of land some 200 miles wide stretching across the northern tier of states from New York down to Maryland and across to the Mississippi River being known as the "German belt."

Political turmoil in Germany, culminating in the 1848 Revolution, caused many German intellectuals to flee to America. The "forty-eighters," as they became known, contributed significantly to the liberal movement in states where they settled. Even though they numbered only about 10,000, this cohort of immigrants wielded influence far beyond their numerical strength. They started German-language newspapers, reading societies, theaters, and other cultural activities. Though the full extent of their influence is debated, the forty-eighters provided important leadership in the American labor movement. In the newly emerging conservation movement, the forty-eighter Carl Schurz led the drive to save virgin forestland and became the first Secretary of the Interior in 1877. Further, they were prominent in the antislavery movement and instrumental in the founding of the Republican Party, where they took credit—undoubtedly an inflated claim—for the election of Lincoln, who had invested in a German-language paper.

During and after the Civil War, German immigrant labor filled desperately needed slots in the northern industrial labor force opened up by the war. The booming economy drew them to areas of high demand, and this became a major factor in their rapid absorption into mainstream American life. The largest wave of German immigrants came after the Civil War period. The Homestead Act of 1862 offered free land to the overcrowded population of Germany. Western states advertised for German farmers, who had a reputation of being hardworking and highly productive. State governments joined the railroads in sending agents to induce German immigrants to settle and develop the abundant lands. An additional draw was that America became a haven from the military conscription during the years of the German wars of unification.

German immigrants did face some opposition, most notably from the Know Nothing Party of the 1850s. German Catholics competed with the large wave of Irish Catholics, who dominated the hierarchy of the Catholic church in America until the early 1900s, when German clergy finally began to fill some leadership roles in the church. World War I resulted in a temporary setback in their assimilation. They initially opposed the war, which resulted in a period of heightened nationalism. Once the United States was formally involved in the war, however, opposition ceased and the German-American community gave its support to the war effort.

Another issue that united the German-American community was their opposition to Prohibition. The importance of beer to their cultural heritage, and the fact that America's brewing industry was nearly exclusively in their hands, accounted for their opposition. Prohibition threatened the brewers with financial disaster.

In 1916, Congress established the Council of National Defense to speed up the assimilation of German and other nationality groups. While debatable as to its impact, the act was extended to the states where several midwestern state legislatures enacted comparable statutes granting the state government, and often local and county councils, sweeping powers to investigate and punish for contempt. The councils forbade the use of the German language in schools, churches, over the telephone, and in semipublic places. While forced acculturation is problematic at best, the banning of the use of German probably sped up the process of acculturation. Postwar isolationism reflected a phobia against everything foreign. Isolationist voting was strongest in those states with heavy German-American populations. Perhaps the disillusion after World War I turned them inward.

After President Franklin D. Roosevelt's election in 1936, his administration adopted a distinctly anti-German foreign policy, triggering a substantial defection of German Americans from the Democratic Party at all levels. While as a group they demonstrated their loyalty to the nation by their sons' conduct in the war effort, in the privacy of the voting booth they voted anti-Roosevelt. After his death they came back to the party in the 1948 election in significant enough numbers that they contributed to President Truman's surprise victory. After World War II, their bloc voting largely disappeared. Today, they are part of the Anglo-Teutonic white stock that composes the majority society.

The German-American pattern of assimilation was closely followed by immigrants from Scandinavia, which we discuss next.

Scandinavian Americans

According to 1990 census data, 679,000 persons claim "Scandinavian" ancestry. In addition, 1,635,000 identify themselves as Danish, 3,869,000 as Norwegian, and 4,681,000 as Swedish. Thus nearly 11 million Americans claim that background.

Scandinavians were among the first European people to explore the New World. Viking explorations and tiny settlements have been traced back to the period of 800 to 1050. In the mid-1600s, several settlements from the region were established in what is now Delaware. A few immigrants continued to come from Norway, Sweden, and Denmark, but their numbers were not substantial until after the Civil War. From then on, motivated by such factors as religious dissension, voting disenfranchisement, crop failures, and related economic factors, Scandinavians emigrated in large numbers. Total Scandinavian immigration to the United States exceeds 2.5 million. The Swedes hit their peak in 1910 and the Norwegians in the 1920s. Although the Norwegians, Swedes, and Danes came from countries with diverse governments, traditions, and languages, their physical characteristics and a tendency to settle together in the United States led to the use of the term "Scandinavian" to refer to all three groups.

On the whole, Scandinavians were a very successful group of immigrants. They were willing to work hard. They arrived in better financial shape than most groups, which enabled them to escape the poverty, slums, and resulting stereotyping and social stigma of the eastern seaboard cities with their "teeming immigrant masses." By 1880, the average Scandinavian immigrant arrived with $60 to $70. Such sums enabled them to reach the Midwest and its abundant and cheap land on which their farming skills could be put to good use. Farming was not their only trade. They went into business, commerce, manufacturing, finance, and the professions. In the frontier settlements they succeeded in setting up their own stores, shops, factories, and banks. Before the 1890s, they were concentrated in the midwestern states whose soil and climate reminded them of their homelands, and where their successful settlements attracted others. Minnesota, Wisconsin, Iowa, Illinois, and the Dakotas all saw dramatic increases in their populations due to this influx. By the 1890s, they were increasingly attracted to the industrial opportunities in the Northeast and to the lumber industry of the Pacific Northwest. By 1920, Chicago had the largest number of Swedes of any city but Stockholm and more Norwegians than any city but Oslo.

Scandinavian assimilation proved comparatively easy. They entered the majority society largely through the economic path. Their political involvement generally followed economic and social success. Several factors account for the relative ease of their assimilation. They did not have to overcome the stigma of some "undesirable" trait. They were Caucasian and escaped racial prejudice. They were strongly Protestant, avoiding anti-Catholic sentiment. They came in relatively small numbers over a long period of time, compared to the huge waves of Irish and Italians, who came by the millions in a decade. Thus, Scandinavians did not suffer the scapegoat effect. Anti-immigrant hatred was directed toward the Irish and Italians arriving at the same time who were feared as job competitors and as "papists." Coming in smaller waves and with sufficient money and job skills to reach the Midwest, they were not viewed as threats to dominant culture's labor force. They also worked hard at becoming "Americans." Strongly desiring to assimilate, they mastered English as quickly as possible. Schools were very important in their settlements, and they insisted on schools that could teach English.

Being overwhelmingly Protestant, their religion gave them a common bond with the majority. They were mostly Lutherans and were considered more devout and straitlaced than the German Lutherans. Their stern faith frowned on drinking, dancing, and levity and stressed piety and the work ethic. Many were anti-Catholic and were accepted more readily by a native stock with whom they shared a common enemy. Unlike the Irish and Italian groups whose loyalty to a unified Catholic church kept them tied to the old country and customs, earning them the suspicion and enmity of the Protestant native stock, the Scandinavians formed numerous new churches often based on American ideas, again easing their assimilation.

Financial success helped them to be more socially accepted. The Homestead Act of 1862 provided cheap land, so they became established without going heavily into debt. Their standard of living was soon comparable to that of the dominant society located in frontier settlements. Describing Norwegian settlers in the Dakotas in the late 1890s, one writer said: "Most of them came with just enough money to buy government land and build a shack. Now they loan money to their neighbors . . . every county has Norwegians worth $25,000 to $50,000, all made since settling in Dakota" (cited in Dinnerstein and Reimers 1988: 97–98).

By the turn of the century they had a fairly clear understanding of American-style politics with its numerous points of access: elections, representation, constitutions, and fragmented political power distributed among many local governments. They were patriotic. They organized political groups to get information on laws and elections, and learned American-style politics through organizing new townships, working on town government, levying and collecting taxes, and laying out new roads. In the early stages of their political development, sometimes more than a fifth of the men participated in town affairs.

The first Scandinavian-born politician to enter state-wide politics was a Norwegian, James Reymert, who represented Racine County in the second constitutional convention of Wisconsin in 1847. After the Civil War Scandinavians became more visible in state-level politics. Norwegian-born Knute Nelson was the first state governor. He was elected, in succession, to the legislatures of Wisconsin and then Minnesota, to the U.S. Congress, and as governor of Minnesota on the Republican ticket in 1892. By the turn of the century, many Scandinavians served in the state legislatures of Wisconsin, Minnesota, and the Dakotas. They tended to be Republicans, whose stand against slavery and status as the party of "moral ideas" appealed to them. By the mid-1900s, they had ceased to be thought of as a foreign ethnic group. Third-generation Scandinavians were firmly part of the WASP majority. Since the 1970s, only a few thousand have emigrated from the Scandinavian countries to the United States. Those coming today tend to be highly skilled craftsmen, professionals, or prospective business executives. They tend to assimilate quickly and easily. They are less likely than those of the past to have feelings of ethnic community.

Another group of immigrants, coming to the United States in massive numbers between 1880 and 1920, are categorized as the "new" immigrants. They came in larger waves and mostly from South, Central, and Eastern Europe. They came for various reasons, responding to several push factors compelling them to migrate. Their greater variety in immigration patterns shows a propensity to use several coping strategies. The next section of this chapter discusses groups who use both economic and political tactics to accommodate. Here we examine Greek Americans and their use of the economic route. Chapter 4 addresses their use of the political route.

Greek Americans

Over 1.1 million Americans claimed Greek ancestry in the 1990 census, 177,000 of whom were born in Greece. They made up 13 percent of the legal immigrants coming to the United States during the 1980–1990 decade.

Greeks have been coming to America since colonial times. A scattering came as explorers, sailors, cotton merchants, gold miners, and as settlers of the ill-fated Smyrna colony in Florida in 1768. They did not arrive in significant numbers until after 1880. Between 1900 and 1920, they reached their peak immigration when 350,000 arrived. Although they came from all parts of Greece, the majority were young, unskilled males from the villages in the south.

As with other groups from South, Central, and Eastern Europe, various push factors led to their migration. Although political persecution played a role, economic conditions in Greece were the most compelling push factor. The rapid rise in population led to an excess the islands could simply no longer support. By 1931, for example, even after decades of extensive emigration, there were 870 persons for every square mile of cultivated land (Thernstrom 1980). Another push factor was the ongoing state of war between Greece and Turkey. The Balkan War of 1912–1913 caused the peak period of Greek immigration to the United States, when many fled the compulsory military service in what they considered to be a Turkish tyranny. Many Greeks, like the Italians and Chinese, came as "sojourners," young men intending to earn enough money to provide a substantial dowry for the prospective brides in their families. The fact that about 95 percent of the early Greek immigrants were young males meant that many returned home for brides.

The opportunity for better jobs was the single most important pull factor drawing Greeks to the United States. Greek immigrants who arrived in the 1880–1920 period settled in one of three major areas: the West, to work on railroad gangs and in the mines; New England, to work in the textile and shoe factories; and New York, Chicago, and other large cities, to work in factories or as busboys, dishwashers, bootblacks, and peddlers.

Greeks used and were exploited by a **padrone system**. The padrone found jobs for the immigrants, assisted with language problems, and settled disputes. Often the padrone's "clients" were young boys sent directly to the padrone, who arranged for their room and board and a small wage. The wage was prearranged and agreed to by the parents. What they did not know was the conditions under which the boys lived—squalid and crowded basement rooms in the heart of the tenement slums. They worked 18 hours a day with no time set aside for lunch. The system was highly profitable for the padrone, who made an average of $100 to $200, and in some cases as much as $500, per year per boy. The boys themselves would receive about $100 to $180 annually in wages. The padrone system has been described as a modernized version of the indentured servant system of the late seventeenth and early eighteenth centuries (Soloutos 1964).

Although the majority of Greek immigrants were young and unskilled, some educated and skilled Greeks also immigrated. They met with unforeseen problems here. Greek lawyers could only practice law after learning English, studying for one year in an American law school, and then passing the bar exam. Greek physicians had it somewhat better; they were able to take a qualifying exam in Greek. Unless they were able to master a reasonable amount of English, however, their practice was confined to serving other Greek Americans. Many college graduates caught the emigration fever, but had few opportunities to proceed in their various interests. For the educated Greeks, it was difficult to find employment equal to their educational qualifications, and they felt it was beneath their dignity to work as unskilled laborers.

A fairly sizable number did manage to start their own businesses. They concentrated on confectioneries, candy stores, and restaurants. After World War I, for instance, there were an estimated 564 Greek restaurants in San Francisco alone. After World War II there were 350 to 450 Greek-American confectionery shops and 8 to 10 candy manufacturing concerns in Chicago alone (Moskos 1980; Parrillo 1985).

Many Greeks went back and forth several times before finally staying in the United States. This back-and-forth migration pattern undoubtedly slowed their acculturation and assimilation rate. It led to a mutual lack of understanding (with the majority society) and often severe conflict. In 1904, for instance, a strike broke out in the diesel shops of Chicago. Heated union–management conflict left the city in a bad situation. Unaware of the conditions of the strike, inexperienced Greek immigrants served as strike-breakers. Since they broke the strike, they were considered the enemy by local unions. A period of severe anti-Greek press followed. Eventually the strike ended with the regular employees returning to work. By then, a strong anti-Greek sentiment developed. In the West, a virulent nativist reaction directed at Greek immigrants erupted. In McGill, Nevada, three Greeks were killed in a 1908 riot. In Utah, where Mormons seemed particularly antiforeign and anti-Greek, they were characterized in the Utah press as a vicious element unfit for citizenship and as ignorant, depraved, and brutal foreigners. A 1917 riot in Salt Lake City almost led to the lynching of a Greek immigrant accused of killing Jack Dempsey's brother. In Price, Utah, local citizens rioted and attacked Greek stores, forcing the American girls who worked in them to return home. The Ku Klux Klan was very active in Utah in the early 1920s, and Greeks were singled out as special targets (Moskos 1980). In Omaha, in 1909, a sizable Greek community of seasonal workers led to a strike-breaking situation that resulted in an ugly riot that caused thousands of dollars of damage to the Greek section of the city. Even supposedly scholarly work, such as that of sociologist Henry Pratt Fairchild, reflected anti-Greek sentiment. His work stereotyped Greek and Italian immigrants as being disproportionately "criminal types" and despaired of their ever being able to assimilate (see Fairchild 1911).

Greek immigrants tended to settle in small colonies where they could socialize with one another and practice their religion. Since the church and state were not separate in Greece, almost every Greek immigrant was a member of the Greek Orthodox church. An unwillingness to practice their faith with others, even with other branches of the Eastern Orthodox church, tended to isolate Greeks from the mainstream of religious society, also slowing their assimilation rate.

Greek social life also tended to isolate them. In the Greek community, the community council and the coffeehouses played a major role:

> In the Greek community, the *kinotitos,* or community council, was the governing body of the people. It provided for the establishment of churches and schools, hired and fired priests and teachers, and exerted a constant influence on Greek affairs. One could always gauge the feelings of the group by the actions of the *kinotitos.* For recreation, the Greeks flocked to their *kuffenein,* or coffee houses. These served as community social centers where men smoked, drank, conversed, and played games in what became literally a place of refuge after a hard day of work or an escape from the dank and dreary living quarters. No Greek community was without its *kuffenein,* and one chronicler reported that in Chicago before World War I, "every other door on Bolivar Street was a Greek coffee house." (Dinnerstein and Reimers 1988: 54)

The Greek church, the Greek-language press (such as the *Atlantis*), and the more than 100 Greek societies all encouraged cohesiveness and slowed their assimilation. The largest and most notable of the Greek societies was the American Hellenic Educational Progressive Association (AHEPA). It was founded in 1922 to preserve Greek heritage and help immigrants understand the American way of life. Greek family life was close-knit and stressed education, particularly higher education. Law and medicine were especially valued. Greek education impacted the whole family. Greek children went to two schools: the public school and the Greek-language school. Mandatory for most children, the purpose of the latter was to maintain communication between the parent, the child, and the church, and to preserve the Greek heritage in the new land. These schools were usually taught by priests to ensure the church's lifelong influence on the new generation. Children went to public school until midafternoon, then the Greek-language school until early evening. This process of dual education made it impossible for Greek children to participate in the after-school activities of the public schools, slowing their own assimilation and that of their families. As of 1978, some 400 Greek-language schools were operating in the United States (Moskos 1980).

The beginnings of their change from sojourners to Greek Americans can be traced to the 1920s, when Congress passed restrictive immigration laws. The quota system set up in 1924 limited Greek immigration to 100 per year. This number contrasted sharply with the 28,000 Greeks who arrived in 1921, the last year of open immigration. In 1929, the Greek quota was changed to 307, where it stayed for the next 30 years. Nonquota immigration allowing families to reunite resulted in a yearly average of about

2,000 entering between 1924 and 1930. Closing the door had a profound impact on Greek America. Initially there was a scramble to acquire citizenship, for only naturalized citizens could bring over family members or be assured of returning if one visited Greece. Without the continued arrival of new immigrants, American-born Greeks soon became the majority within their group, and their ascendancy was inevitable. The new immigration policy set in motion forces that affected both individuals and demographic forces that shaped the entire Greek-American community.

Another important event was World War II. Italy's invasion of Greece in 1940 brought Greece into the war. The initial and heroic success of the Greek army in throwing back the Italian invasion had an exhilarating effect on the Greek American community. Very favorable coverage of "Greek heroism" by the American mass media allowed Greek Americans to bask in unaccustomed glory. A Greek American War Relief Association was immediately formed. It raised $5 million in five months, helping to save an estimated one-third of the Greek population. When the United States entered the war in 1941, Greek-American support of the war effort was overwhelming. With Greece and the United States joined in the struggle against the Axis powers, Greek and American interests came together as never before. AHEPA joined in the drive to sell war bonds and eventually sold a half-billion dollars worth. One AHEPA member, Michael Loris, was named the U.S. Champion War Bond Salesman in 1943 for selling 24,142 individual bonds. The Andrew Sisters, whose "support our boys" tunes made them the most popular singing group during the war years, were second-generation Greek Americans. World War II became a watershed in Greek America. The war effort became a matter of Greek pride combined with American patriotism.

That war effort, plus American involvement in the civil war in Greece that broke out after the war, deepened the tie. The 1947 Truman Doctrine capped a number of foreign policy moves that tied Greece to the American sphere and made President Truman a hero within the Greek-American community. At a White House gala in 1948, Truman became the only President to be initiated into AHEPA, and in 1963 the association erected a statue in Athens memorializing him.

The changed attitude among Greek Americans was reflected in a changed attitude within majority society toward them as well. Today, few negative comments about Greek Americans are heard. When they are singled out, it is to serve as a model of a nationality group that has been accepted, achieved economic security, and become Americanized while retaining a strong pride in their heritage. The postwar years saw increasing numbers of Greek Americans entering the middle class, with a majority of them in white-collar and professional occupations. According to the 1990 census, Greek-born residents, who made up nearly 13 percent of the legal immigrants coming during the 1980–1990 decade, were well educated with over 50 percent having high school degrees and 15 percent college degrees. Among them, 11 percent were in professional occupations. Their median household income of $33,500 exceeded the national average of $28,314.

The postwar years saw renewed efforts to change their limited quotas. In the 1950s, nonquota Greeks coming to the United States numbered over 17,000, and by additional "borrowing on future quotas," some 70,000 Greeks entered between 1945 and 1965. The Immigration Act of 1965 abolished the quota system and led to a new wave contributing to a lingering of Greek ethnic consciousness and a pluralistic adaptation to American life.

Today's Greek-American community numbers over 1,250,000. It is overwhelmingly urban, with over 94 percent of Greek Americans residing in urban areas, as compared to 73 percent of the total population. Nearly half of them live in or near about a half-dozen cities: New York, Chicago, Boston, Detroit, Los Angeles, Philadelphia, Cleveland, and Pittsburgh.

The central Greek-American institution today remains the Orthodox church. Remarkably, the American-born generations are in many ways more Greek Orthodox than their contemporaries of the middle-class youth in urban Greece. The introduction of English into the service exemplifies the process of Americanization of the church. That acculturation is reflected to a lesser degree in new architectural design and other aesthetic aspects, in the changing role of women in the church, and in the number of non-Greeks joining the church through marriage. In the 1960s, mixed-marriage couples accounted for three out of ten church marriages. By the late 1970s, about half of all such marriages were mixed. The Greek Orthodox church stands midway between an ethnic religion and a mainline church in its status. Its ethnicity is self-evident, but a striving for mainline status is apparent in its acceptance of the legitimacy of other religions based not on sufferance or tolerance but as a tenet of its own religion in the pluralism of America (Moskos 1980).

As a summary, Table 3.4 presents the socioeconomic standing among the major Euro-American ethnic groups as of 1990, comparing their median family incomes and percentages of college graduates.

TABLE 3.4   Socioeconomic Status of Euro-American Ethnic Groups, 1990

Group	Median Family Income	Percent College Graduates
Russian	$58,826	49%
Dutch	43,415	18
Greek	43,330	28
Scottish	43,293	34
Hungarian	42,778	27
Italian	42,242	21
Polish	41,700	23
English	40,875	28
Swedish	40,459	27
Slovak	40,072	22
Scotch-Irish	38,816	28
Portuguese	38,370	12
German	38,216	22
Irish	38,101	21
French	36,237	18

SOURCE: Adopted from Martin N. Marger, *Race and Ethnic Relations,* 4th ed. (Belmont, CA: Wadsworth, 1997), p. 174. © 1997. Reprinted with permission of Wadsworth Publishing, a division of International Thomson Publishing.

HISPANIC AMERICANS

In the Southwest many Hispanics can trace their ancestry back to generations before Anglo Americans ever set foot in the area. They are nonetheless viewed as Mexicans and are seen as Catholics, as are virtually all Hispanics, even those who are Protestant or nonpracticing. Many are treated as racially different from Caucasians despite the fact that a majority are indeed Caucasian. They are, in fact, quite diverse, as our discussion will illustrate. They are many in number, so it should not be surprising that they vary in the strategies they employ to cope with their status. Chapter 4 will discuss their political route. Here, we describe their economic route to accommodation.

Since the mid-1950s, immigration to the United States has shifted dramatically from European countries to those of North, Central, and South America and Asia. From 1956 to 1976, while Asian immigration rose by a spectacular 369 percent and South American by 27 percent, those from European countries declined by 27 percent. Of foreign-born residents in the 1990 census, less than 18 percent of Europeans came to the United States during the 1980–1990 decade. In contrast, just over 56 percent of Asian-born residents came during the past decade. Nearly 50 percent of Mexican-born immigrants residing in the United States came during the past decade, as did over 67 percent of Central American-born residents and 52 percent of South Americans.

A troublesome characteristic for the various Hispanic groups is the Anglo tendency to treat them all alike, when in fact there are considerable differences among them. The 1990 census identified the population by claimed ancestry as follows: Cuban, 860,000; Dominican, 506,000; Hispanic, 1,113,000; Mexican, 11,587,000; Puerto Rican, 1,955,000; Salvadoran, 499,000; and Spanish, 2,024. Among what are treated as "Hispanic" groups, Mexicans are just over 64.3 percent, Puerto Ricans, 10.6 percent, and Cubans, 4.7 percent. All the Central/South American groups make up about 13.4 percent of the total, and all other Spanish-speaking total 7 percent. They are decidedly urban, 90 percent of whom live in metropolitan areas, particularly, Los Angeles, New York, Miami, Chicago, San Antonio, Houston, San Francisco, El Paso, Riverside/Ontario (California), and Anaheim (California). They are concentrated in nine states, listed in order of their percentage of the total Hispanic population: New Mexico, California, Texas, Arizona, Colorado, New York, Florida, New Jersey, and Illinois. The U.S. Bureau of the Census projects that by the year 2020, the Hispanic population will reach 39 million, displacing blacks as the nation's largest minority.[5]

Differences in the tactical approach used by the various Hispanic groups reflect their status and the opportunities open to them. The Cubans, many of whom entered under a protected status of "refugees," tend to be better educated, organized, and equipped to acculturate into the American job market structure. The majority society seems more willing to accept them, and they have been aided by special legislation and resettlement programs. This has eased their transition, enabled them to better employ the economic route, and assimilate more rapidly than any other Hispanic group. By contrast, Mexicans, many of whom have entered the United States illegally, remain almost totally unorganized and at the mercy of an economic system designed to exploit them. Economically, they remain at the lowest level of society, living in a social and cultural world apart from the majority society and lacking a real political voice because of their illegal status. The majority culture rejects them as persons who, at best, will lower wages and depress working conditions and, at worst, will swell the ranks of the welfare and criminal justice systems.

Although success stories are to be found, the majority of Hispanics suffer from low status, high crime, low educational levels, ethnic discrimination, and economic exploitation. Those in rural areas (about 10 percent of the total) typically live in run-down shacks provided for migrant workers in an economic system akin to slavery. Those in urban areas are frequently limited to slum areas. A quarter of all Hispanic families live below the poverty level. Gang life is rife among urban Hispanics, and gang-related violence is the major cause of death among their youth.

Hispanic poverty is linked to their low occupational backgrounds. They continue to have among the highest levels of unemployment in the United States. Of those employed, a majority are in low-status, low-paying blue-collar jobs. Hispanic poverty is also linked to their lower levels of educational achievement. Mexican-born residents in the 1990 census data exemplify the Hispanic situation. Some 4,300,000 residents identified themselves as Mexican-born. Among them, 50 percent had come during the 1980–1990 decade. Just over 24 percent of those had high school degrees, and only 3.5 percent were college educated. Their employment status reflects those facts: only 2.6 percent were professionals, 21 percent were in service jobs, and 32 percent worked in factories and related blue-collar jobs. Their median income, $23,912 annually, was well below the $40,420 non-Hispanic white national average.

Each of the three major subgroups comprising the Hispanic population will be briefly examined next. Table 3.5 compares their income and education status as of 1997 with non-Hispanic white, black, and Asian national averages.

Chicano Americans

The nearly 12 million residents of the United States claiming Mexican ancestry are heavily concentrated in California, Texas, New Mexico, Arizona, and Colorado. About 90 percent of all Chicanos reside in those states. Although Chicanos are the largest Hispanic group, at over 64 percent, even they can more accurately be discussed in two subgroups: the Spanish Americans, who trace their ancestry back to the settlers

TABLE 3.5   A Comparison of Hispanic, Non-Hispanic White, Black, and Asian Income/ Employment/Education, 1997

	Income	Poverty Level	Unemployed	High School Graduates	College Graduates
Non-Hispanic white	$44,756	8.6%	4.2%	83.0%	24.6%
Black	26,522	26.1	10.0	74.9	10.3
Asian	49,105	11.9	3.2	84.9	42.2
Hispanic	26,179	29.4	11.7	54.7	10.3

SOURCE: U.S. Bureau of the Census, *Statistical Abstract of the United States, 1998* (Washington, DC: U.S. Government Printing Office, 1998), Tables 51, 52, 55.

of the area now comprising northern New Mexico, and Mexican immigrants who have come in large measure since 1900 and more particularly since 1965.

The heritage of the Spanish-American subgroup is different from that of the Mexican immigrant. The ancestors of Spanish Americans arrived in what is now the Southwest United States while Mexico was still a Spanish colony. They mixed in varying degrees with Pueblo Indians of the area. They lived for generations as farmers, cattle ranchers, and sheepherders, isolated from both more modern Mexican and Anglo cultural influences. They thought of themselves as more Spanish than Mexican, and have preferred to be called Spanish Americans. To most Anglos they are "Mexicans," and are treated as such in intergroup relations. They tend to have higher formal educational patterns than other Spanish-surnamed persons in the Southwest, although they do not exhibit greater income or occupational mobility. They tend to be distributed more evenly throughout the economic strata. They became a minority by absorption after Texas became independent and sought union with the United States. Spanish Americans have ancestors who lived in the area for almost a century and a half prior to its annexation in 1848.

The Mexican-American War ended with the Treaty of Guadalupe-Hidalgo in 1848. Mexico lost about 45 percent of its land. This treaty guaranteed that the Mexicans who remained in the conquered territories would retain their civil, political, and religious rights, among which were specified equal protection and treatment under the U.S. Constitution and the freedom to maintain their culture, language, and property. With the exception of religion, little was done to honor those rights.

The gold rush in 1849 induced a great migration of Anglos into the region. In 1850, New Mexico, Utah, and California were designated territories. Anglos soon achieved economic domination of the area. In Sante Fe a ring of notorious land grabbers operated with "abuses so flagrant that they invoked the wrath of President Grover Cleveland" (Stoddard 1973: 12). Spanish Americans evidenced the pattern of traditional colonialism—in California, as economic colonialism, and in Texas, as "conquest colonialism" (Acuna 1972).

Large-scale immigration to the United States from Mexico is a phenomenon of the twentieth century, during which more than 1.5 million legal immigrants entered the country. While some were pushed north by the violence and turmoil associated with the Mexican Revolution, most were induced by a pull factor—the economic growth of the United States and a need for cheap labor.

In the first decade of the century Mexican immigration was used to fill the void created by the increasing restrictions on Asian migration. The Chinese Restriction Acts of the 1880s and 1890s and the gentlemen's agreement of 1907 restricting immigration from Japan created a void that Mexican laborers soon filled. By 1909, 98 percent of the crews employed by the Atchison, Topeka, and Sante Fe Railways west of Albuquerque were Mexicans, and the Southern Pacific Railroad employed a similar percentage.

Although the Immigration Act of 1917 placed a head tax on Mexican immigrants and applied literacy provisions to them, these laws were seldom enforced and had little impact on the steady flow of Mexicans drawn by the post–World War I economy and the need for "temporary farm workers." During the 1920s, Mexican immigration reached a peak of one-half million. Opposition toward unrestricted Mexican immigration solidified. Restrictionists first attempted to have them covered by the 1921 and 1924 Immigration Acts, but in both cases they were excluded from the quotas. In 1926, restrictionists launched another effort to apply the quota system to the whole of the Western Hemisphere. Again they failed because of agricultural interests in cheap migrant labor. In 1928, the fight loomed again. Congressional hearings were held, but the bills died in committee. The antirestrictionists were more powerful economic opportunists. Growers in the Southwest forced the Departments of State, Agriculture, and Interior to form a united front that overwhelmed the restrictionists. Their efforts were aided in part by the tapering off of immigration, when the Great Depression slowed it to nearly half. The 1940s and 1950s saw another surge in response to the war-generated boom that continued until 1964.

The **bracero program** legally brought in tens of thousands from Mexico annually. Just over 4,000 workers entered under contract with the bracero program in 1942. The annual total rose steadily until its peak year of 1956, when 445,197 entered. During the period 1953 to 1960, the average annual influx was about 300,000. The programs coincided with a new wave of illegal migrants known as **wetbacks**. "Operation Wetback" in the 1960s entailed a concerted effort to deport the illegal immigrants. Over a five-year period, some 3.8 million illegals were apprehended and returned to Mexico.

This wave of illegals from Mexico resurrected the opposition, who finally succeeded with the passage of the Immigration Act of 1965. This law imposed a regional quota system that allowed only 170,000 from the entire Western Hemisphere. The measure passed in no small measure due to the support of organized labor, which feared the impact of cheap labor from Mexico. The discrimination Mexican Americans faced was both intense and pervasive. They were referred to by a variety of derogatory slang terms: "cholo," "spik," "Mex," "beaner," "pachuco," and "greaser." They faced discrimination in jury selection, voting rights, and school enrollment. Until as recently as 1970, Houston had a plan to "integrate" African and Mexican Americans into their schools and have whites attend their own. Next to the Native American, the Chicano ranks lower than any other group in American society in such areas as education, housing, and economic conditions. They are still highly segregated in housing, show low levels of intermarriage, and manifest highly ethnic-related friendship patterns. Their degree of assimilation more nearly resembles a "mixing bowl" than it does a "melting pot." "Both in rate and degree of acculturation and assimilation, Mexican Americans are among the least 'Americanized' of all ethnic groups in the U.S." (Burma 1970: 20).

Three factors inhibited their assimilation: their continued pride in their Mexican culture, heritage, and language; their poor education; and the racial bias they face (about 40 percent are full-blooded Indians and approximately 95 percent have at least some Indian blood). Their close proximity to Mexico means their culture survives more intact than does that of most other minority groups. Conquest, racism, nativism, and the continued dependence of Mexico's economy on the United States have all played a part in keeping Chicanos in the role of servants. They make up a "secondary labor force"—concentrated in such unskilled jobs as laundry workers, packers,

Illegal aliens must go.

and taxi drivers or in such semiskilled crafts as masons, painters, plasterers, and bakers. Over 60 percent are unskilled or semiskilled blue-collar workers, and the Chicano male is even more underrepresented in white-collar jobs than is the female. Only recently have they improved their economic opportunities, and then rarely are these opportunities open to the first-generation immigrant.

The political movement against illegal aliens came to a climax with passage of the Immigration Reform and Control Act of 1986 (IRCA). This act made it against the law to knowingly hire illegal aliens. Its "employer sanctions" approach sought to "demagnetize" the attraction to illegal aliens of the American labor market. Apprehensions of attempted border crossings dipped in the months after its enactment, but the numbers began climbing again and by 1990 were up to pre-IRCA levels. Continued agitation to do something about illegal aliens culminated in enactment of California's Proposition 187, which eliminated such incentives as welfare, education, and health benefits to illegal aliens and their children.

Puerto Rican Americans

The second largest subgroup among Hispanics, at 10.6 percent, are the Puerto Ricans. In the 1990 census nearly 2 million claimed that ancestry. Migrants to the mainland and their descendants are more than that number, as they are undoubtedly undercounted in the census. Estimates run as high as over 3 million (DeLeon 1974). Migration to the mainland has been a factor for the past 30 years, and since they are legally

United States citizens, their movement back and forth is unrestricted. Between 1940 and 1960, the island lost over a million in population due to out-migration. Their movement has been largely a post–World War II phenomenon. Puerto Ricans are heavily concentrated in New York but found in every state, including Alaska and Hawaii. The cities in which they are most heavily settled are New York, Chicago, Bridgeport (Connecticut), Miami, Newark, Paterson/Jersey City, Boston, New Orleans, Lorain (Ohio), and Philadelphia.

The Puerto Rican mainland population is overwhelmingly urban, over 90 percent, and young; the median age is 19 years compared to a median age of 28 for the total American population. It is poor, with a median family income about six-tenths that of the general population. In New York City about 85 percent live in low-income areas. Puerto Rican families headed by a male earned about $4,000 per year less than the national median.

Their highly urban background is reflected in the fact that 30 times as many Puerto Ricans work in manufacturing as in agriculture. One in three of their families depend on two or more wage earners. Puerto Rican workers are concentrated in such blue-collar factory jobs as machine operators, garage workers, and laundry workers. In service jobs they are concentrated in hotels, restaurants, and cafeterias. As craftsmen they often work as repairmen and cabinetmakers. Their educational level is low, trailing both blacks and whites in years of formal education. Among Puerto Ricans 25 years old or older, the median school years completed is only 8.7. Just over 23 percent are high school graduates.

The primary motivation to migrate to the mainland is to seek work. They migrate young, usually between 15 and 39 years of age, and over half are less than 21 years of age. They suffer from racism in the United States, manifested in discrimination in hiring and training programs. Their unemployment rate typically runs two to three times the national rate. They are typically worse off in the job market than are blacks, trail them in voter registration and turnout, and in education and housing. In New York City they are scattered among five boroughs. In Chicago they are concentrated in "el barrio," Spanish Harlem. Spatial segregation leads to social isolation and a slower acculturation, as well as restricting their employment opportunities. Working females are better able than males to get white-collar jobs as clerks, secretaries, and operative positions.

Cuban Americans

With over 900,000 in population, Cuban Americans are the third largest Hispanic group, just under 5 percent of the total. Like Puerto Ricans, their migration has been a recent phenomenon. They came in two large waves. Some 700,000 refugees came after the fall of the Batista regime in 1959 and prior to the most recent influx, and are known as the "Golden Exiles." The post-1980 wave includes the 123,000 who came in 1980 in what was known as the "freedom flotilla." The Cuban boat people of 1980 came at a rate of 3,000 per month, part of an estimated 1 million immigrants who entered the United States in 1980 alone, some 700,000 of whom were illegal.[6] Of foreign-born in the 1990 census claiming Cuban birth, over 25 percent came in 1980–1990.

The initial wave was a flood that approached chaos. Following Castro's seizure of power in 1959, the first to flee were typically people of some measure of wealth. Being a select group of government officials, army officers, bankers, and the like, they had little trouble blending into the pattern of a culture where money constituted an international language and where anonymity meant safety. The latter part of that wave followed the agrarian reforms and land confiscations in Cuba in 1960–1961. These events sent middle-class doctors, lawyers, architects, and disillusioned white-collar workers to seek refuge in the United States. They were soon followed by farmers, peasants, and fishermen until the social strata of the refugees reflected Cuba itself. They came by air and boat, both legally and illegally, until 1960, by which time there were some 40,000 Cuban refugees in Miami alone.

In December 1960, President Eisenhower appointed Tracey Voorhees as his special representative to assess the situation. The President made available $1 million under the Mutual Security Act, which declared Cuba a communist country, to be used for resettlement, registration, and as aid to unaccompanied children. These funds became the seed money to start the Cuban Refugee Emergency Center in Miami. Various government agencies worked with the center: the INS, the U.S. Public Health Service, the U.S. Employment Service, and the Florida State Welfare Agency. These various agencies worked with and were supplemented financially by a variety of volunteer associations, such as the Catholic Relief Services of the National Catholic Welfare Conference, the Children's Service Bureau, the Church World Service Immigration Services, the National Protestant Committee on Cuban Refugees, and the Task Force of the Protestant Latin American Emergency Committee.

The Cuban Refugee Resettlement program really got underway in February 1961, when President Kennedy began the program designed to provide relief, rehabilitation, and resettlement. The program was based on a cooperative venture of the federal agencies and four volunteer agencies: the Catholic Relief Services of the National Catholic Welfare Conference, the United HIAS (Jewish), the International Rescue Committee (nonsectarian), and the Church World Service (Protestant).

The failure of the Bay of Pigs Invasion, in April 1961, drove home the point to the refugees that they could not go back to Cuba for a long time. This compelled them to accept that they would have to make permanent homes in the United States. After the failed invasion attempt, the rate at which new refugees entered rose to nearly 2,000 per week. By the end of 1961, there were more than 100,000 Cuban refugees here, heavily concentrated in Miami, and bringing severe problems to the city in handling the massive influx.

The Cuban Refugee Emergency Center launched a resettlement program to find them homes and jobs elsewhere in the United States. A series of "freedom flights" began in February 1962 and lasted until December 1963. A total of 69 flights resettled 3,802 persons. The single largest such flight carried 118 persons to Kansas City. By March 1963, the center had registered 161,941 Cuban refugees, of whom the various organizations assisted 60,000 to resettle. The center also developed programs for the influx of Cuban refugees who came via Jamaica, Mexico, and Spain.

The next large wave came in the mid-1960s. On September 28, 1965, Castro allowed all who wanted to leave the island for the United States to do so. A few days later, October 3, 1965, President Johnson, at the signing of the new Immigration Act at the Statue of Liberty, indicated that "those who seek refuge will find it" (Stanley 1966: 42). These events spurred an armada of refugees. In less than a month over 500 boats carrying over 3,000 persons arrived. In November 1965, another 2,000 boat people arrived. The greatest numbers came with an airlift organized by the United States from December 1, 1965 to August 5, 1966, bringing an additional 30,487 Cuban refugees. The various resettlement centers were being flooded with 4,000 refugees monthly. In January 1966, nine denominational Cuban Refugee Welfare Centers merged to form a single corporate venture, the Christian Community Service Agency. Working out of two main centers, they processed 165 refugees a day. The total number of refugees resettled from June 1961 to July 1966 was 114,416 (Stanley 1966).

Outside Miami, their reception was not always so welcome. Often, conflict among minorities, especially blacks, Asians, and other Hispanics, has sometimes been intense, particularly when one minority already in an area saw the "refugees" as getting special treatment and as constituting an immediate threat in the job market. In Denver, for example, Hispanics reacted violently to 24 Vietnamese refugee families being given apartments in a Chicano housing project with a long waiting list of Hispanic families. Rock- and bottle-throwing incidents forced the agency to find other housing for the Asians. State officials in Colorado made it clear that they wanted no Cuban refugees (McClellan 1981).

Although the resettlement program involved a significant number of Cuban refugees, the vast majority—over 80 percent—remained in the Miami metropolitan area. They assimilated mostly through the route of economic success. Their success has been attributed to several factors. They were greatly aided by the government-sponsored and related assistance programs. As special "refugees" from a communist-dominated country, they were received by the majority society with far less antipathy than were many other immigrant groups. A far higher percentage of them came from middle-class backgrounds, and even when starting at a lower level here, they rose more quickly to that status than did many older European immigrant groups. Today, some 20 percent of Cuban Americans are professional or managerial, and over 15 percent have college degrees. Their unemployment rate is consistently lower than the national average.

Their economic success led to growing political activity and success. Although originally their political efforts were directed largely at foreign policy issues pertaining to Cuba, increasingly they concern local politics. (Their use of the political route is discussed in Chapter 4.) This chapter closes with a discussion of yet another group that used a variety of strategies, including both economic and political paths to accommodation: black Americans.

BLACK AMERICANS

Only black Americans experienced the problems and status of slavery. Most black Africans who migrated to the United States prior to 1808, when the slave trade was officially ended, were forced to come as slaves. In recent years, voluntary migration has averaged about 65,000 annually. At over 27 million, black Americans are 12 percent of the total population. Two hundred plus years of slavery not only slowed their acculturation and assimilation, it shaped the majority society's norms and attitudes in ways relevant today.

In the South the existence of slavery led to an elaborate caste system with clear and strongly delineated norms for interaction. The repression, prejudice, and discrimination against blacks was exceptionally strong. Even the free blacks of the South, of whom there were nearly one-quarter million prior to the Civil War, faced rigid discrimination because of the caste system. They lived at the margins of society, virtual slaves without masters, and had few legal rights. With few exceptions they could not vote; they were banned from schools, the militia, public places, and many types of occupations. While they could make contracts and be married, sue, and hold property, they could not testify against whites in courts or sit on juries. They faced harsh penalties if convicted of crimes.

For the millions of slaves living in the South by 1860, conditions were far worse. The interstate trade was among slavery's most inhumane aspects. Prior to the Civil War there were an estimated 4 million slaves in the United States. This practice not only degraded the individual in particular, it had profound and lasting impact on the African-American population in general by greatly influencing their acculturation. It destroyed existing links to their native culture and groupings, often destroyed family units, and dispersed their population throughout the South. The harshness of slave life was an important ingredient in subsequent African-American development, as slaves were highly limited in their occupational training and education. Slave status contributed to the development of a sense of racial superiority among whites. The antebellum slave codes were very repressive, designed to cause fear of the white man among the slaves.

Slaves were both legally and culturally considered as property and, by definition, were subhuman. They could be bought, sold, given away, or killed at the will of their master. Slave women could be sexually used by their masters or for breeding purposes. Discipline was strict, as slaves were taught to be submissive yet productive. Slaves were fearful of and dependent upon whites. This was done to ensure their submission and loyalty. Family life was unstable to nonexistent. Morbidity and mortality rates among slaves were very high. Illness, filth, and disorder were common aspects of the slaves' everyday life. Since they were owned and maintained solely for their labor, equal social interaction with whites was unknown. Such status depressed the need for achievement. It developed a *matrifocal* (mother-centered) family life tradition that not only led to higher rates of female-headed households among blacks but also a weakening of the male role.

The effects of the slave system were not limited to the black population. Whites were also, if differentially, affected. Southern whites were obliged to defend slavery against outsiders whom they felt were incapable of understanding their peculiar problem. They also felt an ever-present need to defend themselves against slave revolt. This fear conditioned otherwise compassionate men to accept and overlook excessive brutality against blacks. It encouraged a sense of a common bond among all white men that became the basis for a unified South of one-party politics and a common perspective on national politics that had its roots deeply planted in the slave period (Dye 1971).

The Civil War and the end of slavery brought a promise of peace and equality in the **reconstruction period**, but reconstruction was short-lived, lasting but a decade. The radical Republicans gained control of Congress in 1867. The southern states, under military rule, adopted new constitutions that assured blacks the vote and other civil liberties. Blacks were elected to the Congress and to various state legislatures. A prominent black politician was governor of Louisiana for 40 days. The Reconstruction Congress passed the Thirteenth, Fourteenth, and Fifteenth Amendments, summarized in Box 3.1.

Between the end of the Civil War and the late 1870s, blacks enjoyed considerable success. They voted throughout the South, and many were elected to federal and state-level offices. They were treated nearly equally in theaters, restaurants, hotels, and public transportation facilities as guaranteed by the Civil Rights Act of 1875. By 1877, though, these gains began to recede.

The Compromise of 1877 ended the military occupation of the South. More importantly, a series of U.S. Supreme Court decisions spelled the collapse of reconstruction. The *Slaughterhouse* cases of 1873 nullified the privileges and immunities clause of the Fourteenth Amendment. The *Civil Rights* cases of 1883 declared the Civil Rights Act of 1875 unconstitutional. In 1884, the *Hurtado* vs. *California* ruling severely restricted the due process clause of the Fourteenth Amendment. Finally, in *Plessy* vs. *Ferguson,* in 1896, the Court approved the segregation of society through application of the "separate-but-equal doctrine" that essentially nullified the equal protection clause of the Fourteenth Amendment.

Even during reconstruction, southern whites used campaigns of violence and intimidation. The Ku Klux Klan led the movement to suppress the emergence into society of the new black citizens. Major riots occurred in Memphis, Tennessee, where 46 blacks were killed and 75 wounded, and in Colfax and Coushatta, Louisiana, where more than 100 blacks and white Republicans were massacred.

Segregation in its full-blown **Jim Crow** form took shape gradually, aligned with the rise of populism in the South. Southern blacks voted well into the 1880s. They held office, served on juries, on local government councils, and in the U.S. Congress. Blacks and whites rode the railroads in the same cars, ate in the same restaurants, and sat in the same theaters and waiting rooms. As southern whites regained control over government, a program of relegating blacks to a subordinate place in society accelerated. Beginning in Virginia as early as 1869 and spreading throughout the South, the use of Jim Crow laws and Klan intimidation characterized the "new South's" approach to the end of reconstruction.

Disenfranchisement was the initial step taken. Blacks who defied Klan pressure and tried to vote were met with an array of deceptions and obstacles. Polling places were changed at the last minute without notice to blacks. Severe time limits to complete long and complex ballots were imposed on blacks. Votes cast incorrectly in a maze of ballots were nullified. State constitutions were rewritten to disenfranchise blacks who could not read, understand, or "correctly interpret" complex and obscure

BOX 3.1: The Civil War Amendments

AMENDMENT XIII (RATIFIED ON DECEMBER 6, 1865)

Section 1

Neither slavery nor involuntary servitude, except as a punishment for crime whereof the party shall have been duly convicted, shall exist within the United States, or any place subject to their jurisdiction.

Section 2

Congress shall have power to enforce this article by appropriate legislation.

AMENDMENT XIV (RATIFIED ON JULY 9, 1868)

All persons born or naturalized in the United States, and subject to the jurisdiction thereof, are citizens of the United States and of the State wherein they reside. No State shall make or enforce any law which shall abridge the privileges or immunities of citizens of the United States; nor shall any State deprive any person of life, liberty, or property, without due process of law; nor deny to any person within its jurisdiction the equal protection of the laws.

Section 2

Representatives shall be apportioned among the several States according to their respective numbers, counting the whole number of persons in each State, excluding Indians not taxed. But when the right to vote at any election for the choice of electors for President and Vice President of the United States, Representatives in Congress, the Executive and Judicial officers of a State, or the members of the Legislature thereof, is denied to any of the male inhabitants of such State, being [twenty-one] years of age, and citizens of the United States, or in any way abridged, except for participation in rebellion, or other crime, the basis of representation therein shall be reduced in the proportion which the number of such male citizens shall bear to the whole number of male citizens twenty-one years of age in such State.

Section 3

No person shall be a Senator or Representative in Congress, or elector of President and Vice President, or hold any office, civil or military, under the United States, or under any State, who having previously taken an oath, as a member of Congress, or as an officer of the United States, or as a member of any State legislature, or as an executive or judicial officer of any State, to support the Constitution of the United States, shall have engaged in insurrection or rebellion against the same, or given aid or comfort to the enemies thereof. But Congress may by a vote of two-thirds of each House, remove such disability.

Section 4

The validity of the public debt of the United States, authorized by law, including debts incurred for payment of pensions and bounties for services in suppressing insurrection or rebellion, shall not be questioned. But neither the United States nor any State shall assume or pay any debt or obligation incurred in aid of insurrection or rebellion against the United States, or any claim for the loss or emancipation of any slave, but all such debts, obligations and claims shall be held illegal and void.

Section 5

The Congress shall have power to enforce, by appropriate legislation, the provisions of this article.

AMENDMENT XV (RATIFIED ON FEBRUARY 3, 1870)

Section 1

The right of citizens of the United States to vote shall not be denied or abridged by the United States or by any State on account of race, color, or previous condition of servitude.

Section 2

The Congress shall have power to enforce this article by appropriate legislation.

SOURCE: The Constitution of the United States.

sections of the constitution. Yet state constitutions permitted those who failed the test to vote "if their ancestors had been eligible to vote on January 1, 1860, when no Negro could vote anywhere in the South."[7] In 1896, black registered voters in Louisiana totaled 130,344. In 1900, after the state rewrote its suffrage laws, only 5,320 blacks remained on the registration books. In 1883, the Supreme Court declared the 1875 Civil Rights Act void. In 1896 *Plessy* vs. *Ferguson* promulgated the "separate-but-equal doctrine." Legal segregation reinforced social custom. Soon, blacks and whites were segregated by law on public transit, in all places of public accommodation, even hospitals and churches. Blacks and whites swore their oaths on separate Bibles in courthouses. They were even buried in separate cemeteries. Segregation meant discrimination, since the facilities, school conditions, and salaries were invariably worse for blacks. They were always separate but never equal.

Conditions in the North were not much better. Blacks were crowded by local ordinances into one section of a city where housing and public services were invariably substandard. Discrimination in employment was rampant. Blacks were limited to menial jobs. Labor unions excluded them from membership, or granted them membership only in separate and mostly powerless Jim Crow locals. Yet if blacks took jobs during strikes, they were castigated for undermining the principles of trade unionism.

Northern whites also resorted to violence. Antiblack riots took place in New York in 1900; in Springfield, Ohio, in 1904; in Greensburg, Indiana, in 1906; and in Springfield, Illinois, in 1908. The latter riot, a three-day rampage initiated by a white woman's charge of being raped by a black man, left six persons dead and extensive property damage. Many blacks fled the city permanently, most migrating to Chicago. Throughout the nation about 100 lynchings occurred every year in the 1880s and 1890s. One hundred sixty-one blacks were lynched in 1892 alone. "A virtual reign of terror began in the 1890s and extended to the beginning of World War I. A pioneering study by the NAACP, appropriately entitled 'Thirty Years of Lynchings in the United States, 1889-1918,' lists the names of 3,224 lynch victims" (Dye 1971: 18–19).

Those blacks who fled from Springfield to Chicago found they had left the frying pan for the fire. In 1919, the nation was embroiled in the "Red Summer" race riots, the worst of which shook Chicago, which had experienced an immigration of 60,000 blacks from the South in the 1910–1919 decade. The riot began when an 18-year-old black drifted across the imaginary line segregating black and white swimmers. White rock throwers caused him to drown. Soon after, blacks mobbed a policeman who refused to arrest the whites responsible. Then a crowd of Italian Americans killed the first black they saw, starting a riot that left 38 dead, 1,000 homeless, and 537 injured (Levy and Kramer 1973).

As more blacks migrated north, race riots became almost commonplace. Northern whites increasingly accepted the South's views on race relations. Social customs followed public policy in the North. Soon little signs reading "white only" or "colored" were everywhere. Although these lacked the sanction of law, black children were taught in their segregated schools to obey those signs. Segregation replaced slavery as society's method of keeping blacks "in their place." The vast majority of blacks remained mired at the bottom of the social and economic system. Segregation was supported by state law, by social practices, and by most institutions. Blacks were segregated throughout their lives, from birth in a segregated hospital, to attendance at segregated schools, to living in segregated neighborhoods, to employment in a segregated and limited job, to burial in a segregated cemetery.

Black response to these conditions was varied. At various times and led by various leaders, some faction of black Americans tried all three of the strategies discussed above. The economic accommodation strategy was a commonly used approach following the example of national-origins minorities. The best-known black advocate of accommodation was Booker T. Washington.

Widely known and respected by both blacks and whites, Washington served as an informal adviser to Presidents Theodore Roosevelt and William Howard Taft, and was the founder and president of Tuskegee Institute. His philosophic approach to race relations exemplifies the accommodation strategy. It is summarized in his famous Atlanta Compromise Address (see Case Study 3.1). He advocated that blacks should basically accept a subordinate position in society but quietly and slowly begin to improve their position and status by an economic route through filling a niche that whites would accept as nonthreatening. He stressed training in vocations such as farming, preaching, and blacksmithing. He felt blacks should remain in the South, acquire land, and build their own homes. They should educate themselves to the point where they could eliminate the ignorance and poverty that so plagued them, and then they would be accepted by white society. Among Tuskegee's most outstanding faculty members was George Washington Carver, whose research and various inventions and innovations in crop practices and farming devices earned him a national reputation. Several other black colleges and universities, for example, Fisk and Howard, developed from the Tuskegee Institute model. According to the U.S. Advisory Commission on Civil Disorders (1968):

> Self-help and self-respect appeared a practical and sure, if gradual, way of ultimately achieving racial equality. Washington's doctrines also gained support because they appealed to race pride—if Negroes believed in themselves, stood together, and supported each other, they would be able to shape their destinies.[8]

Black Americans at the turn of the century were so large a group that they could not easily find an economic niche, as did Asian Americans, to successfully pursue this

Booker T. Washington (1856–1915), founder of the Tuskegee Institute.

route. They did not move north soon enough in large numbers to secure nonthreatening jobs. When they did, they largely followed after and had to compete with the wave of South, Central, and East European immigrants, who tended to take the majority of unskilled labor jobs available. By the time they had improved their educational backgrounds sufficiently to move up the ladder, the opportunities were increasingly closed to them. Unlike Scandinavians or Germans, most could not get to the free land being given away by the Homestead Act. They never successfully used the economic tactic and soon had to turn to other strategies.

SUMMARY

This chapter explained and exemplified the use of the economic route to the accommodation strategy. Both racial and national-origins ethnic minorities have employed—to varying degrees of success—this path to accommodation. Asian Americans offer a sort of prototype case for the successful use of the economic tactic. Coming to the United States in small enough numbers and early in the period of United States economic development, the Chinese, Japanese, and Korean immigrant groups were able to find economic niches in the labor system and achieve middle-class status.

The chapter discussed examples of the "old" immigrant groups, northwestern Europeans who successfully relied on the economic path to accommodation. German Americans served as their prototype. They came early enough to enter the frontier farmlands. They enjoyed access to skilled trades and often founded industries that provided their economic niche. Likewise, Scandinavian Americans came at an opportune time. The Homestead Act provided abundant free land. They arrived with sufficient resources to escape the urban immigrant slums and ethnic enclaves and to get out to the frontier regions where their cultural similarities and economic success enabled them to quickly assimilate into the dominant culture.

Greek Americans offer a mixed approach.

Coming somewhat later, they represent the "new" immigrant groups who came mostly from South, Central, and Eastern Europe. Many attempted the economic path with some success. They came in small enough numbers and were sufficiently dispersed to avoid the trap of ethnic enclaves. They relied on special economic niches such as restaurants, confectioneries, and candy stores. Later Greek immigrants pursued professional occupations as their path to middle-class status and to economic accommodation.

Hispanic Americans—Mexican Americans, Puerto Rican Americans, and Cuban Americans—illustrated the economic approach. Differences in the traits, the timing of their entrance, and the sizes of their immigrations accounted for their varied success in employing the economic tactic of the accommodation strategy. The smaller size, special refugee status, and better economic backgrounds of the Cuban Americans account for their greater success in using this approach.

The chapter closed with a brief discussion of black Americans, focusing on the effects of the special slave status on their experience in the United States. The philosophic approach of Booker T. Washington as the foremost advocate among black Americans of economic accommodation was highlighted.

KEY TERMS

Bracero program: a 1942–1964 program of legally imported "temporary agricultural workers," mostly from Mexico.

Community cohesion theory: a theory accounting for the rapid rate of Japanese-American assimilation, stressing the organizational features of their community.

Jim Crow: use of public laws in the South to segregate all aspects of life, begun around the 1870s and lasting until the 1960s.

Padrone system: a "boss" or patron who sponsors and assists, for a price, an immigrant. Used mostly by Greeks and Italians; a type of modern indentured servant system.

Reconstruction: a period (1867–1877) of U.S. history when the Radical Republicans attempted to "reconstruct" the South; it instituted civil rights to the former slaves.

Sojourner: an immigrant who intends to stay only a short while before returning to the country of origin.

Value-compatibility theory: a theory that explains the rapid rate of assimilation of an immigrant group, stressing the values of its culture common with middle-class Anglo-American culture.

Wetback: term for illegal aliens, mostly from Mexico.

REVIEW QUESTIONS

1. Describe an "occupational niche." What factors make it more or less useful to a group in pursuing economic accommodation?

2. Discuss the immigration laws first used to restrict Asian immigration.

3. What law revised the U.S. immigration policy of national-origins quota system by first allowing token quotas for immigrants from Asian nations?

4. Describe the approach of the law that replaced the national-origins quota system with a preference system.

5. What U.S. law provided the cheap land that enabled many "old" immigrant groups to achieve economic success? Relate it to other pull factors influencing immigration.

6. Describe the Greek padrone system.

7. Discuss the effort to "demagnetize" the U.S. labor market as a pull factor by enactment of the Immigration Reform and Control Act in 1986. Why wasn't it successful?

8. Briefly describe the Cuban Refugee Resettlement program. Why did it give Cuban immigrants an advantage in economic accommodation that Mexicans and Puerto Ricans lacked?

9. Describe the use of Jim Crow laws and compare and contrast them with slavery.

10. Who was the foremost advocate of the economic route to accommodation among black Americans? What are the main tenets he advocated? Why were they not successful?

NOTES

1. For more on this topic, see, for example, Kitano (1976), Parrillo (1985), and McLemore (1982).

2. See, for instance, Eugene Rostow, "Our Worst Wartime Mistake," *Harpers Magazine,* September 1945, pp. 193–201; and Ken Ringle, "What Did You Do Before the War, Dad?" *Washington Post Magazine,* December 6, 1981, pp. 54–62. See also McLemore (1982). This assessment is also reached by other scholars: Hosokawa (1969), Simpson and Yinger (1965), and Kitano (1997).

3. See "Disguised Blessing," *Newsweek,* December 29, 1958, p. 23. See also others who make this point: Kitano (1997), Hosokawa (1969), Parrillo (1985), McLemore (1982), as well as "Success Story: Outwhiting the Whites," *Newsweek,* June 21, 1971, pp. 24–25.

4. U.S. Census Bureau, *Statistical Abstract of the United States, 1998* (Washington, DC: U.S. Government Printing Office, 1998). See this source for demographic information for all groups discussed in this chapter.

5. U.S. Census Bureau, Population Reference Bureau, *Current Population Reports,* P25-1082 (Washington, DC: U.S. Government Printing Office, 1998).

6. *Newsweek,* July 7, 1980, p. 27.

7. U.S. Advisory Commission on Civil Disorders, *Report of the Commission* (New York: Bantam, 1968), p. 214.

8. Ibid., p. 216.

SUGGESTED READINGS

CHENG, LUCIE, AND EDNA BONACHICH, EDS. *Labor Immigration Under Capitalism.* Berkeley: University of California Press, 1984.

FEAGIN, JOE, AND CLAIRICE FEAGIN. *Racial and Ethnic Relations,* 5th ed. Englewood Cliffs, NJ: Prentice Hall, 1996.

HOSOKAWA, WILLIAM. *Nisei: The Quiet Americans.* New York: William & Morrow, 1969.

HURH, WOU MOO. *Comparative Study of Korean Immigrants in the United States: A Typological Approach.* San Francisco: R. & E. Associates, 1977.

KITANO, HARRY. *Race Relations,* 5th ed. Upper Saddle River, NJ: Prentice Hall, 1997.

LEHRER, BRIAN. *The Korean Americans.* New York: Chelsea House, 1988.

MOSKOS, CHARLES C. *Greek Americans.* Englewood Cliffs, NJ: Prentice Hall, 1980.

PARRILLO, VINCENT. *Strangers to These Shores,* 2nd ed. New York: Wiley, 1985.

STANLEY, FRANCES. *The New World Refugee—The Cuban Exodus.* New York: Church World Service, 1966.

U.S. Advisory Commission on Civil Disorders. *Report of the Commission.* New York: Bantam, 1968.

WHITE, JOHN. *Black Leadership in America,* 2nd ed. New York: Longman, 1990.

CASE STUDY 3.1

Booker T. Washington's Atlantic Compromise Address

Mr. President and Gentlemen of the Board of Directors and Citizens: One-third of the population of the South is of the Negro race. No enterprise seeking the material, civil, or moral welfare of this section can disregard this element of our population and reach the highest success. I but convey to you, Mr. President and Directors, the sentiment of the masses of my race when I say that in no way have the value and manhood of the American Negro been more fittingly and generously recognized than by the managers of this magnificent Exposition at every stage of its progress. It is a recognition that will do more to cement the friendship of the two races than any occurrence since the dawn of our freedom.

Not only this, but the opportunity here afforded will awaken among us a new era of Industrial progress. Ignorant and inexperienced, it is not strange that in the first years of our new life we began at the top instead of at the bottom; that a seat in Congress or the state legislature was more sought than real estate or industrial skill; that the political convention or stump speaking had more attractions than starting a dairy farm or truck garden.

A ship lost at sea for many days suddenly sighted a friendly vessel. From the mast of the unfortunate vessel was seen a signal, "Water, water; we die of thirst!" The answer from the friendly vessel at once came back, "Cast down your bucket where you are." A second time the signal, "Water, water; send us water!" ran up from the distressed vessel, and was answered, "Cast down your bucket where you are." And a third and fourth signal for water was answered, "Cast down your bucket where you are." The Captain of the distressed vessel, at last heeding the injunction, cast down his bucket, and it came up full of fresh, sparkling water from the mouth of the Amazon River. To those of my race who depend on bettering their condition in a foreign land or who underestimate the importance of cultivating friendly relations with the Southern white man, who is their nextdoor neighbor, I would say: "Cast down your bucket where you are"—cast it down in making friends in every manly way of the people of all races by whom we are surrounded.

Cast it down in agriculture, mechanics, in commerce, in domestic service, and in the professions. And in this connection it is well to bear in mind that whatever other sins the South may be called to bear, when it comes to business, pure and simple, it is in the South that the Negro is given a man's chance in the commercial world, and in nothing is this exposition more eloquent than in emphasizing this chance. Our greatest danger is that in the great leap from slavery to freedom we may overlook the fact that the masses of us are to live by the productions of our hands, and fail to keep in mind that we shall prosper in proportion as we learn to dignify and glorify common labor and put brains and skill into the common occupations of life; shall prosper in proportion as we learn to draw the line between the superficial and the substantial, the ornamental gewgaws of life and the useful. No race can prosper till it learns that there is as much dignity in tilling a field as in writing a poem. It is at the bottom of life we must begin, and not at the top. Nor should we permit our grievances to overshadow our opportunities.

To those of the white race who look to the incoming of those of foreign birth and strange tongue and habits for the prosperity of the South, were I permitted I would repeat what I say to my own race, "Cast down your bucket where you are." Cast it down among the 8 millions of Negroes whose habits you know, whose fidelity and love you have tested in days when to have proved treacherous meant the ruin of your firesides. Cast down your bucket among these people who have, without strikes and labor wars, tilled your fields, cleared your forests, builded your railroads and cities, and brought forth treasures from the bowels of the earth, and helped make possible this magnificent representation of the progress of the South. Casting down your bucket among my people, helping and encouraging them as you are doing on these grounds, and to education of head, hand, and heart, you will find that they will buy your surplus land, make blossom the waste places in your fields, and run your factories. While doing this, you can be sure in the future, as in the past, that you and your families will be surrounded by the most patient, faithful, law-abiding, and unresentful people that the world has seen. As we have proved our loyalty to you in the past, in nursing your children, watching by the sickbed of your mothers and fathers, and often following them with tear-dimmed eyes to their graves, so in the future, in our humble way, we shall stand by you with a devotion that no foreigner can approach, ready to lay down our lives, if need be, in defense of yours, interlacing our industrial, commercial, civil, and religious life with yours in a way that shall make the interests of both races one. In all things that are purely social we can be as separate as the fingers, yet one as the hand in all things essential to mutual progress.

There is no defense or security for any of us except in the highest intelligence and development of all. If anywhere there are efforts tending to curtail the fullest growth of the Negro, let these efforts be turned into stimulating, encouraging, and making him the most useful and intelligent citizen. Effort or means so invested will pay a thousand percent interest. These efforts will be twice blessed—"blessing him that gives and him that takes."

There is no escape through law of man or God from the inevitable:

The laws of changeless justice bind
    Oppressor with oppressed;
And close as sin and suffering joined
    We march to fate abreast.

Nearly 16 millions of hands will aid you in pulling the load upward, or they will pull against you the load downward. We shall constitute one-third and more of the ignorance and crime of the South, or one-third its intelligence and progress; we shall contribute one-third to the business and industrial prosperity of the South, or we shall prove a veritable body of death, stagnating, depressing, retarding every effort to advance the body politic.

SOURCE: Booker T. Washington, *Up from Slavery* (New York: Dover Publications, 1995), pp. 105–113.

CHAPTER FOUR

THE STRATEGY OF ACCOMMODATION
The Political Route

Chapter Three discussed an economic route to accommodation. For some groups, it simply is not an attractive strategy. They may enter majority society at an inopportune time, during a major recession or depression, for example, lacking expanding job opportunities. They may not have the resources in capital or job skills to enter the occupational structure of the dominant society in sufficient numbers to make headway in climbing the socioeconomic ladder. It takes capital to open one's own restaurant, retail store, garment factory, and the like. It takes farming skill and the money to get to where cheap land is available to own a farm and thereby thrive economically and socially.

When a group desires assimilation but finds its economic route blocked, the tactic of choice becomes political action. As with the economic route, political accommodation is favored by a group as its overall strategy only when certain conditions are evident. This chapter examines groups who used the political route. Political accommodation requires racial or ethnic minorities to have both the organizational skills and the experience to develop and deliver a consistent bloc vote. It needs a leadership capable of articulating specific goals to bargain with a faction of majority culture in return for bloc vote support. The majority society must be split into factions, at least some of whom desire to form a coalition with racial and ethnic minorities to win consistently in the electoral struggle with other majority factions. When the minority demonstrates its ability to deliver bloc votes to provide the winning margin in elections, it becomes a highly prized coalition partner. The majority faction is then willing to grant rewards. This enables the minority to use politics to climb the socioeconomic structure of society. Irish Americans are a classic example of political accommodation. They developed the prototype that others followed. This chapter begins with the use of political accommodation by Irish Americans. It proceeds to discuss subsequent use of the tactic by Italians, by factions of the Greeks, other South/Central/

East European groups, and by factions of Hispanic-American groups. It closes with a discussion of how black Americans are now successfully using this route to accommodation.

IRISH AMERICANS

At 38,736,000, residents claiming Irish-American ancestry in the 1990 census rank second only to German Americans in number and percentage of the total population. They are evenly balanced in their regional distribution throughout the country: 24 percent reside in the Northeast, 25 percent in the Midwest, 33 percent in the South, and 17 percent in the West. Among them, 170,000 are foreign-born, nearly 20 percent of whom came to the United States during the 1980–1990 decade. Of those recently immigrated Irish Americans, nearly 64 percent were high school graduates, 15 percent were college graduates, 17 percent were in professional occupations, 19.5 percent were in service occupations, and 9 percent were in factory or related blue-collar work. At $31,562 in median household income, Irish Americans exceed the national average of $28,314. They have achieved middle-class status and a high degree of assimilation.

Irish immigration can be traced back to colonial times, when they settled mostly in the colonies of Pennsylvania and Maryland. By 1790, they were about 2 percent of the nation's total population of nearly 3 million. They trailed German immigrants but were a significant minority, generating strong and overt discrimination. Irish immigrants after 1830 and before the Civil War were fleeing political and religious persecution under British rule. By late 1840, Irish immigration became a flood.

The potato famine precipitated a massive migration. For many Irish the choice was emigrating or starving to death. Between 1847 and 1854, approximately 1.2 million Irish arrived in the United States. That wave peaked in 1851, when nearly a quarter-million arrived. This famine-induced immigration was important because it meant a deluge of poor Irish immigrants settled on the East Coast, which activated existing prejudice. Their sheer numbers, religion (Catholicism), and openly anti-British sentiment contributed to the antipathy toward them evident in the native stock. Perhaps equally important for understanding their failure to use the economic route and their ability to develop the political path was their poverty. It trapped them within the nation's explosively expanding Eastern seaboard cities. That concentration enhanced the effect of bloc voting.

The Irish immigrants' high rates of illiteracy and general lack of job skills forced them into unskilled work. They were of lower-class status precisely when the United States developed class consciousness.[1] They were seen as a particular threat, a great concentration of "indigent foreigners," and a lower class of people who formed the first huge pool of manual labor (O'Grady 1973). The Irish were the first ethnic group to face overt job discrimination. Job advertisements in New York, Boston, and other eastern cities for some time included the line "No Irish Need Apply." They accepted whatever jobs were open to them—unskilled jobs such as stevedores, teamsters, ditchdiggers, dockers, and terriers. They formed construction gangs who razed or erected the buildings of the explosively expanding cities. They built the roads, canals, and railroads connecting the East with the Midwest and beyond. Much to their dismay, not only were the streets of America not paved with gold; they discovered the streets were unpaved and they would do much of the paving!

These jobs were seasonal, low-paying, and periodic. They were subject to constant job threat and labor competition from the Chinese or blacks. Irish immigrants became trapped in an existence that was depressingly grim. Social barriers and meager and insecure incomes forced them to live in enclaves in the slums. Many "escaped" such conditions by abusing alcohol. This contributed to the stereotypical image of the Irish as excessive drinkers.

They broke the vicious cycle and moved up the socioeconomic ladder by their involvement in the beginnings of the American labor movement and by use of politics to enter local government bureaucracies. It was the only route realistically open to them. While few Irish immigrants had experience in labor union affairs, their precarious economic position led them into labor associations. They were early leaders in the formation of unions from New York to San Francisco. These included the gambit from skilled craftsmen to longshoremen to simply "unskilled laborers." In the 1850s, unions operated solely at the local level, but by the 1860s, they appeared at the national level. In 1861, Martin Burke helped form the American Miners Association. By the late 1870s, a second-generation Irish American, Terrence Powderly, gained control of the first truly effective national level labor union, the Knights of Labor. Peter J. McGuire, the "Father of Labor Day," helped form the American Federation of Labor in 1886.

A massive urbanization between 1840 and 1850 required rapidly increasing local government work forces, especially police departments. The Irish were quick to join, and some rose rapidly to levels of responsibility. By 1863, a John A. Kennedy led New York City's police force. In 1870, a new detective, Michael Kerwin, became police commissioner. The police job was especially attractive to the Irish immigrants. The status of the uniform and the steady employment were magnets, as was the potential power of the position. In Ireland they had been oppressed by the police—evicted, taxed, seized for questioning, imprisoned, and even killed. In America, they exercised such power.

> The Irish policemen exercised wide discretion in apprehending violators and as upholders of the law, they interpreted the law with a latitude and flexibility appropriate to their interests and those of the politicians they served, and the political morality they inherited justified this practice. (Levine 1966: 123)

Since politicians controlled appointments to the police force, Irish immigrants soon realized job security rested on the success of the growing urban machine's slate at primaries and on the party's victory on general election day. Irish-dominated police departments became the mainstays of ward and district organizations of the Democratic political party.

Politics set the pattern of immigrant minority group/majority society relations that served as the model for most of the "new" immigrant groups. It served as the prototype for many subsequent groups, none of whom were able to employ it quite as successfully as did the Irish. Social conditions changed by the time later groups emulated the Irish model.

Huge numbers of Irish living in enclaves formed an ethnic voting bloc that provided the margin of victory. Ward leaders and precinct captains of the urban political party machine were often Irish immigrants. Using church and related ethnic organizations, they established the machine apparatus that gradually controlled the electoral machinery. By the 1870s, they gained control of the Democratic Party machine in Brooklyn. Irish Americans served as mayors in Richmond, Memphis, Baltimore, Wilmington, and Scranton. In 1871, an Irishman entered Congress as a representative from New York; in 1876 another won a seat from Pennsylvania. The highly influential Irish Catholic Benevolent Union (ICBU) sent several of its prominent members to seats on the city council of Philadelphia in the 1870s. One of them, William Harrity, served as chairman of the Philadelphia Democratic City Committee. He later served as chairman of the Democratic National Committee during President Cleveland's 1892 campaign. This set the precedent for a long tradition of Irish Democratic Committee chairmen. The ICBU also provided eight men who held judgeships during the 1870s, and by 1880 its founder, Dennis Dwyer, won a seat on New York State's Supreme Court.

This success was duplicated in various parts of the nation, but the early political clout of the Irish reached its zenith in New York City through their 50-year control of Tammany Hall, the first of the classic urban machines. As Senator Daniel Patrick Moynihan so aptly describes it:

> "Dick" Connolly and "Brains" Sweeny had shared power and office with Tweed, as had any number of their followers, but with few exceptions the pre-1870s Irish had represented the canaille. With the dawning of the Gilded Age, however, middle-class and upper-class Irish began to appear; thus ranging across the social spectrum, the Irish appeared to dominate a good part of the city's life for half a century. They came to run the police force and the underworld; they were evident on Wall Street as on the Bowery; Irish contractors laid out the subways and Irish laborers dug them. The city entered the era of Boss Croker of Tammany Hall and Judge Goff of the Lexow Committee, which investigated him; of business leader Thomas Fortune Ryan and labor leader Peter J. McQuire; of reform mayor John Purroy Mitchel and Tammany Mayor "Red Mike" Hylan. It was a stimulating miscellany, reaching its height in the Roaring Twenties with Al Smith and Jimmy Walker. (cited in Fuchs 1990: 79–80)

Successive waves of immigrants caused the nation's cities to virtually explode upward and outward. By 1920, immigrant groups made up 44 percent of New York, 41 percent of Cleveland, 39 percent of Newark, and 24 percent of Pittsburgh, Detroit, Boston, Buffalo, and Philadelphia. Successive waves of immigrants coming after 1880 had similar low levels of skills and resources that characterized the Irish peasants. Like the Irish, they used politics to cope with their minority status. However, they used it less successfully because of changing conditions and because the Irish, who arrived before them, were more reluctant to budge from their newly acquired middle-class "rung" than were the Yankees before them.

ITALIAN AMERICANS

Italian-American immigration occurred almost exclusively after 1870. At 5.5 million immigrants, Italy is second only to Germany in the total number of immigrants coming to the United States. In the 1990 census, some 14,655,000 Americans claimed Italian ancestry. Today they remain concentrated in the East, where over 51 percent reside; the remaining are distributed at 17 percent in each of the Midwest and the South and 15 percent in the West. They continue to come. In the 1990 census, over a half-million people acknowledged being born in Italy, among whom over 6 percent came in the 1980–1990 decade. These newest immigrants are better educated than their earlier compatriots, although they lag far behind both Asian and Irish immigrants. Among Italian-born immigrants, 39 percent were high school graduates and 8.6 percent claimed college degrees. In occupations, 8.5 percent of them are professionals, over 17 percent are in services, and just 18 percent are operators, laborers, and fabricators. At just over $29,000, their median family income level is just slightly more than the national average of $28,314.

There was some colonial and pre–Civil War immigration from Italy. As early as the 1620s, the Virginia colony had a few Italian wine growers. Pre–Revolutionary War immigration from Italy was lightly scattered among Virginia, Georgia, the Carolinas, New York, and Florida. Repression in Europe in the 1870s forced a number of Italian intellectuals and revolutionaries to emigrate. Although small in number, those pre-1880 immigrants, mostly from the northern provinces of Italy, had a considerable impact on the areas where they settled. They founded the opera in the United States during the 1830s and 1840s. From the 1820s to the 1870s, Italian artists were brought in by the federal government to create commissioned public artwork. By 1848, two Italian immigrants had been elected to the Texas state legislature. A year later, in New York, Secchi de Casali founded *L'Eco d' Italia,* a prominent Italian-language newspaper that supported the Whig Party and later the Republicans.

By the 1850s, there was an Italian settlement in Chicago, where they served as saloon keepers, restaurateurs, fruit venders, and confectioners, as well as common ditchdiggers and commissioned artists. They were also being lured to California by the gold rush. Instead of mining, however, most became wine growers, vegetable farmers, and merchants, giving rise to "the Italian American folklore that 'the miners mine the mines, and the Italians mined the miners'" (Iorizzo and Mandello 1971: 13). Early Italian Americans were often skilled craftsmen who were of middle to upper class in background and who came seeking better economic opportunity. This changed radically after the 1870s.

The Risorgimento, resulting in the unification of Italy in 1870, sparked a mass exodus of nearly 9 million Italians who crossed the Atlantic to both North and South America to seek better economic conditions denied them by the very movement they had supported at home. The trickle of northern Italians became a flood from the south. From 1881 to 1910, more than 3 million Italians came to the United States. Most settled in the cities of the industrial Northeast. By 1930, New York City's Italian-American immigrants numbered over 1 million and were 15.5 percent of its total population.[2]

This flood of immigrants was by no means a static bloc. There was considerable mobility after their arrival, as they moved back and forth between Italy and America. They lived in enclaves known as "Little Italys" here. Data from 1910 to 1914 show that about half of those who arrived here returned to Italy to winter there, working the remainder of the year in America (Nelli 1970).

Several push and pull factors influenced Italian immigrants to undertake the arduous and uprooting migration to the United States. Most left Italy because of economic factors, fleeing the economic shackles of poverty. During the 1890s, agricultural workers in Italy earned between 16 and 30 cents per day, and during the winter season that fell to 10 to 20 cents per day. Italian miners received from 30 to 56 cents per day. General laborers received $3.50 for a six-day workweek, compared to $9.50 for a 56-hour workweek in the United States. Carpenters in Italy earned 30 cents to $1.40 per day, or $1.80 to $8.40 for a six-day week. That same worker in the United States received an average $18 for a 50-hour workweek.[3] Floods, volcanic eruptions, and earthquakes plagued the country and contributed to its bleak agricultural outlook, especially in the south. That region was also especially hard hit by phylloxera, a disease that killed off agricultural plants on a scale similar to the potato blight of the 1840s. Southern Italy was further troubled by frequent and severe epidemics of malaria. Others fled compulsory military service.

Far more important were the pull factors. The development of the steamship lines made the journey cheaper, faster, and easier. The glowing reports of relatives and acquaintances about the wealth of opportunity drew others. Returning "Americani," some of whom made the trip back and forth, had sufficient money not only to return to Italy temporarily for brides but also to attract many others to emulate their success in America. State governments, such as those of Illinois, New York, Pennsylvania, California, and Louisiana, hired agents to contract for laborers. And come they did. From 1890 to 1914, they arrived in excess of 100,000 per year. Between 1900 and 1914, a total of 3 million came. So massive was the out-migration that

> one author told the humorous and probably apocryphal tale of a mayor who greeted the Prime Minister of Italy then touring the provinces: "I welcome you in the name of five thousand inhabitants of this town, three thousand of whom are in America and the other two thousand preparing to go. (Iorrizzo and Mondello 1971: 48)

The southern Italian was often a "sojourner" in his mentality, undoubtedly associated with the cultural and social background of the peasant, as opposed to the background of the earlier immigrating northern Italians. For historical reasons, the Mezzogiorno (the south) was more traditional, more backward, and poorer than the north. The *contadini* (peasants) were at the bottom of a still largely feudal society. Oppressed and exploited by signori and borghesi alike, they were despised as *cafoni* (boors). Illiterate, unschooled, lacking in self-confidence, the peasantry was preindustrial in culture and mentality—not a very good preparation for life in America's teeming tenement slums!

The peasant's motive to immigrate was not only to escape grinding poverty, it was to improve his family's lot by earning money to buy land in his village in Italy. Many came intending to work, save, and return after several years with a few hundred dollars. Like the Chinese, to whom they were often compared, the Italians were sojourners: predominantly male and youthful. Of the millions who emigrated, about half in fact did return to their villages, having accomplished their mission or having met with defeat. Even those who remained in America often nourished thoughts of the day they could return. The persistence of that mentality was an important condition affecting their adjustment. Why learn English, why become a citizen, why Americanize, if one were going back to the old country, if not this year, then next?

Italians settled into the teeming cities where they managed to find jobs in a variety of occupations: common laborers on the railroads, digging canals and waterways, digging the sewer systems, and laying the pipes for the water supply. Many took up fruit vending and vegetable farming. In contrast to their experiences in Italy, truck farming in the United States was a good investment. Match and shoe factories recruited laborers and soon found that "chain" migration (depending on the personal word of mouth or letters from one relative or friend to another) was so effective that they no longer needed agents to recruit the laborers.

Some settled into more rural areas and occupations. In San Francisco they dominated the fruit and vegetable truck farming business; they were so prominent in that market in California that "Del Monte" became a household word. In 1881, the Italian-Swiss colony established at Asti in Sonoma County sparked the development of the wine industry. A smaller but comparable role was played in the wine industry in upstate New York. Other important agricultural settlements included Vineland and Hammonton, New Jersey, and Geneva, Wisconsin. In 1850, Louisiana had more Italians as laborers in the cotton fields than any other state, and New Orleans had a larger population of Italians than any other city. By 1920, however, New York City led the nation with its more than one-half million Italian residents.

They arrived by the hundreds of thousands precisely when the United States was experiencing an economic downturn. The turbulent socioeconomic unrest following the Panic of 1873 and the subsequent crippling depression led to rising anti-Semitism, the emerging Jim Crow movement, and growing antipathy toward European immigrants, especially those coming from South, Central, and Eastern Europe. The latter were viewed by the native stock as radicals and criminals who filled the ever-growing slums, fueled class conflicts, and contributed to the developing urban machine and its blatant political corruption.

They did seem to be filling the cities. According to the 1910 census, Italian immigrants accounted for 77 percent of Chicago's foreign-born population, 78 percent of New York's, and 74 percent of Boston's, Cleveland's, and Detroit's. In the late 1880s and 1890s, depression-induced violence swept the country and was frequently directed at the Italians.

Intense discrimination against Italian-American immigrants affected their living conditions. Nearly 90 percent lived in "Little Italy" enclaves of the major cities where conditions were grim. Jacob Riis describes the slums in and around "The Bend," "Bandit's Roost," and "Bottle Alley." They characterized the Mulberry Street–Mulberry Bend area composing New York City's first Little Italy section. He says about the area:

Half a dozen blocks on Mulberry Street there is a rag-pickers settlement, a sort of over-flow from "the Bend," that exists today in all its pristine nastiness. Something like forty families are packed into old two-story and attic houses that were built to hold five, and out in the yards additional crowds are, or were until very recently, accommodated in shacks built of all sorts of old boards and used as drying racks by the Italian stock. (Riis 1971: 49)

Conditions like those described by Riis were all too common. Other studies documented similar conditions. One survey found that 1,231 Italians were living in 120 rooms in New York. Another report stated they could not find a single bathtub in a three-block area of tenements. In Chicago, a two-room apartment often housed an Italian family of parents, grandparents, several children, cousins, and boarders. A 1910 survey in Philadelphia noted that Italian families had to live, cook, eat, and sleep in the same room, and many tenants shared outhouses and a water hydrant—the only plumbing facilities available—with four or five other families. In addition, many kept chickens in their bedrooms and goats in their cellars (Dinnerstein and Reimers 1988: 48).

Concentration in enclaves helped them to cope. One way was the **padroni** system. Although probably exaggerated as to its exploitive nature and extensiveness, this "boss" system was nonetheless an important mechanism for the immigrant. The padroni, the bosses, knew individual employers, spoke English, and understood American labor practices. They were invaluable to American business in need of gangs of laborers. The newcomers depended on them for jobs and other services—collecting wages, writing letters, acting as a banker, supplying room and board, and handling dealings between workers and employers.

Although the Foran Act of 1885 forbade contract labor, the golden era of these padroni was from 1890 to 1900. Conditions of poverty drove many families to work long and hard and forced their young to forgo school and to work at very early ages. In 1897, an estimated two-thirds of the Italian workers in New York City were controlled by padroni. Though exploitive, the padroni system, nonetheless, helped them find jobs and eased the acculturation process. After 1900, it declined rapidly when others provided social services previously done by the padroni. Railroad and construction officials investigated and became aware of the worst abuses. They found laborers without the padroni. Finally, the sheer massive numbers of immigrants pouring into the settlements exceeded what the padroni could handle. Later immigrants were less dependent on bosses for housing, jobs, and persons to assist them with English or with contacts with government or labor officials.

One mechanism that helped Italian immigrants rise on the employment ladder was involvement in the American labor movement. Their role was rather a mixed one. Initially Italians were used as scabs and strikebreakers. This gave rise to the commonly accepted view that they were anti-union or hard to organize because they were too conservative. In places where they were barred from union membership and activity, they often did play such a role. But where unions were open to them, and where such organization looked likely to succeed, Italians provided a significant number of members and local leadership. By the early 1890s, Italians ranked second only to Poles in percentage of white ethnics belonging to blue-collar, working-class, organized labor unions.

Unlike the Irish, the Italians found the church less useful in their assimilation process. Their anti-Irish attitudes spilled over into their relations with the church, whose hierarchy was usually Irish-dominated. Gradually, however, Italian-American priests were ordained who better met their needs, and inroads into the upper levels of the hierarchy were achieved by the 1930s. After that, the church did prove useful as a means of their assimilation.

Also aiding them to adjust to life in America was a wide variety of mutual aid or benevolent societies. These self-help associations began early in the Italian-American experience. San Francisco, for instance, had a Italian Mutual Aid Society in 1858. The Italian Union and Fraternity was started in New York in 1857. By 1912, there were 212 such societies in New York City alone; by 1919, Chicago had 80 societies. They often began as burial societies or as groups to help their members find jobs and housing. They soon developed into organizations providing insurance, a host of social services, and the basis of the social life of many immigrants.

Mafia and crime-related organizations emerged in similar fashion. The mob violence and discrimination directed against Italian immigrants contributed to the rise of criminal activities, in part as self-protective associations. Careers in crime became "a curious ladder of social mobility" (Vecoli and Lintelman 1984: 205). When the urban machines and crime organizations linked in the 1910–1930 period, crime organizations provided leaders to political clubs and party activity, especially in Chicago, where Colosimo, Torrio, and Al Capone emerged. Crime became a source of the derogatory stereotyping of all Italians as criminals. That image, plus the 1913 depression, undoubtedly played a part in the revival of anti-Italian immigrant fervor by such groups as the Ku Klux Klan in the early 1900s and to a resurgence in the use of pejorative terms like "wop" and "dago."

War influenced Italian-American assimilation as well. Although to a lesser degree than was the case with the Irish, Italian Americans saw initial, if short-lived, benefit to their image and acceptability to Anglo America by their service in the Civil War. New York City sent a regiment, the Garibaldi Guard, to fight with the Union forces. Their war record was substantial. In addition to the Guard, 100 Italians from New York served with Union forces, and three reached the rank of general. The effects of World War I, in which some 300,000 Italian Americans served, were also profound.

In politics, the Italians used the Irish model but less successfully so. They moved into the political arena more slowly and often came into conflict with the Irish politicians, who had arrived before them and were reluctant to share power or to move over to make room for the newcomers. Such Irish–Italian conflict was common, often severe, and occasionally violent.

Initially, Italian-American politicians emerged from the various clubs and societies. They ran as Democrats, Republicans, Socialists, Independents, and Progressives. The Progressive and Republican parties, however, were the most popular among them. Before the 1920s, most of their political activity was at the local level. They typically supported machine candidates. In New York, their political activity included the creation of the Italian Federation of Democratic Clubs. In 1925, they established the Fascist League of America. Political leadership emerged out of the padroni system. In upstate New York, these included several notable leaders with connections to the Republican Party: Marnel, D'Angelo, Lapetino, Gualtieri, and later LaGuardia in New York City. In Chicago, a varied pattern was evident. The first state-level Italian-American politician in Illinois was a Democrat, Charles Cois, who was elected to the State House in 1918. At the same time, on the Republican ticket, Camile Volini was elected county commissioner, and Bernard Barasa a municipal judge. Nationally, they at times supported and worked with Democratic machines, but often as not they clashed with the Irish leadership of the party. In Chicago, for example, they had running battles with ward boss John Powers (Gianni Pauli).

> In the words of Oscar Durante, the election of 1928 equaled a declaration of war against Gianni Pauli on the part of the 19th Ward Italians. More than any other ethnic group, they resisted his blandishments and supported Jane Adams . . . and the Progressive Reform movement against him. (Nelli 1970: 99)

In 1919, anti-Wilson views swung many of them away from the Democrats. In New York, Republican Fiorello LaGuardia emerged as their political leader. He was elected to the U.S. House of Representatives in 1915 and, after a distinguished war service, again in 1918. In 1920, he won the seat vacated by Al Smith, the Irish American who was the Democratic Party nominee for President. In 1933, LaGuardia was elected the "reform" mayor of New York City. During the 1920s, Italian Americans split their votes, with a slight edge going to Republicans, but with their usually "wet" vote over "dry" vote on Prohibition no matter what the candidate's party affiliation. In 1932, they returned solidly to the Democratic fold, as they have been ever since, with a 60 percent vote for Roosevelt.

During the 1930s, increasingly prominent Italian-American politicians were working themselves up to state-wide and even national-level offices. By 1937, for example, three Italian-American judges served on New York's Supreme Court. Angelo Rossi, LaGuardia, and Robert S. Maestri were, respectively, the mayors of San Francisco, New York, and New Orleans. Three U.S. congressmen from New York were prominent Italian Americans of the day: Vito Marcantonio, James Lanzetta, and Alfred Santangelo. Through judicious "behind the scenes" politics and his own business acumen, another Italian American stood at the pinnacle of success in American business: Amadeo Peter Giannini, chairman of the board of the Bank of America. By 1945, his bank had surpassed the Chase National Bank of New York as the largest commercial bank in the world.

During the interwar years, a faction of Italian Americans flirted with Fascism, although both pro- and anti-Fascist groups emerged within the Italian-American communities. In part, Il Duce (Benito Mussolini) became a source of ethnic pride, reflecting a sort of communal hero-worship. Humbert Nelli cites a "strongly anti-Fascist Italian American girl," who said, despite her opposition to Mussolini and his program, "You've got to admit one thing: he has enabled four million Italians in America to hold up their heads, and that is something. If you had been branded undesirable by a quota law, you would understand how much that means" (1970: 241).

After World War II, Italian Americans remained aligned with the Democratic Party, when measured by national, and especially presidential, voting behavior. Despite the occasional notable Republican politician of Italian heritage, such as John A. Volpe in Massachusetts, they are overwhelmingly Democratic. They will cross party lines to vote for one of their own. While 85 percent of the Italian-American voters in Massachusetts supported John Kennedy for President in 1960, 50 percent crossed over to vote Republican for Volpe in his gubernatorial bid.

Republicans have made some very concerted efforts to woo the Italian-American voter—most notably the two Richard Nixon presidential campaigns. Their results have been far from realigning since two-thirds of Italian Americans identify themselves with the Democratic Party, significantly above the rate of the general public.

GREEK AMERICANS

Many Greek Americans used the tactic of economic accommodation, but a significant number relied on political action, increasingly using that strategy after achieving a modicum of economic success. Their political involvement closely parallels that of other "new" immigrant groups, especially the Italian Americans. Like them, by the 1940s, most Greek Americans voted for the Democratic Party. First the New Deal, then Roosevelt's and Truman's foreign policies during and immediately after World War II solidified Greek-American loyalty to the Democratic Party.

Some inroads were made by Republicans during the 1960s. These inroads reflected the weakened hold of the Democratic urban organizations, the movement of the Greek-American middle class into the suburbs, and the appearance of Spiro Agnew as vice-presidential candidate in 1968 and 1972. Yet second- and third-generation Greek Americans still vote Democratic at a greater rate than one would expect based solely on economic indicators of class status. Greek Americans self-identify their political party affiliation as 48 percent Democratic, 24 percent Republican, and 29 percent Independent, which reflects almost exactly the party identification of the population nationally.

Greek-American impact on American politics comes from the visibility of second-generation Greek Americans in relatively high electoral office. Although the mainstream Greek-American group is socially conservative, some prominent politicians have emerged from the liberal wing of the Democratic Party. Maryland, for example, elected Paul Sarbanes to the U.S. Senate in 1976, and he was comfortably reelected in 1982, 1988, and 1994. Senator Sarbanes, the son of a Greek immigrant café owner, is a graduate of Princeton University, holds a law degree from Harvard Law School, and was a Rhodes scholar. In 1978, he was joined in the Senate by Paul Tsongas, a Massachusetts Democrat, who was the son of a Greek tailor. Senator Tsongas graduated from Dartmouth and received his law degree from Yale University. He briefly challenged Bill Clinton for the Democratic presidential nomination in 1992.

The Ninety-sixth Congress had five Greek Americans holding seats in the House of Representatives: John Brademas (D.–Ind.), the then majority whip who was also a

Rhodes scholar; Gus Yatron (D.–Pa.); Nicholas Mavroules (D.–Mass.), the son of Greek immigrants who worked in the mills and who was later elected mayor of Peabody; L. A. Bafalis, a conservative Republican from Florida; and Olympia Snowe (R.–Maine), who in 1978 was the youngest woman ever elected to the House. Other Greek Americans who held seats in the House in the 1970s were Peter Kyros (D.–Maine) and Nick Galifianakis (D.–N.C.), who ran unsuccessfully for the Senate.

The most notable Greek-American politician, and a clear indicator that as a group they have "arrived" politically speaking, is former Massachusetts Governor Michael Dukakis, who ran for President on the Democratic ticket in 1988. He lost to George Bush. His success in capturing the party's nomination for the highest elected office in the land indicates the strength and status of Greek Americans in politics. Other Greek Americans who served as governors in their respective states during the 1970s include Republican Nicholas Strike of Utah in 1972; Democrat Harry Spanos of New Hampshire in 1976; and Democrat Michael Bakalis of Illinois in 1978. Many Greek Americans have served in various state legislatures and on state judicial benches. Several dozen have been elected mayors of their cities, including George Christopher of San Francisco; Lee Alexander of Syracuse, New York; George Athanson of Hartford, Connecticut; Helen Boosalis of Lincoln, Nebraska; and John Roussakis of Savannah, Georgia. Scores more have been elected mayors in the small mill towns of New England.

This electoral record is all the more impressive since, with few exceptions, none of these cities has a truly sizable Greek ethnic voting bloc on which to build a base for electoral success. All the candidates had to pitch their campaigns to the general electorate. They received substantial contributions, however, from the Greek-American community. Senator Sarbanes, in his successful bids to the U.S. Senate, raised one-fourth of his total campaign budget from Greek-American contributors from across the nation.

Perhaps the lack of a sizable ethnic bloc allowed them to remain unconstrained by a parochial ethnic base and to run with no special appeal to an ethnic loyalty. Such was the case of former Vice President Spiro Agnew. Emerging rapidly from a school board chairmanship to become governor of Maryland on the Republican ticket, the relatively unknown Agnew burst upon the national scene at the 1968 Republican National Convention. His vice-presidential election in 1968 and reelection in 1972 made him a leading contender for the 1976 presidential nomination until his resignation in disgrace in 1973 ended his political career.

Nonetheless, Agnew exemplifies the case of an assimilated ethnic. Greek American on his father's side, his name was anglicized from Agagnostopoulos. Spiro Agnew spoke no Greek and was Episcopalian rather than Greek Orthodox, but his father had been the owner of a small lunchroom, an active member of the American Hellenic Educational Progressive Association (AHEPA), and a pillar of Baltimore's Greek-American community. Not only could he be called a Greek American, Agnew articulated how most of them felt about law and order, family integrity, and upward social mobility based on one's own efforts. His was an "up-by-your-own-bootstraps" mentality. He personified the 1968 and 1972 Republican Party strategy of appealing to the white ethnic vote.

Agnew's resignation after pleading no contest to charges of income tax evasion shocked the Greek-American community. But a survey of that community shortly after revealed an ambiguity of opinion typical of ethnic minority groups when confronted with examples of corruption among their own. Some retreated to the rationale that he was never really a Greek anyway. Others responded with: "He may be an S.O.B., but at least he's our S.O.B." Most, however, acted with dismay at his betrayal of his middle-class constituency. Agnew quickly became a nonperson within the Greek-American community (Moskos 1980).

Any inroads the Republicans may have made into the Greek-American community during the Nixon years were reversed during the Ford Administration due to the Cyprus crisis. In July 1974, a Greek-led coup overthrew President Mihail Makarios of Cyprus. Turkey responded by invading Cyprus. By August, after numerous cease-fire agreements had failed, Turkey gained control of about 40 percent of the land area, displacing about a third of the nearly 180,000 Greeks on the island. Greek Americans organized a huge relief effort. Angered by the Ford/Kissinger tilt toward Turkey and by the Turkish invasion of Cyprus, the Greek-American community was politically mobilized as never before. Led by the Greek Orthodox Archdiocese and by AHEPA, they exerted great influence on Congress. The press began covering them as one of the most effective lobbies in Washington. Congress responded by imposing an embargo on arms to Turkey in February 1975, although restrictions were later modified.

The incident led to the emergence of the American Hellenic Institute–Public Affairs Committee (AHI-PAC). An association to promote trade between Greece and the United States, the PAC operated as the lobby arm on the Cyprus question and sought to activate the Greek-American community to become even more politically involved. Also active were the United Hellenic American Congress, headquartered in Chicago and linked to the Archdiocese, which served as its umbrella organization to coordinate Greek-American efforts, and the Hellenic Council of America, a New York–based organization that enlisted professional and academic Greek Americans to the cause.

The Cypress issue united the Greek Americans to a degree unprecedented since the Greek War Relief of World War II. These efforts reflected the political maturation of Greek Americans and demonstrated the value of working within the American political system. The political mobilization, by then staunchly "anti-Ford/Kissinger," led them back to the Democratic Party. Greek-American newspapers endorsed Carter. An estimated 87 percent of the Greek-American vote went to the ticket. The effectiveness of their lobby now rivals the reputation of the famed Jewish lobby:

> In Greek-American discussion it is common to contrast the perceived weak Greek influence on foreign policy with that of the strong Jewish influence in support of Israel. Indeed, the Jewish precedent was frequently cited as the appropriate model for Greek-American efforts in behalf of Cyprus in Washington. It was something of a reversal to read a 1977 letter in the *New York Times* defending the Jewish pressure against Carter's Middle-East policies: "We (American Jews) were only acting in the American tradition, just as the American Greeks attacked American foreign policy on the Cyprus issue." Such a testament is a fitting footnote on the Greek-American entrance into the political system. (Moskos 1980: 122)

It shows the importance of the "other nation" loyalty for racial/ethnic minority groups in activating them politically to seek to influence U.S. foreign policy on behalf of their homeland's politics. Other "new" immigrant groups, such as the Slavic immigrant groups and the American-Jewish community, exhibit similar patterns and concerns in their use of the political route to accommodation. Not only is it a means to rise socially and economically in American society, it is a primary way to influence foreign policy on behalf of one's ethnic heritage.

SLAVIC AMERICANS

Immigrating overwhelmingly in the late nineteenth and early twentieth centuries, East European groups traditionally discussed as the Slavic peoples were often treated alike and experienced many similarities in their emigration, acculturation, and assimilation patterns. Like the Irish, Italian, and Greek Americans discussed, they used politics as their main route to accommodation.

They can be grouped into three regions: the Eastern Slavs, the Western Slavs, and the Southern Slavs. The Eastern Slavs include the Russians, White Ruthenians, and Ukrainians. The Western Slavs include the Poles, Czechs, Slovaks, and Lusatin Serbs. The Southern Slavs, located in southwestern Europe, primarily in the Balkan Peninsula, are Slovenians, Croatians, Montenegrins, Serbs, Macedonians, and Bulgarians.

Their migration is almost completely a phenomenon of the post-1870s. Increasingly large numbers arrived from 1890 until 1921, when the Immigration Act sharply curtailed them. During colonial times a few Slavic settlers reached the New Amsterdam and New Sweden colonies, and some Moravians joined the Quaker colony in Pennsylvania. The earliest Russian colonists date back to 1747, when a group settled in Alaska's Kodiak Island. Some colonial-period Ukrainian immigrants were missionaries in California. Polish Americans proudly stress the role of Generals Pulaski and Kosciusko as heroes of the American Revolutionary War.

Slavic immigrants who came after 1880 tended to settle in the industrial centers of the Northeast, some 80 percent of whom were in an area roughly bounded by Washington, D.C., in the southeast, St. Louis in the southwest, and the Mississippi River, Canada, and the Atlantic Ocean. Two-thirds of them can be found in New York, New England, Pennsylvania, and New Jersey, with sizable numbers also in Illinois and Ohio. The major cities in which they settled are New York, Chicago, Detroit, Cleveland, Boston, Philadelphia, Milwaukee, Buffalo, Baltimore, Pittsburgh, Providence, San Francisco, and Los Angeles.

Slavic immigrants tended to replace German and Irish immigrants in the mines and factories of Pennsylvania and the Midwest and in the slaughterhouses of Chicago. Like the Italians and Greeks, Slavic immigrants were often sojourners, making up the majority of more than 2 million aliens who returned to Europe between 1908 and 1914. They all experienced severe segregation, frequently manifested in ghettoization and considerable economic hardship. The fact that their young boys began work at an early age, typically for a six-day, 10-hour-per-day workweek, meant that they climbed the socioeconomic ladder slowly. Their peasant backgrounds, longer periods of economic deprivation, which led to child labor and, therefore, lesser formal educational achievements among the second generation, are all factors that contributed to their slower assimilation rates.

Polish Americans

Estimates as to the number of Polish immigrants vary since official records were not always counted separately and the area itself varied, at times being part of Germany, Austria-Hungary, or Russia. Thomas and Znaniecki estimate their number at over 875,000, while others place their number at over one million.[4] In the 1990 census, 9,366,000 persons claimed Polish ancestry, and 388,000 of the foreign-born cited Poland as their homeland, 30 percent of whom immigrated during the 1980–1990 decade. Among those foreign-born Polish Americans, just over 58 percent were high school graduates, and just over 16 percent were college graduates. In terms of their occupations, 12 percent were professionals, 18 percent in service occupations, and nearly 20 percent in blue-collar jobs. Their median family income was just about at the national average ($28,948 compared to $28,314).

About three-fourths of Polish immigrants were farm laborers, unskilled workers, and domestic servants. Less than 12 percent were classified as skilled. A fourth of them were illiterate, and virtually all came with less than $50 in their possession. Polish immigrants tended to be young male sojourners. Their attachment to the homeland was perhaps enhanced by the fact that the ills of life in Poland could be blamed on foreign occupations. Resentment of the Polish upper class seemed less than was typical among other Slavic groups.

Some Polish immigrants got into farming in the Northeast and Midwest, concentrating in truck farming in Long Island and the Connecticut Valley, and in corn and wheat farming in the north-central Midwest and in the Panna Maria settlement in Texas, which was founded in 1854 entirely of Polish immigrant families. Most concentrated in Buffalo, Chicago, Milwaukee, Pittsburgh, Detroit, and New York. Chicago ranks after Warsaw and Lodz as the third largest Polish center in the world.

Men and boys shared common labor jobs, such as working in the coal mines for ten hours per day, six days per week for less than $15 per week. It was common for children to complete but two years of high school before working full time. That pattern perhaps explains why first- and second-generation Polish Americans were slower in upward mobility than so many other immigrant groups. It is not until they reach the third and fourth generations that Polish Americans start closing the gap. They are heavily blue-collar workers, 40 percent of whom are unionized.

The most influential institutional mechanism in the Polish-American community is the church. Numerous scholars have noted it as the unrivaled instrument for the organization and unification of the Polish-American community.[5] As with Italians and the other Slavic groups, Polish immigrants had difficulty adjusting to the Irish-dominated Catholic church. Protests against that power structure took several forms: parish mutual aid societies joining with the Polish Roman Catholic Union (PRCU), which was organized in 1873; the Polish National Alliance, founded in 1880; and the

Polish National Catholic Church (PNCC), begun in 1897 and re-formed in 1904. Today there are 50 independent Polish parishes unified into the PNCC, plus an unknown number of isolated parishes split from Rome but which have not yet joined the PNCC. The majority of Polish Americans, however, remain faithful to the Catholic church, and since 1970, inroads into the hierarchy have been made with a number of bishops and archbishops now of Polish descent. And, of course, a Pole is now the Roman Pontiff.

Polonia—the term used to designate the total Polish-American population—still maintains an estimated 800 Polish-American Catholic parishes. Closely linked to the church are the parochial schools. In the late 1950s, an estimated 250,000 elementary school students were being taught by Polish-American Catholic nuns, and over 100,000 more students were in catechism classes. As of the end of the 1970s, there were still more than 600 Polish parochial schools.

During and after World War II, the link between Polonia and Poland weakened. While Polish Americans continued to send money and humanitarian aid, they sent few men. Polonia did push hard to get the Displaced Persons Act passed, which granted exceptions to the quota laws and allowed an estimated 162,400 Poles to enter the United States between 1945 and 1969. They also pressured the government against the Yalta agreement and tried to influence foreign policy to help rid Poland of its communist government and to aid the new government once that came about.

Polish Americans banded together to cope with political and social prejudice, especially against their stereotypical image of being illiterate and mentally deficient, as in the "dumb Polack" jokes. Initial reaction in Polonia was to ignore American culture and turn attention to Poland. This was followed by mixed feelings of anger, withdrawal, and inferiority. Since World War II, however, Polonia reacted by developing an ideology of America as a pluralistic society rather than as a melting pot. They have attempted to counter prejudice by stressing Polish-American national heroes and contributions to American culture, such as Revolutionary War heroes Pulaski and Kosciusko, and by spotlighting outstanding sports figures and film stars, successful businessmen, artists, and scientists of Polish-American descent. They also formed a Committee for the Defense of the Polish Name (Anti-Defamation Committee) to counter Polish jokes.

Their political activity developed slowly. In the 1920s in Chicago, for instance, only about 25 percent of Polish Americans turned out to vote. Their political impact was weakened further by splitting their vote rather than voting in a cohesive bloc. Since World War II, however, they have been consistently and highly Democratic, reflecting their blue-collar and unionized status. Today, among all white ethnic voters, they are the most likely to vote Democratic. Over 75 percent self-identify as Democrats nationally, and 80 percent do so in the Midwest. From 1958 to 1964, in a study of 57 elections for such offices as U.S. senator, governor, or President, the Democratic percentage of their vote was 65 percent or higher in 54 of those 57 elections, and in one third (19 elections) of those, it exceeded 80 percent. At any level of office, the typical Democratic candidate can expect to receive about two-thirds of the Polish vote. In 1960, John Kennedy received 80 to 85 percent of the Slavic vote, and that dropped off by only 2 percent for Johnson in 1964. President Nixon succeeded in wooing away about 7 percent more in his 1968 and 1972 elections, but the Slavic and Polish-American vote is still about two-thirds loyal to the Democratic Party. A few Polish-American politicians have achieved prominence on the national scene, most notably former Senator Edmund Muskie (D.–Maine), who sought the Democratic presidential nomination, and the late Clement Zablocki (D.–Wis.) and former Congressman Dan Rostenkowski (D.–Ill.).

The most successful Republican candidates with Polish-American voters are those who are moderate to liberal, such as the former Senators Case, Percy, and Mathias. The first, and so far, only Republican to win a clear majority of the Slavic vote in a state-wide race was William Cahill of New Jersey, who in his successful bid for governor in 1969 received an estimated 60 percent of their vote.

Russian Americans

The earliest Russian immigration to the United States goes back to Alaska and California in the mid-1700s. In 1792, the first Russian Orthodox church was built in America, and as early as 1812 a sizable settlement was founded in Sonoma, California, which lasted for 30 years before the entire group of several hundred returned to Russia at the request of the czar. The headquarters of the Russian church in America moved to San Francisco in 1872. It was after the 1870s, however, before the first sizable wave of Russian immigrants came. Those coming in the early 1870s were Mennonites, who fled to the Great Plains area and numbered over 40,000. During 1900–1913, some 51,500 Russian immigrants arrived, about 45 percent of whom were Jews fleeing persecution in Russia. Their peak period was between 1880 and 1914. Most were peasants seeking better economic opportunity. The 1917 Russian Revolution virtually stopped emigration until about 1970. In the 1990 census, 2,953,000 residents claimed Russian ancestry, heavily concentrated in the Northeast. Some 334,000 claimed Russian ancestry, over 39 percent of whom came during the 1980–1990 decade. Of those, 64 percent were high school graduates, and 27 percent were college graduates. Russian immigrants are 20 percent professionals, 12 percent in service, and 11 percent in blue-collar jobs. Their median family income was significantly below the national average ($19,125 compared to $28,314).

Earlier Russian immigrants worked in coal and other mines and in the iron and steel mills of Pennsylvania and the slaughterhouses of Chicago. In New York City they worked in the clothing industry and in cigar and tobacco manufacturing. They held unskilled jobs in construction and with the railroads. Except for the United Mine Workers and the Industrial Workers of the World, they tended to be non-unionized, and their pay was typically low-scale. In 1909, they worked for an average of 12 hours per day for just over $2. As late as 1919, Russian immigrants in Chicago earned only $12 to $30 per week.

A few Russians did establish agricultural settlements, which tended to be small and scattered. Most lived in enclaves in the cities, crammed into substandard housing. Conditions for construction gangs were grim; typically 36 men slept in three-tier bunkhouses. In the congested Slavic ghettos in the mining and iron and steel mill towns, health problems were especially severe.

JEWISH AMERICANS

Data regarding immigration of Eastern European Jews to the United States are sketchy. About 40 to 45 percent of all South, Central, and East Europeans entering the United States during the 1870–1930 period were Jewish. Estimates of their immigration data are presented in Table 4.1.

East European Jews immigrated for many of the same push and pull factors that motivated the other Slavic groups, plus an added push of religious/political oppression that ultimately became the most compelling cause of their emigration.

By the 1860s, the serfs, or peasant class, were attaining a degree of freedom and slowly began to develop a small middle class. By 1860, about 5 percent of Russia's labor force was Jewish. Of that segment, 11 percent were employed in industry and 36 percent in commerce. By law, Jews were forbidden to own land, so they became merchants, tailors, administrators, and other commerce-oriented businessmen. Consequently many European Jews were urbanites.

The czarist government used the Jews as scapegoats for long-festering social, economic, and political grievances. They openly encouraged ethnic minorities, particularly the Jews, to emigrate. Jewish immigration to the United States can be directly correlated with historical events in Russia, particularly the **pogroms** that swept Russia during the 1880s up to World War I. In the Pale of the Settlement area of Russia—the land between the Baltic and the Black seas—those pogroms were especially violent, involving looting, pillaging, riots, murders, and, in some cases, total destruction of the Jewish ghettos. Government troops would sit idly by or even join in these ventings of frustrations upon the hapless Jews. Such pogroms were often followed by educational restrictions and eventually by expulsion. Since the Jews fled both religious and political persecution, leaving Russia was not as traumatic an experience for them as for other Russian immigrants. Indeed, to remain in the homeland was to risk life and limb, to remain confined within legal limitations on education and occupational opportunities, and to suffer conscription of their youth at the age of 12 for 31 years of compulsory military service. Jewish immigrants were not sojourners as were many other Slavic groups.

TABLE 4.1 Jewish Immigration to the United States, 1899–1973

Period	Number	Percentage of Total Immigration
1899–1900	98,179	NA
1901–1910	976,263	11%
1911–1920	491,165	8
1921–1930	339,954	8
1931–1940	137,525	26
1941–1950	159,518	15
1951–1960	71,847	3
1961–1970	83,177	2.5
1971–1973	17,670	1.5
Total	2,381,298	8.5

SOURCE: Leonard Dinnerstein and David M. Reimers, *Ethnic Americans,* 3rd ed. (New York: Harper & Row, 1988), pp. 172–174.

Their main ports of entry were New York, Philadelphia, and Baltimore, where they often settled in large numbers in the low-rent areas adjacent to the city's business district. These areas quickly developed into ghetto areas.

Jewish immigrants differed from the other South, Central, and East European groups in several respects. They tended to immigrate in whole family units with every intention of remaining. They also came with better and more suitable job skills and a more urban background, which eased their acculturation, especially into American economic life. Sixty-seven percent of Jewish males entering the United States were classified as skilled workers, as compared to the average of 20 percent for all other groups.

They were quickly active in unionization, especially in the garment industry. The Amalgamated Clothing Workers and International Ladies Garment Workers Union (ILGWU) were predominantly Jewish and Italian. By World War II, over 60 percent of the ILGWU was Jewish, and the Dressmakers Local 22 of New York City was 75 percent Jewish. About half of the city's Jewish labor force worked in the trade. Other occupations included cigar manufacturing, bookbinding, distilling, printing, and skilled carpentry. In unskilled work, they tended toward being pushcart peddlers and salesmen. A 1900 census study by the Immigration Service, however, found that the proportion of Jewish immigrants in the professions was the highest of all the non-English-speaking immigrants.

They experienced considerable and growing prejudice here, but nothing like the pogroms of Europe. In colonial America they were often disenfranchised, such restrictions lasting until 1877 in New Hampshire, the last state to end such restrictions. Anti-Semitic attitudes were prevalent, and stereotyping was common. Jews were often portrayed as scoundrels on the American stage.

While their numbers were small, anti-Semitism was easily dealt with by the German Jews who were often middle class. They were at first fearful of the large-scale immigration of East European Jews and rejected the newcomers as a potential source of more virulent outbreaks of anti-Semitism. They were correct in their assessment of the results of such large-scale immigration. When anti-Semitism did escalate, however, they closed ranks and helped the newcomers adjust.

In the 1870s, largely latent anti-Semitism broke out into the open. In 1877, Jews were blackballed from the New York Bar Association, and in 1878, New York college fraternities followed suit. The Saratoga Springs resort began barring them, and soon a host of clubs, resorts, and private schools were doing likewise. The Ku Klux Klan, revived in the late nineteenth century, became the leading nativist group that was especially anti-Semitic.

Pogroms, which broke out again in Russia in 1903 and 1906, led to Jewish efforts to help their brethren. The American Jewish Committee, made up primarily of Americanized German Jews, actively helped the East European Jews raise money for those still suffering in Europe. In 1913, the B'nai B'rith's Anti-Defamation League (ADL) was formed. By 1909, there were over 2,000 Jewish charities operating in the United States, which spent over $10 million in that year alone. By the 1970s, annual Jewish philanthropy exceeded a billion dollars. These charities organized orphanages, educational institutions, and homes for unwed mothers and delinquent children. They established hospitals and a wide variety of recreational facilities. They supported the Jewish Theological Seminary, which trained rabbis, and Yiddish-language newspapers. Between 1883 and 1915, they started 150 such papers, including the highly influential *Jewish Daily Forward.*

In both their religious institutions and their strongly cohesive family life, Jewish immigrants stressed formal education. Advanced learning was particularly emphasized for males. Professional jobs were held up as the ideal, highly valued for their secure incomes and their social prestige not only within the Jewish community but in the broader culture as well. By 1915, they made up 85 percent of the student body of New York's City College, a fifth of those attending New York University, and one sixth at Columbia. Education became *the* route to middle-class status and *the* means of acculturation and assimilation.

Politics followed gains in economics. Jews were slow to enter the classic urban machine, although some Jewish immigrants played prominent roles in city politics. Their slowness in political involvement reflected a lack of political experience in their homelands. Jews were often uncomfortable with the big-city machine politicians with their strange skills, codes, vulgarities, and corruption. But politics was the key to power, and power was needed to protect their economic gains and to influence U.S. foreign policy.

The broader story of their involvement in American politics, a success story to be sure, and their use of politics to influence public policy both to ensure their security here and to aid Israel through foreign policy, is left for Chapter 9. Their use of politics shows some similarities with another group that used both the economic and political routes to accommodation, the Hispanic groups, to whom we next turn our attention.

HISPANIC AMERICANS

Rapidly increasing numbers of Hispanic Americans led to greater political electoral strength. A number of Latino politicians became mayors of their respective large cities, an office to which they could achieve election only with the help of non-Hispanic voters. Miami elected Maurice Ferre. Henry Cisneros, mayor of San Antonio, was considered for a while as a possible vice-presidential candidate in 1984, and served in the Clinton Administration as secretary of Housing and Urban Development. Denver elected Frederico Peña, who also served in President Clinton's cabinet. Robert Martines was elected mayor of Tampa, and Louis Montano served as mayor of Santa Fe.

The Hispanic Congressional Caucus, made up of the various Hispanic members serving in the House, has had a fair degree of influence over some issue areas, such as immigration policy. It has declined in numbers and influence with the Republican-controlled Congress, however, and has yet to give rise to a national-level candidate who is considered "presidential timber."

Hispanic political success is a recent phenomenon. Traditionally, the Hispanic vote has been weak. Splintered and with low turnout, it was not a bloc of voters to be vigorously courted by the major parties. Some of their potential for political strength was diluted because of the large number of illegal aliens within the community. Their lack of political efficacy seems related to a high proportion of working-class members and a common sojourner attitude, a prominent feeling of political apathy and ineffectiveness, a pattern of discrimination, a violation of their civil rights, an often dispersed population, internal quarrels, and a general distrust of government. Until recently few Spanish-speaking people achieved, nor even sought, positions of political leadership. Their relative lack of political power reflects a low level of voter turnout. When they do vote, they are so overwhelmingly Democratic in their voting affiliation that they constitute a virtual "captive voting bloc."

They have begun to mobilize and organize more effectively since the late 1970s. Hispanics are still highly fragmented both in terms of nationality and philosophic view toward dealing with the majority society. Although the majority society sees Hispanics as alike, the Cuban, Puerto Rican, Mexican, and Central American groups see themselves as different. They conflict with one another, and unity among them is largely illusionary, despite "La Raza Unida." Nevertheless, their potential for political clout is significant, particularly in the six states in which they are concentrated (California, Florida, Illinois, New Jersey, New York, and Texas). Together, these states account for 173 electoral votes, three-fifths of the 270 needed to elect a president.

Assimilation is stronger among young Chicanos. Their **exogamy** rate (marrying outside the group) has been rising; the third generation is the most exogamous. Another indicator of assimilation is their growing political involvement. Politically active Chicano organizations include the older and more conservative or traditional organizations formed after World War I, like the League of United Latin American Citizens formed in 1929; the Community Service Organization, begun in Los Angeles after World War II, in 1947; and the American GI Forum, started in Texas in 1948. More recent and more militant are such organizations as the Mexican-American Political Association (MAPA), founded in California in 1958; the Political Association of Spanish Speaking Organizations (PASSO), begun in Texas in 1959; the American Coordinating Council of Political Education (ACCPE), begun in Arizona in 1959; and Cesar Chavez's union, the United Farm Workers Association that arose in Delano California in 1965.

The latter group launched Chavez to national prominence and as a leading force in the Hispanic civil rights movement. Another major Chicano leader was Reies Lopez Tijerina, known as El Tigre, who started the Alianza Federal de Mercedes (Federal Alliance of Land Grants) in 1963. Using radical tactics inspired by the success of the black civil rights movement, the Alianza led several demonstrations and takeovers. In 1968, Tijerina ran for governor of New Mexico on the Independent People's Constitution Party ticket. In 1969, the group briefly seized the Tierra Amarilla courthouse. San Antonio was the site where the Mexican American Nationalist Organization (MANO) began at about the same time. In 1965, a "barrio youth" leader emerged on the national scene—Rodolfo "Corky" Gonzales. He started the Crusade for Justice in 1967, based in Denver, Colorado. He was also instrumental in establishing La Raza

Unida Party in 1970. He ran for several state and local offices. A fourth major Chicano leader to emerge during this period was Jose Angel Guitierrez. He was another youth leader instrumental in the founding of La Raza Unida. He led the Mexican American Youth Organization (MAYO), also begun in 1967. Other Chicano groups with political action agendas included United Mexican American Students (UMAS), Mexican American Student Association (MESA), Movemento Estudiantial Chicano de Aztlain (MECHA), National Organization of Mexican American Students (NOMAS), and the Association of Mexican American Educators (AMEA).

The 1970s saw the development of La Raza Unida and a voter registration drive (the Southwest Voter Education Project). In 1971, President Nixon made a concerted effort to woo the Chicano vote through such appointments as Romana Banuelos as secretary of the Treasury, and Phillip Sanchez as head of the Office of Economic Opportunity and then as director of the Immigration and Naturalization Service. In 1980, President Reagan appealed to the Chicano vote, capturing about 30 percent in 1980 and just over that in 1984. Still, the Chicano vote is more potential than actual, with a typical turnout in the low 40 percent of their registered voters. The 1980s saw them win mayoral positions, and Anthony Ayaya elected governor of New Mexico.

Puerto Rican political activity is a limited and recent development. Their youth, low status, and tradition contribute to low registration and turnout patterns. Several groups make up the major community development forces among them on the mainland. The Puerto Rican Forum started in the mid-1950s. Another important group is the Puerto Rican Family Institute. Of all the grass-roots organizations, Aspira has been the most effective. One of the most articulate spokespersons among Puerto Ricans was the director of the Commonwealth of Puerto Rico office in New York, Joseph Monserrat. Other groups include the Puerto Rican Educators Association, the Puerto Rican Legal Defense and Education Fund, the Puerto Rican Institute for Democratic Education, and the National Association for Puerto Rican Civil Rights.

Puerto Ricans have voted overwhelmingly Democratic, usually in the low 90 percentile range. They have voted so solidly Democratic that in 1968, Hulan Jack, a black Democrat, received 88 percent of their vote against the 14 percent cast for a Puerto Rican running on the Republican ticket.

Since the 1970s they have joined other Hispanics in La Raza Unida, and have organized for more standard electoral action and success. They, too, stress voter registration drives. These drives resulted in the election of some prominent Puerto Rican politicians: Baltasar Corrado, the Puerto Rican commissioner; Judge John Carro, the first mainland Puerto Rican to become a federal judge; Teodoro Moscoso, head of the Alliance for Progress under President Kennedy; and Robert Garcia, a Democrat from New York, member of the Hispanic Caucus, and the first New York–born Puerto Rican to serve in the U.S. Congress.

As Hispanic political activity and clout grows, it does so at times in direct clash with black Americans. While Hispanics follow the lead of the black civil rights movement and often work closely with the black Congressional Caucus on bills of mutual interest—for example, on immigration policy—they also come into conflict with one another on efforts to control local politics. It is to black American political activity we next turn our attention.

BLACK AMERICANS

Chapter 3 examined the use of the economic route to accommodation as practiced by blacks following the leadership and philosophy of Booker T. Washington. While they made some gains in the Reconstruction era, those were largely overturned in the Jim Crow era. Most political gains by black Americans have been recent, post-1970, developments.

One of the earliest leaders using the political strategy was the brilliant W.E.B. Du Bois, a historian and sociologist at Atlanta University. In 1905, he and a small group of black intellectuals met in Niagara Falls, Canada. The Niagara movement rejected the moderation and compromise advocated by Booker T. Washington and called for radical change ending black inferior status, the loss of voting and civil rights, and the Jim Crow laws, segregated schools, inhumane conditions in southern prisons, denial of equal job opportunities, and segregation in the armed forces. Out of this came the establishment, on February 12, 1909, on the 100-year anniversary of Lincoln's birthday, of the National Association for the Advancement of Colored People (NAACP). Over the years, the NAACP led the campaign for black civil rights through legal action. In 1915, it achieved its first major victory in one of hundreds of cases pursued at all levels of government. The U.S. Supreme Court declared unconstitutional the grandfather clause of the Oklahoma constitution. In 1954, the NAACP won an even greater victory in *Brown* vs. *Board of Education of Topeka, Kansas,* which finally overturned the "separate-but-equal" doctrine established in *Plessy* vs. *Ferguson* (1896). The *Brown* decision gave a constitutional blessing to the movement to desegregate the United States, effectively beginning the end to de jure segregation (segregation by law).

From World War II through the mid-1960s, a period of new-style radicalism involving the use of direct-action protest predominated, a tactic discussed more fully

W.E.B. Du Bois, Cofounder of the NAACP.

in Chapter 8. The successes of the civil rights movement in the 1960s paved the way for some substantial gains being made using standard electoral politics. The culminating actions of the movement were passage of the Civil Rights Act of 1964 and the Voting Rights Act of 1965. The impact of these two laws can be seen in the closing of the voting gap between whites and blacks. These two laws, strongly supported by a Democratic Administration and a Democratic-controlled Congress, resulted in continued strong electoral support for the Democrats by black voters throughout the 1970s and 1980s, even as that party's white coalitions weakened and fell. Voting loyalty was often significant. Presidents Carter and Clinton owed their electoral success to the margins they received from African-American voters. The percentage of black voting turnout rose dramatically after 1965. Electoral success followed, with thousands of blacks in public office at all levels and in all regions.

For example, in 1947, there were only two black representatives in the Eightieth Congress. Their number remained under a half dozen through 1963. It reached double digits (12) in 1968, rose to 20 in 1980, to 39 in 1992, and 40 in 1998. The Black Congressional Caucus now has 80 white associate members. Since 1880, only two blacks have been elected to the U.S. Senate, Edward Brooke (R.–Mass.) in the 1970s and Carol Moseley-Braun (D.–Ill.) from 1992 to 1998.

Blacks achieved symbolically important firsts in 1983. Although these events may not rank with the 1964–1965 acts, they validated the opening of doors previously closed to blacks. Guion Bluford became the first black astronaut in space, and Miss New York, Vanessa Williams, became the first black Miss America. Important

Vanessa Williams, first African American Miss America.

strides were made in politics as the civil rights movement shifted from protest politics to elective office. In part, this change in strategy reflected a change in black leadership. Some 1960s' black leaders were assassinated: Dr. Martin Luther King, Jr., Medgar Evers, and Malcolm X. Others were imprisoned: Stokeley Carmichael, Huey Newton, and Bobby Seale. Still others went into exile (Eldridge Cleaver). The newer leadership (Andrew Young, Jesse Jackson) had new political resources. By 1980, the total number of black elected officials had risen to 4,890. Three hundred served in the various state legislatures and the U.S. Congress. Over 2,800 held city and county offices. Gains were made in the nation's largest cities. In 1966, no large American city had a black mayor. By 1984, two dozen cities in excess of 100,000 in population had one, and there were 245 black mayors in cities of all sizes.

The 1984 election demonstrated the dramatic impact of the black vote. The Reverend Jesse Jackson made a credible run for nomination to the presidency by the Democratic Party. In 1983, public opinion polls by the Gallup, Harris, and Washington Post/ABC News showed 77 percent of the public said they would vote for a well-qualified black candidate for President, a higher percentage than those who, in 1960, said they would vote for a Catholic. Jesse Jackson won 18.3 percent of the primary votes cast in 1984, earning a total of 384 delegates and playing a role at the Democratic National Convention. In 1988, he ran again, his percentage growing to 29 and his delegate count to 1,218.

The Jackson candidacy augmented an impressive voter registration drive. The Voter Education Project, based in Atlanta, led a drive netting over 1 million new black voters across the nation. In the 1980 election, black turnout increased by 18 percent, and in some districts it, for the first time, exceeded that of white voters. In 1982, black turnout rose by 5.8 percent over the previous off-year election, which was more than double the increase in white voter turnout. In 1984, the gap between white and black registration was only 3.3 percent, and turnout was only 6.9 percent. The turnout gap in 1996 was only 5.4 percent, the lowest of any national election in history. Black voting remains consistently Democratic. Table 4.2 presents their voting registration and turnout in presidential elections since 1968. Table 4.3 shows blacks' party identification rates for presidential election years since 1964.

TABLE 4.2 Black/White Registration and Voting Turnout, Presidential Elections, 1968–1996

Presidential Election	Registration			Voting			Proportion of Votes Cast by Blacks
	Black	White	Gap	Black	White	Gap	
1968	66.2%	75.4%	−9.2%	57.6%	69.1%	−11.5%	8.0%
1972	65.5	73.4	−7.9	52.1	64.5	−12.4	8.2
1976	58.5	68.3	−9.8	48.7	60.9	−12.2	8.4
1980	60.0	68.4	−8.4	50.5	60.9	−10.4	8.9
1984	66.3	69.6	−3.3	55.8	61.4	−5.6	10.1
1988	64.5	67.9	−3.4	51.5	59.1	−7.6	10.0
1992	63.9	70.1	−6.2	54.0	63.6	−9.6	10.0
1996	63.5	67.7	−4.2	50.6	56.0	−5.4	10.8

SOURCE: Lucius Barker, Mark H. Jones, and Katherine Tate, *African Americans and the Political System,* 4th ed., p. 243. © 1993. Reprinted by permission of Prentice Hall, Inc.

TABLE 4.3   Party Identification, by Race, in Presidential Elections, 1964–1996

Presidential Election Years	Democrats		Independents		Republicans	
	Black	White	Black	White	Black	White
1964	82 %	58%	6 %	8 %	8 %	32%
1968	92	53	3	11	3	37
1972	75	49	12	13	11	36
1976	84	47	8	15	5	37
1980	81	49	7	14	8	37
1984	77	44	11	11	7	44
1988	81	40	6	12	11	46
1992	78	45	12	12	8	42
1996	80.5	48	10.5	8.5	8.5	44

SOURCE: Adapted from Lucius Barker, Mark H. Jones, and Katherine Tate, *African Americans and the Political System,* p. 216. © 1993. Reprinted by permission of Prentice Hall, Inc.

These tables illustrate black American weakness and minority status in the use of political power. The very failure of the Jackson campaign to create a powerful "rainbow coalition" capable of electing a black to the highest office, or even to dramatically impact on national policy, demonstrates the need for alternative strategies and tactics for some racial minority groups. Black Americans have employed all three strategies and all six tactics. Chapters 5 and 6 illustrate the use of physical and psychological separatism, each of which was pursued by significant factions of black Americans.

SUMMARY

This chapter explained and illustrated the strategy of accommodation and how various groups used the political tactic of that strategy. It discussed the Irish Americans as the prototype example of political accommodation and how they helped create the urban political machine and then used machine politics to climb the socioeconomic ladder of society. The chapter discussed other groups who employed that tactic, albeit less successfully than did the Irish: Italian Americans, Greek Americans, and some Slavic American groups, as well as East European Jews. The chapter then discussed its use by factions of Hispanic Americans, focusing especially on the Chicano and Puerto Rican groups. The chapter closed with a discussion of how a faction of black Americans, particularly as illustrated by the leadership of Jesse Jackson and the Black Congressional Caucus, showed success in employing the political approach to accommodation.

KEY TERMS

Exogamy: marrying outside of one's ethnic group.

Padroni: Italian "boss" system.

Pogrom: violent outbreaks of looting, pillaging, riots, and murders in Eastern Europe directed at Jews with the government's tacit approval.

Polonia: term referring to the total Polish-American population.

REVIEW QUESTIONS

1. Which groups provide good examples of the tactic of political accommodation?

2. What was the first, and the classic, example of the urban machine? Why have machine politics declined since the 1930s?

3. What groups make up Slavic Americans? Where in the United States do they tend to concentrate?

4. Compare and contrast how the "new" immigrants relied heavily on their churches and mutual-aid societies for their assimilation process.

5. Why were East European Jewish immigrants *not* sojourners?

6. Specify any three prominent Hispanic political leaders, and discuss the organizations they founded. Characterize the style of politics of each such leader/organization.

7. What are some advantages and disadvantages for a minority group of being closely allied with a particular political party organization?

8. Which black American leader has been the foremost advocate of standard political electoral behavior as a means to develop black political clout? What are some advantages and disadvantages to blacks voting according to their race?

9. Name two black Americans who serve(d) on the U.S. Supreme Court.

10. What barriers to electoral success have minority groups had to overcome?

NOTES

1. See, for example, Parrillo (1985). Dinnerstein and Reimers (1988) cite the fact that by 1860 some two-thirds of the domestics in Boston were Irish.

2. Federal Writer's Project, *The Italians of New York* (New York: Arno Press, 1969), p. viii.

3. Luciano Iorizzo and Salvatore Mondello, *The Italian Americans* (New York: Twayne, 1971), p. 48.

4. Other sources estimate their number at over 1 million (Dinnerstein and Reimers 1988; Parrillo 1985; Dinnerstein and Jaher 1977). Lopata puts the maximum at 1,670,000 for the number who emigrated and remained here from 1885 to 1972; estimates for the total Polish-American group (Polonia) range from 6 million to 15 million (Levy and Kramer 1973).

5. See, for instance, Thomas and Znanieki (1977), Parrillo (1985), Lopata (1976), and Dinnerstein and Reimers (1988). As with the Italians and the other Slavic groups, the Polish immigrants had difficulty adjusting to the Irish-dominated Catholic church.

SUGGESTED READINGS

BARKER, LUCIUS, MARK H. JONES, AND KATHERINE TATE. *African-Americans and the American Political System,* 4th ed. Upper Saddle River, NJ: Prentice Hall, 1999.

CALLOW, ALEXANDER B., JR., ED. *The City Boss in America.* New York: Oxford University Press, 1975.

DAVIS, JERÔME. *The Russian Immigrant.* New York: Arno Press, 1969.

DINNERSTEIN, LEONARD, ROGER NICHOLS, AND DAVID REIMERS. *Natives and Strangers.* New York: Oxford University Press, 1990.

FITZPATRICK, JOSEPH. *Puerto Rican Americans.* Englewood Cliffs, NJ: Prentice Hall, 1971.

FUCHS, LAWRENCE, ED. *American Ethnic Politics.* New York: Harper, 1968.

GOSNELL, HAROLD F. *Machine Politics: Chicago Model.* Chicago: University of Chicago Press, 1987.

HOWE, IRVING. *World of Our Fathers.* New York: Simon & Schuster, 1976.

LEVY, MARK, AND MICHAEL KRAMER. *The Ethnic Factor.* New York: Simon & Schuster, 1973.

LIEBERSON, STANLEY. *A Piece of the Pie.* Berkeley: University of California Press, 1980.

LITT, EDGAR. *Ethnic Politics in America.* Glenview, IL: Scott, Foresman, 1970.

LOPATA, HELEN ZNANIECKI. *Polish-Americans.* Englewood Cliffs, NJ: Prentice Hall, 1976.

MOSKOS, CHARLES. *Greek Americans.* Englewood Cliffs, NJ: Prentice Hall, 1980.

NELLI, HUMBERT C. *Italians in Chicago: 1830–1930.* New York: Oxford University Press, 1970.

PARRILLO, VINCENT. *Strangers to These Shores.* Boston: Houghton Mifflin, 1985.

PRPIC, GEORGE. *South Slavic Immigration in America.* Boston: Twayne, 1978.

SMITH, ROGERS M. *Civic Ideals.* New Haven, CT: Yale University Press, 1997.

SOLOUTOS, THEODORE. *The Greeks in the United States.* Cambridge, MA: Harvard University Press, 1964.

WHITE, JOHN. *Black Leadership in America,* 2nd ed. New York: Longman, 1991.

CASE STUDY 4.1

Urban Machines and Ethnic Minorities

A classic example of the use of the urban machine to incorporate primarily Euro-ethnic Americans into the body politic, greatly enhancing their assimilation process, was New York City's famous Tammany Hall. Founded as the New York Society of Tammany in 1785, it began as a patriotic society but soon developed into a private political club. It became the most important exponent of Thomas Jefferson's doctrines in New York City, and carried the city and the state for the Jeffersonians under the leadership of Aaron Burr in 1800. By 1815, Tammany controlled state politics. The urban machine it established reached its zenith—called its golden age—after the Civil War, when it was led by William Marcy Tweed. Tweed entered politics as a volunteer fireman, became better known and involved in ward politics, then in 1857 was elected to the New York County Board of Supervisors. He sold his business (chair making) and began his career as a full-time politician.

By 1860, Tweed established the "Tweed Ring," based on the Board of Supervisors, which controlled for the Democratic Party the appointment of inspectors of elections. By 1861, Tweed was elected chairman of the Tammany General Committee, then chosen as Grand Sachem of Tammany Hall—becoming "Boss Tweed." By 1863, he also served as deputy street commissioner, a post that enabled him to attract thousands of followers through the patronage

jobs he dispensed. In 1868, he was elected state senator, where he could personally supervise the operations of the New York state legislature. In 1870, he managed to get passed a new charter for New York City, reportedly costing $2 million in bribes, but relieving the ring of any state government authority.

By the late 1870s, the Tweed Ring's fortunes were on the decline. When Tweed's chief of finance, James Watson, was injured, one Matthew O'Rourke became county bookkeeper. He amassed evidence of fraud and had it published in the *New York Times*. The exposé led to the collapse of the Tweed Ring. Boss Tweed was arrested and indicted for a felony, losing his position as Grand Sachem. In 1873, he was tried and found guilty and sentenced to prison, but was released on a technicality after one year. During his retrial, he escaped and fled to Cuba and then Spain. He was later arrested by Spanish authorities upon request by the U.S. secretary of state, Hamilton Fish. He was imprisoned in the Ludlow Street jail, where he died. The remaining Ring members were also tried and jailed. Their total graft was estimated at about $200 million.

The urban machine continued, however, and Tammany Hall reasserted itself under new leadership. The machine attracted loyalty from its supporters by dispensing patronage. Leaders of the machine often enriched themselves through graft, such as payoffs for city contracts that were awarded in return for the machine's backing of public works projects and of candidates for police, fire, and similar city commissioners. The excesses of the machine drove reform movements that occasionally and often temporarily managed to oust the machine-backed politicians from office.

Perhaps most famous of its bosses, and known as the "philosopher" of the machine, was George Washington Plunkitt, the Tammany leader who became a millionaire through machine politics and who wrote, as his epitaph: "He Seen His Opportunities and He Took 'Em." He distinguished between dishonest and honest graft. Blackmailing saloon keepers or stealing from the public treasury (as the Tweed Ring did) he labeled as "dishonest graft." Honest graft, by contrast, was making money through insider knowledge and business foresight. Much of the money acquired through such "honest graft" lined the pockets of machine politicians. But some of it was used to dispense welfare-type services to the needy immigrants who became the voting bloc that kept the machine in political office and political power.

Using an elaborate and decentralized system of ward and precinct clubs, the Tammany Hall machine, under such bosses as John Kelly and Richard Croker, strengthened power in the central party organization, controlled the excesses of corruption, and obtained the allegiance of voters by delivering emergency and social services when no other institutions were providing them. They spent millions of public money or from "honest graft" sources serving citizens in need through Catholic, Protestant, and Jewish church and school charities. Tammany Hall also assisted in the naturalization of many immigrants and organized both public aid and private charities to help them. It later involved immigrants and their children in an elaborate system of balanced ethnic "slates"—running various ethnic politicians for public office and appealing to blocs of ethnic voters in various wards dominated by one or another nationality or ethnic group.

The urban machine also gained the support of business by granting public contracts, by favorable tax policy, and by assisting speculators such as Jay Gould, Jim Fiske, Cornelius Vanderbilt, and John Jacob Astor, all of whom enriched themselves through corrupt government officials who approved their projects.

Tammany's control of New York City politics continued well into the twentieth century, interrupted by the occasional victory by reformers such as Fiorello LaGuardia. Tammany's control was broken once and for all in 1961. Then Tammany leader Carmen DeSapio chose not to slate incumbent Mayor Robert Wagner for a third term, replacing him with State Comptroller Arthur Levitt. Wagner ran on the Liberal Party ticket, won, and eventually regained the Democratic Party nomination by campaigning against the evils of "bossism." Wagner's victory marked the end of machine dominance in New York City.

In its prime, however, the urban machine did more than corrupt city politics and enrich ethnic politicians and corrupt business associates. It provided for the needy, giving immigrants needed emergency assistance and relief, as well as a government of "sympathetic" officials who were more understanding and congenial than an impersonal bureaucracy. It provided immigrants with an important channel of social mobility. Immigrant numbers and bloc voting assured them power in the political arena. Immigrant groups took pride in "one of their own" rising up the ladder of political power.

The machine aided business and was supported by it. Many businesses cooperated with the machine whose political privileges gave them immediate economic gains. The machine provided business with a political organization able to provide them a secure and predictable political environment. Contributions and patronage jobs were readily exchanged for exclusive contracts, licenses, and other preferential treatment that limited their competition and maximized their profits.

The machine centralized power. This often was essential for businesses to expand or develop new ventures that needed myriad licenses, zoning variances, and various permissions from a host of city boards, agencies, committees, and commissions. Machine approval of a project resulted in quick approvals. This process was critical to the city's growth. A city growing at an explosive rate required new streets, sewers, housing, streetcar lines, schools, fire stations, and many other facilities. The centralizing power of the urban machine made sure the necessary permissions were granted, and often that immigrant workers got the unskilled and semiskilled jobs the contracts

generated. Businesses expanded, the city grew, and the machine gained bloc votes.

Crime groups (gamblers, racketeers) also gained benefits from machine officials. In return for graft, the machine guaranteed there would be no "undue" government interference in their activities. Police and court officials were bought off and controlled by the machine politicians. For many ethnic immigrant groups (most notably Jews and Italians in New York City), the crime organizations became another avenue for social mobility.

In machine-controlled cities, the political party apparatus played a conciliating role that kept ethnic groups living together in more or less harmony and kept the city free from violent labor disputes, hunger riots, and class warfare. By individualizing politics and muting class antagonisms, the machine helped undermine class-based political strife. The Socialist, Fascist, and Communist parties, as we will see in Chapter 7, failed to make extensive political gains in part because of the machine's ability to deliver benefits to the disadvantaged that undercut the radical party's political appeal.

CHAPTER FIVE

THE STRATEGY OF SEPARATISM
Physical Separatism

On occasion, an ethnic or racial minority will reject the value system of the majority society. The minority group desires to be left alone rather than to assimilate. It does not seek to impose its values and views on the majority society but wants the majority society to respect its differing values and allow the group to hold its values, norms, and customs without suffering discrimination. Often such groups come into sustained contact with the majority culture in some largely involuntary manner. Forced migration can bring two such cultures into contact, as in the case of the black slaves forcibly brought to America. The minority group rejects major aspects of the new and dominant culture. It also rejects its minority status and position in the new society. Internally developed minority subcultures, such as a new religious minority, may also come to reject the value system of the dominant culture. The Mormons provide a classic example of this type. Sometimes a subculture finds itself in minority status through military suppression, as in the case of Native Americans.

The social withdrawal of the Amish and Mennonites from the secular requirements of American society led them to live in rural communities as far and as separated from the majority as was possible. The emergence of Zionism, the separatist views of the Hasidic Jews, and the development of Black Nationalism are cases where an ethnic group turns inward, creating its own institutions to replenish social, psychological, and cultural values that cannot be fulfilled in the dominant society. In doing so, they develop a strategy of separatist politics, developing distinct organizations and cultural practices to compensate for disenchantment with the ongoing political and social order. When a subculture, for whatever reason, wants to pursue a strategy of separatism, it may attempt to do so in one of two ways: physical separatism (isolation) or the psychological separation of its members from the norms, customs, and values of the rejected majority society.

This chapter discusses and illustrates physical separatism. The choice of this route depends on the group being able to isolate itself physically from the majority culture. This may be done by seeking out frontier or rural areas with low enough density of settlement that the minority group members settle the area as the numerically superior group. The Amish and Mennonites, clustering in rural enclaves, exemplify this route. They reduce their contact with members of the majority culture to a minimum. They reject the media, reinforcing the isolating effect of their rural settlement. The initial fleeing of the Mormons to ever-more isolated frontier regions in response to persecution is another classic example of this route. A small faction of black Americans, following the separatist philosophy of Marcus Garvey's Back to Africa movement, represents an attempt at this approach.

Sometimes physical separatism is not a matter of choice by the minority racial or ethnic group. Sometimes it is to varying degrees forced on a group when the majority treats them in a manner that physically isolates them. The Chicanos in the Southwest are often forced into barrios, much as the Chinese were relegated to Chinatowns. The military forced survivors of Native American tribes of an earlier policy of annihilation to ever-decreasing areas of reservations. The use of physical separatism is typically restricted to minority groups small enough to make isolation a realistic tactic.

This chapter discusses the following groups in relation to the use of physical separatism: the Amish and Mennonites, the Mormons, Native Americans, and, finally, that faction of black Americans who followed Marcus Garvey.

THE AMISH AND MENNONITES

Two ethnoreligious subcultures that provide good examples of a minority following the strategy of physical separatism are the Amish and Mennonites. They reject the values of the majority culture, live in as rural and isolated a setting as they can find, reduce their contact with the majority culture to a minimum, and have struggled for over 400 years to maintain their separate culture. As a scholar of the Mennonites says: "There is almost unanimous agreement within the sect that the regulation of their total physical and spiritual lives is necessary for the unity and continuity of their spiritual culture (Boyton 1986: vii). Likewise, scholars of the Amish characterize them as "a people of separation. Indeed, their entire history can be called a struggle to be separate. They are one of several Anabaptist groups that trace their origins to the Radical Reformation of sixteenth century Europe" (Kraybill and Olshan 1994: 1).

The **Anabaptists**, or "rebaptizers," began as a reformation movement in 1525 in Zurich, Switzerland, preaching adult baptism as a public sign of Christian faith and stressing a double separation: church and state and the separation of the church from the evils of the larger culture. The movement soon encountered severe persecution, as it seemed to threaten the very fabric of sixteenth-century society. Thousands were killed as both civil and religious authorities sought to repress the movement.

Anabaptists eventually became known as Mennonites, after Menno Simons, one of their prominent leaders, a bishop who united with a Dutch group of Anabaptists in 1536. After Zurich, the Netherlands became a second cradle of the movement. Today, Mennonites, Hutterites, and the Amish trace their religious heritage to the Anabaptist movement.

The Amish split off as a separate sect in 1693, in what is today the Alsace region of France. The Anabaptist leader, Jacob Ammann, began a new practice of community life that included social avoidance—shunning—of persons who had been excommunicated from the church, as well as advocating other practices that enforced even greater separation between the church and the majority society.

Both the Amish and the Mennonites migrated to the United States and Canada in the eighteenth century, frequently settling in the same geographic areas. Old Order Mennonites emerged as a conservative subgroup in the late nineteenth century when growing modernization led to schism in the church. Old Order Mennonite and Old Order Amish share similarities, including horse-and-buggy travel, plain dress, a conservative lifestyle, and the use of one-room parochial schools.

Amish society is organized on three levels: settlement, district, and affiliation. A settlement encompasses the general geographic area where Amish families live in proximity, varying considerably in size. Some 25 to 35 families compose a church district, the basic social unit of a settlement. Families within a district worship together in each other's homes. When the number of families grows too large to hold services in the home, it branches into two smaller districts. Thus, the church district becomes the primary social/religious unit—sort of parish, precinct, tribe, and club all wrapped up into a single social package. Church districts that are in fellowship with one another make up an affiliation, sharing similar church practices and exchanging ministers in their worship services. Congregational autonomy and loosely coupled affiliation engender considerable diversity in practice among the Amish churches. But they all share some common aspects of Amish identity:

> These common badges of Amish identity include the Pennsylvania German dialect, the use of horse-drawn transportation, the rejection of electricity from public utility lines, the use of homes for worship, plain dress, beards for men, a prayer cap for women, an eighth-grade education, and the use of horses for field work. There are of course many other distinctive markers of Amish lifestyles but these public symbols of identity are shared by most Amish groups across North America. What is remarkable, yes astonishing, is that the Amish have been able to preserve these common badges of separation without a centralized national structure to link the more than 900 congregations across more than 230 different geographic settlements in North America. (Kraybill and Olshan 1994: 4)

The Holdeman Mennonites and the Old Order Mennonites are more conservative than other Mennonite groups, having retained more of the original beliefs and behaviors of their sixteenth-century ancestors. The Holdeman Mennonites are named after John Holdeman, who with his followers, left the Old Mennonite church in 1859 to set about restoring "the true church." It now has more than 10,000 persons in 100 congregations in the United States and Canada. Their beliefs and social practices serve as cultural markers: "Cultural boundary markers are merely restrictive behaviors which function symbolically to unify a subculture and separate it from the dominant society" (Boynton 1986: 11).

The first Amish settlement in the United States, the Northkill Settlement, was in Berks County, Pennsylvania, a group of about 500. At about the same time another settlement began in Lancaster County, which soon developed into a major area of

Amish children walking home from school.

settlement for Amish and Mennonite groups. These two settlements became the **mother colonies** of the Amish in America. Other settlements came about as both Amish and Mennonite groups expanded both west and east, and a few to the south (Virginia and North Carolina). The Mennonites, who arrived first in 1710, tended to purchase unimproved property. The Amish more often bought land cleared by non-Amish. While there was some advantage to acquiring the somewhat improved farmland, the Mennonite communities tended to be on land of richer soil, and by the late 1700s were generally wealthier than the Amish (Nolt 1992).

A combination of high birth rates and low dropout rates resulted in vigorous growth, as illustrated by Table 5.1, which shows the growth in the Amish population throughout North America from 1900 to 1992.

Amish immigration from Europe came in four distinguishable periods: 1736–1770, when they settled mostly in Pennsylvania; 1804–1810, settling mostly in the Midwest and moving to areas also settled by groups expanding out from the Penn-

TABLE 5.1   Growth of Amish Population in North America, 1900–1992

Year	Estimated Population	Number of Church Districts
1900	4,800	32
1910	8,550	57
1920	12,450	83
1930	16,500	110
1941	23,100	154
1951	30,300	202
1961	40,350	269
1971	55,050	367
1981	83,350	569
1991	134,700	898
1992	139,500	930

SOURCE: Adapted from data in Donald Kraybill and Marc Olshan, eds., *The Amish Struggle with Modernity* (Hanover, NH: University Press of New England, 1994), p. 9.

sylvania area; 1817–1860, when about 3,000 migrated directly to Ohio, Illinois, Indiana, Iowa, and New York; and 1860–1900, when some 50 families came and settled among established Amish communities. The Mennonites of Indiana are descendants of Mennonite families who went there about 1840, except for three congregations who were composed wholly of people who came directly from Europe in 1838 (Wenger 1961). Figure 5.1 shows the Mennonite migrations both to and within North America.

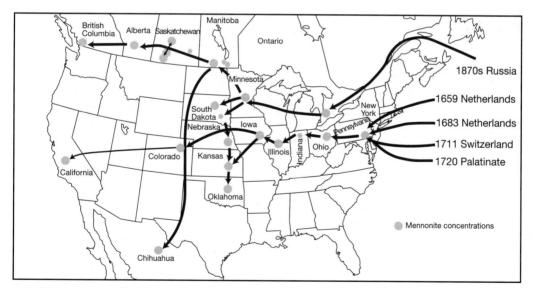

FIGURE 5.1 Mennonite Migrations to and within North America

SOURCE: Donald Kraybill, *The Riddle of Amish Culture,* p. 15. © 1989 The Johns Hopkins University Press.

The Amish and Old Order Mennonites remain separate through a well-defined moral order and lifestyle. Amish use the **Ordnung**, the "understandings," to prescribe expectations of Amish life; the "do's" and "don'ts" articulating Amish practices. They form a major part of a comprehensive program of social control.

These techniques of social control keep individuals in line with group goals and serve as cultural barricades against the encroachment by the larger society's culture. Separatist groups, such as the Amish and Mennonites, employ at least five defensive tactics: symbolization of core values; centralized leadership; social sanctions; comprehensive socialization; and controlled interaction with outsiders (Kraybill 1989). The Amish and Mennonites not only resisted modernization, they also negotiated with it, adopting a process of cultural or structural bargaining wherein they sometimes compromised and at other times refused to concede.

The strains of coping with these strategies led to three internal divisions among the Old Order Amish in 1877, 1910, and 1966. In 1877, following some Amish divisions in the Midwest, two factions formed independent congregations using a meeting house for their worship services. The traditional Amish then became known as the Old Order Amish, or House Amish, because they continued to worship in their homes. The splinter groups, called Amish-Mennonite, or "Meeting House Amish," held their services in a church building, eventually becoming full-fledged Mennonites. A second division occurred in 1910 over the use of cars, telephones, and electricity. A liberal faction became known as the Beachy Church, affiliated today with the Beachy Amish Church. The third division came in 1966, when a group of so-called New Order Amish split over differences in the use of modern farm technology These changes are illustrated in Figure 5.2.

Coordination among Amish groups, often involving matters dealing with law or policy viewed as detrimental to all, led to the creation of six organizations with loosely coordinated activities that go beyond the scope of local districts. These organizations are unlike the formal bureaucratic structures of majority society. They are informal, flat, decentralized, small, and traditional.

Another example of the Amish coping with the broader culture is the dramatic change in their work patterns, especially since 1960. The pressures of suburbanization, declining farmland, rising land prices, and a burgeoning Amish population have made it increasingly difficult for young Amish couples to enter farming. The stereotypical image of the Amish is the farmer. Until 1970, nearly all of the Amish in Lancaster County were engaged in farming or in small crafts and enterprises linked to farming. Since 1970, the Amish have been creating small businesses and cottage industries that have flourished and provide much needed employment in the Amish communities. Now less than half the Amish are in farming. Amish and Mennonites in Indiana have left their farms for factory work in the recreational vehicle and mobile home industries (Kraybill and Olshan: 165–181).

This transformation of Amish employment from farms to business will have a profound impact on Amish life, as well as on their relationship with the outside world.

> No longer barefoot farmers, whose peculiar ways can be attributed to rural naivete, Amish entrepreneurs will be subject to the same legal and regulatory restrictions as their non-Amish competitors without the public indulgence they have sometimes enjoyed in the past. The power brokers of modern life and all their functionaries will no doubt

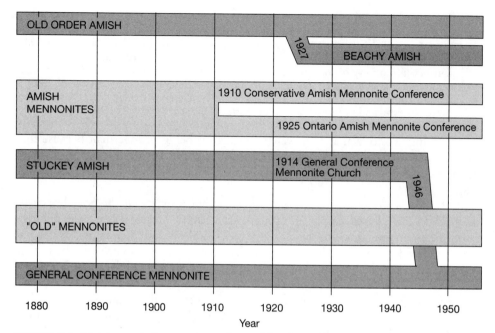

FIGURE 5.2 Division and Merger among the Amish Mennonites and Old Order Amish, 1880–1950

1888 Indiana Michigan Amish Mennonite Conference 1917
1890 Western District Amish Mennonite Conference 1920
1893 Eastern Amish Mennonite Conference 1927

SOURCE: Steven M. Nolte, *A History of the Amish* (Intercourse, PA: Good Books, 1992), p. 163. © Good Books. Used by permission.

insist that the Amish play on a level playing field despite the implications of their religious convictions. Many of the legal and political concessions that have been forged over the years have been based on the assumption that they were innocent farmers seeking to preserve a sharp separation from the world. That assumption will surely erode as they enter the fray of business. What, for example, might have been the outcome of the Supreme Court's 1972 decision in *Wisconsin* vs. *Yoder* if less than half of the Amish had been farming at the time? (Kraybill and Nolt, in Kraybill and Olshan 1994: 162–163)

Conflict with the majority culture and the Amish and Mennonites centered around aspects of their beliefs that clash with the broader culture in ways the majority deems dangerous. Their pacifism caused them no end of problems during the time of the Civil War, when they refused to fight. The pressure was even greater during World War I, when the draft was employed. A few who were drafted served in noncombatant roles. Most, however, refused to participate at all.

Despite the threats and pressure, young Amish draftees remained unwilling to fight, wear military uniforms or perform certain jobs which they felt were aiding the army's war-making ability. . . . Amish conscientious objectors received verbal abuse, beatings and wire-brush treatments. In addition, soldiers sometimes forcibly shaved the beards of the Amish. Many COs were made to stand for long periods of time in the sun, without refreshment. Those who refused to wear military uniforms were at times left in cold, damp cells with no clothing at all. Officers occasionally "baptized" Amish COs in camp latrines in mockery of their Anabaptist beliefs. COs were stuck in abusive camp situations from the time of their induction until well after the war was over and demobilization began. For the Amish men who endured World War I camp experiences, the memories were powerful and unforgettable. (Nolt 1992: 226; see also Wenger 1961: 38-39)

During World War I, they were suspected of being pro-German because they used German in their services and community life. They were hounded, two Mennonite meeting houses were torched, and others were vandalized or posted with American flags.

Another conflict arose in 1955, when Congress extended the Social Security program to include self-employed farmers. The Amish had never taken part in the Social Security program, but suddenly participation became mandatory. When the Amish refused to pay to the fund, the IRS collected funds through their bank accounts. Some Amish closed their accounts. The government then foreclosed and sold several Amish farms to recover lost Social Security funds. The IRS forcibly collected from 130 Amish households. In 1965, Congress finally addressed the problem by including a provision of the Medicare Act that exempted self-employed Amish from both the Medicare and the Social Security systems.

The issue that aroused the most conflict was compulsory education. Old Order Amish and Old Order Mennonite parents refused to send their children to large, consolidated elementary schools or to high school. During the 1950s and 1960s, they had repeated run-ins with the law and were forced to pay fines and serve jail terms. Nearly every state that had Amish or Mennonite settlements experienced such clashes.

The Amish increasingly began to operate their own private schools. Such programs expanded rapidly. Sometimes compromises were negotiated with school officials. In Pennsylvania, the Amish were allowed, after completing eighth grade, to work at home and report to a special "vocational school" one morning per week until age 15. Several other states copied this method. The conflict was finally resolved by the U.S. Supreme Court. In 1967, a Lutheran pastor in Iowa, the Reverend William Lindholm, founded an interest group (the National Committee for Amish Religious Freedom) to work for Amish rights. They backed a case out of Wisconsin. Although they lost before the county court and the Wisconsin Supreme Court, they appealed to the U.S. Supreme Court and won their case in *Wisconsin* vs. *Yoder* (1972). Since then, all states must allow the Old Order Amish the right to establish their own schools or to withdraw from compulsory public schools after the eighth grade. See Box 5.1, which presents excerpts from the *Wisconsin* vs. *Yoder* case.

BOX 5.1:   Excerpts from *Wisconsin* vs. *Yoder et al.* (May 15, 1972)

In May 1972, the U.S. Supreme Court, with seven justices hearing the case, unanimously held that Wisconsin could not force Amish children to attend high school over religious objections. Chief Justice Warren Burger wrote the majority opinion and several justices wrote concurring opinions. Justices Lewis Powell, Jr., and William H. Rehnquist did not take part in consideration of the case. Excerpts from Justice Burger's opinion are as follows.

Amish objections to formal education beyond the eighth grade is firmly grounded in . . . central religious concepts. They object to high school and higher education generally because the values it teaches are in marked variance with Amish values and the Amish way of life. . . . The high school tends to emphasize intellectual and scientific accomplishments, self-determination, competitiveness, worldly success, and social life with other students. Amish society emphasizes learning through doing, a life of "goodness," rather than a life of intellect, wisdom, rather than technical knowledge, community welfare rather than competition, and separation rather than integration with contemporary wordly society.

As the record so strongly shows, the values and programs of the modern secondary school are in sharp conflict with the fundamental mode of life mandated by the Amish religion; modern laws requiring compulsory secondary education have accordingly engendered great concern and conflict. The conclusion is inescapable that secondary schooling, by exposing Amish children to worldly influences in terms of attitudes, goals and values contrary to beliefs, and by substantially interfering with the religious development of the Amish child and his integration into the way of life of the Amish faith community at the crucial adolescent state of development, contravenes the basic religious tenets and practices of the Amish faith, both as to the parent and the child. . . .

The State's requirement of compulsory formal education after the eighth grade would gravely endanger if not destroy the free exercise of respondents' religious beliefs.

The State attacks respondents' position as one fostering "ignorance" from which the child must be protected by the State. No one can question the State's duty to protect children from ignorance, but this argument does not square with the facts disclosed in the record. Whatever their idiosyncrasies as seen by the majority, this record strongly shows that the Amish community has been a highly successful social unit within our society even if apart from the conventional "mainstream.". . .

It is neither fair nor correct to suggest that the Amish are opposed to education beyond the eighth grade level. What this record shows is that they are opposed to conventional formal education of the type provided by a certified high school because it comes at the child's crucial adolescent period of religious development. . . . There can be no assumption that today's majority is "right" and the Amish and others like them are "wrong." A way of life that is odd or even erratic but interferes with no rights or interests by others is not to be condemned because it is different.

SOURCE: 406 U.S. 205.

THE MORMONS

Among religious minority groups, the Church of Jesus Christ of the Latter-day Saints, commonly known as the Mormons, undoubtedly experienced the most repressive discrimination, if measured by use of violence against them, legal restrictions imposed upon them, and their ultimately being forced to change an important tenet of their faith because of majority society pressure. The case of the Mormons is a clear example of religious discrimination since, initially at least, it was a native-born minority faith and therefore experienced no "antiforeign" prejudice. As a noted scholar of the Mormon church noted:

The appearance of such a new religious or social movement, like an invasive organism, presents a challenge to the normative order of the surrounding host society. This challenge will be the more serious, of course, the more militant and deviant the movement is; and survival itself might of necessity preoccupy the new movement. That so many new movements of all kinds fail to survive even one generation testifies clearly enough to their usual fragility. . . . If survival is the first task of the movement, the natural and inevitable response of the host society is either to domesticate [it] or to destroy it. In seeking to domesticate or assimilate it, the society will apply various kinds of social control pressures selectively in an effort to force the movement to abandon at least its most unique and threatening features. To the extent that the society succeeds . . . the result will be eventual assimilation of the movement. Failing to achieve sufficient domestication, the host society will eventually resort to the only alternative: persecution and repression. Movements which, like Mormonism, survive and prosper are those that succeed in maintaining indefinitely an optimum tension . . . between the two opposing strains: the strain toward greater assimilation and respectability, on the one hand, and that toward greater separateness, peculiarity, and militance on the other. (Mauss 1994: 4–5)

Its founder, Joseph Smith, was born in Vermont in 1805. His family moved to Palmyra, New York, in 1816, and it was near there that Smith says he first received his revelations from God, claiming his first visit by an angel, Moroni, began in 1823. In 1827, Smith claimed he "discovered the tablets," which he published in 1829, known as *The Book of Mormon.* On April 6, 1830, Smith and six of his followers formally established the Church of Jesus Christ of the Latter-Day Saints.

Moving from New York to Ohio and then on to Missouri because of severe persecution, Smith was killed by a mob storming the jail in which he was being held in Carthage, Missouri, on June 28, 1844. In the words of one historian of the Mormons: "It is not surprising that the first, and until the assassination of Malcolm X in 1965 the only, American religious leader to be murdered was a Mormon, for the Saints have always inflamed passions" (Hirshon 1969: 50).

Discrimination against the Mormons developed early and involved the reactions of expulsion through the use of violence, as well as applying the force of law to pressure the minority to change its tenets to be more acceptable to the views of the majority society.

Brigham Young, first Mormon president.

John Taylor, second Mormon president.

The tenet of faith that caused the Mormons so much trouble was *polygamy,* or the plural marriage principle, described by them as **celestial marriage**. Early Mormons stressed "speaking in tongues" and faith healing. Its Catholic-like dogmatism aroused animosity, although that aspect of the faith attracted many of its early converts who came from the lower classes and were probably attracted because its dogmatism provided a sense of security in the pre–Civil War period so wracked with disorder. The Mormons revered a "priesthood." Every adult male loyally adhering to the faith was considered a priest. Mormons quickly developed a group of Melchizedek priests, the Council of Seventies, every bit as militant as the Jesuits. Mormonism was more than a church, it was a total way of life. "As much as a church, moreover, the Saints created a society. In specifically designated communities they gathered and became in every sense a people. Often migrating in groups, they proved a new society following some model could even be moved physically from one part of the world to another" (Hirshon 1969: 18–19).

Wilford Woodruff, third Mormon president.

Since the plural marriage tenet was initially a well-kept secret, it was probably those other aspects that caused the initial hostile reactions to the Mormon sect in New York State. There skeptics frequently broke up Mormon meetings with jeering and by throwing stones at the faithful. It was in New York, in 1832, that Brigham Young was converted. The church, and Young, moved to Kirtland, Ohio, where many Mormons assembled in 1832–1833. The plural marriage principle, supposedly revealed to Smith in 1831, was being secretly practiced among the elite of the church by the 1840s. The Mormons built their first temple in Kirtland in 1833, but abandoned it almost upon completion. Hit by the Panic of 1837, they fled Ohio because of financial difficulties, a rather shaky financial venture, some degree of persecution, and a desire to aid the Mormon community in Missouri (Hardy 1992).

It was in Missouri that the most violent conflict broke out between the Mormons and the majority society, called gentiles by the Mormons. Smith had announced the church's intention to start a New Zion in the Carthage/Panock/Nauvoo triangle of Mormon settlements in Missouri/Illinois. In 1833, Nauvoo was a malaria-ridden dot of a town of 240 settlers. By 1842, it had 7,000 people. The initial conflict broke out in Jackson County, Missouri. The area around Independence witnessed a virtual state of war between Mormons and gentiles. Some 1,200 Mormons were engaged in pitched battles. Gentiles burned down Mormon homes, destroyed a Mormon paper, and tarred and feathered several Saints. The governor called for their expulsion. Mormon response was the creation of the militant Legion of Nauvoo. Several battles ended with the killing of Mormon women and children.

In 1840, Brigham Young was sent with several others to serve as missionaries in England. Their first year resulted in nearly 9,000 converts, many of whom migrated to New Zion when Young returned there in July 1841.

Celestial marriage was increasingly being practiced by the upper elite of the Mormons. Polygamy was looked upon with horror by the majority society, and increasing conflict led to Smith's arrest and death in 1844. His martyrdom led to the last great migration of the Mormons to Utah. The polygamy issue was frequently raised because apostates revealed the practice after having left the church.

In 1845, some 150 Mormons were burned to death in Missouri. The conflict, however, was not one-sided. Mormons committed violent acts against their neighbors as well. "If the Mormons had behaved like other people, they would never have been driven from Illinois and Missouri; but they stole, robbed, and plundered from all their neighbors and all the time" (Hirshon 1969: 63). By 1846, Nauvoo was a virtual city-state. The Mormon temple in Nauvoo was finished. There Brigham Young married 35 women in Nauvoo after Smith's death. Young ultimately had 70 wives and fathered 56 children. This practice, more than any other, made him a symbol of evil to the majority society, even in death.

In February 1846, Young left Nauvoo with about 4,000 people to establish winter quarters near what is now Omaha, Nebraska. In April 1847, he led a party of 148 Mormons in 73 wagons to what was then the far frontier. On July 21, 1847, they saw Salt Lake Valley, stopping on July 23 at the site that became Salt Lake City. A second group of nearly 500 joined them soon after. John Nelson, a gentile frontiersman who guided the first of the Mormon parties to Salt Lake City and who joined the church for a while, described them as follows:

> The class of people who made up these Mormon caravans were generally very poor and ignorant. Some, however, amongst them belonged to a better class, and I always fancied these had joined to save their necks from the gallows of the district from which they migrated. . . . The secret of polygamy amongst the Mormons was this. They thought that if each man had ten wives, and each wife had from three to five children, in twenty years time they would be strong enough to protect themselves from the gentiles. (Nelson 1963: 118)

The death of founder Joseph Smith led to a crisis in the movement's leadership and ultimately to the first of many church schisms. This development was not surprising, since the movement arose in a crisis of authority. The Mormon movement was a divisive and ringing dissent from all the existing churches and theologies of the time, and its early attempts to develop a communal utopia under theocratic control in the 1830s and 1840s led to dissenters within. Smith's death created the major split in the summer of 1844, the main line following Brigham Young west, and a minor line remaining in the Midwest. The differences concerned doctrine as well as leadership (Launuis and Thatcher 1994: 3–16).

Several groups developed out of early Mormonism: the Strangites, the Cutlerites, and the Reorganized Church of Jesus Christ of the Latter-Day Saints of Josephites. The Strangites remained in Wisconsin and Michigan. Sidney Rigdon led the Church of Christ, which lasted from its inception in 1845 until after his death to 1876 and was found mostly in Pennsylvania and Iowa. The Utah-based church of the Reorganized Church of Jesus Christ of the Latter-day Saints was headquartered in Independence, Missouri. It was headed for some 40 years by Joseph Smith III, the son of the founder of the Mormon church.

Life on the frontier was harsh for the early Mormon settlers. Certainly their polygamous lifestyle, which Young extended from the elite to the rank-and-file members of the faith, seemed strange and threatening to the majority society. Although only the leaders had many wives, an estimated 20 percent of the Saints were polygamists. The practice of plural marriage acquired added momentum among the migrants during their passage west. The practice, though, was not formally made public by the church until 1852, and was not actually printed in the Mormon *Doctrine and Covenants* until 1876. It was abandoned in 1890, after it was legally banned by the United States, in a church manifesto that marked the end of Mormon separatism and the beginning of an uneasy compromise with non-Mormons (Hardy 1992; O'Dea 1957; Schaefer 1998). The territory of Utah was admitted as a state in 1896.

The pressure of public law against the Mormons was upheld in three U.S. Supreme Court cases. The first, in 1879, upheld the validity of an act by Congress proscribing the advocating of polygamy against the Mormon claim of freedom of religious practice. Chief Justice Waite, writing for an unanimous Court, first expounded the "wall of separation" doctrine with regard to church and state relations. The case ruled that religious beliefs did not justify polygamy as a practice. The final case, rendered in

1890, upheld the validity of an 1887 congressional act that annulled the charter of the Mormon church and declared all of its property forfeited save for a small portion used exclusively for worship. This case was necessitated by the fact that the Mormons ignored the earlier ruling and continued to practice polygamy despite the law.

The manifesto did lead to some schisms and splinter groups who broke away from the main body of Mormonism to continue the practice of plural marriage. Even in the main body, polygamous marriages continued after the manifesto of 1890 with the consent of general authorities. Within the main body, however, the practice increasingly withered under the pressures of the dominant society.

The Mormon settlement in Utah grew rapidly. In 1848, there were only 5,000 Mormons in the territory, virtually all in Salt Lake City. By 1850, there were over 11,000, and by 1852, they numbered 32,000. By 1855, there were some 60,000 Mormons in the territory, over 15,000 of whom resided in Salt Lake City alone.

Flight to the frontier did not end Mormon conflict with the majority society. In December 1848, the Council of Elders of the church created a territorial government with Young at its head. He began colonizing beyond Salt Lake City. This colonization process led to conflict with gentile settlers in the territory. Likened to the czar of Russia, Young ruled with absolute power.

The development and expansion of the Mormon domain was not without conflict, occasionally even violently so. In the presidential election of 1856, the National Republican Party platform, reflecting the sentiment of most easterners and midwesterners, declared opposition to the "twin relics of barbarism"—slavery and polygamy. Tensions rose during the 1856–1858 period of "reformation," and violence erupted. The church leadership had petitioned for statehood as the State of Deseret in 1849, but anti-Mormon sentiment in Washington, D.C., as well as fear and concern over Young's theocratic and czar-like power, resulted in it being given territorial status under the name of Utah, as part of the Compromise of 1850 (while the nation was split among free state and slave state positions). When gold was discovered in California in 1848 and more and more gentile settlers traversed the Mormon-dominated territory, conflict arose between gentile settlers and Mormons. The territorial government was split, with the judiciary being held by non-Mormons. Tensions mounted.

In September 1857, a party of 120 gentiles was massacred by Mormons disguised as Indians. The Mountain Meadows massacre became enough of a national issue that President Buchanan sent a force of soldiers into Utah to suppress a "rebellion." More tension and atrocities followed.[1] John Nelson, who had earlier joined the church and led the Mormons to Salt Lake City, later served as a guide for the Union expedition. He described the events leading up to the use of military force against the church: "Brigham Young and his Saints had outgrown their discretion, and suddenly took to murdering immigrants who did not belong to their denomination, to robbing trains, and to killing people who were bound for California" (p. 117).

As the Union forces advanced upon them, the Mormons abandoned and burned down many of their settlements, fleeing to the stronghold of the Wasatch at Provo. The Union force and the Mormon military reached a virtual standoff without blood being shed. After weeks of tension, a compromise was reached by which the garrison of troops was stationed at Salt Lake City, showing the federal presence in the Mormon region. President Buchanan, in June 1858, granted Young and the Mormon leadership "free and full" pardon, and Young returned to Salt Lake City in July 1859. John D. Lee, a leading Mormon in its military force, was ultimately tried, convicted, and executed by firing squad at the very site of the Mountain Meadow massacre.

One of the California settlements was Fort San Bernardino, erected in 1851. It became the site of the city of San Bernardino, one of 250 Mormon settlements (colonies) in the West. In 1857, just as it was being firmly established, Brigham Young suddenly summoned the settlers back to Salt Lake City. The withdrawal of a majority of its leading citizens was orderly and demonstrated their dedication to the Mormon cause. Fully two-thirds of the population returned to Utah. Some remained and embraced the Reorganized Church of Jesus Christ of the Latter-day Saints, the Missouri-based church without allegiance to Brigham Young or to plural marriage. The persecution of the Mormons certainly tested their dedication and undoubtedly contributed to their sense of "peoplehood."[2]

During the 1858–1860 period of occupation, the soldiers interfered little with Mormon life and tensions eased. The Mormons reaped a sizable economic benefit from the occupying army (Arrington and Bitton 1992: 169). When Young died in 1877, the extensive practice of polygamy began to die with him. After the 1890 manifesto, the Mormon and American value systems gradually grew increasingly congruent, especially between 1900 and 1920, so that by the time of the Great Depression, Utah politics had become thoroughly Americanized. The Mormons' People's Party was disbanded, with the church rank and file and the leadership becoming Republicans and Democrats.

Mormons used politics almost from their inception. Members of the church, being native-born, could and did participate in politics without restrictions. They were active in Ohio politics to the point where their activities led to their being forced to flee. Smith was able to deliver the votes of his members as a bloc. Though small, they were a sizable minority in local politics and aroused much fear in Ohio, especially during the Panic of 1837. When they fled to Illinois and Missouri, Smith again entered politics, with his flock voting en mass for the Democrats. After the move to the far west, the church split into factions. By 1870, there were three main factions whose phenomenal growth made them a force to be reckoned with. In 1850, Mormons had over 10,000 members in 16 branches. By 1870, they had 171 branches and over 87,800 members. The leader of each of the factions could and did deliver his members' votes as blocs. The largest faction, led by Young, established the State of Deseret in January 1862. It set up its own government and for eight years petitioned Congress for admission. The Congress ignored them. Young became obsessed with establishing the "Kingdom of God" with its principles of violence, unquestioned obedience, and a holy war against the gentiles. Once statehood was achieved, the Mormons dominated Utah politics.

Currently, no overwhelming party linkage is evident, although they more often favor Republicans. There is some difference among the leadership and the rank-and-file Mormon membership in party identification. By 1960, while the general members identified themselves as 40.8 percent Republican and 38.3 percent Democrat (and 20.9 percent "other"), bishops of the church were 55.6 percent Republican and

22.2 percent Democrat (and 22.2 percent "other"), and "stake presidents" were 89.3 percent Republican and only 10.7 percent Democrat (none identified as "other"). The Ninety-seventh Congress had two Democrats and five Republicans who were Mormons, and in the Senate, one Republican and three Democrats were Mormons.

During their early days the Mormons' public policy focus was defensive, attempting to achieve statehood without relinquishing their tenet of polygamy. That practice was the one over which most conflict evolved. Their clinging to the tenet was more than theological. A practical reason Mormon leaders urged men to marry often was that a practicing polygamist rarely apostatized, having no other place to go. It was a logical means to massively and rapidly increase the size of the church membership.

While Young was governor of the territory, he used public policy to accumulate personal wealth as well as to build up the property of the Mormon church. Also, he used his appointive power to rid himself of unwanted rivals. Young and the church leadership often fought with presidential appointees who were gentiles assigned to the territorial judiciary. They also tried to develop the region agriculturally, industrially, and through control of railroad development. These developments reflected a tension between the "angel and the beehive." The angel, atop the famous Tabernacle in Salt Lake City, was the symbol of the otherworldly heritage of Mormonism. The beehive, fixed to many Mormon enterprise buildings, was the symbol of the worldly enterprises throughout the Mormon heartland (Mauss 1994).

Young, in part as a result of the Panic of 1873, had initiated the Second United Order, and between 1873–1874 created over 100 United Orders in communities throughout the intermountain west. The community operated several cooperative enterprises, shared proceeds and dividends, and allowed the Mormon people a greater degree of self-sufficiency. This period marked the gradual change in the Mormon movement from a utopian sect into a corporate church.

Figure 5.3 shows the spread of their influence, depicting the core area, the area of greatest density of occupation, intensity of organization, and strength and homogeneity of the Mormon culture. The Mormon's vital center contains about 40 percent of the total Mormon population in the United States. The domain refers to an area markedly less intense and complex than the core. Here the bonds of culture are fewer and more tenuous, and regional peculiarities are clearly evident. By 1952, the domain had about 28 percent of the total Mormon population but has declined gradually since. The core and domain areas make up about 90 percent of the Mormon population. The sphere denotes the zone of outer influence of the Mormon cultural region. It is an area of peripheral nuclear groups within gentile country, or where they are of long-standing local numerical significance.

Anti-Semitic and antiblack attitudes among many Mormons led them to very conservative positions on civil rights and welfare policy. Their view of women made them active opponents of the ERA. Today, their conservatism reflects the defensive posture of a minority faith. They support policy that they feel will benefit them as a group and oppose any policy that they believe threatens them as a group.

The tendency toward schism has continued within the Mormon movement. A Levite Sect, known as the Aaronic Order, emerged during the 1930s and was formally organized in 1940. It was considered a "revitalization" movement by its followers.

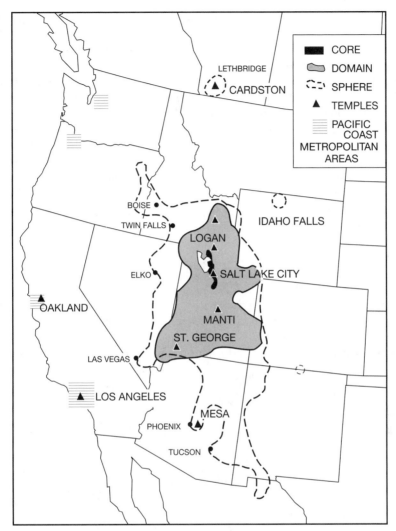

FIGURE 5.3 The Mormon Cultural Region

SOURCE: D. W. Meinig, "The Mormon Cultural Region," *Annals of the Association of American Geographers* 55, 2 (June 1965): 214.

They established several communal settlements: one in Alton, Utah, near Bryce Canyon National Park; the Alpha Colony and sawmill business near Springville, Utah; Partoun, the first in western Utah as a desert community; and Eskdale, their largest and most successful Levite desert community, established in 1955 and still surviving today. The Aaronic Order has a high priesthood and maintains the integrity of polygamist marriages. They have virtually complete endogamy, allowing only a few "out marriages" to other Mormons. They are similar to the Amish and Mennonites in that they wear distinctive garb or "uniforms," even to using a woman's cap modeled after the Mennonite cap.[3]

Since that split the main Mormon church has become increasingly assimilated. A 1980s study of various religious denominations in the United States found that on matters pertaining to racial justice and civil liberties the Mormons, contrary to their racist and conservative image of the 1960s, were closer to liberal mainline denominations, such as Episcopalians, Presbyterians, and even the very liberal Unitarians, than they were to conservative fundamentalist denominations such as Baptists, Methodists, and the various Evangelicals/Fundamentalists. On lifestyle matters (abortion, extramarital and premarital sex, divorce, women's rights, etc.), however, the Mormons joined the Baptists, Assemblies of God, and other fundamentalist denominations on the conservative side. Case Study 5.1, at the end of this chapter, discusses the church to present times, demonstrating its cohesiveness but also its increasingly "mainline church" status.

NATIVE AMERICANS

The 1990 census recorded 1.5 million Native Americans, about 40 percent of whom live off reservations in the nation's cities. Despite some $3 billion a year in federal aid, they have the lowest income and education levels and the worst housing and health conditions of any minority group in the nation. They are truly the poorest of the poor. They have the dubious distinction of topping the nation in unemployment. Native American children are the most poorly prepared students in the nation, exhibit the highest dropout rates, the lowest test scores, and the worst alcoholism and suicide rates of any student group.

Like black Americans, they represent a racial case that is unique in some respects. Despite their being the only truly native population in the nation, they were not legally declared citizens with the right to vote until 1924. They are the only minority group legally segregated into reservations. They are the only minority that suffered from an avowed policy of annihilation. No other minority in the country's history has the unfortunate distinction of having experienced actual genocide.

National policy toward the Native American has taken many approaches over the years. Those policy shifts have ranged from avowed friendship, recognizing their independence to expulsion and to genocide, forced geographic segregation, and forced acculturation through termination, to attempts to allow for cultural pluralism. In the process of these policy shifts, hundreds of treaties were made and broken. Indian affairs have been shifted and parceled out among various agencies housed within several departments of the federal government.

The decimation of the Indian population because of contact with European whites, whether intentional or not, is well established. At the time of the first European settlement of the North American continent, the number of Indians residing in that territory has been estimated at 1 to 10 million. Those residing in what is now the United States numbered about 1.5 million. By 1800, their population had fallen to around 600,000. By 1850, the ravages of malnutrition and disease, coupled with the policies of expulsion and genocide, had reduced the Native American population to around 250,000. Their population has climbed upward from that low point of 1850, reaching just over 2,386,000 today.

Native Americans were initially treated as sovereign nations, and despite some violent clashes between white colonists and the tribes, official government policy was peaceful. Native American tribes had treaty relations with Spain, France, and England. British policy was to protect them. When the American Revolution commenced, both sides attempted to win over and use friendship and alliance with the tribes through treaties.

After the war, the new government followed the British tradition and continued an avowed policy of "friendship" based on treaties with independent nations. But just as the British could not stop the colonies from developing their own relations with the Indians, the new federal government could not stop the states from making their own treaties with the tribes, despite the fact that the federal government was supposed to have sole jurisdiction over trade and treaty relations with Native American tribes. In any event, although supposedly friendly, most of the treaties resulted in the taking of Indian lands by white settlers. From 1778, when the first treaty was signed, until 1871, when the United States officially stopped recognizing Native American tribes as independent nations, 389 treaties were ratified. In a sense, all were broken. The Northwest Ordinance, passed in 1787, promised the Indians that their lands could not be taken without consent, except in case a war was declared by Congress. Since no war was ever really declared, the numerous conflicts with Indians that resulted in whites seizing their lands were illegal.

Henry Knox, Washington's secretary of war, was the first government official to speak of assimilating the Native Americans. Knox felt the best way to do this was to introduce them to the concept and custom of private property. President Washington spoke to a delegation of Indians about learning the white man's ways of farming and raising stock. Even when the official policy considered the tribes as independent nations, the idea of assimilation and acculturation, whether benign or forced, was begun. The friendly policy did not last long.

> The tribesmen presented the federal government with a cruel dilemma. On the one hand, responsible officials wanted to maintain peace; on the other hand, they wanted to satisfy the host of westward-moving land seekers. Unfortunately, any policy likely to satisfy the Indians outraged the pioneers. As a result the government seemed to follow conflicting and contradictory practices; but in reality the policy changed little. (Dinnerstein, Reimers, and Nichols 1990: 36)

By the early 1800s, problems with Native American tribes had become acute, especially in the South. While technically the Indians could choose either to take a portion of land and farm as did the whites or move west, in reality few were given any choice, as greedy miners, lumbermen, and farmers pushed them aside. Federal officials soon began to demand that they migrate.

Policy seemed to vacillate for a time. Under Presidents Jefferson and Madison, a policy of removal was begun. In 1804, a provision was included in the Louisiana Territory Act for the exchange of lands; Indians were to be moved west of the Mississippi River. In 1809, 100 million acres were "appropriated" through some 15 treaties by which William Harris, then governor of the Indiana Territory, received lands purchased from the Indians at one cent per acre. The Indians agreed to these treaties under the threat of force.

In 1815, Congress established the Indian Civilization Fund to educate Native Americans. Between 1783 and 1815, some tribes learned English, and Euro-style farming and business. The Cherokee tribe of North Carolina became bicultural. They were literate, articulate, and fully bilingual. By the mid-1820s, they owned 22,000 cattle, 1,300 slaves, 31 grist mills, 10 saw mills, and 8 cotton gins. They ran 18 schools and published the *Cherokee Phoenix,* a bilingual newspaper. Most Native Americans, however, retained their allegiance to tradition and refused to acculturate.

After the War of 1812, relations began to deteriorate. As the threat of British intervention faded, the federal government felt less need to conciliate Indian tribes. White settlers kept pushing westward and desired Indian lands. The government was forced to oblige them. A removal policy was formally adopted, although between 1816 and 1848 the pretense of "Independent Nations" continued. An Indian removal policy was first officially adopted by President James Monroe in 1825. Federal officials envisioned Indian territories and states in the far west. Apparently no one at the time anticipated the spectacular speed with which white settlers pushed beyond the Mississippi. The rapidly advancing frontier prevented any chance of the removal policy actually succeeding. President Andrew Jackson wholeheartedly approved of the policy of removal, although he felt it "absurd" to continue to deal with the Indians as independent nations. In 1830, Jackson pushed passage of the Indian Removal Act, which provided $300,000 for "an exchange of lands, compensation for improvements, and aid in the removal and initial adjustment to their new homes." Most often, force was used.

Even those who went "voluntarily" suffered greatly in the migration. White officials oversaw the transportation and resettlement of the Indians in their new lands west of the Mississippi. Exploitation was common. Contractors supplying transportation and food bought condemned meat and spoiled flour to feed their charges. For transportation, they rented cheap and untrustworthy boats to get the Indians across major rivers, sometimes with fatal results. One steamboat crossing the Mississippi River sank, drowning 311 Indians. Nearly 4,000 of the 15,000 Cherokee who started west at gunpoint died on what the Indians called the Trail of Tears or during the first few months in what is now Oklahoma.

The Cherokee, being the most acculturated of the tribes, sought legal redress. They appealed to the U.S. Supreme Court. In *Cherokee Nation* v. *Georgia* (1831) and *Worcester* v. *Georgia* (1832), the Court ruled in favor of the Indians. President Jackson simply ignored the ruling, allegedly remarking, "John Marshall has made his decision. Now let him enforce it." In the *Worcester* case, the Court referred to the Indians as "Wards of Washington," which later became the basis for the approach of the Bureau of Indian Affairs. The refusal by Jackson to comply with the Court's ruling dashed hopes for a peaceful and legal resolution to the conflict.

Sometimes geographic separatism is forced upon a racial minority. Such is the case of the Native American on reservations. For American society, they constitute the best example of internal colonialism. In the words of General William Sherman, the typical reservation was "a parcel of land set aside for Indians, surrounded by thieves."[4]

BOX 5.2:   Federal Laws Regulating Indian Affairs

INDIAN REMOVAL ACT (4 U.S. STATUTE 411; MAY 28, 1830)

The president was authorized to trade lands belonging to the United States and west of the Mississippi for lands in the east where Native Americans resided. The president was empowered to compensate Native Americans for any improvements they had made on their eastern lands and also for the costs of moving westward. The exchanges were to be "voluntary." The United States was to guarantee that the new lands would forever belong to the Native Americans. Congress appropriated $500,000 to implement the act.

ORGANIZATION OF DEPARTMENT OF INDIAN AFFAIRS (4 U.S. STATUTE 735; JUNE 30, 1834)

In 1824 the secretary of war, without congressional approval, set up a Bureau of Indian Affairs. This act formalized the organizational structure of the operations. The act designated areas for appointments of superintendents, agents, and sub-agents for Indian affairs. The secretary of war was authorized to distribute treaty funds and goods to Natives, and employees of the Indians Affairs Department were prohibited from having a personal interest in any trading with the Native Americans. In 1849 (9 U.S. Statute 395; March 3, 1849) the functions of the Indian Affairs Department were transferred from the War Department to the newly established Interior Department.

SOURCE: William Thompson, *Native-American Issues* (Santa Barbara, CA: ABC-CLIO, 1996), p. 148.

The Bureau of Indian Affairs was established by the U.S. Congress in 1824, charged with administering all relations with Native Americans. The first reservation was created in 1830 in the Oklahoma territory (see Box 5.2). Between then and 1880, numerous others were established, mostly in Oklahoma, Arizona, and New Mexico. In all cases they were removed "from the path of progress," that is, out of the way of white settlers. They were closely supervised and controlled by the federal government. Lands set aside for reservation were routinely selected as sites judged to have no value or economic potential in the future. They were on barren land well off the main routes of travel west and useless for settlement or agricultural purposes, worthless for farming, and even marginal for ranching. Most had no visible natural resources.

The reservation program was designed to strip Native Americans of their dignity, of any means of supporting themselves, and of their traditional way of life and culture. They were kept powerless and totally dependent on the government for their sustenance. During the administration of President Grant, Congress created a Board of Indian Commissioners under the secretary of the interior. Relations with the tribes shifted legally from "treaties" to "agreements," symbolically reducing the status of Native Americans. Reservation programs accelerated in numbers, yet reduced their lands considerably. In the late 1860s and throughout the 1870s tribes across the nation, from the Dakotas to New Mexico, up to Puget Sound, resisted in a series of wars. Cynical soldiers referred to this policy as "feed 'em in the winter, and fight 'em in the summer."

The reservation system formed the basis of the relationship between Native Americans and the federal government from the 1830s to the present day. In many ways, the reservation program is an ironic misnomer. Far from "reserving" land, it directly led to their loss of land, in millions of acres. In 1879 a policy of **forced assimilation** began. Then Secretary of Interior Carl Schurz outlined his goals in relation to Native Americans: To help them become self-supporting and break them of their "savage ways," he would turn them into farmers. Forced education would introduce the next generation to "civilized" ideas and aspirations. Individuals would get title to their farms, fostering pride of ownership rather than tribal dependence. Once individual allotments had been made, the remaining tribal lands would be sold, the proceeds of which would be set aside to meet future Indian needs, thereby reducing the federal government's obligation to support them. When all this was done, Native Americans would, he concluded, be treated like everyone else. In short, they were to be forcibly assimilated.

From 1887, with the enactment of the General Allotment Act (better known as the Dawes Act), to 1934, when Congress enacted the Indian Reorganization Act (often called the Wheeler-Howard Act), native lands decreased from 138 million acres to 90 million acres (see Box 5.3). Between 1871 and 1983, Native American tribal

---

BOX 5.3: Reservation Policy: Congress and the Supreme Court

GENERAL ALLOTMENT ACT (24 U.S. STATUTE 388; FEBRUARY 8, 1887)

Congress mandated surveys to be taken of Native lands. The president was authorized to divide the lands that could be farmed into parcels that could be distributed to individual Native Americans and their families. The parcels would then be held as private lands, which after 25 years could be sold to non-Natives. In the meantime, the parcels could be leased. Excess lands, left over after each Native family was given its "share," were sold by the government with the proceeds going to members of the tribe. Between 1887 and 1934, more than two-thirds of Native lands were allotted and lost to the tribes. This amounted to over 90,000,000 acres. The act did not apply to the tribes of Indian Territory (Oklahoma). The purpose of the act was to assimilate Natives into the land-owning farming population. Citizenship rights were given to Native Americans making the desired transition to self-sufficiency. The act was modified with several amendments. In 1891, for instance, lands were permitted to be sold before 25 years lapsed (26 U.S. Statute 794; February 28, 1891).

LONE WOLF V. *HITCHCOCK*, 187 U.S. 553 (1903)

The 1867 Treaty of Medicine Lodge stipulated that the lands of the Kiowa Commanche reservation could not be reduced without a three-fourths approval vote of the adult males. However, under the Dawes Act, lands were allotted to individual tribal members, and excess lands were placed up for sale to outsiders. The tribe charged that the treaty had been violated. The Supreme Court disagreed. The justices held that Congress had "plenary authority over the tribal relations . . . from the beginning, and the power has always been deemed a political one, not subject to be controlled by the (courts)." Included in the power is "the power to abrogate the provisions of an Indian treaty."

SOURCE: William Thompson, *Native-American Issues* (Santa Barbara, CA: ABC-CLIO, 1996), pp. 138, 150.

lands declined from over 120 million acres to just over 52 million acres, a reduction of more than 60 percent. Today, tribal lands are located within 35 states and total just over 56 million acres (see Tables 5.2 and 5.3).

Forced assimilation involved more than turning them into farmers. Native American religions came under attack as well. Using "Bibles, not bullets," religious practices were undermined by Christian missionary groups. Specific reservations were assigned to the various denominations so they would not have to compete; they also gained access to a captive audience teeming with potential converts. Indian reservation schools were established at which native languages and cultures were forbidden. The founder of the Carlisle Indian Industrial School in Pennsylvania observed that the school "has always planted treason to the tribe and loyalty to the nation at large." Its philosophy was to "kill the Indian to save the man."

Strict regulations, the use of school uniforms, and marching in formation were intended to move the youth from the desolation of the reservation to assimilation with the national culture. By separating them from their native roots, transporting them hundreds, even thousands, of miles away to distant schools in the East, many children of even grade-school ages were forced to assimilate. Reservation Indians were wards of the government in all aspects of life, controlled by the government. Today, some half-million Native Americans live on 314 reservations, where massive and persistent unemployment keeps the population in a state of dependency. Unemployment figures for reservations run three times the national average, from 23 to 90 percent.

An unanticipated consequence of the residential schools was the intermingling of children of diverse tribes who then developed a camaraderie from being thrown together into such a scary, alien environment. When they became adults, their friendships sometimes blossomed into marriages, intertribal visits, and political alliances.

TABLE 5.2   Tribal Lands in the United States, 1871–1983

Year	Tribal Lands (Acres)	Total Acres
1871	111,761,558	121,993,283
1881	139,006,794	155,632,312
1887	119,375,930	136,394,895
1890	86,540,824	77,865,373
1900	52,455,827	72,535,862
1920	35,501,661	72,660,316
1933	29,481,685	47,311,099
1945	37,288,768	54,646,308
1953	42,785,935	50,577,234
1962	38,814,074	50,577,234
1974	40,772,934	51,017,415
1983	42,385,031	52,611,211

NOTE: Tribal lands are common lands held in trust for tribes; total acres include allotted lands within boundaries of reservations but are privately owned by individuals who may or may not be tribal members.

SOURCE: Bureau of Indian Affairs, *Annual Reports of Indian Lands* (Washington, DC: U.S. Government Printing Office, 1983).

TABLE 5.3   Tribal Lands Under Jurisdiction of the Bureau of Indian Affairs, 1996

Acreage Recapitulation by State	Tribal	Individually Owned	Total Trust	Government Owned	Total
Alabama	2,933.75	0.00	2,933.75	0.00	2,933.75
Alaska	83,879.83	1,056,530.13	1,140,409.96	0.00	1,140,409.96
Arizona	20,370,974.73	256,765.64	20,627,740.37	90,466.48	20,718,206.85
California	520,327.86	71,555.66	591,883.52	152.74	592,036.26
Colorado	797,594.51	2,699.68	800,294.19	12.24	800,306.43
Connecticut	5,028.10	0.00	5,028.10	980.00	6,008.10
Florida	165,267.39	0.00	165,267.39	189,333.30	354,600.69
Idaho	450,269.87	270,841.57	721,111.44	32,631.88	753,743.32
Iowa	7,270.99	0.00	7,270.99	5.00	7,275.99
Kansas	10,840.72	23,335.02	34,175.74	36.00	34,211.74
Louisiana	2,527.77	0.00	2,527.77	0.00	2,527.77
Maine	265,234.00	0.00	265,234.00	0.00	265,234.00
Massachusetts	467.30	0.00	467.30	0.00	467.30
Michigan	15,898.24	9,268.55	25,166.79	0.00	25,166.79
Minnesota	975,714.76	50,217.61	1,025,932.37	88.05	1,026,020.42
Mississippi	22,772.07	0.00	22,772.07	82.50	22,854.57
Missouri	0.00	374.37	374.37	0.00	374.37
Montana	2,534,379.10	2,850,445.40	5,384,824.50	94,535.96	5,479,360.46
Nebraska	23,174.00	43,288.37	66,462,37	6.79	66,469.16
Nevada	1,149,492.08	78,528.56	1,228,020.64	4,978.71	1,232,999.35
New Mexico	7,500,567.57	668,839.71	8,169,407.28	179,739.96	8,349,147.24
New York	53,188.40	0.00	53,188.40	35,341.00	$88,529.40
North Carolina	51,166.11	0.00	51,166.11	112.16	51,278.27
North Dakota	245,629.60	619,337.66	864,967.26	1,927.71	866,894.97
Oklahoma	104,290.72	957,204.51	1,061,495.23	849.88	1,062,345.11
Oregon	666,106.28	130,465.87	796,572.15	16.24	796,588.39
Rhode Island	2,335.25	0.00	2,335.25	0.00	2,335.25
South Carolina	720.00	0.00	720.00	0.00	720.00
South Dakota	2,617,894.54	2,381,515.92	4,999,410.46	2,645.45	5,002,005.91
Tennessee	168.04	0.00	168.04	0.00	168.04
Texas	5,250.33	0.00	5,250.33	0.00	5,250.33
Utah	2,297,770.10	33,236.69	2,331,006.79	87.45	2,331,094.24
Washington	2,170,345.68	431,748.36	2,602,094.04	160.08	2,602,254.12
Wisconsin	352,515.39	82,969.23	435,484.62	335.65	435,820.27
Wyoming	1,794,589.22	93,646.98	1,888,236.20	1,296.15	1,889,532.35
Total	45,266,584.28	10,112,815.49	55,379,399.77	635,821.38	56,015,221.15

SOURCE: U.S. Department of the Interior (http://www.doi.gov/bia/realty/state.html).

Ironically, "The phenomenon later called **Pan-Indianism**, a sense of shared identity that transcended tribal boundaries, arose at least partly from these schools—the very institutions designed to erase the idea of "Indianness" from modern American life" (Marger 1997: 344).

The reservations evolved as well. Beginning as little more than outdoor prisons or holding pens that were administered by heavy-handed agents controlling barren and isolated acreage to which unwilling groups of people had been banished, they were gradually developed into tribal lands with self-governing bodies. The numbers of Native Americans also began to rebound. In 1890, their population in the United States was just over 270,000. By the 1990 census it had exceeded 2 million (just under 1 percent of the total population). Between 1980 and 1990, Native Americans became the fastest growing sector of the U.S. population, registering an increase of 72.4 percent.

The Indian Reorganization Act of 1934 required that persons living on the Native American **trust lands** (i.e., reservations) have at least one-half Native American bloodline. As of 1997, their growth rate has been more than double that of the white rate, at 15.4 per 1,000 versus 6.3 per 1,000. Their median age is much younger than the national average (26 years versus 33 years for the population generally), so a higher birth rate is likely to continue for the foreseeable future.

Currently at over 56 million acres and representing about 2.5 percent of the total U.S. land base, the reservations are home to about 42 percent of the total Native American population. Within the 48 contiguous states there are 325 tribal nations with trust lands, and Alaska has more than 200 Native American communities, and over 100 others are seeking official recognition. They speak about 100 recognized tribal languages. Conditions on the reservation are still well below the standards for the nation as a whole. As of 1997, over 27 percent of Native American families living on reservations were below the poverty level. Nationally, 23 percent of reservation housing, which was three times the national level, lacked complete plumbing facilities, and 49 percent of those on the Navajo reservation, one of the nation's largest, lacked plumbing facilities. Native American family income level hovers at 35 to 40 percent below that of the general population. In 1990, Native American median family income was $21,619, compared to the national average for the total population at $39,066. Their formal education is far below average: in 1997, the percentage of Native Americans who had completed high school was 65.6 percent, compared to 77.6 percent for the total population; and the percentage with college degrees was 9.4 versus the 24.6 percent of the white population.

Native American assimilation and a greater acceptance and tolerance of them were influenced by war. When the United States entered World War I in 1917, Congress passed the Selective Service Act. Many American Indians joined the armed services despite the fact that as non-citizens they were deferred from the draft. By war's end, some 17,000 had enlisted, close to 30 percent of adult Indian males and double the national average. Congress gave citizenship to honorably discharged Indian veterans in 1919 and, finally, universal Indian citizenship in 1924. In World War II, likewise, their rate of service exceeded the national average. As citizens they were eligible for the draft. By 1945, over 25,000 Native American men and 1,000 women had served, with some tribes sending as many as 70 percent of their men between the ages of 18 and 50 (Thompson 1996). Box 5.4 highlights their special contribution as **code-talkers**. Nearly twice as many as those who donned uniforms, some 46,000, served the war effort by leaving their tribal homelands to work in war-related industry jobs, including 12,000 Indian women who took off-reservation jobs. For many of them, it was the first time they had seen a city or experienced life off-reservation as a member of a minority group.

BOX 5.4:   The Unbreakable Code

The U.S. Marine Corps had a secret weapon against Japan in World War II: the 420 Navajo code talkers who fought all the way from Guadalcanal to Okinawa. Using a blend of everyday Navajo speech and some 400 specially devised code words, they transmitted messages that completely baffled the enemy. Bombers were *jaysho* ("buzzards"); bombs, *ayeshi* ("eggs"); battleship was *lotso* ("whale"); destroyer, *calo* ("shark"); submarine, *beshlo* ("iron fish"). In a coded alphabet the Navajo word for "ant" was the letter *A,* the word for "bear" was *B,* and so on; thus, a place such as Bloody Ridge was spelled out with the Navajo words for Bear, Lamb, Onion, Dog, Yucca, Rabbit, Ice, Dog, Goat, and Elk. In keeping with a language that was rarely written, there was no code book. Until trained, even new Navajo recruits could not break encrypted messages.

Initially skeptical about the unconventional code, Marine officers finally had to acknowledge its effectiveness. "Without the Navajos," said one, "the Marines would never have taken Iwo Jima." In addition to the Navajo, there were Hopi, Lakota, Sauk and Fox, Oneida, Chippewa, and Comanche code talkers in Europe and the Pacific.

SOURCE: *Through Indian Eyes* (Pleasantville, NY: Reader's Digest, 1995), p. 358. Copyright © 1995 by the Reader's Digest Association, Inc.

As with the Indian school programs, an unanticipated consequence of the World War II experience was the development of Pan-Indianism. In 1944, the National Congress of American Indians was founded in Denver, Colorado. It began lobbying in Washington, D.C., adopting tactics similar to those of the NAACP. It was instrumental in the enactment of the Indian Claims Commission law and in convincing the Bureau of Indian Affairs to abandon the practice of treating Native Americans as wards of the state.

In 1946, Congress created the Indian Claims Commission to settle grievances, including treaty disputes, conflicts over Indian trust funds, and unresolved land claims, some dating back to colonial times. Originally the three-member commission was to work for five years, but so many claims were filed that Congress expanded it to a five-member commission, and it operated until 1978, with hundreds of complex cases still unresolved. For a summary of these laws, see Box 5.5.

In 1952, the Bureau of Indian Affairs (BIA) began programs designed to assist Native Americans in relocating off-reservation. The 1962 Employment Assistance Program, for example, set up job assistance centers in a dozen major metropolitan areas, and by 1968, over 100,000 Native Americans had participated; over 200,000 had moved to urban areas, although about one-fourth of those returned to their reservations. One effect was to create a "brain drain" problem for reservations.

Also in the 1950s, the Eisenhower Administration adopted the policy of *termination* (see Box 5.5). This policy remained in effect until it was halted by the Indian Self-Determination and Education Assistance Act of 1975, but by then, 109 tribes were dissolved.

BOX 5.5:   Major U.S. Statutes Regarding Native Americans, 1946–1990

INDIAN CLAIMS COMMISSION ACT (60 U.S. STATUTE 1049; AUGUST 13, 1946)

This act was passed because Congress was being besieged with requests to settle claims for lands wrongfully taken from tribes. Congress set up a commission that met until 1978. Native American tribes having claims settled by the commission could not raise the issues again. Claims could be settled only for financial compensation for the value of lands when they were wrongfully taken. The commission could not order the return of the lands. For this reason many tribes decided not to present claims to the commission. The act also provided funds for expert witnesses to be used by the tribes and allowed tribal attorneys to be paid on a contingency basis.

TERMINATION RESOLUTION (HOUSE CONCURRENT RESOLUTION 108; 67 U.S. STATUTE B132; AUGUST 1, 1953)

The wording of the Termination Resolution is as follows: "It is declared to be the sense of Congress that, at the earliest time, all of the Indian tribes and the individual members thereof located within the state of California, Florida, New York, and Texas, and all the following named Indian tribes . . . should be freed from federal supervision and control and from all disabilities and limitations specifically applicable to Indians. (For these tribes) offices of the Bureau of Indian Affairs . . . should be abolished . . . Whereas it is the policy of Congress as rapidly as possible, to make the Indians . . . subject to the same laws and entitled to the same privileges and responsibilities as are applicable to other citizens . . . to end their status as wards. . . ."

PUBLIC LAW 280 (67 U.S. STATUTE 588; AUGUST 15, 1953)

This act of Congress gave several states jurisdiction over offenses committed on Native lands. States included California, Nebraska, Minnesota (except Red Lake reservation), Oregon (except Warm Springs reservation), and Wisconsin (except Menominee reservation). Other states could later request the jurisdiction. States also acquired some civil jurisdiction over disputes upon Native lands. However, they were not given regulatory authority nor taxation authority over the Native lands. The Indian Civil Rights Act of 1968 allowed states to withdraw this authority and required that tribes give approval before new states take over the authority.

THE INDIAN CIVIL RIGHTS ACT OF 1968 (87 U.S. STATUTE 77; APRIL 11, 1968) (TITLES II–VIII OF THE 1968 CIVIL RIGHTS ACT)

The Bill of Rights and the Fourteenth Amendment offered protections against the actions of the federal government and the state governments. This act filled a gap by giving individuals civil rights protections against tribal government actions, particularly actions by tribal judicial systems. Included in the protections were: the free expression of religion, freedom of speech, the right to a speedy trial, the right to confront witnesses, and the ability to seek habeas corpus remedies. The act also prohibited illegal searches, excessive bail, cruel and unusual punishments, bills of attainder, ex post facto laws, and self-incrimination.

ALASKA NATIVE CLAIMS SETTLEMENT ACT (85 U.S. STATUTE 688; DECEMBER 18, 1971)

Congress found that "there is an immediate need for fair and just settlement of all claims by Native groups of Alaska." The act provided for the enrollment of Natives and their organization into 12 regional corporations. United States citizens with one-quarter or more Alaskan Native blood were qualified to be enrolled. Each of the corporations was divided into villages (200 in all), which were given grants of lands. Forty million acres were distributed to the villages. The lands were not placed into trust. The regional corporations were collectively given $962,500,000, which in turn was distributed to members as stock shares. The moneys came from the U.S. treasury and from future revenues from Alaskan oil deposits. This amount was four times the total given all tribes in the 32-year period of the Indian Claims Commission. In 1988 the act was amended to increase individual control over their share of the settlement (101 U.S. Statute 1788; February 3, 1988).

continued

INDIAN FINANCING ACT (88 U.S. STATUTE 77; APRIL 12, 1974)

This act extends the authority of the Indian Reorganization Act by increasing funding of a revolving loan fund for Native American business ventures and also establishing a program for business grants. Such financial help is necessitated by the reluctance of banks to give loans to tribal businesses that could not be collateralized with lands and buildings held in trust by the federal government.

INDIAN SELF DETERMINATION AND EDUCATION ASSISTANCE ACT (88 U.S. STATUTE 2203; JANUARY 4, 1975)

Tribal organizations were authorized to enter into contracts with federal agencies to directly administer educational and other service programs on reservations. Grants were authorized for tribes so that they could operate school and health programs. Funds could be given to public schools for education of Native American children only if they demonstrated that they had "objectives that adequately addressed the educational needs" of the students. Also the Native American parents had to be given a voice on school boards that accepted such grants. The program was enlarged with the Tribally Controlled Schools Act of 1988 (Public Law 102-385; April 28, 1988). Also in 1978 Congress passed an act to give grants to Native community colleges (Tribally Controlled Community College Assistance Act, Public Law 92-1325 [October 17, 1978]).

INDIAN HEALTH CARE IMPROVEMENT ACT (90 U.S. STATUTE 1400; SEPTEMBER 30, 1976)

This act seeks to improve Native American health by encouraging Native Americans to seek education and training in the health professions. The act also increases funding for Native health facilities and for water and sanitary waste facilities. The act also encourages the establishment of health services for urban Natives and authorizes a feasibility study for the creation of a Native American School of Medicine.

AMERICAN INDIAN RELIGIOUS FREEDOM ACT (92 U.S. STATUTE 469; AUGUST 11, 1978)

This "act" was really a joint resolution of both houses of Congress. The resolution proclaims a policy "to protect and preserve" the "inherent right (of Native Americans) to freedom to believe, express, and exercise the traditional religions . . . including but not limited to access to sites, use and possession of sacred objects, and the freedom to worship through ceremonials and traditions." The president was directed to inform all federal agencies of the resolution and require that they adjust any of their policies adverse to it. In 1994 Congress amended the "act" to provide that Native Americans could use peyote in traditional ceremonies without fear of enforcement of state or federal drug laws (108 U.S. Statute 3125; October 6, 1994).

INDIAN CHILD WELFARE ACT (92 U.S. STATUTE 3069; NOVEMBER 8, 1978)

Many Native American children were being placed up for adoption in white homes. This practice was considered to be very destructive of Native cultures. The act seeks the "best interests" of children by promoting the stability of Native family ties. Standards are set for adoptions, and preference is first given to adoptions within the child's extended family, then within the tribe, and next to Native foster homes.

THE INDIAN GAMING REGULATORY ACT (102 U.S. STATUTE 2467; OCTOBER 17, 1988)

The act provides a mechanism for regulating gambling on Native American lands. A tribe may pass an ordinance and have a form of gambling if that form is permitted for any purpose by any organization by a state. There are three classes of gambling under the act. Class one includes traditional Native games with low-stakes prizes. These games are regulated exclusively by the tribes offering the games. Class two includes bingo, pull tabs, and nonbanked card games (those contested among players only). These games are initially regulated by a National Indian Gaming Commission (NIGC). Later the tribes may be certified to self-regulate the games. Class three games include most casino games, race betting, and lotteries. These games are regulated in accordance with agreements negotiated by tribes and state governments. If states refuse to negotiate, the tribes may sue the states in federal court to force negotiations. In 1996 this provision was ruled unconstitutional. The NIGC approves contracts between tribes and management companies. The commission has three members, two of whom must be Native Americans.

NATIONAL MUSEUM OF THE AMERICAN INDIAN ACT (103 U.S. STATUTE 1336; NOVEMBER 28, 1989)

Congress established within the Smithsonian Institution a "living memorial to Native Americans and

continued

their traditions . . . known as the National Museum of the American Indian." In addition to collecting and preserving Native American objects, the museum will provide for research and study programs. A facility is being constructed on the National Mall at Independence and Fourth Street, S.W., in the District of Columbia. The federal government will pay two-thirds of the building costs, private donors one-third.

NATIVE AMERICAN LANGUAGES ACT (104 U.S. STATUTE 1153; OCTOBER 30, 1990)

This act recognizes traditional languages as integral parts of Native American cultures. The policy of the United States is to preserve rights of Native Americans to use and develop languages. Use of the languages is encouraged in Native American educational programs both as an object for study and as a medium for study. The use of Native languages shall not be restricted in any public proceedings.

NATIVE AMERICAN GRAVES PROTECTION AND REPATRIATION ACT (104 U.S. STATUTE 3048; NOVEMBER 16, 1990)

This act seeks to protect Native American grave sites and human remains. All Native American cultural items excavated on public lands are to be the property of the appropriate tribal organization. Trafficking in such human remains and cultural items becomes a federal offense. In addition, all museums holding such objects or remains must make an inventory of them, and tribes from which the items came shall be entitled to have them returned upon request.

INDIAN CHILD PROTECTION AND FAMILY ABUSE PREVENTION ACT (104 U.S. STATUTE 4544; NOVEMBER 28, 1990)

This act recognizes the growing problem of family violence. Reports of abused Native children are to be made to appropriate authorities. A central registry of cases is established. The act creates grants so that the tribes may set up counseling and treatment programs. Each office of the Bureau of Indian Affairs is authorized to set up an Indian Child Resource and Family Service Center.

SOURCE: William Thompson, *Native-American Issues* (Santa Barbara, CA: ABC-CLIO, 1996), pp. 152–157.

The increased urbanization of the Native American population contributed to the Pan-Indian movement with such developments as the National Indian Youth Council (NIYC), the American Indian Movement (AIM), and the Council of Energy Resource Tribes (CERT).

The 1970s witnessed a spate of national legislative victories won by Native Americans. During the Nixon Administration, two major laws were enacted: the Indian Education Act of 1972 and the Indian Financing Act of 1974. The Indian Self-Determination and Educational Assistance Act of 1975 was passed during the Carter Administration. In 1978, Congress enacted the American Indian Religious Freedom Act, the Tribally Controlled Community College Assistance Act, and the Indian Child Welfare Act. In 1979, it passed the Indian Archaeological Resources Protection Act (see Box 5.5). In 1988, Congress passed the Indian Gaming Regulatory Act, resulting in 97 tribes in 22 states operating more than 200 casinos.

Nearly 60 percent of the native population now lives off-reservation, with their political activism and success in courts and statutes increasing considerably. More will be said of those developments in Chapter 8. Urbanization also contributed to higher rates of assimilation, exemplified by the fact that by 1995 more than half of all Indians, both on- and off-reservation, were marrying non-Indians.

Today, the states with the highest Native American populations are California, Oklahoma, Arizona, New Mexico, Alaska, and Washington—each with 100,000. The metropolitan areas with the largest populations are, in rank order, Los Angeles–Anaheim–Riverside, Tulsa, New York, Oklahoma City, San Francisco, Phoenix, Seattle–Tacoma, Minneapolis–St. Paul, Tucson, and San Diego. Despite the large migration to urban areas, reservations are unlikely to disappear. On the contrary, some 100 tribal groups are seeking official recognition, so the number of reservations is likely to increase in the future.

BLACK NATIONALISM: MARCUS GARVEY AND "BACK TO AFRICA"

A portion of black Americans advocated a strategy of physical separatism. This chapter will focus on the most important such instance, the movement headed by Marcus Garvey, active in the United States during the 1920s.[5]

While Garveyism is a prototype case of **Black Nationalism**, he certainly was not the first to argue the case for physical separatism, nor for a back to Africa tactic. An earlier if lesser known case involved a free black Quaker from Philadelphia who was captain of a trade ship, the *Traveller*. Captain Paul Cuffe visited Sierre Leone in Africa in April 1811 to establish trade between the United States and Africa that did not involve the slave trade.

After that first trip, Captain Cuffe met with President James Madison, in May 1812, to discuss his plans to begin trade with the ultimate goal of enabling free blacks to return to Africa. President Madison, as did Thomas Jefferson, preferred a plan to remove blacks to Africa as a means of ending slavery in America. Cuffe declared that blacks "might rise to be a people in Africa, something they could not do in America" (Lamont:108). He helped found the African Institution of Philadelphia to promote such a plan, working mostly with the Quakers. He promoted Pan-Africanism. In 1816, the American Colonization Society began using him to promote racial separation in America, however, and he ceased promoting the plan. The black Quaker captain has been characterized as an early "voice from within the Veil," which was W.E.B. Du Bois's expression for oppressive white society.

A century later, Marcus Garvey's movement, the Universal Negro Improvement Association (UNIA), became the first mass movement among blacks in the United States, one that indeed had worldwide scope. As one of his biographers said: "Garvey's UNIA had collected more money and claimed a larger membership than any other Negro group either before or since" (Cronon 1969: 3).

Garvey was born in St. Ann's Bay, Jamaica, on August 17, 1887, the youngest of 11 children and descended from Maroons, African slaves who had successfully defied the Jamaican slave regime and set up virtually independent communities in the island's mountain regions from 1664 to 1765. In his teens he moved to Kingston and began work in a print shop where, at age 20, he became the youngest foreman printer at a time when British and Canadian immigrants usually held such jobs. He was elected union leader during a strike that failed, and he was then fired and blacklisted. This experience made him skeptical of the labor movement and of Socialism. He then began to work for a government printing office. It was during this period that he became increasingly aware of the injustices to blacks and began his opposition to British colonial rule.

In 1910, at age 23, he began publishing his first newspaper, *Garvey's Watchman,* a small weekly. Thus began a career in journalism that continued for most of his life. He went on to Costa Rica, where he started a second paper, *La Nacion,* and also worked for *The Bluefield Messenger.* After a brief stint he moved to Panama, where he began publishing *La Prensa.* He traveled throughout South America, observing the poor treatment of blacks everywhere.

Garvey migrated to Europe and settled for a brief time in London, where he met an Egyptian nationalist, Duse Mohammad Ali, who expanded his knowledge of black subjugation throughout the world and who introduced him to the work of Booker T. Washington and his autobiography, *Up from Slavery.* It had a profound impact upon Garvey, and he determined to become a race leader. In 1914, he returned to Jamaica where, on August 1, he formed an international black organization designed to establish an independent black state—the Universal Negro Improvement and Conservation Association and African Communities League (known simply as the UNIA). Its motto was: "One God! One Aim! One Destiny!" As one of his biographers noted:

> The specifically racial character of Garveyite nationalism was a reaction to centuries of slavery, colonialism, and capitalist exploitation. This process involved the brutal enslavement of African people, their loss of territory, their arbitrary dispersal throughout the new world, the suppression of language, culture and kinship patterns and their victimization under the inhuman conditions of plantation slavery and the pernicious stigma of racial inferiority. (Lewis 1988: 125)

In 1916, at age 28, Garvey visited the United States, a move that was to be the decisive factor in his political career. He visited Tuskegee to pay his respects to his by then dead hero, Booker T. Washington. He toured 38 states before settling in New York City, where he remained and worked, in Harlem, until 1927.

Initially, Garvey intended to raise funds in the United States and return to Jamaica and set up a school similar to Tuskegee. His oratorical skills attracted followers and attention. He faced immediate opposition from Harlem's black leadership, and he decided to remain in Harlem to build the UNIA chapter there. Within three weeks he claimed to have recruited 2,000 members, and by 1921, he estimated the worldwide membership of the UNIA at 6 million, though his figures have been much disputed and undoubtedly were inflated. In 1923, W.E.B. Du Bois stated that the UNIA had fewer than 20,000 members. Yet, by 1923, Garvey could reasonably claim to have many more members in the UNIA than all other Negro organizations combined.

In 1919, he began his weekly paper, *The Negro World,* the official organ of the UNIA. With a weekly circulation estimated as high as 200,000, it was his greatest propaganda device and by far his most successful publishing venture. It appeared in

English, French, and Spanish editions and lasted until 1933. It led to a new militancy in the Negro press during the 1920s.

In July 1919 Garvey bought a large auditorium in Harlem that he called Liberty Hall. It became the headquarters of the UNIA, and soon other branches opened their own Liberty Halls. These halls served multiple functions; Sunday morning worship, afternoon Sunday schools, public meetings at nights, and concerts and dances were held there. Notice boards were put up where one could look for a room, a job, or a lost article. In localities where there were many people out of work during the winter, Black Cross nurses would organize soup kitchens. On freezing winter days stoves were kept going to accommodate the cold and homeless until they "got on their feet again." In 1919–1920, Garvey's UNIA and related ventures experienced a period of remarkable growth. The peak of his influence was a 1920 UNIA worldwide convention held at Liberty Hall in Harlem.

Garvey began a number of ventures. The Negro Factories Corporation was established to build and operate factories in major urban areas in the United States, South and Central America, the West Indies, and Africa. It developed a chain of grocery stores, a restaurant, a tailor shop, a hotel, a printing press, a doll factory, and a steam laundry in Harlem that employed 300 people. The UNIA established a motor corp, an African Legion, and the Black Cross nurses. A long-term goal of these ventures, and especially of the Black Star Shipping Line and the Liberia scheme, was to advance the organization of the UNIA and to aid ultimately in the "repossession of Africa by Africans."

His most notable undertakings, and the ones that gave basis to his movement being referred to as the Back to Africa movement, were the Black Star Steamship Line and the Liberia scheme. Garvey's plan was to build an all-black steamship company that could link all the colored peoples of the world in commercial and industrial exchange. Begun in 1919, it was capitalized at one-half million dollars, with 100,000 shares selling for $5 each. The venture reflected Booker T. Washington's philosophy of blacks becoming independent of white capital. Its stock circulars appealed to racial pride.

Although connected to his Liberia scheme, the Black Star Line (BSL) was not for the purpose of mass transportation of blacks back to Africa but was a commercial venture to enhance justifiable racial pride and demonstrate black entrepreneurial and nautical skills. In promoting the BSL and the Negro Factories Corporation, Garvey made a clear statement on the "back-to-Africa" interpretation of his movement that his enemies on the right and left used to characterize the UNIA:

> It is a mistake to suppose that I want to take the Negroes to Africa. I believe that the American Negroes have helped to establish the North American civilization and, therefore, have a perfect right to live in the U.S. and to aspire to equality of opportunities and treatment. Each Negro can be a citizen of the nation in which he was born or that he has chosen. But I foresee the building of a great state in Africa which, featuring in the concert of the great nations, will make the Negro race as respectable as the others. . . . Cuban Negroes will be favored by the building of this African state because when this state exists they will be considered and respected as descendants of this powerful country which has enough strength to protect them. (Cited in Lewis 1988: 109; see also Cronon 1969)

His wife described the intention of the BSL enterprise:

> The main purpose of the formation and promotion of the Black Star Line was to acquire ships to trade between the units of the Race—in Africa, the U.S.A., the West Indies, and Central America, thereby building up an independent economy of business, industry, and commerce, and to transport our people on business and pleasure, without being given inferior accommodation or refusal of any sort of accommodation. (cited in White 1992: 86)

The 1920 UNIA convention, however, provided fodder for his critics to label his movement the "back to Africa movement" by electing Garvey the "provisional president of the African Republic."

It was in connection with the Liberia scheme that his movement came to be known in the international press as the Back to Africa movement. In 1920, 1923, and 1924 the UNIA sent delegations to conduct negotiations with the Liberian government, first to establish trade and commerce ventures, but ultimately to create a black nation in Africa that could become the base of a worldwide black nationalism. The UNIA convention created a nobility, the "Knights of the Nile," with honors such as the "Distinguished Service Order of Ethiopia," and they issued a "Declaration of the Rights of the Negro Peoples of the World," which demanded that "Negro" be spelled with a capital N and which condemned European imperialism in Africa and lynchings in America.

Garvey himself traveled extensively to promote the BSL and the UNIA, including visits to Cuba, Jamaica, Costa Rica, Panama, and British Honduras. In 1922, he went to Georgia to meet with Edward Young Clarke, the Imperial Kleagle of the revived Ku Klux Klan, in an attempt to elicit Klan support for the UNIA's African program. Despite their opposing perspectives, they shared a common belief in racial purity and racial separation. Garvey stated: "Whilst the Ku Klux Klan desires to make America absolutely a white man's country, the UNIA wants to make Africa absolutely a black man's country" (cited in White 1992: 88).

In the mid-1920s, the UNIA grew extensively. Returning veterans from World War I, in which some 400,000 blacks served in the U.S. armed forces, proved to be fertile grounds for his appeal to Black Nationalism and black pride.

Marcus Garvey as President General of the African Republic.

His Liberia scheme and his support for white segregationists such as the Ku Klux Klan and Mississippi Senator Theodore Bilbo, who actively opposed racial intermixing and also espoused the repatriation of black Americans to West Africa, demonstrated that in his zeal for black separatism, Marcus Garvey badly disregarded the sensibilities of the majority of American blacks. That misjudgment, and the repeated financial and legal difficulties of the BSL, which was economically unsound, led to his decline. The BSL's first ship, the S.S. *Yarmouth,* which became the S.S. *Frederick Douglass,* was never seaworthy and was in constant financial trouble. Purchased at an inflated price of $165,000, it was in need of constant repairs. Two other ships purchased by the line never realized a fraction of their purchase prices. The aptly named *Shadyside,* with less than five months of active service, cost the BSL $11,000 in operating losses. Likewise, the *Kanawha,* a steam yacht, was overpriced and operated briefly at a huge loss.

It was his promotion of the stock when the BSL's financial status was so clearly unable to match his promises that led to Garvey and three associates being arrested and charged with using the mails to defraud. His trial began in mid-May 1923, and he acted as his own lawyer, despite no law degree or legal training. His conceit and inexperience cost him dearly. Although the presiding judge gave him wide latitude and assistance in the conduct of the trial, he was found guilty and sentenced to five years in prison and a fine of $1,000.

Released on bond pending appeal, he continued his work with the UNIA, founded the Black Cross Navigation and Trading Company, and attempted to obtain permission from the Liberian government to establish a UNIA base there. The Firestone Rubber Company, which did extensive business in Liberia, put economic and political pressure on the Liberian government. The Liberian government changed its attitude toward Garvey and opposed his African colonization plan. In 1924, the federal government indicted him on perjury and income tax evasion charges as well. His 1925 appeal on the mail fraud conviction was rejected by the U.S. Circuit Court of Appeals, and he was sent to the federal penitentiary in Atlanta, where he remained from 1925 to 1927. His imprisonment earned him a martyr's image, but upon his release (with a presidential commutation of his sentence to time served), he was deported.

From 1927 to 1940 he tried to rebuild the UNIA, including developing new branches in Paris and London, where he set up an office in West Kensington. He held the 1929 UNIA convention in Kingston, Jamaica, but disputed with the American delegation when he refused to accept its demand to keep the headquarters in Harlem. His influence in the United States rapidly declined after that convention.

Marcus Garvey died on June 10, 1940, in West Kensington, England, at the age of 52, impoverished and without ever having set foot in Africa. Largely forgotten through the 1940s and 1950s, he was rediscovered in the 1960s, when a renewal of Black Nationalism inspired a reassessment. "Garvey's reputation as the outstanding father of Negro nationalism has grown in the years since his death" (Cronon 1969: 212).

Garvey promoted a zionist vision of Black Nationalism, an attempt to unite Negroes throughout the world. He, more than the black power theorists of the 1960s, deserves credit for the slogan "Black Is Beautiful." His significance was in demonstrating that a mass-membership organization of blacks was possible. He articulated the grievances of those blacks for whom the civil rights goals of desegregation and political rights were largely meaningless. The nationwide interest in the UNIA and its charismatic leader both aroused and reflected the disillusionment of blacks for whom "the promised land of the American city had turned into the squalid ghetto" (White 1992: 102). On a visit to Jamaica in 1965, Martin Luther King, Jr., perhaps best summed up the leadership role of Marcus Garvey when he stated:

> Marcus Garvey was the first man of color in the history of the United States to lead and develop a mass movement. He was the first man on a mass scale and level to give millions of Negroes a sense of dignity and destiny, and make the Negro feel he is somebody. You gave Marcus Garvey to the United States of America, and gave to millions of Negroes . . . a sense of personhood, a sense of manhood, a sense of somebodiness. (Cited in White 1992: 104; see also Sewell 1990)

SUMMARY

This chapter discussed the strategy of physical separatism employed by racial/ethnic minorities who reject the norms, values, and customs of the majority society and desire to be physically isolated. Such groups seek frontier or rural areas with low enough density of population that they can fill in the area as a substantial numerical group of settlers. Often it is the very rejection by the majority society that determines their adoption of the separatist strategy. The actions of the majority certainly reinforce their isolation. Sometimes the majority forces them, as in the case of Native Americans, into isolation. Physical separatism is a tactic and strategy followed by groups who are small in size, making isolation viable. They are often an ethnoreligious group.

This chapter reviewed the experiences of the Amish and Mennonites, Mormons, Native Americans, and that faction among African Americans who followed Marcus Garvey during the 1920s.

KEY TERMS

Anabaptists: "rebaptizers," a Protestant Reformation sect that developed in Switzerland in the sixteenth century.

Black Nationalism: a separatist ideology that projects a collectivist economy and the cultural and political independence of a black nation-state, similar to Jewish Zionism.

Celestial marriage: the practice of plural marriages (male polygamy) as a tenet of the Mormon church.

Code talkers: Native Americans who served in the U.S. armed forces during World War II and were communication specialists.

Forced assimilation: the use of law and formal government policy to deliberately suppress the culture of a minority group in order to force it to acculturate to the dominant society.

Mother colonies: the source colonies of the Amish and the Mennonites in America in Northkill and Lancaster, Pennsylvania.

Ordnung: the "understandings" that prescribe the do's and don'ts of Amish life; part of their method of social control.

Pan-Indianism: a sense of shared identity among Native Americans that transcends tribal boundaries; the movement to unify all "Indians" for common political action in dealing with the majority culture.

Trust lands: term referring to American Indian reservations.

REVIEW QUESTIONS

1. Discuss the periods of Amish immigration from Europe to the United States. How did their reasons for coming influence their separatist strategy?

2. What distinguishes the Old Order Amish from the New Order Amish?

3. What is the significance of *Wisconsin* vs. *Yoder* (1972)?

4. Discuss why the Mormon church/movement has splintered so often.

5. Compare and contrast the schism tendencies of the Amish and Mennonite communities with those of the Mormon community.

6. When, where, and why was the first Indian reservation established?

7. What was the General Allotment Act? Why did it lead to the loss of so much Indian land?

8. Describe Pan-Indian organizations. Compare and contrast their various styles of coping with the majority society.

9. What was the UNIA, and when, where, and by whom was it founded?

10. Identify three of the commercial ventures started by Marcus Garvey. Why did they lead to his movement being labeled as a back to Africa movement?

NOTES

1. For more on the massacre and its aftermath, see Fuoniss (1960), Hirshon (1969), and Nelson (1963).

2. Lyman (1996: 19–21, 371).

3. For more on modern-day schisms, see Baer (1988).

4. See Readers Digest, *Through Indian Eyes,* 1995, for an in-depth discussion of reservations and reservations policy.

5. On Garvey and black nationalism, see Cronon (1969), Lewis (1988), Sowell (1990), White (1992).

SUGGESTED READINGS

ARRINGTON, LEONARD, AND DAVIS BITTON. *The Mormon Experience,* 2nd ed. Chicago: University of Chicago Press, 1992.

BOYNTON, LINDA L. *The Plain People: An Ethnography of the Holdeman Mennonites.* Salem, WI: Sheffield, 1986.

GONZALES, JUAN, JR. *Racial and Ethnic Groups in America,* 3rd ed. Dubuque, IA: Kendall/Hunt, 1996.

HARDY, B. CARMON. *Solemn Covenant: The Mormon Polygamous Passage.* Chicago: University of Chicago Press, 1992.

HOSTETLER, JOHN A. *Amish Society,* 4th ed. Baltimore: Johns Hopkins University Press, 1993.

KRAYBILL, DONALD B., AND MARC O. OLSHAN, EDS. *The Amish Struggle with Modernity.* Hanover, NH: University Press of New England, 1994.

LAUNIUS, ROGER D., AND LINDA THATCHER, EDS. *Differing Visions: Dissenters in Mormon History.* Urbana: University of Illinois Press, 1994.

LEWIS, RUPERT. *Marcus Garvey: Anti-Colonial Champion.* Trenton, NJ: Africa World Press, 1988.

MARGER, MARTIN M. *Race and Ethnic Relations: American and Global Perspectives,* 4th ed. Belmont, CA: Wadsworth, 1997.

MAUSS, ARMAND. *The Angel and the Beehive: The Mormon Struggle with Assimilation.* Urbana: University of Illinois Press, 1994.

PRUCHA, FRANCIS P. *Documents of United States Indian Policy.* Lincoln, NE: University of Nebraska Press, 1990.

SCHAEFER, RICHARD T. *Racial and Ethnic Groups,* 7th ed. New York: HarperCollins, 1998.

SEWELL, TONY. *Garvey's Children: The Legacy of Marcus Garvey.* Trenton, NJ: Africa World Press, Inc., 1990.

WHITE, JOHN. *Black Leadership in America,* 2nd ed. New York: Longman, 1992.

WIGGINS, ROSALIND COBB, ED. *Captain Paul Cuffe's Logs and Letters, 1807–1817.* Washington, DC: Howard University Press, 1996.

CASE STUDY 5.1

Kingdom Come

David Van Biema

In Salt Lake City, Utah, on a block known informally as Welfare Square, stands a 15-barreled silo filled with wheat: 19 million pounds, enough to feed a small city for six months. At the foot of the silo stands a man—a bishop with the Church of Jesus Christ of Latter-day Saints—trying to explain why the wheat must not be moved, sold, or given away.

Around the corner is something called the bishop's storehouse. It is filled with goods whose sole purpose is to be given away. On its shelves, Deseret-brand laundry soaps manufactured by the Mormon Church nestle next to Deseret-brand canned peaches from the Mormon cannery in Boise, Idaho. Nearby are Deseret tuna from the church's plant in San Diego, beans from its farms in Idaho, Deseret peanut butter and Deseret pudding. There is no mystery to these goods: they are all part of the huge Mormon welfare system, perhaps the largest nonpublic venture of its kind in the country. They will be taken away by grateful recipients, replaced, and the replacements will be taken away. . . .

For more than a century, the members of the Church of Jesus Christ of Latter-day Saints suffered because their vision of themselves and the universe was different from those of the people around them. Their tormentors portrayed them as a nation within a nation, radical communalists who threatened the economic order and polyga-

mists out to destroy the American family. Attacked in print, and physically by mobs, some 30,000 were forced to flee their dream city of Nauvoo, Illinois, in 1846. Led by their assassinated founder's successor, they set out on a thousand-mile trek westward derided by nonbelievers as being as absurd as their faith.

This year their circumstances could not be more changed. Last Tuesday, 150 years to the week after their forefathers, 200 exultant and sunburned Latter-day Saints reached Salt Lake City, having re-enacted the grueling great trek. Their arrival at the spot where, according to legend, Brigham Young announced, "This is the right place" was cheered in person by a crowd of 50,000—and observed approvingly by millions. The copious and burnished national media attention merely ratified a long-standing truth: that although the Mormon faith remains unique, the land in which it was born has come to accept—no, to lionize—its adherents as paragons of the national spirit. It was in the 1950s, says historian Jan Shipps, that the Mormons went from being "vilified" to being "venerated," and their combination of family orientation, clean-cut optimism, honesty, and pleasant aggressiveness seems increasingly in demand. Fifteen Mormon Senators and Representatives currently trek the halls of Congress. Mormon author and consultant Stephen R. Covey bottled parts of the ethos in *The Seven Habits of Highly Effective People,* which has been on best-seller lists for five years. The FBI and CIA, drawn by a seemingly incorruptible rectitude, have instituted Mormon-recruitment plans.

The Mormon Church is by far the most numerically successful creed born on American soil and one of the fastest growing anywhere. Its U.S. membership of 4.8 million is the seventh largest in the country, while its hefty 4.7 percent annual American growth rate is nearly doubled abroad, where there are already 4.9 million adherents. . . .

University of Washington sociologist Rodney Stark projects that in about 83 years, worldwide Mormon membership should reach 260 million.

The church's material triumphs rival even its evangelical advances. . . . Its current assets total a minimum of $30 billion. If it were a corporation, its estimated $5.9 billion in annual gross income would place it midway through the *Fortune* 500, a little below Union Carbide and the Paine Webber Group but bigger than Nike and the Gap. And as long as corporate rankings are being bandied about, the church would make any list of the most admired: for straight dealing, company spirit, contributions to charity (even the non-Mormon kind), and a fiscal probity among its powerful leaders that would satisfy any shareholder group, if there were one.

Historian Leonard J. Arrington says the church, along with the values it represents, "has played a role, and continues to play a role, in the economic and social development of the West—and indeed, because of the spread of Mormons everywhere, of the nation as a whole." And in a country where religious unanimity is ever less important but material achievement remains the earthly manifestation of virtue, their creed may never face rejection again.

The top beef ranch in the world is not the King Ranch in Texas. It is the Deseret Cattle & Citrus Ranch outside Orlando, Fla. It covers 312,000 acres; its value as real estate alone is estimated at $858 million. It is owned entirely by the Mormons. The largest producer of nuts in America, Ag-Reserves, Inc., in Salt Lake City, is Mormon-owned. So are the Bonneville International Corp., the country's 14th largest radio chain, and the Beneficial Life Insurance Co., with assets of $1.6 billion. There are richer churches than the one based in Salt Lake City: Roman Catholic holdings dwarf Mormon wealth. But the Catholic Church has 45 times as many members. There is no major church in the U.S. as active as the Latter-day Saints in economic life, nor, per capita, as successful at it.

The first divergence between Mormon economics and that of other denominations is the tithe. Most churches take in the greater part of their income through donations. Very few, however, impose a compulsory 10 percent income tax on their members. Tithes are collected locally, with much of the money passed on informally to local lay leaders at Sunday services. . . .

Last year $5.2 billion in tithes flowed into Salt Lake City, $4.9 billion of which came from American Mormons. By contrast, the Evangelical Lutheran Church in America, with a comparable U.S. membership, receives $1.7 billion a year in contributions. So great is the tithe flow that scholars have suggested it constitutes practically the intermountain states' only local counterbalance in an economy otherwise dominated by capital from the East and West coasts.

The true Mormon difference, however, lies in what the LDS church does with that money. . . .

The Mormons are stewards of a different stripe. Their charitable spending and temple building are prodigious. But where other churches spend most of what they receive in a given year, the Latter-day Saints employ vast amounts of money in investments that *Time* estimates to be at least $6 billion strong. Even more unusual, most of this money is not in bonds or stock in other peoples' companies but is invested directly in church-owned, for-profit concerns, the largest of which are in agribusiness, media, insurance, travel, and real estate. Deseret Management Corp., the company through which the church holds almost all its commercial assets, is one of the largest owners of farm- and ranchland in the country, including 49 for-profit parcels in addition to the Deseret Ranch. Besides the Bonneville International chain and Beneficial Life, the church owns a 52 percent holding in ZCMI, Utah's largest department-store chain. . . .

The explanation for this policy of ecclesiastical entrepreneurism lies partly in the Mormons' early experience of ostracism. Brigham Young wrote 150 years ago that "the kingdom of God cannot rise independent of Gentile nations until we produce, manufacture, and make every article of use, convenience or necessity among our people." By the time the covered wagons and handcarts had concluded their westward roll, geographic isolation had reinforced social exclusion: the Mormons' camp on the Great Salt Lake was 800 miles from the nearest settlement. . . .

In the first century of corporate Mormonism, the church's leaders were partners, officers, or directors in more than 900 Utah-area businesses. They owned woolen mills, cotton factories, 500 local co-ops, 150 stores, and 200 miles of railroad. Moreover, when occasionally faced with competition, they insisted that church members patronize LDS-owned businesses. Eventually this became too much for the U.S. Congress. In 1887 it passed the Edmunds-Tucker Act, specifically to smash the Mormons' vertical monopolies.

But there is an additional aspect to the Mormons' spectacular industry and frugality. Their faith, like several varieties of American Protestantism, holds that Jesus will return to earth and begin a thousand-year rule, this glory preceded by a period of turmoil and chaos. . . . From the beginning, the Saints' millennial strain was modulated by a delight in the economic nitty-gritty. Of some 112 revelations received by the first Prophet and President of the church, Joseph Smith, 88 explicitly address fiscal matters. And although the faithful believe the "End Times" could begin shortly, their actual date is (to humankind) indefinite, and certain key signs and portents have not yet manifested themselves. Rather than wild-eyed fervor, most church moneymen project a can-do optimism. . . .

Or, in their higher echelons, a case-hardened if amiable professionalism. A primary reason for the church's business triumphs, says University of Washington sociologist Stark, is that it has no career clerics, only amateurs who have been plucked for service from successful endeavors in other fields. . . . Rodney Brady, who runs Deseret Management Corp., has a Harvard business doctorate, served as executive vice president of pharmaceutical giant Bergen Brunswig, and from 1970 to 1972 was Assistant Secretary of the U.S. Department of Health, Education and Welfare. Similar figures fill the church's upper management: Tony Burns, a "stake president" (the rough equivalent of an archbishop), is chairman of Miami-based Ryder Systems, the truck-rental empire.

And then there is Jon Huntsman. Currently a powerful "area authority," Huntsman may at some point make official church fiscal policy. But right now he is exemplary of the Mormon gift for not only making a buck but also spending it on others. An enthusiastic missionary as a young man, at age 42 he was asked to serve as "mission president" for a group of 220 young prose-lytizers in Washington. He took leave from his company and moved his wife and nine children with him. When his stint was up, they headed back to Utah, and Huntsman resumed building the $5 billion, 10,000-employee Huntsman Chemical Corp., which he owns outright. Ten years ago, Huntsman shifted his company's mission from pure profit to a three-part priority: pay off debt, be a responsible corporate citizen, and relieve human suffering. Thus far, his company has donated $100 million of its profit to a cancer center at the University of Utah. It has also built a concrete plant in Armenia to house those rendered homeless by the 1988 earthquake, and it is active in smaller charities ranging from children's hospitals to food banks. . . .

Mormon theology recognizes the Christian Bible but adds three holy books of its own. It holds that shortly after his resurrection, Jesus Christ came to America to teach the indigenous people, who were actually a tribe of Israel, but that Christian churches in the Old World fell into apostasy. Then, starting in 1820, God restored his "latter-day" religion by dispatching the angel Moroni to reveal new Scriptures to a simple farm boy named Joseph Smith near Palmyra, N.Y. Although the original tablets, written in what is called Reformed Egyptian, were taken up again to heaven, Smith,

who received visits from God the father, Jesus, John the Baptist, and saints Peter, James, and John, translated and published the *Book of Mormon* in 1830. He continued to receive divine Scripture and revelations. One of these was that Christ will return to reign on earth and have the headquarters of his kingdom in a Mormon temple in Jackson County, Missouri. (Over time, the church has purchased 14,465 acres of land there.)

There is a long list of current Mormon practices foreign to Catholic or Protestant believers. . . . Marriages are "sealed," not only until death doth part, but for eternity. And believers conduct proxy baptisms for the dead: to assure non-Mormon ancestors of an opportunity for salvation, current Mormons may be immersed on their behalf. The importance of baptizing one's progen-itors has led the Mormons to amass the fullest genealogical record in the world, the microfilmed equivalent of 7 million books of 300 pages apiece.

Members of the church celebrate the Lord's Supper with water rather than wine or grape juice. They believe their President is a prophet who receives new revelations from God. These can supplant older reve-lations, as in the case of the church's histor-ically most controversial doctrine: Smith himself received God's sanctioning of poly-gamy in 1831, but 49 years later, the church's President announced its recision. Similarly, an explicit policy barring black men from holding even the lowest church offices was overturned by a new revelation in 1978, opening the way to huge missionary activity in Africa and Brazil.

Mormons reject the label polytheistic pinned on them by other Christians; they believe that humans deal with only one God. Yet they allow for other deities presiding over other worlds. Smith stated that God was once a humanlike being who had a wife and in fact still has a body of "flesh and bones." Mormons also believed that men, in a process known as deification, may become God-like. Lorenzo Snow, an early President and Prophet, famously aphorized, "As man is now, God once was; as God now is, man may become." Mormonism excludes original sin, whose expiation most Christians understand as Christ's great gift to humankind in dying on the Cross.

All this has led to some withering denominational sniping. . . . The Mormons have responded to such challenges by downplaying their differences with the mainstream. In 1982 an additional subtitle appeared on the covers of all editions of the *Book of Mormon:* "Another Testament of Jesus Christ." In 1995 the words Jesus Christ on the official letterhead of the Church of Jesus Christ of Latter-day Saints were enlarged until they were three times the size of the rest of the text. In Salt Lake City's Temple Square, the guides' patter, once full of proud references to Smith, is almost entirely Christological.

It would be tempting to assign the Mormons' success in business to some aspect of their theology. The absence of original sin might be seen as allowing them to move confidently and guiltlessly forward. But it seems more likely that both Mormonism's attractiveness to converts and its fiscal triumphs owe more to what Hinckley terms "sociability," an intensity of common purpose (and, some would add, adherence to authority) uncommon in the non-Mormon business or religious worlds. There is no other major American denomination that officially assigns two congregation members in good standing, as Mormonism does, to visit every household in their flock monthly. Perhaps in consequence, no other denomi-

nation can so consistently parade the social virtues most Americans have come around to saying they admire. . . .

Yet it is hard to argue with Mormon uniformity when a group takes care of its own so well. The church teaches that in hard times, a person's first duty is to solve his or her own problems and then ask for help from the extended family. Failing that, however, a bishop may provide him or her with cash or coupons redeemable at the 100 bishops' storehouse depots, with their Deseret-brand bounty. The largesse is not infinite: the system also includes 97 employment centers, and Mormon welfare officials report that a recipient generally stays on the dole between 10 and 12 weeks, at an average total cash value of $300. Perhaps the most remarkable aspect of the system is its funding, which does not, as one might expect, come out of tithes. Rather, once a month, church members are asked to go without two meals and contribute their value to the welfare system. The fast money is maintained and administered locally, so that each community can care for its own disadvantaged members. . . . The church authorities have removed the tithe from the authority of local administrators and pulled every penny of it back to Salt Lake City for delegation by a more select and internationally minded group of managers.

No one thinks the push abroad, and the complementary balancing act domestically, will be easy. . . .

Will it succeed? Will the generations of young Mormon men who have so avidly evangelized beyond the borders of their country be followed by a fiscal juggernaut that will make the church as respected a presence in Brazil or the Philippines as it is in Utah, Colorado or, for that matter, America as a whole? Assessing the church's efforts at overseas expansion, author Joel Kotkin has written that "given the scale of the current religious revival combined with the formidable organizational resources of the church, the Mormons could well emerge as the next great global tribe, fulfilling, as they believe, the prophecies of ancient and modern prophets.". . .

SOURCE: David Van Biema, *Time,* August 4, 1997, pp. 51–57. © 1997 Time Inc. Reprinted by permission.

CHAPTER SIX

THE STRATEGY OF SEPARATISM
Psychological Separatism

Closely related to the racial and ethnic groups discussed in Chapter 5 are groups espousing separatism but adopting a tactical approach of psychological means rather than physical isolation. The use of psychological separatism is often by **millennial movements**, whose strong religious ideology provides the means by which the individual can develop a sort of psychological shell to isolate himself or herself from the influence of the majority society, even while living in its midst.

This chapter focuses on two prime examples of psychological separatism: the Nation of Islam, or Black Muslims, and the Hasidic Jews. Brief references are made to other religious separatist movements, but these two cases best exemplify the tactic and the difficulty of employing this tactic to retain separatism amidst the constant pressure from the majority culture to conform to its value system.

THE BLACK MUSLIMS

The Muslims exhibit distinct organizational and cultural norms that are specifically designed to compensate for the effects of discrimination. The group withdraws from the ongoing polity. Black Muslims are given a myth that accounts for their past in a manner that overcomes the psychological damages of racial discrimination while providing a glorious image of the future. One scholar describes the Nation of Islam (NOI) as follows:

> Whether the prophet is Treitschke, Doestoevsky, Hitler, Moses, Mazzini, Mussolini or Elijah Muhammad, the myth of the past and the illusion of the future remain a remarkably consistent, nationalistic, mass movement formula. To convince an alienated people of their worth and unity, one must remind them of their sacred origin. To explain the disheartening realities of their present plight, one must convince them of their natural superiority and ferret out corruptors and devils. To gird them for the trials ahead, one

must reveal a glorious destiny ordained from the beginnings of time. Past, present, and future must intermingle in one expression of Divine Intent. The rehabilitative effects of the movement on many members of the sect have been remarkable. From the nation's prisons and slums, the Muslims have recruited drug addicts and pushers, prostitutes and pimps, alcoholics, criminals and the despairing ghetto residents alienated from society. These men and women have been transformed by the Muslims into employees of value in honest jobs, who conscientiously marry and raise a family. They obey the laws, save money, and tithe to their faith. They no longer drink, use drugs or tobacco, gamble, engage in sexual promiscuity, dance, take long vacations, steal, lie, nor exhibit idleness or laziness. Their women are models of domesticity: thrifty, keeping fastidiously clean homes, devoted to their mates and children. Instead of buying expensive clothes or cars, they pool their resources to help each other. Muslim families, even in the midst of the nation's worst slums, exhibit a healthy living standard. The movement has, in its own strange way, repaired some "irreparable" damages and saved some of the damned. (Litt 1970: 78–79)

The **Black Muslims** began in the 1930s. During the depression, various mystic black nationalist sectarian cults arose in the nation's urban ghettos. One of the precursors to the Black Muslims was the Moorish-American Science Temple movement, started by Noble Drew Ali in Newark, New Jersey, in 1913. It had temples in Chicago, Detroit, and Pittsburgh, and gained from an influx of Garveyites in the late 1920s. Another was the Peace Mission movement of Father Divine, established on Long Island in 1919. He also instituted a collectivist economy that attracted many former Garvey followers to his blend of social and religious Black Nationalism. Father Divine's movement peaked between 1931 and 1936 with an estimated following of 1 million. The Ethiopian Pacific movement, founded in Chicago in 1932, attracted some 300 ex-Garveyites with a program of emigration and repatriation. All these movements echoed the Negro Convention movement of 1830 to 1860, which met annually and advocated repatriation or the possible creation of a black nation-state in Haiti. That movement ended with the Civil War.

The Black Muslims, also known as the Nation of Islam (NOI), were first introduced to black Americans in 1930 with the arrival of Wali D. Fard, also called Mr. W. Fard Muhammad, in Detroit's black ghetto. Under the leadership of Elijah Muhammad, Fard's most trusted follower and his successor when Fard disappeared mysteriously in June 1934, the Nation of Islam developed into a well-known if controversial organization. The Black Muslims are America's foremost Black Nationalist movement, with 69 temples in 27 states.

Fard was a disciple of Noble Drew Ali's Moorish-American Science Temple. His identity remains a mystery. He is thought to have been an Arab, claiming to have come from Mecca, but his true racial and even national origin is still undocumented. Claiming to be Allah Incarnate, Fard assumed the leadership of the Noble Drew Ali's movement when the latter died in 1929. Fard went to Detroit in 1930, and between 1930 and 1933 he attracted a following of about 8,000 persons before he disappeared.

With his disappearance, leadership of the movement passed to Elijah Poole, who changed his name to Elijah Muhammad, declaring he was "Allah's Prophet," the "Messenger of Allah" come to awaken the sleeping black nation and rid it of the whites' age-old domination. An early faction of Fard's movement followed Abdul Muhammad, another of his disciples, but that faction did not prosper. The Nation of Islam grew slowly but steadily during the 1930s and 1940s, appealing mostly to the black lower class. Temples were established in Chicago, Milwaukee, and Washington, D.C. The black **underclass** provided fertile ground for the new movement's growth.

> Behind the ghetto's crumbling walls lives a large group of people who are more intractable, more socially alien and more hostile than almost anyone imagined. They are the unreachables: the American underclass. . . . Their bleak environment nurtures values that are often at odds with those of the majority—even the majority of the poor. Thus the underclass produces a highly disproportionate number of the nation's juvenile delinquents, school dropouts, drug addicts and welfare mothers, and much adult crime, family disruption, urban decay, and demand for social expenditures.[1]

Black Muslims preached that whites were devils created by a black scientist named Yakub. Whites were considered to be mentally, physically, and morally inferior to blacks. Blacks were the "original man," the first people to inhabit the earth. Yakub's work was met with anger by Allah, who ordained that the white man would rule for 6,000 years over blacks. In this process blacks would suffer but thereby gain a greater appreciation of their spiritual worth by comparing themselves to whites. Blacks were members of the tribe of Shabazz. Black Muslims desired to free blacks from white influence and secure land for themselves within the continental United States. Preaching an assertive, militant separatism, they advocated a very Garvey-like form of group economy and black pride.

Elijah Muhammad addresses his followers during the annual convention in the Coliseum.

Black Muslims advocated racial separatism and self-determination in a brand of black economic nationalism. They rejected the use of the term "Negro," favoring the use of "Afro-American." They discarded black surnames as slave-names. They substituted the suffix X or a Muslim name, for example, Muhammad. Their Black Nationalism blended the economic nationalism of Booker T. Washington and the cultural nationalism of W.E.B. Du Bois's "Negro-Americanism."

> The so-called American Negro group . . . while it is in no sense absolutely set off physically from its fellow Americans, has nevertheless a strong, hereditary cultural unity born of slavery, of common suffering, prolonged proscription, and curtailment of political and civil rights. . . . Prolonged policies of segregation and discrimination have involuntarily welded the mass almost into a nation within a nation. (Du Bois, cited in Lincoln 1994: 43)

Black Muslims rejected both white society and the Judeo-Christian heritage underpinning the dominant culture and its value system. In their words:

> As long as the Negro is in America there is no hope for him. The white man takes one Negro and kills the aspirations of a million others. The white man has successfully made the Negro into an individual for himself, and denied a nation of his own to the Negro. The Negro's worst enemy is his religion. The acceptance of Christianity killed his nationalism. Christianity is his worst poisonous enemy. There are over 700 denominations among Negroes and yet the Negroes have not founded a single denomination of their own. They get together to serve white gods. The Negro will never unite until the religious struggle is won. Ask a Negro what his problem is, he says, unity. He agrees with you but that is all. His case in America is hopeless. The NAACP is the Big Niggers' organization. It was founded by whites, the bosses are whites and Jews—the biggest thief there ever was. The Big Niggers, the NAACP, don't want Langer's Bill passed. The Jews don't want it passed. The Big Niggers want to get jobs here. They are not nationalists. They have no national program. They are not interested in the plight of the masses. The Big Niggers as a class don't think. Of course they get their diplomas and stand around like any other Negro for a job from the white man. Once a Negro reaches college level he is no good for anybody. They were brought here slaves, have remained slaves, and will remain slaves. (cited in Essien-Udom 1962: 55)

Temple 2, established in Chicago in 1934, functioned as the headquarters of the Nation of Islam, the "Mecca" of the movement. Chicago was a hotbed of Black Nationalism in the 1930s. It was home to the Abyssinian movement. This offshoot of Garvey's movement, the Peace Movement of Ethiopia, and the Moorish-American Temple movement was taken over by the Black Muslim movement. The Chicago temple experienced remarkable growth between 1946 and 1960. By 1960, it was a nationwide movement, growing from about 10,000 members to over 250,000 members.

The Black Muslim movement demands total commitment.[2] Black Muslims are not just a "Sunday religion"; they require a whole lifestyle change. For Black Muslims, their "Zion" is wherever whites are absent. In the words of Malcolm X, America's blacks are the "Lost Nation of Islam in North America." For them *black* is the ideal, the ultimate value. The black man is the primogenitor of *all* civilization, the "Chosen of Allah," and the rightful rulers of the planet earth.

In return for a total commitment to Islam, the movement provides its converts with an elaborate organization capable of maintaining a variety of institutional supports that radically change the member's lifestyle. Members are immersed in the new Muslim culture. The movement provides the temple, schools for children and adults, a well-disciplined security force known as the Fruit of Islam, and numerous daily or weekly publications filled with inspirational messages and Black Muslim ideology. The Nation of Islam publishes or published *Dispatch, Islamic News, Salaam,* and *Muhammad Speaks,* the latter of which claimed a circulation of 600,000.

Women's auxiliaries teach homemaking skills, child care, and women's "proper role." Muslim children attend grade school and summer camps. Teenagers are provided with Muslim community centers. The movement offers employment training and runs a variety of retail and service businesses. Black Muslims have created their own "University of Islam" (actually no more than a high school). They strengthen the sense of collective identity by symbols that furnish deified objects for mass loyalty and expressions of aspirations. All nationalistic movements have flags or gods around which the faithful rally. For the Black Muslims, there are Allah, the star and crescent, their version of the Koran, and the Islamic tongue.

These cultural symbols, and the norms and values they embody and reinforce, help establish their **ethnic boundaries**. Such boundaries define the group. The ethnic boundary "canalizes social life—it entails a frequently quite complex organization of behavior and social relations" (Barth 1969: 15). The ethnic boundary both enables some relationships to exist and constrains or limits others. It is the device to distinguish the respective character of both intra- and intergroup relationships.

These boundary markers are important to the separatist movement's success in creating that psychological shell about each of its members. Black Muslim men adopt the Muslim name, are clean-shaven, and dress in dark, conservative suits, white shirts and ties, and with a small star and crescent button on their lapels. Black Muslim women wear a nunlike garb with full headdress and habit covering their arms and legs.

Changes in clothing style serve several identification functions. They reject the stereotypical flamboyant appearance of lower-class blacks. The sober neatness expresses strength and a new sense of dignity. The nunlike garb of the women again rejects the flashy and wild colors of the stereotypical black female. Their new dress stresses the protected, sequestered, and obedient role that women play in the Muslim life and family. The uniformity of both men and women heightens a sense of group cohesion and affords a readily detectable commonality that sets them apart from non-Muslims. Brothers and sisters are differentiated from all others.

Racial pride is stressed. Black features are upheld as the highest human representation of Allah. "Black Is Beautiful" is the prevailing aesthetic. Self-composure and control are maintained at all times. Young men conduct themselves with military-like bearing. Loud and boisterous behavior is forbidden, and displays of emotion are discouraged. A Black Muslim is told to listen to music quietly, without swaying or crooning. All these norms of behavior reject stereotypical images.

Black Muslims have numerous prescribed foods (see Box 6.1). A Muslim is forbidden to eat pork, seafood, or scavenger creatures. All "soul food" is held to be

BOX 6.1: Dietary Restrictions of Black Muslims and Laws of Prescribed Behavior

Some of the Foods We Eat and Do Not Eat

Some We Do Eat	*Foods We Do Not Eat*
Small navy beans	Lima beans
Small pink beans	Butter beans
Stringbeans	Black-eyed peas
June beans	Green cabbage
White cabbage (not Green)	Collard greens
Cauliflower	Pinto beans
Eggplant	Kidney beans
Okra	Brown field peas
Carrots	Cornbread
Mustard greens	
Turnips (white)	
Spinach	
Tomatoes	
Celery	
Lettuce	
Green and hot peppers	
White potatoes (be careful they are easy to put on weight)	
Fresh corn (milk corn)	
Radish	
Asparagus	
Whole wheat bread	

Meats We Do Eat	*Meats We Do Not Eat*
Of course no meat is good for us; but if we are going to eat meat the best is:	Pig (Hog–Swine) The Hog Meat is divinely Forbidden by Almighty God
Lamb	Rabbit
Beef	Possum
Squabs (young pigeons, we eat chickens but they are not good for us)	Squirrel
	Coon and any other animal of the family
	No wild games (sic), that which walks, crawls, runs, or flies

Fish We Do Eat	*Fish We Do Not Eat*
White fish	Carp
Trout	Catfish
Bass	Buffalo
Salmon	Eat no fish without scales weighing over 50 lbs.
Pike	Eat no fish that sucks its food (Sucker fish)
	No seafood such as Lobster, Crabs, Oysters, Shrimp, Frogs, Clams, etc.

BOX 6.1:   Dietary Restrictions of Black Muslims and Laws of Prescribed Behavior
(*continued*)

"In the name of Allah, the Beneficent, the Merciful:" Violations of these laws are subjected to 30 days to indefinite suspension from the Temple:

1. Sleeping in the Temple

2. Keeping late hours

3. Using narcotics (dope, heroin, marijuana)

4. Married and taking up time with other Sisters

5. Abusing your wife

6. Socializing with Christians

7. Drinking alcoholic juices

8. Unclean homes

9. Personal hygiene

10. Watching the movements of the Sisters

11. Lying and stealing from one another

12. Gambling (shooting pool, dice, cards, etc.)

13. Eating pork

14. Gossiping on one another

15. Fornication

16. Adultery

17. Disobeying your officers

18. Disrespecting Ministers and the Supreme Captain

19. Talking about your Leader and Teacher

20. Misrepresenting the teachings of Islam

21. Disrespecting the Messenger of Allah

The rules which govern the conduct of Muslim Sisters are similar. In addition, Sisters are required to wear clothes which do not expose their legs or arms. They do not wear lipstick or conspicuous cosmetics. The headtie is required for all Sisters. Dresses and colors are prescribed for boys and girls at the University of Islam. Detailed requirements of conduct are numerous.

SOURCE: E. U. Essien-Udom, *Black Nationalism: A Search for an Identity in America* (Chicago: University of Chicago Press, 1962), pp. 205–207. © 1962 University of Chicago Press.

---

reminiscent of the slave past, so cornbread, black-eyed peas, collard greens, and 'possum are prohibited. These dietary norms bolster members' new identity and help to eradicate the old. The result is a new sense of black self-worth. Black Muslims are taught that feeling inferior results in acting inferior, in accepting the white man's view of the black. Rejecting the stereotypes is their way of liberating the individual from the "slave mentality." As Elijah Muhammad stated it: "Love yourself and you will not need the white man's love."[3]

The Black Muslim movement distinguishes itself from the civil rights groups by its stress on the individual rather than changes in the majority society's laws, policies, or customs. It teaches that responsibility for the betterment of the individual rests with the black man, not with white society. Black Muslims demand absolute separation of the black and white races. They are psychologically indrawn. They feel responsible only to each other and derive their satisfaction from their own mutual self-approval.

Black Muslim membership remains predominantly male and young. About 80 percent of its members are between 18 and 35 years of age. Older persons who joined the movement tended to be ex-Garveyites or ex-Moorish Science Muslims.

Converts to the Black Muslims, besides following a strict code of personal conduct, were forbidden to be involved in any political activity of the white dominant society, including service in the armed forces. Until they achieve their separate state, Black Muslims were to avoid any social or religious or political contact with whites. Even during the Great Depression, they refused to accept relief checks, Social Security numbers, or any form of federally sponsored employment (White 1991).

These tenets led to the first clash between the Black Muslims and the legal system of white society. In May 1942, Elijah Muhammad was arrested, charged with sedition for inciting his followers to resist the draft and for tax evasion. He and 62 followers were convicted and sentenced to five years in the Federal Corrections Institute in Michigan. Eventually 100 of his followers were incarcerated for draft resistance. This incident resulted in the Black Muslim's outreach to recruit new members among criminals, delinquents, drug addicts and pushers, prostitutes and pimps, and the black underclass. They recruited recent immigrants to the northern cities from the deep South, most of whom were illiterate. As the movement developed temples in some dozen cities, it began to appeal to a broader spectrum of blacks.

Among the young, black male prisoners the Black Muslims recruited was its most successful proselytizer and effective preacher, Malcolm Little. He became Malcolm X. He was born in Omaha, Nebraska, in 1925, the son of a West Indian mother and a black American Baptist preacher, both ardent followers of Marcus Garvey. When Malcolm was very young, the family moved to Michigan, and he often went with his father to Universal Negro Improvement Association (UNIA) missions. His father died when Malcolm was six. In his autobiography Malcolm claimed that his father was beaten and thrown to his death under a tram car by members of a local white supremacist group called The Black Legion. Allegedly, they had earlier burned the Little house. Subsequent biographers have disputed that story. The Detroit police listed his death as accidental.

Malcolm's budding oratorical skills were quickly noted and developed. He became the minister of the Philadelphia temple and then went on to Harlem, New York. In June 1954, he assumed command of the New York City temple. At Harlem's Temple 7, Malcolm X preached orthodox Black Muslim doctrine. He attracted followers by his militant condemnation of the civil rights movement's push for integration through nonviolent protest. He likened himself and Black Muslim leadership to slavery's "field Negro," and the civil rights leadership to the "house Negro." He called them "Uncle Toms" to his "new Negro." By 1964, Malcolm was the second most requested speaker on college campuses across the nation. He frequently wrote and was quoted in the Nation of Islam's national newspaper, *Muhammad Speaks.* Its circulation rose to about 900,000.

Malcolm X, Black Muslim orator, addresses a Harlem rally.

In the early 1960s, a strain developed between Malcolm X and the Nation of Islam, reflecting a growing envy by Elijah Muhammad of Malcolm X for his increasing popularity. It also reflected the increasing ideological differences that Malcolm X had with the Nation of Islam. Elijah Muhammad's innermost circle of leadership at the Chicago headquarters was distrustful of Malcolm X and viewed him as a rival for leadership in the Nation of Islam to Elijah's chosen heir-apparent, his seventh son, Wallace Deen Muhammad.

Malcolm X's thoughts and perspectives went through three periods. From 1952 to 1962, he espoused the orthodox theology of Black Nationalism. From 1962 to 1964, he went through a period of transition, increasingly to one of secular Black Nationalism. From 1964 to his assassination, he advocated **pan-African internationalism**. By the early 1960s, Malcolm X questioned the theology of Elijah Muhammad, the Nation of Islam's programs, its refusal to become politically active, and its patriarchal attitude toward women. The Black Muslim program was politically and economically conservative, much like that of Booker T. Washington. Malcolm X advocated a more militant and politically activist stance. He was attracted to African socialism, and his view of whites shifted from that of "devils" to simply "hypocrites."

His open split with the Nation of Islam began in 1963, when he spoke out after the assassination of President John Kennedy, about which he had been ordered to refrain from public comment. He described the assassination as reaping what Kennedy had sown—in reference to the Administration's involvement in the attempted assassination of Castro in Cuba and the assassinations of Patrice Lumumba in Africa and Ngo Dinh Diem in South Vietnam. In March 1964, Malcolm X announced his separation from the Nation of Islam. He set up his own movement, Muslim Mosque, Inc., to promote a more activist, direct-action approach to the racial problem. Disavowing nonviolence, he stated that if provoked by violence from whites, there would be retaliation. Elijah Muhammad called Malcolm X a "Judas," "Traitor," "Apostate," "Brutus," and "Benedict Arnold." But the open split dismayed many Black Muslims (Kivisto 1995: 319).

Malcolm toured the Middle East and Africa (Ghana and Nigeria) and made a pilgrimage to Mecca, where he discovered "True Islam," and returned to the United States as a Sunni Muslim, adopting the name El Hajj-Malik El Shabazz. He openly changed his earlier positions and moved toward dealings with whites and with the mainstream civil rights movement. On his return he stated:

> Every time you see another nation on the African continent become independent, you know that Marcus Garvey is alive. All the freedom movement that is taking place right here in America today was initiated by the philosophy and teachings of Garvey. The entire Black Nationalist philosophy here in America rested upon the seeds that were planted by Marcus Garvey. (cited in White 1991: 156)

Malcolm's break with the Nation of Islam won him many admirers but few followers. In June 1964, he formed the **Organization of Afro-American Unity (OAAU)**. It reflected Marcus Garvey's pan-Africanism. Malcolm took a second trip to Africa in 1964, attending a conference of the Organization of African Unity in Cairo. He flirted with Socialism as an economic approach and articulated a strong anti-imperialism message.

The OAAU attracted a small following of about 900 persons, including some old-line Latino Garveyites, mostly Cubans and Panamanians. It published a newsletter, mostly a four-page mimeographed sheet with a circulation of only 200 to 300 copies, a far cry from the days when Malcolm's messages in *Muhammad Speaks* reached literally tens of thousands.

Malcolm articulated his pan-African internationalism in words that directly reflected the influence of Marcus Garvey:

> I believe that a psychological, cultural, and philosophical migration back to Africa will solve our problems. Not a physical migration, but a cultural, psychological and philosophical migration back to Africa—which means restoring our common bond—will give us the spiritual strength and the incentive to strengthen our political and social position here in America . . . and at the same time this will give incentive to many of our people to also visit and even migrate physically back to Africa, and those who stay here can help those who go back, and those who go back can help those who stay here, in the same way as the Jews who go to Israel. (cited in White 1991: 164)

After his split with the Nation of Islam, Malcolm was less prominent, certainly less so than his rival for leadership of the black civil rights movement, Dr. Martin Luther King, Jr. After Dr. King was awarded the Nobel Peace Prize, Malcolm X said: "He got the Peace Prize; we got the problem. I don't want the white man giving me medals." He also recognized the varying roles that the black leadership played. In his final period he moved closer to the position of the civil rights movement. He realized that the more radical rhetoric of the Black Nationalists helped the King movement by contrast. "On another occasion, he looked a perceptive reporter in the eye and told him that the white power structure would turn a deaf ear to the demands of black moderates unless black extremists continued to threaten from the wings" (cited in Perry 1992: 349).

Like King, Malcolm X feared and anticipated his own assassination. The growing tension with his split from the Nation of Islam led to ever increasingly strong denunciations of Malcolm X by the NOI. His home was firebombed on February 14, 1965. Malcolm suspected but the police could not prove it was by the Nation of Islam's followers. Malcolm X was assassinated on February 21, 1965 by three NOI followers at a rally in New York City, at a ballroom in Harlem.

The call for a separate black state both by Malcolm X's OAAU and by the NOI, like Marcus Garvey's advocacy of such a state either in Africa or in some fenced-off portion of the United States, was unfathomable to most whites. To Garvey's followers and disciples, it remains a reasonable goal. In 1968, Malcolm's followers called for the creation of the Republic of New Africa.

> In the Black Belt, running through the five states that the Republic claims as the national territory of the Black Nation (Louisiana, Mississippi, Alabama, Georgia, and South Carolina), we have met all the criteria for land possession required of us by international practice, international law. We have incidentally met these tests too in many cities of the North . . . we give up these claims to these cities as *national* territory . . . in exchange for the five states of the deep South. (cited in Sales 1994: 176–177)

Malcolm X and his teachings were "rediscovered" in the 1990s. Today black youth searching for a "politics of liberation" have set Malcolm X as an icon equal to Dr. King in the pantheon of black heroes. Malcolm's evolution from Black Nationalism to pan-African internationalism, reflected in the OAAU, addressed the dilemma of the civil rights movement at the end of its first decade, the crucial period of 1963–1965. A more complete discussion of that period follows in Chapter 8.

After Malcolm's assassination, the Nation of Islam continued to be plagued by factionalism. In 1970, another prominent Black Muslim leader and rival to Elijah's son, Hamass Abdul Khaalis, was expelled from the group. He, too, set up a rival sect. He was denounced as a false prophet. The "Messenger's" triggermen shot his wife and daughter and drowned three of his children.

The Nation of Islam evolved in the 1970s. The Elijah Muhammad branch called itself the African Muslim Mission. After the death of Elijah Muhammad and his son's selection as his successor, membership declined from over 250,000 to around 100,000. W. Deen Muhammad opened the faith to people of all races, but it remains an African-American organization. In 1985, he dissolved the sect, leaving 200 mosques and worship centers to operate locally.

Its image changed as well. As the NOI stressed separatism less, elements within white society changed their view of the Black Muslims. A growing respect for the Nation of Islam's impressive use of capitalism to the organization's advantage, and for the strict moral code that its members follow, is evident in the mass media's coverage of the organization.[4] Much of that change and the new image of the Black Muslims can be attributed to the rise of Minister Louis Farrakhan. His faction is now the most visible among the various Muslim groups within the black community. Farrakhan broke with Wallace Deen Muhammad in 1977. He named his faction the Nation of Islam, adopting the name and the orthodox ideals of Elijah Muhammad. He stresses black moral superiority. He continues the strong tradition of Garveyism by stressing: black economic self-reliance; nontolerance for oppression and self-hatred; the belief that you cannot love your neighbor as yourself without first liking yourself and knowing who you are; and a belief that the sin of the Negro was that he failed to know himself.

Like Malcolm X, Minister Louis Farrakhan modified the Nation of Islam's isolation from politics. His endorsement of the Reverend Jesse Jackson in Jackson's bid for the Democratic Party's presidential nomination in both 1984 and 1988 exemplifies dramatically the change. It thrust Minister Farrakhan into the national limelight—and his anti-Semitic taint and rhetoric kept him there. His strong stands against drugs, abortion, and homosexuality emphasize anew the social conservatism of the Black Muslim tradition, as does his stress on self-help and bootstrap capitalism. In 1995, he called for and led the "Million Man March," which actively encouraged blacks to vote and to work for positive change.

Black Muslims showed a typical softening of their separatism over time, as they changed from a revolutionary to an institutional force. They followed a path typical of millennial movements that are too weak to achieve their dreams of paradise, yet too strong and structured simply to wither away. By attaining structural stability and longevity, the movement began a process of transformation from separatism to accommodation. The very success of the movement in turning its members into "haves" rather than "have-nots," and the organizational structures that tend over time to undercut the charismatic leadership of the movement, work to take the edge off the movement's separatist fervor. Instead of becoming a more radical sect, it is becoming more of a "conservative, black self-improvement" group, more interested in material advances than in sacrificing the life of the movement for the sake of a black supremacist doctrine. As it increasingly developed its organizational structures—temples, schools, farms, stores, newspapers, and clothing businesses—the needs of those organizational structures modified the charismatic and separatist aspects of the sect toward a more accommodational approach.

Minister Louis Farrakhan at a news conference, 1994.

Eric Hoffer, the street corner philosopher, observed: "We are less willing to die for what we have or are than for what we wish to have and to be. It is a perplexing and unpleasant truth that when men already have something worth fighting for they do not feel like fighting" (Hoffer 1963: 134).

Black Muslims have shown increasing signs of accommodation since the mid-1970s. Instead of viciously attacking other civil rights groups that advocate an integrationist approach, as it had done in the early years of the movement to the mid-1960s, the Muslim press now gives such groups fair coverage. It decreased its emphasis on separatism in its publications. Accounts of integrationist battles now are often treated sympathetically and positively. The movement aligned itself with avowedly integrationist groups advocating a full-scale attempt to elect black officials, backing black candidates from mayors to Jesse Jackson's campaign for the presidency. The movement modified its stance regarding the "white devil." Increasingly, its press stresses "black pride" rather than "white hatred." This trend toward a less strident version of separatism that now characterizes the Nation of Islam is illustrated in Case Study 6.1.

HASIDIC JEWS

Another example of separatism in a religious sect whose members, like the Black Muslims, are immersed in the heart of urban America is the Hasidic Jews of Brooklyn, New York. Like the Black Muslims, they exemplify a psychological approach to separatism and have successfully maintained a religious/ethnic subculture while living amidst the majority culture for hundreds of years.

It should not be surprising to most readers that Jews would be classified as a minority group. This recognizes that, nationally, Jews are a small percentage of the total population—about 3 percent. Jewish immigration prior to 1880 was small. Most Jews came from Germany, among whom were the prominent "forty-eighters" discussed in Chapter 4. The first big wave of Jewish immigration came between 1880 and 1920, mostly from Eastern Europe.

Jews can be divided by religious affiliation into three subgroups: Orthodox, Reformed, and Conservative. Orthodox Jews sometimes contain distinct "sects," such as the Hasidim, who are highly visible because of their distinctive dress, hairstyle, the character of their worship, a strong sense of "peoplehood," and a dogma that operates as a self-segregating force and a divisive factor between gentile and Jew. Their sense of peoplehood figures both in the discrimination they have experienced and in their manner of coping with it.

Their "in-group" sense is reflected in strongly cohesive family units, a cultural opposition to marriage to gentiles, a high proportion of self-employment and avoidance of economic contact with the gentile society, and their being stereotyped by majority society as "excessively clannish" (Marden and Meyer 1968).

Negative stereotyping is among the more pronounced forms of anti-Semitism in the United States. Gordon Allport (1958), in his classic *The Nature of Prejudice*, lists the most common stereotypical images ascribed to Jews in the United States: shrewd, mercenary, industrious, grasping, intelligent, ambitious, sly, loyal to family ties, persistent, talkative, aggressive, and very religious. Jews are often viewed as clannish, in control of everything, underhanded in business, overbearing, dirty, sloppy or filthy, energetic and smart, and loud and noisy.

In the United States, anti-Semitism ebbs and flows with social conditions that increase or decrease levels of fear among non-Jews. Chronic fear raises anxiety; anxiety causes prejudice to rise, manifested in increased discrimination against Jews. Any strong emotions can trigger anti-Semitism. Greed leads to desiring what belongs to others. If a group's self-esteem falls, it can be raised by making them seem better than Jews. Anti-Semitism can be traced to the post–Civil War period of economic displacement. The 1870s were an economically troubled decade in which many of the old upper-class families were being replaced by a new industrial elite. By the 1880s, when such displacement was considerable, the waves of East European Jews provided a convenient scapegoat for a society undergoing the pangs of industrialization.

After World War I, a strong and open anti-Semitism appeared. Such feelings were at their height in the 1920s and 1930s, when World War I and then the Great Depression upset so many socioeconomic positions. Much of the agitation for passage of the Immigration Act of 1921 and the Reed-Johnson Act of 1924 (the Quota Acts) was clearly anti-Semitic in nature. The only lynching of an American Jew—Leo Frank, a manager of an Atlanta pencil factory—took place in 1915. Although the lynching was attributed to Tom Watson, a Georgia Populist, the more intense anti-Semitism of the 1920s was a product of the revived Ku Klux Klan. Klan publications *Searchlight* and *Fiery Cross* linked communism to Jewishness. This same era linked anti-Semitism with anti-Bolshevik and anti-German attitudes of the World War I era. The infamous *Protocols of the Elders of Zion,* a fabrication of czarist Russia, were widely distributed by the Fellowship Forum. Henry Ford contributed to this anti-Semitic campaign through publication of the *Dearborn Independent,* described as "the most consistent and widespread anti-Semitic agitation that America has yet known. It touched off other movements and gave aid and comfort to lesser demagogues" (Janowsky 1964: 190).

In 1877, the prominent New York banker and President Grant's nominee for secretary of the treasury, Joseph Seligman, was refused accommodations at the Grand Hilton Hotel in Saratoga Springs. By the 1920s, discrimination in social clubs, hotels, and resorts was commonplace. A popular ditty sung by members of college fraternities around the turn of the century reflects this type of social anti-Semitism: "Oh, Harvard's run by millionaires, And Yale is run by booze, Cornell is run by farmer's sons, Columbia's run by Jews. So give a cheer for Baxter Street, Another one for Pell, And when the little sheenies die, Their souls will go to hell."

Discrimination against Jews in the United States has been pervasive and persistent. While undoubtedly more moderate than in Europe, American anti-Semitism has sometimes been more intense if less violent than against other religious minorities. No violent mob actions of burning down synagogues, attacking rabbis, or lynching Jews have occurred in the United States, even during times of intense anti-Semitism marked by desecration of Jewish cemeteries and synagogues. It has been more subtle, if nonetheless pervasive. It was into that background of more general anti-Semitism that Hasidic Jews migrated when they came to the United States during World War II.

Hasidic Jews in the United States are most notably settled in Brooklyn, New York. They are viewed as being ultra-orthodox Jews from Eastern Europe who continue to use their Old World garb and customs. Survivors of the Holocaust, they are seen largely as a "sect" by the broader American culture and even by many Reform Jews.

The Hasidic movement began in the mid-eighteenth century in what is today Poland, Belorussia, and Ukraine. At the time these areas had the largest concentrations of Jews anywhere in the world. Living in Jewish **shtetls** (villages), they were generally very poor and forbidden by law to own land. Hasidism began with a small group of rabbis searching for a way to renew the fervor of the Jewish people, among whom was Israel ben Eliezer, who came to be known as Baal Shem Tov. He first rose to prominence as a healer and miracle worker. He was 36 years old in 1734, when he began traveling from village to village as his fame for mysticism and miracles spread. Using parables and talmudic folktales, he brought the classical Jewish mystical themes to stories that even uneducated people could understand. Shortly before his death, in 1760, he selected certain disciples to succeed him in spreading Hasidism, generating a group of remarkable leaders who became known as **rebbes**.

The institution of the rebbe was central to the expansion of the Hasidic movement. Each rebbe was close to Baal Shem Tov and highly influenced by his daily routines and devotion. They provided Hasidic guidance in every sphere of daily life. Viewed as intercessors in the heavenly courts and as teachers of mysteries through study and meditation, they became figures of wisdom in each community they founded. Each Hasidic group evolved into a dynastic court composed of the rebbe and his followers.

Eventually, nearly half of East European Jewry became allied with the movement (Mintz 1968). Among the leading rebbes emerged Rabbi Schneur Zalman of Liady, who became the founder of the Lubavitch Hasidim—today the largest group of Hasidic Jews. Despite a period of sustained persecution that saw him twice imprisoned by the czar's government, Rabbi Zalman refused to leave Russia. When some 300 Hasidim fled to the Holy Land in 1777, Rabbi Zalman remained. He used his organizational skills to establish a pattern of leadership that became the model for successive generations of Lubavitcher rebbes and, indeed, the Hasidic movement more generally. Leadership was transmitted through lineage. Rebbes were the sons or sons-in-law of their predecessors. The new generation of Hasidic rebbes provided mystical-oriented writings and tales.

In the early 1800s, when all of Europe was undergoing massive change, the Hasidic Jews remained unswerving in their allegiance to traditional Judaism and its laws. Even after World War I and the Communist revolution in Russia, which shattered the Hasidic way of life, Rabbi Yosef Schneersohn, the sixth Lubavitcher rebbe, refused to leave. During the period of severe Communist government repression, he became the unofficial head of all Russian Jewry.

In 1927 he was arrested as a "counterrevolutionary" and imprisoned. International protest succeeded in winning his release and permission to leave Russia. He moved first to Latvia and then to Poland. Seeing no hope for Judaism to flourish in Russia, he encouraged all Hasidim to emigrate if possible. With the Nazi invasion of Poland in 1939, Rabbi Schneersohn fled to New York in 1940.

Rabbi Menachem Schneerson, Lubavitcher leader of the Hasidic Jews, speaking in Brooklyn, New York.

He established what became the world headquarters of the Lubavitch Hasidic group in Crown Heights, Brooklyn. He appointed his son-in-law, Rabbi Manachem Schneerson, to organize three Chabad (Hasidic movement) divisions: publishing, educational outreach missions, and social services. A small nucleus of young Chabad-trained rabbis founded yeshivas in a dozen cities across the country, circulating Hasidic texts, prayer books, and periodicals. After the death of Rebbe Yosef Schneerson in 1950, Rabbi Manachem Schneerson, at the age of 46, reluctantly accepted the position of the seventh Lubavitcher rebbe. For the next 40 years he led the Hasidic group through a period of rapid growth.

Other Hasidic courts were established as rebbes fled the Holocaust in Eastern Europe. Groups of Hasidic Jews settled in London, Montreal, Jerusalem, and Benei Brak in Israel. But for most, Brooklyn, New York, became the end of their exodus from war-torn Europe. Several surviving rebbes became the heart of new settlements in the United States: the Satmar and Klausenberger rebbes in Williamsburg; the Lubavitcher and Bobover rebbes in Crown Heights, and the Stoliner rebbe in Boro Park. In all, some 40 courts began to function. To keep their beliefs intact, they were aware that they had to resist the acculturating pressures that had reshaped the lives of earlier Jewish immigrants who were becoming increasingly secularized. The courts continued to grow. By 1970, an estimated 50,000 Hasidic Jews resided in New York, with courts ranging from the Satmar with over 1,300 families to several courts of between 100 and 500 families. In 1967, the Lubavitcher rebbe, Manachem Schneerson, was the leader of an estimated 250,000 people, the world's largest Hasidic group. Worldwide, there are courts in Israel, Canada, England, South America, and Russia.

The first attempt to found a Hasidic village in the United States was New Square, in the Rockland County township of Ramapo, New York, just over an hour's drive from New York City. Started in 1956, it is a suburban village of about 130 families and a population of under 1,000, accepting the leadership of Rebbe Squarer. It was officially incorporated as a village in 1961. Although none of the villagers were followers of Rebbe Squarer in Europe, they joined the new Squarer court after becoming attracted to the rebbe or to the idea of living in a completely Hasidic village. Rebbe Squarer died in March 1968, and his son was proclaimed his successor at the funeral.

Whether in the midst of Brooklyn, New York, or in a small village of 1,000, the Hasidic Jews live in a world apart. They establish strong communities of believers who interact mostly within the community, are generally self-employed in various trades, and live and marry within the Hasidic culture. They maintain their cultural identity by living apart from the broader culture, even if living within its midst.

Orthodox Jewish children attend special schools to meet minimal educational requirements. Their strong devotion to religious study is reflected in the following comment of a Hasidic Jew: "Look at Freud, Marx, Einstein—all Jews who made their mark on the non-Jewish world. To me, however, they would have been much better off studying in a **yeshiva** [a Jewish religious school]. What a waste of three fine Talmudic minds" (cited in Schaefer 1998: 414).

Although they maintain strict cultural separatism, Hasidic Jews participate in local elections and some are employed at jobs outside their ethnic enclave. All such activities are shaped by their self-reliance and orthodoxy. Like the Amish and Mennonites, they maintain a high degree of cultural identity despite living within the heart of the majority culture.

The relationship between Jews and black Americans was severely strained by events that highlighted alleged black anti-Semitism, as well as antiblack feelings among Jewish Americans. The strain developed when the Black Muslim and Black Panther movements supported Arabs in the Middle East, to the point of calling for Israel to surrender. The relationship was strained further during Jesse Jackson's presidential campaign when his off-the-record reference to Jews as "hymies" and the openly anti-Semitic remarks by the Nation of Islam Minister Louis Farrakhan were reported in the media. In his 1988 campaign, Jesse Jackson purposively distanced himself from Farrakhan and the Nation of Islam rhetoric by avowing that the "sons and daughters of the Holocaust and the sons and daughters of slavery must find common ground again." In 1991, an incident in New York City added fuel to the fires of tension between blacks and Jews when a Hasidic Jew ran a red light, killing a black child, and the ambulance that normally served the Hasidic community failed to pick up the child. Tempers in the black neighborhood rose to a fever pitch, and an Australian Jew was stabbed to death. That was followed by several days of rioting in the Brooklyn neighborhood of Crown Heights.

Hasidic Jews have been remarkably successful in their use of psychological separatism by maintaining a degree of involvement in the majority society while retaining their distinctive subculture to an amazing degree. Their strained relationship with black Americans and the effort by Minister Farrakhan to reduce tensions between the two groups is reflected in Case Study 6.1.

SUMMARY

This chapter examined the use of psychological separatism as a tactic of religious/ethnic subcultures to cope with their minority status. It examined the cases of Black Muslims and Hasidic Jews. It stressed their use of ethnic boundary markers to create a psychological shell around individual members both to set themselves apart from the majority culture whose values they reject and to protect themselves from the psychological harm that can be caused by the prejudice and discrimination they endure. Both Black Muslims and Hasidic Jews show remarkable persistence in maintaining their identity from the acculturation pressures of the majority society. Both exhibit the difficulty of this tactical approach to separatism, and resulting signs of increased accommodation among their members. Neither subculture has escaped a degree of acculturation among its members. The religious nature of sects like the Black Muslims and Hasidic Jews, much like the Amish and Mennonites, is an essential element in their ability to maintain a subculture over a long time, as well as a source of their rejection of the value system of the majority society.

KEY TERMS

Black Muslims: also known as the Nation of Islam; a religious Islamic sect advocating Black Nationalism, founded in Detroit in 1930.

Ethnic boundaries: the aspect of an ethnic group subculture that defines it and sets it apart from all other cultures; a complex organization of behaviors and social relationships that control intra- and interethnic social relations.

Millennial movement: a religious movement with a myth of the past and glorious vision of the future with a prescribed plan for the present designed to bring the future vision to fruition.

OAAU: Organization for Afro-American Unity, a group founded by Malcolm X in 1964 just before his assassination.

Pan-African internationalism: the ideology to which Malcolm X evolved in his political thinking at the time of his assassination.

Rebbes: the leadership group of the Hasidic Jewish sect; a leading rabbi around whom a "court" is formed in a Hasidic community.

Shtetls: Jewish villages or ghettos of Eastern Europe, mostly in Russia and Poland.

Underclass: an economic class of people, mostly minority, who are unemployed in the dominant economy and lack job skills needed to be viable in the above-ground economy.

Yeshiva: a Jewish religious school of Orthodox Jewry formed to study the Talmud.

REVIEW QUESTIONS

1. When and where did the Black Muslim movement begin? How is it related to Garveyism?

2. What ethnic boundary markers distinguish Black Muslims? Which ones characterize the Hasidic Jews?

3. What is the OAAU? How is it philosophically similar to or different from the NOI?

4. Discuss the three major subgroups of American Jews. Why is American Jewry fragmented?

5. When and where did the Hasidic movement begin? How does it maintain its identity in the highly secular world of New York City?

NOTES

1. "The American Underclass," *Time,* August 19, 1977, p. 140.

2. For accounts of the Black Muslim movement, see Essien-Udom (1962), Lincoln (1994), Perry (1996), and White (1991).

3. See Litt (1970); see also LeMay (1985) and Lincoln (1994).

4. See Bill Turque, "Playing a Different Tune," *Newsweek,* June 28, 1993, pp. 30–31; and Don Terry, "Minister Farrakhan: Conservative Militant," *New York Times,* March 3, 1994, pp. A-1, A-10.

SUGGESTED READINGS

BARTH, ERNEST, AND LAWRENCE NORTHWOOD. 1965. *Urban Desegregation: Negro Pioneers and Their White Neighbors.* Seattle: University of Washington Press.

ESSIEN-UDOM, E. U. 1962. *Black Nationalism: A Search for an Identity in America.* Chicago: University of Chicago Press.

HOFFMAN, EDWARD. 1991. *Despite All Odds: The Story of Lubavitch.* New York: Simon & Schuster.

JACOBSON, SIMON. 1995. *Towards a Meaningful Life: The Wisdom of the Rebbe.* New York: William Morrow.

JANOWSKY, OSCAR, ED. 1964. *The American Jews: A Reappraisal.* Philadelphia: Jewish Publication Society of America.

KITANO, HARRY. 1997. *Race Relations,* 5th ed. Upper Saddle River, NJ: Prentice Hall.

LEMAY, MICHAEL. 1985. *The Struggle for Influence.* Lanham, MD: University Press of America.

LINCOLN, C. ERIC. 1994. *The Black Muslims in America,* 3rd ed. Trenton, NJ: Africa World Press.

MINTZ, JEROME. 1968. *Legends of the Hasidim.* Chicago: University of Chicago Press.

PERRY, BRUCE. 1992. *Malcolm: The Life of a Man Who Changed Black America.* Barrytown, NY: Station Hill Press.

SALES, WILLIAM H., JR. 1994. *From Civil Rights to Black Liberation: Malcolm X and the Organization of Afro-American Unity.* Boston: South End Press.

SCHAEFER, RICHARD. 1998. *Racial and Ethnic Groups,* 7th ed. New York: HarperCollins.

WHITE, JOHN. 1990. *Black Leadership in America,* 2nd ed. New York: Longman.

CASE STUDY 6.1

The Nation of Islam Reaches Out

For much of white America, he remains a fearful image frozen in political time: a black David Duke in bow tie and starched white shirt, menacing Jewish critics of his friend Jesse Jackson nearly a decade ago. But Louis Farrakhan has long been a more complex figure in the African-American community. In stadiums and campus auditoriums, the spiritual leader of the Nation of Islam finds receptive audiences for his iconoclastically conservative gospel of black self-reliance. Now Farrakhan is trying to reintroduce himself to a wary white mainstream. His campaign began in April [1993] with a startling gesture. In a surprise North Carolina concert appearance, he played the Violin Concerto of Jewish-born composer Felix Mendelssohn. "I'm not this ugly fellow you would like to make people think I am," he said during an interview with *Newsweek* in his Chicago home. "It's necessary for the garbage to be cleared away so that a new and better relationship can be structured between blacks and Jews."

The musical peace offering is only part of Farrakhan's bid for a broader audience. Later this year he'll publish a new book, "A Torchlight for America," recasting the spiritual teachings of his late mentor Elijah Muhammad as remedies for drug addiction and crime in black and white communities. He's made overtures to Jewish leaders, dining last month at the home of a prominent Chicago rabbi. And his new outreach isn't limited to whites. Farrakhan recently joined Coretta Scott King, Andrew Young and the Rev. Joseph Lowery of the Southern Christian Leadership Conference at a gathering of African and African-American leaders in Gabon. "There are more things we agree on than disagree on," says Lowery.

SET OFF: While maintaining his perennial call for an African homeland for American blacks, the man who called Hitler "wickedly great" and allegedly described Judaism as a "gutter religion" says he is more optimistic about prospects for racial harmony. "We don't want to be set off to the side for people to look at and say, 'They're the haters, they're the anti-Semites'," he says.

Why is Farrakhan reaching out? One reason is political pragmatism. He realizes that unless he sheds his image as an antagonist from the racist fringe, his hopes of reaching large black and white middle-class audiences with his message are remote. He also believes that repairing relations with Jews will make it more acceptable for influential blacks in sports, entertainment and business worlds to associate with him. But friends say the shift also signals more personal changes. They wonder whether advancing age—he turned 60 last month—and a recent brush with prostate cancer has stirred a sense of mortality. And while he has crusaded against drug abuse, one of his sons is "struggling" with substance abuse (he won't elaborate). It all suggests, friends say, a tempering of passions. "He's reached the same point

Malcolm X reached," says Vincent Lane, chairman of the Chicago Housing Authority. "No man is an island. Racial hate doesn't work. It's a change, and he's trying to signal it with music."

Farrakhan's fence-mending efforts are getting a mostly frosty reception. "Sorry, but I don't think a few musical notes would be enough to soothe my rage as an African-American if someone talked about my people the way Farrakhan has talked about Jews," wrote *Chicago Tribune* columnist Clarence Page, who has covered Farrakhan for years. Chicago Jewish leaders complain that *The Final Call,* his Nation of Islam newspaper, is still filled with anti-Jewish invective. National Jewish leaders are also unenthusiastic. "Playing the music of a dead convert from Judaism [Mendelssohn converted to Christianity] will not repair the depth of hurt, insult and damage that Reverend Farrakhan has spewed," says Abraham Foxman, national director of the Anti-Defamation League of B'nai B'rith.

Farrakhan's new benign rhetoric grows sharp again when confronted with resistance from his old enemies. "Some of my detractors want apology before dialogue," he thundered in his interview with *Newsweek.* "[They] want me to say to my people that Louis Farrakhan has come on bended knee and capitulated. That you will never see if you live 10,000 years!" Farrakhan says his most notorious phrases come from polemics taken out of context in the culture of the 30-second sound bite. He insists that the "gutter religion" comment was a condemnation of Israel for persecuting Palestinians in the name of Judaism. "I *never* meant to slander the Jewish faith," he says. "I was speaking of Israel."

Farrakhan's attempts to allay white suspicion are causing him problems among longtime supporters. Black nationalists who viewed him as an unwavering spokesman against white oppression are disenchanted. "My radio callers are asking, 'What's happened to Farrakhan?'" says Lu Palmer, a prominent black call-in host and a friend. "They're concerned that a voice that was uncompromising has now been softened."

CALYPSO SINGER: White America first heard Farrakhan's voice in defense of Jackson, who referred to New York City as "Hymie-town" while running for president in 1984. By then, Farrakhan had been a fixture in the black community for 20 years. Raised in Boston as Louis Eugene Walcott, he worked as a guitarist and nightclub calypso singer (stage name: The Charmer) before joining the Nation of Islam at the urging of Malcolm X. Farrakhan eventually denounced the Muslim leader for accusing Nation founder Elijah Muhammad of extramarital affairs, but he denies any role in Malcolm's 1965 assassination. He broke with the sect in the late '70s when Muhammad's son steered it from racial separatism toward orthodox Islam. Farrakhan founded a reconstituted Nation based on Muhammad's original doctrines of nationalism and self-renewal through strict behavioral and dietary codes.

Farrakhan works from a heavily secured, Syrian-style home in an integrated neighborhood on Chicago's South Side, rising before dawn to answer mail and work out for two hours (with a trainer) on a treadmill and weights. For the last two years, he's also spent three hours a day with a violin teacher preparing for his concerts. His nearly unbroken layoff of 40 years showed in his April 18 performance, but critics were nonetheless impressed. "Mr. Farrakhan's sound is that of the authentic player," said *The New York Times.* Music critics may be the only skeptics Farrakhan can win over. The repressive character of

Nation culture, especially its antipathy toward feminism and gay rights, is certain to limit his audience. And those he has savaged in his rhetoric are waiting for larger signs of contrition than Farrakhan may ever be willing or able to provide. Playing a concerto is one thing. Facing the music is another.

SOURCE: "Playing a Different Tune," *Newsweek,* June 28, 1993, pp. 30–31. © 1993 Newsweek. All rights reserved. Reprinted by permission.

CHAPTER SEVEN

OLD-STYLE RADICALISM

Some racial and ethnic minorities neither accept the values of the dominant culture and seek to acculturate and eventually assimilate into it, nor reject the value system and seek to isolate themselves from it by psychological or physical means. Some groups not only reject the value system of the majority society, they seek to radically alter that value system. They seek to replace some part of the dominant culture's values with their own. This chapter explores three radical ideologies that are prominent examples of groups reaching out to recruit from among the nation's minorities converts to their value system: Socialists, Communists, and Fascists. They viewed minorities as potentially fruitful sources of adherents so they could gradually build their movements to where they could seize power and impose their values as dominant ones. Although none succeeded, they all made a valiant effort and had an impact, if only indirectly, on the dominant culture.

This chapter explores their cases, starting with Socialism, then Communism, and closing with an examination of Fascism, in both the Italian and German variations. What is particularly interesting is that while they proposed what was for their time a radical ideology that, if accepted, would have drastically altered American culture and society, they pursued that goal using standard political behavior and methods. These "isms" sought mass followings by using standard political behavior targeted at the nation's racial and ethnic minorities.

SOCIALISM

The earliest *ism* to develop in America was Socialism.[1] It sought converts especially among immigrant groups, particularly Germans, Russians, Scandinavians, Slavs, and East European Jews. While it also appealed in areas where radical agrarianism was strong, its weakness was in being perceived as a foreign ideology. Perhaps equally important to its ultimate failure was the factional strife that split and weakened the Socialist movement throughout its history. The earliest stages of the movement in the United States were characterized by a struggle between Marxist Socialists and Lassalleans. The Lassalleans were Socialist followers of the German Socialist Ferdinand Lassalle and advocated reform rather than a revolutionary change.

Among the 1848 immigrant wave were German immigrants who espoused Marxism. They were the most decisive force in developing Marxist thought within American society in the nineteenth century. Forerunners of both the Socialists and Communists in the United States, they settled in large numbers in a half-dozen large cities in which Socialist and labor organizations arose: New York, Philadelphia, St. Louis, Milwaukee, Cincinnati, and Chicago.

The first distinctly Marxist-Socialist organization was the Proletarian League, founded in New York City in June 1852 by two German immigrants, Joseph Weyde-meyer and F. A. Sorge. After an economic crisis in 1857, several Marxist-Socialist organizations arose calling themselves Communist clubs in New York City, Chicago, Milwaukee, and Cincinnati, all of which had large German immigrant settlements.

In 1873, an economic crisis took place followed by large-scale and at times violent labor unrest. In the Pennsylvania mines, a radical Irish immigrant group, the Molly McGuires, arose. Extensive labor strife, including massive railroad strikes in 1877, helped bring about the Socialist Labor Party. It lasted from 1876 to 1890. The Socialist Labor Party was handicapped in achieving broad social appeal by the very basis of its organizational strength—its highly German immigrant composition. Its peak membership was about 3,000. The party quickly split into factions when those advocating anarchosyndicalism established the Revolutionary Socialist Labor Party.

The labor movement was struggling to become national. In 1869, the Knights of Labor was formed. It peaked at about 700,000 members in 1886. On May 4, 1886, the Haymarket Square bombing killed seven policemen and injured sixty people. An immediate reaction resulted in the Knights of Labor losing over 178,000 members. The press linked trade unionism, Socialism, and anarchism in the minds of many.

In 1881, the American Federation of Labor (AFL) was formed in Pittsburgh, and the Knights of Labor gradually died out as the AFL grew to nearly 600,000 members by 1900. The Workingman's Party of the United States began in 1876, and the Social Labor Party of North America in 1877. In the 1890s, the Western Federation of Miners became one of the strongest and most radical of American unions. As America industrialized, social upheaval, labor strife, and the struggle to adjust to millions of immigrants fed the Socialist movement: "American socialism flourished in a few decades after the time of the robber barons, the brutalities of Social Darwinism, rapid industrialization, shameless strikebreaking, labor spying. Coarsely primitive in its accumulations, early industrial capitalism could easily be taken as the enemy by everyone within, and a good many without, the Party" (Howe 1985: 16).

German workers in Milwaukee, Chicago, Detroit, and Cincinnati, and Jewish workers in New York provided the shock troops of the Socialist Party. They remained the most loyal, supplied the party most of its money and manpower, showed the fewest number of defections, and provided most of its leadership. Finns, Russians, and Slavs supplied important contingents to the party. The Socialist Labor Party included

Jews, Germans, Poles, Czechs, Slavs, Hungarians, South Slavs, and Russians. The Jewish and Germans were the most important in overall numbers and in leadership positions in the party. These groups formed a solid base upon which industrial trade unions and Socialist parties developed. Given historical backgrounds of persecution in their homelands, they were accustomed to organizing. By World War I, Jewish needleworkers were solidly organized into the International Ladies' Garment Workers Union; the furriers and the hatters unions were notably Socialist. Union members read Socialist newspapers. German workers dominated several trade unions, for example, printers, bakers, and brewers. They forged an iron combination of organization and ideology.

In 1890, Daniel DeLeon joined the Socialist Labor Party, serving as editor of its paper, *Weekly People.* A dominant force in the party, he oversaw its decline in the decade 1890–1900. DeLeon organized the Socialist Trades and Labor Alliance, whose membership was heavily foreign-born (German, Jewish, Scandinavian, and Polish). By 1900, it slipped to less than 6,000 members in 26 states and mustered less than 80,000 votes in the 1900 election.

The Socialist Labor Party was weakened by its position on the "**Negro question**." Both its leaders and its rank-and-file members simply believed Negroes were inferior to whites. They did not attempt to recruit black members.[2] Rather, DeLeon developed the tactic of "boring from within." Socialist members joined trade unions to take them over. When that failed, they attempted to form a rival to the American Federation of Labor, the Socialist Trades and Labor Alliance.

In 1900, the Socialist Labor Party split. One faction continued to follow DeLeon; the other led to the creation of the Socialist Party, formally established in St. Louis in 1901, with Leon Greenbaum as its national secretary and Eugene Debs as its outstanding mass personality and perennial presidential candidate.[3] The Socialist Democratic Party, as it was called in 1900, picked Debs to run for President, with Job Harriman for vice-president. Other leaders of the new party were Morris Hillquit, a Russian-born attorney and ardent Socialist in New York, and Victor Berger, a German Socialist active in Milwaukee.

Eugene Debs was born in Terre Haute, Indiana, on November 5, 1855.[4] His parents were immigrants from Alsace (in present-day France) who came to the United States in 1849. Debs was fluent in French and German, as well as his native English. Debs lost his railroad fireman job during the depression that followed the Panic of 1873. In 1875, he became a labor organizer of the Brotherhood of Locomotive Firemen (BLF). By 1879, he was active in Democratic politics and was elected to the Indiana state legislature in 1883. In 1880, he became editor of the union magazine and national secretary/treasurer. In 1893, Debs organized the American Railway Union (ARU), pushing the concept of forming an industry-wide union for all railroad workers.

The unsuccessful Pullman strike in 1894 was a disaster that essentially ended the union. Debs was jailed for six months for violating an injunction. In 1897, Debs became a Socialist, beginning a 30-year career of carrying the dual message of industrial unionism and Socialism to Americans. He constantly stressed that the movement had to be economic and political in character.

A 1912 Socialist Party campaign poster.

Debs was a spellbinding speaker. A Socialist follower described him: "I was a young man at the time and had heard a good many speakers before," he avowed, "but Debs was something out of the ordinary. He held the audience in a trance with his tall figure and long arms waving" (cited in Brommel 1978: 63). Debs pushed various Progressive Era reform measures. His ideas, considered so radical in his day, eventually became standard American political values: the abolition of child labor; the right of women to vote; the graduated income tax; the direct election of U.S. senators; unemployment insurance; employer liability laws; establishment of national departments of education and of health; attacks on Jim Crowism; support of equal rights for blacks; and prison reform.

The American Socialist Party depended heavily on and actively sought immigrants as converts to its cause. These immigrant groups formed associations linked to the Socialist parties of their respective native countries. Federations of the foreign-language workers played a special role in American Socialism. Pathbreakers in linking language federations and the American Socialist Party were the Finnish Socialists. Socialism was part of their immigrant baggage, involving a radical break with old traditions: Finnish Socialists preached atheism and science as well as Socialism. Their membership strength grew from anticlericalism as much as from specific labor grievances. The various foreign-language federations of the Socialist Party are shown in Table 7.1, which lists the year when each was admitted.

TABLE 7.1 **Membership in Foreign-Language Sections of Workers Party, 1922–1925**
(Yearly Averages)

	1922	1923	1924	1925
Armenian	—	59	61	132
Czecho-Slovak	169	431	353	295
Estonian	42	73	73	70
Finnish	5,846	6,583	7,099	6,410
German	463	461	442	350
Greek	88	142	203	256
Hungarian	313	374	469	509
Italian	138	412	581	331
Jewish	975	1,055	1,368	1,447
Lettish	597	417	443	434
Lithuanian	677	929	901	815
Polish	110	210	165	121
Roumanian	—	81	65	47
Russian	379	959	941	870
Scandinavian	33	259	248	211
South Slavic	1,077	1,158	1,290	1,109
Slovenian	—	—	—	14
Ukrainian	87	623	781	622
English	1,269	1,169	1,906	2,282
Total	12,058	15,395	17,377	16,325

This table is from the unpublished doctoral thesis of Francis X. Sutton, "The Radical Marxist" (Harvard University, 1950). It is based on Workers (Communist) Party of America, *The 4th National Convention* (Chicago: Daily Worker Publishing Co., 1925), pp. 27–37.

SOURCE: Nathan Glazer, *The Social Basis of American Communism* (New York: Harcourt Brace and World, 1961), p. 42.

Debs sought to recruit blacks, but both he and the party considered the "Negro problem" one of class, not race, a view dictating a strategy of working-class organizations. As Debs said:

> The Socialist Party is the party of workers regardless of race, color, creed. In mill and mine, shop and farm, office and school, the workers can assert their united power, and through the Socialist Party establish a cooperative commonwealth forever free from human exploitation and class rule. (cited in Record 1951: 101)

Debs, however, failed to gain widespread support within the party for recruiting blacks. The party was unsuccessful in efforts to attract a large number of blacks to the cause:

> Negroes were too preoccupied with staying alive and praising God (in that order) to give time to the building of a new society. Coupled with this was their reluctance to invite the stigma of radicalism when the stigma of race was already overwhelming. The fact that it (the Socialist Party) did proper defense to southern mores by organizing separate locals below the Mason-Dixon line did not enhance its appeal to Negroes. (Record 1951: 11)

Despite Debs's untiring efforts, the American Socialist Party was never able to gain mass appeal. In its presidential bids, for example, the party never got more than 6 percent of the vote, that in its high-tide year of 1912. In 1912, Debs received his largest electoral support, over 80,000 votes for President, representing one tenth of his total national vote, from Oklahoma, Texas, Arkansas, and Louisiana. Oklahoma had the strongest state party organization in the Socialist Party, with over 961 locals and 12,000 dues-paying members. In 1914, they had over 100 people elected to local office and even six to the state legislature.

The Socialist Party's inner diversity developed schismatic factionalism that led to catastrophe after 1912. The party split began at the 1912 convention when the left wing, enraged over the question of the party's position on the United States entering World War II in 1917, left the party. It split further when the Communist Party was established in 1919–1920.

The party's decline was also influenced by Debs's evangelism. His very fervor allowed him to see only two choices: capitalism, which he characterized as the devil's spawn, and Socialism, his angelic promise. He could never breach the gap between factions of the party advocating violent activism (the syndicalists/anarchists) and those advocating political reform and close cooperation with the trade/skilled craft unionism movement. The 1912 split was partly over relations with the AFL and the labor union movement generally. In 1912, the AFL had fewer than 1 million members and confined itself to skilled craftsmen. The Socialists called Samuel Gompers a "reactionary." Both Debs and Victor Berger attacked him for his "class collaboration." This threatened a labor movement that included anti-Socialist elements, especially large numbers of Catholics.

By 1912, factions within the Socialist Party were increasingly unwilling or unable to work together. One faction, the so-called "**Sewer Socialists**," were largely German Americans in Milwaukee. Their leftist critics sneeringly called them by that title. They had little of the millennial zeal that marked the Debsian cadres in the West and Southwest. They lived in close and effective harmony with their local trade unions. Ironically, these often "foreign-born" (German) immigrants showed a keener appreciation of changes in American society than such completely indigenous radicals as the "Texas Reds," the "Oklahoma Rebels," and the "Colorado syndicalists." Sewer Socialists proved they knew how to win elections.

Another faction involved Jewish immigrant socialists in New York. They were Yiddish-speaking and distinctively Jewish in the flavor of their organization. They were militant garment workers. Their leader, Morris Hillquit, tried to steer the movement between the extremes of antipolitical syndicalism and incoherent reform. A third faction were Christian Socialists of Populist agrarianism.

A more fundamentalist and radical faction was the Western syndicalists. In 1905, they formed the Industrial Workers of the World (IWW), known as the **Wobblies**. This group was addicted to verbal violence and advocated "direct action"—the use of violence and force to further the revolution. Its leaders were William Haywood, Charles Ruthenberg, and William Foster, all of whom later became Communists.

The IWW led a textile strike in 1912. Its radicalism prevented its establishment as a lasting union. In 1912, its membership exceeded 14,000; a year later it had declined to 700. It reached out to blacks, attempting to organize both unskilled and semiskilled workers with no racial lines. Very critical of the AFL for its racial policies, the Wobblies trained and used Negro organizers, such as Ben Fletcher, who recruited both blacks and whites. Despite its efforts to do so, however, it never achieved a large black membership. Blacks were never more than 5 to 10 percent of its members.

After the split in 1912, the Socialist Party made a concerted effort to win over blacks. It played a central role in the formation of the NAACP, began to organize black dockworkers in New Orleans, and recruited blacks into the United Mine Workers. In 1915, it helped organize the International Trade Union Educational League to organize Negro workers. In 1917, it made its most serious effort when A. Philip Randolph and Chandler Owen established *The Messenger* and served as its editors. These outreach efforts were less successful in attracting new members than those lost by Debs's antiwar position, which damaged the party's chances to win additional support, led to the imprisonment of many of its leaders, and to the eventual decline of the party.

Just as the industrial labor union movement divided into two major factions, the American Federation of Labor and the Congress of Industrial Organizations, so the Socialist Party split in two in 1912. Haywood and Foster left the party in 1912, forming the Syndicalist League of North America in Chicago. After a brief attempt to keep them in the party, Debs shifted his support to mend differences with Hillquit and Berger in 1913. During 1912–1915, as World War I raged in Europe, Debs became a militant pacifist and led the Socialist Party to become an antiwar movement.

When the United States entered World War I, on April 6, 1917, the Socialist Party held its convention in St. Louis and opposed the war in a statement known as the "Majority Report" and by a national referendum of its members who voted for the antiwar resolution by a vote of 11,041 to 782. The party had been slowly recovering from the 1912 split. Its membership rose from just over 79,000 in 1915, to over 80,000 in 1917, and to just short of 105,000 in 1919. By the end of the war, however, almost every Socialist leader was prosecuted under the Espionage Act: Victor Berger, Kate Richards O'Hare, Adolph Geuner, Charles Ruthenberg, and Eugene Debs. Only Hillquit, stricken with tuberculosis, was spared.

The Socialist Party was attacked as being pro-German. Debs was arrested following an anti-war speech he gave in 1918, and sentenced, under the Espionage Act, to ten years in prison. In March 1919 his conviction was upheld by the U.S. Supreme Court. The party was further split when its left wing walked out, held its own convention, and voted to affiliate with the Communist Internationale, forming the Communist Party.

In 1920, the Socialist Party again nominated Debs for President. Although he was serving his term in a federal prison, he was allowed to issue a once-per-week statement for the campaign. He won nearly 1 million votes. The party launched a campaign to have him pardoned. President Harding ordered Debs released (a commutation, not a pardon) at Christmastime in 1921. In 1922, Debs tried to revive the Socialist Party of America, which by then was down to a mere 7,793 members, almost half of whom were foreign-language affiliates. He specifically rejected joining the Communist Party. In 1924, Debs supported Robert La Follette and the new Progressive Party.

In 1926, he wrote a pamphlet appealing to American labor in defense of Sacco and Vanzetti. Eugene Debs died on October 20, 1926. The Socialist Party continued its factional strife. In 1934, Upton Sinclair, the novelist who had run for office as a Socialist, entered and won the California Democratic primary for governor. Norman Thomas followed Debs as the party's leader. He ran for President six times, but never received the votes of Debs's high point. Like Debs, Thomas was unable to heal the factional strife. The party was torn between support of President Roosevelt and the New Deal evolutionary programs in support of labor, or whether, along with the Popular Front period of Communism, it should ally itself with local union groups, the American Labor Party, the Farmer-Labor Party, and the like. In these allied groups, the party was never a dominant force, although it played a significant role in some coalitions.

COMMUNISM

The Communist Party in America grew out of the Socialist Party movement, with members drawn from the mostly foreign-language affiliations of the Socialist Labor Party. Nathan Glazer describes its birth:

> The most important step to a proper understanding of the question "who" became Communists and "why" is to realize that for certain social groups, for certain milieux, it was neither eccentric nor exceptional to become a communist. The great majority of these members came from the Socialist Party. In January 1919, this party had almost 110,000 members. In May and June of that year, great blocs of the membership were expelled or suspended for allegiance to the Left Wing that was forming in response to the Bolshevik revolution. By July 1919, the membership was down to 40,000. . . . As the entire [Communist] party emerged from the underground, it had about 12,000 members. At this time, in 1922, the Socialist Party had about the same number of members. (1961: 39)

The Communist Party in America was always small. At its peak it had fewer than 100,000 members, and its card-carrying membership was never more than 35,000 to 40,000. Numbers and votes were not the critical aspects of the movement. It targeted for recruitment the most exploited and oppressed because they were considered potentially the best, most loyal, and most dependable workers: white Euro-ethnic immigrants and the American Negro.[5]

Two American Communist parties were formed in 1919. One emerged from the left wing of the Socialist Party (the IWW) and the Socialist Labor Party. The other arose in the Workers International Industrial Union and responded to the appeal of the Communist Internationale. The Communist Labor Party was the foreign-language-federation-dominated faction from the Socialist Labor Party. It met in Chicago and claimed about 10,000 members. The Communist Party of America was the Michigan federationist group claiming about 58,000 members. A partial merger between the groups was effected when the United (or Centrist) Communist Party was set up in July 1920 in New York City.

All the factions were driven underground when Attorney General A. Mitchell Palmer led hundreds of raids during the "Red Scare" summer of 1919. These raids resulted in over 10,000 persons being arrested in 70 cities. Over 500 aliens were deported, 249 alone aboard the "Soviet Ark" ship, the *Buford*. In the hysteria of 1919, the Socialist congressman from Milwaukee, Victor Berger, was refused his elected seat in the House of Representatives. Five Socialist assemblymen were denied their seats in the New York state legislature. In the delirium of anti-Communism, Palmer even claimed that the Communist Party had 1 million members. The various surviving Communist Party factions met in New York City in 1922 and formed the Worker's Party of America. It claimed a membership of 25,000 by 1923.

The most striking characteristic of the Communist Party in the 1920s was its overwhelmingly new-immigrant membership. The Communist Party worked with the foreign-language groups active in the Socialist movement and in the industrial union movement because they provided the party with three key elements: money, access to the industrial worker class, and the movements' cadres of rank-and-file members.

While the white ethnic predominance of party membership caused white-black membership strains, it reflected the predominance of such white ethnics in the primary target group of the party, the "American industrial proletariat." As a report of the Sixth Convention noted: "We face the fact that the working class of this country, in its national composition, consists of a majority of foreign born. For example, we find that 67% of the oil workers are foreign born, 62% of the packing house workers, 61% of the miners. We find textile workers over 60%, steel workers over 60%. . . . The party was a working class party because the greater part of its membership came from certain immigrant communities" (cited in Glazer 1961: 76).

After World War I, the Third Internationale of the Communist Party, as did the party in the United States, believed that world revolution was at hand, European nations were collapsing, and the United States was on the eve of a social revolution.

The left wing of the Socialists, in June 1920, organized the Proletarian Party of America, but the new party was expelled from the Communist Party. The two factions of the party failed to effectively unite, and by 1921 the movement experienced a multiplication of Communist sects and organizations: the Industrial Communist Party, the Rummager League, the Worker's Council, the American Labor Alliance, the United Communist Party, and the African Black Brotherhood (which did not survive the year, as only a few Communists were initially attempting to carry on agitation among the nation's Negro workers). Of the twelve Communist organizations that began in 1921, eight of which were political, seven died or merged, so that at the end of 1921 only six remained: the Communist Party, the United Communist Party, the Proletarian Party, the American Labor Alliance, the Worker's Council, and the Arbeiter Bildungs Vereine (former German Socialists).

American Communists of all types were profoundly affected by the barren results. American labor simply was not responding to their propaganda and policies. After World War I, all labor organizations declined: the IWW declined rapidly from its peak of about 60,000; the AFL had 4 million members in 1920 but was down to 2.9 million by 1923; the Socialist Labor Party, which only had 11,000 members in 1912, was down to 2,000 by 1920; and the Socialist Party, likewise, fell from over 80,000 before World War I to just over 26,000 by 1920.

The American Communist Party, which the Worker's Party began to call itself by 1923, had a decidedly middle-class membership, which differentiated it from almost every other Communist Party in the Western world. This reflected the middle-class status of its Jewish members, which by 1925 were second only to the Finnish members. Although Communist Party members were but a miniscule percentage of American Jews, those Jews who were Communist were a significant (about 9) percentage of the party.

By the early 1920s, the party was making a concerted effort to attract African Americans. The founders of the American Communist Party were radicals of European origin, and their initial expectation had been that they would first revolutionize white workers and then go on to bring the gospel of Marx and Lenin to people of color. They considered the Negro an organizing asset and were anxious to enlist the support of the African-American organizers in the IWW. Taking their lead from Lenin's analysis of imperialism and the national and colonial question, they proposed to direct much of their energy toward developing the oppressed Negroes into a revolutionary force. Since blacks were clearly the most oppressed group in the United States, the party thought them to be one of the greatest potential resources for its program, and it actively tried to recruit black leadership, consistently made the "Negro question" a major issue in its program, and issued a stream of special books and pamphlets on the subject.

At the Fourth Congress of the Comintern, in 1922, American Communists John Reed and Claude McKay contributed resolutions on Garveyism, recognizing the legitimacy of the black anticolonial and anti-imperialist struggle. The congress put a high priority on recruitment of African Americans to the party:

> In their efforts during the 1920s and 1930s to appeal to blacks and to progressive whites troubled by the flagrant racial injustices of American and South African society, Communists enjoyed a special advantage. No one else in those decades was fighting so intently and assertively for the abolition of segregation and the complete equality of the races. (Frederickson 1995: 180)

Despite the party's overtures and attempts to infiltrate the UNIA, Marcus Garvey, by 1925 and while in prison, explicitly rejected working with them:

> Communism among Negroes in 1920–1921 was represented in New York by such Negroes as Cyril Briggs, and W.A. Domingo, and my contact and experience of them and their methods are enough to keep me shy of that kind of communism for the balance of my natural life. . . . The American Negro is warned to keep away from communism, as it is taught in this country. (cited in Lewis 1988: 134)

While the Communist Party had an advantage in its uncompromising position of antiracism, its major liability was the approach it used. The party shifted directions in its appeal to the black struggle in response to changes in the party line coming from Moscow. In two decades, from the late 1920s to 1950s, it adopted five major strategy shifts, giving the American party the image of being mere agents of Moscow, tools of the Soviet Union. Rupert Lewis (1988) argues that the conflict between the rank-and-file white and black members of the party and the party's stumbling over how to deal with the Garvey movement were significant reasons for the party's failure to win over a large black following.

Its main source of African-American members was the **African Blood Brotherhood (ABB)**, created in 1919 after the Socialist Party split. Most of the Brotherhood leaders were Socialists drawn to the promise of the Bolshevik revolution. The Brotherhood specifically rejected Garvey's program. Instead, it favored organizing a militant program to win black freedom in the United States. Although the Brotherhood supplied relatively few party members, it was among the first to join the party and made up the core of the black Communist leadership for many years.

The Worker's Party members were unofficially involved in the Federated Farmer–Labor Party founded July 3, 1923 in Chicago. It had an estimated 600,000 members—miners, machinists, needleworkers, carpenters, metalworkers, the 87,000-strong West Virginia Federation of Labor, and the 210,000-strong AFL-affiliated unions. The Federated Farmer–Labor Party endorsed Senator Robert La Follette, who made one of the strongest third-party efforts of the twentieth century, polling 4,826,382 votes, or 16.5 percent of the total cast. The Worker's Party refused to endorse him and instead ran its own candidate, William Foster. He received 33,316 votes in the 13 states where the party was on the ballot.

Among the earliest of the members who rose to become prominent within the Worker's Party was Cyril Briggs, who founded the African Blood Brotherhood, edited *The Crusader,* a monthly magazine of the left, and was a regular contributor to *The Messenger,* the Socialist magazine edited by Chandler Owen and A. Philip Randolph. Another was poet Claude McKay, the most notable black intellectual associated with the party in the early 1920s and who was associate editor of *The Liberator.* Another ABB member who became an early Communist leader was Harry Haywood, of the IWW. Edward Doty commanded the Chicago post and organized independent unions in Chicago. Other members included Richard Moore, Otto Huiswood, Grace Campbell, Otto Hall, and N. V. Phillips. The ABB never had more than 2,000 members, about 150 to 200 of whom joined the party.

In 1924, an All-Race Assembly, also known as the **Sanhedrin**, met in Chicago. It had 250 delegates from 20 states representing 61 national black organizations. It was the first united front of blacks in which the Communist Party participated officially. The Worker's Party sent Lovett Fort-Whiteman, Gordon Owens, and S. V. Phillips; the African Blood Brotherhood was represented by Otto Huiswood.

The party was instrumental in establishing the American Negro Labor Congress in 1925, the first significant effort by the party to organize the black masses. Convened in October, also in Chicago, six of the seventeen signers were Communist Party members. The strategy of using the Sanhedrin and the American Negro Labor Congress exemplified the "bore from within" tactic of the party. But organized labor and the Communist Party were essentially using one another in this strategy.

In 1928, the Communist Party launched its "Negro self-determination" phase, a shift that certainly surprised most black Communists in the United States. This effort was led by Cyril Briggs. In *The Crusader,* Briggs called for self-determination for blacks in an independent society in the nation, while continuing to advocate cooperation with radical whites to overthrow capitalism. The other leading advocate of self-determination was Harry Haywood, another leading force in the ABB, who joined the Young Communist League in 1923 and the Communist Party in 1925. He was sent to

Moscow in 1926 for training. He characterized African Americans as members of an "oppressed nation," and argued for "self-determination for the black belt." The Sixth Congress of the International voted that Negro self-determination must be a party goal in the United States and South Africa. It ruled out working with the NAACP, UNIA, or the ANLC (American Negro Labor Congress). Communists were to denounce such movements and to discredit them in any way they could.

This new strategy was in part a response to the failure to recruit a significant black following during the 1920–1928 period. Their lack of success in attracting black unionists differed little from that of their fellow white members. In 1925, they set up the International Labor Defense (ILD) and selected a black lawyer, William L. Patterson, as its executive secretary. The American Negro Labor Congress was mostly a paper organization of sweeping promises but little performance. By 1928, it claimed a membership of 14,000, but its total black membership was between 150 and 200.

James Allen succinctly described the **black belt** to which the struggle for self-determination was aimed:

> The national-liberation movement centering in the struggle for the right of self-determination among the Negro masses will necessarily be concentrated in the Black Belt of the South, an area roughly designated as East Virginia and North Carolina, the state of South Carolina, central Georgia and Alabama, the delta regions of Mississippi and Louisiana, and the coastal regions of Texas. In this area there are 264 counties in which the Negroes make up the majority of the population, and two states—Mississippi and South Carolina—in which they form the majority of the whole population. (Foner and Allen 1987: 63)

The self-determination phase was the party's attempt to attract a mass following among America's black population. It had noted the success of Marcus Garvey's movement in attracting a mass following among lower- and lower-middle-class blacks, the very classes it was targeting, who had found in Garvey's promises of a new land an escape from the harsh realities of segregation. After his imprisonment, Garvey's organization began to deteriorate, and the Communists shifted from their original position of not opposing him and his movement to one of being increasingly critical of him and of "Negro Zionism."

When the Sixth World Congress laid down its program of self-determination, the CPA responded with its black belt program, defining the basis for a separate Negro nation: "In the economic and social conditions and class relations of the Negro people there are increasing forces which serve as a basis for the development of a Negro nation (a compact mass of farmers on a contiguous territory, semi-feudal conditions, complete segregation, common traditions of slavery, the development of distinct class and economic ties, etc." (Record 1951: 59)

Despite its criticism of the Garvey movement as "Negro Zionism," the party's self-determination and black republican program had a distinctly Garvey look. Both the new Communist view and the UNIA stressed the distinct culture of the Negro; both held that common racial features were a basis for a nation-state, and both noted that the Negro had a "natural area" for the location of a state—in Africa according to Garvey and in the black belt of the United States for the Communists. And both programs were ultimately defeated by a basic African-American attitude that Ralph Bunche so aptly described:

> It is conceivable that conditions might become so intolerable for Negroes in the United States that the black man would seek refuge on other shores. It is extremely doubtful that any significant support for a colonization or repatriation movement could be developed among Negroes under present conditions. However, the glamour of a black state, either here as a 49th state or in Africa, as an independent nation, has not caught the imagination of the Negro—either of the Negro intellectual or the Negro in the mass. The Negro in his customs, in his thinking, and in his aspirations is an American, and he regards America as his home. He lacks even those religious ties which would attract the Jewish refugee to Palestine. If the Negro is to be gotten out of America he will have to be driven out. Only when racial persecution becomes so efficiently brutal, so thoroughly institutionalized that life for the Negro will become impossible here, will there be any likelihood that the black American will seek refuge elsewhere. (cited in Record 1951: 42)

During the 1928–1935 phase, Communists, with a revolutionary self-determination program, stood in opposition to practically all the Negro betterment, interracial, and nationalist organizations. The party failed to see merit in any of their programs. It lumped them together as conscious conspiracies to defeat the potentially radical Negro masses. The party alone was right, the party alone had the correct theory, the party alone had a program of action—according to the party. Communists blessed only those extensions of themselves: the League for the Struggle of Negro Rights, the International Labor Defense, and the Trade Union Unity League.

In some respects, the 1930s witnessed the biggest success the Communist Party experienced in winning credibility among black Americans. It set up the League of Struggle for Negro Rights in 1930. Although its obvious character as a front organization of the party prevented it from developing true mass support, the depression released radical impulses that had been held in check during the prosperity and conservative pro-business climate that prevailed during the 1920s. The Communist-led **Sharecropper's Union of Alabama** had no chance of reaching the bulk of the black farmers in the state, but it persisted in some counties for several years despite horrendous violence and intimidation against it. At its peak, in 1935, it may have had as many as 10,000 members. Its leader, Hosea Hudson, was one of a few black Alabamians able to substitute Marx and Lenin for Christ or the dictatorship of the proletariat for the millennium. Unquestionably, the party's greatest gains were made in the large urban industrial centers where relief programs were more acute and where the large concentrations of the unemployed provided a solid base for the party's organizational efforts.

The party recruited and developed some key black leaders. Negro journalists, intellectuals, and trade unionists went to Moscow for training. Among them were James W. Ford, the party's vice-presidential candidate in 1932; Eugene Gordon, a journalist; and William L. Patterson, who became the secretary of the International Labor Defense. Young Negro trade unionists were targeted by the Trade Union Educational League. The American Negro Labor Congress selected and trained radical Negro unionists. James Ford entered the party in 1926 and was a delegate to the

Fourth World Congress of the Red International Labor Unions. In 1928, he was a delegate to the Sixth World Congress of the Communist Internationale. Shortly afterward, he assumed the post of Negro Organizer for the Trade Union Unity League. In 1932, the Foster/Ford ticket received 102,991 votes.

The most successful effort by the party in increasing its visibility and its credibility among blacks was its role in the defense of the Scottsboro Boys, led by the International Labor Defense (ILD).[6] (See Case Study 7.1.) Its involvement helped develop a conviction among blacks by the mid-1930s that the Communists were the boldest and most effective advocates of equal citizenship for African Americans. Although the case won it no judicial victory or mass membership, it enabled the Communist Party to develop a much more favorable image. As Nathan Glazer points out, by "capturing" the Scottsboro case, the party could, for the first time, enter Negro churches and other organizations to raise money for the defense. The sums raised were considerable, and most of it could go to support a staff of Communist organizers and fund-raisers. The ILD was on the constant lookout for victims of injustice who might allow them to take over their defense.

The Scottsboro case significantly aided black recruitment. A big recruiting drive in 1930 brought in 6,197 new members, including the first big wave of Negro members, at 1,300. But turnover of Negro members was particularly high, and it took a few years before Negro membership rose above 1,000. Chicago was particularly effective in recruiting Negro members; New York lagged. In May 1935, the party reported 2,227 Negro members, 8 percent of the party membership at the time. Among recruits, 15 percent were blacks. This was the pattern of Negro recruitment into the

James Ford, Communist Party vice-presidential nominee, 1936.

party for many years. The party steadily recruited about twice as many Negro members as the rolls showed at any time. In a big recruiting drive in 1938, it was announced that 2,890 (17 percent of all new recruits) were Negro and that the Negro membership of the party was 5,000. Yet, in 1942, the party still had only 3,200 Negro members, about 7 percent of total membership. It is doubtful that the Negro membership ever rose much above this percentage. The party made continuous efforts to recruit and retain blacks. It aimed at a high percentage of blacks at its conventions as delegates, committee chairs, and national standing committee members. Nonetheless, it failed to achieve a high percentage of black members at any time.

A 1953 study by the FBI determined that of the 5,395 "leading members of the Communist Party," 411 were black, about 8 percent of the leadership. While a sizable proportion (about their proportion of the total population), it was not "high." Still, no other predominantly white party, or, indeed, any social movement in the United States, had that percentage of blacks among its leadership. The party faced a difficulty in reaching out to blacks, cited by analysts of the party and recognized in its official organs as well—the attitudes of many of its members. This problem was called the "sin" of **white chauvinism**.

Throughout the 1920s, the party struggled with the white chauvinism issue. There was feuding in its day-to-day operations at the local branch level to carry over a biracial pattern. In the mid-1920s the party tried, for a time, to organize separate black and white unions, such as the American Negro Labor Congress. As Philip S. Foner and James Allen describe it:

> The other major effort to reach outward occurred in 1925, with the organization of the American Negro Labor Congress. Its central objective was to generate a movement directed toward the organization of Black labor and to overcome its exclusion from the established unions. The formation of separate Black unions was to be supported where necessary, but this was not to be seen as a diversion from the main task of uniting white and black workers in the same unions. The program approved at the Congress went beyond the labor question to cover the broad field of Black rights in all aspects—including demands that were to be recognized in law years later. The Congress aroused considerable interest around the country, both from those who were fearful of Black militancy, and from Blacks who looked hopefully to radical initiatives to advance the cause of freedom and equality. It is indicative of the times that in back of both attitudes was the expectation that, given the Black condition, communism would have great appeal to Black Americans. (1987: x)

The congress failed to attract a mass following among blacks. A major lesson to be learned from both the Sanhedrin and the congress was that the Negro question could not be relegated to a separate compartment, even if placed in the hands of black Communists.

In the mid-1930s, the party launched a new strategy and effort—the United Front phase. The American Communist Party decided it could work with middle-class black reform groups. It sought to work with unions and organizations like the NAACP and the National Negro Congress. During this phase it made a significant contribution to the cause of African-American liberation through its success in helping to influence organized labor to open its ranks to blacks. The party transformed the

Trade Union Educational League into the Trade Union Unity League (TUUL). Its task was to create a trade union center that could unite all revolutionary unions, minority groups, and individual militants, and to infiltrate the "reformist" unions against the AFL bureaucracy.

The Popular Front period of Communism (1936–1938) saw the party infiltrate the institutions and organizations of the New Deal, and it allied itself with local political groups, with the Socialist Party, the American Labor Party, the Farmer-Labor Party, and the like. While in none of these efforts was it dominant, it did become a significant force. Its greatest success during the period of the Popular Front was in the newly formed CIO unions, which at one time had 60 Communists among 200 full-time organizers. This phase not only represented a shift in strategy, it was a period when the party itself changed in its composition. As Nathan Glazer noted: "During the thirties, the party was transformed from a largely working-class organization to one that was one-half middle-class. . . . In 1938, the breakdown of the occupations of a large group of new recruits (17,000) showed 22 percent in middle-class categories. In 1941, no less than 44 percent of the party was reported as professional and white collar" (p. 114).

What success the Popular Front policy had can be attributed to its leader, Earl Browder. In the election of 1940, the Communist Party ticket of Earl Browder for President and James Ford for vice-president garnered only 46,251 votes, but he was an effective proponent of the Popular Front line. In the Popular Front era, while working cooperatively with other groups, especially the union movement and particularly the CIO, the party enjoyed some success and access that until then had eluded all its efforts. Glazer describes some very human aspects of that development:

> Let us not forget a simple fact that some historians of American communism do tend to forget; communists, even communist leaders, remain human beings—often enough fanatical, often enough with moral sensibilities coarsened, but, still, human beings susceptible to the desires and needs that most of us experience. A second-level party leader who had been section organizer, say, in Cleveland during the early thirties and had led demonstrations that brought him stitches in his head and months in jail, might now find it exceedingly pleasant to be leading a party that had opened an attractive headquarters, enjoyed good relations with local politicians and trade-union leaders, and could attract seven or eight thousand people to a rally when Earl Browder came to Cleveland. A section organizer in Harlem, where the Party had counted a mere straggle of comrades during the early thirties, might now find it decidedly pleasant to be able to reach Adam Clayton Powell on the phone whenever he chose, to enroll hundreds of new black members, and to lure a brilliant array of Harlem talent when the party ran a big social event. An old, battered activist could now feel a sense of growing authority in heading, say, a large Massachusetts local of the electrical workers' union, or a local of the California maritime workers' union, sheltered within the CIO and favored, more or less, by John L. Lewis. As for the top union leaders who belonged or were close to the Communist Party, men like Julius Emspak, Joseph Curran, Harry Bridges, and Mike Quill—they were starting to enjoy the taste of real power. They were negotiating contracts that covered thousands of members; were disposing of significant sums of money (some of it drained off to the party and its front groups); were dealing and wheeling with other union leaders and political figures who wanted their support. Respectability, comfort, secretaries, good salaries, docile staffs, admiring followers—all came together to soften and allure. (pp. 100–101)

The sea change in membership in the party from old-line, working-class radicals to middle-class and lower professional workers contributed to a new phase that appealed to blacks by purging its members of the "sin" of white chauvinism, and by selecting a black, James Ford, as its vice-presidential nominee.

Earl Browder led the party into the early 1940s in a revisionist phase he called "organized capitalism," and by 1944 the party reached its peak in official membership. In the 1944 convention, Foster claimed 80,000 members, about 14 percent of whom were blacks. He claimed they became about 33 percent of the party by 1945. Glazer notes the relationship of that trend to its white ethnic, and particularly Jewish, base.

> The development of such groups in the party is largely to be explained in terms of the ethnic origin of those being recruited into these professions in the twenties and thirties. Many second-generation Jews then moved into these occupations. The doctors and lawyers in the Communist Party were no random sample of doctors and lawyers in general, but were predominantly drawn from these newcomers. Certainly they suffered the fate of newcomers—difficulties in establishing practices, making a decent living, achieving status. The fact that some of them joined the Communist Party may be explained with equal justice in terms of the special difficulties of newcomers in an occupational role, with the accompanying frustrations and resentment, or in term of the ethnic background which may have made more radical politics familiar to them, and thus made them more accessible to Communist influence. In either case, very much the same people were involved; the doctors and dentists and lawyers in the Communist Party were generally Jewish doctors, dentists, and lawyers. (pp. 146–147)

In 1940, A. Philip Randolph, then the Democratic Socialist president of the National Negro Congress, resigned over the peace resolution passed that year. This was a turning point in the development of the black protest movement, since it turned one of the most effective and charismatic protest leaders into an uncompromising anti-Communist. Randolph called for and began to organize a March on Washington, which, although it did not take place because World War II developments derailed it, nonetheless was important in that it foreshadowed the growth of the more militant, nonviolent civil rights movement of the post–World War II era from which the Communists were excluded. The party savagely attacked Randolph and suffered greatly as a result in its image among African Americans.

The party line, and its appeal, held only while the United States and the Soviet Union were allies against Nazism during World War II. After the war, and the rise of the Iron Curtain and the Cold War, the Communist Party in the United States shifted its line yet again. William Foster opposed Browder, and the party expelled Browder in 1946, adopting a stronger leftist line and developing new leadership. The party underwent critical self-evaluation, again focused to a great degree on the Negro question. Harry Haywood published his book, *Negro Liberation,* and the party went through another phase of rooting out white chauvinism.

In 1948, the Communist Party backed the Progressive Party and its nomination of Henry Wallace for President (against Harry Truman). Wallace's campaign was supposedly controlled by the Communist Party, which is a major reason why the NAACP would not be associated with it, and why black "revolutionary antagonists" like W.E.B. Du Bois and Paul Robeson were attracted to it.[7] The Progressive Party aggressively sought, yet failed to achieve, a significant black vote, winning less than 14 percent of the votes in Harlem.

Paul Robeson was the expatriate black artist and avowed Communist who had returned from France to the United States in 1939 to fight Fascism. He created the Council on African Affairs. It was labeled as a subversive organization and placed on the U.S. attorney general's list of such organizations after the war. W. E. B. Du Bois, as discussed earlier, was a former NAACP leader who increasingly moved to the left in the 1940s. In 1950 he was indicted for "failure to register as an agent of a foreign principal" (i.e., Moscow) for his work with another Communist front group, the Peace Information Center. He was tried on those charges in November 1951 but was acquitted.

In July 1948, 12 members of the Communist Party, including William Foster and Eugene Dennis, were indicted for violation of the Alien Registration Law of 1940, better known as the Smith Act. They were convicted and sentenced to five years in prison and fined $10,000 each. The Federal Court of Appeals affirmed those convictions in 1951, and the U.S. Supreme Court upheld them in October 1951. After the Supreme Court decision, the FBI arrested many other Communists, announcing that it had "43,000 communists under surveillance." It used the McCarren Walter Act of 1952 to deport foreign-born Communists.

In terms of its appeal to blacks, the American Communist Party staggered into the postwar era with a number of handicaps. Due to its party line shifts and its attacks on the NAACP and Randolph's March on Washington, it was seen as less militant than those organizations. Its position on "self-determination for the black belt," restored to party prominence by Harry Haywood, was rejected by an increasingly urbanized black population that during the war had moved to the urban industrial North in a mass migration that then made the black belt strategy seem unreal. The failure of all but a tiny minority of blacks to vote for the Progressive Party in 1948 showed clearly that the party carried little weight in the black community.

The foreign-language members of the party shared in its general postwar decline, although at a slower pace. Being more isolated, socially, linguistically, and by age, from the mainstream of American public opinion, their rate of defection from the party was slower. Some clung to the party in fear, since many had belonged to the International Workers Order and other such organizations judged to be subversive in the 1950s. Others had never become citizens and were being deported or feared deportation and separation from their families. The party characterized itself as the defender of the rights of the foreign-born. By the 1950s, the foreign-language groups had little to offer the party. They were aged and no longer dominated the work force, having declined in size and proportion of those working in heavy industry. Their sole virtue for the party was that they were faithful, but that faithfulness was greatly taxed by developments in the mid-1950s.

The Communist Party made a strong appeal to white ethnics, especially from South, Central, and East European countries, and it had a small degree of success in attracting membership from those groups. These were the members who dominated the party and its cadres throughout its history in America. Party membership, nonetheless, was never more than a tiny percentage of those foreign-born, at its height never more than tens of thousands among tens of millions. Likewise was the case of its appeal to black Americans. In the late 1960s and early 1970s, the Marxist-Leninist perspective would again inform the thinking of a few black radicals, as we shall see more fully in Chapter 8. It was a major element in the ideology of the Black Panther Party, for instance; but with the conspicuous exception of Angela Davis, no prominent black activist or black intellectual formally affiliated with the remnant of the diehard loyalists that were the American Communist Party after 1960.

FASCISM

Our last example of old-style radicalism appealing to ethnic minorities in the United States is Fascism, whose appeal was limited to three white ethnic target groups: Italians, Germans, and White Russians. This section briefly examines Italian Fascism and German Nazism.

The Italian Fascist movement was launched in Italy in 1919.[8] It had the support of industrialists and stressed government policy that favored big business. It endorsed and relied on a totalitarian method of ruling society. As in Nazi Germany, Italian Fascists glorified war and adopted an expansionist foreign policy. The Italian Fascist dictator, Benito Mussolini, stated: "War alone brings to their maximum tension all human energies and stamps the seal of nobility on those people who have the virtue to face it."

In America, Fascism arose after World War I, responding to the economic dislocations of the postwar economy, particularly the Great Depression. In October 1922, after Mussolini came to power in Italy, his government established a Secretariat General of the Fasci Abroad to use consuls of the foreign office to spread Fascism abroad. It targeted particularly the huge Italian population in the United States (some 5 million immigrants by then). In 1923, it entrusted the fascio of New York with acting as the central fascio of the Italian **fasci** (fascist organization) in North America.

The director of the Bureau of Italians Abroad, who later served as a consul of the Italian government to the United States, described its tactics:

> The Bureau of Italians Abroad, faithful to the directions by which the Duce wanted to reattach the Italian Communities abroad to the life of our nation, has devised new instruments and sharpened and perfected those already on hand. Each Fascio abroad . . . is a center of the faith which has . . . put Italy back on the map among the peoples of the world. The Fascist Regime has increased the number and scope of the Italian schools abroad. . . . Lectures in the Italian language in foreign universities and regular courses in Italian language for foreigners not only help to spread our language and culture, but fan the spark of Fascist thought in the modern world. (Salvemini 1977: 190)

The bureau worked with the Dante Alighieri Society to coordinate action. It used a foreign section of the National Union of Discharged Officers to create and maintain a bond of national and military solidarity among the ex-officers to be intimately united to the Fascist fatherland. Through its propaganda, the Bureau for Italians Abroad coordinated the tools to keep alive in the communities of emigrants love for the fatherland and faith in the Fascist regime, and to stress the achievements of Fascist Italy. The bureau maintained strict watch over the Italian newspapers abroad as potential centers of loyalty. Orators were sent from Rome to inspire fellow Italians, bring them support, and maintain ties to Italy. The Bureau of the Consuls organized annual celebrations like the birthday of Fascism, the March on Rome, and Victory Day in Italian communities abroad, always with orators selected by or sent over from Rome. It organized group excursions of Italian émigrés to Italy and published school textbooks, purposely edited, illustrated, and printed for Italian schools abroad.

The Bureau of the Consuls immediately began to infiltrate the many Italian-American organizations in the United States. The **Order of the Sons of Italy** was first established in New York in 1914, with 316 lodges. By 1918, it had grown to 590 lodges and a membership of 125,000. By 1924, in New York alone, it had 1,110 lodges with 160,000 members and claimed a nationwide membership of 300,000. After Mussolini came to power, his government financially backed its growth (Salvemini 1977). Giovanni Di Silvestro, a "Venerable" of the Sons of Italy, declared in 1922 that the "Order of the Sons of Italy is today a Fascio for the safety of Italy and America." He remained a pillar of Fascism in the United States until 1935, when he suddenly left the Order under suspicion of having embezzled funds.

From 1922 to 1923, the Italian fascio of New York directed all of the Fascist movement in the United States. By 1923, however, it became clear that the directors in New York were incapable of coping with the multiplying local fasci. The national directorate of the Fascist Party in Italy dissolved the Fascio of New York and reorganized it. It delegated the job of controlling the Fascist organizations all over North America to a Fascist Central Council, made up of 11 members.

Agostino De Biasi, editor of the Fascist magazine *Il Carroccio,* in the January 1923 issue, described the goal of the Italian fasci in the United States:

> Fascism will watch carefully over Italian foreign policy in Washington. When we have organized fasci in all our communities as scouts and observatories of our fatherland, then our ambassador will find in the masses with whom he will come in contact, a more intelligent readiness to work with him. We, the vanguard on this side of the Ocean of irresistible Fascism, make this promise to our Italy. (Cited in Salvemini 1977: 52)

In July 1925 the fascio established a Fascist League of North America, which lasted until December 1929. It set up several subordinate organizations: a Court of Discipline, a Central Committee for Press and Propaganda, and a National Fascist Party in the United States. It published *Il Carrocio,* edited by Agostino De Biasi. The Directorate of the League was appointed from Rome, and the league was clearly acting as an agent of the Fascist government. The Italian-American Fascist movement was soon publishing several daily newspapers, *Progresso Italo-Americano, Opinione, Il Bulletino della Sera,* and *Il Corriere d'America;* the weekly *Nuova Italia* and *Bulletin of the Fascist League of America;* and several monthly magazines, *Il Grido, Grido della Stirpe, Giovinessa, Il Vittoriale, Italia Madre, L'Italia Nostra,* and *Noi.*

The Fascist League and its successor, the Lictor Federation, created organizations or had its members serve as officers in already established organizations that were then used to promote the Fascist movement: Fascist Italian Union of America, the Italian War Veterans Federation, the Italian Chamber of Commerce, the Italian Historical Society of Rhode Island, the New York Fascio Benito Mussolini, the Fascist Association of Italian Journalists, the Yearbook of Italian Press, the Order of the Sons of Italy, the Dante Alighieri Society, the Victor Emmanuel III Foundation, the Fascist Longshoremen Federation of North America, the Italian Medical Association, the Italy-America Society, and the Black Shirts. All became sources of Fascist propaganda in America.

Italian Americans who joined a Fascist organization took an oath: "In the name of God and Italy, I swear to carry out the orders of my Duce and to serve with all my strength, and if necessary with my blood, the cause of the Fascist revolution." During the period 1928–1929 there was wide sympathy for Mussolini among Italian Americans. Gaetano Salvemini estimated that among American-born Italian Americans around five percent were "out and out Fascists."

The triumphal year for Fascism in America was 1929, when the movement had grown beyond the capabilities of the Fascist League of North America to direct it, and it was disbanded and replaced by the Lictor Federation. The league claimed 12,000 members in 1929, although that claim was probably exaggerated. The Sons of Italy claimed 300,000 at the time, when their actual number was closer to 150,000.

The Black Shirts youth organization first appeared in New York City in July 1923. By 1927, at their Brooklyn meeting, they were 2,000 strong. By the late 1930s, anti-Fascists Salvemini and Girolamo Valenti reported to the U.S. Congress, in a hearing before the Un-American Activities Committee, on a decade-long study of Fascist activities abroad. Valenti produced a briefcase of documents and affidavits proving that Italian consular officials were intimidating Italian Americans reluctant to go along with the Fascist party line. Valenti told the committee:

> Italian-American Black Shirt legions, 10,000 strong, are marching in America with the same resounding tread as those of the goose-stepping detachments of German-American Bund storm troopers. Behind this Black Shirt parade are more than 100,000 Americans of Italian descent who are willing to be seen at the public manifestations of some 200 Fascist organizations throughout the United States. . . . Another 100,000 fall within the influence of the powerful organs of propaganda emanating from well-knit and centralized fascistic forces which are mind-conditioning American citizens and swerving their allegiance to Italian dictatorship under the thumping fist of Mussolini. (Salvemini 1977: xxxiii)

The appeal of Fascism, particularly after the post–World War I economic dislocations and the Great Depression, went beyond Italian Americans. By the 1930s, a number of "American" organizations developed or took on increasingly fascist tones. In 1932, an openly Fascist magazine, *The American Guard,* was launched by the Swastika Press. Terrorist organizations like the Black Legion, the White Legion, and the White Crusaders joined the revived Ku Klux Klan as reactionary groups composed mostly of native-born whites. Other American groups supporting the Fascist line were the Liberty League, the Sentinels of the Republic, and the Southern Committee to Uphold the Constitution. American-born Lawrence Dennis became the theoretician of American Fascism, and Father Charles Coughlin, characterized as an American version of Paul Goebbels, Hitler's propagandist, established the National Union for Social Justice, openly preaching a Fascist message.

In 1934, the Liberty League was founded, backed by the DuPonts, Lloyds, Mellons and other wealthy businessmen. The Sentinels of the Republic, founded in 1922, was an anti-Semitic organization revived in the 1930s with the financial backing of the Liberty League. The Crusaders, founded in 1929, were organized along pseudo-military lines, with a "national commander," "battalions," and "battalion commanders." In 1935, the Farmer's Independence Council, an extreme right group appealing to farmers, was formed.

The Ku Klux Klan, revived in 1915, grew from a few thousand to several million members nationwide by 1932. The Black Legion used terrorism and had an estimated 40,000 members in Michigan in 1931. The Silver Shirts, begun in Asheville, North Carolina, by William Dudley Pelley, blended anti-Semitism and antiblack sentiment into a Nazi-inspired terrorist group.

The Reverends Coughlin and Gerald Smith used demagoguery during the 1936 election campaign. As described by A. B. Magil and Henry Stevens:

> The anti-New Deal diatribes of the Hearst press were mild in comparison [to] two men of God, Father Coughlin and Reverend Gerald Smith. Smith is a truly remarkable rabble-rouser, and during the campaign he ripened his fascism by adding those ingredients which Huey Long had lacked: extreme national chauvinism, anti-Semitism and, above all, Red-baiting. His and Coughlin's speeches had a bloodthirstiness reminiscent of the days when Hitler was promising that the heads of the Weimer Republic "Marxists" would roll in the sand. . . . A United Press dispatch of September 25, 1936 quoted [Coughlin] as saying: "When any upstart dictator in the United States succeeds in making this a one-party form of government, when the ballot is useless, I shall have the courage to stand up and advocate the use of bullets." Since Coughlin and his Liberty League allies had already discovered the "dictator" occupying the White House, his meaning was clear. The statement shocked the country and was undoubtedly instrumental in losing many votes for Lemke. (p. 190)

By 1930, German and Italian Fascist movements linked several organizations designed to promote Fascism, notably the American National Socialist Leagues, the Friends of New Germany, and the United States Fascists. Russian "White Guard" Fascism was the target of the National Revolutionary Fascist Party, begun by a naturalized American citizen, Anatase Vonsiatsky. Avowedly Fascist organizations worked through English-speaking front organizations serving as "transmission belts" to the broader American culture and society. Prominent among those from the Italian Fascist movement were the Italy-America Society, the Institute of Italian Culture, and the Italian Historical Society.

During the Great Depression, influential American politicians adopted a demagogue approach, promoting an extreme right wing ideology as the way to solve the ills of American society. Most notable were Huey Long, Francis Townsend, and Theodore Bilbo. Senator David Reed (R.–Pa.), known as the "Mellon Man," an acknowledged spokesman for big business, announced on the floor of the Senate that "if this country ever needed a Mussolini, it needs one now." Demarest Lloyd, a wealthy businessman and financial supporter of the Liberty League, published in his magazine, *Affairs,* a call for Congress to abdicate to a small group of "patriotic men" (the American Fascist Party).

A British journalist, commenting on the high society of Washington, D.C., at the time noted: "At that time, you could scarcely walk into a club or drawing room anywhere in Washington, without hearing something like Senator Reed's prayer for a Mussolini. Everywhere amateur fascists and parlor Whites were damning democracy between drinks" (cited in Magil and Stevens 1938: 79).

The early 1930s witnessed an assault on civil liberties and democratic rights. Growing numbers of workers and farmers were driven to loudly demand relief, and government authorities increasingly resorted to force in dealing with such demonstrations. In scores of cities, unemployment demonstrations were broken up with police bullets and tear gas. Armed troops were sent out against strikers. Negro sharecroppers attempting to organize unions were hunted down, and hundreds were lynched. Waves of aliens were deported. State governments revived old criminal syndicalism and sedition statutes, and professional patriots clamored for new repressive laws.

Italian-American Fascism reached its peak of activity during 1933–1934, when Mussolini appointed Antonio Grossardi the Italian consul general. Under his auspices, Fascist celebrations and demonstrations increased rapidly in number, size, and significance. The movement was especially active in trying to influence United States foreign policy vis-à-vis Italy. As did the party in Italy, the Fascist Party in the United States created a dual hierarchy of party and government officials and leaders to direct efforts to influence U.S. policy and politics.

> Ambassadors, consuls and consular agents, as official representatives of the Italian government, were bound by rules of diplomatic behavior. The secretaries of the fasci, although also representatives of the Fascist regime, had no diplomatic character, and were free to carry on activities forbidden to the former. The abnormal situation of the fasci in America and in all foreign countries, consisted precisely in the fact that, according to the law of the countries where the fasci were established, they were only private associations, whereas according to the Italian law they were organs of the Fascist regime . . . their constitutions were dictated by the head of the Italian government, and they had as their basic duty, "obedience to the Duce and to Fascist law." (Salvemini 1977: 61)

There was an anti-Fascist movement in the Italian-American community, most notably the Mazzini Society, created by Gaetano Salvemini; serious opposition to Fascism also formed within the labor union movement. But this was by no means a cohesive and unified resistance. As early as 1923, various radicals of Communist, Socialist, syndicalist, and anarchist persuasion formed the Anti-Fascist Alliance of North America (AFANA). It was supported by the New York Federation of Labor, Amalgamated Clothing Workers of America, and the International Ladies' Garment Workers Union.

In 1925, Frank Ballanco of the ACWA and Girolamo Valenti launched *Il Nuovo Mondo,* a daily newspaper aimed at reconciling the divisive factions with the anti-Fascist left. Efforts to create a unified front proved unsuccessful, and by 1926, the Socialist-liberal elements split from AFANA and created the Anti-Fascist Federation for the Freedom of Italy.

The turning point for the Fascist movement in the United States came with the Italo-Ethiopian war. Until late 1935 and early 1936, the Fascists controlled a majority of Italian-American organizations, as discussed earlier. With Italy's invasion of Ethiopia, however, Mussolini lost America in a few weeks, and all the prestige he had managed to build up over the many years of Fascist propaganda was dissipated. The movement managed to hold a few huge demonstrations in early 1936, and the Fascists claimed allegiance of 250,000 members in all of their various organizations in 1936, but by the fall of that year the movement was clearly dying.

> The American people, however, did not take the road of Father Coughlin in the 1936 elections. Nor did they take the road of Communism since this was not an issue in the balloting despite the strenuous efforts of Coughlin, Hearst and the Liberty Leaguers to identify Roosevelt and every progressive idea with Communism. But the American people did indicate unmistakably their rejection of all that the Coughlin-Hearst-Liberty League crowd represented and their desire to retire Father Coughlin permanently from political life. In place of the 9,000,000 votes which the radio priest had, in the height of self-intoxication, promised personally to deliver for Lemke, the latter received a total of only 891,858 and did not carry a single state. Four days after the election, Coughlin, in a nationwide broadcast, announced his retirement. Admitting that more than 90 percent of his own followers had deserted him on election day, he said: "The National Union, as a result of this Presidential election, is thoroughly discredited in the face of the tremendous vote of confidence which Mr. Roosevelt obtained. Therefore, our organization ceases to be active." (Magil and Stevens 1938: 191)

The 1936 election showed dramatically the decline of Fascism's appeal in the United States. After World War II it was ended completely.

> As long as Mussolini remained nonbelligerent and no clash with the policies of the United States seemed possible, the Fascist-pacifist attitude could be maintained without undue difficulty. The end of Mussolini's non-belligerency, the harsh condemnation uttered by President Roosevelt against him, and the consent given by the overwhelming majority in this country to the president's judgement, have brought about a serious dislocation in Fascist activities. (Salvemini 1977: 245)

After Pearl Harbor, when the United States entered the war against the Axis Powers, Italian-American Fascism was finished as a viable political ideology that could appeal to Americans of Italian descent. By early in the war, military necessity forced the Germans into Italy and Mussolini was seen as a mere flunky of Hitler. Italy became, in fact, occupied German territory.

NAZISM

As Italian Fascism sought to develop a mass movement among Italian immigrants, the Nazi movement appealed to German immigrants, White Russian immigrants, and their American-born children. Since there were more immigrants to the United States from Germany than from any other single nation (over 6 million), its potential was enormous. As with Fascism, however, Nazism's appeal was short-lived and never very successful. It, too, was quickly seen as a mere tool of a foreign power.[9]

The largest and most influential Nazi organization in the United States was the German-American Bund. It began in July 1933 as the Association of the Friends of New Germany. Working with the United German Societies of Chicago and of New York, it was re-formed as the German-American Bund in 1936, under the leadership of Fritz Kuhn, a naturalized citizen born in Munich in 1896. He was soon replaced, however, by Gerhardt Kunze, a Nazi spy. White Russians formed a significant part of the Bund. That section was headed by James Wheeler-Hill, who, despite his decidedly non-Slavic name, was a White Russian. In 1936, the FBI reported the membership of the Bund at 8,000.

Through the Bund, parties were held on German steamships while they were in U.S. ports, where German Americans were wined and dined and addressed by representatives of various Nazi organizations. Hitler followed Mussolini's example by creating a Foreign Division of the National Socialist Party (Gau Ausland) under its director, Ernst Wilhelm Rohle. Its official purpose was to bring all those of German citizenship living outside Germany into the ranks of the National Socialist Party. The Nazi government took over the League of German Societies Abroad, established in 1892, to promote cultural relations between Germany and other countries, and fashioned it into an agency of propaganda. This organization, and a number of others, were coordinated into the League for Germans Abroad, which sought allegiance among all so-called "Volksgenossen," or racial comrades. Stuttgart was officially designated as the city of foreign Germans. Annual conventions held there attracted 70,000 or more persons from all over Europe and America.

Various other agencies of the German government, the Student Exchange Service, the Academic Exchange Service, and lecture bureaus and travel organizations established German racial groups devoted to the interests of the German Reich. German newspapers in the United States were supplied with free news services, German schools with free educational materials, and German radio listeners with special short-wave broadcasts. This propaganda was directed toward one goal: to instill in the American citizen of German descent a consciousness of the German "race" and a feeling of allegiance toward the German Reich.

The Bund faced a problem in appealing to German Americans or even to their parents who were German immigrants, however, in that so many had come to America to escape the very totalitarianism that the Bund was peddling. The Nazi movement quickly established organizations to appeal to German-American youth. The Brown Shirts began a summer camp for youth, Camp Hindenberg, in Grafton, Wisconsin. Others were set up outside Philadelphia, in Detroit, and on Long Island. Children attending the camps were taught to regard Hitler as their leader and to believe that the principles of government espoused by him were superior to those of the democratic American government.

The Nazis worked with and financially supported America First, a propaganda campaign to keep the United States out of the war in Europe. The FBI, however, immediately infiltrated the Nazi movement and began tracking it. Frederich Aughagen, a Nazi agent who was arrested in September 1941, testified that America First was an agency of the German government. FBI Director J. Edgar Hoover agreed. The Detroit headquarters of Henry Ford and Father Coughlin were the center of the activities of the America First campaign, which by 1941 had a membership list of 25,000 names. Henry Ford and James D. Mooney, then chairman of General Motors, were so valued for their work with America First that they were awarded the Order of Merit of the Golden Eagle by Adolf Hitler himself.

German propagandists in America sought to soothe public opinion and encourage isolationism. They established the German Library of Information as a front to promote an isolationist line. More significantly, they used a German agent, George Sylvester Viereck, who was a press officer with the German embassy, to secretly manage the pro-Nazi and anti-British U.S. senator from Minnesota, Ernest Lundeen. He was under the direct pay of the Nazis and used his free mailing privileges as a member of Congress to distribute isolationist propaganda financed directly by the German embassy. Lundeen served as chair of the Make Europe Pay Its War Debts Committee, which sought to make U.S. foreign policy insist that Great Britain and France pay their World War I debt to the United States. His ideas and articles were published through a German propaganda publisher, Flanders Hill, in Scotch Plains, New Jersey. This was part of a Nazi conspiracy to infiltrate and influence Capitol Hill.

The most strongly Fascist intellectual in the pro-Nazi American movement was Lawrence Dennis, a U.S. Department of State employee and close friend of Senator Burton K. Wheeler, U.S. senator from Montana. Dennis wrote the book *The Coming American Fascism.* The American Nazi movement promoted the cause of Major General George Van Horn Moseley for president as the "solution to America's problems," and briefly attempted to launch him as a candidate to oppose Roosevelt. For his role in the "Capitol Hill conspiracy," Dennis and 27 others working for the government were indicted, in July 1942, on sedition charges.

Using front organizations, Nazi propaganda was published through various outlets. Through the German-American Alliance of Chicago, the party put out a Nazi paper, *Free American.* It also regularly fed information to the flagrantly Nazi magazine *Social Justice,* published by Father Charles Coughlin. In it, Father Coughlin recommended that the United States become a "fascist corporate state" in which democracy would be perfected. A regular contributor was "Leon Hamilton," whose real name was Father Jean Baptiste Duffee. Duffee was the contact between Father Coughlin and Boris Brasal, the White Russian forger who was the true author of the "Protocols of the Learned Elders of Zion." This famed anti-Semitic forgery was reprinted in *Social Justice* and was widely circulated through the publishing house of William Dudley Pelley, the leader of the Gestapo-like Silver Shirts.

Another Nazi front organization, the American Fellowship Forum, established the magazine *Today's Challenge.* It regularly published the writings of Charles Lindbergh and members of America First. These propaganda efforts were directed by several Nazi agents: George Sylvester Viereck, Manfred Zapp, Hans Thomsen, and Friedrich Aughagen.

The Bund was badly damaged by events in Europe. Krystallnacht, the "Night of the Broken Glass," when Nazis looted and destroyed Jewish temples, proved a disaster for Fritz Kuhn, the Bund's head. He continued to organize public displays, even after the German government had ordered him to downplay such activity. On February 22, 1939, George Washington's birthday, he organized the "single most striking display of Nazism in the history of the United States": a huge rally at Madison Square Garden in New York City which 22,000 people attended. Kuhn's self-indulgence led the Nazi government to have him replaced. They exposed him for misappropriation of

Bund funds, and in December 1939 he was sent to Sing Sing prison for two and a half years for embezzlement.

In 1939, after the German invasion of Poland, the Nazi occupation force found files in the Warsaw office of the Polish Foreign Ministry clearly indicating that President Roosevelt intended to push the United States into World War II against the Axis and on the side of the Allies. The German government published the documents in a "White Book" designed to undercut President Roosevelt's reelection in 1940. The report of the German Foreign Office was published throughout the world and caused an immediate sensation. The White Book showed conclusively that the American President planned to bring the country into the war at a time when the majority of the population, and of the Congress, supported peace and neutrality. Roosevelt denounced the documents as forgeries, as did Secretary of State Cordell Hull. The Nazis also leaked embarrassing documents and statements by Joseph Kennedy, then ambassador to the Court of St. James. In early 1940, the German charge d'affairs, Hans Thomsen, leaked the documents to the press through pro-Nazi publishers like Ralph Strassburger, owner of the *Norristown Times Herald*. The leaks, however, failed to impede Roosevelt's reelection.

When the United States declared war against Japan and Germany, the FBI swept up and arrested many German spies. It uncovered plots to kill President Roosevelt and the king and queen of England. The bureau linked John Koos, a Ukrainian White Russian who worked for Henry Ford, to a Ukrainian terrorist group in Detroit, connecting them to Father Coughlin and Marion Stevens Vonsiatsky, wife of a White Russian count who was a financial supporter of America First. It arrested Lucy Boehmler, an American woman who was a Nazi spy and had smuggled, through the Nazis to Japan, the secret U.S. defense plans and installations for Pearl Harbor.

World War II completely ended Nazi influence in the United States as a political movement to appeal to German Americans. By 1943, America First was discredited and could do little more than express its annoyance with the war.

In the 1960s, a brief neo-Nazi political movement, led by the "sixties Führer," George Lincoln Rockwell, surfaced in reaction to the civil rights movement. Today, neo-Nazi skinheads carry on the tradition, but the movement is small and largely an expression of antiblack racism rather than a fully Fascist political ideology.

SUMMARY

This chapter examined the approach of old-style radicalism. Sometimes racial and ethnic groups reject the value system of the dominant society and seek to replace its values with their own. The chapter focused on three such cases, the radical ideological "isms": Socialism, Communism, and Fascism.

Socialism attempted to win over a mass following primarily among ethnic groups comprising white Euro-Americans, particularly those immigrants who came from Scandinavia and from South, Central, and Eastern Europe. Developing in the late 1800s, the Socialist movement in America peaked in the American Socialist Party during the 1912 election, when Eugene Debs attracted 6 percent of the total vote cast in the presidential election, when the party elected over 1,000 local officials, and when the party's official membership exceeded 100,000.

Socialism failed to attract a true mass following in part because of the basic conservatism of the very immigrants it was trying to organize and because of its own internal factionalism and tendency to schism. By the end of the 1920s, Socialism ceased to be a significant political movement. Although it lost its electoral battles, in a sense it won its war in that, subsequently, Progressive and liberal Democratic Party reforms enacted most of its proposals for reform. Many of its values have become part of the American political mainstream.

Communism arose in the 1920s. Like the Socialist movement from which it emerged, it targeted immigrants from South, Central, and Eastern Europe and native Americans who were involved in the radical industrial union movement. It aggressively sought to win a mass following among black Americans. As with Socialism, Communism failed to win over any significant following among its targeted groups due to their basic cultural, eco-nomic, and religious conservatism. It failed to develop a good organizational base from which to work with blacks. Its reliance on ethnic foreign-language associations to reach white Euro-Americans foundered on factionalism, schism, and bewildering shifts in tactical approaches following the changing party line of the Communist Internationale. The Communist Party never achieved even half the size of the Socialist Party. It was suppressed and simply withered away by the 1950s.

Fascism was a movement of even shorter duration, existing in America only during the interwar years (1920–1945). Italian Fascism appealed to Italian immigrants and Italian Americans. Nazism worked with White Russians and Germans. Fascism never overcame its image of being the mere tool of a foreign power and never attracted more than 1 to 5 percent of its targeted groups. Fascism and Nazism died out with the entrance of the United States into World War II.

KEY TERMS

African Blood Brotherhood (ABB): a radical black organization that had strong Communist Party ties in the 1920s.

Black belt: the area of the United States advocated for the establishment of a separate black republic composed of parts of Virginia, North and South Carolina, Georgia, Alabama, Mississippi, and Texas.

Fasci: plural for Fascist; persons who adhered to the Fascist ideology.

"Negro question": term used by the Communist Party as to how best to appeal to American Negroes and what was the appropriate role of blacks in the United States.

Order of the Sons of Italy: the largest Italian-American ethnic organization, strongly infiltrated by the Fascists during the 1920s and 1930s.

Sanhedrin: the All-Race Assembly, a conference held in Chicago in 1924.

Sewer Socialists: the German Socialists of Milwaukee who won local office by stressing practical political reforms and services.

Sharecroppers Union of Alabama: a failed attempt by the Communist Party to win support of rural blacks in the South during the 1930s.

White chauvinism: a "sin" within the Communist Party during the late 1930s and 1940s in which white ethnic Communist members were opposed to working closely and equally with black Communist members.

Wobblies: members of the radical industrial union, the International Workers of the World (IWW).

REVIEW QUESTIONS

1. Describe the struggles among competing factions that characterized the earliest stages of Socialism in the United States.

2. Discuss the reforms advocated by the Socialist Eugene Debs that eventually became accepted as mainstream American policy. Why did they fail to win widespread support in the 1920s?

3. Describe the factors over which the Socialist Party split.

4. What white Euro-American ethnic groups were the strongest foreign-language components of the Socialist and the Communist parties of America?

5. Discuss three major reasons why the Communist Party, despite vigorous efforts, failed to win significant support among black Americans.

6. What was the peak or triumphal year for Fascism in America? Why did it have appeal at that time?

7. Name three prominent American national elected officials who became associated with the American Fascist movement.

8. What event proved to be the turning point leading to the decline of the American Fascist movement?

9. Discuss the American industrialists prominently allied with the American Nazi movement. What organizations and media outlets did they found or use to spread Nazi propaganda?

10. Who was the "sixties Führer"? What vestiges of Nazism still linger in the United States?

NOTES

1. For in-depth discussions of Socialism and other radical movements in the United States, see Aveling (1969), Foster (1952), and O'Neal and Warner (1947).

2. See Record (1951) for blacks and radical movements in the United States.

3. Eugene Debs was the Socialist Party's presidential candidate in 1900, 1904, 1908, 1912, and 1920. (He declined to run in 1916, instead making a failed attempt to be elected to Congress.)

4. See Brommel (1978), Constantine (1995), and Tussey (1970) on Debs.

5. See note 1; see also Buhle (1987).

6. See Frederickson (1995: 201); Glazer (1961: 173–174); Record (1951), Foster (1952), and Ford (1938).

7. See Wynn (1955).

8. See Magil and Stevens (1938) and Salvemini (1977).

9. See note 1; see also Higham (1985).

SUGGESTED READINGS

BROMMEL, BERNARD. 1978. *Eugene V. Debs: Spokesman for Labor and Socialism.* Chicago: Charles H. Kerr.

CONSTANTINE, J. ROBERT, ED. 1995. *Gentle Rebel: Letters of Eugene V. Debs.* Urbana and Chicago: University of Illinois Press.

CROSS, THEODORE. 1984. *The Black Power Imperative.* New York: Faulkner.

FONER, PHILIP S., AND JAMES ALLEN, EDS. 1987. *American Communism: A Documentary History, 1919–1929.* Philadelphia: Temple University Press.

FONER, PHILIP S., AND HERBERT SHAPIRO, EDS. 1991. *American Communism and Black Americans: A Documentary History, 1930–1934.* Philadelphia: Temple University Press.

FORD, JAMES W. 1938. *The Negro and the Democratic Front.* New York: International Publishers.

FOSTER, WILLIAM Z. 1952. *History of the Communist Party of the United States.* New York: International Publishers.

FREDERICKSON, GEORGE M. 1995. *Black Liberation.* New York: Oxford University Press.

GLAZER, NATHAN. 1961. *The Social Basis of American Communism.* New York: Harcourt, Brace & World.

HIGHAM, CHARLES. 1985. *American Swastika.* New York: Doubleday.

HOWE, IRVING. 1985. *Socialism in America.* New York: Harcourt Brace Jovanovich.

MAGIL, A. B., AND HENRY STEVENS. 1938. *The Peril of Fascism.* New York: International Publishers.

RECORD, WILSON. 1951. *The Negro and the Communist Party.* Chapel Hill: University of North Carolina Press.

SALVEMINI, GAETANO. 1977. *Italian Fascist Activities in the United States.* New York: Center for Migration Studies.

The Communist Party and the Scottsboro Defense

Perhaps the most effective instrument employed by the Communist Party in its Negro program during the 1928–34 period was the International Labor Defense (ILD). This organization had not been widely known among Negroes or whites until its participation in the famed Scottsboro cases, beginning in 1931. The Scottsboro trials grew out of the indictment of nine Negro youths for the alleged rape of two white women (who were later shown to be of unsavory repute) on a freight train bound from Chattanooga to Huntsville, Alabama, in late March of 1931.

The chances for a fair trial, always slim for Negroes in Alabama, in this instance were practically non-existent. The NAACP quickly intervened in the case, and its attorneys were assigned to handle the defense. During the first trial the Party and the ILD carried on an intensive propaganda campaign in which southern injustice and the ineptness of the NAACP defense were the principal themes. As the trial neared its close the ILD in New York addressed a telegram to the presiding judge in which it advised him that he would be held "personally responsible unless the defendants were immediately released." The boys were summarily convicted, and eight were given the death sentence. Then began the first of a long series of appeals to the higher courts.

While the appeals were pending the ILD sent its representatives to the parents of the condemned boys and persuaded them that the ILD rather than the NAACP should thereafter handle the cases. This maneuver, perhaps more than any other act of the Communists, indicated the contempt in which they held the moderate organizations; it indicated also the extent to which the Party was willing to go in obtaining participation in trials of such obvious propagandistic value. "It was a sorry spectacle," said Henry Lee Moon—

—the scramble of the Communists to wrest the defense of the hapless boys from the control of the NAACP. To accomplish this end the whole propaganda machinery of the party was turned loose in a campaign to discredit the Association's leadership. Stunned by the violence of this attack, not only upon the principles and policies of their organization, but also upon their personal integrity, the leaders of the NAACP were bewildered and in the end relinquished the defense to the ILD. The Communists maintained that legal defense had to be supplemented by international propaganda. American consulates, legations and embassies were picketed and stoned in many parts of the world. Mass meetings of protest were held in the capitals of Europe and Latin America at which resolutions demanding the freedom of the Scottsboro boys were passed. Letters, telegrams and cablegrams poured in upon the President of the United States, the governor of Alabama, the presiding judge, and other state officials, demanding the immediate release of the boys. This propaganda was effective in exposing the hypocrisy of American justice, but it did not gain the freedom of the boys. Only after it had ceased was a compromise effected which resulted in the release of four of the accused.

Having withdrawn from the case, the NAACP had nothing further to do with the Scottsboro matter until 1935. At this time, with the ILD facing failure in its efforts to obtain the freedom of the defendants, and with the new line of cooperation having been laid down to the Party and the ILD by the Communist International, the Communists agreed to share the case with the NAACP and other organizations; out of this grew a new Scottsboro defense committee. Among the participating organizations were the American Civil Liberties Union, Methodist Federation for Social Service, League for Industrial Democracy, Church League for Industrial Democracy, and the National Urban League, the latter in an advisory capacity.

During some four years in which the ILD had almost exclusive control of the Scottsboro defense, it widely employed the technique of "mass pressure" described in the previous chapter. The general position of the Party among Negroes was undoubtedly strengthened as a result, although it is highly doubtful whether its efforts were of any direct benefit to the defendants in the case. Scottsboro was not only publicized by the Communists among Negroes in the United States but, because of the ILD's connections with Communist agencies throughout the world, it became a global *cause célèbre*. In the fund-raising campaigns and at the protest rallies staged from San Francisco to New York, the ILD had an excellent opportunity to explain its larger program and the Communist cause to Negroes. "To the Communists," said Henry Lee Moon,

the whole campaign was much more than a defense of nine unfortunate lads. It was an attack upon the system which had exploited them, fostered the poverty and ignorance in which they were reared, and finally victimized them by legal proceedings which were a mockery of justice. It was a case made to order for the Communists and well worth the scramble they made for the privilege of representing the defendants. They made the most of it.

For the Communist Party no intrinsic issues of justice were involved. It viewed the Negroes as victims of a capitalist economic order and the courts as one of its institutional extensions. The Scottsboro victims could be liberated only by an effective challenge to the economic order outside the limits of the regular judicial process. It is significant, however, that the ILD retained exceptionally able lawyers to handle the actual court proceedings. But basically, the Communists regarded Scottsboro as only a steppingstone for organizing the unemployed, recruiting Negro workers and sharecroppers, and building a mass Communist organization among colored Americans.*

Scottsboro had values for the Party outside the propaganda field; one of these values could be expressed in cash. How many of the thousands of dollars raised by the ILD, the Communist Party, and other

---

*Ford, for example, as late as 1935 declared: "Properly brought forward not by liberal humanitarian methods, but as a support to the struggles of the working class, the correctness of our fight for Scottsboro can be shown to even the most backward worker. Similarly, among liberal groups who still believe in democracy and civil rights, support will be gained when the fight for Scottsboro is presented as inseparably bound up with the rights of the Negro people and the maintenance of civil rights. Scottsboro is bound up with the national liberation of the Negro people and with the struggle of the entire American working class for the dictatorship of the proletariat—Soviet Power." (James W. Ford, "The United Front in the Field of Negro Work," *Communist*, Vol. XIV, No. 2, February, 1935, 174.) Such statements as the above indicated also the confusion within Party ranks concerning the pursuit of revolutionary as opposed to united front objectives during the first phase of the 1934–1939 period.

Communist organizations involved with the Scottsboro defendants actually went for defending them we have no way of knowing. The Party's ideological bookkeeping was frequently confused with the more regular forms of financial accounting. A thousand dollars raised for the Scottsboro boys' defense could be just as legitimately spent for pamphlets advocating self-determination for Negroes in the black Belt as for the payment of lawyers' fees. And we have no way of estimating how much of these funds were used for activities having an even remoter connection with the Scottsboro case.

The Party also reaped an organizational windfall from the case. It attempted to follow up protest and fund-raising meetings with the building of local branches of the Communist Party and the Young Communist League. Party functionaries were instructed to employ the Scottsboro trials as a means for building Communist strength in the various communities. It was possible to get a hearing in the name of Scottsboro when a reference to self-determination would have been hooted down or tolerated in stony silence. The Party was aware of the organizational implications of the case, even if few other organizations were.

In trying to pass final judgment on the role of the Communists and the ILD in the Scottsboro case from the standpoint of their effectiveness in obtaining legal justice for the defendants, we are involved largely in speculation. It is not possible to predict what would have happened had the ILD not intervened, or, having intervened, if it had not attempted to employ the technique of mass pressure. The extremes of complete exoneration or the death penalty were possible; where the verdict would have to come to rest between these two poles is a conjectural matter. How effective the propaganda campaign of the Party was in influencing the courts we have no way of knowing.

SOURCE: C. Wilson Record, *The Negro and the Communist Party,* pp. 86–88. Copyright © 1951 by the University of North Carolina Press. Used by permission of the publisher.

CHAPTER EIGHT

NEW-STYLE RADICALISM

Some racial and ethnic minority groups not only reject the values and norms of the majority society, they seek to change those norms and values by radically altering the majority's culture. Chapter 7 discussed those groups espousing a radical ideology who sought to bring about such change through the standard tactic of electoral politics. They pursued a tactic of a "third party" movement. This chapter focuses on groups seeking change by espousing and practicing radical political behavior—from nonviolent civil disobedience to the use of radical rhetoric to even physical violence. It exemplifies this strategy and tactical approach by discussing the black, brown, and red power movements of the late 1950s through the early 1970s.

Various proponents of this approach have used somewhat different tactics to reach their goal of resistance and protest designed to drastically change public policy. One of the earliest leaders to advocate this strategy was the brilliant W. E. B. Du Bois, a historian and sociologist at Atlanta University. In 1905, he and a small group of black intellectuals met in Niagara Falls, Canada. The Niagara movement rejected moderation and compromise. It called for radical change that would end black inferior status, loss of voting rights, Jim Crow laws, segregated schools, inhumane conditions in southern prisons, denial of equal job opportunities, and segregation of blacks in the federal armed forces. Out of this meeting came the establishment, on February 12, 1909, the one-hundredth anniversary of Lincoln's birth, of the National Association for the Advancement of Colored People (NAACP). Over the years, the NAACP has led various campaigns to establish black rights through legal action. In 1915, it achieved its first major victory in one of hundreds of cases pursued at all levels of government when the U.S. Supreme Court declared unconstitutional the grandfather clause of the Oklahoma state constitution.

THE MODERN BLACK CIVIL RIGHTS MOVEMENT

In many respects the modern black civil rights movement grew out of events precipitated by World War II.[1] Black soldiers served in the war, especially after President Harry Truman integrated the armed forces by Executive Order 9981 in 1948. Upon their return to the States they were not willing to return to the status of the prewar years. During the war years large numbers of blacks moved North to work in industry and other jobs opened up by the war effort. Blacks from the deep South experienced a lifestyle of far less severe racial discrimination and segregation. They would not easily return to those conditions and meekly accept Jim Crowism.

By 1940, a host of black organizations united to demand full and equal service in the military, as well as an end to discrimination in employment in the defense industries. The March on Washington signaled a change in black protest thought and strategy. In early 1941, A. Philip Randolph issued a call and began to plan for 10,000 Negroes to march on the nation's capitol to demand their rights. The march was conceived as an all-black action by and for the black masses, anticipating the black protest actions of the 1950s and 1960s. The march was never held because President Franklin Roosevelt established a federal Fair Employment Practices Commission in 1941.

In 1943, Randolph began to plan a campaign of civil disobedience, following the Gandhi movement in India, to expressly attack segregation and discrimination in the northern states. The Congress on Racial Equality (CORE), founded in 1942–1943, grew out of a pacifist organization, the Fellowship of Reconciliation. Its founder was James Farmer, a black Louisianan. Combining the nonviolent, direct-action techniques of Gandhi with the sit-down strikes of the 1930s, it developed the "sit-in." CORE concentrated on attacking discrimination in places of public accommodation. It engaged in its first sit-ins in 1943, using the tactic against a segregated restaurant in Chicago. In 1947, it sponsored a "journey of reconciliation," a forerunner to the freedom rides of 1961. The integrated bus trip through the upper South tested compliance with a decision, *Morgan* v. *Virginia* (1946), that had banned segregation in interstate transportation.

In many respects the black civil rights movement was propelled forward by the 1954 Supreme Court decision, *Brown* v. *Board of Education of Topeka, Kansas.* In that decision the NAACP won its greatest legal battle against de jure (by law) segregation when the Court finally overturned the separate-but-equal doctrine of *Plessy* v. *Ferguson* (1896). Where the *Plessy* case established a constitutional principle that served to underpin Jim Crowism and the pervasive use of de jure segregation, the *Brown* case gave constitutional blessing to the effort and policy of racial desegregation. *Brown* failed to be immediately enforced, and little practical change resulted from it. More than a decision by the nine justices of the Supreme Court would be needed to seriously alter the norms, values, and institutionalized racism of a nation. Such change required a truly national mass movement.

> Reaction to the *Brown* decision showed how deeply prejudice was imbedded in the South. Whites called for the impeachment of the Justices. Cities closed schools rather than comply with Court-ordered desegregation. The Governor of Arkansas used his state's militia to block blacks from entering Little Rock's all-white high school. Missis-

sippi state troopers faced-off with federalized state National Guard troops when James Meredith was admitted to the University of Mississippi in 1962. (Schaefer 1998: 204)

The direct-action approach was ignited into a truly national mass movement with the 1955–1956 bus boycott in Montgomery, Alabama. The protest action was precipitated in early December 1955, when Mrs. Rosa Parks, a 43-year-old black seamstress, refused a bus driver's order to give up her seat to a white man. She had been ejected several times before for refusing to obey the Alabama segregation ordinance requiring that blacks give up their seats to whites when ordered to do so by a white bus driver. This ordinance enacted provisions of a 1945 Alabama state law requiring the Alabama Public Service Commission to enforce racially segregated seating on all bus companies under its jurisdiction. Mrs. Parks was arrested, charged with breaking the law, and fined $14. The bus boycott ensued, and the Reverend Dr. Martin Luther King, Jr., eventually emerged out of this action, becoming a national figure. His organization, the Southern Christian Leadership Conference (SCLC), which he began in 1957, moved to the forefront of the civil rights movement.

Nonviolent, direct-action protest became a popular tactic to fight segregation across the nation. Its most effective use was in the South against de jure segregation. The 1960s saw new groups and leaders emerge. In April 1960, the Student Nonviolent Coordinating Committee (SNCC) was organized in Raleigh, North Carolina, and CORE began its freedom rides into Alabama and Mississippi in 1961.

The Montgomery bus boycott was launched when Mrs. Jo Ann Robinson, an English teacher at Alabama State College, an active member of the Dexter Avenue Baptist Church, and president of the Women's Political Council, a local black women's organization founded in 1946, and Edgard Nixon, president of the local chapter of the International Brotherhood of Sleeping Car Porters and a leading force in the Montgomery chapter of the NAACP, activated a group of black ministers to form the Montgomery Improvement Association (MIA) to direct and coordinate what became a 382-day boycott of the City Lines bus company. The city's black churches united behind the boycott, providing crucial meeting places and fund-raising efforts for a city that did not have a black-owned radio station or newspaper. The vast majority of the city's bus passengers were blacks, and the bus line stood to lose $3,000 a day in revenues, and the city its part of $20,000 a year in taxes from the bus line. Downtown merchants could anticipate in excess of $1 million in lost sales if the boycott proved effective.

At first, the MIA's demands were a modest modification of the city's bus segregation practices. The group asked for no more concessions than had been granted by other southern cities, notably by Baton Rouge, Louisiana, two years earlier. It simply demanded seating on a first-come, first-served basis within segregated seating areas. It asked for greater courtesy from bus drivers, the hiring of black bus drivers for predominantly black routes, the seating of blacks from the back of the bus forward, and the seating of whites from the front of the bus backward, without a designated section always to be kept clear for each race. King, then a 26-year-old minister who had arrived in Montgomery only a year before, was unanimously elected president of the MIA.

Montgomery's black churches became the organizational base for an elaborate car-pool system for blacks who refused to use the bus line. King was arrested for an alleged speeding offense, and in January 1956 his home was bombed. A grand jury indicted 115 blacks for breaking a 1921 antilabor law by supporting the bus boycott. King continued to preach nonviolent civil disobedience and began to work closely with Dr. Ralph Abernathy, pastor of the First Baptist Church. According to King's own account, he was first alerted to the parallels between their bus boycott and Gandhi's strategy in India by a white woman, Miss Juliette Morgan. In a letter to the editor of the *Montgomery Advertizer,* she wrote:

> The Negroes of Montgomery seem to have taken a lesson from Gandhi—and our own Thoreau, who influenced Gandhi. Their task is greater than Gandhi's, however, for they have greater prejudice to overcome. One feels that history is being made in Montgomery these days. It is hard to imagine a soul so dead, a heart so hard, a vision so blinded and provincial as to not be moved with admiration at the quiet dignity, discipline and dedication with which the Negroes have conducted this boycott. (cited in White 1991: 121)

In June 1956, a federal district court ruled that the city ordinance violated the U.S. Constitution. The boycott continued while the city appealed. The U.S. Supreme Court, in *Gales* v. *Browder,* declared Alabama's state and local laws upholding segregation on buses to be unconstitutional. The MIA prepared the black community for desegregation, urging them to behave courteously and to "Pray for guidance and commit yourself to complete non-violence as you enter the bus. Be quiet but friendly; proud but not arrogant; joyous but not boisterous. If cursed, do not curse back. If pushed, do not push back. If struck, do not strike back, but evidence love and goodwill at all times" (cited in White, p. 121).

The desegregation of Montgomery's buses was followed by retaliatory violence against blacks, including fire-bombing of Negro churches. Blacks did not respond to violence with violence. They accepted the MIA's approach of relying upon the power of moral suasion.

> Once a man, or a human institution, decides to use coercive weapons or pressures, a moral judgement will be made about the act of power. An important consequence of this is that one's success in using pressure or coercion of any kind will depend, to a considerable extent, on whether or not the people affected by the action, as well as society as a whole, judge the use of power to be fair, moral, or just. Particularly, society tends to approve of those exercises of human power that it regards, for one reason or another, as "legitimate." This means that the efficiency and force of any exercise of power is automatically enhanced if its use is seen as proper or legitimate, whereas even the most forceful and commanding measures lose their strength if they are perceived as illegitimate or improper uses of power. (Cross 1984: 47)

In 1957, King, Abernathy, and other black clergymen, with advice from Bayard Rustin and Stanley Levison, began the Southern Christian Leadership Conference (SCLC). Its strategy was to use nonviolent protest throughout the South to oppose racial segregation in all its forms. Stanley Levison, an early adviser to Martin Luther King, Jr., was a white, Jewish lawyer and an alleged Communist. He was the target of J. Edgar Hoover and the F.B.I.'s campaign to discredit King. Bayard Rustin was a black intellectual and man of letters, publisher of the Socialist magazine *Liberation*. An early and key adviser to Martin Luther King, Jr., he was openly gay, and this caused much criticism for King's tolerance of homosexuals.

Dr. King's nonviolent philosophy rested on six key principles: active resistance to evil, attempts to win over one's adversaries through understanding, attacking forces of evil rather than people, willingness to accept suffering without retaliation, refusing to hate one's opponent, and the conviction that the universe is on the side of justice.

King spoke in Washington, D.C., in May 1957, joining other more prominent black leaders in a "Prayer Pilgrimage." He authored a book, *Stride Toward Freedom*, describing the Montgomery boycott and articulating his nonviolent civil disobedience philosophy. He was stabbed in 1959 by a deranged black woman, while signing copies of his book in a New York City bookstore. He traveled to India, visiting Gandhi's shrine. In November 1959 he resigned as pastor of the Dexter Avenue Church and moved to Atlanta to concentrate entirely on the SCLC movement.

North Carolina college students stage a sit-in strike at a Woolworth store in Greensboro.

In 1960, a sit-in tactic was pioneered at Greensboro, North Carolina, when a group of students from the Agricultural and Technical College sat in at a Woolworth's segregated lunch counter and demanded service. These sit-in demonstrations were soon followed by "wade-ins" at city swimming pools and segregated beaches, by "stand-ins" at segregated churches, and by the famous freedom rides on interstate buses. Students at Raleigh, North Carolina, led by Ella Baker, met in April 1960 and formed the Student Nonviolent Coordinating Committee (SNCC), an organization that King tried to mold in the image of the SCLC. The students accepted and used his nonviolent philosophy but they maintained a separate identity. They soon moved beyond King's cautious approach, which they considered too conciliatory and unrealistic.

SNCC first sought to create a rationale for activism by eclectically adopting ideas from the Gandhian independence movement, from American traditions of pacifism, and from Christian idealism as formulated by the Congress of Racial Equality (CORE), Fellowship of Reconciliation (FOR), and Southern Christian Leadership Conference (SCLC). SNCC was less willing than other civil rights groups to impose its ideas on local black leaders or to restrain southern black militancy. Viewed as the shock troops of the civil rights movement, SNCC activists worked in areas, such as rural Mississippi, considered too dangerous by other organizations. SNCC developed a new phase when its members resolved their differences by addressing the need for black power and black consciousness, by separating themselves from white people, and by building black-controlled institutions. After his election as chairman of SNCC in May 1966, Stokeley Carmichael popularized the organization's new separatist orientation. He and other workers, however, were less able to formulate a set of ideas that could unify blacks.

During the 1960 presidential campaign, when King was given a four-month prison sentence for an alleged driving offense in Georgia, Democratic candidate Senator John F. Kennedy intervened and won his early release. In gratitude, Martin Luther King, Sr., quietly backed the senator and urged blacks to support him. Kennedy narrowly won; his 68 percent of the black vote provided a crucial margin in that victory. President Kennedy, however, was slow to push civil rights. In 1961, CORE sponsored a series of freedom rides into the South to test compliance with the Supreme Court's decision on desegregating interstate travel. They were met with violence in Alabama and Mississippi. CORE's and SNCC's more militant tactics drew King into the fray as he attempted to regain leadership of the civil rights coalition.

From the winter of 1961 to the summer of 1962, King led a mass direct-action campaign in Albany, Georgia, to integrate its public facilities and its police department. The campaign stalled, in part due to the rivalry among SNCC, SCLC, and the local black leadership. James Foreman, of SNCC, did not want King in Albany, believing it should be a grass-roots led campaign. King was arrested and jailed, but later released. The local police chief avoided using violence against the protestors, avoiding media exposure and possible federal intervention. Attorneys for the city secured a federal court injunction halting the demonstration for ten days and thus draining the momentum from the demonstrations. The city closed its parks rather than integrate them. When the library was integrated, the city simply removed all its

A CORE-sponsored Freedom Ride bus was set afire by a white mob.

chairs. The Albany campaign failed, although King and SCLC did learn some valuable lessons from it.

King's next campaign, in Birmingham, Alabama, in 1962–1963, was better organized and conducted. New staff members were brought in who had practical experience in voter registration drives and the freedom rides. They made the organization more effective and efficient. They and King realized that protest was an effective tactic only if it elicited brutality and oppression from the white power structure, creating what King called "creative tension." Attacks by whites on peaceful, nonviolent protestors attracted media coverage, resulting in national outrage and federal intervention. The South's major industrial city, Birmingham, was a fortress of racial segregation pledged to resist change. Eugene "Bull" Connor exercised total power and had earlier closed city parks rather than integrate them. Seventeen black churches and homes of civil rights leaders had been bombed and no arrests made. Local college students began a boycott of Birmingham stores and staged sit-ins at segregated restaurants. King and SCLC were invited to direct the campaign. They issued three demands: integration of lunch counters, fitting rooms, rest rooms, and drinking fountains in department stores; increased hiring of blacks in the local labor market; and the creation of a biracial committee to work out a timetable to desegregate other areas of the city.

Boycotts, sit-ins, and street demonstrations were all used in Birmingham. King was arrested and jailed without being allowed to contact his wife or a SCLC lawyer. President Kennedy intervened again. King's activities were harshly criticized by a group of eight local white clergymen, describing him as an outsider and extremist. King's response was to write what became the classic statement and the most eloquent justification of civil disobedience and use of nonviolent protest. See his famous "Letter from a Birmingham Jail" in Case Study 8.1. It is both an emotional and a philosophical explanation for the strategy of new-style radicalism. Summarizing why racial and ethnic groups might be compelled to use civil disobedience, it moves the reader to see how such attempts to awaken the conscience of a nation can be a powerful means of effective protest politics.

After his release, King left Birmingham while the protest continued. Hundreds of black schoolchildren were used in direct confrontation with white authorities. Bull Connor met them with fire hoses, police dogs, clubs, and electric cattle prods. Over 20,000 persons participated in Birmingham's demonstrations, many of whom were arrested and jailed. Ten lost their lives. Some 35 homes and churches were bombed. The reports by the national press and television coverage shocked the nation. Bull Connor was viewed as a bigot, and the federal government sent in Burke Marshall, head of the Civil Rights Division of the Justice Department, to negotiate a settlement with the city. Only some SCLC goals were met, and King was criticized for accepting the compromises. The Birmingham case illustrates well the difficulty of sustaining a nonviolent protest effort.

Martin Luther King, Jr., acknowledges the crowd at the Lincoln Memorial after his "I Have a Dream" speech.

Before his assassination, President Kennedy, prodded by the Birmingham demonstrations, introduced sweeping civil rights legislation to the Congress. The Birmingham campaign put King back into the leadership of the civil rights coalition. In August 1963, the various national civil rights groups organized a March on Washington. An estimated quarter-million people, some 20 percent of whom were white, converged on the nation's capital to demand passage of the civil rights bill. During the march King delivered, from the steps of the Lincoln Memorial, his "I Have a Dream" speech, now widely considered one of the greatest speeches of the twentieth century.

The FBI undertook a campaign of spying, wiretapping, and disinformation designed to discredit King, but it failed to dissuade or discredit him. In 1964, King made the cover of *Time* magazine when he was awarded the Nobel Peace Prize.

SCLC launched a protest campaign in St. Augustine, Florida. The local campaign ended in stalemate, but the SCLC leadership believed it pushed President Lyndon Johnson to secure enactment of the 1964 Civil Rights Act, the most sweeping civil rights law ever passed by the Congress. The "Freedom Project," a voter registration drive in Mississippi, was directed by a coalition of SNCC, CORE, NAACP, and SCLC. It challenged the all-white Mississippi delegation to the Democratic National Convention. President Johnson refused to allow the "Freedom Democrats" voting rights at the convention, but negotiated a compromise covering future conventions and allowing two Freedom Democrats to sit in the convention as delegates-at-large with full voting rights. King and SCLC, Roy Wilkins and NAACP, James Farmer and CORE, and Bayard Rustin all favored accepting the compromise. SNCC, angered by the treatment of the Mississippi Freedom Democratic Party (MFDP), increasingly drew away from King and SCLC, viewing them as too conservative. In 1965, however, SCLC joined CORE and SNCC in a voter registration drive in Selma, Alabama.

King led a march from Selma to Montgomery, drawing national media attention. SNCC leadership was upset when he refused to break through a police barricade. King's presence dramatized an already violent confrontation. Sheriff James Clark was provoked into violence against the demonstrators. On "Bloody Sunday," at the Edmund Pettis Bridge, the demonstrators were tear-gassed and beaten by mounted police. C. T. Vivian of SCLC had been publicly assaulted by Clark, and the murder of a white Unitarian minister, James Reeb, by Selma whites moved President Johnson to call Congress into special session to enact a new voting rights bill.

A federal court approved the Selma-to-Montgomery march, and President Johnson activated the Alabama state militia to protect the procession. On March 25, 1965, Dr. King spoke to a crowd of 25,000 from the capital steps in Montgomery, bringing the civil rights movement back to the scene of the bus boycott a decade earlier. The Selma march culminated the civil rights movement in the South and was King's finest hour. President Johnson signed the Voting Rights Act into law on August 6—a direct result of the Selma campaign.

The 1964 and 1965 laws resulted in a dramatic closing of the gap between black and white voter turnout. The Civil Rights Acts of 1964 and 1965 solidified black voting support for Democrats. Table 8.1 shows that black support for Democratic presidential candidates remained strong from the 1960s into the 1990s, even as that party's white coalition weakened and fell.

TABLE 8.1   Black/White Voting Patterns, by Party, 1964–1996

Year	Race	Democratic	Republican	Other
1964	Black	94%	6%	—
	White	59	41	—
1968	Black	85	12	—
	White	38	47	—
1972	Black	87	13	—
	White	32	68	—
1976	Black	85	15	—
	White	46	52	—
1980	Black	86	10	3
	White	36	56	8
1984	Black	87	13	—
	White	34	66	—
1988	Black	86	12	—
	White	40	59	—
1992	Black	82	11	7
	White	39	41	20
1996	Black	64	30	6
	White	43	46	9

SOURCE: Adapted from Steffen Schmidt, Mack Shelly II, and Barbara Bardes, *American Government and Politics Today* (Belmont, CA: West/Wadsworth, 1998), pp. 346–347.

Passage of the 1964 and 1965 acts meant only the end of de jure (by law) segregation, not of de facto (by custom) segregation. Racial separation and inequality continued. Black leaders, aware of the discrepancy between what had been accomplished versus legal discrimination and the lack of improvement in the day-to-day lives of blacks, increasingly shifted their focus to the Northeast and Midwest. In 1966, King led SCLC demonstrations in Chicago, attempting to end its status as the "most segregated city in America." The Reverend Jesse Jackson launched "Operation Breadbasket," using consumer boycotts against white employers that practiced hiring discrimination. SCLC soon discovered its tactics did not transfer easily from the rural South to the urban North. Black ministers lacked the prestige they enjoyed in the South, and black churches were less efficient at organizing protests. Ill-prepared and inadequately briefed, SCLC workers were not even dressed for Chicago's harsh winters. Black street gangs rejected King's philosophy of nonviolent protest. The SCLC campaign achieved little and called King's philosophy, strategies, and leadership into question.

The growing split between SNCC and the SCLC deepened in 1966. James Meredith began his one-man "March Against Fear." When Meredith was shot, Martin Luther King of SCLC, Stokeley Carmichael of SNCC, and Floyd McKissick of CORE finished his march. Carmichael's use of the slogan "black power" became a source of tension between him and King, who opposed it because of its connotations of racial separatism and apparent acceptance of violence. In 1967, King began speaking out against the war in Vietnam, arousing hostile press commentary. The FBI intensified its surveillance of SCLC and of King.

In February 1968, black sanitation workers in Memphis, Tennessee, went on strike to win union recognition and improve working conditions. King viewed the strike as the beginning of a SCLC project, the "Poor People's Campaign." He went to Memphis in support of the strikers. On April 3, he delivered a speech to a small but enthusiastic audience, referring to the increasing number of threats made on his life. His speech became known as the "I've Been to the Mountaintop" address. On April 4, he was shot and killed by a white sniper on the balcony of his motel. His martyrdom touched off a wave of violence across the nation in which 20 people died. Following King's death, 300 black and white ministers marched on city hall in Memphis demanding recognition of the union. Local businessmen urged a settlement. The passage of the 1968 Civil Rights Act, incorporating a fair housing proposal, was eased through Congress in the period of sympathy King's assassination provoked. Eighteen years later, Dr. King was recognized as only the second citizen (George Washington was the first) to be celebrated in a personal national holiday.

After King's assassination, the leadership of SCLC shifted to Dr. Ralph Abernathy. Its overall influence and visibility quickly declined as rival leaders, organizations, and approaches advanced to the forefront of the civil rights movement.

Social and economic gains did not keep pace with political change. De facto segregation in schools, ongoing occupational discrimination, and much slower change in the social norms gave rise to frustration and to increasingly radical tactics.

As black protest groups proliferated and more varied tactics were used, the advances made by blacks fell short of expectations. Frustrations grew. The ideology and rhetoric of the movement became angrier. Radical protest leaders like H. Rap Brown decried nonviolence, chanting "Burn, baby, burn" during urban riots. Malcolm X of the Black Muslims exemplified the belief that racism was so deeply ingrained in white America that appeals to conscience would fail to bring fundamental change. From this mood the rhetoric of black power emerged in the summer of 1966. It expressed disillusionment and alienation from white America and pride in black independence and self-respect. Phrases like "black power," "black is beautiful," and "black consciousness" were soon expressed by the full range of black organizations. Black Power became associated with fringe groups emerging from CORE and SNCC. The Black Panthers illustrate this trend.

The late 1960s witnessed an increase in violent behavior as well as rhetoric. From 1963 through 1968, hundreds of riots rocked the cities of America, in sharp contrast to the previous 50-year period when there were only 76 major racial disturbances. Moreover, the very nature of the urban violence—in its scope, intensity, and targets—was far different from the earlier riots of this century, 1900–1940.

One study for 1967 alone identified 257 "disorders" in 173 cities that resulted in 87 deaths, injury to over 2,500, and 29,200 arrests. After King's assassination more cities (369) erupted in riots than in all of 1967. They reached small as well as large cities; one fourth of the riots took place in cities under 25,000 in population.

The riots were more intense and destructive. The Watts riot of 1965 lasted five days, destroyed $40 million in property, left a burned area in excess of 45 square miles with 34 dead, of whom 31 were black. Over 1,100 were injured and 1,600 arrested. The national guard used 3,000 troops, with local police providing 1,400 officers and the state sending 500 state troopers. More than 10,000 demonstrators confronted over 15,500 police and national guard troops. The Newark riot of 1967 required 4,000 officers to quell it. Twenty-six persons, of whom 21 were black, perished in that riot. Detroit erupted in 1967. Its five-day riot was the worst of all. Of the 43 dead, 39 were black. Fifteen thousand police officers were used to restore order. Some 1,300 buildings were destroyed and 2,700 business looted; property damage exceeded $500 million. The army and national guard were called into 15 cities. The property damage alone in eight riots that year amounted in excess of $250 million. In July 1967, President Johnson created a National Advisory Commission on Civil Disorders to study the riots, determine what happened, why, and what could be done to prevent them.

Within the majority society a popular explanation for the outbreak of the riots was called the "riffraff," or "rotten apples" theory. This view saw riot participants as unemployed youth with criminal records who vastly outnumbered the African Americans who repudiated the looting and the arson. This theory, of course, left white society untouched. The black community viewed the riots and rioters with more sympathetic understanding. Rioters were often not merely the poor and uneducated, but also working-class and even middle-class and educated residents of the black ghetto areas in which the riots took place.

Another explanation for the riots involves a theory of **rising expectations** coupled with **relative deprivation**. In this view, the riots are seen as emerging from frustrations that resulted as the standards of blacks improved after World War II and as the civil rights movement promised increased change. Black expectations for progress rose exponentially. Black incomes rose, but so did white incomes. The gap between black and white income did not close. This situation caused an increased sense of relative deprivation—the conscious feeling of negative discrepancy between legitimate expectations and present actualities. Not only were black lives relatively unchanged, the existing social structure seemed to hold no prospect for improvement. When their frustration levels reached a flash point, incidents such as the assassination of Dr. King set off the riots.

Yet another explanation has been termed a developing national consciousness. Media coverage of the civil rights movement, especially on national television, created a national interest and racial identity that transcended community boundaries. Blacks had become acutely aware not of deprivation unique to their own neighborhood but of the deprivation characteristic of all urban ghettos. Nearly every black community became a powder keg ready to explode.

In the late 1960s, a more militant phase of the black civil rights movement emerged, one advocating if not using violent behavior to bring about a radical change in majority society. Its adherents espoused and used the term **black power**, which came to symbolize this end of the spectrum of new-style radicalism. The term itself was not new. It can be traced back to the early 1900s, for example, in Garvey's movement. Its renewed usage, however, was popularized during the SNCC-CORE-SCLC campaign in Mississippi in 1966. It is generally attributed to Stokeley Carmichael, who became its chief advocate. He defined it as "the ability of black people to politically get together and organize themselves so that they can speak from a position of strength rather than a position of weakness" (cited in Kitano 1997: 131). Within the black community, the black power ideology came to mean a sense of black control over the community and an effort to instill self-pride. The term gained wide acceptance among blacks, although whites tended to view it and its usage as a form of **reverse discrimination** or reverse racism.

The black power term and ideology was explained and developed in a book by that title written by Stokeley Carmichael and Charles V. Hamilton (1967). It was more popularly associated with two divergent groups: the Nation of Islam and the Black Panther Party. The Black Muslims used the term in an avowedly separatist movement. They used it to justify their goals of political and economic separatism. Black power was a "dramatically defiant" term that came to symbolize the more militant phase of the civil rights movement. It increasingly represented a rejection of integrationist objectives.

The Black Panther Party popularized the term as but one aspect of its symbolic radicalism and militancy. In 1966, the party arose in Oakland, California, founded by Huey Newton and Bobby Seale. In their radical rhetoric, the Black Panthers condemned capitalism, defied white racist society, and promised to respond to violence with violence. Wearing black leather jackets and berets, adopting paramilitary titles (minister of defense), and sporting rifles over their shoulders, they were seen as the leading black nationalist group in the country. In their programs, however, they were clearly reformist rather than revolutionary. They developed many community service programs, such as breakfast programs for schoolchildren. Their service to the black community inspired emulation by the Chinese Americans, Chicanos, and Puerto Ricans.

The Black Panthers were willing to work within the political system. Cofounder Bobby Seale ran for mayor of Oakland (unsuccessfully), and Eldridge Cleaver, their minister of information (propaganda), ran for President of the United States. Their former defense minister, Bobby Rush, eventually became the deputy chairman of the Illinois State Democratic Party. In 1992, he was elected to the U.S. Congress. The Black Panthers were willing to form alliances with other groups, including political reform and integration groups, as well as with more radical organizations: Students for a Democratic Society, the Peace and Freedom Party, the Communist Party of the United States, the Young Lords, and the Young Patriots.

The Black Panthers exemplify the fate that often awaits a racial or ethnic minority group that is "defiantly militant" and uses the radical rhetoric of violence. The majority culture responds with repression rather than reform. Because of their militancy, the Black Panthers became the target of both local and federal police agencies. The FBI conducted an extensive campaign of surveillance against them, and secretly plotted and executed a campaign of disinformation to discredit them publicly. Local police departments simply suppressed them. Between 1968 and 1970, dozens of Black Panthers were killed and thousands of others arrested. "One notorious case was the 1969 killing of Mark Clark and Fred Hampton by the Chicago police, who fired between 800 and 1,000 rounds of ammunition into the victims' apartment" (Kivisto 1995: 320). By 1971 the party split. Eldridge Cleaver went into exile in Algiers. Another faction concentrated on less radical rhetoric, pushing black pride and service to the black community instead.

It is arguable that this more militant phase of the black civil rights movement, despite its brief period, proved to generate some results. Just as the ending of de jure segregation in the form of Jim Crowism can be attributed to the nonviolent civil disobedience phase, certain economic gains can be attributed to the more violent phase of the urban riots and the radical rhetoric used by groups such as the Black Panthers and the Symbionese Liberation Army (SLA). Frances Fox-Piven and Richard Cloward, in their book *Regulating the Poor* (1971), argue that the expansion of the welfare rolls and the social service programs of the Johnson Administration's War on Poverty was a "political response to political disorder." Economic progress was significant: From 1965 to 1970, black incomes gained 13 percent on whites'. Black elected officials in the South increased ninefold in ten years, although black gains, power, and influence slid backward during the 1980s and the Reagan and Bush Administrations.

BROWN POWER: THE HISPANIC PROTEST MOVEMENT

Although there is some reluctance by them to admit it, the brown power movement resulted from Hispanics' adoption of the black civil rights movement's strategy and tactics.[2] Brown power advocates learned from the experience of black militants. The success of their movement unquestionably had much to do with the Chicano adoption of brown power and the tactics of protest politics, including boycotts, marches, and building take-overs.

In the early 1960s, Mexican Americans were even lower than black Americans in terms of income, housing, and formal educational status. The brown power and Chicano movement erupted across the nation and manifested itself in farm workers' strikes in California, in the land grant struggle in New Mexico, in the revolt of the young Chicano electorate in Crystal City, Texas, and in school walkouts in Denver and Los Angeles. Just as the black civil rights movement gave rise to newly formed civil rights organizations and new leaders, the Hispanic movement was led by new leaders and new groups.

In its early years, the black power movement was led by groups tactically conservative and accommodationist (NAACP, Urban League, etc.). So too was the Hispanic movement. Among the earliest such organizations were the League of United Latin American Citizens (LULAC), the G.I. Forum, the Order of the Sons of America (La Orden de los Hijos de America), and the Community Service Organization (CSO).

In 1918, the Order of the Sons of America (OSA) was organized in San Antonio, Texas, and was open only to U.S. citizens. LULAC began in 1928–1929 in Corpus Christi, Texas, and was strongly assimilationist. It began in the wake of a racial attack by the Ku Klux Klan that spread across Texas, just after World War I. LULAC began as a self-proclaimed defensive and patriotic organization. The Klan held sway over much of East Texas, and the previously staunchly Democratic state had voted for Herbert Hoover in the presidential election of 1920 because of the Klan's hatred of the Catholic "papist" nominee on the Democratic ticket, Al Smith. LULAC used the name "Latin American citizens" in order to avoid using "Mexican American," then decidedly not in vogue. LULAC soothed jittery anti-Mexican sentiment then evident in much of Texas by a pledge of loyalty. Reflecting the "Four Freedoms" of World War II, LULAC set goals of reverence for their racial heritage; equal protection under the law; eradication of discrimination, and political unification by participating in all local, state, and national elections.

After the war, several Hispanic or Latino organizations developed, most notably the Community Service Organization (CSO), from which arose Congressman Eduardo Roybal and Cesar Chavez, the G.I. Forum, the Council of Mexican-American Affairs, and the Mexican American Political Association.

The Community Service Organization can be traced to the pioneer of nonviolent confrontation politics, Saul Alinsky. His Chicago-based Industrial Areas Foundation had a West Coast organizer, Fred Ross, who served as a guiding spirit to the budding CSO. Congressman Roybal described its founding when, in 1947, he first ran for the Los Angeles City Council. Although he lost that race, he and his campaign forces decided they needed a community group, which became the CSO. In his words, "We thought of it and we organized it. Of course, others helped. But we did it" (Steiner 1969: 180).

In the postwar era, returning veterans organized to elect Chicanos. Middle-class Chicanos used CSO as a political lever to help elect Roybal. It became innovative yet cautious, tempering its boldness with politeness. The barrio youth looked upon the CSO as too middle class and mainline. Its membership dropped off markedly during the 1960s—by 300 percent, from 12,000 to 4,000. Its membership was elderly. Young Chicanos were joining other, more militant groups.

The Chicano movement began using the term *Chicano* as a matter of self-pride, much as blacks began referring to themselves as blacks or African Americans instead of Negroes. Like the black civil rights movement, it was a national, mass membership movement evident in both the rural areas and the urban barrios.

The rural movement began with a union-led campaign to organize migrant workers. Its leader, Cesar Chavez, went on to become the best known Chicano leader. Like Dr. Martin Luther King, Jr., he was an authentic "man of the people" in the traditional sense of those words—a charismatic leader who came from a rural migrant working-class background and who understood and commanded the loyalty of those he led.

Chavez's movement, often referred to as "La Causa," began in September 1965. In Delano, California, a strike by Filipino workers harvesting grapes and who belonged to the Agricultural Workers Organizing Committee (AWOC) expanded to include Mexican migrant workers. The migrant workers earned an annual average income of $1,378. **La Huelga**, the strike, soon developed into La Causa, a social movement that used the strike and boycotts against lettuce and grape growers. The others joined in coalitions with organized labor, liberal clergy, radicals, and student groups when Cesar Chavez formed the National Farm Workers Association (NFWA). Even the city of Boston experienced a symbolic demonstration, a "Boston Grape Party" that evoked the revolutionary spirit of the Boston Tea Party. The beginnings of the NFWA are described in Box 8.1.

The striking grape pickers took on powerful economic forces with but $85 in their treasury. They were arrayed against the multi-billion-dollar giants of California's

BOX 8.1:   Beginnings of the National Farm Workers Association (NFWA)

"On the edge of the Mojave Desert, in the Coachella Valley, the local grape pickers demand the same pay as the braceros. Early in the summer of 1965 they go on strike. Within ten days the growers, fearing the ripe grapes will shrivel to raisins in the desert heat, raise wages from $1.10 to $1.40 per hour. . . . It was the young Filipino boys that started the strike. These young boys have a lot of violence in them, and when they had a picket line at the field all of the workers left. . . . But these Filipino boys started the strike. . . . With the grapes rotting on the vines, the growers began to hire scabs, mostly Mexicans. The farm workers are divided. Not merely do they speak different languages, but they belong to different groups. In the AWOC of Itilong are the Filipinos, and in the NFWA of Chavez are the Mexicans. Itilong goes to Chavez for help. Both men know that if they do not get together, the strike will be lost. Chavez is hesitant. He had not come to Delano to organize a strike. He had come to organize the barrios. The NFWA is not even a union, but an "association." He says, "The strike was not the normal function of the association." He is not an experienced union leader. "We didn't feel we were ready for a big strike," he says. He has "some misgivings.". . .

On the Mexican Independence Day, September 16, a meeting is held in a Catholic church hall in Delano. More than one thousand campesinos crowd the hall to vote on whether to strike. Under the red flag with the Aztec eagle, and a portrait of Zapata, the band plays the Mexican National Anthem, a priest gives an invocation, and Chavez invokes the spirit of Father Hidalgo—the George Washington of Mexico—and $1.40 an hour. 'Huelga! Huelga! Huelga!' the crowd yells. The vote to strike is unanimous.

Huelga! The word means "strike," but it means much more to the campesinos. Strike is a cruel word that means to lash out, to attack. In the old Anglo-Saxon there is the word *strican,* that like the Hoch German, *strihhan,* means to row a boat, to strike the water, to flow and go forward. In the Spanish the meaning is different. The old word, huelga, meant a time of rest and relaxation and merry-making—a little fiesta. The new word *huelga* is more vigorous and joyous still. Luis Valdez has sought to capture the new meaning of *huelga.* "*Huelga* means strike. With the poetic instinct of La Raza, the Delano grape strikers have made it mean a dozen other things. It is a declaration, a challenge, a greeting, a feeling, a movement. We cry, '*Huelga!*' It is the most significant word in our entire Mexican-American history. If the Raza in Mexico believe in *La Patria,* we believe in *La Huelga.*" "Under the name of *huelga* we had created a Mexican American *patria,* and Cesar Chavez was our first *presidente,*" says Valdez.

SOURCE: Stan Steiner, *La Raza: The Mexican Americans* (New York: HarperCollins, 1969), pp. 282–283. Copyright 1969, 1970 by Stan Steiner. Reprinted by permission of HarperCollins Publishers, Inc.

agribusiness. The union grew dramatically. By fall, over 2,000 workers in the Delano area alone had joined the NFWA, and 5,000 workers signed to have NFWA or AWOC represent them. By winter, the strike expanded to a national boycott. The AFL-CIO gave them $5,000 a month so the strikers could receive their $5 per week strike pay. In March 1966, they organized a three-hundred-mile march, the Pilgrimage to Sacramento. The strike evolved into a movement when university students and barrio youth joined the workers, and La Huelga became a crusade that literally changed lives.

Like the black civil rights campaigners, striking migrant workers faced violence. One striking worker suffered broken legs when he was run over with a truck driven by a strike-breaker. Three strikers riding in a car were run off the road. Picketers were

Cesar Chavez leads farm workers on the Pilgrimage to Sacramento March.

beaten, and they had guns discharged over their heads. Forty-four strikers were arrested for refusing to remain silent on the picket line. The sheriff's officer from Kern County came to the picket lines and said they could not use the word *huelga*. The strikers refused to give up using the word. Forty-four were jailed.

Like King and SCLC, Chavez and UFW were committed to nonviolence. He testified before a special subcommittee of labor that investigated the strike. "The only reason that there has not been any bloodshed in Delano is because we have not responded to attacks on us by the opposition. Mr. Congressman, it seems to us that there will be very few people who will be against unions, but it seems to me that most of them are in Delano," Chavez said. His remarks were greeted with laughter (Steiner 1969: 370).

When the Chicano youth began using the term **La Raza**, which though translated as "the race" was used by them in the sense of "our people," Cesar Chavez was quick to distinguish its meaning as other than a racist term. "When *La Raza* means or implies racism, we don't support it. But if it means our struggle, our dignity, or our cultural roots, then we're for it" (Chavez 1984: 137).

During the five-year strike against the growers, the "association" evolved into a union, then into a social protest movement, a mass protest civil rights group (by 1967, it had 17,000 members in California alone), and eventually into a community organizing force. The strike went from the grape fields to the lettuce fields, and the "Plan of Delano" of 1966 spread across California to the entire Southwest and then to the nation.

Just as SCLC inspired the development of SNCC and contributed to the increased militancy of CORE and the Black Panthers, so did La Causa. The strike got everyone excited. University students organized. Chicano leaders in the cities and universities struck out in new directions. Out of the upheavals came dozens of new barrio and university clubs. The Brown Berets was an organization of young Chicanos from the barrios of Los Angeles. They styled themselves after the Black Panthers and were a militant Chicano group. University students were especially outspoken and active. The United Mexican American Students (UMAS) in California and the National Organization of Mexican American Students (NOMAS, literally, "no more") in Texas were but two of more than thirty groups organized on campuses. University and barrio youth talked and marched together. David Sanchez, prime minister of the Brown Berets, talked to students at UCLA, while the members of UMAS walked the picket lines of the campesinos of Delano and beside the Brown Berets protesting school conditions in East Los Angeles.

A similar sense of inspiring militancy arose from the New Mexico land grant movement and its colorful leader, Reies Lopez Tijerina, known as "El Tigre" (the Tiger). A native Texan, he began the militant Alianza Federal de Mercedes on February 2, 1962. He first tried to work through the courts, asserting claims to land taken illegally from Mexicans living in Texas and New Mexico after the Treaty of Guadalupe Hidalgo. His movement was inspired by the black civil rights movement. "We are expecting this great change. The Negroes are expecting this great change, they feel it. That's why they are jumping, breaking the barriers, and yelling, and respecting *nothing* that gets in their way. Because the Negroes can *feel* the future. And so can we, the New Breed" (cited in Steiner 1969: 88).

The Treaty of Guadalupe Hidalgo guaranteed the land rights to Mexicans living in what became California and New Mexico. Tijerina argued that those treaty rights, "consecrated by the law of nations," were stolen in land grabs after the Mexican-American War. Those lands ranged across Texas, New Mexico, Arizona, California, Nevada, Utah, Colorado, and north into Wyoming. They made up an area larger than any of the nations of Europe except Russia, and larger than most other nations of the world. Property rights guaranteed by the treaty if held to be legally valid were no small real estate matter.

Records of the land grants were destroyed, but they were known to number over 1,700. Profits from Anglos' seizing land grant property were enormous, as the grants covered an estimated 20 million acres in Texas and New Mexico and 10 million acres in California. Tijerina argued the lands were stolen by Anglos, such as Thomas Catron, the "king of the Santa Fe ring." By filing a "patenting" and paying some well-placed bribes, he acquired some 593,000 acres with a single piece of paper. Some 34,653,340 acres of land grants land were brought to the Court of Private Land Claims. It validated only 1,934,986 acres, about 6 percent.

In launching his land grant movement Tijerina argued that Chicanos had to demand their rights, to fight for them, to be willing if need be to die for them. "Look at the black man. He has become free, free in spirit. He has lost his fear of the 'white power.' He is clean of fear and terror. And when you are free of these things you become filled with anger. You strike out for freedom. Anger is a manifestation that you know you are right and you wish to tear down the system that enslaved you" (Steiner 1969: 64).

The barrios' newspaper in Los Angeles, *La Raza,* voiced a growing sentiment for Tijerina and Corky Gonzales: "'We've been waiting since 1846 for real men.' The barrio newspaper hails 'El Tigre' and 'Corky,' Reies Tijerina and Rodolfo Gonzales, as a 'new and militant type of leadership' that youth 'admire and respect.'. . . These men 'have said and done things Chicanos have only mumbled and have said under their breath, but didn't have the 'Guts' or the 'Machismo' to say out loud.' These men are real men: They are both *machos.*" (Steiner 1969: 195).

The newspaper *El Grito de Norte* described the farmers of Tierra Amarilla (a small town in New Mexico) setting up a farmer's co-op which had near its door the defiant slogan "Che is alive and farming in Tierra Amarillo." In the near-by city of Santa Rosa, a Chicano student helped rural villagers construct a stone schoolhouse. He described his work as follows: "School? It is not just a school. It is one battle in our fight for self-determination. 'La Raza Arriba!' the student says. 'Our people arise!' " (Steiner 1969: 41).

El Tigre was an evangelical minister and spoke with the fiery intensity of a preacher using the podium as his pulpit. When court action failed to restore lands, he adopted the tactics of civil disobedience. In October 1966, he led a group that occupied the Echo Amphitheater at Kit Carson National Forest. In protest, they burned down a guard post, and Tijerina was arrested for vandalism. In November 1967, he and four members of Alianza were convicted on one or more counts for the Echo Amphitheater takeover. Tijerina was convicted of assaulting two forest rangers and burning two national forest signposts (in retaliation for Anglos burning down the barns of two co-op farmers). On June 5, 1967, while out on bail awaiting appeal, he led an attack on the courthouse of the county seat at Tierra Amarilla, New Mexico. The state government sent 400 national guardsmen, 200 state troopers, 2 tanks, and several helicopters. He was arrested and charged with wounding two officers, and kidnaping for taking two hostages. The kidnaping charge was reduced to false imprisonment. Though released on bail, none of his fiery oratory was quenched. Tensions were high during his trial for the Tierra Amarilla takeover. On the wall of an abandoned gas station near the court someone had written, "If Tijerina goes to jail—WAR!" After a brief deliberation the jury found him not guilty. Released, he participated in the Poor People's March on Washington in 1968.

In 1969, Tijerina was sent to federal prison for two years for the Kit Carson National Forest incident. His health declined. He was released early after promising not to hold any office with the Alianza movement. While Tijerina was in jail, Alianza suffered attacks. In April 1968, a former sheriff's deputy bombed the Alianza headquarters, but bungled the job and blew off his right hand. The police, following a trail of blood, arrested him in his blood-spattered car, finding yet another stick of dynamite in a lunch box in the car. Charges of using a "deadly weapon" were dismissed, and a grand jury cleared him of a "dangerous use of explosives charge." He was sentenced to a mere 16 hours of community service at the county medical center.

In the winter of 1968, rifle shots from a speeding car shattered the headquarters' office windows. There were no arrests. In June 1969, terrorists shot up a crowded hall during an Alianza meeting. Again, no arrests were made. Repeated bombings, rock throwing, and shooting amounted to a campaign of terror against Alianza. Cars were burned. Arsonists set fire to the villagers' health clinic. Tijerina's children were threatened with kidnaping and murder. An Alianza car was tear-gassed with members in it—but again, no arrests were made.

The Minutemen are a paramilitary, white extremist group who are racist and advocate the violent overthrow of the United States government. During the campaign of terror, an extremist Minutemen leader, Robert DePugh, and his chief assistant, Walter Peyson, were caught by the FBI in a small New Mexico town near Albuquerque. Their cache of arms and bombs was so large its description filled 24 typed pages in the police report. Maps of the land grant villages were found, as well as thousands of rounds of ammunition. A list of Minutemen membership found there suddenly vanished amid rumors that local law enforcement officers were in on it. A security chief of Alianza was warned that opponents of Tijerina were going to assassinate him. After their arrest, the Minutemen leaders were taken out of state. Tijerina's office was bombed three times, once while his wife and children were present, although no one was injured. Like Martin Luther King, Jr., Tijerina was accused of being a Communist. District Attorney Alfonso Sanchez, with whom Tijerina fought in the Tierra Amarilla incident, implied that Alianza villagers were training for a revolution. Tijerina scoffed at such charges: "I don't know much about Communism or Marxism. Communism is just another European political system to me, just as corrupt as any other political system. We don't need it. . . . The old powers are dying . . . we are being born. The Communists are no threat to the rich, the oppressors, in New Mexico. We are a threat to them" (Steiner 1969: 89).

The Alianza movement crumbled without Tijerina's active leadership. In 1979, the courts did consider the land grant issue, but no victories were won. Tijerina now lives a lonely and isolated life in a small New Mexico town. Nonetheless, he activated ethnic pride and inspired new leadership.

Another Chicano leader was Rodolfo "Corky" Gonzales, founder of the Crusade for Justice, a Chicano youth group centered in Denver, Colorado. In the 1960 presidential election, Gonzales had been a district captain of the Denver Democratic Party, as its Viva Kennedy coordinator. He worked for the War on Poverty Program in Denver from 1961 through 1965, when he resigned to begin the Crusade for Justice. He helped organize the Poor People's March on Washington, D.C., and he and Reies Tijerina led the delegation of Chicanos from the Southwest. The Crusade started as a civil rights group but quickly developed into a wide-ranging barrio group stressing self-defense. It had its own security force whose aim was not only to protect the barrio but to safeguard its activists. It was praised by the Washington, D.C., police force for its work in maintaining good order during the Poor People's March. By 1967, the Crusade claimed a membership of 1,800.

Corky Gonzales adopted the term **Aztlan** at the first national Chicano conference, held in Denver in 1969. He used the term and popularized it. Many scholars believe the Aztlan of the Aztecs was actually within present-day Mexico. Nonetheless, the term came to be used to refer to the "lost lands" of northern Mexico that are now the southwestern United States. Aztlan became a kind of Utopia or Eden. The Chicano activists converted that ancient idealized landscape into an ideal of a modern homeland where they hoped to fulfill their people's (La Raza) political, economic, and cultural destiny.

Gonzales inspired the Crusade for Justice with the fervor of nationalism. On Palm Sunday, 1969, he convened a national gathering of barrio youth at the Chicano Youth Federation Conference to the cries of *"Raza! Raza! Raza!"* From the conference various campus groups merged into the more militant Estudiantil Chicano de Aztlan (MECHA), the Chicano Student Movement of Aztlan. Corky Gonzales and the conference inspired groups such as UMAS, MAYO, and the Brown Berets.

Corky Gonzales rejected integration as fruitless. He characterized it as the "small end of a funnel" wherein a few Chicanos may make it, but the rest of the people stay behind at the bottom. He praised the youth for demanding a revolutionary change, not merely putting water on fire. He challenged them to teach their people, rather than trying to educate a racist majority; to be proud of their values and their culture. Perhaps his most lasting contribution was helping to organize La Raza Unida. At the Denver, Colorado, conference he issued a ringing declaration of independence for Mexican Americans: "We have to start judging our lives with new values. . . . The Anglos consider us conquered citizens, but we are not second class citizens. We must declare that our rights under the Treaty of Guadalupe Hidalgo be recognized, that the educational system be changed and include bilingual teaching and the history of the Mexican American. Que viva la raza y la revolucian!" (Steiner 1969: 324).

The La Raza Unida Conference in 1967 in El Paso, Texas, inspired numerous new leaders and groups.[3] Jose Angel Gutierrez, who helped organize La Raza Unida, led a Chicano voter revolt in 1970 in Crystal City, Texas. Although the small city had a population that was 80 percent Mexican American, it had a 100 percent Anglo government. Organizing La Raza Unida as a third party, Gutierrez and La Raza ran candidates for local office, organized community co-ops, supported Chicano business, and led boycotts against hostile merchants. The **La Raza Unida Partido** (the People's Party or LRU) won numerous city offices, essentially capturing the government of Crystal City.

Like black youth in SNCC and CORE, militant Chicano youth challenged their leaders and showed little patience with the efforts of the veteran Chicano leaders. Jose Angel Gutierrez of San Antonio, president of the Mexican American Youth Organization (MAYO), challenged the crowds in the barrio gym: "We are going to march and you can join us. But if you don't, you will be left behind." Another young leader, Phil Castruita of the United Mexican American Students (UMAS), a California State University group, remarked matter of factly, "The young Chicanos see this conference [the hearings and La Raza Unida] as the last chance you older Chicanos have to come through. If nothing happens from this you'll have to step aside or we'll walk over you" (Steiner 1969: 238–239).

The **barrio** of Los Angeles is the third largest city of Mexican residents in the world, exceeded only by Guadalajara and Mexico City. Over 1 million Mexicans live in Los Angeles. By themselves they would constitute one of the ten largest cities in the United States. Los Angeles is the capital of La Raza. It is to the Chicano what Boston is to the Irish American and New York City is to the American Jew (Steiner 1969).

In March 1968 the barrio of Los Angeles experienced student protest when some 15,000 Chicano students walked out of five Los Angeles high schools and staged what they called a "blowout." Their "strike" had closed classes throughout the barrio. Police and sheriff's deputies blockaded the neighborhood, arresting both students and some teachers. The teenagers held up hastily drawn posters voicing their frustrations: "Education not contempt," "Education not eradication," "Teachers si, bigots no!" "Que paso? Free speech!" "We are not 'Dirty Mexicans,'" "Our kids don't have blue eyes, but they do go oversees," "School, not prison," and "Is this a holiday?"

Student leaders issued a list of demands ranging from textbook and curriculum revisions to show Mexican contributions to America, to the transfer of teachers who evidence prejudice, to the building of swimming pools in all East Los Angeles schools, to unlocked rest rooms, and to all campuses being open and fences removed. The Los Angeles Teachers Association and Local 1021 of the American Federation of Teachers supported their demands for more bilingual and bicultural training of school personnel, more Spanish-language library materials and textbooks, and better food in the cafeterias.

The city responded by arresting 13 student leaders of the blowout and their teacher, Sal Castro. Charged with conspiracy to disturb the educational process, they were jailed. The barrio newspaper, *La Raza,* chortled that there were "thirteen Aztec gods," that those arrested were a select and prophetic number, and their arrest showed the ignorance of the Board of Education of the Chicano heritage. The paper called the students the "cream of their crop" who were "pushed out" of their schools. Numerous groups came to the defense of those arrested: the Congress of Mexican American Unity, UMAS, Cesar Chavez's United Farm Workers, the Council of Churches of Southern California, the Pacific Southwest Council of the Union of American Hebrew Congregations, the local American Federation of Teachers, the NAACP, and the Black Congress. After a year's delay, protests by thousands of barrio residents, and dozens of subsequent arrests, the "thirteen" were brought to trial, convicted, fined, and placed on three-years probation forbidding them to enter any barrio school unless on official business. When the Board of Education voted to suspend the teacher, students and parents staged a week-long sit-in at the board offices. Upon their return, the bemused members of the board voted to reinstate the teacher. Students were appeased but still angry, promising more blowouts if the board did not act on their demands.

In the fall of 1969, Chicano students across the country declared a national walkout in celebration of Mexican Independence Day on September 17. In Denver, Colorado, school officials agreed to the students' demand by holding a special assembly in a high school that had been the site of a riot the previous spring, allowing the blowout student leaders to address the student body, an unprecedented action by the school board in recognition of the Chicano students' views. There were numerous walkouts, blowouts, and student marches from Texas to California. Student activists demanded community control of barrio schools and new curricular changes to recognize the teaching, language, and cultural heritage of Mexican Americans. The barrio classroom became an arena of the movement's struggles. In the streets, Chicano youth organized the Brown Berets. Wearing berets and gun belts and slinging rifles on their shoulders, barrio militants embraced the style and tactics of the Black Panthers. Just as the Black Panthers popularized the term "black power," the Brown Berets used their version, "brown power."

While Reies Tijerina was free on bond, he visited Los Angeles and spoke at a MAPA meeting. He appeared several times in the area, flanked by Brown Beret body-guards. He embraced and praised Black Nationalist leaders and stirred young mili-tants with hints of violence and calls for valor, for a willingness to die, if need be, for La Causa. Louis Valdez, then a young Chicano leader of MAPA and a disciple of Cesar Chavez, spoke to the same rally. Wearing a Che Guevara outfit, he attacked the *"baga-chos"* (a Chicano term for Anglos), showing a militancy more typical of the fiery Tije-rina and the Brown Berets than of Cesar Chavez.

The Brown Berets supported high school student blowout demonstrations, eco-nomic boycotts, political drives, and street demonstrations. Their motto was "To Serve, Observe, Protect." They monitored especially the Los Angeles police depart-ment, which they accused of harassment and having an agenda to destroy their group. Like the Black Panthers, they adopted paramilitary titles. "Field Marshall" Jose is quoted on the misperception of La Raza as a racist expression: "You are using the white people's words. English, you see . . . English is a racist language. That is why they sound the same, brown power, black power. In Spanish we don't say a color. We say the power of the people—La Raza" (Steiner 1969: 116–117).

The chairman of the Mayor's Youth Advisory Council became the "prime minis-ter" of the Brown Berets. When asked, "Who organized them?" he replied, "The police organized them." The Brown Berets saw their struggle with the police as "fight-ing like the Indian fought—for motherland." The Los Angeles police arrested 65 members of the Brown Berets. White police were characterized as bigots with guns who saw Chicanos as brown faces, not human beings. Chicanos perceived the police as having the attitude that they could treat Chicanos any way they wanted and get away with anything; as creating violence not preventing it; and as building commu-nity animosity rather than community relations. "More Chicanos are killed by cops on the streets in the Southwest than any other minority group in the population," wrote a young man in the barrio newspaper. He called it "Chicano birth control."

In the 1970s, paralleling the development of the Black Panthers, the Brown Berets evolved into a community service movement. Many of its members hung up their berets and guns and became part of La Junta, whose manifesto stated:

> It is the purpose of La Junta to spread cultural consciousness among our people by set-ting up Chicano libraries in the barrios which will carry books dealing with the History, Heritage and Culture of La Raza; by setting up educational classes; by setting up pro-grams of community involvement; by working in the creative arts such as the Teatro Chicano, Music, Poetry, Painting, and Film. . . . We will stress pride in our people not only by teaching and learning our history, but by showing the great contributions of La Raza to civilization. In working towards our goals we will conduct ourselves and La Junta in a free and democratic manner, in keeping with the great traditions of the Amer-icas." (Steiner 1969: 111–112)

In New York City and Chicago, the Puerto Rican community formed its version of the Black Panthers and the Brown Berets: the Young Lords. In the Puerto Rican area of Manhattan known as "El Barrio," or Spanish Harlem, Puerto Rican power arose among students in 1968–1969. They were concerned with many of the same issues that agitated New York's Black Harlem: poor schools, bad housing, and widespread poverty. The Puerto Rican Young Lords of New York and of Chicago adopted a radically militant paramilitary style. In 1968, they occupied a church in Harlem and staged militant actions around two city hospitals. In the spring of 1969, they demonstrated at Queens College and City College, supporting militant Puerto Rican college students in their demonstrations in association with black youth demonstrations. In April 1969, they took over the Second City-Wide Puerto Rican Conference of New York. In June 1969, they marched in the streets.

Despite its militancy and celebration of brown power, the reality of Hispanic power is more potential than actual. Since 1980, the more radical groups have given way to Hispanic organizations following a more political accommodationist route: PASSO, MAPA, MASA, MAYO, and UMAS all used standard electoral politics. MECHA continues its more militant voice, but it too organizes campus and community groups and stresses Chicano pride more than violent or radical reform. The Mexican-American Legal Defense and Education Fund (MALDEF), founded in 1967, developed a strategy based on court cases and voter drives, developing into an Hispanic version of the NAACP. Likewise, the American Coordinating Council on Political Education (ACCPE) launched a nationwide Hispanic voter registration drive.

Political organization and action brought measurable results. From 1970 to 1988, Hispanic elected officials increased from less than 800 to over 3,400. Hispanic elected officials served prominently in the Clinton Administration, such as Henry Cisneros, secretary of housing; Frederico Peña, White House chief of staff; and Antonia Novella, surgeon general.

RED POWER: THE NATIVE AMERICAN PROTEST MOVEMENT

Like Hispanics, the Native American movement turned to a more radical and militant strategy by using a variation of the tactics developed by the black civil rights movement. Like Hispanics, the Native American civil rights movement began in the early 1960s.

The "red power" theme did not develop until the pan-Indian movement arrived (creating organizations that crossed or spanned tribal or "national" boundaries). Again, World War II played a key role in the organizational development of the pan-Indian movement. In 1944, the National Congress of American Indians was organized in Denver, Colorado, the first truly viable national pan-Indian organization. This organization was integrationist rather than radical. Like the NAACP, it used the courts and lobbied for legislation. At a June 1961 national conference held in Chicago, 500 delegates from 90 communities attended. Four young militants addressed the conference, calling the leadership "Uncle Tomahawks."

Ten young leaders split off and met in Gallup, New Mexico, to form the National Indian Youth Council, led by Mel Thom, a Pauite graduate student. While stressing the spirit of red power, tactically they first pointed to the 370 existing treaties and simply advocated that the government enforce laws already on the books.

Gradually, however, they began using more active protest actions. From 1961 through 1970, various groups staged 194 instances of Native American protest.

Like SNCC and the black power movement, the young and more militant Indian leaders began their first use of direct-action protest, in this case by organizing "fish-ins" in 1964 in the Seattle, Washington, area. In 1968, the U.S. Supreme Court upheld their treaty rights to fish. They led a similar fish-in campaign in Wisconsin from 1968 through 1991 to gain traditional (and treaty-protected) rights through a combination of demonstrations (spear fishing) and court actions. In Wisconsin, the Chippewas started the dispute by asserting their spear-fishing rights. A number of Wisconsin "anti-native" groups developed: the Wisconsin Alliance for Rights and Resources and Protect American Rights and Resources. Soon whites were sporting racist signs that proclaimed "Save a Walleye, Spear an Indian," and "Spear a Pregnant Squaw, Save a Walleye," and bumper stickers that read "Indian Niggers" and "Red Niggers." The Chippewas waged a nine-year legal battle to ensure their treaty rights to fish and hunt.

What became the best known of the radical protest pan-Indian groups, the American Indian Movement (AIM), began in the summer of 1968 in Minneapolis, Minnesota. Its founders were Clyde Bellencourt, a Chippewa; Dennis Banks, an Anishinabe Ojibwa; and Russell Means, an Oglala Lakota Sioux. They were born on reservations but lived in urban areas. They began by stressing community service programs: monitoring police violence against Indians, alcohol rehabilitation programs, and school reform.

Their militant protests began when they linked up with a group calling itself the Indians of All Tribes, which staged what became a 19-month (November 1969 through May 1971) takeover of Alcatraz Island in San Francisco Bay. Red Power was truly born with this action. The radical youth castigated all Indians who sympathized with the Bureau of Indian Affairs as "Uncle Tomahawks," and "apples" (red on the outside but white on the inside). They laid claim to the island with the takeover, asserting rights under an 1868 treaty that promised to return unused federal property to Indian control. This protest action drew worldwide attention to their cause.

AIM had a knack for selecting an appropriate symbolic gesture that would maximize the power of publicity. On Thanksgiving Day 1970, they seized the *Mayflower* replica and painted Plymouth Rock red. On the Fourth of July they organized a "counter-celebration" at Mount Rushmore in the sacred Black Hills of South Dakota. In 1972, AIM and eight other Native American organizations began the extensive protest they called the "Trail of Broken Treaties." It started on the West Coast and picked up Native Americans at various reservation stops along the way. On November 1, 1972, it ended at Washington, D.C., where 500 demonstrators seized the Bureau of Indian Affairs headquarters, occupied its offices for six days, and rummaged through and released embarrassing files.

By far their most militant protest action occurred in 1973 when they staged a "takeover" of Wounded Knee, South Dakota. The ten-week siege began when Dennis Banks and Russell Means organized demonstrations at the Pine Ridge and Rosebud reservations to protest the failure of authorities to arrest the suspected murderers of Raymond Yellow Thunder. He was a 51-year-old Sioux who had been stripped of his pants and assaulted by a group of drunken whites at the local American Legion Hall.

His frozen body was later found in the back of a pickup truck. Wounded Knee was the site of the 1890 massacre of 250 Sioux old men, women, and children at what white soldiers had termed the last "battle" of the Plains Indians Wars.[5]

The dispute leading to the siege began when Richard Wilson and the tribal elders banned AIM activities at the Pine Ridge Reservation. In February 1973, Banks and Means led a group of 300 AIM members who took over the tiny hamlet, which they occupied for 70 days, during which time two of their members were killed. The FBI arrested the demonstrators, and although AIM's goals were not met, the incident did focus national attention on conditions of reservation life.

AIM's radicalism spurred Indian pride. Even assimilated Indians began to return to their native culture: "I watched what they were doing, and I could see the pride in these young men and women. . . . Then I looked at myself. I was making money and living in white suburbia. . . . I started letting my hair grow long, and I stopped wearing a tie and started to sort of de-program myself" (*Through Indian Eyes,* p. 366).

Although arrested and charged for the Wounded Knee siege, Means and Banks were cleared of any crimes for it. They were later imprisoned for other crimes, however, and AIM's protest actions quieted down in the mid-1970s. AIM spent much time and effort during the period 1976–1994 to win the release of one of their leaders, Leonard Peltier, who was sentenced to two consecutive life terms for the murder of two FBI agents on the Pine Ridge Reservation. In 1994, these efforts culminated in the "Walk for Justice."

Like the black and Hispanic civil rights movements, the Native American movement shifted its focus and tactics during the late 1970s and throughout the 1980s to the court and legislative arenas.[6] It scored some significant victories in both areas. Native Americans fought legal battles over lands they claimed were taken in direct violation of treaty agreements. Over the course of two decades various Indian tribes sued

Chief Big Foot lying dead in the snow at the Wounded Knee battlefield.

a number of states over land, often settling the disputes when the courts awarded them millions of dollars in compensation for the lost land. They used court action in Maine, Massachusetts, Rhode Island, New York, South Carolina, Washington, South Dakota, Alaska, and even against the South Pacific Transportation Company, which settled with the Walker River Paiutes for $1.2 million over a land dispute.

The Alaska dispute exemplifies many of these long, drawn-out court battles over land. In 1970, the Alaskan Federation of Natives (AFN) took court action to stop what they termed the biggest land-grab in the history of the United States. They were disputing state seizure of 53,000 million acres of land. The 1971 Alaskan Claims Settlement Act awarded 44 million acres to the Inuits, Aleuts, and Eskimos and a cash settlement of nearly $1 billion. Further reforms in 1988 helped safeguard the original act, but as a major trade-off, the Alaskan Native Americans surrendered future claims to all aboriginal lands.

In 1974, a new pan-Indian organization was formed, the Council of Energy Resource Tribes, to press legal claims and to protect Indian lands from exploitation. It fought to ensure a fair return to tribes when natural resources were developed. It began with the 25 largest tribes; by 1990, over 45 tribes had joined. In 1991, funds awarded to the Sioux tribes over a Black Hills land suit amounted to $330 million. As of 1995, however, the Sioux had refused to accept payment, insisting on control of the land rather than taking the cash settlement.

This period also saw Native Americans securing a number of legislative victories:

1. Indian Civil Rights Act of 1968, which reversed the termination policies of the 1950s and increased the number of Native Americans serving in the Bureau of Indian Affairs and other related federal agencies

2. Indian Education Act of 1972

3. Indian Self-Determination and Education Assistance Act of 1975

4. Indian Child Welfare Act of 1978, which halted the long-standing practice of forcing assimilation of Native Americans by mandatory attendance at boarding schools

5. Indian Religious Freedom Act of 1978, designed to protect sacred sites and allow certain religious practices (use of eagle feathers, the use of peyote), but rendered nearly ineffective by subsequent (1990s) court rulings

6. 1988 Indian Gaming Regulation Act, which resulted, by 1994, in 23 states having Native American–operated gaming on their reservations netting some $600 million for the 200 tribes involved.

The Clinton Administration appointed Ada Deer, a Menominee Indian leader who had led the fight against the Termination Act, director of the Bureau of Indian Affairs. In 1994, in a symbolic show of support for Native Americans, President Clinton hosted a conference of 547 leaders of the federally recognized tribes. It was the largest Native American meeting with a U.S. President. Box 8.2 presents a summary of Supreme Court decisions relating to Native American Indian rights handed down during the period.

BOX 8.2:   Native American–Related Supreme Court Decisions, 1973–1988

McCLANAHAN V. ARIZONA STATE TAX COMMISSION, 441 U.S. 164 (1973)

McClanahan was a member of the Navajo tribe. All her 1967 income was earned on the reservation. Arizona withheld state income tax from her. She sued for a tax refund. The Arizona courts denied the refund, and she appealed. Justice Thurgood Marshall wrote for a unanimous court in reversing Arizona and ordering the refund. Marshall analyzed treaties with the Navajos and found no provisions allowing state taxation. Instead the treaties implied that the Navajos would be under federal protection. Arizona had decided not to seek Public Act 280 control over reservations and hence had no claim to levy taxes.

UNITED STATES V. MAZURIE, 419 U.S. 544 (1975)

In 1953 Congress passed a local option law for alcoholic beverages in Indian Country—all lands within the outer boundaries of reservations, if state law permitted. The Wyoming Wind River reservation permitted sales if distributors followed state licensing laws. Mazurie was given a state license to operate a tavern on fee lands (private lands) within the reservation boundaries. Later the Wind River tribes passed an ordinance requiring a tribal license to sell alcoholic beverages. Mazurie applied for a tribal license for the tavern. He was turned down following a public hearing. Mazurie closed the tavern, but later reopened it and was charged with violating the tribal ordinance. Mazurie appealed. Lower federal courts overturned the tribal conviction; however, the Supreme Court reversed and upheld the conviction. Justice William Rehnquist defended the 1953 congressional delegation of power to the tribe as being consistent with tribal sovereignty to regulate tribal internal affairs.

BRYAN V. ITASCA COUNTY, 426 U.S. 373 (1976)

Bryan, a Chippewa, owned a mobile home on the Leech Lake reservation in Minnesota. The local county government (non-Native) assessed a personal property tax against Bryan's home (which he personally owned). Bryan objected, but the Minnesota courts upheld the tax. Bryan appealed. Minnesota claimed that as a state covered by Public Act 280

(except for another reservation) it could tax "private" property of tribal members. Public Act 280 gave states jurisdiction over criminal matters and matters of general civil law, an exception being taxation on tribal property. The court held that neither the taxation authority nor matters of civil regulation were covered by the act. The justices reasoned that the taxation exception was not limiting but that the power to tax would have required a very specific positive statement. The tax was nullified.

SANTA CLARA PUEBLO V. MARTINEZ, 436 U.S. 439 (1978)

Mrs. Martinez, a member of the Santa Clara Pueblo, married a Navajo. Her children were denied membership in the Pueblo and denied tribal benefits because their father was not from the Santa Clara Pueblo. On the other hand, the children of a Santa Clara Pueblo father and a non-Pueblo mother would be considered a member of the patriarchal Pueblo community. The Martinez children sued the Pueblo for membership on the basis of the Indian Civil Rights Act (1968), which guarantees equal protection of the law. The Pueblo's claims of sovereignty immunity (the fact that the Pueblo's rules could not be reviewed by outside courts) were disregarded by the Supreme Court on the grounds that the Indian Civil Rights Act provided legal mechanisms for assuring rights. However, the Supreme Court reversed lower courts and denied relief to the Martinez family. The court maintained that the definition of tribal (Pueblo) membership was clearly a matter of tribal sovereignty that preceded the writing of the U.S. Constitution and the Indian Civil Rights Act. The membership criteria could be altered only with very specific legislation from Congress.

CALIFORNIA V. CABAZON, 480 U.S. 94 (1987)

The Cabazon band was operating bingo and poker games in manners not permitted by California gaming regulations. California allowed the games with certain restrictions as to hours and prize limits. These restrictions were not followed by the Cabazon band. The court ruled that California—a Public Act 280 state—could not prohibit the Native gaming, as the gaming restrictions were "regulatory" and not "prohibitory." If they were prohibitory, nobody would be allowed to have bingo and poker games in California. The case ruling meant, in essence, that a tribe could offer a game that was legal within a state, and they could operate the gaming totally unregulated by the state. The fear of unregulated Native American gaming enterprise and the possibilities of organized crime involvement led to the passage of the Indian Gaming Regulatory Act of 1988.

LYNG V. NORTHWEST INDIAN CEMETERY PROTECTIVE ASSOCIATION, 485 U.S. 439 (1988)

The federal government sought to build a 75-mile paved road through national forest lands outside of all reservations but near three reservations. Three tribes (the Association) protested that the road and its traffic would disturb their religious practices. They engaged in meditations at spiritual places within the forest. An initial environmental statement suggested that the road would violate the Natives' free exercise of their religion. The U.S. Forest Service took this into consideration but decided to build the road anyway. The tribes challenged the decision. A split Supreme Court ruled in favor of the Forest Service. Justice Sandra Day O'Connor wrote that the construction of the road in no way coerced the Native Americans or anyone else regarding religious practices, even though it would interfere with the practices. However, the government could not operate if it were required to satisfy every citizen's religious needs and desires.

SOURCE: William Thompson, *Native American Issues* (Santa Barbara, CA: ABC-CLIO, 1996).

The 1980s saw Native American organizations split in their goals. Some were largely "reformative" in their goals. They were accommodationist and sought to "improve" the conditions of life for Native Americans through reforms won by legislation or court action. This approach is exemplified by Senator Ben Nighthorse Campbell (R.–Colo.), who in 1992 became the first Native American elected to the U.S. Senate. In contrast were the **transformative goals** of anti-assimilationist and anti-acculturationist groups (such as AIM), who sought a fundamental restructuring of Native American–white relations. In the 1990s, AIM again attracted national media attention with a series of protests against the various national sports franchises (baseball, basketball, football) that use Native American logos and mascots in racially offensive ways. They objected to the use of the tomahawk chop and degrading caricatures that embody mocking stereotypes. Although spokespersons for the teams responded that such usage was not racist or intentionally offensive, AIM leaders such as Russell Means argued they clearly were racist. Box 8.3 presents an article by Ward Churchill that strongly states their case as to the offensive and racist nature of such majority society cultural practices.

Senator Ben Nighthorse Campbell addresses a news conference.

BOX 8.3:   Sticks and Stones . . . and the Hurt of Name Calling

In recent years Native Americans have protested the use of Indian names, logos, and mascots by various professional and university sports teams—names like the Atlanta "Braves," the Washington "Redskins," the Kansas City "Chiefs," the Florida State "Seminoles," or the Lamar Colorado High School "Savages." They object to mascots with head dress and beads, spears, and "warpainted" faces using gestures like the "tomahawk chop." Team owners, university officials, team players, and a great many fans disagree with the Native American position taken by Russell Means of the American Indian Movement and by the related American Indian Anti-Defamation Council that he founded. They insist that such use of these terms, logos, and mascots is just "good, clean fun," and not intended to be offensive.

But the point is that such behavior naturally *is* offensive. Imagine the uproar in society if we used comparable names and symbols for other racial and ethnic groups. As Indian author Ward Churchill noted, would society tolerate a football team called the "Niggers," with a half-time show featuring a simulated stewing of the opposing team's coach in a pot of boiling water while players danced around it garbed in leopard skins and wearing fake bones in their noses? Would society accept a baseball team being called the San Francisco "Sambos"? How about a hockey team called the New Jersey "Jungle Bunnies"? What would be the reaction to such names as the Galveston "Greasers," or the San Diego "Spics," or the Wisconsin "Wetbacks"? How about a college basketball team called the Gonzaga "Gooks"? Would Jews accept the use of the Kansas City "Kikes"? How would Italian Americans react to the Daytona "Dagos," or Polish Americans to the Pittsburgh "Polacks"? What would be the reaction to rechristening the Fighting Irish of Notre Dame the "Drunken Irish," or the "Papist Pigs"? Would society think it was just "good, clean fun" to call a women's professional basketball team the Detroit "Dykes"?

Clearly, the offensive nature of these examples illustrates why Native Americans are concerned. What is unacceptable for other racial and ethnic minorities ought to be equally unacceptable in their case.

In 1946, after World War II, the Nuremberg Trials prosecuted, convicted, and hanged a Nazi, Julius Streicker, for what it termed "crimes against humanity." His offense? He published a tabloid titled *Der Sturmer* in which he penned a long series of virulently anti-Semitic editorials, "news" stories, and cartoons graphically depicting Jews in derogatory fashion. He was prosecuted for propaganda designed to "dehumanize" Jews in the German public's mind, thereby creating the atmosphere that contributed to the horrors of the holocaust wherein some six million Jews as well as several million Gypsies, Poles, Slavs, homosexuals, and other "untermenschen" (subhumans) were exterminated.

Russell Means and Ward Churchill have pointed out the parallels to the United States' policy to "exterminate red savages." They note that from the year 1500, when Europeans arrived, the indigenous American Indian population was reduced from about 12.5 million to 250,000 at the beginning of the twentieth century. The majority society accepted the opinion that "the only good Indian was a dead Indian." The United States Army perpetrated numerous massacres of Indians—at Horsehoe Bend, Bear River, Sand Creek, Washita River, Marias River, Camp Robinson, and Wounded Knee. Native Americans were forcibly removed from the east and force-marched (in the Trail of Tears) two-thousand miles to the west in what today we would justifiably refer to as "ethnic cleansing." Native Americans were forcibly "assimilated." Their native culture was suppressed on reservation schools, where children were forced to adopt the white (Anglo) culture. Indeed, for over a century the United States government implemented a national policy that today would fit actions specifically prohibited by Article II of the United Nations Genocide Convention.

Data published by the United States government document that Native Americans have the lowest annual and lifetime per capita incomes of any group in the population. They suffer the highest rates of infant mortality, as well as death by exposure and malnutrition and diseases related to alcoholism and substance abuse. Native American men living on reservations have a life expectancy of only 45 years, and women of just 48 years.

Thus, Native Americans are justly concerned that the American public think about the implications of the "fun and games" use of derogatory images and terms. People need to think about it the next time they witness a gaggle of face-painted and war-bonneted fans doing a "tomahawk chop" dance at a ballgame, or when the grade-school teacher dresses children in turkey feathers to celebrate Thanksgiving Day. The public need to be aware of the damage and the hurt these practices entail the next time they watch a John Wayne cowboy movie on television in which he kills a dozen "savages" with a few shots of his blazing six-gun.

Native Americans urge that the public think about the real situation of American Indians and understand that the treatment of Indians in American popular culture is not "cute," "amusing," or "good, clean fun." Such cultural practices cause real pain and real suffering to real people and are as much a crime against humanity as was the treatment of the Jews in Nazi Germany. They have every right to expect, even to demand, that such practices are brought to a halt.

SOURCE: This box is an adaptation of ideas raised by Ward Churchill in "Crimes Against Humanity," *Z Magazine,* March 1993: 43–47.

SUMMARY

Not all minority groups choose assimilation or the accommodationist approach. This chapter reviewed three groups that pursued new-style radicalism: blacks, Hispanics, and Native Americans. The black civil rights movement arose during the late 1950s and 1960s. It developed new tactics and organizations to pursue nonviolent protest politics. The chapter explored such groups as SCLC, SNCC, CORE and their use of sit-ins, freedom rides, and protest marches that peacefully confronted de jure segregation and Jim Crowism. It focused on the groups and leaders who developed and articulated the strategy of new-style radicalism, setting the model with black power that inspired subsequent movements. It discussed the use of more radical protest politics, focusing on the Black Panthers and on urban riots of the late 1960s as political protests.

The chapter then went on to the development of brown power, emphasizing the Chicano protest movement. It discussed both rural and urban variations, drawing close parallels between the Hispanic movement and the black civil rights movement. It described various groups and leaders who promoted strikes, boycotts, land grant protests, and the young urban Chicano groups that sprang up in the nation's barrios.

Finally, it described the red power protest movement of Native Americans. Describing the various protest organizations of the pan-Indian movement, it showed how they modified and adapted protest politics to suit their needs and aspirations. It assessed the failures and accomplishments of the red power movement.

KEY TERMS

Aztlan: the "lost land" of Mexico, the present-day Southwest of the United States.

Barrio: the neighborhood or urban village; the Hispanic section of a major urban area in the United States.

Black power: ability of black people to get together politically and organize to speak from a position of strength rather than weakness.

La huelga: "the strike."

La Raza: "the race" or "the people," the Chicano term for Mexicans, Mexican Americans.

La Raza Unida (Partido): "the united race" or "united people." It also refers to the political party formed by Chicanos, mostly in Texas.

Relative deprivation: sociological theory; mostly refers to black income relative to white income.

Reverse discrimination: programs of preference toward minorities, held to constitute discriminatory treatment of the white majority.

Rising expectations: the conscious feeling of negative discrepancy between legitimate expectations and present actualities.

Transformative goals: goals seeking a fundamental restructuring of Native American–white relations.

REVIEW QUESTIONS

1. Discuss two pre–World War II black civil rights organizations that were accommodationists. Compare them to two more militant organizations formed in the 1960s.

2. Which U.S. Supreme Court decision established the separate-but-equal doctrine? Discuss its role in inspiring the new black civil rights movement.

3. What was the most sweeping civil rights law ever enacted by the U.S. Congress? What protest actions were critically instrumental in its enactment?

4. Describe the assimilationist Hispanic groups of the pre-1960s era.

5. Which Chicano leader became the best known, often characterized as the Martin Luther King, Jr., of the Chicano movement? What organization did he found and lead? What tactics did he use?

6. What takeover protest brought the New Mexico land grant protest to national attention? When and why did it die off?

7. In the Chicano movement, to what does Aztlan refer? What militant Chicano youth organization did this concept inspire? What tactics do they use?

8. Specify any two pan-Indian organizations. Compare and contrast them in style and tactics with black or Chicano groups.

9. What is the most notably militant pan-Indian organization? Discuss its style and tactics. What black and Chicano groups does it resemble?

10. What pan-Indian group has successfully been using the U.S. courts to press cases for Native American land claims associated with treaty rights? Discuss the Native American loss of land. What laws, policy, and court decisions contributed to that great loss?

NOTES

1. The volumes on the civil rights movement and its personalities are too numerous to cite here, but see, in particular, Branch (1988), Cross (1984), and White (1991). See also Carson (1981), Gonzales (1996), Kitano (1997), Kivisto (1995), LeMay (1985), Marger (1997), and Schaefer (1998).

2. See note 1. See also, for in-depth treatments of the struggle, Burma (1970), Chavez (1984), and Steiner (1969).

3. For a list, see Burma (1970).

4. See Howard (1983) and Fitzpatrick (1968) for accounts of the activities of Puerto Ricans in New York City.

5. See Brown (1970).

6. See Cornell (1988).

SUGGESTED READINGS

BARKER, LUCIUS J., MACK JONES, AND KATHERINE TATE. 1999. *African Americans and the American Political System,* 4th ed. Upper Saddle River, NJ: Prentice Hall.

BRANCH, TAYLOR. 1988. *Parting the Waters: America in the King Years, 1954–1963.* New York: Simon & Schuster.

BURMA, JOHN H. 1970. *Mexican-Americans in the United States.* New York: Harper & Row.

CARMICHAEL, STOKELEY, AND CHARLES V. HAMILTON. 1967. *Black Power: The Politics of Liberation in America.* New York: Vintage.

CARSON, CLAYBORNE. 1981. *In Struggle: SNCC and the Black Awakening of the 1960s.* Cambridge, MA: Harvard University Press.

CHAVEZ, JOHN R. 1984. *The Lost Land: The Chicano Image of the Southwest.* Albuquerque: University of New Mexico Press.

CORNELL, STEPHEN. 1988. *The Return of the Native: American Indian Political Resurgence.* New York: Oxford University Press.

GONZALES, JUAN. 1996. *Racial and Ethnic Groups in America,* 3rd ed. Dubuque, IA: Kendall/Hunt.

JAMES, M. ANNETTE, ED. 1992. *The State of Native America: Genocide, Colonization, and Resistance.* Boston: South End Press.

JOSEPHY, ALVIN, JR. 1971. *Red Power.* New York: McGraw-Hill.

KING, MARTIN LUTHER, JR. 1958. *Stride Toward Freedom: The Montgomery Story.* New York: Harper & Brothers.

KITANO, HARRY. 1997. *Race Relations,* 5th ed. Upper Saddle River, NJ: Prentice Hall.

KIVISTO, PETER. 1995. *Americans All.* Belmont, CA: Wadsworth.

LEMAY, MICHAEL. 1985. *The Struggle for Influence.* Lanham, MD: University Press of America.

MARGER, MARTIN N. 1997. *Race and Ethnic Relations.* Belmont, CA: Wadsworth.

SCHAEFER, RICHARD. 1998. *Racial and Ethnic Groups.* New York: HarperCollins.

STEINER, STAN. 1973. *La Raza: The Mexican Americans.* New York: Random House.

WEATHERFORD, J. 1991. *Native Roots: How the Indians Enriched America.* New York: Fawcett Books.

WINKELMAN, MICHAEL. 1993. *Ethnic Relations in the U.S.* Minneapolis, MN: West.

CASE STUDY 8.1

Martin Luther King, Jr.,
"Letter from a Birmingham Jail"

My dear fellow clergymen:

While confined here in the Birmingham city jail, I came across your recent statement calling my present activities "unwise and untimely." Seldom do I pause to answer criticism of my work and ideas. . . . But since I feel that you are men of genuine good will and that your criticisms are sincerely set forth, I want to try to answer your statement in what I hope will be patient and reasonable terms. . . .

I think I should indicate why I am here in Birmingham, since you have been influenced by the view which argues against "outsiders coming in.". . . I am here because I have organizational ties here. . . . But more basically, I am in Birmingham because injustice is here. . . .

Moreover, I am cognizant of the interrelatedness of all communities and states. I cannot sit idly by in Atlanta and not be concerned about what happens in Birmingham. Injustice anywhere is a threat to justice everywhere. We are caught in an inescapable network of mutuality, tied in a single garment of destiny.

Whatever affects one directly, affects all indirectly. Never again can we afford to live with the narrow, provincial "outside agitator" idea. Anyone who lives inside the United States can never be considered an outsider anywhere within its bounds.

You deplore the demonstrations taking place in Birmingham. But your statement, I am sorry to say, fails to express a similar concern for the conditions that brought about the demonstrations.

I am sure that none of you would want to rest content with the superficial kind of social analysis that deals merely with effects and does not grapple with underlying causes. It is unfortunate that demonstrations are taking place in Birmingham, but it is even more unfortunate that the city's white power structure left the Negro community with no alternative.

In any nonviolent campaign there are four basic steps: collection of the facts to determine whether injustices exist; negotiation; self-purification; and direct action. We have gone through all these steps in Birmingham.

There can be no gainsaying the fact that racial injustice engulfs this community. Birmingham is probably the most thoroughly segregated city in the United States. Its ugly record of brutality is widely known. Negroes have experienced grossly unjust treatment in the courts. There have been more unsolved bombings of Negro homes and churches in Birmingham than in any other city in the nation. These are the hard, brutal facts of the case. . . .

On the basis of these conditions, Negro leaders sought to negotiate with city fathers. But the latter consistently refused to engage in good-faith negotiation. Then, last September, came the opportunity to talk with leaders of Birmingham's economic community. In the course of the negotiations, certain promises were made by the merchants—for example, to remove the stores' humiliating racial signs.

On the basis of these promises, the Reverend Fred Shuttlesworth and the leaders of the Alabama Christian Movement for Human Rights agreed to a moratorium on all demonstrations. As the weeks and months went by, we realized that we were the victims of a broken promise. A few signs, briefly removed, returned; the others remained.

As in so many past experiences, our hopes had been blasted, and the shadow of deep disappointment settled upon us. We had no alternative except to prepare for direct action, whereby we would present our very bodies as a means of laying our case before the conscience of the local and the national community.

Mindful of the difficulties involved, we decided to undertake the process of self-purification. We began a series of workshops on nonviolence, and we repeatedly asked ourselves: "Are you able to accept blows without retaliation?" "Are you able to endure the ordeal of jail?"...

You may well ask, "Why direct action? Why sit-ins, marches, and so forth? Isn't negotiation a better path?" You are quite right in calling for negotiation. Indeed, this is the very purpose of direct action. Nonviolent direct action seeks to create such a crisis and foster such a tension that a community which has constantly refused to negotiate is forced to confront the issue. It seeks so to dramatize the issue so that it can no longer be ignored.

My citing the creation of tension as part of the work of the nonviolent resister may sound rather shocking. But I must confess that I am not afraid of the word "tension." I have earnestly opposed violent tension, but there is a type of constructive, nonviolent tension which is necessary for growth.

Just as Socrates felt that it was necessary to create a tension in the mind so that individuals could rise from the bondage of myths and half-truths to the unfettered realm of creative analysis and objective appraisal, so must we see the need for nonviolent gadflies to create the kind of tension in society that will help men rise from the dark depths of prejudice and racism to the majestic heights of understanding and brotherhood.

The purpose of our direct-action program is to create a situation so crisis-packed that it will inevitably open the door to negotiation. I therefore concur with you in your call for negotiation. Too long has our beloved Southland been bogged down in a tragic effort to live in monologue rather than dialogue.

One of the basic points in your statement is that the action that I and my associates have taken in Birmingham is untimely. Some have asked: "Why didn't you give the new city administration time to act?" The only answer that I can give to this query is that the new Birmingham administration must be prodded about as much as the outgoing one, before it will act. . . .

We have not made a single gain in civil rights without determined legal and nonviolent pressure. . . . Lamentably, it is an historical fact that privileged groups seldom give up their privileges voluntarily. Individuals may see the moral light and voluntarily give up their unjust posture; but, as Reinhold Niebuhr has reminded us, groups tend to be more immoral than individuals.

We know through painful experience that freedom is never voluntarily given by the oppressor. It must be demanded by the oppressed. Frankly, I have yet to engage in a direct-action campaign that was "well timed" in view of those who have not suffered unduly from the disease of segregation.

For years now I have heard the word "Wait!" It rings in the ear of every Negro with piercing familiarity. This "Wait!" has almost always meant "Never." We must come to see, with one of our distinguished jurists, that "justice too long delayed is justice denied."

We have waited for more than 340 years for our constitutional and God-given rights. The nations of Asia and Africa are moving with jetlike speed toward gaining political independence, but we still creep at horse-and-buggy pace toward gaining a cup of coffee at a lunch counter. Perhaps it is easy for those who have never felt the stinging darts of segregation to say, "Wait."

But when you have seen vicious mobs lynch your mothers and fathers at will and drown your sisters and brothers at whim;

when you have seen hate-filled policemen curse, kick and even kill your black brothers and sisters;

when you see the vast majority of your twenty million Negro brothers smothering in an airtight cage of poverty in the midst of an affluent society;

when you suddenly find your tongue twisted and your speech stammering as you seek to explain to your six-year-old daughter why she can't go to the public amusement park that has just been advertised on television, and see tears welling up in her eyes when she is told that Funtown is closed to colored children, and see ominous clouds of inferiority beginning to form in her little mental sky, and see her beginning to distort her personality by developing an unconscious bitterness toward white people;

when you have to concoct an answer for a five-year-old son who is asking, "Daddy, why do white people treat colored people so mean?";

when you take a cross-country drive and find it necessary to sleep night after night in the uncomfortable corners of your automobile because no motel will accept you;

when you are humiliated day in and day out by nagging signs reading "white" and "colored";

when your first name becomes "nigger," your middle name becomes "boy" (however old you are) and your last name becomes "John," and your wife and mother are never given the respected title "Mrs.";

when you are harried by day and haunted by night by the fact that you are a Negro, living constantly at tiptoe stance, never quite knowing what to expect next, and are plagued with inner fears and outer resentments;

when you are forever fighting a degenerating sense of "nobodiness"—then you will understand why we find it difficult to wait.

There comes a time when the cup of endurance runs over, and men are no longer willing to be plunged into the abyss of despair. I hope, sirs, you can understand our legitimate and unavoidable impatience.

You express a great deal of anxiety over our willingness to break laws. This is certainly a legitimate concern. Since we so diligently urge people to obey the Supreme Court's decision of 1954 outlawing segregation in the public schools, at first glance it may seem rather paradoxical for us consciously to break laws.

One may well ask: "How can you advocate breaking some laws and obeying others?" The answer lies in the fact that there are two types of laws: just and unjust. I would be the first to advocate obeying just laws. One has not only a legal but a moral responsibility to obey just laws. Conversely, one has a moral responsibility to disobey unjust laws. I would agree with St. Augustine that "an unjust law is no law at all."

Now, what is the difference between the two? How does one determine whether a law is just or unjust? A just law is a man-made code that squares with the moral law or the law of God. An unjust law is a code that is out of harmony with the moral law.

To put it in the terms of St. Thomas Aquinas: An unjust law is a human law that is not rooted in eternal law and natural law. Any law that uplifts human personality is just. Any law that degrades human personality is unjust.

All segregation statutes are unjust because segregation distorts the soul and damages the personality. It gives the segregator a false sense of superiority and the segregated a false sense of inferiority. . . .

Let us consider a more concrete example of just and unjust laws. An unjust law is a code that a numerical or power majority group compels a minority group to obey but does not make binding on itself. This is *difference* made legal. By the same token, a just law is a code that a majority compels a minority to follow and that it is willing to follow itself. This is *sameness* made legal.

Let me give another explanation. A law is unjust if it is inflicted on a minority that, as a result of being denied the right to vote, had no part in enacting or devising the law. Who can say that the legislature of Alabama which set up that state's segregation laws was democratically elected?

Throughout Alabama all sorts of devious methods are used to prevent Negroes from becoming registered voters, and there are some counties in which, even though Negroes constitute a majority of the population, not a single Negro is registered. Can any law enacted under such circumstances be considered democratically structured?

Sometimes a law is just on its face and unjust in its application. For instance, I have been arrested on a charge of parading without a permit. Now, there is nothing wrong in having an ordinance which requires a permit for a parade. But such an ordinance becomes unjust when it is used to maintain segregation and to deny citizens the First-Amendment privilege of peaceful assembly and protest.

I hope you are able to see the distinction I am trying to point out. In no sense do I advocate evading or defying the law, as would the rabid segregationist. That would lead to anarchy.

One who breaks an unjust law must do so openly, lovingly and with a willingness to accept the penalty. I submit that an individual who breaks a law that conscience tells him is unjust, and who willingly accepts the penalty of imprisonment in order to arouse the conscience of the community over its injustice, is in reality expressing the highest respect for law.

Of course, there is nothing new about this kind of civil disobedience. It was evidenced sublimely in the refusal of Shadrach, Meshach, and Abednego to obey the laws of Nebuchadnezzar, on the ground that a higher moral law was at stake. It was practiced superbly by the early Christians, who were willing to face hungry lions and the excruciating pain of chopping blocks rather than submit to certain unjust laws of the Roman Empire.

To a degree, academic freedom is a reality today because Socrates practiced civil disobedience. In our own nation, the Boston Tea Party represented a massive act of civil disobedience.

We should never forget that everything Adolf Hitler did in Germany was "legal" and everything the Hungarian freedom fighters did in Hungary was "illegal."

It was "illegal" to aid and comfort a Jew in Hitler's Germany. Even so, I am sure that, had I lived in Germany at the time, I would have aided and comforted my Jewish brothers. If today I lived in a Communist country where certain principles dear to the Christian faith are suppressed, I would openly advocate disobeying that country's anti-religious laws.

I must make two honest confessions to you, my Christian and Jewish brothers. First, I must confess that over the past few years I have been gravely disappointed with the white moderate. I have almost reached the regrettable conclusion that the Negro's great stumbling block in his stride toward freedom is not the White Citizen's Counciler or the Ku Klux Klanner, but the white moderate, who is more devoted to "order" than to justice; who prefers a negative peace which is the absence of tension to a positive peace which is the presence of justice; who constantly says, "I agree with you in the goal you seek, but I cannot agree with your methods of direct action"; who paternalistically believes he can set the timetable for another man's freedom; who lives by a mythical concept of time and who constantly advises the Negro to wait for a "more convenient season."

Shallow understanding from people of good will is more frustrating than absolute misunderstanding from people of ill will. Lukewarm acceptance is much more bewildering than outright rejection.

I had hoped that the white moderate would understand that law and order exist for the purpose of establishing justice and that when they fail in this purpose they become the dangerously structured dams that block the flow of social progress.

I had hoped that the white moderate would understand that the present tension in the South is a necessary phase of the transition from an obnoxious negative peace, in which the Negro passively accepted his unjust plight, to a substantive and positive peace, in which all men will respect the dignity and worth of human personality.

Actually, we who engage in nonviolent direct action are not the creators of tension. We merely bring to the surface the hidden tension that is already alive. We bring it out in the open, where it can be seen and dealt with. Like a boil that can never be cured so long as it is covered up but must be opened with all its ugliness to the natural medicines of air and light, injustice must be exposed, with all the tension its exposure creates, to the light of human conscience and the air of national opinion, before it can be cured.

In your statement you assert that our actions, even though peaceful, must be condemned because they precipitate violence. But is this a logical assertion? Isn't this like condemning a robbed man because his possession of money precipitated the evil act of robbery? . . .

We must come to see that, as the federal courts have consistently affirmed, it is wrong to urge an individual to cease his efforts to gain his basic constitutional rights because the quest may precipitate violence. Society must protect the robbed and punish the robber.

I had also hoped that the white moderate would reject the myth concerning time in relation to the struggle for freedom. . . . Actually, time itself is neutral; it can be used either destructively or constructively. More and more I feel that the people of ill will have used time much more effectively than have the people of good will. We will have to repent in this generation not merely for the hateful words and actions of the bad people, but for the appalling silence of the good people.

Human progress never rolls in on wheels of inevitability; it comes through the tireless efforts of men willing to be co-workers with God, and without this hard work, time itself becomes an ally of the forces of stagnation. We must use time creatively, in the knowledge that the time is always ripe to do right.

Now is the time to make real the promise of democracy and transform our pending national elegy into a creative psalm of brotherhood. Now is the time to lift our national policy from the quicksand of racial injustice to the solid rock of human dignity.

You speak of our activity in Birmingham as extreme. At first I was rather disappointed that fellow clergymen would see my nonviolent efforts as those of an extremist. I began thinking about the fact that I stand in the middle of two opposing forces in the Negro community.

One is a force of complacency, made up in part of Negroes who, as a result of long years of oppression, are so drained of self-respect and a sense of "somebodiness" that they have adjusted to segregation; and in part of a few middle-class Negroes who, because of a degree of academic and economic security and because in some ways they profit by segregation, have become insensitive to the problems of the masses.

The other force is one of bitterness and hatred, and it comes perilously close to advocating violence. It is expressed in the various black nationalist groups that are springing up across the nation, the largest and best-known being Elijah Muhammad's Muslim movement. Nourished by the Negro's frustration over the continued existence of racial discrimination, this movement is made up of people who have lost faith in America, who have absolutely repudiated Christianity, and who have concluded that the white man is an incorrigible "devil."

I have tried to stand between these two forces, saying that we need emulate neither the "do-nothingism" of the complacent nor the hatred and despair of the black nationalist. For there is the more excellent way of love and nonviolent protest. I am grateful to God that, through the influence of the Negro church, the way of nonviolence became an integral part of our struggle.

If this philosophy had not emerged, by now many streets of the South would, I am convinced, be flowing with blood. And I am further convinced that if our white brothers dismiss as "rabble-rousers" and "outside agitators" those of us who employ nonviolent direct action, and if they refuse to support our nonviolent efforts, millions of Negroes will, out of frustration and despair, seek solace and security in black-nationalist ideologies—a development that would inevitably lead to a frightening racial nightmare.

Oppressed people cannot remain oppressed forever. The yearning for freedom eventually manifests itself, and that is what has happened to the American Negro. Something within has reminded him of his birthright of freedom, and something without has reminded him that it can be gained. Consciously or unconsciously, he has been caught up by the Zeitgeist, and with his black brothers of Africa and his brown and yellow brothers of Asia, South America and the Caribbean, the United States Negro is moving with a sense of great urgency toward the promised land of racial justice.

If one recognizes this vital urge that has engulfed the Negro community, one should readily understand why public demonstrations are taking place. The Negro has many pent-up resentments and latent frustrations, and he must release them. So let him march; let him make prayer pilgrimages to the city hall; let him go on freedom rides—and try to understand why he must do so.

If his repressed emotions are not released in nonviolent ways, they will seek expression through violence; this is not a threat but a fact of history. So I have not said to my people, "Get rid of your discontent." Rather, I have tried to say that this normal and healthy discontent can be channeled into the creative outlet of nonviolent direct action. And now this approach is being termed extremist.

But though I was initially disappointed at being categorized as an extremist, as I continued to think about the matter I gradually gained a measure of satisfaction from the label.

Was not Jesus an extremist for love: "Love your enemies, bless them that curse you, do good to them that hate you, and pray for them which despitefully use you, and persecute you."

Was not Amos an extremist for justice: "Let justice roll down like waters and righteousness like an ever-flowing stream.". . .

And John Bunyan: "I will stay in jail to the end of my days before I make a butchery of my conscience."

And Abraham Lincoln: "This nation cannot survive half slave and half free." And Thomas Jefferson: "We hold these truths to be self-evident, that all men are created equal. . . ."

So the question is not whether we will be extremists, but what kind of extremists we will be. Will we be extremists for hate or for love? Will we be extremists for the preservation of injustice or for the extension of justice? . . . Perhaps the South, the nation, and the world are in dire need of creative extremists.

I had hoped that the white moderate would see this need. Perhaps I was too optimistic; perhaps I expected too much. I suppose I should have realized that few members of the oppressor race can understand the deep groans and passionate yearnings of the oppressed race, and still fewer have the vision to see that injustice must be rooted out by strong, persistent, and determined action.

I am thankful, however, that some of our white brothers in the South have grasped the meaning of this social revolution and committed themselves to it. They are still all too few in quantity, but they are big in quality. Some—such as Ralph McGill, Lillian Smith, Harry Golden, James McBride Dabbs, Ann Braden, and Sarah Patton Boyle—have written about our struggle in eloquent and prophetic terms.

Others have marched with us down nameless streets of the South. They have languished in filthy, roach-infested jails, suffering the abuse and brutality of policemen who view them as "dirty nigger-lovers." Unlike so many of their moderate brothers and sisters, they have recognized the urgency of the moment and sensed the need for powerful "action" antidotes to combat the disease of segregation.

Let me take note of my other major disappointment. I have been so greatly disappointed with the white church and its leadership.

Of course, there are some notable exceptions. I am not unmindful of the fact that each of you has taken some significant stands on this issue. I commend you, Reverend Stallings, for your Christian stand on this past Sunday, in welcoming Negroes to your worship service on a nonsegregated basis. I commend the Catholic leaders of this state for integrating Spring Hill College several years ago.

But despite these notable exceptions, I must honestly reiterate that I have been disappointed with the church. I do not say this as one of those negative critics who can always find something wrong with the church. I say this as a minister of the gospel, who loves the church; who was nurtured in its bosom; who has been sustained by its spiritual blessings and who will remain true to it as long as the cord of life shall lengthen.

When I was suddenly catapulted into the leadership of the bus protest in Montgomery, Alabama, a few years ago, I felt we would be supported by the white church. I felt that the white ministers, priests and rabbis of the South would be among our strongest allies. Instead, some have been outright opponents, refusing to understand the freedom movement and misrepresenting its leaders; all too many others have been more cautious than courageous and have remained silent behind the anesthetizing security of stained-glass windows.

In spite of my shattered dreams, I came to Birmingham with the hope that the white religious leadership of this community would see the justice of our cause and, with deep moral concern, would serve as the channel through which our just grievances could reach the power structure. I had hoped that each of you would understand. But again I have been disappointed.

I have heard numerous southern religious leaders admonish their worshipers to comply with a desegregation decision because it is the law, but I have longed to hear white ministers declare: "Follow this decree because integration is morally right and because the Negro is your brother."

In the midst of blatant injustices inflicted upon the Negro, I have watched white churchmen stand on the sideline and mouth pious irrelevancies and sanctimonious trivialities. In the midst of a mighty struggle to rid our nation of racial and economic injustice, I have heard many ministers say: "Those are social issues, with which the gospel has no real concern." And I have watched many churches commit themselves to a completely otherworldly religion which makes a strange, un-Biblical distinction between body and soul; between the sacred and the secular. . . .

I hope the church as a whole will meet the challenge of this decisive hour. But even if the church does not come to the aid of justice, I have no despair about the future. I have no fear about the outcome of our struggle in Birmingham, even if our motives are at present misunderstood. We will reach the goal of freedom in Birmingham and all over the nation, because the goal of America is freedom.

Abused and scorned though we may be, our destiny is tied up with America's destiny. Before the pilgrims landed at Plymouth, we were here. For more than two centuries our forebears labored in this country, without wages; they made cotton king; they built the homes of their masters while suffering gross injustice and shameful humiliation—and yet out of a bottomless vitality they continued to thrive and develop.

If the inexpressible cruelties of slavery could not stop us, the opposition we now face will surely fail. We will win our freedom because the sacred heritage of our nation and the eternal will of God are embodied in our echoing demands.

Before closing I feel impelled to mention one other point in your statement that has troubled me profoundly. You warmly commended the Birmingham police force for keeping "order" and "preventing violence."

I doubt that you would have so warmly commended the police force if you had seen its dogs sinking their teeth into unarmed, nonviolent Negroes. I doubt that you would so quickly commend the policemen if you were to observe their ugly and inhumane treatment of Negroes here in the city jail; if you were to watch them push and curse old Negro women and young Negro girls; if you were to see them slap and kick old Negro men and young boys; if you were to observe them, as they did on two occasions, refuse to give us food because we wanted to sing our grace together. I cannot join you in your praise of the Birmingham police department.

It is true that the police have exercised a degree of discipline in handling the demonstrators. In this sense they have conducted themselves rather "nonviolently" in public. But for what purpose? To preserve the evil system of segregation.

Over the past few years I have consistently preached that nonviolence demands that the means we use must be as pure as the ends we seek. I have tried to make clear that it is wrong to use immoral means to attain moral ends. But now I must affirm that it is just as wrong, or perhaps even more so, to use moral means to preserve immoral ends. . . . As T. S. Eliot has said, "The last temptation is the greatest treason: To do the right deed for the wrong reason."

I wish you had commended the Negro sit-inners and demonstrators of Birmingham for their sublime courage, their willingness to suffer, and their amazing discipline in the midst of great provocation. One day the South will recognize its real heroes. They will be the James Merediths, with the noble sense of purpose that enables them to face jeering and hostile mobs, and with the agonizing loneliness that characterizes the life of the pioneer. They will be old, oppressed, battered Negro women, symbolized in a seventy-two-year-old woman in Montgomery, Alabama, who rose up with a sense of dignity and with her people decided not to ride segregated buses, and who responded with ungrammatical profundity to one who inquired about her weariness: "My feets is tired, but my soul is at rest."

They will be the young high school and college students, the young ministers of the gospel and a host of their elders, courageously and nonviolently sitting in at lunch counters and willingly going to jail for conscience' sake. One day the South will know that when these disinherited children of God sat down at lunch counters, they were in reality standing up for what is best in the American dream and for the most sacred values in our Judaeo-Christian heritage, thereby bringing our nation back to those great wells of democracy which were dug deep by the founding fathers in their formulation of the Constitution and the Declaration of Independence.

Never before have I written so long a letter. I'm afraid it is much too long to take your precious time. I can assure you that it would have been much shorter if I had been writing from a comfortable desk, but what else can one do when he is alone in a narrow jail cell, other than write long letters, think long thoughts and pray long prayers? . . .

Yours for the cause of peace and brotherhood,

Martin Luther King, Jr.

SOURCE: *Why We Can't Wait.* © 1963, 1964 Martin Luther King, Jr. Copyright renewed 1991 by Coretta Scott King. Reprinted by arrangement with the heirs of the Estate of Martin Luther King, Jr., c/o Writers House, Inc. as agent for the proprietor.

CHAPTER NINE

ARENAS OF THE STRUGGLE

Whenever a majority and a minority culture come into sustained and intimate contact with one another, a degree of conflict is inevitable. Certain public policy areas move to the forefront of relations between the two cultures. A minority group can be seen to be relegated to minority status in a given society because it lacks the political power to influence certain policy areas to its benefit or by its inability to restrain certain factions of the majority culture from using public policy to its detriment. Majority society employs public policy to treat members of the minority in a negatively differential manner. The majority society develops a degree of structural or institutionalized discrimination against the minority which is reflected in public policy.

When a minority group seeks to cope with and change its status, whether through accommodation, separatism, or radicalism, it must do so by using those strategies to influence public policy. A number of policy areas can be seen as the more important arenas of conflict in minority/majority relations. While virtually any policy area can be used by the majority society to "keep a minority in its place," and while a minority may seek to influence any number of policy areas as being more likely to respond to its particular needs, capabilities, or resources, this chapter focuses on six policy areas traditionally important to the struggle: education, employment, housing, immigration, law enforcement, and political participation.

The chapter highlights how aspects of each area were used by factions of the majority to discriminate against minority groups in American society. It shows how some minority groups have sought to influence those policy areas to redress their minority status and mitigate related problems. Once a portion of the majority society is convinced that a "problem" exists and change is needed, they advocate or support specific proposals for change in one or more of these areas.

EDUCATION

Of all the areas of critical import to majority/minority relations, none is more basic or significant in its impact than that of education. Discrimination in educational opportunities is the primary method by which minority status is enforced, since poor educational background influences occupational and income opportunities, related housing options, and the social status of the individual.

Segregation in schools has been the most pronounced and longstanding form of institutionalized discrimination against minorities. The segregation of Native Americans within special reservation schools was discussed in Chapter 5, as was the segregation of Chinese and Japanese students from the 1880s to 1920s in California. These incidents exemplify de jure segregation; that is, formal segregation based on law. The most significant use of de jure segregation, both in terms of numbers and of impact, was directed against black Americans.

Despite the Fourteenth Amendment, the reconstruction effort had clearly failed by 1877. Southern states increasingly enacted Jim Crow laws that legally segregated all aspects of life, including education, and effectively kept blacks in second-class citizenship status. Although the Fourteenth Amendment states: "No State shall make or enforce any law which shall abridge the privileges or immunities of citizens of the United States; nor shall any State deprive any person of life, liberty or property, without due process of law; nor any person within its jurisdiction the equal protection of the law, . . ." the Supreme Court ruled state laws segregating the races were constitutional as long as persons in each of the segregated races were protected equally. This "separate but equal" doctrine became the Court's interpretation of the Fourteenth Amendment with its decision in *Plessy* v. *Ferguson* (163 U.S. 537, 1896). This doctrine gave a constitutional blessing to de jure segregation, to Jim Crow laws. It led to extensive segregation of all public facilities, especially schools. Segregated facilities are seldom, if ever, equal in reality. Black schools, as were Indian and Asian schools in the West, were poorer in physical aspects. They had dilapidated and overcrowded buildings, smaller libraries and gyms, and fewer supplies. Their teachers were paid lower salaries, were often less qualified, and taught restricted curriculum.

Figure 9.1 shows the status of de jure segregation as of 1954. Seventeen states *required* segregation by law. Even Congress required segregation of public schools in the District of Columbia. Four states had enabling laws allowing local school districts to impose segregation. Only 16 states *prohibited* segregation; 11 states were simply silent on the matter.

The NAACP fought to overturn *Plessy* and end de jure segregation by using federal power via the courts to overrule the states. Prior to the 1950s, the NAACP achieved very limited success: two cases which ruled that blacks must be admitted to white law schools because comparable black law school facilities were not available (*Missouri ex rel. Gaines* v. *Canada* [1938], and *Sepuel* v. *University of Oklahoma* [1948]).

The first real dent in the separate but equal doctrine's wall of separation came with the *Sweatt* v. *Painter* (1950) ruling. Although the Court refused to overturn *Plessy* directly, it ordered the admission of black students to the University of Texas law school on the grounds that segregated *professional* schools were necessarily unequal.

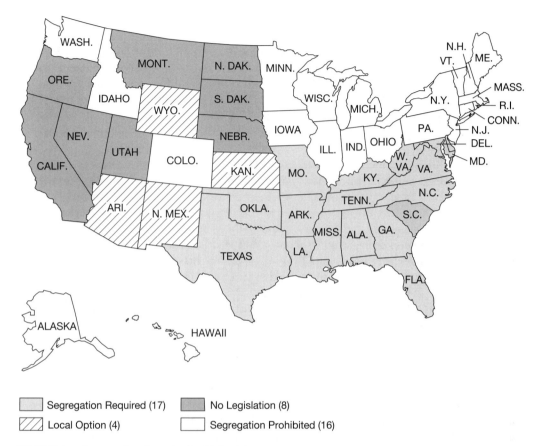

FIGURE 9.1 Segregation Laws in the United States, 1954

Segregation Required (17)   No Legislation (8)
Local Option (4)   Segregation Prohibited (16)

SOURCE: Thomas R. Dye, *Understanding Public Policy,* 9th ed., p. 45. © 1998. Reprinted by permission of Prentice Hall, Upper Saddle River, NJ.

The Court's test of "true equality" included such factors as the school's reputation, the experience of the faculty, and the school's traditions, prestige, and standing in the community. The Court stopped short of a full reversal of *Plessy.* A question remained as to whether such tests—virtually impossible to meet—would apply also to the primary and secondary school levels. The *Sweatt* decision led to immediate and significant improvements in black schools in the South, as southern states scrambled to upgrade their black schools to come closer to apparent equality in conditions and facilities.

The NAACP pressed on with its frontal attack on *Plessy.* It backed litigation in five border area school districts where the conditions were fairly equal (Delaware, District of Columbia, Kansas, South Carolina, and Virginia). They sought a ruling upholding their contention that segregation per se was unconstitutional. On May 17,

1954, the Court so ruled in its famous *Brown* v. *Board of Education of Topeka, Kansas* decision. The *Brown* case was historic in several respects. Not only was *Plessy* overturned, but in arriving at its decision, the Court deliberately underplayed the importance of legal precedent. Instead, it used social and psychological evidence to determine the detrimental effects of segregation on black children. The decision stated that in the field of public education the doctrine of separate but equal had no place. Segregated facilities were *inherently unequal.* The Court held that segregation laws deprived those segregated of the equal protection of the law guaranteed by the Fourteenth Amendment.

The ruling became a watershed case. Just as *Plessy* gave a constitutional underpinning to segregation based on the separate but equal doctrine, the *Brown* ruling that segregation was inherently unequal gave the constitutional basis to overturning Jim Crow laws. The Court moved thereafter to end legal segregation in transportation, public parks, playgrounds, golf courses, and bathing beaches. The *Brown* ruling did not immediately end segregation in schools, but it struck the death knell for de jure segregation. The victory precipitated the black civil rights movement. It legitimated their concerns and protests over second-class citizenship implicit in a segregated society. It sparked the use of mass political protest actions to seek true equality in public and private life. While the significance of the historic decision was tremendous—in a single blow it struck down the laws of 21 states and the District of Columbia—its effects were less immediate. In allowing for its implementation to proceed "with all deliberate speed," the Court opened the door to the use of litigation, obstruction, and delays by those states continuing to resist desegregation.

Nine states (Arizona, Delaware, Kansas, Kentucky, Maryland, Missouri, New Mexico, Oklahoma, and West Virginia) and the District of Columbia decided not to resist desegregation, and progress proceeded fairly well in those places. The 11 states of the deep South, however, resisted and employed a number of delaying tactics. Only 2 percent of their black students were attending integrated schools by late 1964.

Some states passed new laws creating an endless series of litigation. Other states established "private" schools in which the state paid the tuition of white students attending such schools. Still others revised their compulsory attendance laws so that no child was compelled to attend integrated schools. Some resisted on the grounds of protecting public safety by interposing the state between the schools and federal authority. Most successful of all was the tactic of revising "pupil placement law." Each child was guaranteed freedom of choice in selecting his or her school. Most students chose to attend the school they had previously attended. In effect, this ploy maintained the segregated system using de facto rather than de jure methods to achieve segregation. Resistance also took the form of violence. Some prominent examples of violent resistance to court-ordered desegregation occurred in Clinton, Tennessee, in 1956; in Little Rock, Arkansas, in 1957; in New Orleans in 1960; and at the University of Mississippi at Oxford in 1962. Both Presidents Eisenhower and Kennedy countered violence with the use of federal troops to ensure compliance with the law.

Real change came about only after passage of the 1964 Civil Rights Act and the 1965 Elementary and Secondary Education Act (ESEA). Title VI of the Civil Rights Act specified the termination of federal aid to states and communities that resisted compliance with court-ordered desegregation. ESEA provided sufficient funding to public schools to make this threat a compelling one. The monetary "club" sped up desegregation faster than all prior federal court actions. The U.S. Office of Education (then within the Department of Health, Education, and Welfare) required desegregation plans from 17 states that used de jure segregation. In three years desegregation of schools in those states increased eightfold. By 1970, the South had more black students attending integrated schools than did the states of the North. This situation demonstrated that the real issue was de facto segregation, which was far more difficult to overcome.

A 1967 Commission on Civil Rights Report found that 75 percent of black elementary school children in 75 large cities attended schools whose enrollment was 90 percent or more black. Ending or even reducing such segregation would be no easy task. Attempts to reduce the level of de facto segregation required that school officials classify their students on the basis of race and use race as a category in school placement decisions. Effective reduction of de facto racial segregation seemed to necessitate busing. Opposition to busing, however, was widespread and often violent. Boston, for instance, was the site of long and violent confrontations over busing. Black parents often opposed busing as much as did white parents. The nation witnessed the revival of the Ku Klux Klan and its spread north as cities across the country grappled with busing plans to desegregate school systems of central city and suburb.

In *Swann v. Charlotte-Mecklenberg Board of Education* (402 U.S. 1, 1971), the U.S. Supreme Court ruled that where no present or past actions of state and local governments were used to create the racial imbalance, there was no affirmative duty to correct the racial imbalance. Where such imbalance was the result of discriminatory laws by states or local school district governments, then school officials had a duty to eliminate vestiges of segregation, and that duty could entail busing and deliberate racial balancing to achieve greater integration of their schools. The *Swann* decision impacted southern schools. In the North, where no history of de jure segregation was evident, the Court ruled 5–4 (in *Milliken v. Bradley* [418 U.S. 717, 1974]) that the Fourteenth Amendment does not require busing across city/suburban school district lines to achieve integration. *Milliken* meant that the nation's mostly black central cities surrounded by white suburbs would remain segregated de facto because there simply were not enough white students living in the central city boundaries to achieve anything near a balanced integration. In 1991, the Supreme Court ruled that since "state sanctioned discrimination" (de jure) has been removed "as far as practicable," lower federal courts could dissolve racial balancing plans even though some imbalances caused by racially separate housing patterns continued to exist (in *Board of Education v. Dowell* [U.S. 1991 111 S.Ct. 630]; see also *Missouri v. Jenkins* [1995]). Table 9.1 demonstrates that school segregation of blacks is greatest in the North and of Hispanics is greatest in the North and Southwest.

Many educators attribute the significant rise in achievement levels among blacks, while similar levels for whites have run slightly higher or held steady, to the integration of schools. Progress has been most dramatic where past segregation had been most deeply rooted. In most communities opposition remains intense. Although busing about half of Boston's 94,000 students has been underway since 1974, school

TABLE 9.1   States with Schools with 50 Percent or More Minority Enrollment

State	Percent Black	State	Percent Hispanic
Illinois	89%	New York	86%
New York	86	Illinois	85
Michigan	85	Texas	84
New Jersey	80	New Jersey	84
California	79	California	79
Maryland	76	Rhode Island	78
Wisconsin	75	New Mexico	74
Texas	68	Connecticut	72
Pennsylvania	68	Pennsylvania	67
Connecticut	66	Arizona	57

SOURCE: Gary Orfield and Franklin Montfort, "Status of School Desegregation: The Next Generation," in Karen DeWitt, "The Nation's Schools Learn a 4th R: Resegregation," *New York Times,* January 19, 1992, p. E5.

vehicles are still stoned, and several empty ones have been overturned and set afire. Many whites simply fled the public school system. White enrollment dropped from 70 percent in 1974 to 27 percent by 1985 (Dye 1998). Proponents of mandatory busing argue that it is the only efficient way to achieve integration, since most residential areas remain so strongly segregated. Opponents charge that forced busing is divisive, costly, and counterproductive, since it prompts white flight from the public school system, leaving those schools even more segregated.

The Reagan Administration advocated using voluntary plans like those used in Buffalo and Milwaukee. Its Justice Department led the anti-busing drive. The administration favored voluntary systems that offer special programs, called *magnet schools,* that provide intensive instruction in subjects like the fine arts, as being ultimately more effective. Such programs are costly. Federal support for desegregation has been cut drastically. Voluntary plans have not worked in many large cities. Courts have sometimes dismissed them as ineffective. White resistance to school integration, while still in the majority, has been declining since the *Brown* decision, as shown in Table 9.2.

While blacks have closed the gap in formal educational levels that existed relative to white levels since the 1960s, a gap still remains, as evident in the data shown in Table 9.3.

TABLE 9.2   White Attitudes Toward School Integration

Question: "Would you, yourself, have any objection to sending your children to a school where more than half the children are blacks?"

	1958	1965	1970	1975	1980	1985	1990	1994
Percent Objecting	70	68	66	66	62	60	59	54

SOURCE: General Social Survey and Gallup Reports, in Harold Stanley and Richard Niemi, *Vital Statistics on American Politics,* 5th ed. (Washington, DC: CQ Press, 1995), p. 368. Reprinted with permission.

TABLE 9.3   Educational Attainment of Persons 25 Years or Older by Race, 1960–1997

Year	Total	White	Black
	Completed 4 Years of High School or More		
1960	41.1	43.2	20.1
1965	49.0	51.3	27.2
1970	52.3	54.5	31.4
1975	62.5	64.5	42.5
1980	66.5	68.8	51.2
1985	73.9	75.5	59.8
1990	77.6	79.1	66.2
1995	80.9	82.0	73.8
1996	81.7	82.8	74.3
1997	82.1	83.0	74.9
	Completed 4 Years of College or More		
1960	7.7	8.1	3.1
1965	9.4	9.9	4.7
1970	10.7	11.3	4.4
1975	13.9	14.5	6.4
1980	16.2	17.1	8.4
1985	19.4	20.0	11.1
1990	21.3	22.0	11.3
1994	22.2	22.9	12.9
1995	23.0	24.0	13.2
1996	23.6	24.3	13.6
1997	23.9	24.6	13.3

SOURCE: U.S. Bureau of the Census, *Statistical Abstract of the United States, 1998,* Table 260, p. 167.

EMPLOYMENT

From the days of slave labor through the era of "No Irish Need Apply" to the present, discrimination in employment opportunity has been a recurrent aspect of majority/minority relations. Job discrimination has been institutionalized, sometimes manifested in formal policy, such as specific laws. Usually it is enforced through labor union training practices (apprenticeships), educational entrance barriers, and informal hiring practices of majority member employers. The "last hired, first fired" norm has always been a problem for the nation's minorities and continues to be so today.

The Irish were initially limited to periodic or seasonal work, low pay, and constant job threat explicitly implemented by the common use of the "No Irish Need Apply" signs, as were Jews, who experienced both the signs and job advertisements that read "Christians Only" or "Gentiles Only." The use of the padrone constituted a formalized system of occupational discrimination for Greeks and Italians. Even the Foran Act of 1885, which forbade contract labor and was intended to counteract the padrone system, constituted a formalized pattern of discrimination.

Institutionalized racism was based on formal acts of job discrimination. Blacks were legally enslaved for a time. Even after slavery was abolished, blacks were kept out of many jobs by Jim Crow legislation that reinforced informal norms. In California, racism led to the Foreign Miners Tax of 1885, which, when coupled with violence, kept the Chinese out of the mine fields. The Chinese and Japanese were restricted from certain occupational endeavors by the California Alien Land Act of 1913. That law was upheld as constitutional in *Ozawa v. the United States* (1921). In 1923, California strengthened the legal restrictions by plugging several loopholes in the 1913 act. Similar laws were enacted in Arizona, Idaho, Louisiana, Montana, New Mexico, and Oregon. The reservation policy of the 1870s legally forced occupational restrictions on Native Americans. As with race, formal or legal barriers in the job market have been used for gender, age, and sexual preference as well. Women and persons over 65 years of age face legal barriers in occupational opportunity in the Social Security laws. The firings of gays from certain jobs has been legally upheld, even when the sole basis for the dismissal was the individual's sexual preference.

Most job discrimination against minorities has been and continues to be informally enforced. Informal mechanisms include: (1) restrictions in job training conducted by labor unions; (2) educational barriers that denied certain minorities the educational backgrounds required for many jobs; and (3) informal hiring practices of majority employers. These informal mechanisms have been used to enforce society's norms by denying equal opportunity in employment. Because these norms are informally enforced, they cannot be directly measured. That they have operated and continue to operate, however, cannot be denied.

Indirect evidence of informal discrimination is both pervasive and persuasive. Patterns of minority employment demonstrate discrimination unmistakably if indirectly. Exceptionally large percentages of minority group members in specific and limited occupations indicate **occupational niches** typical of minority groups. Employment discrimination is channeling large numbers of such persons into those jobs. While minority members voluntarily enter such occupations, they are jobs that are inordinately attractive because a pattern of informal discrimination has closed off access to alternative occupations of equal or better opportunity. Box 9.1 shows the types of niches common to various minorities. It is but one indirect measure of pervasive job discrimination. Subsequent data show additional evidence.

Another indicator of occupational discrimination is presented in Table 9.4, which shows the status of several racial and ethnic minorities in relation to that of the total population based on 1990 census data. The racial and ethnic minorities are clearly underemployed as managers, professionals, and executives, and disproportionately employed in low-paying service occupations. Likewise, unemployment rates for blacks continue to be higher than for whites, consistently being about twice the rate of whites. In 1994, for example, black unemployment rates were 11 percent, compared to only 5 percent for whites. Black unemployment in relation to white unemployment has remained remarkably consistent over the past 35 years, as shown in Table 9.5. The various government programs designed to mitigate systematic discrimination against minorities apparently have done little to change that picture. During the recessions of the 1980s and early 1990s, minorities bore the brunt of the unemployment burden.

BOX 9.1: Employment Discrimination: Special Occupational Niches

NATIONAL ORIGIN GROUPS

Greeks	Restaurants, confectionaries, candy stores, construction
Hispanics	Migrant farm work, low-skilled blue-collar urban jobs
Hungarians	Unskilled labor in heavy industry—steel, rubber, mines
Irish	Unskilled—mines, railroads, police, fire, stevedores, domestic service
Italians	Truck farming, restaurants, wine, barbers
Poles	Truck gardening, domestics, unskilled labor in mines, steel
Russians	Unskilled labor—mines, construction, tailors, furriers

RELIGIOUS GROUPS

Amish and Mormons	Agriculture
Jews	Garment and cigar industries, retail sales, theater, music

RACIAL GROUPS

Blacks	Blue-collar unskilled jobs to low-skilled menial jobs, migrant farm work, tenant farming, domestic service
Chinese	Restaurants, laundries, domestic service, import/export gift shops
Japanese	Gardening, truck farming, fishing

OTHER GROUPS

Gender: Women	Nursing, elementary school teachers, typists, data entry, secretaries, hairdressers, waitresses, telephone operators
Sexual preference	Bookkeeping, dress design, window display, hairdressers, interior decorating, art, theater, music

The nation took steps to reverse the effects of occupational discrimination. A series of congressional actions and Supreme Court decisions attempted to address the problems of informal but structured job discrimination. Congress took action with various War on Poverty programs in the 1960s, some of which were designed to provide training to aid the underemployed and the unemployed to develop needed job skills. Examples of this approach include the Job Corps and the Neighborhood Youth Corps projects conducted by the Office of Economic Opportunity, the Comprehensive Employment Training Act (CETA), and Public Service Employment (PSE).

The most significant action regarding employment discrimination was the Civil Rights Act of 1964, which created the Equal Employment Opportunity Commission (EEOC). It was charged with implementing policy to end discrimination by any employer or labor union with 25 or more persons. While the EEOC could not require specific quotas or even preferential treatment from the mere fact of racial imbalance, the commission used imbalance as evidence of discrimination. The law assumes that if discrimination were not at work, members of the targeted groups (e.g., blacks, Hispanics, women) would be present in various sectors of society in rough proportion to

TABLE 9.4   Occupational Status of Various Ethnic Minorities Compared to Whites, 1997

By Occupation	Employed Persons Age 16 or Older						
	Female	Black	Hispanic				
Managerial/Professional	48.9%	7.3%	5.0%				
Technical/Sales	64.1	10.5	7.9				
Service	59.4	17.6	14.6				
Farming	2.0	1.2	2.4				
By Category, 1995	*Female*	*Black*	*Hispanic*	*White*			
Skilled, blue-collar	15.0%	2.5%	18.5%	2.1%			
Unskilled, blue-collar	30.7	10.8	19.3	6.8			
Managers/Executives/ and Professionals	*Total*	*Black*	*Hispanic*	*Chinese*	*Japanese*	*Korean*	*Asian Indian*
	26%	*7%*	*4%*	*36%*	*37%*	*26%*	*44%*
Other	61%	76%	85%	47%	52%	49%	48%
Services	13%	17%	11%	17%	11%	15%	8%

SOURCE: U.S. Bureau of the Census, *Statistical Abstract of the United States, 1998,* pp. 418–419. See also Martin N. Marger, *Race and Ethnic Relations,* 4th ed. (Belmont, CA: Wadsworth, 1997), p. 248.

their numbers in society at large. This **proportionality criterion** served as the basis for the EEOC treatment plans and represented a shift in the conceptualization of what constitutes "equality" from equality under the law to equality of opportunity to equality of well-being.

The policies that attempted to attain this goal of equality of material well-being came to be collectively known as **affirmative action**, a search for compensatory justice for the persisting effects of past institutionalized discrimination. Affirmative action includes any program designed to get minority persons past institutionalized barriers that previously would have stopped them. These programs are concentrated in educational and employment structures where such barriers existed. The logic of affirmative action is that a cycle of discrimination affects minority persons, and that cycle must be broken. If poor education leads to poor jobs, to low income and poor housing, which leads back to poor education, then one might improve the whole chain by breaking

TABLE 9.5   Unemployment Rates of Persons Age 16 or Older, by Race, 1960–1997

Year	Blacks	Whites	Black/White Ratio
1960	10.2%	4.9%	2.1
1970	8.2	4.5	1.8
1980	14.3	6.3	2.2
1990	11.3	4.7	2.4
1994	11.5	5.3	2.2
1997	10.0	4.2	2.4

SOURCE: Based on data in U.S. Bureau of the Census, *Statistical Abstract of the United States, 1998,* Table 677, p. 423.

one link. A better job leads to better housing, a more middle-class lifestyle, and better schools, which all lead to better education and a new generation that would no longer need affirmative action. The cycle has been broken. Affirmative action is an attempt to force structural assimilation.

Attempts to achieve better racial and gender balance in employment and in higher education led to various plans for preference. These plans were challenged in a number of cases: *Bakke* (1978), *Weber* (1979), *Stotts* (1984), and *Crosen* (1989). The Office of Federal Contract Compliance and the EEOC began a process of court battles by setting guidelines that held any test for employment, promotion, or membership in a union, for example, that disproportionately failed members of designated groups constituted evidence of illegal discrimination unless the job relevance of the test could be shown. The employer has the burden of proof to show that those who scored higher on the test or selection criteria actually performed better in the role for which they were being selected.

In *Griggs* v. *Duke Power* (401 U.S. 424, 1971), the Court upheld those guidelines and threatened the legality of virtually every performance criteria. Three "suspect" categories were identified by the Court: race, gender, and alienage. In *Craig* v. *Boren* (429 U.S. 190, 1976), the Court set standards for when gender may be used to classify people. The government has to convince the Court that its purpose is an important one and that gender classification is "substantially related" to achieving that purpose. In *Washington* v. *Davis* (44 LW 4789, 1976), the Court further muddied the waters in a case concerning a Washington, D.C., police officer test. Although four times as many blacks as whites failed to pass the written test, the Court nonetheless decided that this failure rate was not in and of itself sufficient evidence to invalidate the test. Unlike the *Griggs* decision, this one was not argued under Title VII, which did not apply to governmental units. It was decided under the due process clause. The Court ruled a test is presumed valid unless the intent to discriminate is shown.

The situation was further complicated by several challenges to various racial preference plans. In *DeFunis* v. *Odegaard* (416 U.S. 312, 1974), the Court essentially dodged the question by ruling that the DeFunis challenge of the University of Washington's Law School preferential admissions program was a moot question, since, by the time the case had reached the Court, DeFunis, who had been ordered admitted by the state trial court, was ready to graduate. In the case of *Bakke* v. *Regents of the University of California, Davis* (438 U.S. 265, 1978), the Court decided upon the admission criterion and procedures of the medical school at Davis. Alan Bakke had been denied admission even though he clearly had higher scores on his GPA and Medical College Aptitude test than did a number of minority applicants who were admitted under the school's set-aside quota system of 16 placements out of 100 to be used for nonwhites. The *Bakke* decision, in a 5–4 split in which the deciding opinion of Justice Powell hinged on a different basis than the other four justices composing the majority, found the school's program invalid on equal protection grounds. It objected to the fixed-quota system. In *Firefighters Local Union* v. *Stotts* (1984), the Supreme Court decided that a city could not lay off white firefighters with greater seniority in order to retain black firefighters with less seniority. In *Richmond* v. *Crosen* (1989), it ruled that Richmond, Virginia's set-aside program mandating 30 percent of all city construction contracts must go to specified racial minorities violated the equal protection clause of the Fourteenth Amendment. In *Wards Cove* v. *Antonio* (1989), the Court reiterated its *Bakke* position that any rigid numerical quota was suspect of reverse discrimination. It held that the burden of proof of unlawful discrimination should be shifted from the employer (the defendant) to the plaintiff (the person claiming to have suffered discrimination).

During the Reagan and Bush administrations the executive branch also shifted on affirmative action. Under President Reagan, the budgets and staffs of key civil rights agencies were cut dramatically, busing was opposed, and the EEOC filed 50 percent fewer discrimination suits against employers. Government cases against school desegregation and housing discrimination dropped to a fraction of previous administrations. Under Reagan, the Justice Department terminated suits based on statistical evidence of discrimination and focused only on individual cases where intent to discriminate could be proven. President Bush vetoed the Civil Rights Act of 1990 as a "quota bill" (although he signed essentially the same bill in 1991). He appointed conservative judges to the federal bench, including Justice Clarence Thomas, an adamant opponent of affirmative action, as his sole appointment to the Supreme Court.

In 1991, Congress passed the Civil Rights Act, which shifted the burden of proof back to employers, but the Supreme Court, in *Adarand Constructors* v. *Pena* (1995), weakened affirmative action by ruling that race-based policies, such as preferences given to minority contractors, must survive strict scrutiny, placing the burden on the government to show that affirmative action programs serve a compelling government interest and are narrowly tailored to identifiable past discrimination.

The cumulative effect of these Court cases was to maintain a highly modified affirmative action structure. While strict quotas in preference plans may violate either the Civil Rights Act or the Constitution, other uses of race or gender for the "benign" purpose of achieving racial or gender balance seem acceptable. Critics of affirmative action, however, continue to press their case. They hold such plans to be a denial of meritocracy, inconsistent with equality under the law, and penalizing competitive success by its performance standards.

The problem involves the conflict among rights and the difficulty of pursuing group goals at the expense of the individual. When society seeks a goal of social policy involving the redistribution of material well-being, it involves a **zero-sum situation** wherein whatever new benefits are accorded to some must be taken away from others. What one group gains another must lose. Although the history of discrimination against groups clearly establishes an argument for some form of compensatory justice, the confusion between bigotry and discrimination of groups and of individuals within groups muddies the concept of justice. The white race in the aggregate may be guilty of discrimination, but individuals—Alan Bakke, Brian Weber, or Marco DeFunis— pay the debt, even though they may not have personally discriminated. Nor do the benefits of affirmative action necessarily flow to the most disadvantaged individuals in society. The hard-core unemployed seldom get to professional schools under such programs. These programs benefit middle-class members of the designated groups. To change the rules of the game and deny benefits to the Bakkes of society, benefits to which they were entitled under the old rules, is perceived by many as the denial of their rights.

Racial preferences were further muddied when Angel Luevano challenged, under Title VII of the Civil Rights Act, the use of the Professional and Administrative Career Examination (PACE) by the Office of Personnel Management on the grounds that a disproportionate number of blacks and Hispanics failed the test. The failure rate for all applicants on PACE was about 60 percent, while the failure rate for blacks was around 95 percent. Recall that *Griggs* held that the employer must show the job relevance for any hiring criteria that disproportionately failed targeted groups, while the *Davis* precedent held that when the due process clause of the Constitution is used, no such requirement exists. Accordingly, the plaintiffs in *Luevano* v. *Campbell* (1981) relied on Title VII even though the employer in this case was the federal government. The case was settled out of court by the Reagan Administration with an agreement to phase out the PACE test and replace it with "alternative examining procedures" that have no "adverse impact" on blacks and Hispanics. In the agreement, *adverse impact* was defined to mean a failure to be hired at the same rate as whites. The government agreed to hire certain categories of individuals without reference to test scores (for example, Spanish-speaking people when knowledge of Spanish is an asset), and to strive to have blacks and Hispanics make up at least 20 plus percent of the work force at the GS-5 level and higher. Clearly, this amounts to a quota of the sort that *Bakke* seemed to forbid and that has been alleged to constitute reverse discrimination against whites explicitly banned by Title VII.

Box 9.2 demonstrates that a wide gap on race and gender still remains in the U.S. work force. Using 1995 annual salary data from the U.S. Census Bureau, the National Committee on Pay Equity shows the continued impact of race and gender discrimination in the arena of employment.

The pay/employment gap is further evident in median income data. Figure 9.2 shows the median incomes of various racial, ethnic, and gender groups as of 1997. It reveals rather striking differences between white men and all other minority groups. It also shows the "double jeopardy" suffered by women of color. Moreover, the gap in earning power remains even when holding the effect of education constant, as shown in Table 9.6.

TABLE 9.6   Median Income, by Race and Gender, Holding Education Constant, 1995

Per capita income, 1995 dollars			
Male		**Female**	
White, non-Hispanic origin	$26,290	All females	$12,815
White male	23,834	White, non-Hispanic origin	13,514
Black male	16,491	White female	12,961
Hispanic male	15,437	Black female	11,772
Asian male	23,374	Asian female	14,634
High school graduate	24,814	Hispanic female	9,484
College graduate	44,161	High school graduate	12,702
		College graduate	27,556

SOURCE: U.S. Bureau of the Census, *Statistical Abstract of the United States, 1998,* p. 476.

BOX 9.2: Report of the National Committee on Pay Equity Data, 1996

1. THE UNITED STATES LABOR FORCE IS OCCUPATIONALLY SEGREGATED BY RACE AND SEX

- In 1995, women constituted 46.0 percent of all workers in the civilian labor force (over 57 million women).[1]
- People of color constituted 14.7 percent of all workers (over 18 million workers).[2]
- Labor force participation is almost equal among white women, black women, and women of Hispanic origin. In 1995, 59.5 percent of black women (7.6 million), 52.6 percent of Hispanic women (4.8 million), and 59.0 percent of white women (50 million) were in the paid labor force.[3]

In 1995, women were:
98.5 percent of all secretaries
93.1 percent of all registered nurses
96.8 percent of all child care workers
88.4 percent of all telephone operators
74.7 percent of all teachers (excluding colleges and universities)
82.9 percent of all data entry keyers

Women were only:
13.4 percent of all dentists
8.4 percent of all engineers
26.2 percent of all lawyers and judges
12.9 percent of all police and detectives
8.9 percent of all precision, production and craft and repair workers
24.4 percent of all physicians[4]

2. ECONOMIC STATUS

- Over 12 million women work full-time in jobs which pay wages below the poverty line (in 1995 for a family of three the poverty line was $12,158 per year). They work in jobs such as day care, food counter, and many service jobs. Many more women than men are part of the working poor (125 percent of the poverty level) and work in jobs such as clerical, blue collar, and sales positions.[5]

- In 1995, married couple families had a median income of $47,062 while female-headed families had a median income of only $19,691.[6]

3. THE WAGE GAP IS ONE OF THE MAJOR CAUSES OF ECONOMIC INEQUALITY IN THE UNITED STATES TODAY

In 1995, all men working year-round full-time were paid a median salary of $31,496 per year.

All women, working year-round full-time, were paid a median salary of $22,497 per year.

On average, women earned only 71.4 cents for each dollar that a man earned.

Year-Round Full-Time Earnings, 1995

Race/Sex	Earnings	Percentage of White Men's Earnings
White men	$32,172	100%
White women	$22,911	71.2
Black men	$24,428	75.9
Black women	$20,665	64.2
Hispanic men	$20,379	63.3
Hispanic women	$17,178	53.4

SOURCE: U.S. Census Bureau, *Current Population Reports,* Series P-60-193, September 1996.

1. U.S. Department of Labor, Bureau of Labor Statistics, 1995 Annual Average Tables, from the January 1996 issue of *Employment and Earnings,* Table 2.

2. Ibid., Table 3.

3. Ibid., Tables 3 and 4.

4. Ibid., Table 11.

5. *Poverty in the United States,* U.S. Department of Commerce, Bureau of the Census, Current Population Reports, Consumer Income, Series P-60-194, Table 1; and *Money Income in the United States: 1995,* Current Population Reports, Consumer Income, Series P-60-193, Table 10.

6. *Money Income in the United States: 1995,* U.S. Department of Commerce, Bureau of the Census, Current Population Reports, Consumer Income, Series P-60-193, Table 5.

SOURCE: Paula Rothenberg, *Race, Class, and Gender in the United States,* 4th ed. (New York: St. Martin's Press, 1998), pp. 234–236.

4. THE WAGE GAP HAS FLUCTUATED BUT HAS NOT DISAPPEARED IN THE LAST SEVERAL DECADES

Comparison of Median Earnings of Year-Round, Full-Time Workers by Sex (Selected Years)

Year	Median Earnings		Women's Earnings as a Percentage of Men's	Year	Median Earnings		Women's Earnings as a Percentage of Men's
	Women	Men			Women	Men	
1946	$1,710	$2,558	66.1%	1975	$7,504	$12,758	58.8
1955	$2,719	$4,252	63.9	1976	$8,099	$13,455	60.2
1956	$2,827	$4,466	63.3	1977	$8,618	$14,626	58.9
1957	$3,008	$4,713	63.8	1978	$9,350	$15,730	59.4
1958	$3,102	$4,927	63.0	1979	$10,151	$17,014	59.7
1959	$3,193	$5,209	61.3	1980	$11,197	$18,612	60.2
1960	$3,293	$5,317	60.8	1981	$12,001	$20,260	59.2
1961	$3,351	$5,644	59.4	1982	$13,014	$21,007	61.7
1962	$3,446	$5,974	59.5	1983	$13,915	$21,881	63.6
1963	$3,561	$5,978	59.6	1984	$14,780	$23,218	63.7
1964	$3,690	$6,195	59.6	1985	$15,624	$24,195	64.5
1965	$3,823	$6,375	60.0	1986	$16,232	$25,256	64.3
1966	$3,973	$6,848	58.0	1987	$16,909	$26,008	65.0
1967	$4,150	$7,182	57.8	1988	$17,606	$26,656	66.0
1968	$4,457	$7,664	58.2	1989	$18,780	$27,430	68.5
1969	$4,977	$8,227	60.5	1990	$20,656	$28,843	71.6
1970	$5,323	$8,966	59.4	1991	$20,553	$29,421	69.9
1971	$5,593	$9,399	59.5	1992	$21,375	$30,197	70.8
1972	$5,903	$10,202	57.9	1993	$21,747	$30,407	71.5
1973	$6,335	$11,186	56.6	1994	$22,205	$30,854	72.0
1974	$6,772	$11,835	57.2	1995	$22,497	$31,496	71.4

SOURCE: National Committee on Pay Equity tabulations of U.S. Census Bureau data (September 1996).

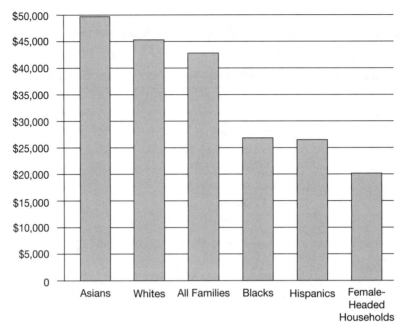

FIGURE 9.2 Median Income of Families by Race, Ethnicity, and Gender, 1997 (in 1996 Constant Dollars)

SOURCE: U.S. Bureau of the Census, *Statistical Abstract of the United States, 1998,* Table 748, p. 473.

HOUSING

Housing is another area that has a high degree of discrimination. This pattern is particularly evident regarding racial minorities. Housing remains highly segregated despite federal government action by the courts and Congress designed to end de jure segregation in housing. This section reviews how segregation became the established pattern, as well as efforts passed to mitigate it.

Spatial isolation (segregation) is a powerful indicator of a group's general position in society, influencing a wide variety of social phenomena such as intermarriage, linguistic assimilation, and even the maintenance of a group's distinctive occupational composition. Most minorities in the United States have experienced housing segregation. Some have done so largely through self-segregation for security; others through de jure segregation, such as Native Americans on reservations. Be it the "Little Italy" of East Coast cities, the Chinatowns of Los Angeles, San Francisco, or New York, or the black ghettos of the nation's major cities, most minorities have experienced some combination of voluntary and forced housing segregation.

The concentration of minorities in central cities is a product of the availability of low-priced rental units in the older, run-down sections of the central city; the heavy outflow of the middle-class white population to the surrounding suburbs; and the policies of public and private real estate owners and developers.

Black isolation was not always so intense. At the turn of the century, according to Stanley Lieberson's study (1980), there were higher levels of segregation among the South, Central, and East European groups than among blacks in the North. Italians and Russians, for example, were more isolated than blacks. Lieberson found black isolation to be rather slight in 1890 among the 17 leading cities of the North and West. The average black, frequently working as a domestic servant and living in the white home, lived in a ward where over 90 percent of the population was not black. Although black isolation increased in the next decade, in five or six cities there were actual declines in the degree of black isolation. From 1910 to 1930, however, massive increases in black isolation occurred. A massive migration of blacks from the rural South to the urban North caused a sharp increase in antiblack sentiment and attempts by whites to maintain the degree of isolation existing before that migration began. The isolation of new immigrant groups declined as second and third generations were able to move out of ethnic enclaves. Those enclaves developed into black ghettos.

The sharp increase in black isolation severely affected jobs and education and indicates that the social position of blacks in the North deteriorated drastically at the turn of the century. Historian Allan Spear (1967), in his study of the growth of Chicago's black ghetto, distinguishes it from ethnic enclaves:

> The Chicago experience, therefore, tends to refute any attempt to compare Northern Negroes with European immigrants. Unlike the Irish, Poles, Jews, or Italians, Negroes banded together not to enjoy a common linguistic, cultural, and religious tradition, but because a systematic pattern of discrimination left them no alternative. . . . The persistence of the Chicago Negro ghetto, then, has not been merely the product of a special historical experience. From its inception, the Negro ghetto was unique among the city's ethnic enclaves. It grew in response to an implacable white hostility that has not basically changed. In this sense it has been Chicago's only true ghetto, less the product of voluntary development within than external pressure from without. (pp. 228–229)

Several policy devices ensured black isolation. The restrictive covenant used by real estate agencies and enforced by the courts typically read as follows: "No part of the land hereby conveyed shall ever be used or occupied by or sold, demised, transferred, conveyed unto, or in trust for, leased or rented or given to Negroes, or to any person or persons of Negro blood or extraction, or to any person of the Semitic race, blood, or origin which racial description shall be deemed to include Armenians, Jews, Hebrews, Persians, and Syrians" (cited in Dye 1971).

Other practices leading to the ghetto included large lot zoning, which keeps lower income (i.e., nonwhite) families out of suburbs; illegal collusion among real estate agents, who refuse to sell to blacks; and the lack of enforcement of housing codes, which virtually encourages slum development. Municipal property tax policy penalizes improvements and rewards slum landlords who poorly maintain their properties. The use of "earnings power" as a measure of determining the value of a property in condemnation proceedings favors those who overcrowd their buildings. Capital gains taxes and depreciation policies favor slum owners. The location of public housing projects concentrated in central city neighborhoods helps maintain the ghetto pattern.

From late 1930 to mid-1960, the federal government encouraged the ghetto by requiring "homogeneous neighborhoods" in its mortgage policies within Federal Housing Administration, Federal National Mortgage Association, and G.I. bill programs. These programs helped finance white flight to the suburbs. Although the making of a ghetto was not an intended impact, it was the direct consequence of programs subsidizing white flight to the suburbs. In 1962 alone, "the federal government spent $820 million to subsidize housing for the poor (this includes public housing, public assistance, and tax deductions). That same year at least an estimated $2.9 billion was spent to subsidize housing for the middle and upper income families" (Schon 1968: 208).

Once developed, the economics of the ghetto encouraged their continuation. Segregation was the single most important factor making slums profitable. Slum profits depend on collusion between city agencies and slum landlords. In return for nonenforcement of codes, slum lords take the blame for the slums and enable the city to evade the political ire of the ghetto residents (Tabb 1970). Economist David Gorden (1977) notes the effects of economic colonization:

> What kind of housing do black people have? One index of the quality of housing available is the completeness of plumbing facilities. In 1910, while 5% of white housing lacked some or all plumbing facilities, 17% of Negro housing was that way. In 1970, the median value of Negro housing was $10,700; for housing occupied by whites it was $17,400. The degree of overcrowding (defined as more than one person per room) of Negroes varied from 2.5 to 8 times as much as that for non-Negroes. (p. 157)

Black ghettos reflect the shift of blacks from the rural South to the urban North, where discrimination practices forced them into the central city locations. From 1950 to 1970, black population grew by 25.4 percent, compared to a white growth rate of 17.6 percent. Where 87 percent of the nation's blacks lived in the South in 1900, less than half live there today. Although blacks make up just over 12 percent of the population, they make up a much larger share of the nation's large cities. Table 9.7 shows the most segregated metropolitan areas as of 1990. The segregation index is a measure of the extent of residential segregation between two groups. It indicates the percentage of one group that would have to move in order to achieve total integration, that is, a population mix that corresponds to each group's proportion of the population of a designated area. The index can range from 100, indicating total segregation, to 0, indicating total integration. The higher the index, the greater the degree of segregation.

High residential segregation has consequences for a wide variety of related events: school isolation; restrictions of opportunities because of minimal contacts with whites, marking the racial population as distinct and different; and the restricted opportunities to live near all sorts of employment found at great distance from the black ghettos. Racial residential isolation reinforces differences between whites and racial minorities and intensifies ethnic bonds.

Despite several decades of policy attempts to redress segregation, little real change has taken place. The 1948 Supreme Court decision *Shelly* v. *Kramer* overturned the use of restrictive covenants as unconstitutional. Southern community attempts to legalize zoning for the purpose of residential segregation were ended by subsequent court action.

TABLE 9.7   The Nation's Most Segregated
             Metropolitan Areas, 1990

Blacks from Whites	Segregation Index Score
1. Gary	89
2. Detroit	88
3. Chicago	86
3. Cleveland	86
5. Milwaukee	83
5. Buffalo	83
7. St. Louis	81
8. Philadelphia	80
9. Birmingham, AL	79
9. Cincinnati	79

Hispanics from non-Hispanics	
1. Chicago	66
2. Miami	56
2. Bergen-Passaic, NJ	56
4. Los Angeles	53
4. San Antonio	53
4. Oxnard, CA	53
4. El Paso, TX	53
4. Bakersfield, CA	53

Asians from non-Asians	
1. Stockton, CA	52
2. San Francisco	47
3. Los Angeles	45
3. Vallejo, CA	45
5. Honolulu	41

SOURCE: Data from Reynolds Farley and William Frey, *Changes in the Segregation of Whites from Blacks During the 1980s: Small Steps Toward a More Racially Integrated Society* (Ann Arbor: Population Studies Center, University of Michigan).

But while Jim Crow de jure segregation in housing may have ended, blacks and whites are still largely segregated de facto.

Black attempts to integrate previously all-white areas adjacent to predominantly black areas elicit white flight. Generalizing this reaction, known as the **tipping mechanism**, led to uncovering the principal dimensions of such expected behavior. Attempts to alter the way in which the housing market currently operates to enforce the concentration of blacks into inner city enclaves remains politically explosive.

In 1966, President Johnson first requested open housing legislation. His bills died in the House in 1966 and 1967, in part because of entrenched opposition from the real estate industry that lobbied against enactment of any fair housing law. The

National Association of Real Estate Boards published a "Property Owners Bill of Rights" opposing those bills. The Civil Rights Act of 1968 finally established a fair housing law. Coming after the assassination of Dr. Martin Luther King, Jr., the measure was passed in part as a memorial to him. It prohibited the following forms of discrimination: (1) the refusal to sell or rent a dwelling to any person because of race, color, religion, or national origin; (2) discrimination against a person in terms, conditions, or privileges of the sale or rental of a dwelling; (3) indicating a preference or discrimination on the basis of color, race, creed, or national origin in advertising the sale or rental of a dwelling; and (4) inducing **block-busting** techniques of real estate selling. The law covered all apartments and houses rented or sold by real estate developers or agents. It exempted private homes sold without real estate agents and apartments with less than five rental units where the landlord maintained his or her own residence in the building.

Yet the federal government worked at cross-purposes to this law by concentrating public housing projects in central city locations. Only one of the nation's 24 largest cities—Cincinnati—built public housing units outside the central city. The Department of Transportation spends billions of dollars constructing metropolitan expressways that encourage urban sprawl and promote white flight to the suburbs, in addition to promoting the outflow of commercial interests that follow the white middle-class exodus. This leads to further racial segregation and reduces the number of jobs available to minorities trapped in central cities. FHA mortgage programs encouraged white flight to the suburbs. HUD, by tearing down slum housing and replacing it with civic centers and upper-middle-class developments, displaced the poor. Despite decades of efforts to end segregation and promote fair housing, contradictory policy action and inaction resulted in ghetto areas remaining virtually untouched.

IMMIGRATION

Immigration policy is important in race relations because it is *intermestic* policy—one that blends both international and domestic policy concerns. Immigration to the United States is a primary source of minority groups in the United States. Immigration policy plays a **gatekeeping** role significantly determining the composition of the flow (LeMay 1989). It has long been an area of intense struggle. Since the nation began keeping count of immigration in 1820, well over 60 million persons have immigrated here, making the United States by far the largest immigrant-receiving nation in the world. Figure 9.3 shows the levels of immigration from 1901 to 1997.

This section discusses various phases in immigration policy and the link between policy and the resulting composition of the flow. Immigration policy reflects the perceived needs of the nation as those needs shift over time in response to changing economic and social conditions. Immigration policy reflects reactions to the changing nature and composition of immigrant waves. Various economic, ethnic, cultural, and foreign policy issues played key roles in the debates over immigration policy.

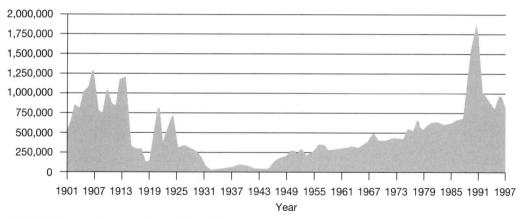

FIGURE 9.3 Legal Immigration, 1901–1997

SOURCE: Statistics Branch, Immigration and Naturalization Service, U.S. Department of Justice, *Annual Report, 1997,* p. 1.

Shifts in policy reflect conflicting value perspectives that tug and pull at one another, causing policy to oscillate between them. On the one hand, immigrants are valued as a source of industry and renewed vigor, a desirable infusion of new blood into the American stock, enriching the heritage and spurring new economic growth. This perspective forms the traditional base for a more open immigration policy. Almost every president, from George Washington to William Clinton, has affirmed that we are a nation of immigrants, a nation of asylum for which immigration expresses and confirms the American spirit of liberty for all. The other perspective calls for varying degrees of restrictions. Its proponents fear strangers who cannot, or in their view should not, be assimilated. They fear the dilution of American culture. They fear so vast an influx will destroy the economy or severely depress wages and working conditions. They advocate restrictive immigration policy to avoid such dire effects.

Changes in immigration policy can often result in dramatic shifts in the size and composition of the flow. The gatekeeping function suggests the use of "door" imagery to characterize U.S. immigration policy. Figure 9.4 graphically portrays the changing nature of immigration as to source of origin, demonstrating changes from 1820 to 1990 in terms of which regions of the world served as the primary sources of immigration to the United States. Figure 9.5 shows the nature of the composition, focusing on the decades since 1965, in which the shift from Europe to Latin America and Asia occurred.

We distinguish five phases in immigration policy. Phase 1, from 1820 to 1880, we term the **open-door era**. During this phase, policy had few restrictions on immigration; almost all who sought entrance were allowed in. Indeed, some state governments sent agents to Europe to recruit immigrants. Phase 2, the **door-ajar era**, lasted from 1880 to 1920. This phase saw the beginnings of effective restrictions, although the door was open to most. Phase 3, the **pet-door era**, lasted from 1920 to 1950,

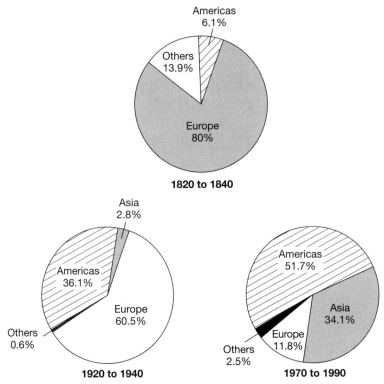

FIGURE 9.4 Changing Sources of Immigration by Region, 1820–1990

SOURCE: *Statistical Yearbook of the Immigration and Naturalization Service, 1994,* p. 126.

when the national origins quota system formed the basis of U.S. immigration policy. A highly restrictive approach to immigration, it allowed in only a favored few. Phase 4, the **dutch-door era**, lasted from 1950 to 1985, establishing more open policy than during the quota years, allowing for an increase in total immigration, but favoring those who entered "at the top" by allowing large refugee flows under special provisions. Phase 5, the **revolving-door era**, characterizes the policy from 1985 to date. It both responds to and allows an increased number, many of whom come and go in large numbers often annually.

The "asylum" view determined policy making in the first phase, the open-door era. With the successful establishment of an independent nation and then its newly revised Constitution in the late 1790s, the official policy was to be open to all. Little opposition to this policy was even voiced at first. In 1790, when the nation took its first census, it recorded a population of 3,227,000, mostly the descendants of seventeenth- and eighteenth-century arrivals or recent immigrants themselves. More than 75 percent were of British origin; about 8 percent were of German origin; the remainder were Dutch, French, or Spanish in origin, or black slaves and Native Americans. This popu-

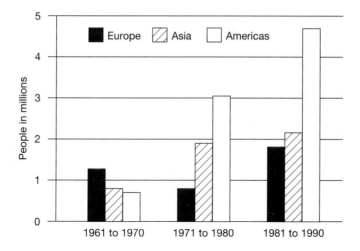

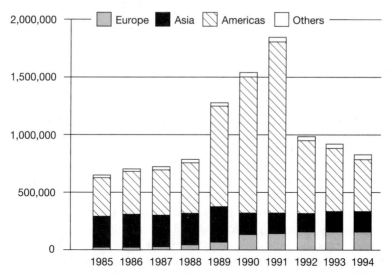

FIGURE 9.5   Three Decades of Immigration and the Origins of 10 Million Immigrants, 1985–1995

SOURCE: *Statistical Yearbook of the Immigration and Naturalization Service, 1994,* pp. 132 and 133.

lation occupied a vast, sparsely settled land obviously rich in soil and natural resources. The population density in 1790 was only 4.5 persons per square mile.

There was an obvious need for labor to build cities and clear farms on the frontier. Additional population was desired to strengthen the defense against Indians and

European colonial powers. President Washington summed up the prevailing view and policy when he stated: "The bosom of America is open to receive not only the opulent and respectable stranger, but the oppressed and persecuted of all Nations and Religions; whom we shall welcome to a participation of all our rights and privileges, if by decency and propriety of conduct they appear to merit the enjoyment" (cited in Rischin 1976: 43).

Congress passed laws regulating naturalization. The first act (1 Stat. 104, 1790) was very liberal, requiring only a two-year residency and the renunciation of former allegiances. In 1795, turmoil in Europe raised fears and Congress passed a more stringent act requiring five years' residency and a renunciation of foreign titles as well as allegiances. In 1798, Congress, then under the control of the Federalists, raised the residency to 14 years (1 Stat. 566). It passed the Alien Acts allowing the President to deport any alien considered to be a threat to the nation. These acts were permitted to expire when the Jeffersonian Democratic Republicans replaced the Federalists in power. In 1802, an act reinstated the five-year provisions of the 1795 law. In 1819, Congress passed a law requiring the listing of all entering ship passengers which indicated their sex, occupation, age, and country to which they belonged (3 Stat. 489).

During the 1830s and 1840s, a wave of largely Catholic immigrants set off a dramatic xenophobic reaction. They were easy scapegoats to blame for problems of a rapidly urbanizing and industrializing country. They were alleged to be importing crime and drunkenness. Social reformers desiring to preserve the nation's institutions and Protestant evangelicals seeking to save the nation's "purity" joined forces to form anti-immigration associations like the Secret Order of the Star Spangled Banner, which became the Know Nothing political party. These groups advocated restrictive immigration policy and more stringent naturalization laws. Xenophobia led to violent attacks on churches and convents and inflamed anti-Catholic literature. Such nativist sentiment did not prevail over public policy, however, as the more politically and economically powerful of the native stock continued supporting more open immigration to supply cheap labor for the explosively expanding cities and factories. Economic needs, coupled with the philosophic idealism regarding America as the land of opportunity and freedom, prevailed over the narrow views of the anti-Catholic movement.

The discovery of gold in California in 1848 drew a vast population west. The post–Civil War period created an insatiable need for immigrants. The transcontinental railroad building boom opened up vast lands to settlement. Massive numbers of unskilled laborers were needed to mine the coal and ore, work the mills, and staff the factories of Civil War-generated production. These forces drew Chinese immigrants to the West Coast. The composition of European immigrants also began to change, with those from South, Central, and Eastern Europe outnumbering those from Western Europe.

The changing flow of immigration, coupled with economic recessions and a depression during the 1870s, renewed political pressures for restrictions. A law banning the immigration of convicts and prostitutes was passed in 1875, and the 1880s ushered in a new phase in immigration policy, the "door-ajar era." Ironically, at the very time the Statue of Liberty was erected symbolizing the nation being open to the "poor and the oppressed" of the world, the "new" immigrants were raising fear and dislike among many in the native stock. The more "alien" characteristics of the newcomers—

strange coloring, physiques, customs, and languages—renewed fears that such strangers were unable to assimilate. A spate of pseudo-scientific studies by historians, sociologists, and biologists attacked the new immigrants as biologically and racially inferior. Racist fervor led to the first blatantly restrictionist immigration law, the Chinese Exclusion Act of 1882 (22 Stat. 58; 8 U.S.C.). Racist and nativist fervor led to restrictive immigration policy reflecting four historical trends that culminated in the 1880s and 1890s: (1) the burgeoning cities and rapid industrialization, which led to visibly corrupt urban political machines catering to the ethnic immigrants as ethnic voting blocs; (2) the official closing of the frontier; (3) the persistence among the "new" immigrants to maintain their culture and traditions far longer than did the "old" immigrants largely of northwestern European origin; and (4) the greater religious diversity among the new immigrants, who were overwhelmingly Catholic, Jewish, or Orthodox (Russian/Greek).

Passage of the 1882 immigration acts did not satisfy the restrictionists. The continued large flow of immigrants during the 1880–1890 decade resulted in further efforts to change immigration policy, focusing on a new device—literacy. The first literacy bill was introduced in Congress in 1895, where it quickly passed both houses but was vetoed by President Cleveland. In 1906, another comprehensive immigration act was proposed that included both a literacy test for admission and an English-language test for naturalization. Nativist forces were joined by labor unions in advocating this policy. The budding unionization movement feared the economic threat to wage scales and working conditions implicit in unrestricted immigration. Business leaders opposed the new law, wanting to avoid any limitation of new and cheap labor.

Restrictionists succeeded in passing the literacy requirements for entrance and the language requirement for naturalization, but again the law was vetoed. In 1907, Congress established the Dillingham Commission to study the impact of immigration. The Dillingham Commission adopted pseudo-scientific, racist theories prevalent at the time. Its recommendations, published in 1911, called for a literacy test and other highly restrictive legislation. The war in Europe, however, generated economic growth and labor demands, both of which ran counter to restrictive policy. The growing political power of the new immigrant groups, coupled with business demand for new labor, preserved a more free entry policy. In 1912, Congress again passed a literacy bill, and President Taft successfully vetoed it. In 1915, another bill passed, this time being vetoed by President Wilson. After the United States entered World War I, Congress passed and successfully overrode yet another veto. The 1917 law finally made literacy an entrance requirement (39 Stat. 874; 8 U.S.C.). It codified a list of aliens to be excluded, virtually banned all immigration from Asia, and culminated in restrictive policy being accepted broadly throughout society.

A frenzy of anti-German activity resulted in an "Americanization" movement to educate the foreign-born in American language and customs. Between 1919 and 1921, 20 states passed laws creating Americanization programs. Even industry, for the first time, took a more restrictionist view, resulting in a new phase of immigration policy, the national origins quota system. When industry, exemplified by such groups as the National Association of Manufacturers, industrial giants like the International Harvester Company, and such prominent business leaders as Henry Ford joined labor unions and nativist groups in calling for restrictionist immigration policy, a change in policy became inevitable.

Two restrictionist groups—organized labor and the nativist "100 Percenters"—called for the suspension of all immigration. Labor feared the job competition of immigrants who enhanced the realignments occurring in the postwar economy. The 100 Percenters simply feared the European ideas, most notably the "red-menace of Bolshevism," that would contaminate society's institutions and customs. The Senate led the way, designing a bill to reduce total immigration and to change the composition of those who were allowed to enter. The Quota Act of 1921 (42 Stat. 5; 8 U.S.C. 229) contained many of the ideas proposed by the Dillingham Commission. It was designed to ensure access for immigrants from northwestern Europe while restricting those from South, Central, and Eastern Europe and continuing the total ban on Asian immigration. In 1921, Congress passed and President Harding signed into law a measure introducing the national origins quota device. In 1924, this concept was expanded by enactment of the Johnson-Reed Act, known as the National Origins Quota Act (43 Stat. 153; 8 U.S.C. 201). It established an annual immigration limit of 150,000 Europeans, a total ban on Japanese, the issuance of visas against set quotas rather than upon arrival, and quotas based on the number of each nationality in the overall population, providing for the admission of immigrants until 1927 by annual quotas of 2 percent of the proportion of the United States population based on the 1890 census. It was amended in 1929 when the quotas were permanently set.

The Immigration Act of 1924 remained in force until 1952. It rejected the open-door tradition. The reduction in emigration influenced by the worldwide Great Depression of the 1930s and the National Origins Act dramatically reduced overall immigration for nearly three decades. In 1925, Congress established the Border Patrol in an effort to halt illegal aliens, an estimated half-million of whom entered during the 1920s.

The first pressures to revise the immigration policy of the quota system began during the 1940s in reaction to World War II. The need for alien labor resulted in enactment of the "bracero" program, a temporary workers program that imported labor mostly from Mexico to fill wartime needs. Congress responded to our wartime alliance with China to repeal the 60-year ban of Chinese immigration. News of the Holocaust at the end of the war helped induce President Truman to issue a directive admitting 40,000 war refugees. Congress reacted to the problems of soldiers who had married overseas by passing the War Brides Act in 1945 (59 Stat. 659; 8 U.S.C. 232) allowing 120,000 alien wives, husbands, and children of members of the Armed Forces to immigrate to the United States separate from the quota system. Truman initiated a refugee law, the Displaced Persons Act (62 Stat. 1009). It was pushed by such groups as the American Jewish Committee and Citizens Committee for Displaced Persons, and was even supported by the American Federation of Labor. Passed by Congress in 1948, it allowed the admission of over 400,000 displaced persons through the end of 1951 by "mortgaging" their entry against future quotas. It served as the precursor to the next phase of immigration policy, the "dutch-door era," when special provisions allowed for the easier entry of various favored groups.

In 1952, Congress passed the Immigration and Nationality Act, also known as the McCarran-Walter Act (66 Stat. 163). It consolidated previous immigration laws into a single statute, retained aspects of the national origins quota system, but also set up a system of preferences for certain skilled labor and for the relatives of U.S. citizens and permanent resident aliens. It set a limit of 150,000 on immigration from the Eastern Hemisphere and retained the unlimited number for the Western Hemisphere. It set a small quota for Asian immigration, a "Pacific Triangle" provision. President Truman vetoed the act, but Congress overrode him. In 1953 he appointed a commission to study immigration and naturalization policy. It recommended a liberalized approach, harkening back to the more open-door era.

During the cold war period of foreign policy, Congress enacted measures in response to that issue. In 1956 and 1957, it passed laws allowing Hungarian "refugee-escapees" displaced by their failed revolution to enter and established a category for refugees fleeing Communist-dominated countries or countries in the Middle East (72 Stat. 419). In 1960, Congress passed the Refugee Fair Share Act providing a temporary program for World War II refugees and displaced persons still in United Nations refugee camps (74 Stat. 504). In 1962, Congress enacted the Migration and Refugee Assistance Act to aid the President in these matters (responding to refugees fleeing Communist Cuba).

Congress more extensively revised immigration policy when it passed the Immigration and Nationality Act of 1965 (79 Stat. 911). This new law reflected the civil rights era in much the same way as the McCarran-Walter Act reflected the cold war period. A healthy and expanding economy eased fears of job competition among organized labor forces, enabling organized labor to favor more liberal immigration policy. The new law abolished the national origins quota system, replacing it with an overall limit of 160,000 to be distributed on the basis of a limit of 20,000 persons per country for all nations outside the Western Hemisphere and an overall limit of 120,000 on Western Hemisphere nations without individual national limits. It established a seven-category system of preferences for the Eastern Hemisphere, giving first preference to reuniting families and a high preference for certain desired occupational skill categories. The ending of the open-door policy for Western Hemisphere nations was a compromise to get the bill passed. The bracero program was ended in 1964. That, coupled with the closing of the open door to Western Hemisphere countries, led to a backlog of applicants from Latin America and to renewed problems of undocumented (illegal) aliens coming in from those countries. In 1976, Congress reacted to such pressures by passing an amendment to the 1965 law. It set immigration limits for both hemispheres to 20,000 per country, on a first-come, first-served basis. It set a worldwide limit of 290,000 and retained the seven-category preference system of the 1965 act.

Special "parole" programs to handle massive waves of refugees from Cuba, Vietnam, and the Soviet Union were enacted instead of any blanket revisions in overall legal immigration policy, which clearly could not keep up with the pressures by the would-be immigrants to enter. This approach became increasingly inadequate to handle what was becoming a recurring "special" situation, however, and concern over the "refugee problem" led Congress to pass the Refugee Act of 1980 (94 Stat. 102), providing an ongoing mechanism for the admission of and aid to refugees, removal of previous geographic and ideological restrictions, and the setting of a total allocation for such refugee admissions at 50,000 annually through 1982. It set up a system for reimbursement to states and voluntary associations for financial and medical assistance they provided to refugees. It signaled a renewed concern for reexamining immigration policy.

Beginning in 1973, a decade of "stagflation" characterized an economy troubled by both high inflation and high unemployment. These economic conditions, coupled with continued massive illegal immigration, led to calls for a major revision in immigration policy. In 1984 alone, the Immigration and Naturalization Service apprehended over 1.2 million undocumented aliens, an astonishing 34 percent increase over two years. Rather broad support for a new policy and for a bipartisan effort developed in response. It became increasingly clear that the United States could not adequately patrol its more than 5,000 miles of border. The combined illegal and legal immigration rate exceeded the peak years of the early 1900s, representing an estimated 40 to 50 percent of the U.S. annual population increase.

Another commission was established to study the problem—the Select Commission on Immigration and Refugee Policy (SCIRP). Its recommendations formed the basis of the Simpson-Mazzoli bill, which ushered in a new direction in policy exemplified by the Immigration Reform and Control Act (IRCA) of 1986 (100 Stat. 3360). It enacted a new balance in the opposing values pursued over the years. On the one hand, it attempted to control illegal immigration by strengthening the border patrol and cutting down on incentives for new entrants by placing stiff penalties on potential employers—fines and even prison terms for employers who knowingly hire or recruit undocumented aliens for employment. The stiffer and restrictionist-oriented employer sanctions provision was balanced by an amnesty provision. Over 3 million previously illegal aliens were granted amnesty and allowed legal status as resident aliens. Several religious and Hispanic organizations had been openly defying immigration law over the issue of illegal aliens. A sanctuary movement involving hundreds of congregations across the country developed in the late 1970s and early 1980s. The U.S. Committee for Refugees, a private group, protested the unwillingness of the INS to grant asylum to tens of thousands of refugees fleeing civil war in Nicaragua and El Salvador. This approach of attempting to decrease immigration by decreasing the economic incentives for immigration portends a new direction in immigration policy. This approach, plus the new law's provisions to extensively expand a temporary worker program, suggest a phase in immigration policy perhaps best characterized as the "revolving-door era."

Legal immigration was further amended by the Immigration Act of 1990 (104 Stat. 4981), which among other provisions established a sort of lottery for Irish immigrants and set up a new category for persons willing to invest millions into the economy and create new jobs. In 1996, Congress enacted the Personal Responsibility and Work Opportunity Act, a welfare reform act that contained provisions aimed at both legal and illegal immigrants (110 Stat. 2105). Later that same year Congress passed a more restrictive legal immigration law, the Illegal Immigration Reform and Immigrant Responsibility Act (110 Stat. 3009). These laws had a temporary impact on the numbers of illegal and legal immigrants. During the 1990s immigrants admitted to the nation reached levels matching the peak years of 1900–1910. Table 9.8 shows the number of immigrants admitted annually from 1991 to 1997.

TABLE 9.8   Immigration to the United States, 1991–1997

Year	Number of Immigrants Admitted
1991	1,827,167
1992	810,635
1993	880,014
1994	804,416
1995	720,461
1996	915,900
1997	798,378

SOURCE: Immigration and Naturalization Service data posted on the Internet: http://www.ins.usdoj.gov>1999.

Illegal immigration, complex refugee issues, and the continued pressure for high levels of legal immigration to the United States made immigration policy more complex and less predictable. Policy swings between intense moral links to the American creed and an ongoing struggle over who and how many the economy could afford and society could effectively absorb. Immigration policy is an area in the struggle between the nation's racial and ethnic minorities and the majority because it so clearly affects the very nature of what sort of nation of people the United States will be in the future. This brief review of immigration policy illustrates the constant struggle with the immigration process and its periodic attempts at achieving a politically acceptable bal-

No longer welcoming.

ance in procedural justice. Ultimately, the key to understanding the immigration policy process is the disparities in power among the competing groups who seek to influence that balance. The interplay among such groups determines how wide open or closed will be the doors to the nation at any given period of time.

LAW ENFORCEMENT

> The relationship between the police and minority groups in big city ghettos is one of the sorest spots in American life today. In the words of a report by the President's Commission on Law Enforcement and the Administration of Justice, a "wall of isolation" surrounds the police, blocking understanding between them and the dwellers in the slums, permitting the growth of every kind of misunderstanding and hatred. . . . The policeman, whose mission it is to guard the peace, walks uneasy in the ghetto. What worries him is not so much the ordinary criminal; usually he feels he can cope with lawbreakers, whose apprehension is his main job. He fears, rather, the very people he is there to protect. For many otherwise law-abiding ghetto residents are openly hostile to him; many refuse to cooperate with him in maintaining law and order; and on occasion some may attack him. (Edwards 1982: 2)

The relationship between the police and the minority population, particularly blacks in the ghettos, is characterized by a hostility bordering on a "war" mentality on both sides. A leading criminologist, James Q. Wilson, states: "The views of many police officers seem to confirm the 'war' theory of police-community relations. Data gathered at least as far back as 1960 suggest that most big city police officers see the citizenry as a least uncooperative and at worst as hostile" (Stedman 1972: 60). Wilson goes on to note that while his research shows a majority of black and white citizens have a positive attitude toward the police, the most antipolice groups are young adult males, especially young black males. Another police scholar says simply: "Hating and mistrusting the police has become a way of life in the ghetto" (Alexander 1969: 23).

In large measure the animosity between the two reflects racial two-sided prejudice. As we have seen throughout this book, racism runs deep in American society and is a force that can be explosive in nature. When racial prejudice becomes uncontrolled, as during a race riot, racial violence runs loose in the streets. It unleashes a degree of fear and hatred that can turn even warm human beings, black as well as white, into savages. Often it is the innocent who are victims during violent outbreaks. Riots exacerbate the antipathy between police and minorities. Most riots have begun with an encounter between police and ghetto residents, with police serving as the "flash point" for minority anger, the formation of mobs, and disorder.

Minority hostility toward police reflects a long history of discrimination. Blacks remember the mistreatment of their southern past where de jure segregation was enforced by the police, often brutally so. As a former police chief put it: "Many people living today remember far worse things—the worst being the lynchings which were possible only because law enforcement agencies stood aside and let the mobs work their will. From 1882 to 1959, 2595 Negroes were lynched in nine Southern states. No white person was ever punished for these offenses" (Edwards 1982: 25).

Pervasive racial conflict often results from the commonality of anti-minority attitudes among police personnel. When the civil rights movement first arose, the attitude of the police was apparent. It engendered a reciprocal feeling among blacks both North and South. "Every time illegal violence is employed against civil rights demonstrations anywhere, it increases animosity against police everywhere. The dogs which Police Chief T. Eugene "Bull" Connor set on young Negroes in Birmingham, Alabama, in 1963, probably caused more physical injury to police officers in other cities in the long run than to the demonstrators they were pictured as attacking" (Edwards, p. 17).

Numerous studies indicate a widespread prejudice among police against minorities, particularly blacks.[1] A President's Crime Commission Task Force found that 72 percent of the police officers it interviewed in three major cities exhibited prejudice against blacks in their responses to task force observers. Blacks and whites manifest sharply different positions in their attitudes and experience with police. Numerous studies indicate a widespread problem of police abuse and excessive use of force. Reports on police brutality show that it is common and that the lower class bears the brunt of victimization. Officers tend to mistreat citizens of the same race: 67 percent of citizens victimized by white police officers were white, 71 percent of citizens victimized by black officers were black (Lipsky 1970: 74).

In terms of the systematic abuse problems, the commission's most troubling finding was that in a third of the cases where excessive use of force was evident, it took place in the police station after the arrest, when the police officer should have been in control. Highly publicized incidents, like the beatings of Rodney King and Abner Louima, confirm the worst fears among the nation's minorities.

The ghetto setting itself virtually ensures the conflict. Because of residential segregation and density problems, blacks are more likely than whites to come into adversarial contact with the police. A study of 600 police officers in three major cities with large black populations found that three-fourths of white officers working in predominantly black areas expressed prejudiced views of blacks. Twenty-eight percent of black officers in the study did so as well. Mark Levy concludes that the problem is not one of a few bad eggs but rather of a police system that is racist in its recruitment, training, socialization, and assignment patterns (in Ruchelman 1973: 80). The very existence of the ghetto as the center of intense crime aggravates the systematic nature of police/minority conflict. Metropolitan areas have a violent crime rate five times higher and a property crime rate twice as high as those of the smaller city or rural area.

The adversarial relationship is compounded by the role police must play in the ghetto. The police serve as buffers. Their job is to minimize crime where possible and to contain it where it is less likely to be a threat to the person or property of the majority members of society. This means the police officer comes quite literally to personify "the law." The officer becomes the symbol of authority, empowered to use his gun when necessary. He becomes the symbol and agent of the sovereign right of the state to take lives if need be. Ghetto residents react to that role. Their frustrations and anger are directed toward the police like lightening to the rod. The enmity and animosity so pervasive in the ghetto are transferred to the police officer. This enmity provides for ghetto residents a release for their pent-up frustrations that, if left without an object, seethe and boil over into social eruptions such as race riots.

The judicial system is structured to exacerbate the problem. Policy concerning so-called victimless crime enhances the likelihood of police/minority conflict by concentrating many of the resources of the entire judicial system, most especially law enforcement, on the control of such crime. Arrests for prostitution, public intoxication, crimes of "sexual perversions," or drug abuse consume the vast proportion of court time in any large city, time that might otherwise be devoted to more swiftly prosecuting perpetrators of crimes against person or property. Add to the court time the use of the resources of the prosecutor's office, court-appointed defense attorneys, and police time spent on victimless crime, and the total mounts dramatically. These laws demean law enforcement officers who consort with prostitutes, gamblers, and drug pushers in order to catch them. This reinforces them against "social undesirables." Police arrest street-walkers but rarely expensive call girls; blacks, Hispanics, and lower-class whites for public intoxification but seldom middle-class whites unless when driving. Victimless crime encourages organized crime which provides them as a "service."

These laws fail to prevent the conduct they proscribe. It is arguable whether they even reduce such behavior significantly. But the need to enforce such laws puts the police into sustained conflict with minorities. For the police, who often witness the ghetto resident in the context of breaking the law, antiminority attitudes are confirmed and reinforced. To the ghetto resident, the police are viewed as "The Man," whose only contact is when they bust somebody for something often culturally viewed as "not real crime."

Minority persons are more likely to be arrested, prosecuted, and convicted than are members of the white majority. The nation's prison population is disproportionately black. Figure 9.6 compares the incarceration rates among males and females and blacks and whites. What, if anything, can be done to reduce this seemingly inherently conflictual relationship? Several reforms have been commonly suggested after the outbreak of riots to improve police/minority relations:

1. More minority officers. A city's police force should mirror the racial diversity of its citizenry.

2. More sensitivity and stress training.

3. More patrolmen who walk the neighborhood beat and know the people they serve, and vice versa.

Since the 1970s, attempts to implement reforms have resulted in the dramatic increase in minority police officers in the nation's major cities and the sharp decrease in fatal police shootings. But some scholars of police/community relations are less optimistic about how much improvement such "reforms" bring. They argue that the conflict will continue as long as the police must be the buffers, the social brokers and urban colonial guards of society. Police departments, moreover, attract **stratiphiles**, individuals who are extraordinarily disposed to the forces and commitments that flow from social stratification. They are also marginal men. In the ghetto, police are often

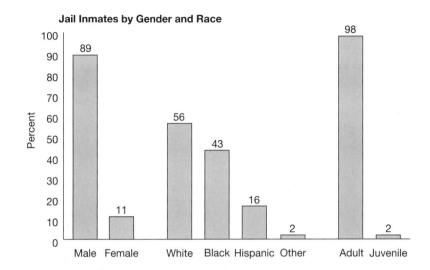

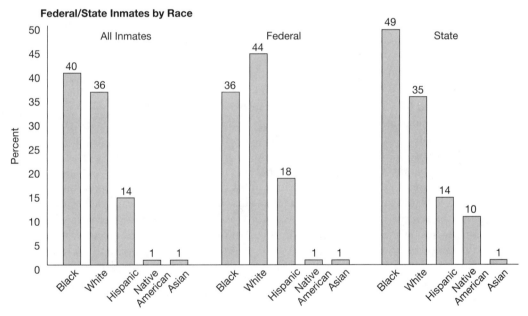

FIGURE 9.6 Incarceration Rates by Groups, 1996

SOURCE: (top) *U.S. Statistical Abstract, 1998,* Table 375, p. 228; (bottom) Department of Justice, Bureau of Justice Statistics, *Census of State/Federal Facilities,* August 1997, p. 1.

viewed as pariahs, judas-goats, and sacrificial lambs. This is doubly so for the black officer, who often feels a double marginality, rejected by both blacks and many white officers, sometimes viewed as traitors to their race. And those officers who regularly work the ghetto, be they black or white, can become ghettoized: coming to feel rejected, abused, exploited, alienated, and even powerless. Even black officers sometimes become abusive toward ghetto residents.

Another common proposal for reform is the civilian review board. Such boards have not been very successful, and few metropolitan areas have established them. They clearly are not panaceas. Where they have been established—Philadelphia and Rochester, for example—they are faulted for being inadequately staffed, relying on the police for the investigation of the police. They have not prevented riots in those cities. They often lack remedial powers, only being able to investigate and advise.[2]

Self-policing can be a sham. Police are rarely convicted and punished on the basis of citizen complaints by internal affairs division investigation or by outside police civilian review boards. The police reform movement has generally persuaded state, local, and even federal authorities that they should handle complaints against the police. Out of a deep concern for the reputation of the department, internal affairs units and special squads have on occasion used reprehensible tactics to discourage citizens from filing complaints against officers. Robert Fogelson (1977) cites a virtual litany of devices used in many major cities: threatening citizens with criminal libel; forcing them to take lie detector tests; employing disorderly conduct charges and resisting arrest charges against them, or threatening to do so; intimidating them or their witness if they do file charges; refusing access to counsel or to files; and developing expensive, complicated, and protracted procedures.

The police reform movement has also called for greater police "professionalism." This approach, however, is very expensive. In New York City, in one decade, the police force increased by 18 percent and its costs rose by 96 percent. Various police scholars and critics are pessimistic about the value of "professionalism" reforms. They have not prevented riots, reduced significantly the allegations of police abuse, or improved ghetto residents' attitudes toward the police. A major federal policy response to the urban riots was the Crime Control and Safe Streets Act of 1968, which created the Law Enforcement Assistance Administration (LEAA). This law poured millions of federal dollars into local police departments with an approach that critics allege is inefficient. Most of the money spent, at least early on, was on expensive "hardware" and on a repressive response to police minority relations.[3] "So long as crime and disorder are disproportionately to be found among young lower-class males, and so long as blacks remain over-represented in (though by no means identical with) such groups blacks—especially young ones—and the police are going to be adversaries" (James Q. Wilson, cited in Stedman 1972).

If the area of law enforcement, like housing, is one that shows precious little improvement in minority/majority relations, political participation is perhaps the one showing the greatest degree of change.

POLITICAL PARTICIPATION

This section traces changes in American public policy regarding political participation. It shows how the United States changed from a society that systematically disenfranchised its minority population to one that now guarantees basic civil rights of participation. It shows that dramatic improvements have been made in the actual participation by minorities—increases in their voting registration and turnout rates and in the success of their electing from among their own officials to public office.

Earlier chapters described varying but consistently low levels of political participation characteristic of minority groups in the United States. Much of that low level of participation is undoubtedly related to low socioeconomic status. Social science scholars studying political participation view **socioeconomic status (SES)** as the most important determinant of political participation. The consensus among scholars about its importance is referred to as the *standard SES model.* Simply put, the higher one's SES, the more likely one is to vote, and vice versa.

But as we shall see, ethnicity can have an independent impact on political participation. Public policy has been consciously used by some factions of the majority society to disenfranchise ethnic minorities and has been instrumental in developing an association between low SES and low levels of participation.

> Of all the rights available to democratic citizens, none is more generally significant than the right to vote. Voting is the primal act of democratic citizens. Without the suffrage all other rights become endangered, since a minority could prevent the enjoyment of these other rights by exerting its power upon government disproportionately. The enjoyment of the right to vote is a test of democracy. . . . At the core of the right to vote is the opportunity for a group to protect itself against injurious governmental policies. The right is available to individuals, but it is also a safeguard for groups. (Sigler 1975: 111, 113)

Majority society uses laws and public policy, as well as informal measures such as violence and intimidation, to deny participation to minority groups. The poll tax, literacy tests, white primary, racial gerrymandering, and registration laws have all been used to disenfranchise minorities.

Women were denied the right to vote until the Nineteenth Amendment passed in 1920. Asian immigrants, denied citizenship by law, were thereby denied the vote. Native Americans could not vote, except for their tribal leadership, until Congress finally passed the Indian Citizen Act in 1924. Even then, some states limited them from participation in state and local elections until the 1940s. The most extensive use of public policy to disenfranchise minorities were the various Jim Crow laws aimed at blacks. So intense was racial (and sex) discrimination that, at one time, 17 states permitted male aliens to vote but denied American women and black citizens doing so.

Immediately after the Civil War, three constitutional amendments passed that abolished slavery and guaranteed citizenship to all persons born or naturalized in the United States, and specifically prohibited the denial of the right to vote to any citizen on the basis of race. Enjoyment of this basic right by blacks was short-lived. When federal troops left the South in the late 1870s, southern whites reestablished political control over the black population in the South, effectively denying them the vote until the mid-1960s. Although southern blacks continued to vote, sometimes in fairly sizable numbers, until well into the 1880s and 1890s, by the 1890s most of the former Confederate states passed laws segregating public facilities and eroding their participation. The first objective of the white supremacy movement was to disenfranchise blacks.

At first, Congress attempted to deal with the South's efforts to curtail black voting rights. Congress passed the Enforcement Act of 1870 to give clear "teeth" to the Fifteenth Amendment. A hostile Supreme Court effectively scuttled the law in 1876 (in *United States* v. *Reese,* 92 U.S. 214). The Court argued that the right to vote was not conferred to anyone by the Fifteenth Amendment since the right to vote was not derived from the states. In 1894, Congress repealed the Enforcement Act, thereby leaving black voting rights to the mercies of the Court. Despite the clear intent of the Fifteenth Amendment, most of the nation's blacks living in the South were denied the right to vote prior to the mid-twentieth century. Several Supreme Court decisions led to that development.

In 1883, the civil rights cases decided that the Constitution gave Congress no expressed or implied powers to pass laws prohibiting discrimination practiced by private individuals. In *Hurtado* v. *California* (1894), the Court ruled that the Fourteenth Amendment's due process clause did not make the Bill of Rights binding on state governments. It took 40 years for the Court to reverse itself.

A common device used in the South to strip blacks of the vote was the **literacy test**. These tests originated in the North—in Connecticut and Massachusetts—and only later came to the South. They were first developed to screen out the new immigrants and deny them the vote. Southern states soon seized on them as effective devices against their black populations. The tests were upheld by the Supreme Court in 1898 (*Williams* v. *Mississippi,* 170 U.S. 218), but they were "fraud, and nothing more" (Key 1949: 576).

Another effective device was the **poll tax**, used by 11 southern states. In several cases the tax was made retroactive—that is, the citizen desiring to vote not only had to pay the poll tax for that year but for past years for which he or she had been eligible to vote. The poll tax prevented large numbers of poor whites as well as blacks from voting in the South. It was upheld by the Supreme Court in 1937 (in *Breedlove* v. *Suttles,* 302 U.S. 277). Only in 1966 did the Court finally reverse itself and declare the poll tax invalid (in *Harper* v. *Virginia Board of Elections,* 383 U.S. 663).

A blatant form of legal disenfranchisement of the black was the **grandfather clause**, used in seven southern states. It allowed a registrant to vote without barriers if one's grandfather could do so. Since the grandfathers of blacks had been slaves legally barred from voting, this device blatantly denied blacks that right. In 1915, the Supreme Court finally struck down such laws, based on an Oklahoma case that exempted whites from a literacy test on the basis of a grandfather clause (in *Guinn* v. *United States,* 238 U.S. 347). Oklahoma quickly passed a new registration law that continued to deny blacks the vote until it, too, was finally overturned in 1939 (in *Lane* v. *Wilson,* 307 U.S. 268, 275).

The **white primary** was a popular disenfranchisement device in many southern states, since Democratic Party turnout was so solid that an aspiring politician effectively had to win the Democratic Party nomination to win office. The primary election became the real election. The general election merely rubber-stamped the selection made in the primary. By legally banning blacks from the primary, southern states denied blacks an effective vote in the general election. The Supreme Court first ruled that there was no national authority to regulate primary elections (*Newberry* v.

United States, 256 U.S. 232, 1921). In 1927, that ruling was modified by *Nixon* v. *Herndon,* which invalidated a Texas law that flatly prohibited blacks from voting in the state's Democratic primary. Texas responded by authorizing the executive committees of the state's parties to prescribe voting qualifications in primary elections. In 1932, that law was struck down in *Nixon* v. *Condon* (286 U.S. 73). Texas then set up the Democratic Party as a "private club," whose members could be limited to whites only. At first, the Court upheld the law, deciding such action was discrimination by a private organization rather than by a state (see *Grovey* v. *Townsend,* 295 U.S. 45, 1935; and *Breedlove* v. *Suttles,* 302 U.S. 277, 280, 1937). The white primary was finally ruled unconstitutional in any form when the Supreme Court reversed itself in the case of *Smith* v. *Allwright* (285 U.S. 355, 1944).

Racial gerrymandering was ruled unconstitutional by the Court in *Gomillion* v. *Lightfoot* (364 U.S. 339, 1960). This decision overturned an Alabama legislative redistricting plan that designed voter districts in a manner the Court ruled was clearly intended to diffuse black votes. With virtually every Jim Crow law being overturned, the white majority turned increasingly to more indirect methods. Registration laws still remained a hurdle to the poor, and intimidation suppressed black registration.

Intimidation worked because of the South's history of violence against blacks who dared to participate. From the 1880s through the 1920s, the Ku Klux Klan used a systematic campaign of violence against blacks to "keep them in their place." From 1889 to 1918, a total of 3,224 blacks were lynched. In the late 1940s, Congress became involved in the process. President Truman supported bills in 1948 that ensured fair employment and fair elections, outlawed the poll tax, cracked down on violence and lynchings, and eliminated segregation in interstate commerce. He also advocated creation of a permanent Civil Rights Commission. The South's power in the Senate blocked passage of his proposals, but clearly the pressure was on the Congress to act.

In 1962, Congress passed the Twenty-fourth Amendment outlawing the poll tax in national elections. It was ratified by the states in 1964. In 1966, the Supreme Court, in *Harper* v. *Virginia Board of Elections,* applied it to state and local elections as well. That decision effectively brought an end to all poll taxes in the United States.

The civil rights movement, through direct-action tactics, pressured Congress to enact legislation ending de jure segregation. In 1963, the Birmingham demonstrations ignited protests across the nation, culminating in the March on Washington in August of that year. More than 200,000 blacks and whites participated. Dr. Martin Luther King, Jr., delivered his famous "I Have a Dream" address. In response to the march, President Kennedy sent a strong civil rights bill to Congress, which passed after his assassination as the Civil Rights Act of 1964. The act was hailed as the most sweeping civil rights law enacted in American history. Its various titles and provisions did much to end all Jim Crow practices in the South. The act contained several provisions touching directly on participation. Title I concerned literacy tests, making it unlawful when determining whether an individual was qualified by state law to vote in any federal election to apply any standard, practice, or procedure different from those applied to other individuals within the same county. It required written literacy tests and exempted any individual who had completed sixth grade in any English-speaking school as being presumed literate.

Title V of the act empowers the U.S. Commission on Civil Rights, first established by the Civil Rights Act of 1957, to investigate deprivations of the right to vote. The law was immediately challenged, but the entire act was upheld as constitutional in *Heart of Atlanta Motel* v. *United States* (379 U.S. 241); and in *Katzenbach* v. *McClung* (379 U.S. 241)—both decided in 1964.

Local registrars in the South still barred blacks by an endless variety of registration barriers. Congress reacted by passing the Voting Rights Act of 1965. This law was the first truly effective tool for protecting the voting rights of minority citizens. Congress extended the act in 1970, 1975, and 1982. It has both permanent and temporary provisions.[4] The permanent or general provisions of the act (1) ensure that length-of-residency requirements will not prevent any citizen from voting in presidential elections; (2) prohibit anyone from denying an eligible citizen the right to vote or from interfering with or intimidating anyone from seeking to register or to vote; and (3) forbade the use of literacy tests or other devices as qualifications for voting in any federal, state, local, general, or primary election. The temporary or special "triggering" provisions applied to those states or counties where (1) literacy tests or similar devices were enforced as of November 1, 1964, and (2) where fewer than 50 percent of the voting-age residents were registered or had cast ballots in the 1964 presidential election. In such jurisdictions, the attorney general of the United States, upon evidence of voter discrimination determined by him, was empowered to replace local registrars with federal examiners who were authorized to abolish literacy tests, waive poll taxes, and register voters under simpler federal procedures. Although quickly challenged, the law was upheld in *South Carolina* v. *Katzenbach* (383 U.S. 301).

A third triggering device was added in 1975 concerning minority languages. It was added to ensure that citizens are not deprived of the vote because they cannot speak, read, or write English. A jurisdiction is covered by the language provision if (1) in November 1972, more than 5 percent of the voting-age population in that jurisdiction were members of a single-language minority (specified as American Indian, Asian Americans—Chinese, Japanese, Filipino, Koreans—Alaskan Natives, or persons of Spanish heritage); and the jurisdiction provided English-only election material and less than 50 percent of the voting-age population registered or voted in the 1972 presidential election; or (2) more than 5 percent of the voting-age population in a jurisdiction are members of a single-language minority and the illiteracy rate for that minority population is higher than the national illiteracy rate, such rate being defined as failure to complete the fifth grade.

The original two trigger provisions brought under their special coverage the entire states of Alabama, Georgia, Louisiana, Mississippi, South Carolina, and Virginia, about 40 counties in North Carolina, and a scattering of counties in Arizona, Hawaii, and Idaho. Hundreds of observers and federal examiners were sent to those jurisdictions under the original act. The special language provisions affected many more jurisdictions in other parts of the country, including local governments in California, Massachusetts, and Kansas.

Section V of the act requires all jurisdictions covered under its first and second trigger provisions to submit in advance any proposed changes in their election laws or procedures to the federal government for approval. The intent of this provision is to prevent new discrimination practices from replacing old ones—a common cycle prior to the 1965 act. Section V further places the burden of proof on covered jurisdictions that neither the purpose nor effect of proposed changes in their election system is discriminatory.

The impact of the 1964 and 1965 laws has been dramatic. Whereas only 5 percent of voting-age blacks were registered to vote in the 11 southern states in 1940, black registration rose to 45 percent in 1964 and to 57 percent in 1968. In Mississippi, before the 1965 act, only 6.7 percent of the voting age blacks were registered. By 1972, that number had jumped to 60 percent. Georgia's rate rose from 27 percent in 1965 to nearly 68 percent in 1972. Overall, black registration rates in the South have approached the level of white rates for the first time since Reconstruction. In the Southwest, after the 1975 language provision was added, Hispanic registration rose from 44 percent in 1976 to 59 percent in 1980. The closing of the gap between white and minority (black and Hispanic) registration and voter turnout from 1972 to 1996 is shown in Table 9.9.

Registration and voting increases showed up in similarly dramatic strides in the number of successfully elected black officials. In 1962, there were only 72 black elected officials in the South. A decade later there were over 2,500, and by 1995 over 8,500. These data are shown in Table 9.10.

TABLE 9.9   **Voter Participation, by Group, 1972–1996**

Group	1972		1992		1996	
	Percentage Registered	Percentage Voted	Percentage Registered	Percentage Voted	Percentage Registered	Percentage Voted
Whites	73.4	64.5	63.6	70.1	67.7	56.0
Hispanics	44.4	37.5	28.9	35.0	35.7	26.7
Blacks	65.5	52.1	54.0	63.9	63.5	50.6
Total population	72.3	63.0	61.3	68.2	65.9	54.2

SOURCE: U.S. Bureau of the Census, *Statistical Abstract of the United States, 1998,* Table 483, p. 296.

TABLE 9.10   **Black Elected Officials, 1972–1994**

Year	Number	Percent Increase Over Prior 4 Years	Percent Increase Since 1972
1972	2,264	NA	NA
1976	3,979	58	58
1980	4,912	23	117
1984	5,700	16	152
1988	7,225	27	219
1992	7,552	5	234
1994	7,984	.06	252

SOURCE: U.S. Bureau of the Census, *Statistical Abstract of the United States, 1998,* Table 479, p. 294.

Hispanic voters in the Southwest still face gerrymandering barriers. *Citizen participation,* a journal on voting behavior, found 66 counties in Texas and California that were racially gerrymandered against Mexican Americans. Increased voter registration drives and voter turnout are less effective when the vote is diluted by gerrymandering. Discriminatory redistricting schemes have plagued Hispanic political advancement for some time, especially in Texas. The Southwest Voter Registration Education Project (SVREP) has been involved in 36 lawsuits alleging gerrymandering in Colorado, New Mexico, and Texas. Most were settled out of court.

Both blacks and Hispanics launched drives to overcome such obstacles. The Voter Education Project (VEP), begun in 1962, was rejuvenated in the 1980s. Jesse Jackson's two presidential campaigns scored impressive gains in new black registrations, with estimates of over 2 million new voters turning out during the primary elections in which he ran.

The potential of such programs is considerable. Hispanics can provide the swing vote in states like Texas and California, which alone account for nearly one-third of the votes needed to be elected President. The SVREP campaign scored considerable success, and the results of its litigation efforts are impressive. In Texas, for example, Medina County had not reapportioned since the turn of the century. When SVREP sued and the district was redrawn, three Mexican Americans were elected to office, the first in the county's history. In Victoria County, where minorities are 30 percent of the population, a county commissioner was elected and the city council forced to go from an at-large to a single-member district structure. Victories such as these set off a chain reaction: when Mexican Americans have a better chance of winning elections, they register and turn out to vote in even greater numbers. The Mexican American Legal Defense Education Fund and the Texas Rural Legal Aid have used suits to challenge at-large election structures and racial gerrymandering in Texas.

Dale Nelson (1982) examined a number of variables that influence political attitudes and communal political participation. He found both ethnicity and SES were the strongest predictors. Ethnic identity, however, was the best single predictor, and its impact was independent of SES. His findings support the proposition that while SES and ethnicity share a certain amount of impact due to their statistical correlation, they have substantial independent influence on communal participation. SES was statistically unrelated to ethnic social cohesion and only slightly related to ethnic social consciousness and ethnic political consciousness. Ethnic identity was the best single predictor of variations in political attitudes—explaining 35 percent of the variance while SES explained only 24 percent.[5]

SUMMARY

This chapter examined public policy in six areas viewed as the arenas in the struggle between majority/minority society: education, employment, housing, immigration, law enforcement, and political participation. In each policy area laws and institutionalized policy were used by the majority culture to relegate certain racial and ethnic groups to minority or second-class citizenship status. It reviewed how minority groups struggled in each of those policy areas to bring about changes to end or reduce de jure or institutionalized discrimination against them.

The chapter documented gains made by minorities in education and employment. The chapter also illustrated that comparatively little progress has been made in coping with ethnic and

racial housing segregation, an arena largely impacted by de facto discrimination through norms and customs rather than de jure segregation. It discussed five phases of U.S. immigration policy, linking each to the flows of immigration and how changes in those policy phases influenced the composition of subsequent immigration flows. It discussed the arena of law enforcement and the nearly warlike relationship that has developed between the police and racial minorities. Finally, the chapter reviewed how Jim Crow laws were used to disenfranchise blacks and other ethnic minorities, and how changes in civil rights laws enacted since the 1960s have resulted in rather dramatic increases in their political participation and electoral success.

KEY TERMS

Affirmative action: government programs designed to get minority persons past prior institutionalized barriers in education and employment in an attempt to force structural assimilation.

Block busting: a device by which real estate agencies promote minority members to purchase homes in a previously all-white neighborhood in order to reach the tipping point and set off white flight, thus generating large-scale sales of real estate in an area.

Door-ajar era: the second phase of immigration policy, from 1880 to 1920, during which the beginnings of restrictive immigration policies were enacted.

Dutch-door era: the fourth phase of immigration policy, from 1950 to 1985, in which the quota system was replaced by the "preference system" and special refugee/asylum laws.

Gatekeeping: the function of immigration policy to determine who is or is not allowed to enter the United States as a permanent immigrant.

Grandfather clause: a device used to disenfranchise blacks in the South; only persons whose grandfathers voted could vote, thus blacks whose grandfathers were slaves and could not vote were denied registration.

Literacy tests: a "test" one had to pass to prove literacy in order to vote; used against blacks in the South.

Occupational niche: jobs in which members of particular racial or ethnic minorities work in highly disproportionate numbers. They serve as indirect evidence of pervasive employment discrimination.

Open-door era: the first phase of U.S. immigration policy, from 1820 to 1880, in which immigration policy was virtually unrestricted.

Pet-door era: the third phase of immigration policy, from 1920 to 1950, during which severe restriction was imposed via the national origins quota system.

Poll tax: a tax one had to pay in order to vote; used mostly in the South to disenfranchise blacks.

Proportionality criterion: a measure of inequality used to establish occupation discrimination; it would look critically at employers or job classifications in which minority members fall far below their proportion of the appropriate labor market.

Racial gerrymandering: drawing electoral district lines in such a way as to diffuse or dilute a certain racial or ethnic group's vote.

Revolving-door era: the fifth phase of immigration policy, from 1985 to date, in which large and massive refugee flows and illegal immigrants enter and leave the United States in massive numbers.

SES: socioeconomic status.

Stratiphiles: individuals who are extraordinarily disposed to the forces of social stratification, such as many police officers.

Tipping mechanism: a factor in racial segregation; the point at which an influx of blacks or another ethnic minority will trigger widespread white flight out of a neighborhood.

White primary: primary elections in the one-party South open to voting by whites only; another device used to disenfranchise blacks during the Jim Crow era.

Zero-sum situations: whenever the benefits accorded to some must be taken away from others; one person's or group's gain is another person's or group's loss.

REVIEW QUESTIONS

1. Discrimination in which policy area is the primary method by which minority status is enforced?

2. Compare/contrast the *Plessy* v. *Ferguson* with the *Brown* v. *Board of Education* cases. How and why did the Supreme Court rule in each case? What were the consequences of these two watershed Supreme Court decisions?

3. Describe the proportionality criterion and how it affects affirmative action programs.

4. Discuss three Supreme Court decisions that concerned reverse discrimination. How has the concept of affirmative action evolved over time?

5. Which public policy area remains today as the most racially segregated area in U.S. society?

6. Describe the five phases of U.S. immigration policy. How did each phase affect the flow of immigration to the United States?

7. Name four anti-immigrant nativist groups. How did they inject concepts of race into U.S. immigration policy?

8. Specify two groups that entered the United States in large numbers under special "parole" status. How has that special status affected their ability to assimilate into U.S. society?

9. Discuss the devices used to "demagnetize" the pull of the U.S. economy in immigration laws enacted during the 1980s and 1990s. Why do they not seem to be working?

10. Describe the policy arena characterized as a "war zone" in racial relations between the majority society and its racial/ethnic minorities. Why have reforms to reduce the "institutional nature" of racism in this arena been so ineffective? Contrast this with the political participation arena that shows rather dramatic improvement since 1964.

NOTES

1. See those cited in Cooper (1980).

2. See Edwards (1982).

3. See the reservations of Gordon Misner and Jerry Wilson in "Reform at a Standstill," in Fogelson (1977); and the criticisms of Burton Levy, Arthur Niederhoffer, and Jerome Skolnick, in Levy (1968). See also Dye (1998), and Sindler (1977).

4. See "Open Door Policy for Voting Rights." *National Voter* (Spring 1981): 1–2; and Dye (1971). See also U.S.

Commission on Civil Rights, *Report of the Commission, 1975* (Washington, DC: U.S. Government Printing Office, 1975).

5. Similar conclusions about the independent impact of ethnicity explaining the persistence of ethnic politics are reached using other methods of analysis and based upon a Buffalo study. See R. Robert Huckfeldt, "The Social Contexts of Ethnic Politics," *American Politics Quarterly* ll, 1 (January 1983): 91–123.

SUGGESTED READINGS

ALEXANDER, NICHOLAS. 1969. *Black in Blue.* New York: Appleton-Century-Crofts.

BARDES, BARBARA, MACK SHELLEY II, AND STEFFEN SCHMIDT. 1998. *American Government and Politics Today.* Belmont, CA: Wadsworth.

BARKER, LUCIUS, MACK JONES, AND KATHERINE TATE. 1999. *African Americans and the American Political System,* 4th ed. Upper Saddle River, NJ: Prentice Hall.

BREWSTER, LAWRENCE, AND MICHAEL BROWN. 1998. *The Public Agenda: Issues in American Politics,* 4th ed. New York: St. Martin's Press.

COCHRAN, CLARKE E., et al. 1999. *American Public Policy,* 6th ed. New York: St. Martin's Press.

KITANO, HARRY. 1997. *Race Relations,* 5th ed. Upper Saddle River, NJ: Prentice Hall.

LEMAY, MICHAEL. 1987. *From Open Door to Dutch Door.* New York: Praeger.

LEMAY, MICHAEL. 1994. *Anatomy of a Public Policy.* New York: Praeger.

LIEBERSON, STANLEY. 1980. *A Piece of the Pie.* Berkeley: University of California Press.

LIPSKY, MICHAEL. 1970. *Law and Order Police Encounters.* Chicago: Aldine.

ROTHENBERG, PAULA. 1998. *Race, Class, and Gender in the United States,* 4th ed. New York: St. Martin's Press.

SCHAEFER, RICHARD T. 1998. *Racial and Ethnic Groups,* 7th ed. New York: HarperCollins.

SPEAR, ALLAN. 1967. *Black Chicago.* Chicago: University of Chicago Press.

TAEUBER, KARL, AND ALMA TAEUBER. 1965. *Negroes in Cities.* Chicago: Aldine.

WELCH, SUSAN, et al. 1998. *American Government,* 6th ed. Belmont, CA: Wadsworth.

CASE STUDY 9.1

American Diversity into the Twenty-first Century

The United States enters the twenty-first century with a population in excess of 275 million, of which over 80 million are considered members of a minority group. The number of legal immigrants to the United States, including those coming as refugees and those seeking asylum, has been about 800,000 annually for the decade of the 1990s. In addition, an estimated 4 million to 5 million undocumented aliens continue to live and work in the United States. These demographic trends pose a number of challenges to American society and raise a number of public policy questions.

As this chapter has demonstrated, American society has made a number of substantial gains and changes in its minority/ majority relationships. As America began the decade of the 1960s, Jim Crowism was alive and well, with numerous legal and other barriers to African-American political participation. Today no legal barriers remain to their participation, and their actual involvement has essentially closed the gap with that of white political participation. The 1960s witnessed a society with few significant protections for minority groups. Today there are many significant protections. The 1960s began with virtually no equal employment opportunity for blacks and other minorities. Today, equal opportunity is the law, and affirmative action programs are in place if under increasing attack. In the 1960s there were no bilingual education programs required and they were seldom available.

Today bilingual education is required in many school districts and by a number of states. The 1960s began with rampant discrimination in housing. Today, such discrimination is illegal if still all too common. In 1960, as this chapter showed, there were few African Americans and other minorities in public office. Today, black, Hispanic, and Asian elected officials number in the many thousands, having been elected to political office at all levels of government. In 1960, minorities were registered at less than half that of whites, and voted at a rate of 20 to 30 percent less than that of whites. Today the voter turnout among many minorities is very close to that of whites. In 1960, women had little or no legislative protection against employment discrimination. Today, women are protected against discrimination in employment by both federal and state laws. Despite these gains, however, as this entire book has shown, racism in America is persistent.

In the nearly 400 years since the first slaves were brought to America, and almost 50 years since Rosa Parks touched off the Montgomery bus boycott, American society remains racially divided. Paradoxically, race both defines and in some ways unites society because racism still matters to so many. Race-based thinking permeates our laws and public policy. Racial grievance impacts our politics in diverse ways. African Americans demonstrate against their role as one of this nation's historical victims even while whites complain and vote to end affirmative action programs they hold constitute reverse discrimination.

A 1997 Gallup poll demonstrated the gap in black and white attitudes. Where less than half of blacks felt that they were treated the same as whites, over 75 percent of whites believed they now were so treated. Whereas only 45 percent of blacks agreed they were treated fairly on the job, over 74 percent of whites agreed. Whereas over 60 percent of blacks agreed that they were treated less fairly by police, only 30 percent of whites so believed. Where 63 percent of blacks agreed that they had as good a chance as whites to get quality education, nearly 80 percent of whites believed they did. Where 58 percent of blacks agreed they had an equal chance with whites to get quality housing, over 86 percent of whites thought they did. Whereas only 33 percent of blacks agreed that the quality of life for blacks had improved over the past ten years, nearly 60 percent of whites felt that it had done so. Where 60 percent of blacks felt government should make every effort to improve conditions for blacks, only 43 percent of whites agreed. When asked, should the government not make any special efforts to aid blacks, that they should help themselves, 30 percent of blacks agreed, while nearly 60 percent of whites agreed (Gallup Poll Social Audit on Black/White Relations in the United States, June 1997). Similarly, a 1995 *Newsweek* poll found that 86 percent of blacks rated race relations in the United States as "only fair" or as "poor."

Yet opinion polls show acceptance of interracial marriage and the willingness to reside in mixed-race neighborhoods has never been higher. America is beginning to change its two-way definition of race. Racial identity is being blurred. The sense that race is physical, fixed, immutable, and primarily a matter of skin color is being replaced with a sense that race is as much a matter of ideology and identity as skin pigmentation, that race is a social construct—a mixture of prejudice, superstition, and myth. And now, some 30 years after the last state antimiscegenation law was struck down, an increasingly interracial generation is demanding its place in American society.

Racial thinking, as this book has shown, has been modified by the changing nature of the racial composition in American society, reflecting the past three decades of immigration from Africa, Asia, and Latin America. The additional 18 million people who came since 1965 have been largely "people of color." Blacks are nearly 13 percent of the total population. Hispanics, at over 25 million, are nearly 10 percent, and are projected to be the nation's largest minority by 2010. Hispanics, however, are themselves a disparate collection of nationalities reflecting various descendants of Europeans, African slaves, and Native Americans. The new (post-1965) immigrants number nearly 4 million from Asia.

All of this means an era of increasing multiethnic and multiracial diversity. It raises questions as to whether American society can absorb the increasingly diverse demographic changes. The arrival of these tens of millions of new immigrants from racially mixed sources undermines the de facto consensus as to what "race" means in American society. Demand for more flexible definitions of race are prevalent. The Association of Multi-Ethnic Americans is a group lobbying in Washington to add a multiracial category to the year 2000 census. Changing the census form helps acknowledge the nation's increasing diversity. In the 1990 census, Americans wrote in the blank on the form to identify "other" with nearly 300 "races," some 600 Indian tribes, over

70 Latin groups, and some 75 combinations of multiracial ancestry.

There will be political consequences should a significant number of Americans check the proposed multiracial block, as census-based formulas are used to distribute federal aid in varied ways and programs. A number of African Americans fear that the biracial category may erode black solidarity and voting clout due to "defections" to the multiethnic status.

This chapter has amply presented the evidence of African-American political gains since 1965. The mere handful of black elected officials then have been succeeded by over 8,000 today. Hispanic officeholders grew from just over 3,000 in 1985 to nearly 6,000 today. Progress in such electoral strength demonstrates that as America enters the twenty-first century, minority group politics will remain persistent and increasingly potent. Clearly, the perennial struggle described throughout this volume will continue vibrantly active into the first decades of the next century. These trends beg the question of whether a black person can be elected president, or whether the American presidency will continue to be held only by white, non-Jewish, and non-Hispanic males. The Gallup polling organization asked, between 1937 and 1987 (since which time it no longer asks the question), the following question: "If your party nominated a generally well-qualified man for president who happened to be black [Jew], would you vote for him?" Or, "If your party nominated a woman for president, would you vote for her if she were qualified for the job?" Whereas nearly 70 percent opposed voting for a black for President in 1937, less than 15 percent admitted to opposing doing so in 1987. Where just less than 50 percent opposed voting for a Jew in 1937, less than 10 percent were opposed to doing so in 1987. Where nearly 55 percent of Americans opposed voting for a woman for President in 1958, less than 15 percent were so opposed in 1987. Perhaps the first decade of the new century will witness the election of the first minority person as President of the United States.

BIBLIOGRAPHY

ABRAHAM, HENRY J. 1967. *Freedom and the Court.* New York: Oxford University Press.

ACUNA, RODOLFO. 1972. *Occupied America: The Chicano's Struggle Toward Liberation.* San Francisco: Canfield Press.

AGUIRRE, JR., ADALBERTO, AND DAVID U. BAKER, eds. 1995. *Sources: Notable Selections in Race and Ethnicity.* Guilford, CT: Dushkin.

ALBA, RICHARD. 1990. *Ethnic Identity: The Transformation of White America.* New Haven, CT: Yale University Press.

ALBA, RICHARD. 1995. "Assimilation's Quiet Tide." *The Public Interest* (Spring): 3–18.

ALEXANDER, NICHOLAS. 1969. *Black in Blue.* New York: Appleton-Century-Crofts.

ALLPORT, GORDON. 1958. *The Nature of Prejudice.* New York: Doubleday.

ANDERSON, CHARLES. 1974. *The Political Economy of Social Classes.* Englewood Cliffs, NJ: Prentice Hall.

ARMOR, JOHN, AND PETER WRIGHT. 1988. *Manzanar.* New York: Times Books.

ARRINGTON, LEONARD, AND DAVIS BITTON. 1992. *The Mormon Experience,* 2nd ed. Chicago: University of Illinois Press.

ASAYESH, GELAREH. 1989. "As Refugees Flood In, Localities Must Foot the Bill for the American Dream." *Governing* 2 (May): 23–31.

AUCHING, EDWARD, AND ELEANOR MARX. 1969. *The Working Class Movement in America.* New York: Arno Press.

BABICS, WALTER. 1972. *Yugoslav Assimilation in Franklin County, Ohio.* San Francisco: R. and E. Research Associates.

"Back to the Melting Pot." 1992. *Governing* 5 (June): 31–35.

BAER, HANS. 1988. *Recreating Utopia in the Desert: A Sectarian Challenge to Modern Mormonism.* Albany: State University of New York Press.

BAHR, HOWARD, AND BRUCE CHADWICK. 1979. *American Ethnicity.* Lexington, MA: D. C. Heath.

BALL, GEORGE. 1982. "American Foreign Policy and American Jews." *Washington Post,* July 11, p. C8.

BANTON, MICHAEL. 1967. *Race Relations.* London: Tavistock.

BANTON, MICHAEL. 1987. *Racial Theories.* New York: Cambridge University Press.

BARDES, BARBARA, MACK SHELLEY II, AND STEFFEN SCHMIDT. 1998. *American Government and Politics Today.* Belmont, CA: Wadsworth.

BARKER, LUCIUS, MARK H. JONES, AND KATHERINE TATE. 1999. *African Americans and the Political System,* 4th ed. Upper Saddle River, NJ: Prentice Hall.

BARTH, ERNEST, AND DONALD NOEL. 1972. "Conceptual Frameworks for the Analysis of Race Relations: An Evaluation." *Social Forces* 50: 333–347.

BARTH, ERNEST, AND LAWRENCE NORTHWOOD. 1965. *Urban Desegregation.* Seattle: University of Washington Press.

BARTH, FREDRIK. 1969. *Ethnic Groups and Boundaries.* Boston: Little, Brown.

BASKIN, JANE, et al. 1971. *Race Related Civil Disorder: 1967–1969.* Waltham, MA: Lambery Center for the Study of Violence, Brandeis University.

BAYLOR, RONALD. 1978. *Neighbors in Conflict.* Baltimore: Johns Hopkins University Press.

BERLE, ADOLPH. 1959. *Power Without Property.* New York: Harcourt, Brace & World.

BERRY, BREWTON. 1958. *Race and Ethnic Relations.* Cambridge, MA: Addison-Wesley.

BETTELHEIM, BRUNO, AND MORRIS JANOWITZ. 1950. *The Dynamics of Prejudice.* New York: Harper & Row.

BIAL, RAYMOND. 1995. *Visit to Amish Country.* Urbana, IL: Phoenix.

BLALOCK, HUBERT M. 1967. *Towards a Theory of Minority Group Relations.* New York: Wiley.

BLAUNER, R. 1969. "Internal Colonialism and Ghetto Revolt." *Social Problems* 16: 393–408.

BLAUNER, R. 1972. *Racial Oppression in America.* New York: Harper & Row.

BOGARDUS, E. S. 1930. "Race Relations Cycle." *American Journal of Sociology* 35 (January): 613.

BOGARDUS, E. S. 1950. "Stereotypes vs. Sociotypes." *Sociology and Social Research* 34 (March): 286–291.

BONACICH, EDNA. 1973. "A Theory of Middleman Minorities." *American Sociological Review* 38: 583–594.

BONACICH, EDNA. 1976. "Advanced Capitalism and Black/White Race Relations in the U.S.: A Split Labor Market Interpretation." *American Sociological Review* 41 (February): 34–51.

BONACICH, EDNA, AND JOHN MODELL. 1980. *The Economic Basis of Ethnic Solidarity: Small Business in the Japanese-American Community.* Berkeley: University of California Press.

BOND, JULIAN. 1986. "Black Equality—An Elusive Goal." *American Visions* (January/February): 12–13.

BORRIE, W. D. 1959. *The Cultural Integration of Immigrants.* Paris: UNESCO.

BOYTON, LINDA. 1986. *The Plain People: An Ethnography of the Holdeman Mennonites.* Salem, WI: Sheffield.

BRANCH, TAYLOR. 1988. *Parting the Waters: America in the King Years, 1954–1963.* New York: Simon & Schuster.

BREWSTER, LAWRENCE, AND MICHAEL BROWN. 1998. *The Public Agenda: Issues in American Politics,* 4th ed. New York: St. Martin's Press.

BROMMEL, BERNARD. 1978. *Eugene V. Debs: Spokesman for Labor and Socialism.* Chicago: Charles H. Kerr.

BROWDER, EARL. 1938. *The People's Front.* New York: International Publishers.

BROWN, DEE. 1971. *Bury My Heart at Wounded Knee.* New York: Holt, Rinehart & Winston.

BUGELSKI, B. R. 1961. "Assimilation Through Intermarriage." *Social Forces* 40: 148–153.

BUHLE, PAUL. 1987. *Marxism in the United States.* London: Verso.

BURGESS, THOMAS. 1913. *Greeks in America.* Boston: Scherman, French.

BURKEY, RICHARD. 1978. *Ethnic and Racial Groups.* Menlo Park, CA: Cummings.

BURMA, JOHN H., ed. 1970. *Mexican-Americans in the United States.* New York: Harper & Row.

BURNETTE, ROBERT, AND JOHN KOSTER. 1974. *The Road to Wounded Knee.* New York: Bantam.

CALLOW, ALEXANDER B., JR. 1966. *The Tweed Ring.* New York: Oxford University Press.

CALLOW, ALEXANDER B., JR. 1975. *The City Boss in America.* New York: Oxford University Press.

CARMICHAEL, STOKELEY, AND CHARLES V. HAMILTON. 1967. *Black Power: The Politics of Liberation in America.* New York: Vintage.

CARSON, CLAYBORNE. 1981. *In Struggle: SNCC and the Black Awakening of the 1960s.* Cambridge, MA: Harvard University Press.

CASTRO, TONY. 1974. *Chicano Power.* New York: Dutton.

CATTON, WILLIAM R., AND SUNG CHICK HONG. 1962. "The Relation of Apparent Minority Ethno-Centrism to Majority Antipathy." *American Sociological Review* 27 (April): 190.

CHAVEZ, JOHN R. 1984. *The Lost Land: The Chicano Image of the Southwest.* Albuquerque: University of New Mexico Press.

CHENG, LUCIE, AND EDNA BONACICH, eds. 1984. *Labor Immigration Under Capitalism.* Berkeley: University of California Press.

CHISWICK, BARRY, ed. 1982. *The Gateway: U.S. Immigration Issues and Policies.* Washington, DC: American Enterprise Institute.

CHURCH, WARD. 1993. "Crimes Against Humanity." *Z Magazine* (March): 43–47.

COCHRAN, CLARKE, et al. 1999. *American Public Policy,* 6th ed. New York: St. Martin's Press.

COLBY, DAVID. 1982. "A Test of the Relative Efficiency of Political Tactics." Paper presented at the American Political Science Association Meeting, Denver, September.

COLLINS, BARRY. 1970. *Social Psychology.* Reading, MA: Addison-Wesley.

CONSTANTINE, J. ROBERT, ed. 1995. *Gentle Rebel: Letters of Eugene V. Debs.* Urbana: University of Illinois Press.

COOPER, JOHN R. 1980. *The Police and the Ghetto.* New York: Kennikat Press.

CORNELL, STEPHEN. 1988. *The Return of the Native: American Indian Political Resurgence.* New York: Oxford University Press.

COX, OLIVER C. 1948. *Caste, Class and Race: A Study in Social Dynamics.* New York: Doubleday.

CRONON, E. DAVID. 1969. *Black Moses: The Story of Marcus Garvey and the Universal Negro Improvement Association.* Madison: University of Wisconsin Press.

CROSS, THEODORE. 1984. *The Black Power Imperative.* New York: Faulkner.

DAHL, ROBERT. 1960. *Who Governs.* New Haven, CT: Yale University Press.

DAHRENDORF, RALF. 1939. *Class Conflict in Industrial Society.* Stanford, CA: Stanford University Press.

DANIELS, ROGER, AND HARRY KITANO. 1970. *American Racism.* Englewood Cliffs, NJ: Prentice Hall.

DANZGER, HERBERT. 1989. *Returning to Tradition.* New Haven, CT: Yale University Press.

DASHEFSKY, ARNOLD, ed. 1976. *Ethnic Identity in Society.* Chicago: Rand McNally.

DAVIS, JEROME. 1967. *The Russian Immigrant.* New York: Arno Press.

DAVIS, KINGSLEY, AND WILBERT E. MOORE. 1945. "Some Principles of Stratification." *American Sociological Review* 10: 242–249.

DAVISSON, WILLIAM, AND JOHN J. UHRAN, JR. 1976. "Modeling and Simulation: A Systems Science Approach." Mimeo. Notre Dame, IN: University of Notre Dame.

DELEON, SHIRLEY. 1974. *Puerto Ricans in America.* Chicago: Claretian.

DELORIA, VINE, JR. 1969. *Custer Died for Your Sins: An Indian Manifesto.* New York: Avon.

DEVOS, GEORGE, AND LOLA ROMANUCCI-ROSS. 1975. *Ethnic Identity.* Palo Alto, CA: Mayfield.

DINNERSTEIN, LEONARD, AND FREDERICK C. JAHER. 1977. *Uncertain Americans.* New York: Oxford University Press.

DINNERSTEIN, LEONARD, ROGER NICHOLS, AND DAVID REIMERS. 1990. *Natives and Strangers,* 2nd ed. New York: Oxford University Press.

DINNERSTEIN, LEONARD, AND DAVID M. REIMERS. 1988. *Ethnic Americans,* 3rd ed. New York: Harper & Row.

"Disguised Blessing." 1958. *Newsweek,* December 29, p. 23.

DOLLARD, JOHN. 1937. *Caste and Class in a Southern Town.* New Haven, CT: Yale University Press.

DOLLARD, JOHN, et al. 1939. *Frustration and Aggression.* New Haven, CT: Yale University Press.

DRAPER, THEODORE. 1957. *The Roots of American Communism.* New York: Viking Press.

DRAPER, THEODORE. 1960. *American Communism and Soviet Russia.* New York: Viking Press.

DURKHEIM, EMILE. 1964. *The Study of Sociology.* New York: Free Press.

DYE, THOMAS. 1971. *The Politics of Equality.* Indianapolis, IN: Bobbs-Merrill.

DYE, THOMAS, 1998. *Understanding Public Policy,* 9th ed. Upper Saddle River, NJ: Prentice Hall.

EASTON, DAVID. 1965. *A Framework for Political Analysis.* Englewood Cliffs, NJ: Prentice Hall.

EDWARDS, GEORGE. 1982. *The Politics of the Urban Frontier.* New York: Institute of Human Relations Press.

EHRLICHMAN, JOHN. 1982. "An American Struggle." *Parade,* March 14, pp. 4–8.

ESSIEN-UDOM, E. U. 1962. *Black Nationalism: A Search for an Identity in America.* Chicago: University of Chicago Press.

FAIRCHILD, HENRY. 1911. *Greek Immigration.* New Haven: Yale University Press.

FAIRCHILD, H. 1949. "Public Opinion and Immigration." *Annals of the Academy of Political and Social Sciences* 262 (March): 185–192.

FARLEY, REYNOLDS, AND WILLIAM H. FREY. 1992. *Changes in the Segregation of Whites from Blacks During the 1980s: Small Steps Toward a More Racially Integrated Society.* Ann Arbor: Population Studies Center, University of Michigan.

FEAGIN, JOE R., AND CLAIRICE FEAGIN. 1996. *Racial and Ethnic Relations,* 5th ed. Englewood Cliffs, NJ: Prentice Hall.

FEAVER, G. 1975. "Wounded Knee and the New Tribalism." *Encounter,* March.

FEDERAL WRITER'S PROJECT. 1969. *The Italians of New York.* New York: Arno Press.

FICHTER, JOSEPH. 1954. *Social Relations in an Urban Parish.* Urbana: University of Illinois Press.

FITZPATRICK, DANIEL R. 1953. *As I Saw It.* New York: Simon & Schuster.

FITZPATRICK, JOSEPH P. 1968. "Intermarriage of Puerto Ricans in New York City." *American Journal of Sociology* 71: 395–406.

FITZPATRICK, JOSEPH P. 1971. *Puerto Rican Americans.* Englewood Cliffs, NJ: Prentice Hall.

FOGELSON, ROBERT M. 1977. *Big City Police.* Cambridge, MA: Harvard University Press.

FONER, PHILIP S., AND JAMES ALLEN, eds. 1987. *American Communism: A Documentary History, 1919–1929.* Philadelphia: Temple University Press.

FONER, PHILIP S., AND HERBERT SHAPIRO, eds. 1991. *American Communism and Black Americans: A Documentary History: 1930–1934.* Philadelphia: Temple University Press.

FORBES, JACK. 1964. *The Indians in America's Past.* Englewood Cliffs, NJ: Prentice Hall.

FORD, JAMES. 1938. *The Negro and the Democratic Front.* New York: International Publishers.

FOSTER, WILLIAM Z. 1952. *History of the Communist Party in the United States.* New York: International Publishers.

FOX-PIVEN, FRANCES, AND HOWARD CLOWARD. 1971. *Regulating the Poor.* New York: Random House.

FOX-PIVEN, FRANCES, AND HOWARD CLOWARD. 1975. *The Politics of Turmoil.* New York: Vintage.

FREDERICKSON, GEORGE M. 1995. *Black Liberation.* New York: Oxford University Press.

FREEMAN, HAROLD. 1982. *Toward Socialism in America.* Cambridge, MA: Schenkman.

"Fresh Faces for an Old Struggle." 1983. *Time,* August 22, pp. 32–33.

FREUD, SIGMUND. 1950. *Group Psychology and the Analysis of the Ego.* New York: Boni and Liverright.

FUCHS, LAWRENCE H., ed. 1968. *American Ethnic Politics.* New York: Harper & Row.

FUCHS, LAWRENCE. 1990. *The American Kaleidoscope: Race, Ethnicity, and Civil Culture.* Hanover, NH: University Press of New England.

FURNISS, N. F. 1960. *The Mormon Conflict: 1850–1859.* New Haven, CT: Yale University Press.

FUSHFIELD, DANIEL R. 1973. *The Basic Economics of the Urban Racial Crisis.* New York: Holt, Rinehart & Winston.

GALLAGHER, CHARLES A. 1999. *Rethinking the Color Line.* Mountain View, CA.: Mayfield.

GLAZER, NATHAN. 1961. *The Social Basis of American Communism.* New York: Harcourt, Brace & World.

GLAZER, NATHAN, AND DANIEL MOYNIHAN. 1975. *Ethnicity: Theory and Experience.* Cambridge, MA: Harvard University Press.

GONZALES, JUAN. 1996. *Racial and Ethnic Groups in America,* 3rd ed. Dubuque, IA: Kendall/Hunt.

GORDON, DAVID. 1977. *Problems in Political Economy and Urban Perspectives.* Lexington, MA: D. C. Heath.

GORDON, MILTON. 1964. *Assimilation in American Life.* New York: Oxford University Press.

GOSNELL, HAROLD F. 1987. *Machine Politics: Chicago Model.* Chicago: University of Chicago Press.

GRANT, JOANNE. 1970. *Black Protest: History, Documents and Analysis, 1600 to Present.* New York: Fawcett.

GREENE, VICTOR R. 1987. *American Immigrant Leaders: 1800–1910.* Baltimore: Johns Hopkins University Press.

GREENSTEIN, FREDERICK. 1970. *The American Party System and the American People.* Englewood Cliffs, NJ: Prentice Hall.

GREER, EDWARD. 1971. *Black Liberation Politics.* Boston: Allyn & Bacon.

HAGAN, WILLIAM. 1949. *American Indians.* Chicago: University of Chicago Press.

HAMAMOTO, DARRELL. 1992. "Black-Korean Conflict in Los Angeles." *Z Magazine,* July 1, pp. 61–62.

HANDLIN, OSCAR. 1951. *The Uprooted.* Boston: Little, Brown.

HARDY, B. CARMON. 1992. *Solemn Covenant: The Mormon Polygamous Passage.* Chicago: University of Illinois Press.

HARLICH, WASYL. 1933. *Ukrainians in the United States.* Chicago: University of Chicago Press.

HAWKINS, HUGH. 1974. *Booker T. Washington and His Critics.* Lexington, MA: D. C. Heath.

HENRY, NICHOLAS. 1980. *Governing at the Grass Roots.* Englewood Cliffs, NJ: Prentice Hall.

HERNSTEIN, RICHARD. 1971, "I.Q." *Atlantic Monthly,* September, pp. 43–64.

HERSHKOWITZ, LEO. 1978. *Tweed's New York: Another Look.* New York: Anchor Press/Doubleday.

HESS, STEPHEN, AND SANDY NORTHROP. 1996. *Drawn and Quartered: The History of American Political Cartoons.* Montgomery, AL: Elliott and Clark.

HIGHAM, CHARLES. 1985. *American Swastika.* New York: Doubleday.

HIRD, JOHN A. 1995. *Controversies in American Public Policy.* New York: St. Martin's Press.

HIRSHON, STANLEY. 1969. *The Lion and the Lord.* New York: Knopf.

HOFFER, ERIC. 1963. *True Believer.* New York: Harper and Row.

HOFFMAN, EDWARD. 1991. *Despite All Odds: The Story of Lubavitch.* New York: Simon & Schuster.

HOLLIFIELD, JAMES. 1989. "Migrants to Citizens: The Politics of Immigration in France and the United States." Paper delivered at the Annual Meeting of the American Political Science Association, Atlanta, August 31–September 3.

HOSOKAWA, WILLIAM. 1969. *Nisei: The Quiet Americans.* New York: William Morrow.

HOSTETLER, JOHN A. 1952. *Amish Life.* Scottsdale, PA: Herald Press.

HOSTETLER, JOHN A. 1993. *Amish Society,* 4th ed. Baltimore: Johns Hopkins University Press.

HOWARD, JOHN R., ed. 1983. *Awakening Minorities.* New Brunswick, NJ: Transaction Books.

HOWE, IRVING. 1976. *World of Our Fathers.* New York: Simon & Schuster.

HOWE, IRVING. 1985. *Socialism in America.* New York: Harcourt Brace Jovanovich.

HOWE, IRVING, AND LEWIS COSER. 1957. *The American Communist Party.* Boston: Beacon.

HUCKFELDT, R. ROBERT. 1983. "The Social Contexts of Ethnic Politics." *American Politics Quarterly* 11, 1 (January): 91–123.

HURH, WON MOO. 1977. *Comparative Study of Korean Immigrants in the United States: A Typological Approach.* San Francisco: R. and E. Research Associates.

"Immigration Law Revised: May Be Derailed in House." 1982. *Washington Post,* December 5, pp. A12, A15.

"Intermarried . . . With Children." 1993. *Time Special Issue* 142 (November): 64.

IORRIZZO, LUCIANO, AND SALVATORE MONDELLO. 1971. *The Italian Americans.* New York: Twayne.

JACOBSON, SIMON. 1995. *Towards a Meaningful Life: The Wisdom of the Rebbe.* New York: William Morrow.

JAMES, M. ANNETTE, ed. 1992. *The State of Native America: Genocide, Colonization and Resistance.* Boston: South End Press.

JANOWSKY, OSCAR. 1964. *The American Jews: A Reappraisal.* Philadelphia: Jewish Publication Society of America.

JENSEN, ARTHUR. 1969. "How Much Can We Boost IQ and Scholastic Achievement?" *Harvard Educational Review* 39 (Winter): 1–123.

JONES, M. 1960. *American Immigration.* Chicago: University of Chicago Press.

JOSEPHY, ALVIN, JR., ed. 1971. *Red Power.* New York: McGraw-Hill.

KATZ, DANIEL, AND KENNETH BRALEY. 1958, "Verbal Stereotypes and Racial Prejudice." In Eleanor Mausby, Theodore Newcomb, and Eugene Hartley, eds., *Readings in Social Psychology,* pp. 40–46. New York: Holt, Rinehart & Winston.

KILLIAN, LEWIS M. 1975. *The Impossible Revolution, Phase II: Black Power and the American Dream.* New York: Random House.

KIM, HYUNG-CHAU, ed. 1977. *The Korean Diaspora.* Santa Barbara, CA: ABC-CLIO.

KING, MARTIN LUTHER, JR. 1958. *Stride Toward Freedom: The Montgomery Story.* New York: Harper & Brothers.

KING, MARTIN LUTHER, JR. 1986. "Letter from a Birmingham Jail." *American Visions* (January/February): 52–59.

"Kingdom Come." 1997. *Time,* August 4, pp. 48–59.

KINLOCH, GRAHAM. 1974. *The Dynamics of Race Relations: A Sociological Analysis.* New York: McGraw-Hill.

KINLOCH, GRAHAM. 1979. *Sociology of Minority Group Relations.* Englewood Cliffs, NJ: Prentice Hall.

KITANO, HARRY. 1976. *Japanese-Americans: The Evolution of a Subculture.* Englewood Cliffs, NJ: Prentice Hall.

KITANO, HARRY. 1997. *Race Relations,* 5th ed. Upper Saddle River, NJ: Prentice Hall.

KIVISTO, PETER. 1995. *Americans All.* Belmont, CA: Wadsworth.

KLEG, MILTON. 1993. *Hate, Prejudice, and Racism.* Albany: State University of New York Press.

KOTTAK, CONRAD PHILLIP, AND KATHRYN A. KOZAITIS. 1999. *On Being Different.* Boston: McGraw-Hill.

KRAYBILL, DONALD. 1989. *The Riddle of the Amish Culture.* Baltimore: Johns Hopkins University Press.

KRAYBILL, DONALD, AND MARC OLSHAN, eds. 1994. *The Amish Struggle with Modernity.* Hanover, NH: University Press of New England.

KRITZ, MARY M. 1983. *U.S. Immigration and Refugee Policy: Global and Domestic Issues.* Lexington, MA: Lexington Books.

KUNG, SHIEN WOO. 1962. *Chinese in American Life.* Seattle: University of Washington Press.

KUROKAWA, MINAKO, ed. 1970. *Minority Responses.* New York: Random House.

LAUNIUS, ROGER. 1988. *Joseph Smith III: Pragmatic Prophet.* Urbana: University of Illinois Press.

LAUNIUS, ROGER, AND LINDA THATCHER, eds. 1994. *Differing Visions: Dissenters in Mormon History.* Urbana: University of Illinois Press.

LEAGUE OF WOMEN VOTERS. 1981. "Open Door Policy for Voting Rights." *National Voter* (Spring): 1–2.

LEHRER, BRIAN. 1988. *The Korean Americans.* New York: Chelsea House.

LEMAY, MICHAEL. 1985. *The Struggle for Influence.* Lanham, MD: University Press of America.

LEMAY, MICHAEL. 1987. *From Open Door to Dutch Door.* New York: Praeger.

LEMAY, MICHAEL. 1989. *The Gatekeepers.* New York: Praeger.

LEMAY, MICHAEL. 1994. *Anatomy of a Public Policy.* New York: Praeger.

LEVINE, EDWARD M. 1966. *The Irish and the Irish Politicians.* Notre Dame, IN: University of Notre Dame Press.

LEVINE, ROBERT A., AND DONALD CAMPBELL. 1972. *Ethnocentrism.* New York: Wiley.

LEVY, BURTON, ed. 1968. *Riots and Rebellion: Civil Violence in the Urban Community.* Beverly Hills, CA: Sage Publications.

LEVY, MARK, AND MICHAEL KRAMER. 1973. *The Ethnic Factor: How American Minorities Decide Elections.* New York: Simon & Schuster.

LEWIS, OSCAR. 1968. *A Study of Slum Culture.* New York: Random House.

LEWIS, RUPERT. 1988. *Marcus Garvey: Anti-Colonial Champion.* Trenton, NJ: Africa World Press.

LIEBERMAN, ROBERT C. 1998. *Shifting the Color Line.* Cambridge, MA: Harvard University Press.

LIEBERSON, STANLEY. 1980. *A Piece of the Pie.* Berkeley: University of California Press.

LIEBMAN, CHARLES. 1973. *The Ambivalent American Jew.* Philadelphia: Jewish Publication Society of America.

LINCOLN, C. ERIC. 1994. *The Black Muslims in America,* 3rd ed. Trenton, NJ: Africa World Press.

LIND, A. W., ed. 1955. *Race Relations in World Perspective.* Honolulu: University of Hawaii Press.

LINTON, RALPH. 1936. *The Study of Man.* New York: Appleton-Century-Crofts.

LIPSET, SEYMOUR M., AND EARL RAAB. 1995. *Jews and the American Scene.* Cambridge, MA: Harvard University Press.

LIPSKY, MICHAEL. 1968. "Protest as a Political Resource." *American Political Science Review* (December): 1144–1158.

LIPSKY, MICHAEL. 1970. *Law and Order Police Encounters.* Chicago: Aldine.

LITT, EDGAR. 1970. *Ethnic Politics in America.* Glenview, IL: Scott, Foresman.

LOMAX, LOUIS. 1962. *The Negro Revolt.* New York: Harper.

LOPATA, HELEN Z. 1976. *Polish-Americans.* Englewood Cliffs, NJ: Prentice Hall.

LYMAN, EDWARD L. 1996. *San Bernardino: The Rise and Fall of a California Community.* Salt Lake City, Utah: Signature Books.

MAGIL, A. B., AND HENRY STEVENS. 1938. *The Perils of Fascism.* New York: International Publishers.

MARDEN, CHARLES, AND GLADYS MEYER. 1968. *Minorities in American Society.* New York: Van Nostrand.

MARGER, MARTIN N. 1997. *Race and Ethnic Relations,* 4th ed. Belmont, CA: Wadsworth.

MARX, HERBERT, ed. 1973. *The American Indian: A Rising Ethnic Force.* New York: W. H. Wilson.

MATHEWS, BASIL. 1949. *Booker T. Washington.* London: SCM Press.

MATHIAS, CHARLES MCC. 1981. "Ethnic Groups and Foreign Policy." *Foreign Affairs,* July 17, pp. 975–998.

MATRAS, JUDAH. 1975. *Social Inequality, Stratification, and Mobility.* Englewood Cliffs, NJ: Prentice Hall.

MAUSS, ARMAND. 1994. *The Angel and the Beehive: The Mormon Struggle with Assimilation.* Urbana: University of Illinois Press.

MCCLELLAN, GRANT S., ed. 1981. *Immigrants, Refugees and U.S. Policy.* New York: H. W. Wilson.

MCLEMORE, DALE S. 1983. *Racial and Ethnic Relations in America,* 2nd ed. Boston: Allyn & Bacon.

MEINIG, D. W. 1965. "The Mormon Cultural Region: Strategies and Patterns in the Geography of the American West, 1847–1964." *Annals of the Association of American Geographers* 55, 2 (June): 217–218.

MELENDY, H. BRETT. 1980. "Filipinos." In Stephen Thernstrom, ed., *Harvard Encyclopedia of American Ethnic Groups,* pp. 354–362. Cambridge, MA: Harvard University Press.

MENCARELLI, JAMES, AND STEVE SEVERIN. 1975. *Protest 3: Red, Black, and Brown Experience in America.* Grand Rapids, MI: William B. Eerdmans.

MERTON, ROBERT. 1949. "Discrimination and the American Creed." In R. M. MacIver, ed., *Discrimination and National Welfare,* pp. 99–126. New York: Harper & Row.

MEYER, MICHAEL. 1995. "No Sex, Just Sales." *Newsweek,* July 17, pp. 39–40.

MIN, PYONG GAP, ed. 1995. *Asian Americans.* Newbury Park, CA: Sage.

MINTZ, JEROME R. 1968. *The Legends of Hasidim.* Chicago: University of Chicago Press.

MONTERO, DARRELL. 1979. *Vietnamese Americans.* Boulder, CO: Westview Press.

MONTGOMERY, PATRICIA A. 1994. *The Hispanic Population of the United States.* Current Population Reports, P-20, N. 475. Washington, DC: U.S. Government Printing Office.

MOORE, JOAN. 1970. *Mexican Americans.* Englewood Cliffs, NJ: Prentice Hall.

MORGANTHAU, TONI. 1993. "America: Still a Melting Pot." *Newsweek,* August 9, pp. 16–25.

MORRISON, TONI. 1993. "On the Back of Blacks." *Time Special Issue* 142 (November): 57.

MOSKOS, CHARLES C. 1980. *Greek Americans.* Englewood Cliffs, NJ: Prentice Hall.

MURPHY, CARYL. 1984. "Sanctuary: How Churches Defy Immigration Law." *Washington Post Weekly Edition,* September 17, pp. 8–9.

NAKAYAMA, THOMAS K., AND JUDITH N. MARTIN, eds. 1999. *Whiteness: The Communication of Social Identity.* Thousand Oaks, CA: Sage.

NELLI, HUMBERT S. 1970. *Italians in Chicago, 1830–1930.* New York: Oxford University Press.

NELSON, DALE. 1977. "Ethnic Sources of Non-Electoral Participation in American Urban Setting." Paper presented at the American Political Science Association Meeting, Washington, DC, September.

NELSON, JOHN. 1963. *Fifty Years on the Trail.* Norman: University of Oklahoma Press.

NOEL, DONALD. 1968. "A Theory of the Origin of Ethnic Stratification." *Social Problems* (Fall): 157–172.

NOLT, STEVEN M. 1992. *A History of the Amish.* Intercourse, PA: Good Books.

O'DEA, THOMAS F. 1957. *The Mormons.* Chicago: University of Chicago Press.

O'GRADY, JOSEPH D. 1973. *How the Irish Became Americans.* New York: Twayne.

OLSON, JAMES S. 1994. *The Ethnic Dimension in American History.* New York: St. Martin's Press.

OMI, MICHAEL, AND HOWARD WINANT. 1994. *Racial Formation in the United States,* 2nd ed. New York: Routledge.

O'NEAL, JAMES, AND G. A. WARNER. 1947. *American Communism.* Westport, CT: Greenwood Press.

"Open Door Policy for Voting Rights." 1981. *National Voter* (Spring): 1–2.

ORFIELD, GARY, AND FRANKLIN MONTFORT. 1992. "Status of School Desegregation: The Next Generation." *New York Times,* January 19, p. E5.

PALMORE, ERDMAN B. 1962. "Ethnophaulism and Ethnocentrism." *American Journal of Sociology* 67 (January): 442–445.

PARK, ROBERT E. 1939. "The Nature of Race Relations." In Edgard T. Thompson, ed. *Race Relations and Race Problems,* pp. 3–45. Durham, NC: Duke University Press.

PARK, ROBERT E. 1950. *Race and Culture.* New York: Free Press.

PARK, ROBERT E., AND ERNEST BURGESS. 1924. *Introduction to the Science of Sociology.* Chicago: University of Chicago Press.

PARRILLO, VINCENT. 1985. *Strangers to These Shores.* New York: Wiley.

PARRILLO, VINCENT, ed. 1991. *Rethinking Today's Minorities.* New York: Greenwood Press.

PARRILLO, VINCENT. 1996. *Diversity in America.* Thousand Oaks, CA: Pine Forge Press.

PARSONS, TALCOTT. 1953. "A Revised Analytical Approach to the Theory of Social Stratification." In Reinhard Bendix and Seymour Lipset, eds., *Class Status and Power: A Reader in Social Stratification.* New York: Free Press.

PARSONS, TALCOTT, AND KENNETH CLARK. 1966. *The Negro American.* Boston: Beacon Press.

PEACH, C. 1980. "Which Triple Melting Pot? A Re-Examination of Ethnic Intermarriage in New Haven, 1900–1950." *Ethnic and Racial Studies* 3: 1–16.

PERRY, BRUCE. 1992. *Malcolm: The Life of a Man Who Changed Black America.* Barrytown, NY: Station Hill Press.

PERRY, THERESA. 1996. *Teaching Malcolm X.* New York: Routledge.

PETTIGREW, THOMAS, et al. 1980. *Prejudice.* Cambridge, MA: Harvard University Press.

PIERCE, RICHARD L. 1973. *The Polish in America.* Chicago: Claretian Press.

"Playing a Different Tune." 1993. *Newsweek,* June 28, pp. 30–31.

"Police and Minorities." 1983. *U.S.A. Today,* January 5, p. A10.

POWELL, THOMAS. 1993. *The Persistence of Racism in America.* Lanham, MD: Rowman and Littlefield.

POWER, PAUL F. 1984. "Ethnic Groups and the National Interest." Paper presented at the American Political Science Association Meeting, Washington, DC, September.

PRPIC, GEORGE. 1978. *South Slavic Immigration in America.* Boston: Twayne.

PRUCHA, FRANCIS P. 1990. *Documents of United States Indian Policy.* Lincoln: University of Nebraska Press.

"Quebec Voters Return Separatists to Power." 1994. *San Bernardino Sun,* September 13, p. A8.

"Raids Nab High-Pay Aliens, Make Jobs, Outrage Clergy." 1982. *Washington Post,* May 2, p. A10.

READER'S DIGEST. 1995. *Through Indian Eyes.* Pleasantsville, NY: Reader's Digest.

RECORD, WILSON. 1951. *The Negro and the Communist Party.* Chapel Hill: University of North Carolina Press.

REUTER, E. B. 1934. *Race and Cultural Contacts.* New York: McGraw-Hill.

REUTER, E. B., AND C. W. HART. 1963. *Introduction to Sociology.* New York: McGraw-Hill.

RIIS, JACOB. 1971. *How the Other Half Lives.* New York: Dover.

RINGLE, KEN. 1981. "What Did You Do Before the War, Dad?" *Washington Post Magazine,* December 6, pp. 54–62.

RISCHIN, MOSES. 1976. *Immigration and the American Tradition.* Indianapolis, IN: Bobbs-Merrill.

ROSE, ARNOLD. 1950. "The Causes of Prejudice." In Francis E. Merrill, ed., *Social Problems.* New York: Knopf.

ROSE, ARNOLD. 1951. *The Roots of Prejudice.* Paris: UNESCO.

ROSE, HAROLD. 1971. *The Black Ghetto.* New York: McGraw-Hill.

ROSE, PETER. 1990. *They and We.* New York: McGraw-Hill.

ROSE, PETER. 1993. *Interminority Affairs in the United States: Pluralism at the Crossroads.* Thousand Oaks, CA: Sage.

ROSEN, BERNARD, AND H. J. CROCKETT, JR. 1969. *Achievement in American Society.* Cambridge, MA: Schenman.

ROSS, BERNARD H., MYRON A. LEVINE, AND MURRAY S. STEDMAN. 1991. *Urban Politics: Power in Metropolitan America,* 4th ed. Itasca, IL: F. E. Peacock.

ROSTOW, EUGENE. 1945. "Our Worst Wartime Mistake." *Harper's Magazine,* September, pp. 193–201.

ROTHENBERG, PAULA. 1998. *Race, Class, and Gender in the United States,* 4th ed. New York: St. Martin's Press.

RUCHELMAN, LEONARD. 1973. *Who Rules the Police?* New York: New York University Press.

SALES, WILLIAM H., JR. 1994. *From Civil Rights to Black Liberation: Malcolm X and the Organization of Afro-American Unity.* Boston: South End Press.

SALVEMINI, GAETANO. 1977. *Italian Fascist Activities in the United States.* New York: Center for Migration Studies.

SCHAEFER, RICHARD. 1998. *Racial and Ethnic Groups,* 7th ed. New York: HarperCollins.

SCHAUFFLER, RICHARD. 1994. "Children of Immigrants." *National Forum: Phi Kappa Phi Journal* 74, no. 3 (Summer).

SCHERMERHORN, RICHARD. 1949. *These Our People: Minorities in American Culture.* Boston: D. C. Heath.

SCHERMERHORN, RICHARD A. 1970. *Comparative Ethnic Relations.* New York: Random House.

SCHMIDT, RONALD. 1989. "The Political Incorporation of Recent Immigrants: A Framework for Research and Analysis." Paper presented at the Annual Meeting of the American Political Science Association, Atlanta, August 31–September 3.

SCHMIDT, STEFFEN, MACK SHELLY II, AND BARBARA BARDES. 1997. *American Government and Politics Today.* Belmont, CA: West/Wadsworth.

SCHON, ALVIN. 1969. *Explorations of Social Policy.* New York: Basic Books.

SCUROS, M. 1982. "The Southwest Voter Registration Education Project." *Citizen Participation* 4, 1 (September).

"Seeking Votes and Clout." 1983. *Time,* August 22, pp. 20–31.

SEWELL, TONY. 1990. *Garvey's Children: The Legacy of Marcus Garvey.* Trenton, NJ: Africa World Press.

SHAHEEN, JACK. 1984. *The T.V. Arab.* Bowling Green, OH: Bowling Green University Press.

SIGLER, JAY A. 1975. *American Rights Policy.* Homewood, IL: Dorsey Press.

SIMPSON, GEORGE E., AND J. M. YINGER. 1965. *Racial and Cultural Minorities.* New York: Harper & Row.

SINDLER, ALLAN, ed. 1977. *America in the Seventies: Problems, Policies and Politics.* Boston: Little, Brown.

SINDLER, ALAN. 1978. *Bakke, DeFunis, and Minority Admissions.* New York: Longman.

SMITH, ROGERS M. 1997. *Civic Ideals.* New Haven, CT: Yale University Press.

SNIPP, MATTHEW. 1989. *American Indians: The First of This Land.* New York: Russell Sage Foundation.

SOLOUTOS, THEODORE. 1964. *The Greeks in the United States.* Cambridge, MA: Harvard University Press.

SPEAR, ALLAN H. 1967. *Black Chicago: The Making of a Negro Ghetto.* Chicago: University of Chicago Press.

SPIEGEL, STEVEN. 1984. "Ethnic Politics and the Formulation of U.S. Policy Towards the Arab-Israeli Dispute." Paper presented at the Annual Meeting of the American Political Science Association, Washington, DC, September.

STANLEY, FRANCES. 1966. *The New World Refugee: The Cuban Exodus.* New York: Church World Service.

STANLEY, HAROLD, AND RICHARD NIEMI. 1995. *Vital Statistics on American Politics,* 5th ed. Washington, DC: CQ Press.

STEDMAN, MURRAY. 1972. *The Police and the Community.* Baltimore: Johns Hopkins University Press.

STEINER, STAN. 1969. *La Raza.* New York: Harper & Row.

STODDARD, ELLWYN. 1973. *Mexican Americans.* New York: Random House.

STODDARD, LOTHROP. 1931. *Master of Manhattan: The Life of Richard Croker.* New York: Longman, Green.

STOWERS, GENIE. 1989. "Cuban Political Incorporation into Miami Politics: A Model for the 'New Immigrants.'" Paper presented at the Annual Meeting of the American Political Science Association, Atlanta, August 31–September 3.

"Success Story: Outwhiting the Whites." 1971. *Newsweek,* June 21, pp. 24–25.

SUMNER, WILLIAM G. 1906. *Folkways.* Boston: Ginn.

TABB, WILLIAM. 1970. *The Political Economy of the Black Ghetto.* New York: W. W. Norton.

TAUBER, KARL, AND ALMA TAUBER. 1964. "The Negro as an Immigrant Group: Recent Trends in Racial and Ethnic Segregation in Chicago." *American Journal of Sociology* 69: 374–382.

TAUBER, KARL, AND ALMA TAUBER. 1965. *Negroes in Cities.* Chicago: Aldine.

TERRY, DON. 1994. "Minister Farrakhan: Conservative Militant." *New York Times,* March 3, pp. A1, A10.

"The American Underclass." 1977. *Time,* August 19, pp. 14–27.

"The New Immigrants." 1980. *Newsweek,* July 7, pp. 26–31.

"The New Slave Trade." 1993. *Newsweek,* June 21, pp. 34–41.

THERNSTROM, STEPHEN. 1980. *The Harvard Encyclopedia of American Ethnic Groups.* Cambridge, MA: Harvard University Press.

THOMAS, WILLIAM, AND FLORIAN ZNANICKI. 1977. "The Polish American Community." In Leonard Dinnerstein and Frederick Jaher, *Uncertain Americans.* New York: Oxford University Press.

THOMPSON, WILLIAM, 1996. *Native-American Issues.* Santa Barbara, CA: ABC-CLIO.

TURNER, JONATHAN H., AND EDNA BONACICH. 1980. "Toward a Composite Theory of Middleman Minorities." *Ethnicity* 7: 144–158.

TUSSEY, JEAN, ed. 1970. *Eugene V. Debs Speaks.* New York: Pathfinder Press.

U.S. COMMISSION ON CIVIL RIGHTS. 1975. *Report of the Commission.* Washington, DC: U.S. Government Printing Office.

U.S. DEPARTMENT OF COMMERCE. BUREAU OF THE CENSUS. 1990. *1990 Census of Population: Social and Economic Characteristics.* Washington, DC: U.S. Government Printing Office.

U.S. DEPARTMENT OF COMMERCE. BUREAU OF THE CENSUS. 1993. *Statistical Abstract of the United States, 1993.* Washington, DC: U.S. Government Printing Office.

U.S. DEPARTMENT OF COMMERCE. BUREAU OF THE CENSUS. 1998. *Statistical Abstract of the United States, 1998.* Washington, DC: U.S. Government Printing Office.

U.S. DEPARTMENT OF COMMERCE. BUREAU OF THE CENSUS. 1995. *Current Population Reports. P-25.* Washington, DC: U.S. Government Printing Office.

U.S. DEPARTMENT OF INTERIOR. BUREAU OF INDIAN AFFAIRS. 1991. *American Indians Today,* 3rd ed. Washington, DC: U.S. Department of the Interior, Bureau of Indian Affairs.

U.S. DEPARTMENT OF JUSTICE. IMMIGRATION AND NATURALIZATION SERVICE. 1994. *Statistical Yearbook of the INS.* Washington, DC: U.S. Government Printing Office.

U.S. NATIONAL ADVISORY COMMISSION ON CIVIL DISORDER. 1968. *Disorders: Report of the Commission.* New York: Bantam.

U.S. PRESIDENT'S SELECT COMMISSION ON IMMIGRATION AND REFUGEE POLICY (SCIRP). 1981a. *U.S. Immigration Policy and the National Interest: Final Report.* Washington, DC: U.S. Government Printing Office.

U.S. PRESIDENT'S SELECT COMMISSION ON IMMIGRATION AND REFUGEE POLICY. 1981b. *U.S. Immigration Policy and the National Interest: Staff Report.* Washington, DC: U.S. Government Printing Office.

VAN DEN BERGHE, PIERRE. 1971. *Race and Racism.* New York: Wiley.

VANDER SLIK, JACK, ed. 1980. *Black Conflict with White America.* Columbus, OH: Charles E. Merrill.

VANDERZANDEN, JAMES. 1983. *American Minority Relations.* New York: Ronald Press.

VECOLI, RUDOLPH, AND JOY K. LINTELMAN. 1984. *A Century of American Immigration, 1884–1984.* Minneapolis, MN: University of Minnesota Continuing Education and Extension.

VILLARREAL, ROBERTO. 1984. "Ethnic Leadership in American Foreign Policy: The Hispanic Experience." Paper presented at the American Political Science Association Meeting, Washington, DC, September.

VOLKERSZ, WILLEM. 1994. *National Forum: Phi Kappa Phi Journal* 74, no. 3 (Summer).

WARNER, LLOYD, AND LEO SROLE. 1945. *The Social System of American Ethnic Groups.* New Haven, CT: Yale University Press.

WARREN, FRANK A. 1966. *Liberals and Communism.* Bloomington: Indiana University Press.

WASHINGTON, BOOKER T. 1977. *Up from Slavery.* New York: Dell.

WEATHERFORD, J. 1991. *Native Roots: How the Indians Enriched America.* New York: Fawcett.

WEBER, MAX. 1946. *Essays in Sociology.* Hans Gerth and C. Wright Mills, trans. New York: Oxford University Press.

WEINBERG, DANIEL. 1977. "Ethnic Identity in Industrial Cleveland, 1900–1920." *Ohio History* 86 (Summer): 13.

WEINSTOCK, S. ALEXANDER. 1963. "Role Elements: A Link Between Acculturation and Occupational Status." *British Journal of Sociology* 14: 144–149.

WELCH, SUSAN, et al. 1998. *American Government,* 6th ed. Belmont, CA: Wadsworth.

WENGER, JOHN. 1961. *The Mennonites in Indiana and Michigan.* Scottsdale, PA: Herald Press.

WESSEL, B. B. 1931. *An Ethnic Survey of Woonsocket, Rhode Island.* Chicago: University of Chicago Press.

"What Americans Think: A Black or a Woman Does Better Today Than a Catholic in 1960." 1983. *Washington Post Weekly Edition,* November 21, p. 42.

WHITE, JOHN. 1991. *Black Leadership in America,* 2nd ed. New York: Longman.

WIGGINS, ROSALIND COBB, ed. 1996. *Captain Paul Cuffe's Logs and Letters, 1808–1817.* Washington, DC: Howard University Press.

WILLIAMS, ROBIN JR. 1947. *The Reduction of Intergroup Tension.* New York: Social Science Research Council.

WILLIAMS, ROBIN. 1994. "The Sociology of Ethnic Conflict: Comparative Perspectives." *Annual Review of Sociology* 20: 49–79.

WILSON, STEPHEN. 1978. *Informal Groups.* Englewood Cliffs, NJ: Prentice Hall.

WILSON, WILLIAM J. 1973. *Power, Racism and Privilege.* New York: Free Press.

WILSON, WILLIAM J. 1987. *The Truly Disadvantaged.* Chicago: University of Chicago Press.

WINKELMAN, MICHAEL. 1993. *Ethnic Relations in the United States.* Minneapolis, MN: West.

WIRTH, LOUIS. 1945. "The Problem of Minority Groups." In Ralph Linton, ed., *The Science of Man in the World Crisis.* Chicago: University of Chicago Press.

WIRTH, LOUIS. 1956. *The Ghetto.* Chicago: University of Chicago Press.

WRIGHT, LAWRENCE. 1994. "One Drop of Blood." *New Yorker,* July 25, pp. 46–50, 52–55.

WYNN, DANIEL WEBSTER. 1955. *The NAACP versus Negro Revolutionary Protest.* New York: Exposition Press.

ZANGWILL, ISRAEL. 1909. *The Melting Pot.* New York: Macmillan.

ZENNER, WALTER. 1991. *Minorities in the Middle: A Cross-Cultural Analysis.* Albany: State University of New York Press.

PHOTO CREDITS

AUTHOR INDEX

Alexander, Nicholas, 323n
Allen, James, 218, 221, 235n
Allport, Gordon, 5, 9, 25n, 197
Anderson, Charles, 25n
Armor, John, 76
Arrington, Leonard, 178n

Banton, Michael, 20–22, 24, 25n
Bardes, Barbara, 248, 323n
Barker, Lucius, 138n, 269, 323n
Barth, Ernest, 62n, 203n
Berle, Adolph, 25n
Berry, Brewton, 25n
Bettleheim, Bruno, 25n
Blalock, Hubert M., Jr., 62n
Bogardus, E. S., 25n, 62n
Bonacich, Edna, 25n, 36, 108n
Branch, Taylor, 269n
Brewster, Lawrence, 323n
Briggs, Cyril, 217
Brommel, Bernard, 235n
Brown, Dee, 62n
Bugelski, B. R., 62n
Bunch, Ralph, 218–219
Burma, John, 269n

Callow, Alexander B., Jr., 138n
Campbell, Donald (with Robert A. Levine), 25n
Carmichael, Stokeley (with Charles Hamilton), 250, 270n
Carson, Clayborne, 270n
Chavez, John, 270n
Cheng, Lucie (with Edna Bonacich), 108n
Cloward, Howard (with Frances Fox-Piven), 25n, 252
Cochran, Clarke (et al.), 323n
Collins, Barry, 25n
Constantine, J. Robert, 235n

Cornell, Stephen, 270n
Coughlin, Fr. Charles, 232
Cox, Oliver, 25n
Cross, Theodore, 235n

Dahrendorf, Ralf, 25n, 36
Davis, Jerome, 138n
Davis, Kingsley (with Wilber Moore), 25n
Davisson, William (with John Uhran), 62n
Debs, Eugene, 209–214, 235n
DeLeon, Daniel, 208–209
Dennis, Lawrence, 232
Dinnerstein, Leonard, 138n
Dollard, John, 25n
DuBois, W. E. B., 18, 134, 172, 173, 188
Durkheim, Emile, 25n
Dye, Thomas, 321n

Easton, David, 62n
Essien-Udom, E. U., 203n

Fairchild, Henry, 91
Farrakhan, Louis, 195
Feagin, Joe (with Clairice), 7, 25n, 109n
Fichter, Joseph, 1–3, 24
Fitzpatrick, Daniel, 62n
Fitzpatrick, Joseph, 138n
Fogelson, Robert, 321n
Foner, Philip S. (with James Allen), 235n
Ford, James, 220, 235n
Foster, William, 235n
Fox-Piven, Frances (with Howard Cloward), 25n, 252
Frederickson, George, 235n
Freud, Sigmund, 25n
Frey, W. H., 319n

Fuchs, Lawrence, 138n
Fushfield, Daniel, 25n

Garvey, Marcus, 18, 53, 144, 171–177, 217
Glazer, Nathan, 35, 214, 220, 222–223, 235n
Glick, E. C., 25n
Gonzales, Juan, Jr., 178n, 270n
Gordon, David, 298
Gordon, Milton, 20–22, 24n, 25n, 31–32, 34–35, 61n, 62n
Gosnell, Harold, 138n
Greenstein, Frederick, 50

Hamilton, Charles V. (with Stokeley Carmichael), 251, 270n
Hardy, B. Carmon, 178n
Haywood, Harry, 224
Hernstein, Richard, 25n
Higham, Charles, 235n
Hoffer, Eric, 196
Hoffman, Edward, 203n
Hosokawa, William, 108n, 109n
Hostetler, John A., 178n
Howe, Irving, 138n, 235n
Huckfeldt, R. Robert, 321n
Hurch, Won Moo, 108n

Jacobson, Simon, 203n
Jaher, F. C. (with Leonard Dinnerstein), 138n
James, M. Annette, 270n
Janowitz, Morris (with Bruno Bettelheim), 25n
Janowsky, Oscar, 203n
Jensen, Arthur, 25n
Jones, Mack (with Lucius Barker and Kathryn Tate), 270n, 323n
Josephy, Alvin, Jr., 270n

King, Martin Luther, Jr., 18, 59–60, 177, 244, 246, 269, 271n, 272–280
Kipling, Rupyard, 1–2
Kitano, Harry, 10, 12, 23, 25n, 45, 62n, 108n, 203n, 271n, 323n
Kivisto, Peter, 271n
Kottak, Conrad (with Kathryn Kozaitis), 62n
Kramer, Michael, 138n
Kraybill, Donald (with Marc Olshan), 178n

Launis, Roger, 178n
Lehrer, Brian, 108n
LeMay, Michael, 25n, 203n, 271n, 323n
Levine, Robert A. (with Donald Campbell), 25n
Levy, Burton, 321n
Levy, Mark (with Michael Kramer), 138n, 322n
Lewis, Rupert, 178n, 217n
Lieberman, Robert, 62n
Lieberson, Stanley, 31, 42–43, 62n, 138n, 323n

Lincoln, C. Eric, 203n
Lind, A. W., 62n
Lipsky, Michael, 55–59, 60, 62n, 323n
Litt, Edgar, 18, 45, 51–52, 54, 62n
Lloyd, Demarest, 228
Lopata, Helen, 138n

Magil, A. B. (with Henry Stevens), 228, 235n
Malcolm X, 188, 190–195
Marger, Martin, 23, 94, 178n, 271
Marx, Karl, 10, 25n
Matras, Judah, 25n
Mauss, Armand, 178n
McLemore, Dale, 33, 108n
Merton, Robert, 13
Min, Ryong Gap, 40
Mintz, Jerome, 203n
Misner, G., 321n
Moore, Wilbur (with Kingsley Davis), 25n
Morgan, Juliette, 242
Moskos, Charles, 108n, 138n
Moynihan, Daniel Patrick, 115
Muhammad, Elijah, 187

Nelli, Humbert, 121–122, 138n
Nelson, Dale, 320
Nelson, John, 154, 156
Nichols, R., 138n
Niederhoffer, A., 321n
Noel, Donald, 35, 62n
Northwood, L., 203n

Olshan, Marc, 178n

Palmore, Erdman B., 25n
Park, Robert E., 25n, 35, 36
Parrillo, Vincent, 36, 108n, 138n
Parsons, Talcott, 25n
Peach, C., 62n
Perry, Bruce, 203n
Plunkitt, George Washington, 51
Prpic, George, 138n
Prucha, Francis P., 178n

Record, Wilson, 235n
Reimer, David M. (with Leonard Dinnerstein), 138n
Reuter, E. B., 25n, 62n
Riis, Jacob, 118–119
Rinder, Irving, 35
Ringle, Ken, 108n
Rose, Peter, 1, 6–7, 14, 25n
Rosen, Bernard (with H. J. Crockett, Jr.), 33
Rostow, Eugene, 108n
Rothenberg, Paula, 323n

Sales, William H., 203n
Salvemini, Gaetano, 235n
Schaefer, Richard T., 178n, 203n, 271n, 323n
Schermerhorn, Richard, 16, 25n, 62n
Schmidt, Steffen (with Mack Shelly and Barbara Bardes), 248, 323n
Sewell, Tony, 178n
Shapiro, H., 235n
Shelly, Mack II (with Steffen Schmidt and Barbara Bardes), 248, 323n
Simpson, George (with J. M. Yinger), 25n, 108n
Sindler, Allan, 321n
Skolnick, J., 321n
Smith, J., 152
Smith, Rogers M., 138n
Soloutos, Theodore, 138n
Spear, Allan, 323n
Srole, Leo (with Lloyd Warner), 36
Stanley, Frances, 108n
Steiner, Stan, 253–254, 256–261, 271n
Stevens, H., 228, 235n

Tabb, William, 25n
Tate, Kathryn (with Lucius Barker and Mack Jones), 138n, 271n, 323n
Tauber, Karl (and Alma), 323n
Terry, Don, 203n
Thatcher, L. 178n

Thomas, William (with F. Znanciki), 126, 138n
Turner, Jonathan (with Edna Bonacich), 62n
Turque, B., 203n

Uhran, J. J., Jr., 62n

Van den Berghe, Pierre, 8, 25n
VanderZanden, James, 44, 62n

Warner, Lloyd (with Leo Srole), 36
Washington, Booker T., 18, 67, 105–106, 134, 188
Weatherford, J., 271n
Weber, Max, 6–7
Welch, Susan, 323n
Wessell, B. B., 62n
White, John, 62n, 109n, 138n, 178n, 203n
Williams, Robin, Jr., 25n
Wilson, J. 321n
Wilson, William, 15, 25n
Winkelman, Michael, 271n
Wright, Lawrence, 76

Yinger, J. M. (with George Simpson), 25n, 108n

Zangwill, Israel, 22
Znaniecki, F. (with William Thomas), 126, 138n

SUBJECT INDEX

Abernathy, Dr. Ralph, 242, 249; *see also* Southern Christian Leadership Conference

Ability to organize function, 39, 42, 44; *see also* LeMay's System Model of Assimilation

Accommodation, 18, 20, 22–23, 35, 45–55, 60, 67, 82, 94, 101, 105–107, 122, 125, 137, 196, 281

Acculturation, 18–20, 23, 30, 31–32, 36, 38, 40, 72, 93, 102, 131, 160–164

  forced, 160, 163–164

Achieved status, 15

Achievement syndrome, 33

Adaptability function, 37, 42

  function of, 42

  rate of, 39

Adarand Construction v. Pena, (1995), 292

Affirmative action, 11, 287, 289, 292–293, 321, 322

African Americans, 67, 102, 135, 177, 195, 217–218, 222, 250, 253

Afro-Americans, 188, 194, 222; *see also* Blacks

African Black Brotherhood (ABB), 215, 216–217, 234

Agnew, Spiro, 123–124

Alabama, 241–242, 244, 317–318

Alaska Claims Settlement Act, 265

Alianza Federal de Mercedes, 132, 257–258; *see also* Tijerina, Reies

Alien Acts, 304

Amalgamation, 20–21

America First movement, 231–233

American Civil Liberties Union, 79–80

American Communist Party, 54, 207, 212–214, 215–225, 235

  Communist Labor Party, 214

  Proleterian Party of America, 215

  Workers Party of America, 215

American Fascist Party, 54, 207, 235

American Federation of Labor, 208–209, 212–213, 215, 222, 255, 306

American Helenic Education Progressive Association (AHEPA), 91–92, 107, 123–124

American Indian Movement (AIM), 59, 263–264, 269; *see also* Pan-Indian Movement

Americanization, 305

American Labor Party, 54, 214, 222

American Party, 41

American Socialist Party, 54, 234; *see also* Debs, Eugene

Amish, 53–54, 143–151, 159, 178, 201–202

Amnesty program, 308

Anabaptist movement, 144–145, 177

Anglo-American culture, 20, 81

Anglo-conformity, 4, 18–19

Anti-Catholic movement, 87–89, 304

Anti-Fascism movement, 229–230

Anti-Fascist Alliance of North America (AFANA), 229

Anti-miscegenation laws, 69, 75

Anti-Semitism, 118, 130–131, 158, 195, 198, 227–228, 232

Arenas of conflict, 281–321

Asian Americans, 45, 67–84, 101, 106–107, 318

Asian Political Alliance, 72

Assimilation, 20–21, 30–33, 35, 44, 67, 73, 84, 86–87, 91, 94–95, 102, 112, 131–132, 138, 143, 152, 163–164, 167, 177, 207, 253, 264, 289, 301, 304

  civic, 40

  cultural, 20

  kinds of, 21

  processes, 31–60

  rates of, 44, 125

  structural, 73, 289

  systems model of, 37–44

  theories of, 33–44

Asylum, 301, 308

Atlantic Compromise Address, 105–106, 110–111; *see also* Washington, Booker T.

Authoritarian personality type, 34

Aztlan, 259, 270

Back to Africa movement, 53, 143, 172–178; *see also* Garvey, Marcus
Bakke v. Regents of the University of California, Davis (1978), 291–293
Barrios, 53, 99, 253, 260, 261, 269
Bay of Pigs invasion, 100
Beachy Amish Church, 148
Biculturalism, 22–23
Bigot, 13, 56, 246
Bill of Rights, 316
Birmingham, Alabama, 245–247, 317
Black belt, 218, 224, 234
Black Congressional Caucus, 133–135, 137
Black is Beautiful, 189, 249
Black Legion, 227
Black Muslims, 54, 59, 185–197, 202, 249–250
Black nationalism, 143, 171–177, 186, 192, 194, 261
Black Panthers, 59–60, 224, 249, 250–252, 255, 260–261, 269
Black power, 59, 176, 239, 248–250, 252, 260, 269
Black pride (consciousness), 197, 249
Blacks, 13–14, 18–19, 31, 42, 46, 54, 56–57, 59, 80, 82, 84, 94, 99, 101–107, 113, 133–136, 160, 189, 202, 211, 212–213, 216, 224, 234–235, 240–255, 262, 267, 282, 284–289, 293, 297, 299, 310, 312, 315–317, 319–321; *see also* African Americans, Afro-Americans
Black shirts, 227
Black Star Line, 176
Black zionism, 218
Bloc voting, 50–51, 112, 114–115, 123, 131
Border patrol, 306
Boston, 53, 76, 92, 97, 116, 118, 126, 253–254, 259, 285–286
Boycott (grape/lettuce), 255–256, 269
Bracero program, 99, 107–108, 307
Brigham Young, 153–154, 156–158; *see also* Mormons
Briggs, Cyril, 217–218; *see also* American Communist Party
Brooklyn, 199–202
Browder, Earl, 222–223; *see also* American Communist Party
Brown v. Board of Education of Topeka, Kansas (1954), 134, 240–241, 282–284, 286, 322
Brown, H. Rap, 249
Brown Berets, 255,258–261
Brown power, 59, 239, 252–262, 269
Brown shirts, 231
Bureau of Indian Affairs, 162, 168, 263, 265
Bus boycott, 241, 246
Busing, 285, 292; *see also* Desegregation, Integration

California, 68–72, 74, 79–82, 95–97, 116–118, 125, 132, 157, 171, 213, 251–256, 260, 282, 304, 319–320
California Alien Land Act, 74–75, 287
Campbell, Ben Nighthorse, 267
Carmichael, Stokeley, 244, 248, 250; *see also* Black power
Caste system, 15–16
Catholics, 1–3, 17, 113, 304
Celestial marriage, 153–156, 177; *see also* Polygamy, Mormons
Chavez, Cesar, 132, 253–256, 260–261
Cherokee, 161–162

Chicago, 50, 79–80, 90–91, 94, 98–99, 101, 116, 118–121, 124–128, 186–188, 192, 207–208, 217, 220, 230, 232, 248, 252–253, 261–262, 297
Chicanos, 17, 28, 95–97, 132–133, 137, 143, 251, 252–262, 269; *see also* Hispanics, Mexican-Americans
Chinatowns, 53, 70–71, 73, 143, 296
Chinese American Citizen League, 72
Chinese Americans, 68–73, 80, 82, 251
Chinese Exclusion Act, 70, 72, 96–97, 305–307
Chinese immigrants, 35, 38–39, 46, 48, 82, 89, 107, 112, 282, 287, 304, 318
Cincinnati, 207–208, 299
Civil disobedience, 239
Civil disorders, 249–250
Civil Rights Acts:
    of 1875, 103
    of 1957, 317
    of 1964, 134, 247–248, 284
    of 1965, 247–248, 289, 319
    of 1968, 248, 299
    of 1990, 292
Civil Rights Cases, 316
Civil Rights movement, 240–253, 255, 262, 264, 269, 284
    commission on, 284, 317–318
    policy of, 314, 321
Civil War, 38, 84, 86–87, 102–103, 112, 116, 120, 149, 153–154, 186, 198
Civil War Amendments, 104, 304, 315
Cleaver, Eldridge, 251–252; *see also* Black Panthers
Closeness of culture function, 40; *see also* LeMay's Model of Assimilation
Cold War, 223, 307
Colonialism, 20, 96–97
Colonization, 16
Community service organization (CSO), 132, 252–253
Communism, 207, 214–224, 233–234, 257
Comprehensive Employment and Training Act (CETA), 287
Concentration camps, 15, 75–76
Confederate states, 315
Congress on Racial Equality (CORE); 60, 240, 244, 247, 249–251, 255, 259, 269
Connor, Bull, 245–246
Conscientious objectors, 149–150
Coolie labor, 73–74
Coughlin, Father Charles, 227–233
Craig v. Boren (1976), 290
Crime Control and Safe Street Act of 1968, 314
Cross-group voting, 60, 122; *see also* Bloc voting
Crusade for Justice, 132, 258–259; *see also* Gonzales, Corky
Cuban Americans, 99–101, 107, 131–132
Cuban Refugee Resettlement program, 100
Cubic Air Act, 71
Cuffe, Captain Paul, 172
Czarist Russia, 10, 129

Dante Alighieri Society, 227; *see also* Fascism
Dawes Act, 164–165; *see also* General Allotment Act

Debs, Eugene, 209–214, 234
Defunis v. Odegaard (1974), 291–292
Democratic Party, 17, 69, 86, 114, 120–124, 127–128,
    131–133, 136, 157–158, 195, 209, 213, 234, 244,
    247–248, 253, 258, 304, 316
Denver, 252, 258–260, 262
Desegregation, 284, 286; *see also* Integration
Detroit, 186, 190, 208, 231, 249
Dillingham Commission, 305–306
Direct action protest, 59, 241; *see also* Civil disobedience,
    Civil rights movement
Discrimination, 1, 4, 11, 13–14, 16–18, 23, 36, 45, 53, 56,
    97, 99, 102, 105, 151, 188, 197–198, 249, 282,
    287–290, 292, 299, 315–316, 320–322
    defined, 11–12, 15
    employment, 105, 289–296
    isolate, small-group, direct, indirect, institutional, 8
    racial, 315
    sexual preference, 287
    theories of, 37
    types of, 15
Disenfranchise, 314–315, 321
Displaced Persons Act, 306
Dominant culture, 31, 33, 67, 82, 112
Door-ajar era, 301, 304, 321
DuBois, W. E. B., 173, 188, 223, 234
Dukkakis, Michael, 122
Dutch-door era, 301, 306, 321

Economic route (to assimilation), 36–37, 67, 94–95,
    107, 112, 122
    niches, 45, 107
Education policy, 282–285, 321
Elementary and Secondary Education Act of 1965 (ESEA),
    384
Elite groups, 17
Employer sanctions, 98, 308
Employment policy, 287–293, 321
Endo v. U.S., 79
Equal Employment Opportunity Commission, 290–292
Ethnic boundaries, 189, 202
Ethnic cleansing, 18–19
Ethnic group, 16, 22–23, 46, 55–57, 67, 129, 143, 207, 239,
    287, 300, 315, 321, 323
Ethnic jokes, 14
Ethnic stratification, 7, 35–36
Ethnicity, 1, 6–7, 93, 315, 320
    model of, 7
Ethnocentrism, 1, 10, 15, 36
Ethnophaulism, 14, 23, 41, 60
Euro-American groups, 93–94
Evacuation order, 79
Exclusion League:
    Asian, 70
    Japanese/Korean, 74
Exogamy, 132
Exploitation, 10, 12

Farmer, James, 240, 247
Farrakhan, Louis, 195, 202, 204–206
Fascism, 121–122, 207, 224–235
    American Fascist Party, 207, 229, 235
    Fascio, 225
    Fascists, 78, 225, 328
    League of America, 120, 226–227
Federal Bureau of Investigation (FBI), 78, 221, 224, 230–
    233, 247–248, 251, 257, 264; *see also*, Hoover, J. Edgar
Fifteenth Amendment, 316; *see also* Civil War Amendments
Firefighters Local Union v. Stotts (1984), 291
Foran Act (1875), 119, 287
Ford, Henry, 231, 233, 305
Ford, James W., 219–220, 222; *see also* Communist Party of
    America
Foreign miners tax of 1855, 70, 287
Forty-eighters, 85, 197, 208; *see also* German Americans
Foster, William, 213, 219, 222–224; *see also* Communist Party
    of America
Fourteenth Amendment, 103–104, 282–283, 285, 291, 316;
    see also Civil War Amendments
Freedom of choice, 284; *see also* Education policy
Freedom rides, 240–241, 244

Ghandi, Mahattma, 240, 242, 244
Garvey, Marcus, 186, 188, 190, 194–195, 217–218, 250;
    see also Back to Africa movement
Garveyism, 216
Garveyites, 186, 190, 195
Gatekeeping function, 300–301, 321
General Allotment Act, 164, 178; *see also* Dawes Act
General DeWitt, 76
General Pulaski, 50, 125, 127–128
Genocide, 160
Gentlemen's Agreement (1907), 75, 96–97
German Americans, 84–86, 230–231
German American Bund, 227, 230–233
Germans, 45, 78, 84–87, 106–107, 112, 116, 125, 130–131,
    197, 207–208, 224, 230, 234
Gerrymandering, 14, 315, 317, 320, 322
    racial, 315, 317, 320, 322
Ghettoization, 14, 15, 17, 125, 128
Ghettos, 187, 296–298, 300, 310, 311–312
G. I. Bill, 298
G. I. Forum, 132, 252–253
Glass ceiling, 13
Golden Exiles, 99; *see also* Cuban Americans
Gold rush, 96–97, 116, 304
Gomillion v. Lightfoot (1960), 317
Gonzales, Rodolfo "Corky," 132, 257–259
Gordon's Continuum, 32
Grandfather clause, 145, 316, 321
Great Depression, 97, 157, 186, 190, 197, 219, 225,
    227–228, 306
Greek Americans, 80–94, 122–125, 137
Greeks, 39–40, 46, 48–50, 53, 88–94, 287
Griggs v. Duke Power (1971), 291–293
Group-relatedness, 1, 3, 33

Groups, 46, 143, 190, 207
Guitirrez, Jose Angel, 133, 259

Hasidic Jews, 54, 143, 185, 197–203
Hawaii, 73–74, 77, 81–82, 98
Harper v. Virginia Board of Education (1966), 317
Haywood, Harry, 212, 217, 223–224; *see also* American
    Communist Party
Heart of Atlanta Hotel v. U. S. (1964), 318
Health, Education and Welfare, Department of (HEW), 284
Hirabayashi v. U. S., 79
Hispanics, 46, 53, 67, 80, 82, 83–84, 262, 267, 289,
    292–293, 319
Hispanic Americans, 94–101, 107–108, 131–134, 137, 252,
    269, 308, 312, 320
Hispanic Congressional Caucus, 131, 133
Hitler, Adolph, 185, 227–228, 230–232
Homestead Act of 1862, 86, 88, 106–107
Hoover, J. Edgar, 231
Housing and Urban Development, Department of (HUD),
    300
Housing policy, 296–300, 321
Huelga, La, 253–255, 269; *see also* Chavez, Cesar
Hurtado v. California (1884), 103, 316

Illegal Immigration Reform and Immigrant Responsibility Act
    (1996), 309
Immigration, 28, 41, 48, 67, 82–83, 91, 94, 96, 300–310
Immigration Acts:
    of 1917, 96
    of 1921, 197, 306
    of 1924, 74–75, 91, 97, 198, 306
    of 1929, 306
    of 1952, 80, 306–307
    of 1965, 92, 101, 307
    of 1986, 98–99, 229–230
    of 1996, 28
Immigration and Naturalization Service (INS), 307–308,
    310
Immigration policy, 17, 133, 300–310, 321–322
Indian Civil Rights Act of 1968, 265
Indian Citizens Act of 1924, 315
Indian Gaming Regulation Act, 265
Indian Removal Act, 162
Indian Reorganization Act (1934), 166–167
Industrial Workers of the World (IWW), 212, 215–217, 234
Intermestic policy, 300
International Labor Defense, 220–221, 234
International Ladies Garment Workers Union (ILGWU), 54,
    130, 208, 229
Internment camps, 75–76
Interstate Commerce Commission (ICC), 241, 317
Institutionalization, 13, 289
Integration, 20–21, 197, 250, 284–285
Irish Americans, 5, 49, 52–53, 87–88, 113–116, 122,
    125–126, 137, 287, 289
Irish model, 120–121

Italian Americans, 116–122, 125, 137, 224–230, 234
Italians, 33, 54–55, 87–89, 105–106, 207, 287, 297

Jackson, Jesse, 136, 195, 248, 320
Japanese American Citizens League (JACL), 79–80
Japanese Americans, 15, 21, 39, 46, 72, 73–82, 282, 287,
    306, 318
Jews, 10, 14, 17–18, 33, 36, 39, 46, 49, 188, 197–203
    Conservative, 197
    Eastern European, 129–131, 136–137, 207
    influence, 54
    lobby, 124
    Orthodox, 197–201
    Reform, 197–199
Jim Crow laws, 11, 14, 15, 59, 103–104, 107, 118, 134, 210,
    239–140, 252, 282, 284, 298, 315, 317, 321; *see also*
    Segregation
Johnson-Reed Act, 306
Justice Department, 286, 292

Katzenbach v. McClung (1964), 318
Kearny, Dennis, 70; *see also* Workingmen's Party
King, Dr. Martin Luther, Jr., 57–59, 135, 177, 194–195,
    241–249, 253, 255, 257, 269, 299, 317
    I Have a Dream, 247, 317
    I've Been to the Mountaintop, 248
    Letter from a Birmingham Jail, 246, 272–280
King, Rodney, 311
Knights of Labor, 208
Know-Nothing Party, 17, 41, 68, 86, 304; *see also* Nativism
Korean Americans, 82–84, 107
Korematsu v. U. S., 79
Ku Klux Klan, 17, 41, 90–91, 103, 130, 175–176, 198, 227,
    253, 285, 317

La Causa, 253, 261
LaFollette, Robert, 213, 217
LaGuardia, Fiorello, 120–121
La Huelga, 253–256
LaRaza Unida, 131–134, 255, 257–261, 269
Lassalleans, 207
Law Enforcement Assistance Administration (LEAA), 314
Law Enforcement policy, 310–314, 321
League of Germans Abroad, 231
League of United Latin American Citizens (LULAC), 132,
    252
LeMay's Model of Assimilation, 38
Levison, Stanley, 242
Liberty League, 227–229
Lindbergh, Charles, 232
Lipsky's Model, 56–57, 60
Literacy bill, 305; *see also* Immigration Act of 1917
Literacy tests, 14, 305, 315–318, 322
Little Italy, 116–118, 296
Little Rock, Arkansas, 284
Little Tokyo, 79

Los Angeles, 73, 83, 92, 94, 125, 132, 171, 252, 259–260, 296

Lubavitch Hasidism, 199–200; *see also* Hasidic Jews

Luevano v. Campbell (1981), 293

Lynchings, 105, 198, 317

Malcolm X, 136, 152, 189, 190–195, 249; *see also* Black Muslims

Manifesto of 1890, 156–157

Manzanar, 76–77

March on Washington (Poor People's), 1968, 223–224, 240, 247, 257–258, 317

Marginal membership function, 38–39, 44, 60; *see also* LeMay's Model of Assimilation

Marxism, 207–208, 216, 257

Majority's fear function, 31, 41, 44, 60; *see also* LeMay's Model of Assimilation

Mazzini society, 229

McCarrin-Walter Act of 1952, 72, 80, 224, 306–307

McKissick, Floyd, 248

Meiji restoration, 73–74

Melting pot, 22–23, 26–27

Memphis, 248

Mennonites, 53, 128, 143–151, 159

Meredith, James, 241, 248

Mexican American Legal Defense Fund (MALDEF), 262, 320

Mexican American Political Association (MAPA), 132, 253, 261–262

Mexican American Nationalist Organization (MANO), 132, 259; *see also* Gutierrez, Jose Angel

Mexican American Youth Organization (MAYO), 133, 258, 262

Mexican American War, 95

Mexican Americans, 252–262, 320; *see also* Chicanos

Mexicans, 39, 94–98, 107, 131–132

Miami, 94, 98, 99–101, 131

Middle-man minority, 46, 83–84

Migration, 16, 153–154

    forced, 143, 161–162

Migration and Refugee Assistance Act, 307; *see also* Cuban Americans

Millennial movement, 185, 202

Milliken v. Bradley, 285

Million Man March, 195

Milwaukee, 54, 85, 125–126, 187, 201, 208–209, 212, 214, 286

Mind-set, 11

Minority group, 1, 4, 6, 10, 17–19, 21, 30–31, 35–36, 38–39, 48–49, 53–54, 59–60, 80, 143, 160, 232, 281, 287, 289, 296, 310, 312

    culture, 149, 151–153, 202

    relations, 43, 312

    society, 6, 38–40, 41, 143–144

    status, 67, 115–116, 281

Mississippi, 240–241, 244, 247, 250, 284, 318–319

Missouri ex rel. Gaines v. Canada (1938), 282

Modal type, 1, 3, 31–32

Molly McGuires, 208

Montgomery, Alabama, 56–57, 241–243, 247

    bus boycott, 56–57, 241–243

    Improvement Association, 241–242

Mormons, 30, 38, 53–54, 143–144, 151–159, 177, 178, 179–183

Mountain Meadow Massacre, 157

Movemento Estudiantial Chicanos de Aztlain (MECHA), 133, 258, 262

Moynihan, Daniel Patrick, 115

Muhammad, Elijah, 185, 186–188, 190, 192–193, 195; *see also* Black Muslims

Multi-ethnic society, 23

Mussolini, Benito, 185, 225–230

Nation of Islam (NOI), 185, 202–203, 250

National Advisory Commission on Civil Disorders, 249–250

National Association for the Advancement of Colored People (NAACP), 59–60, 134–135, 188, 213, 218, 222–24, 239, 241, 247, 252, 260, 262, 282

National Association of Manufacturers (NAM), 305

National Congress of American Indians (NCAI), 262

National Farm Workers Association, 254

National Indian Youth Council (NIYC), 262

National Organization of Mexican American Students (NOMAS), 133, 255

Nationality group, 17

Native Americans, 4, 15, 21, 53, 80, 97, 143–144, 159–171, 262–267, 270, 282, 287, 296, 301, 315

Nativism, 97, 304–305, 322

Naturalization, 304

Nazi, 78, 306

    American Nazi movement, 235

    National Socialist Party, 231

    Nazism, 223, 230–235

Negro, 186, 188, 211–212, 215–221, 228, 253, 256, 297–298

Negro Labor Congress, 217–219, 221–222

Negro question, 208, 216, 221, 234

Negro "Self-Determination," 217–218, 224

New Mexico, 252, 256–258, 287, 320

New York, 48, 71, 73, 79, 85, 92, 94, 98–99, 105, 114, 116–122, 124–126, 128, 130–133, 135, 146, 152, 171, 192, 198–201, 203, 207–208, 212, 214–215, 220, 225–227, 230, 233, 259, 261–262, 296, 313

Nisei, 75, 79–81; *see also* Japanese Americans

Nineteenth Amendment, 315

Nixon v. Herndon (1927), 317

Nuclear type, 1–3, 31–32

Occupational mobility, 36

Occupational niches, 48–49, 62, 107–108, 287, 321

Occupational queuing, 46–47, 62

Office of Economic Opportunity (OEO), 287

Office of Education, 284

Old Order Amish, 145–148, 150, 177–178

Open door policy, 17, 301, 307, 321

Operation Wetback, 97

Order of Caucasians, 70; *see also* Nativism

Organization of Afro-American Unity (OAAU), 194, 202; *see also* Malcom X

Order of the Sons of America, 252; *see also* Nativism

Oriental Exclusion Act of 1924, 80; *see also* Chinese Exclusion Act

Orthodox Church:
  Eastern, 91
  Greek, 91, 93, 123
  Russian, 128

Outgroup, 9, 42

Outmarriage, 80–81, 132, 137

Ozawa v. U. S., 75, 287

PACE test, 292–293

Pacific Triangle, 306

Padrone, 89–90, 107, 287

Padroni, 119–120, 137

Pan-Africanism, 172

Panic of 1873, 39, 69, 118–119, 154, 157–158, 209

Pan-Indianism, 167–168, 177–178; *see also* American Indian Movement

Pan-Indian Movement, 262–263, 265, 269–270

Pariahs, 16

Parks, Rosa, 241

Parole program, 307, 322; *see also* Immigration policy

Paternalism, 20

Patronage, 51, 122

Pennsylvania, 145–146, 148–150, 155

Peoplehood, 6–8, 197

Personal Responsibility and Work Opportunity Act of 1996 (Welfare Reform Act), 308

Pet-door era, 301

Philadelphia, 50, 92, 98, 116, 119, 126, 130, 192, 207, 313

Picture brides, 74, 82

Pittsburgh, 71, 92, 116, 125–126, 186, 208

Plessy v. Ferguson (1896), 103, 134–135, 240, 282, 284, 322

Plunkitt, George Washington, 51; *see also* Tammany Hall

Pluralism, 1, 22–23, 36, 160
  types of, 35

Pogroms, 129–130, 138

Poles, 119, 125, 297 *see also* Polonia

Police, 310–313

Polish Americans, 53–54, 126–128

Political accommodation, 112–128

Political Association of Spanish-Speaking Organizations (PASSO), 132

Political participation policy, 314–321, 323

Poll tax, 14, 315–318, 321
  outlawed, 320

Polonia, 126–128, 137

Polygamy, 153–156, 158–159; *see also* Celestial marriage, Mormons

Popular Front, 214, 222

Post-industrial society, 15

Poston, Arizona, 76, 78

Poverty levels, 48

Power relationship, 4

Preferences, 306–307; *see also* Immigration Act of 1965

Preferment politics, 52–53

Prejudice, 1, 6–7, 10–12, 13, 16, 23, 34, 36,
  attitudes of, 7, 11, 13
  categories of, 10
  dimension of, 6
  institutionalized, 9
  model of, 10
  racial, 310

Presidents:
  George Bush, 122, 252, 292
  Jimmy Carter, 135, 168
  Glover Cleveland, 96, 115, 305
  William Clinton, 28, 122, 131–132, 135, 262, 265, 301
  Dwight David Eisenhower, 99, 168, 284
  Gerald Ford, 124–125
  Ulysses Grant, 163–164, 198
  Herbert Hoover, 253
  Andrew Jackson, 162
  Thomas Jefferson, 161, 304
  Lyndon Johnson, 72, 101, 128, 247, 249, 252, 299
  John F. Kennedy, 72, 100, 122, 128, 133, 193, 244, 247, 284, 317
  James Madison, 161–162, 172
  James Monroe, 162
  Richard Nixon, 122, 128, 133, 168
  Ronald Reagan, 252, 286, 292–293
  Franklin D. Roosevelt, 86, 121, 122, 214, 230, 232–233, 240
  Theodore Roosevelt, 74, 105
  William H. Taft, 305
  Harry S. Truman, 80, 86, 92, 223, 240, 306
  George Washington, 161, 249, 301, 304
  Woodrow Wilson, 305

Progressive party, 120–121, 223–224, 234

Proposition 187, 98

Protocols of the Elders of Zion, 198, 232; *see also* Anti-Semitism

Psychological approach, 33–34, 39

Public policy, 11–12, 17, 281, 314, 321, 322

Puerto Rican Forum, 133

Puerto Ricans, 39, 98–99, 107, 131–133, 137, 251, 261–262

Pull factors (of immigration), 89, 96–97, 117, 129, 301

Push factors (of immigration), 116–117, 129

Quakers, 172

Queu tax, 70–71

Quotas, 11, 97, 291–292; *see also* Immigration Acts of 1921, 1924, 1929

Quota system, 306

Race, 6, 7–8, 24, 322
  defined, 7, 24
  institutionalized, 6

Racial minority group, 8, 17, 21–22, 45, 67, 68, 207, 287, 300

Racism, 1, 7, 97, 99, 287, 310, 323
  defined, 7
  institutionalized, 8, 287, 323
  society, 10
  types of, 11, 305
Race relations cycle, 35
Radical agrarianism, 207, 212
Radicalism:
  behavioral tactics, 56
  new style, 54, 55–60, 134, 239–269
  old style, 54, 207–234
  politics of, 54–60, 102, 212
Randolph, Philip A., 213, 217, 223–224
Rebbe, 199–201, 202; *see also* Hasidic Jews
Robeson, Paul, 223
Reconstruction period, 102–103, 107, 134, 319
Red-lining, 15
Red Power, 59, 239, 262–269
Red Summer riots, (1919), 105, 214
Refugee Act of 1980, 308
Refugees, 94, 99–101, 306–308
Relocation camps, 112–114
Republican Party, 17, 53, 86, 88–89, 102, 116, 120–123,
  128, 131–133, 156–158, 248
Reservations, 15, 53, 160, 162–163, 164–171, 178, 282,
  296; *see also* Native Americans
Restrictive covenant, 297
Revolutionary War, 84, 116, 125, 127, 161
Revolving-door era, 301, 308, 321
Richmond v. Crosen (1989), 291
Roybal, Eduardo, 252–253; *see also* Community Service
  Organization
Rule of Expansion, 52
Russian Americans, 128–129, 224, 297
Rustin, Bayard, 242, 247; *see also* Southern Christian
  Leadership Conference

Salad-bowl image, 22–23
Salt Lake City, Utah, 154–158
San Francisco, 70–71, 74, 114, 118–119, 121–122, 125,
  128, 172, 296
Sarbanes, Paul, 122–123
Scandinavian Americans, 87–89
Scandinavians, 45, 86, 106
Scapegoats, 10, 88, 129, 197
Schurz, Carl, 86, 164
Scotch Irish, 40
Scottsboro defense, 220, 236–238
Segregation, 14–15, 99, 103–105, 125–126, 134, 160, 188,
  242, 245, 249, 282–285, 293, 298, 300, 311–322
  de facto, 14, 249, 284–285
  de jure, 134, 240, 248, 252, 282, 284–285, 296, 298,
  321
  desegregation, 284
  housing, 15, 296–298, 314, 321
Select Commission on Immigration and Refugee Policy
  (SCIRP), 307–308
Selective perception, 10

Separate-but-equal doctrine, 282; *see also Plessy v. Ferguson,*
  Brown v. Bd. of Education.
Separatism, 18–19, 30, 45, 54–55, 60, 105, 152, 155, 185,
  188, 196, 244, 250, 281
  geographic, 162
  physical, 143–177
  psychological, 185–202
Sepuel v. University of Oklahoma (1948), 282
Set-aside provisions, 291; *see also* Quotas
Sharecropper's Union, 219, 228, 234
Shelly v. Kramer (1948), 298
Silver Shirts, 227, 323
Similarities of cultures function, 39, 42–43, 61; *see also*
  LeMay's Model of Assimilation
Sit-ins, 240, 244
Size of minority function, 38, 41, 44, 62; *see also* LeMay's
  Model of Assimilation
Slaughterhouse Cases (1873), 103
Slave codes, 102
Slavery, 10, 102–103, 156, 188, 316
Slavic Americans, 125–131, 137–138
Slavic groups, 40, 124, 129, 208
Slums, 298
Smith Act, 224
Smith, Al, 121, 253
Smith, Joseph, 152–153, 154–155, 158; *see also* Mormons
Smith v. Allwright (1944), 317
Social class, 15, 36
Social Darwinism, 208
Socialism, 207–214, 233–234; *see also* Debs, Eugene
Socialists, 120–121, 207–209
  American Socialist Party, 210, 214, 222
  Sewer Socialists, 212, 234
  Socialist Labor Party, 208–209, 214, 222
  Socialist Party of America, 213, 234–235
Social-psychological approach, 34–35, 37
Social Security, 150, 190
Social stratification, 15, 24
Social variables of assimilation, 35
Sociological approach, 35–36
Socioeconomic status (SES), 320, 321, 325
  Standard SES model, 315
Solidarity, 4–5
Sojourner, 69, 89, 107, 118, 125, 129, 131, 138
Sons of Italy, 226–229, 234; *see also* American Fascist Party
South Carolina v. Katzenbach (1964), 318
Southern Christian Leadership Conference (SCLC), 60,
  241–251, 255–256, 269
Southeast Voter Registration Education Project (SVREP),
  320
Spanish Americans, 95; *see also* Hispanics, Chicanos
St. Louis, 71, 85, 125, 207, 213
Split-labor market, 36–37
Strategies for coping, 45–53
Stereotyping, 1, 9–10, 14, 35, 149, 189, 197
Student Nonviolent Coordinating Committee (SNCC), 60,
  241, 243–245, 249, 255, 259, 269
Subordinate groups, 4, 16
Superordinate groups, 4, 10

Swann v. Charloette-Mecklenberg Board of Education (1971), 285

Sweatt v. Painter (1950), 282

Symbionese Liberation Army (SLA), 59, 252

Symbolic explanations, 11

Symbolic satisfactions, 57

Systems dynamic approach (to assimilation), 37–44 theory, 62

Tammany Hall, 51–52, 115

Target groups, 10, 57–59; *see also* Lipsky's Model

Teamsters, 70

Termination policy, 160–161; *see also* Bureau of Indian Affairs

Texas, 95, 132, 212, 252–253, 256–260, 316, 320

Third party movements, 54

Thomas, Clarence, 292

Thomas, Norman, 214

Tierra Amarilla, New Mexico, 257–258; *see also* Tijerina, Reies

Tijerina, Reies Lopez (El Tigre), 132, 255–258, 261

Time of entry function, 38, 41, 44; *see also* LeMay's Model of Assimilation

Tolerance, 37

Transportation, Department of, 300

Treaty of Guadalupe-Hidalgo (1848), 96, 256, 259

Trukee Raid (1876), 70

Truman Doctrine, 92, 317

Tuskegee Institute, 105–106; *see also* Washington, Booker T.

Twenty-fourth Amendment, 317

Two-party system, 17, 20, 54

Typologies of reaction (to minority status), 45

Underclass, 15, 187, 190, 202

Unemployment, 48, 288

United Farm Workers, 132, 255; *see also* Chavez, Cesar

United Front, 222; *see also* Popular Front

United Mexican American Students (UMAS), 255, 259–260, 262

United Mine Workers, 213

United Negro Improvement Association (UNIA), 172–178, 190, 217–218; *see also* Garvey, Marcus

United Steelworkers v. Weber (1979), 291

Urban machine, 50–52, 115, 120, 131, 138, 140–142

Utah, 154–158

Vietnamese, 101

Voting, 315–317

Voting Rights Act of 1965, 134–135, 317; *see also* Civil Rights Act of 1965

War Brides Act, 306

Wards Cove v. Antonio (1989), 291

War of 1812, 162

War Relocation Authority, 79–80

Washington, Booker T., 173–174, 188, 193; *see also* Tuskegee Institute, Atlantic Compromise Address

Washington, D. C., 187, 263, 284, 290

WASP, 4–5, 88

Watts Riot, 249

Welfare Reform Act of 1996, 29–30; *see also* Personal Responsibility and Work Opportunity Act of 1996

We-ness, 1, 5, 15

Whig Party, 116

White chauvinism, 221, 223, 234

White flight, 298–299

White primary, 14, 315–17, 322; *see also* Jim Crow laws

White Russians, 224, 228, 230, 232–234

White supremacy, 4, 315; *see also* Ku Klux Klan, Nativism

Wilkins, Roy, 247

Willingness to accept acculturation, 44; *see also* LeMay's Model of Assimilation

Willingness to acculturate rate, 44; *see also* LeMay's Model of Assimilation

Wisconsin, 263

Wisconsin v. Yoder, 148, 151, 178, 179–183

Women (as a protected class), 289

Workingmen's Party, 70, 208; *see also* Chinese Exclusion Act

World War I, 74, 86, 89, 96, 105, 120, 124, 132, 149–150, 167, 175, 197, 199, 208, 213, 215, 225, 231, 253, 305

World War II, 15, 37, 40, 72, 75, 76, 86, 89, 92, 98, 122, 124, 127, 130, 132, 134, 167–168, 199, 212, 223, 233, 234, 240, 250, 253, 262, 269, 306

Wounded Knee, 59, 263–264; *see also* American Indian Movement

Xenophobia, 138, 304; *see also* Chinese Exclusion Act

Yellow menace, 70

Yellow Peril, 74

Young Lords, 251, 261–262; *see also* Puerto Ricans